100
KEY
DOCUMENTS
IN
AMERICAN
DEMOCRACY

100
KEY
DOCUMENTS
IN
AMERICAN
DEMOCRACY

Edited by
Peter B. Levy

Foreword by **William E. Leuchtenburg**

Greenwood Press
Westport, Connecticut • London

Library of Congress Cataloging-in-Publication Data

100 key documents in American democracy / edited by Peter B. Levy ; foreword
   by William E. Leuchtenburg.
     p.   cm.
   Includes index.
   ISBN 0–313–28424–5 (alk. paper)
    1. United States—History—Sources. 2. United States—Politics
and government—Sources. I. Levy, Peter B.
   E173.A15   1994
   973—dc20   93–1137

British Library Cataloguing in Publication Data is available.

Library of Congress Catalog Card Number: 93–1137
ISBN: 0–313–28424–5

First published in 1994

Greenwood Press, 88 Post Road West, Westport, CT 06881
An imprint of Greenwood Publishing Group, Inc.

Printed in the United States of America

The paper used in this book complies with the
Permanent Paper Standard issued by the National
Information Standards Organization (Z39.48–1984).

10 9 8 7 6 5 4 3 2

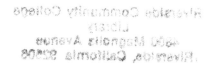

To my wife
Diane Krejsa

Contents

II. The Early Republic

III. Ante-Bellum Reform

Foreword

"The United States," the distinguished historian Richard Hofstadter once observed, "was the only country in the world that began with perfection and aspired to progress." The spirit of that brilliant paradox informs this superb collection of documents. Peter Levy fully understands why American institutions, charters, and ideas became beacons for aspiring democrats and freedom fighters all over the globe. But he also recognizes that even in a republic that "began with perfection," millions of African Americans were in chains, women were denied the most fundamental of rights, Native Americans were harried, and the propertied fared better than the propertyless. Hence, much of his volume is the story of the aspiration to progess, a striving that often, after long struggle, succeeded, but that, even today, is not over.

The student of history can count on finding in this book those fundamental statements of democratic values and individual liberties that undergirded this nation from its earliest days: the Mayflower Compact, the Declaration of Independence, the Constitution, the Seneca Falls Declaration, the Emancipation Proclamation, the Gettysburg Address, John F. Kennedy's civil rights address. Familiar though they are, they are indispensable. We cannot too often be reminded that the Pilgrims, in the storm-tossed waters off Cape Cod, covenanted to frame "just and equal laws" or too often reread Lincoln's resolve at the blood-soaked battlefield at Gettysburg, "that from these honored dead we take increased devotion to that cause for which they here gave the last full measure of devotion." The resolution adopted at Seneca Falls "that woman is man's equal—was intended to be so by the Creator, and the highest good of the race demands that she should be recognized as such"—is as pertinent today as it was in 1848. So, too, are the words President

Kennedy spoke only five months before his murder: "The nation, for all its hopes and all its boasts, will not be fully free until all its citizens are free."

More remarkable is Professor Levy's unerring eye for documents that are not nearly so well known. We are moved to tears by "the humbl petition" in Salem of Mary Easty, falsely accused of witchcraft, "not for my own life for I know I must die and my appointed time is sett," but for assurance that "no more Innocent blood may be shed." Who could not be affected by the dignified and eloquent Appeal of the Cherokee Nation against being expelled from their land: "If we are compelled to leave our country, we see nothing but ruin before us. The country west of the Arkansas territory is unknown to us. . . . It contains neither the scenes of our childhood, nor the graves of our fathers"? We read with a shock of recognition Langston Hughes's proud forecast from *The Weary Blues*:

> Tomorrow,
> I'll be at the table
> When company comes.

And Fannie Lou Hamer's words, following her recounting of her horrifying experience of being battered for trying to register to vote, continue to ring in our ears: "Is this America, the land of the free and the home of the brave, where . . . our lives be threatened daily because we want to live as decent human beings, in America?"

Perusing this volume gives us a deeper comprehension of what our democratic heritage is—not simply a set of tablets handed down to us by bewigged eighteenth-century gentlemen, significant though the Founding Fathers were, but a multifold legacy from people, obscure as well as renowned, who strove generation after generation to create a society in which no one was excluded. We come away from reading it not only knowing more than we did before about this legacy but inspired to ask ourselves what we can contibute to the creation of the documents of democracy that are still to come.

William E. Leuchtenburg
William Rand Kenan Professor of History,
University of North Carolina at
Chapel Hill
Past President, American Historical
Association

Introduction

This book is a collection of 100 key documents on the development and meaning of democracy in America. It can be read as a succinct overview of American history and used as a reference source on the same. It contains classical writings and speeches, such as Abraham Lincoln's "Gettysburg Address," and lesser-known gems, such as Fannie Lou Hamer's "Testimony" before the Credentials Committee of the Democratic Party at its national convention in 1964. The documents were written (or spoken) by Presidents and ex-slaves, by political theorists and poets, by labor leaders and songwriters. It reveals the diversity of the American experience, the contributions made to America's development by both the high and mighty and the common folk. And it depicts the ongoing struggle to achieve the ideals on which the nation was founded.

In making my selections, I have followed several rough guidelines. First, as the title of the book suggests, my central organizing theme or principle has been the concept of democracy. I have selected documents that furthered democracy or arose out of seminal struggles over its meaning and nature. Indeed, the process of selecting documents and writing appropriate introductions compelled me to rethink what is meant by the very term "democracy." And my ultimate selections were the result of much fine-tuning. For instance, at the last minute I substituted a selection from John Woolman's *Journal* for an excerpt from Benjamin Lay's *Slavekeeper's Apostates* because I felt that the former made the antislavery case more succinctly than the latter and it clearly had a greater impact on colonial Pennsylvania society.

Common to most of the documents is the belief that every individual enjoys certain basic or inalienable rights. Some of these rights, such as freedom of expression and religion, were spelled out by the framers of the Constitution. Others were not self-evident at the time of its writing.

Second, I have selected documents that display the diversity of the American experience. This means that I have included items that represent the variety of Americans themselves. It also means that I have selected pieces that vary in form and style, from political speeches and scholarly essays to introspective poems and satirical songs. I do so not to be politically correct but to be historically accurate. Democracy has been the product of all sorts of people, and a documentary history on the subject must reflect this. Those that leave out the works of artists, musicians, philosophers, and poets exaggerate the importance of political leaders. Yet to underestimate the contribution of the latter would also misrepresent American history.

Third, through my selections I have sought to convey the idea that democracy is the ongoing product of struggle, that American history did not begin with a golden age. Rather, democracy has grown because individual men and women courageously pursued the ideal of democracy notwithstanding the personal costs of doing so. Many of the documents in this collection were the products of nonconformists or dissenters, who fought against injustice and for democracy for all, not just for the enfranchised or privileged. And many others were written (or spoken) by radicals, who were well ahead of their time in understanding the true meaning of democracy. For example, Andrew Hamilton and Patrick Henry expressed radical ideas when they challenged English laws that restricted the press and levied taxes on the colonies. Abigail Adams, Frederick Douglass, and Walt Whitman did the same when they criticized tradition, for women, blacks, and artists. Of course, some views that once seemed radical may not seem so today. Mary Easty's claim that she was not a witch and that she should not be convicted on the basis of forced testimony, for one, was not heeded in her time. But few today believe in witchcraft and one of the cardinal principles of democracy today is that evidence obtained by torture is unacceptable.

Fourth, I have sought to show the ways in which democracy has unfolded over time, the ways in which certain groups sought to expand on the principles embodied by the Declaration of Independence and Bill of Rights, so as to make reality and principle square. Those documents that deal with racial and sexual inequality clearly fit this mold. Along the same lines, I have included documents that reflect the ways in which Americans sought to update democracy or make it relevant to a modernizing society. Thus as early as 1840 Orestes Brownson expressed deep concerns over the impact of industrialism on democracy, and many others, from Henry George to Michael Harrington have continued to do so.

Fifth, I have included pieces that deal with several key issues that have been somewhat particular to the development of American history. One of the other great challenges to democracy has been the issue of inclusion of ethnic minorities, and I have included several documents on this subject, from Carl Schurz's critique of nativism to Justice Murphy's dissent in *Korematsu v. United States*. Another theme addressed is that of the impact of America's global role. While I have not presented extensive coverage of this subject, I have included a number of seminal pieces that ponder the dangers of militarism and imperialism, from William Jennings Bryan's criticism of America's colonization of the Philippines to Dwight Eisenhower's warnings about the military-industrial complex.

Last, I have sought to include pieces that would be interesting in terms of content and style. Hence, unlike some of the best-known documentary histories, this one contains no laws, with the exception of the Emancipation Proclamation. Instead, I have given preference to speeches and writings that led to the passage or defeat of certain laws. For example, rather than including the Civil Rights Act of 1964, this book contains President Kennedy's "Address on Civil Rights" and Martin Luther King, Jr.'s "I Have a Dream" speech, which set the stage for the Act.

Let me end by adding that compiling, editing, and annotating this book has been a rewarding and challenging enterprise. Obviously, I had to leave out many important items. A definitive work on the subject of democracy would have to include thousands of documents. And even then its author would have to make hard choices over what to include or exclude. I received ample help and advice from my review board and editors along the way. They alerted me to a number of seminal pieces and steered me away from inappropriate documents. I have also been aided by my colleagues and students at York College who lent me materials and their ears. I owe special thanks to Dean William DeMeester, the Research and Publication Committee, and the Faculty Enhancement Committee for the financial support they provided. Without the help of the staff at York College, from Rosemary Wivagg, the History and Political Science Department's secretary, to the work study students who performed miracles for me on the xerox machine, I never would have completed this book by my publisher's deadline. Likewise, my chairperson, Phil Avillo, has helped me in every way possible. As in the past, I received invaluable encouragement, advice and understanding from my wife, Diane, and from my children, Jessica and Brian, whose democratic spirits fill our home everyday.

PART I
COLONIAL AMERICA

"The Wedding of Pocahontas, with John Rolfe." Lithograph by George Spohni (Library of Congress).

1. Powhatan, "Letter to John Smith" (ca. 1609)

1607   Jamestown founded
1608   Captain John Smith takes command of colony
1609   Powhatan's daughter, Pocahontas, marries John Rolfe
1611   Rolfe cultivates tobacco in Virginia
1619   First African slaves brought to colony; House of Burgesses established in Virginia
1622   Algonquins attack Jamestown
1646   Algonquins officially subjugated to English rule

What if the Americas had been uninhabited when the Europeans first arrived in the fifteenth century? What if Columbus had found only densely forested islands, with no signs of human life? What if the first English settlers in North America had not received aid from the Native Americans? Columbus might have returned to Spain disillusioned, never to return; he might have decided that his search for a new trade route to the East Indies had been in vain. Lacking word of gold, silver, and "lost souls," Spanish conquistadores and missionaries probably would not have ventured across the Atlantic. Similarly, French, Dutch, Portuguese, and English explorers and settlers would have had few reasons to follow. Put another way, American history would have turned out much differently.

Indeed, it is impossible to contemplate the course of American history without considering the impact that Europeans had on the native population and vice versa. America's political, cultural, social, and economic institutions were shaped by the interaction among Europeans, Native Americans, and African slaves. Democracy grew out of their relationships. Paradoxically, as Yale historian Edmund Morgan has argued, democracy developed for whites alongside the repression of nonwhites.

The first piece in the collection, a speech that Powhatan, a leader of the Algonquin tribe, delivered to Captain John Smith, the leader of the Virginia Colony, documents some of the earliest relations between European settlers in North America and Native Americans. Since the speech was recorded by Smith, who did not fully understand the Algonquin language, its accuracy is problematic. Nonetheless, one gains a sense of Powhatan's fears about the future of his people, fears that proved well founded. Even though Powhatan established a détente, of sorts, with Smith, which was reinforced by the marriage of Powhatan's daughter, Pocahontas, to John Rolfe, tensions between the natives and newcomers mounted. Following John Rolfe's successful cultivation of tobacco the Jamestown colony expanded rapidly, impinging on the Algonquins' land. In 1622, Powhatan's brother, Opekankanough, launched a surprise attack on the colony. Nearly one-third of the English settlers were killed. But the colonists gained reinforcements and arms from England and, in time, renewed their westward expansion. Finally, in 1646, Opekankanough signed a treaty that officially subjugated the Algonquins in Virginia to English rule.

I am now grown old, and must soon die; and the succession must descend, in order, to my brothers, *Opitchapan, Opekankanough,* and *Catataugh,* and then to my two sisters, and their two daughters. I wish their experience was equal to mine; and that your love to us might not be less than ours to you. Why should you take by force that from us which you can have by love? Why should you destroy us, who have provided you with food? What can you get by war? We can hide our provisions, and fly into the woods; and then you must consequently famish by wronging your friends. What is the cause of your jealousy? You see us unarmed, and willing to supply your wants, if you will come in a friendly manner, and not with swords and guns, as to invade an enemy. I am not so simple, as not to know it is better to eat good meat, lie well, and sleep quietly with my women and children; to laugh and be merry with the English; and, being their friend, to have copper, hatchets, and whatever else I want, than to fly from all, to lie cold in the woods, feed upon acorns, roots, and such trash, and to be so hunted, that I cannot rest, eat, or sleep. In such circumstances, my men must watch, and if a twig should but break, all would cry out, "*Here comes Capt. Smith*"; and so, in this miserable manner, to end my miserable life; and, Capt. Smith, this *might* be soon your fate too, through your rashness and unadvisedness. I, therefore, exhort you to peaceable councils; and, above all, I insist that the guns and swords, the cause of all our jealousy and uneasiness, be removed and sent away.

Source: Samuel B. Drake, *Biography and History of the Indians of North America* (Boston, 1851), p. 353.

For Further Reading:

James Axtell, "Colonial America Without the Indians: Counterfactual Reflections," *Journal of American History* 73 (March 1987): 981–96.

Francis Jennings, *The Invasion of America: Indians, Colonialism and the Cant of Conquest* (Chapel Hill: University of North Carolina Press, 1975).

Edmund S. Morgan, *American Slavery, American Freedom: The Ordeal of Colonial Virginia* (New York: Norton, 1975).

Aldon Vaughn, *American Genesis: Captain John Smith and the Founding of Virginia* (Boston: Little, Brown, 1975).

2. "The Mayflower Compact" (1620)

1608   Pilgrims flee to Holland
1619   Pilgrims obtain patent to establish colony in North
        America
1620   Pilgrims arrive in Provincetown
1620–21 Starving time
1621   Pilgrims celebrate their first Thanksgiving

Thirteen years after the Virginia Company founded the first English colony in North America, about one hundred men, women, and children, led by thirty-five Pilgrims, set sail for the New World on the Mayflower *with the goal of establishing a colony near the mouth of the Hudson River. While those who settled in Jamestown came largely for economic or material reasons, the Pilgrims arrived hoping to create a community where they could practice their religion without fear of persecution and free from the corrupting influences of the Church of England and Catholicism.*

The Pilgrims were one of many Protestant groups that emerged in northern Europe in the sixteenth century. More radical than many other Protestants, including the better-known and more numerous Puritans, the Pilgrims faced persistent persecution. In 1608 they had fled to Holland, only to return to England a decade later with the goal of winning a "patent" to establish a colony of their own in North America, a wish they were granted.

In mid-November they got caught in the rough winds and currents off Cape Cod—nearby what is today Provincetown. Rather than risk disaster, they cast anchor and decided to search for a suitable place to settle. Before disembarking, however, the Pilgrim leaders wrote the Mayflower Compact. This document served the immediate function of providing political legitimacy to those who would govern. Since the Pilgrims' patent was for land to the north of Cape Cod, not at Provincetown (or subsequently Plymouth), the Pilgrim leaders feared they lacked the right to rule. Moreover, many on board the Mayflower *were not Pilgrims, and there was grave concern among the group's leaders that they would desert the community to pursue their own gain. The compact overcame these two interrelated problems by binding all of the signers together.*

Forty-one males signed the Mayflower Compact—all of the heads of households, every adult bachelor, and nearly every male servant. The document resembled church covenants that were common at the time, especially among English Puritans and Scotch Presbyterians. For example, the Pilgrims had written similar compacts during previous moves. By writing the Mayflower

"Signing the Social Compact in the Cabin of the Mayflower." Painting by Matteson (Library of Congress).

Compact the Pilgrims established several principles fundamental to democracy in America, namely a belief in self-government, rule of law, and government by mutual consent.

In the Name of God, Amen. We, whose names are underwritten, the Loyal Subjects of our dread Sovereign Lord King *James*, by the Grace of God, of *Great Britain, France,* and *Ireland,* King, *Defender of the Faith,* &c. Having undertaken for the Glory of God, and Advancement of the Christian Faith, and the Honour of our King and Country, a Voyage to plant the first colony in the northern Parts of Virginia; Do by these Presents, solemnly and mutually in the Presence of God and one another, covenant and combine ourselves together into a civil Body Politick, for our better Ordering and Preservation, and Furtherance of the Ends aforesaid; and by Virtue hereof do enact, constitute, and frame, such just and equal Laws, Ordinances, Acts, Constitutions, and Offices, from time to time, as shall be thought most meet and convenient for the general Good of the Colony; unto which we promise all due Submission and Obedience. In WITNESS whereof we have hereunto subscribed our names at *Cape Cod* the eleventh of *November,* in the Reign of our Sovereign Lord King *James of England, France,* and *Ireland,* the eighteenth and of *Scotland,* the fifty-fourth. *Anno Domini,* 1620.

Mr. John Carver	Mr. Stephen Hopkins
Mr. William Bradford	Digery Priest
Mr. Edward Winslow	Thomas Williams
Mr. William Brewster	Gilbert Winslow
Isaac Allerton	Edmund Margesson
Miles Standish	Peter Brown
John Alden	Richard Bitteridge
John Turner	George Soule
Francis Eaton	Edward Tilly
James Chilton	John Tilly
John Craxton	Francis Cooke
John Billington	Thomas Rogers
Joses Fletcher	Thomas Tinker
John Goodman	John Ridgate
Mr. Samuel Fuller	Edward Fuller
Mr. Christopher Martin	Richard Clark
Mr. William Mullins	Richard Gardiner
Mr. William White	Mr. John Allerton
Mr. Richard Warren	Thomas English
John Howland	Edward Doten
	Edward Liester

Source: Benjamin Perly Poore, ed., *The Federal and State Constitutions, Colonial Charters and Other Organic Laws of the United States*, 2 vols. (Washington, D.C., 1878), 1: 931.

For Further Reading:

Charles Andrews, *The Colonial Period of American History* (New Haven, Conn.: Yale University Press, 1938).

William Bradford, *Of Plymouth Plantation*, ed. by Samuel Elliot Morrison (New York: Knopf, 1952).

3. John Winthrop, Excerpt from "A Model of Christian Charity" (1631)

1629 Massachusetts Bay Colony chartered
1630 Winthrop sets sail from Southampton, England for New England; arrives in Salem; delivers "Model of Christian Charity"
1630–50 Great Migration to New England

Like the Pilgrims (see document 2), the Puritans were distraught by the religious situation in England in the early decades of the seventeenth century.

They found both the teachings of the Church of England and the operations of the state or government corrupt. To a lesser degree than the Pilgrims, the Puritans also faced persecution for exercising their beliefs. Hence, in 1629, the Puritans, who were much larger in number than the Pilgrims, obtained a charter to establish a self-governing colony in New England. In the spring of 1629 the first Puritans departed for the New World. A year later, a much larger group of approximately 700 men, women, and children sailed from Southampton, England to New England. All together there were eleven ships, including the Arebella, *which carried the Puritans' newly elected leader, John Winthrop.*

Winthrop was a pious, well-respected and well-off landowner, who served as the governor of the Massachusetts Bay Company for most of its early history. Although not a minister, Winthrop set the tone for life in the new colony with a sermon he delivered on the Arebella *shortly before the first passengers disembarked in Salem, Massachusetts. The sermon was entitled "A Model of Christian Charity." Like the Mayflower Compact, it sought to bind the colonists together. By coming to the New World, Winthrop proclaimed, the settlers had made a covenant or agreement with God to establish a Christian community. If they abided by this covenant, God would hold them up high, as examples to the world. But if they broke the agreement, they would feel God's wrath.*

Put another way, Winthrop's sermon planted the idea of American exceptionalism. The Puritans had agreed to establish a "city upon a hill." God had chosen them and they had agreed to be the chosen. This notion of exceptionalism, that the United States was a special land and that its people had a special responsibility, would grow with time. Politicians and writers would continually return to this theme.

God Almighty in his most holy and wise providence hath so disposed of the condition of mankind, as in all times some must be rich, some poor, some high and eminent in power and dignity, others mean and in subjection.

The Reason Hereof

1. Reason: First, to hold conformity with the rest of his works: being delighted to show forth the glory of his wisdom in the variety and difference of the creatures, and the glory of his power, in ordering all these differences for the preservation and good of the whole, and the glory of his greatness, that, as it is the glory of princes to have many officers, so this great King will have many stewards, counting himself more honoured in dispensing his gifts to man by man, than if he did it by his own immediate hand.

2. Reason: Secondly, that he might have the more occasion to manifest the work of his Spirit: first, upon the wicked in moderating and restraining

them, so that the rich and mighty should not eat up the poor, nor the poor and despised rise up against their superiours and shake off their yoke; secondly, in the regenerate in exercising his graces in them: as in the great ones, their love, mercy, gentleness, temperance, etc., in the poor and inferiour sort, their faith, patience, obedience, etc.

3. Reason: Thirdly, that every man might have need of other, and from hence they might be all knit more nearly together in the bond of brotherly affection. From hence it appears plainly that no man is made more honourable than another, or more wealthy, etc., out of any particular and singular respect to himself, but for the glory of his Creator, and the common good of the creature, man. . . .

There are two rules whereby we are to walk one towards another—*justice* and *mercy*. . . . There is likewise a double law by which we are regulated in our conversation one towards another in both the former respects—the law of *nature* and the law of *grace*. . . . By the first of these laws, man as he was enabled so withall [is] commanded to love his neighbor as himself. Upon this ground stands all the precepts of the moral law, which concerns our dealings with men. To apply this to the works of mercy, this law requires two things: first, that every man afford his help to another in every want or distress; secondly, that he perform this out of the same affection which makes him careful of his own good. . . .

The law of grace, or the gospel, hath some difference from the former, as in these respects. First, the law of nature was given to man in the estate of innocency; this of the gospel in the estate of regeneracy. Secondly, the former propounds one man to another, as the same flesh and image of God; this as a brother in Christ also, and in the communion of the same spirit, and so teacheth us to put a difference between Christians and others. Do good to all, especially to the household of faith. Upon this ground the Israelites were to put a difference between the brethren [and] such as were strangers. . . .

It rests now to make some application of this discourse [to] the present design, which gave the occasion of writing of it. Herein are four things to be propounded: first the persons, secondly the work, thirdly the end, fourthly the means.

1. For the persons: We are a company professing ourselves fellow members of Christ, in which respect only though we were absent from each other many miles, and had our employments as far distant, yet we ought to account ourselves knit together by this bond of love, and live in the exercise of it, if we would have comfort of our being in Christ. . . .

2. For the work we have in hand: It is by a mutual consent through a special overruling providence, and a more than an ordinary approbation of the Churches of Christ, to seek out a place of cohabitation and consortship under a due form of government, both civil and ecclesiastical. In such cases as this the care of the public must oversway all private respects, by which

not only conscience, but mere civil policy doth bind us; for it is a true rule that particular estates cannot subsist in the ruin of the public.

3. The end is to improve our lives, to do more service to the Lord, the comfort and increase of the body of Christ whereof we are members, that ourselves and posterity may be the better preserved from the common corruptions of this evil world to serve the Lord and work out our salvation under the power and purity of his holy ordinances.

4. For the means whereby this must be effected: They are twofold—a conformity with the work and end we aim at. These we see are extraordinary; therefore we must not content ourselves with usual ordinary means. Whatsoever we did or ought to have done when we lived in England, the same must we do and more also where we go. That which the most in their churches maintain as a truth in profession only, we must bring into familiar and constant practice, as in this duty of love. We must love brotherly without dissimulation; we must love one another with a pure heart fervently; we must bear one another's burthens; we must not look only on our own things, but also on the things of our bretheren; neither must we think that the Lord will bear with such failings at our hands as he doth from those among whom we have lived. . . .

Thus stands the cause between God and us: we are entered into covenant with him for this work; we have taken out a commission; the Lord hath given us leave to draw our own articles; we have professed to enterprise these actions upon these and these ends; we have hereupon besought him of favour and blessing. Now if the Lord shall please to hear us, and bring us in peace to the place we desire, then hath he ratified this covenant and sealed our commission, [and] will expect a strict performance of the articles contained in it. But if we shall neglect the observation of these articles which are the ends we have propounded, and dissembling with our God, shall fall to embrace this present world and prosecute our carnal intentions seeking great things for ourselves and our posterity, the Lord will surely break out in wrath against us, be revenged of such a perjured people, and make us know the price of the breach of such a covenant.

Now the only way to avoid this shipwreck and to provide for our posterity is to follow the counsel of Micah: to do justly, to love mercy, to walk humbly with our God. For this end we must be knit together in this work as one man; we must entertain each other in brotherly affection; we must be willing to abridge ourselves of our superfluities for the supply of other's necessities; we must uphold a familiar commerce together in all meekness, gentleness, patience and liberality; we must delight in each other, make other's conditions our own, rejoice together, mourn together, labour and suffer together, always having before our eyes our commission, and community in the work, our community as members of the same body. So shall we keep the unity of the spirit in the bond of peace. The Lord will be our God and delight to dwell among us as his own people and will command a blessing upon us in all our ways, so that we shall see much more of his wisdom, power, goodness and truth than formerly we have been acquainted with. We shall find that the God of Israel is among us when ten of us shall be able to resist a thousand of our enemies, when he shall make us a praise and glory, that men shall say of succeeding plantations, "The Lord make it like that of New England."

For we must consider that we shall be as a city upon a hill. The eyes of all people are upon us. So that if we shall deal falsely with our God in this work we have undertaken, and so cause him to withdraw his present help from us, we shall be made a story and a byword through the world; we shall open the mouths of enemies to speak evil of the ways of God and all professors for God's sake; we shall shame the faces of many of God's worthy servants, and cause their prayers to be turned into curses upon us, 'til we be consumed out of the good land whither we are going.

And to shut up this discourse with that exhortation of Moses, that faithful servant of the Lord, in his last farewell to Israel: . . . Beloved, there is now set before us life and good, death and evil, in that we are commanded this day to love the Lord our God and to love one another, to walk in his ways and to keep his commandments and his ordinance and his laws and the articles of our covenant with him, that we may live and be multiplied, and that the Lord our God may bless us in the land whither we go to possess it. But if our hearts shall turn away so that we will not obey, but shall be seduced and worship . . . other gods, our pleasures and profits, and serve them, it is propounded unto us this day, we shall surely perish out of the good land whither we pass over this vast sea to possess it. Therefore, let us choose life, that we and our seed may live, by obeying his voice and cleaving to him. For he is our life and our prosperity.

Source: *Winthrop Papers*, ed. by Stewart Mitchell (Boston, 1931), 2: 289–295.

For Further Reading:

Perry Miller, *The New England Mind*, 2 vols. (Cambridge, Mass.: Harvard University Press, 1963).

Edmund S. Morgan, *The Puritan Dilemma* (Boston: Little, Brown, 1958).

4. Anne Bradstreet, "In Memory of My Dear Grandchild Elizabeth Bradstreet, Who Deceased August, 1665, Being a Year and Half Old" (1665)

1636   Harvard founded
1650   Bradstreet's first work of poetry, *Tenth Muse Lately
          Sprung Up*, published
1660s   Bradstreet writes "Contemplations"; published
          posthumously

Among those to migrate to New England in 1630 was Anne Bradstreet, the daughter of Thomas Dudley, a high official for the Earl of Lincoln in England. Bradstreet was raised in relative comfort and in the highly charged intellectual climate of the 1620s. However, when conditions worsened for religious dissenters, Bradstreet moved with her husband, Simon Bradstreet, to the Massachusetts Bay Colony.

Her life in the New England wilderness was not an easy one. She moved numerous times, settling finally in the frontier town of Andover in 1645. Her husband was away much of the time, busy with political affairs. Like other women in the colony, she was consumed with bearing children, eight in all, and laboring to establish and maintain a household.

In spite of the harshness of her surroundings and a society that confined women to a limited role—Puritans contended that a woman's hands were better suited for knitting needles than pens—Bradstreet managed to become America's first published poet. Most of her early poems were modeled after the works of the great masters. In contrast, in "Contemplations," which she wrote during the 1660s, Bradstreet reflected on some of the travails of early American life, from the death of loved ones to the destruction of homes. The poems displayed Bradstreet's, and to a lesser extent the Puritans', inner strength. Their faith in God's greater plan allowed them to overcome great personal losses. Bradstreet's poetry reminds us of the key role that American women played in establishing democracy in America, from raising children and maintaining homes to creating and nurturing a vibrant intellectual community.

Farewell dear babe, my heart's too much content,
Farewell sweet babe, the pleasure of mine eye,
Farewell fair flower that for a space was lent,
Then ta'en away unto eternity.

Blest babe, why should I once bewail thy fate,
Or sigh thy days so soon were terminate,
Sith thou art settled in an everlasting state.

By nature trees do rot when they are grown,
And plums and apples thoroughly ripe do fall,
And corn and grass are in their season mown,
And time brings down what is both strong and tall.
But plants new set to be eradicate,
And buds new blown to have so short a date,
Is by His hand alone that guides nature and fate.

Source: *The Poems of Mrs. Anne Bradstreet*, introduction by Charles Elliot Norton (New York, 1897), pp. 279–280.

For Further Reading:

J. Hensley, ed., *The Works of Anne Bradstreet* (Cambridge, Mass.: Belknap Press, 1967).
Lyle Koehler, *A Search for Power* (Urbana: University of Illinois Press, 1980).
Samuel Elliot Morrison, *Builders of the Bay Colony* (Boston: Houghton Mifflin, 1930).
Elizabeth C. White, *Anne Bradstreet* (New York: Oxford University Press, 1971).

5. Mary Easty, "Petition of an Accused Witch" (1692)

1688–89   Glorious Revolution
1692   Witchcraft Hysteria in Salem

Over three hundred years after they took place, the Salem witchcraft trials of 1692 remain one of the most famous, fascinating, and controversial events in American history. That individuals would stand accused of witchcraft was not unusual in the seventeenth century, as virtually the entire society believed in witches. Even the most highly educated members of the community believed that witches were the devil's agents. What was unusual about the Salem incident was that the hysteria lasted so long and affected so many. Indeed, by the time the trials were finally halted by the governor in the fall of 1692, twenty men and women had been executed and over a hundred more awaited a similar fate.

Clearly, as historians have recently shown, the witchcraft hysteria in Salem in 1692 demonstrated that New England was torn by social tensions.

"The Witch No. 3." Lithograph by George H. Walker & Company, 1892 (Library of Congress).

Just as clearly, the trials displayed the inadequacies of the judicial system at the end of the seventeenth century. The lawyers, judges, and jurists were all educated people. Still, twenty people were put to death for a crime that they could not have committed, since we know today that they were not witches. One of the problems with the witchcraft trials was that the rules of evidence were weak. Individuals were convicted of witchcraft based on spectral evidence—the alleged statements of ghosts—and individuals were encouraged to make false confessions.

One of the convicted, Mary Easty, addressed the latter problem in her petition to the court. Even though Easty's plea failed to save her life, the trials resulted in the development of fairer procedures in criminal trials. Indeed, the witchcraft hysteria helped establish the principle that it would be better to let the guilty free than to convict the innocent.

The humbl petition of Mary Eastick unto his Excellencyes Sir Wm Phipps and to the honourd Judge and Bench now s[i]tting In Judiacature in Salem and the Reverend ministers humbly sheweth

That wheras your poor and humble Petition[er] being condemned to die Doe humbly begg of you to take it into your Judicious and pious considerations that your poor and humble petitioner knowing my own Innocencye Blised be the Lord for it and seeing plainly the wiles and subtility of my accusers by my selfe can not but Judg charitably of Others that are going the same way of my selfe if the Lord stepps not mightily in   i was confined a whole month upon the same account that I am condemned now for and then cleared by the afflicked persons as some of your honours know and in two dayes time I was cryed out upon by them and have been confined and now am condemned to die   the Lord above knows my Innocencye then and likewise does now as att the great day will be known to men and Angells   I petition to your honours not for my own life for I know I must die and my appointed time is sett but the Lord he knowes it is that if it be possible no more Innocent blood may be shed which undoubtidly cannot be Avoyd[e]d   In the way and course you goe in   I Question not but your honours does to the uttmost of your Powers in the discovery and detecting of witchcraft and witches and would not be gulty of Innocent blood for the world but by my own Innocencye I know you are in the wrong way   the Lord in his infinite mercye direct you in this great work if it be his blessed will that no more innocent blood be shed   I would humbly begg of you that your honours would be plesed to examine theis Aflicted persons strictly and keepe them apart some time and likewise to try some of these confesing wichis I being confident there is severall of them has belyed themselves and others as will appeare if not in this world I am sure in the world to come whither I am now agoing and I question not but youll see an alteration of thes things they say my selfe and others having made a League with the Divel we cannot confesse   I know and the Lord knowes as will thorlly appeare they belye me and so I Question not but they doe others   the Lord above who is the searcher of all hearts knowes that as I shall answer it att the Tribunall Seat that I know not the least thinge of witchcraft therfore I cannot I dare not belye my own soule   I beg your honers not to deny this my humble petition from a poor dying Innocent person and I Question not but the Lord will give a blesing to yor endevers

   Source: Essex County Archives, Essex County Courthouse, Salem, Mass., in "Witchcraft, 1692," 1: 126.

For Further Reading:

Paul Boyer and Stephen Nissenbaum, *Salem Possessed* (Cambridge, Mass.: Harvard University Press, 1974).
John Demos, *Entertaining Satan* (New York: Oxford University Press, 1982).
Carol F. Karlsen, *The Devil in the Shape of a Woman* (New York: Norton, 1987).

6. Jonathan Edwards, Excerpt from "Sinners in the Hands of an Angry God" (1741)

1730s–1760s   Great Awakening
1735   Revival in Edwards' Northampton, Mass. congregation
1739   Reverend George Whitfield arrives in America, revivals spread
1741   "Sinners in the Hands of an Angry God"

By the one-hundredth anniversary of the arrival of the Puritans, religious zeal had waned in New England. It had never been that great in the southern colonies. In the face of such a decline, Jonathan Edwards, the son and grandson of famous New England ministers, delivered his most famous sermon, "Sinners in the Hands of an Angry God," to his congregation in Northampton, Massachusetts. In it, Edwards warned about the dangers of living without faith. While there was nothing particularly new about this argument, the way he presented it, through a strict appeal to the emotions, was new indeed. He encouraged his audience to move beyond traditional Puritan theology, which tended toward a cerebral understanding of God's will, to a more heartfelt faith in God.

Edwards was one of early America's great intellectuals and one of the fomenters of the Great Awakening, a revival in religion that swept across America in the mid-eighteenth century. Old congregations saw their memberships grow; new ones came into existence. Just as importantly, the nature of religion changed. It became more personal, emotional, and, to an extent, anti-elitist.

While the ultimate effect of the Great Awakening on organized religion is unclear, it had a clear impact on American culture and thought. Since many of the revivalists were not ordained ministers and since their message appealed directly to the heart, the Awakening tended to break down deference to authority. "Old Light," or traditional, ministers and institutions tended to be hierarchical, whereas the "New Light" teachings and institutions were more egalitarian or democratic. The Awakening empowered individuals, as individual men and women had to decide whether or not they had experienced God. In turn, some historians have argued, the Great Awakening paved the way for a political revolution, a rebellion against the authority of the king.

The God that holds you over the pit of hell, much as one holds a spider, or some loathsome insect, over the fire, abhors you and is dreadfully provoked; His wrath towards you burns like fire; He looks upon you as worthy of nothing else but to be cast into the fire; He is of purer eyes than to bear to have you in His sight; you are ten thousand times more abominable in His eyes than the most hateful and venomous serpent is in ours. You have offended Him infinitely more than ever a stubborn rebel did his prince; and yet it is nothing but His hand that holds you from falling into the fire every moment; it is to be ascribed to nothing else, that you did not go to hell the last night, that you were suffered to awake again in this world, after you closed your eyes to sleep; and there is no other reason to be given, why you have not dropped into hell since you arose in the morning, but that God's hand has held you up; there is no other reason to be given why you have not gone to hell, since you have sat here in the house of God, provoking His pure eyes by your sinful, wicked manner of attending His solemn worship; yea, there is nothing else that is to be given as a reason why you do not this very moment drop down into hell.

O sinner! consider the fearful danger you are in; it is a great furnace of wrath, a wide and bottomless pit, full of the fire of wrath, that you are held over in the hand of that God, whose wrath is provoked and incensed as much against you, as against many of the damned in hell; you hang by a slender thread, with the flames of divine wrath flashing about it and ready every moment to singe it and burn it asunder; and you have no interest in any Mediator and nothing to lay hold of to save yourself, nothing to keep off the flames of wrath, nothing of your own, nothing that you ever have done, nothing that you can do to induce God to spare you one moment. . . .

How awful are those words, Isaiah 63:3, which are the words of the great God: "I will tread them in mine anger, and trample them in my fury; and their blood shall be sprinkled upon my garments, and I will stain all my raiment." It is perhaps impossible to conceive of words that carry in them greater manifestations of these three things, viz., contempt, and hatred, and fierceness of indignation. If you cry to God to pity you, He will be so far from pitying you in your doleful case, or showing you the least regard or favor, that instead of that He will only tread you under foot; and though He will know that you cannot bear the weight of omnipotence treading upon you, He will not regard that, but He will crush you under His feet without mercy; He will crush out your blood and make it fly, and it shall be sprinkled on His garments, so as to stain all His raiment. He will not only hate you, but He will have you in the utmost contempt; no place shall be thought fit for you but under His feet, to be trodden down as the mire in the streets. . . .

. . . When the great and angry God hath risen up and executed His awful vengeance on the poor sinner and the wretch is actually suffering the infinite weight and power of his indignation, then will God call upon the whole universe to behold that awful majesty and mighty power that is to be seen in it. Isaiah 33:12–14, "And the people shall be as the burnings of lime: as thorns cut up shall they be burnt in the fire. Hear, ye that are afar off, what I have done; and ye that are near, acknowledge my might. The sinners in Zion are afraid; fearfulness hath surprised the hypocrites," &c.

Thus it will be with you that are in an unconverted state, if you continue in it; the infinite might, and majesty, and terribleness of the Omnipotent God shall be magnified upon you in the ineffable strength of your torments; you shall be tormented in the presence of holy angels, and in the presence of the Lamb; and when you shall be in this state of suffering, the glorious inhabitants of heaven shall go forth and look on the awful spectacle, that they may see what the wrath and fierceness of the Almighty is; and when they have seen it, they will fall down and adore that great power and majesty. Isaiah 66:23–24, "And it shall come to pass, that from one new moon to another, and from one Sabbath to another, shall all flesh come to worship before me, saith the Lord. And they shall go forth and look upon the carcasses of the men that have transgressed against me; for their worm shall not die, neither shall their fire be quenched; and they shall be an abhorring unto all flesh."

It is everlasting wrath. It would be dreadful to suffer this fierceness and wrath of Almighty God one moment; but you must suffer it to all eternity. There will be no end to this exquisite horrible misery. When you look forward, you shall see a long forever, a boundless duration before you, which will swallow up your thoughts, and amaze your soul; and you will absolutely despair of ever having any deliverance, any end, any mitigation, any rest at all. You will know certainly that you must wear out long ages, millions of millions of ages, in wrestling and conflicting with this almighty merciless vengeance; and then when you have so done, when so many ages have actually been spent by you in this manner, you will know that all is but a point to what remains. So that your punishment will indeed be infinite. Oh, who can express what the state of a soul in such circumstances is! All that we can possibly say about it gives but a very feeble, faint representation of it; it is inexpressible and inconceivable: For "who knows the power of God's anger?"

How dreadful is the state of those that are daily and hourly in the danger of this great wrath and infinite misery! But this is the dismal case of every soul in this congregation that has not been born again, however moral and strict, sober and religious, they may otherwise be. Oh that you would consider it, whether you be young or old! There is reason to think that there are many in this congregation now hearing this discourse that will actually be the subjects of this very misery to all eternity. We know not who they are, or in what seats they sit, or what thoughts they now have. It may be they are now at ease, and hear all these things without much disturbance, and are now flattering themselves that they are not the persons, promising themselves that they shall escape. If they knew that there was one person, and but one, in the whole congregation, that was to be the subject of this misery, what an awful thing would it be to think of! If we knew who it was, what an awful sight would it be to see such a person! How might all the rest of the congregation lift up a lamentable and bitter cry over him! But, alas! instead of one, how many is it likely will remember this discourse in hell? And it would be a wonder, if some that are now present should not be in hell in a very short time, even before this year is out. And it would be no wonder if some persons, that now sit here, in some seats of this meeting-house, in health, quiet and secure, should be there before tomorrow morning. Those of you that finally continue in a natural condition, that shall keep out of hell longest will be there in a little time! your damnation does not slumber; it will come swiftly, and, in all probability, very suddenly upon many of you. You have reason to wonder that you are not already in hell. It is doubtless the case of some whom you have seen and known, that never deserved hell more than you, and that heretofore appeared as likely to have been now alive as you. Their case is past all hope; they are crying in extreme misery and perfect despair; but here you are in the land of the living and in the house of God, and have an opportunity to obtain salvation. What would not those poor damned hopeless souls give for one day's opportunity such as you now enjoy!

And now you have an extraordinary opportunity, a day wherein Christ has thrown the door of mercy wide open, and stands in calling and crying with a loud voice to poor sinners; a day wherein many are flocking to Him, and pressing into the kingdom of God. Many are daily coming from the east, west, north and south; many that were very lately in the same miserable condition that you are in, are now in a happy state, with their hearts filled with love to Him who has loved them and washed them from their sins in His own blood, and rejoicing in hope of the glory of God. How awful it is to be left behind at such a day! To see so many others feasting, while you are pining and perishing! To see so many rejoicing and singing for joy of heart, while you have cause to mourn for sorrow of heart and howl for vexation of spirit! How can you rest one moment in such a condition? Are not your souls as precious as the souls of the people at Suffield, where they are flocking from day to day to Christ? . . .

And let every one that is yet of Christ, and hanging over the pit of hell, whether they be old men and women, or middle aged, or young people, or little children, now hearken to the loud calls of God's word and providence. This acceptable year of the Lord, a day of such great favors to some, will doubtless be a day of as remarkable vengeance to others. Men's hearts harden, and their guilt increases apace at such a day as this, if they neglect their souls; and never was there so great danger of such persons being given up to hardness of heart and blindness of mind. God seems now to be hastily gathering in His elect in all parts of the land; and probably the greater part of adult persons that ever shall be saved will be brought in now in a little

time and that it will be as it was on the great out-pouring of the Spirit upon
the Jews in the apostles' days; the election will obtain, and the rest will be
blinded. If this should be the case with you, you will eternally curse this
day, and will curse the day that ever you were born to see such a season of
the pouring out of God's Spirit, and will wish that you had died and gone
to hell before you had seen it. Now undoubtedly it is, as it was in the days
of John the Baptist, the axe is in an extraordinary manner laid at the root
of the trees, that every tree which brings not forth good fruit may be hewn
down and cast into the fire.

Therefore, let every one that is out of Christ, now awake and fly from the
wrath to come. The wrath of Almighty God is now undoubtedly hanging
over a great part of this congregation: Let every one fly out of Sodom: "Haste
and escape for your lives, look not behind you, escape to the mountain, lest
you be consumed."

Source: *The Works of President Edwards*, vol. 2 (New York, 1868), pp. 313–21.

For Further Reading:

Richard Bushman, *From Puritan to Yankee* (Cambridge, Mass.: Harvard University
    Press, 1967).
Edward S. Gaustad, *The Great Awakening* (New York: Harper & Row, 1957).
Patricia J. Tracy, *Jonathan Edwards, Pastor* (New York: Hill & Wang, 1980).

7. Andrew Hamilton, Excerpt from "Defense of John Peter Zenger" (1735)

1733   Zenger publishes first issue of *New York Weekly
        Journal*
1734   Zenger publishes offending passages
1735   Zenger's trial
1737   Zenger becomes public printer for New York

*A little over forty years after the Salem witchcraft trials (see document 5),
another court case helped push forward the boundaries of American democracy. This one involved John Peter Zenger, the publisher of the* New
York Weekly Journal, *and an outspoken critic of William Cosby, the governor
of New York.*

*In 1734 Zenger was arrested and tried for seditious libel against the
governor. Zenger had printed articles and a cartoon that satirically criticized
Cosby's administration for its corruption and high-handedness. Since En-*

John P. Zenger Trial (Library of Congress).

glish law defined libel as printing any attack upon a public official, which Zenger had done, he should have been convicted. But Andrew Hamilton, Zenger's eloquent defense attorney, ingenuously argued that Zenger's criticism should not be considered libelous since it was true. On the basis of the law the judge of the Royal Court of New York disagreed with this argument, but to his astonishment the jury returned a verdict of not guilty. If the jury had returned a guilty verdict, Zenger was prepared to deliver a speech that emphasized that Americans had fled Europe in the first place to escape oppression and arbitrary power and that to rule against him violated their creed.

While Hamilton's argument did not convince royal judges to alter their definition of libel, it did establish an important precedent. Over the years the press's freedom and the public's right to speak grew. The Bill of Rights (1791) protected freedom of expression. And in the mid-1960s, in Sullivan v. N.Y. Times, the Supreme Court took Hamilton's argument to its logical conclusion, ruling that a newspaper was not guilty of libel even if its statements were false unless it could be proven that the newspaper had acted with malice.

MR. ATTORNEY. The case before the court is whether Mr. Zenger is guilty of libeling His Excellency the Governor of New York, and indeed the whole administration of the government. Mr. Hamilton has confessed the printing and publishing, and I think nothing is plainer than that the words in the information [indictment] are scandalous, and tend to sedition, and to disquiet the minds of the people of this province. And if such papers are not libels, I think it may be said there can be no such thing as a libel.

MR. HAMILTON. May it please Your Honor, I cannot agree with Mr. Attorney. For though I freely acknowledge that there are such things as libels, yet I must insist, at the same time, that what my client is charged with is not a libel. And I observed just now that Mr. Attorney, in defining a libel, made use of the words "scandalous, seditious, and tend to disquiet the people." But (whether with design or not I will not say) he omitted the word "false."

MR. ATTORNEY. I think I did not omit the word "false." But it has been said already that it may be a libel, notwithstanding it may be true.

MR. HAMILTON. In this I must still differ with Mr. Attorney; for I depend upon it, we are to be tried upon this information now before the court and jury, and to which we have pleaded not guilty, and by it we are charged with printing and publishing a certain false, malicious, seditious, and scandalous libel. This word "false" must have some meaning, or else how came it there? . . .

MR. CHIEF JUSTICE. You cannot be admitted, Mr. Hamilton, to give the truth of a libel in evidence. A libel is not to be justified; for it is nevertheless a libel that it is true. . . .

MR. HAMILTON. I thank Your Honor. Then, gentlemen of the jury, it is to you we must now appeal, for witnesses, to the truth of the facts we have offered, and are denied the liberty to prove. And let it not seem strange that I apply myself to you in this manner. I am warranted so to do both by law and reason.

The law supposes you to be summoned out of the neighborhood where the fact [crime] is alleged to be committed; and the reason of your being taken out of the neighborhood is because you are supposed to have the best knowledge of the fact that is to be tried. And were you to find a verdict against my client, you must take upon you to say the papers referred to in the information, and which we acknowledge we printed and published, are false, scandalous, and seditious. But of this I can have no apprehension. You are citizens of New York; you are really what the law supposes you to be, honest and lawful men. And, according to my brief, the facts which we offer to prove were not committed in a corner; they are notoriously known to be true; and therefore in your justice lies our safety. And as we are denied the liberty of giving evidence to prove the truth of what we have published, I will beg leave to lay it down, as a standing rule in such cases, that the suppressing of evidence ought always to be taken for the strongest evidence; and I hope it will have weight with you. . . .

I hope to be pardoned, sir, for my zeal upon this occasion. It is an old and wise caution that when our neighbor's house is on fire, we ought to take care of our own. For though, blessed be God, I live in a government [Pennsylvania] where liberty is well understood, and freely enjoyed, yet experience has shown us all (I'm sure it has to me) that a bad precedent in one government is soon set up for an authority in another. And therefore I cannot but think it mine, and every honest man's duty, that (while we pay all due obedience to men in authority) we ought at the same time to be upon our guard against power, wherever we apprehend that it may affect ourselves or our fellow subjects.

I am truly very unequal to such an undertaking on many accounts. And you see I labor under the weight of many years, and am borne down with great infirmities of body. Yet old and weak as I am, I should think it my duty, if required, to go to the utmost part of the land, where my service could be of any use, in assist—to quench the flame of prosecutions upon informations, set on foot by the government, to deprive a people of the right of remonstrating (and complaining too) of the arbitrary attempts of men in power. Men who injure and oppress the people under their administration provoke them to cry out and complain; and then make that very complaint the foundation for new oppressions and prosecutions. I wish I could say there were no instances of this kind.

But to conclude. The question before the court and you, gentlemen of the jury, is not of small nor private concern. It is not the cause of a poor printer, nor of New York alone, which you are now trying. No! It may, in its consequence, affect every freeman that lives under a British government on the main[land] of America. It is the best cause. It is the cause of liberty. And I make no doubt but your upright conduct, this day, will not only entitle you to the love and esteem of your fellow citizens; but every man who prefers freedom to a life of slavery will bless and honor you, as men who have baffled the attempt of tyranny, and, by an impartial and uncorrupt verdict, have laid a noble foundation for securing to ourselves, our posterity, and our neighbors, that to which nature and the laws of our country have given us a right—the liberty both of exposing and opposing arbitrary power (in these parts of the world, at least) by speaking and writing truth. . . .

Source: J. P. Zenger, *Own Story* (New York, 1736), pp. 20-41.

For Further Reading:

Bernard Bailyn, *The Origins of American Politics* (New York: Vintage, 1968).
Leonard Levy, ed., *Freedom of the Press from Zenger to Jefferson* (Indianapolis: Bobbs-Merrill, 1966).

8. John Woolman, Excerpt from *Journal* [On Slavery] (1757)

1619   First Africans imported to North America as "bound servants"
1672–1760   Royal African Company imports thousands of slaves to North America
1737   Benjamin Lay, *All Slave-Keepers Apostates*
1774   John Woolman, *Journal* published
1775   Quakers organize antislavery society
1780   Pennsylvania passes first antislavery law

While the Quakers theoretically opposed slavery, since it ran counter to their general belief in the sanctity of every individual and the brotherhood of man, Pennsylvania, under Quaker rule in the early 1700s, had a relatively large slave population. In 1700 nearly one in five persons in Philadelphia, the city of brotherly love, was enslaved. Appalled by this contradiction between their beliefs and practices, in the 1730s Benjamin Lay launched a personal attack on slavery. To emphasize the immorality of the slave trade, Lay kidnapped the children of his fellow Quakers. To raise the public's awareness of the inhuman conditions that slaves endured, Lay stood outside of a Quaker meeting house (church) with bare feet and skimpy clothing in the heart of winter. Just as importantly, he wrote All Slave-Keepers Apostates, *a lengthy treaty on the immorality of the Quakers' acceptance of slavery.*

At the time, Lay's actions and works were not well received. By the 1770s, however, other, more prominent Quakers were making the same arguments with much greater success. John Woolman, one of the most respected Quakers, for example, sharply attacked slavery in his Journal *and helped establish the first antislavery society. During the revolution, with Pennsylvania taking the lead, the northern states passed antislavery legislation. Even if this legislation often contained loopholes, it displayed the ability of idealists like Lay and Woolman to move society.*

Feeling the exercise in relation to a visit to the Southern Provinces to increase upon me, I acquainted our Monthly Meeting therewith, and obtained their certificate. Expecting to go alone, one of my brothers who lived in Philadelphia, having some business in North Carolina, proposed going with me part of the way; but as he had a view of some outward affairs, to accept of him as a companion was some difficulty with me, whereupon I had conversation with him at sundry times. At length feeling easy in my mind, I had conversation with several elderly Friends of Philadelphia on the subject, and he obtaining a certificate suitable to the occasion, we set off in the fifth month, 1757. Coming to Nottingham week-day meeting, we lodged at John Churchman's, where I met with our friend, Benjamin Buffington, from New England, who was returning from a visit to the Southern Provinces. Thence we crossed the river Susquehanna, and lodged at William Cox's in Maryland.

Soon after I entered this province a deep and painful exercise came upon me, which I often had some feeling of, since my mind was drawn toward these parts, and with which I had acquainted my brother before we agreed to join as companions. As the people in this and the Southern Provinces live much on the labor of slaves, many of whom are used hardly, my concern was that I might attend with singleness of heart to the voice of the true Shepherd, and be so supported as to remain unmoved at the faces of men.

As it is common for Friends on such a visit to have entertainment free of cost, a difficulty arose in my mind with respect to saving my money by kindness received from what appeared to me to be the gain of oppression. Receiving a gift, considered as a gift, brings the receiver under obligations to the benefactor, and has a natural tendency to draw the obliged into a party with the giver. To prevent difficulties of this kind, and to preserve the minds of judges from any bias, was that Divine prohibition: "Thou shalt not receive any gift; for a gift blindeth the wise, and perverteth the words of the righteous" (Exodus 23:8). As the disciples were sent forth without any provision for their journey, and our Lord said the workman is worthy of his meat, their labor in the gospel was considered as a reward for their entertainment, and therefore not received as a gift; yet, in regard to my present journey, I could not see my way clear in that respect. The difference appeared thus: the entertainment the disciples met with was from them whose hearts God had opened to receive them, from a love to them and the truth they published; but we, considered as members of the same religious society, look upon it as a piece of civility to receive each other in such visits; and such reception, at times, is partly in regard to reputation, and not from an inward unity of heart and spirit. Conduct is more convincing than language, and where people, by their actions, manifest that the slave-trade is not so disagreeable to their principles but that it may be encouraged, there is not a sound uniting with some Friends who visit them.

The prospect of so weighty a work, and of being so distinguished from many whom I esteemed before myself, brought me very low, and such were the conflicts of my soul that I had a near sympathy with the Prophet, in the time of his weakness, when he said: "If thou deal thus with me, kill me, I pray thee, if I have found favor in thy sight" (Numbers 11:15). But I soon saw that this proceeded from the want of a full resignation to the Divine will. Many were the afflictions which attended me, and in great abasement, with many tears, my cries were to the Almighty for his gracious and fatherly assistance, and after a time of deep trial I was favored to understand the state mentioned by the Psalmist more clearly than ever I had done before; to wit: "My soul is even as a weaned child" (Psalm 131:2). Being thus helped to sink down into resignation, I felt a deliverance from that tempest in which I had been sorely exercised, and in calmness of mind went forward, trusting that the Lord Jesus Christ, as I faithfully attended to him, would be a counsellor to me in all difficulties, and that by his strength I should be enabled even to leave money with the members of society where I had entertainment, when I found that omitting it would obstruct that work to which I believed he had called me. As I copy this after my return, I may here add, that oftentimes I did so under a sense of duty. The way in which I did it was thus: when I expected soon to leave a Friend's house where I had entertainment, if I believed that I should not keep clear from the gain of oppression without leaving money, I spoke to one of the heads of the family privately, and desired them to accept of those pieces of silver, and give them to such of their negroes as they believed would make the best use of them; and at other times I gave them to the negroes myself, as the way looked clearest to me. Before I came out, I had provided a large number of small pieces for this purpose and thus offering them to some who appeared to be wealthy people was a trial both to me and them. But the fear of the Lord so covered me at times that my way was made easier than I expected; and few, if any, manifested any resentment at the offer, and most of them, after some conversation, accepted of them.

Ninth of fifth month.—A Friend at whose house we breakfasted setting us a little on our way, I had conversation with him, in the fear of the Lord, concerning his slaves, in which my heart was tender; I used much plainness of speech with him, and he appeared to take it kindly. We pursued our journey without appointing meetings, being pressed in my mind to be at the Yearly Meeting in Virginia. In my travelling on the road, I often felt a cry rise from the centre of my mind, thus: "O Lord, I am a stranger on the earth, hide not thy face from me." On the 11th, we crossed the rivers Patowmack and Rapahannock, and lodged at Port Royal. On the way we had the company of a colonel of the militia, who appeared to be a thoughtful man. I took occasion to remark on the difference in general betwixt a people used to labor moderately for their living, training up their children in frugality and business, and those who live on the labor of slaves; the former, in my view, being the most happy life. He concurred in the remark, and mentioned the trouble arising from the untoward, slothful disposition of the negroes, adding that one of our laborers would do as much in a day as two of their slaves. I replied, that free men, whose minds were properly on their business, found a satisfaction in improving, cultivating, and providing for their families; but negroes, laboring to support others who claim them as their property, and expecting nothing but slavery during life, had not the like inducement to be industrious.

After some further conversation I said, that men having power too often misapplied it; that though we made slaves of the negroes, and the Turks made slaves of the Christians, I believed that liberty was the natural right of all men equally. This he did not deny, but said the lives of the negroes were so wretched in their own country that many of them lived better here than there. I replied, "There is great odds in regard to us on what principle we act"; and so the conversation on that subject ended. I may here add that another person, some time afterwards, mentioned the wretchedness of the negroes, occasioned by their intestine wars, as an argument in favor of our fetching them away for slaves. To which I replied, if compassion for the Africans, on account of their domestic troubles, was the real motive of our purchasing them, that spirit of tenderness being attended to, would incite us to use them kindly, that, as strangers brought out of affliction, their lives might be happy among us. And as they are human creatures, whose souls are as precious as ours, and who may receive the same help and comfort from the Holy Scriptures as we do, we could not omit suitable endeavors to instruct them therein; but that while we manifest by our conduct that our views in purchasing them are to advance ourselves, and while our buying captives taken in war animates those parties to push on the war, and increase desolation amongst them, to say they live unhappily in Africa is far from being an argument in our favor. . . .

Having travelled through Maryland, we came amongst Friends at Cedar Creek in Virginia, on the 12th; and the next day rode, in company with several of them, a day's journey to Camp Creek. As I was riding along in the morning, my mind was deeply affected in a sense I had of the need of Divine aid to support me in the various difficulties which attended me, and in uncommon distress of mind I cried in secret to the Most High, "O Lord be merciful, I beseech thee, to thy poor afflicted creature!" After some time, I felt inward relief, and, soon after, a Friend in company began to talk in support of the slave-trade, and said the negroes were understood to be the offspring of Cain, their blackness being the mark which God set upon him after he murdered Abel his brother; that it was the design of Providence they should be slaves, as a condition proper to the race of so wicked a man as Cain was. Then another spake in support of what had been said. To all which I replied in substance as follows: that Noah and his family were all who survived the flood, according to Scripture; and as Noah was of Seth's race, the family of Cain was wholly destroyed. One of them said that after the flood Ham went to the land of Nod and took a wife; that Nod was a land far distant, inhabited by Cain's race, and that the flood did not reach it; and as Ham was sentenced to be a servant of servants to his brethren, these two families, being thus joined, were undoubtedly fit only for slaves. I replied, the flood was a judgment upon the world for their abominations, and it was granted that Cain's stock was the most wicked, and therefore unreasonable to suppose that they were spared. As to Ham's going to the land of Nod for a wife, no time being fixed, Nod might be inhabited by some of Noah's family before Ham married a second time; moreover the text saith "That all flesh died that moved upon the earth" (Genesis 7:21). I further reminded them how the prophets repeatedly declare "that the son shall not suffer for the iniquity of the father, but every one be answerable for his own sins." I was troubled to perceive the darkness of their imaginations, and in some pressure of spirit said, "The love of ease and gain are the motives in general of keeping slaves, and men are wont to take hold of weak arguments to support a cause which is unreasonable. I have no interest on either side, save only the interest which I desire to have in the truth. I believe liberty is their right, and as I see they are not only deprived of it, but treated in other respects with inhumanity in many places, I believe He who is a refuge for the oppressed will, in his own time, plead their cause, and happy will it be for such as walk in uprightness before him." And thus our conversation ended. . . .

The sense I had of the state of the churches brought a weight of distress upon me. The gold to me appeared dim, and the fine gold changed, and though this is the case too generally, yet the sense of it in these parts hath in a particular manner borne heavy upon me. It appeared to me that through the prevailing of the spirit of this world the minds of many were brought to an inward desolation, and instead of the spirit of meekness, gentleness, and heavenly wisdom, which are the necessary companions of the true sheep of Christ, a spirit of fierceness and the love of dominion too generally prevailed. . . .

The prospect of a way being open to the same degeneracy, in some parts of this newly settled land of America, in respect to our conduct towards the negroes, hath deeply bowed my mind in this journey, and though briefly to relate how these people are treated is no agreeable work, yet, after often reading over the notes I made as I travelled, I find my mind engaged to preserve them. Many of the white people in those provinces take little or no care of negro marriages; and when negroes marry after their own way, some make so little account of those marriages that with views of outward interest they often part men from their wives by selling them far asunder, which is common when estates are sold by executors at vendue. Many whose labor is heavy being followed at their business in the field by a man with a whip, hired for that purpose, have in common little else allowed but one peck of Indian corn and some salt, for one week, with a few potatoes; the potatoes they commonly raise by their labor on the first day of the week. The correction ensuing on their disobedience to overseers, or slothfulness in business, is often very severe, and sometimes desperate.

Men and women have many times scarcely clothes sufficient to hide their nakedness, and boys and girls ten and twelve years old are often quite naked amongst their master's children. Some of our Society, and some of the society called Newlights, use some endeavors to instruct those they have in reading; but in common this is not only neglected, but disapproved. These are the people by whose labor the other inhabitants are in a great measure supported, and many of them in the luxuries of life. These are the people who have made no agreement to serve us, and who have not forfeited their liberty that we know of. These are the souls for whom Christ died, and for our conduct towards them we must answer before Him who is no respecter of persons. They who know the only true God, and Jesus Christ whom he hath sent, and are thus acquainted with the merciful, benevolent, gospel spirit, will therein perceive that the indignation of God is kindled against oppression and cruelty, and in beholding the great distress of so numerous a people will find cause for mourning.

Source: Albert Bushnell Hart, ed., *American History Told by Contemporaries* (New York, 1889), 2: 302.

For Further Reading:

David Brion Davis, *The Problem of Slavery in Western Culture* (New York: Cornell University Press, 1966).

Gary B. Nash, *Forging Freedom* (Cambridge, Mass.: Harvard University Press, 1988).

Gary B. Nash and Jean R. Soderland, *Freedom by Degree* (New York: Oxford University Press, 1991).

9. James Otis, Excerpt from "Considerations on Behalf of the Colonists" (1765)

1756–63   Seven-Year War or French-Indian War
1765   Stamp Act enacted; Stamp Act Congress assembles; Stamp Act riots
1766   Parliament repeals Stamp Act; enacts Declaratory Act

Parliament's enactment of the Stamp Act in 1765, a tax on paper products such as newspapers, almanacs, and pamphlets, unleashed a wave of protest in the colonies that reached a climax with the American Revolution in 1776. The citizens of Massachusetts were among the most vociferous opponents of the Stamp Act and remained in the forefront of the challenge to British rule.

Boston Massacre, March 5, 1770. Copy of chromolithograph by John Bufford after William L. Champney, ca. 1856 (National Archives).

For example, following the passage of the Stamp Act, riots erupted in Boston. Mobs of workingmen ransacked the homes of Andrew Oliver, the local stamp distributor, and other colonial officials.

One of the leaders of Boston's protests was James Otis. Even before Parliament levied this tax, Otis had earned a reputation as a radical. In 1764, a year before others decried taxation without representation, Otis challenged Parliament's authority to levy direct taxes on the colonies. With the Stamp Act, Otis repeated his attack, writing a number of radical pamphlets. For example, in "Considerations on Behalf of the Colonists," Otis responded to a defense of the tax by Soame Jenys, a member of Parliment and the Board of Trade. In addition, Otis helped organize the Stamp Act Congress, a colony-wide assembly committed to protesting the tax. His words and actions won him the respect of Boston's workingmen and women and, in turn, helped turn them against British rule. By the late 1760s, ironically, Otis became a bit more conservative in his thought and he did not play a major role in the Revolution.

My Lord,

I have read the *Opusculum* of the celebrated Mr. J——s, called "Objections to the taxation of the colonies by the legislature of Great-Britain, briefly considered." In obedience to your lordships commands, I have thrown a few thoughts on paper, all indeed that I have patience on this melancholy occasion to collect. The gentleman thinks it is "absurd and insolent" to question the expediency and utility of a public measure. He seems to be an utter enemy to the freedom of enquiry after truth, justice and equity. He is not only a zealous advocate for pusilanimous and passive obedience, but for the most implicit faith in the dictatorial mandates of power. The "several patriotic favorite words *liberty, property, Englishmen,* &c." are in his opinion of no use but to "make strong impressions on the more numerous part of mankind who have ears but no understanding." The times have been when the favorite terms *places, pensions,* French *louis d'ors* and English *guineas,* have made very undue impressions on those who have had votes and voices, but neither honor nor conscience—who have deserved of their country an ax, a gibbet or a halter, much better than a star or garter. The grand aphorism of the British constitution, that *"no Englishman is or can be taxed but by his own consent in person or by his deputy"* is absurdly denied. In a *vain* and most *insolent* attempt to disprove this fundamental principle he exhibits a curious specimen of his talent at chicanery and quibbling. He says that "no man that he knows of is taxed by his own consent." It is a maxim at this day, that the crown by royal prerogative alone can levy no taxes on the subject. One who had any "understanding as well as ears" would from thence be led to conclude that some men must consent to their taxes before they can be imposed. It has been commonly understood, at least since the glorious revolution, that the consent of the British Lords and Commons, i.e. of all men within the realm, must be obtained to make a tax legal there. The consent of the lords and commons of his majesty's ancient and very respectable kingdom of Ireland, has also been deemed necessary to a taxation of the subjects there. The consent of the two houses of assembly in the colonies has till lately been also thought requisite for the taxation of his majesty's most dutiful and loyal subjects, the colonists. *Sed tempora mutantur. . . .*

Right reason and the spirit of a free constitution require that the representation of the whole people should be as equal as possible. A perfect equality of representation has been thought impracticable; perhaps the nature of human affairs will not admit of it. But it most certainly might and ought to be more equal than it is at present in any state. The difficulties in the way of a perfectly equal representation are such that in most countries the poor people can obtain none. The lust of power and unreasonable domination are, have been, and I fear ever will be not only impatient of, but above, controul. The Great love pillows of down for their own heads, and chains for those below them. Hence 'tis pretty easy to see how it has been brought about, that in all ages despotism has been the general tho' not quite

universal government of the world. No good reason however can be given
in any country why every man of a sound mind should not have his vote in
the election of a representative. If a man has but little property to protect
and defend, yet his life and liberty are things of some importance. . . .

Mr. J——s says, "by far the major part of the inhabitants of Great Britain
are non electors." The more is the pity. "Every Englishman, he tells us, is
taxed, and yet not one in twenty is represented." To be consistent, he must
here mean that not one in twenty, votes for a representative. So a small
minority rules and governs the majority. This may for those in the saddle
be clever enough, but can never be right in theory. What *ab initio* could
give an absolute unlimitted right to one twentieth of a community, to govern
the other nineteen by their sovereign will and pleasure? Let him, if his
intellects will admit of the research, discover how in any age or country this
came to be the fact. Some favourite modern systems must be given up or
maintained by a clear open avowal of these *Hobbeian* maxims, viz. That
dominion is rightfully founded on force and fraud.—That power universally
confers right.—That war, bloody war, is the real and natural state of man—
and that he who can find means to buy, sell, enslave, or destroy, the greatest
number of his own species, is right worthy to be dubbed a modern politician
and an hero. Mr. J——s has a little contemptible flirt at the sacred names
of Selden, Locke, and Sidney. But their ideas will not quadrate with the
half-born sentiments of a courtier. Their views will never center in the
paricranium of a modern politician. The characters of their writings cannot
be affected by the crudities of a ministerial mercenary pamphleteer. He
next proceeds to give us a specimen of his agility in leaping hedge and ditch,
and of paddling through thick and thin. He has proved himself greatly skilled
in the ancient and honourable sciences of horse-racing, bruising, boxing,
and cock-fighting. He offers to "risk the merits of the whole cause on a single
question." For this one question he proposes a string of five or six. . . . True
it is, that from the nature of the British constitution, and also from the idea
and nature of a supreme legislature, the parliament represents the whole
community or empire, and have an undoubted power, authority, and jurisdiction, over the whole; and to their final decisions the whole must and
ought peaceably to submit. They have an undoubted right also to unite to
all intents and purposes, for benefits and burthens, a dominion, or subordinate jurisdiction to the mother state, if the good of the whole requires it.
But great tenderness has been shown to the customs of particular cities and
boroughs, and surely as much indulgence might be reasonably expected
towards large provinces, the inhabitants of which have been born and grown
up under the modes and customs of a subordinate jurisdiction. But in a case
of necessity, the good of the whole requires, that not only private interests,
but private passions, should give way to the public. But all this will not
convince me of the reasonableness of imposing heavy taxes on the colonists,
while their trade and commerce are every day more than ever restricted.

Much less will it follow, that the colonists are, in fact, represented in the house of commons. Should the British empire one day be extended round the whole world, would it be reasonable that all mankind should have their concerns managed by the electors of old Sarum, and the "occupants of the Cornish barns and ale-houses," we sometimes read of? We who are in the colonies, are by common law, and by act of parliament, declared entitled to all the privileges of the subjects within the realm. Yet we are heavily taxed, without being, in fact, represented.—In all trials here relating to the revenue, the admiralty courts have jurisdiction given them, and the subject may, at the pleasure of the informer, be deprived of a trial by his peers. To do as one would be done by, is a divine rule. Remember Britons, when you shall be taxed without your consent, and tried without a jury, and have an army quartered in private families, you will have little to hope or to fear! But I must not lose sight of my man, who sagaciously asks "if the colonists are English when they solicit protection, but not Englishmen when taxes are required to enable *this country* to protect them?" I ask in my turn, when did the colonies solicit for protection? They have had no occasion to solicit for protection since the happy accession of our gracious Sovereign's illustrious family to the British diadem. His Majesty, the father of all his people, protects all his loyal subjects of every complexion and language, without any particular solicitation. But before the ever memorable revolution, the Northern Colonists were so far from receiving protection from Britain, that every thing was done from the throne to the footstool, to cramp, betray, and ruin them: yet against the combined power of France, Indian savages, and the corrupt administration of those times, they carried on their settlements, and under a mild government for these eighty years past, have made them the wonder and envy of the world.

These colonies may, if truly understood, be one day the last resource, and best barrier of Great Britain herself. Be that as it may, sure I am that the colonists never in any reign received protection but from the king and parliament. From most others they had nothing to ask, but every thing to fear. Fellow subjects in every age, have been the temporal and spiritual persecutors of fellow subjects. The Creoles follow the example of some politicians and ever employ a negroe to whip negroes. As to "that country," and "protection from that country," what can Mr. J——s mean? I ever thought the territories of the same prince made one country. But if, according to Mr. J——s, Great Britain is a distinct country from the British colonies, what is that *country* in nature more than this country? The same sun warms the people of Great Britain and us; the same summer chears, and the same winter chills. . . .

I cannot see why the American peasants may not with as much propriety speak of their cities of London and Westminster, of their isles, of Britain, Ireland, Jersey, Guernsey, Sark, and the Orcades, and of the "rivulets and runlets thereof," and consider them all but as appendages to their sheep-cots and goose-pens. But land is land, and men should be men. The property of the former God hath given to the possessor. These are *sui juris*, or slaves and vassals; there neither is nor can be any medium. Mr. J——s would do well once in his life to reflect that were it not for *our* American colonies, he might at this "present crisis," been but the driver of a baggage cart, on a crusade to the holy sepulchre, or sketching caracatura's, while the brave were bleeding and dying for their country. He gives us three or four sophistical arguments, to prove that "no taxes can be exactly equal." "If not exactly equal on all, then not just." "Therefore no taxes at all can be justly imposed." This is arch. But who before ever dreamt that no taxes could be imposed, because a mathematical exactness or inequality is impracticable. . . .

Mr. J——s asks, if "any time can be more proper to impose taxes on their *trade*, than when they are enabled to rival us in our manufactures, by the encouragement and protection we have given them?" Who are WE? It is a miracle he had not affirmed, that the colonies rival Great Britain in trade also. His not asserting this, is the only glimmering of modesty or regard to truth, discoverable through his notable performance. As the colonists are British subjects, and confessedly on all hands entitled to the same rights and privileges, with the subjects born within the realm, I challenge Mr. J——s or any one else to give even the colour of a conclusive reason, why the colonists are not entitled to the same means and methods of obtaining a living with their fellow-subjects in the islands.

Can any one tell me why trade, commerce, arts, sciences and manufactures, should not be as free for an American as for an European? Is there any thing in the laws of nature and nations, any thing in the nature of our allegiance that forbids a colonist to push the manufacture of iron much beyond the making a horse-shoe or a hob nail? We have indeed "files for our mattocks, and for our coulters, and for our forks, and for our axes, to sharpen our goads," and to break our teeth; but they are of the manufacture of Europe: I never heard of one made here. Neither the refinements of Montesquieu nor the imitations of the servile Frenchified half thinking mortals, who are so fond of quoting him, to prove, that it is a law of Europe, to confine the trade and manufactures to the mother state, "to prohibit the colonists erecting manufactories," and "to *interdict* all commerce between them and other countries," will pass with me for any evidence of the rectitude of this custom and procedure. The *Administrator* has worked these principles up to "fundamental maxims of police at this crisis." The *Regulator* hath followed him, and given broad hints that all kinds of American manufactures will not only be discountenanced, but even prohibited, as fast as they are found to interfere with those of Britain. That is, in plain English, we shall do nothing that they can do for us. This is kind!—And what they cannot do for us, we are permitted to do for ourselves. Generous!

Source: James Otis, *Considerations on Behalf of the Colonists in a "Letter to Noble Lord"* (London, 1765).

For Further Reading:

Bernard Bailyn, *Ideological Origins of the American Revolution* (Cambridge, Mass.: Harvard University Press, 1967).

Pauline Maier, *From Resistance to Revolution* (New York: Knopf, 1972).

Edmund and Helen S. Morgan, *The Stamp Act Crisis*, rev. ed. (New York: Collier, 1974).

10. Patrick Henry, Excerpt from "Speech to the Second Virginia Convention" (1775)

1765	Patrick Henry makes radical proposals in Virginia House of Burgess
1767	Townsend Acts
1769	Virginia endorses Nonimportation
1770	Townsend duties repealed; Boston Massacre
1773	Tea Act; Boston Tea Party
1774	Coercive Acts; First Continental Congress, Patrick Henry one of two Virginia representatives
1775	Battle of Lexington and Concord; Second Continental Congress, Henry represents Virginia

Patrick Henry, a leading lawyer and planter from Charlotte County, Virginia, first gained colony-wide fame in 1765 by proposing that the Virginia House of Burgess adopt seven radical resolutions in opposition to the Stamp Act (see document 9). These resolutions not only called for repeal of the tax, they denied Britain's authority to tax Virginians at all. Even though the House of Burgess did not adopt Henry's resolutions, his fiery oratory was recorded by the press and gained him instant recognition as a leading opponent of British rule. Indeed, even if Henry had never uttered the words "Give me liberty or give me death," he would have earned a place in the history books for his 1765 statement: "Caesar had his Brutus—Charles the first his Cromwell—and George the third [the King of England] may profit by their example. If this may be treason, make the most of it."

For over a decade, Henry played a leading role in the push toward independence. He represented Virginia at the First and Second Continental Congresses. Shortly before attending the latter, he delivered his famous "Give me liberty or give me death" speech to a convention of Virginia radicals at Saint Joseph's Church in Richmond. Two months later, Henry was pro-

"Give Me Liberty, Or Give Me Death!" Speech by Patrick Henry, March 23, 1775.
Currier & Ives (Library of Congress).

*claimed an outlaw by Virginia Governor Lord Dunmore. Following the
writing of the Declaration of Independence, ironically, Henry took over
Dunmore's post. After the Revolution, Henry remained active in state politics. And during the fight over ratification of the Constitution he led the
call for the adoption of a Bill of Rights.*

It is natural for man to indulge in the illusions of hope. We are apt
to shut our eyes against a painful truth, and listen to the song of that siren,
till she transforms us into beasts. Is this the part of wise men, engaged in
a great and arduous struggle for liberty? Are we disposed to be of the number
of those who, having eyes, see not, and having ears, hear not, the things
which so nearly concern their temporal salvation? For my part, whatever
anguish of spirit it may cost, I am willing to know the whole truth; to know
the worst and to provide for it.

I have but one lamp by which my feet are guided; and that is the lamp
of experience. I know of no way of judging of the future but by the past.
And judging by the past, I wish to know what there has been in the conduct
of the British ministry for the last ten years to justify those hopes with which
gentlemen have been pleased to solace themselves and the House? Is it that
insidious smile with which our petition has been lately received? Trust it

not, sir; it will prove a snare to your feet. Suffer not yourselves to be betrayed with a kiss. Ask yourselves how this gracious reception of our petition comports with these warlike preparations which cover our waters and darken our land. Are fleets and armies necessary to a work of love and reconciliation? Have we shown ourselves so unwilling to be reconciled, that force must be called in to win back our love? Let us not deceive ourselves, sir. These are the implements of war and subjugation; the last arguments to which kings resort. I ask gentlemen, sir, what means this martial array, if its purpose be not to force us to submission? Can gentlemen assign any other possible motives for it? Has Great Britain any enemy, in this quarter of the world, to call for all this accumulation of navies and armies? No, sir, she has none. They are meant for us; they can be meant for no other. They are sent over to bind and rivet upon us those chains which the British ministry have been so long forging. And what have we to oppose to them? Shall we try argument? Sir, we have been trying that for the last ten years. Have we anything new to offer on the subject? Nothing. We have held the subject up in every light of which it is capable; but it has been all in vain. Shall we resort to entreaty and humble supplication? What terms shall we find which have not been already exhausted? Let us not, I beseech you, sir, deceive ourselves longer. Sir, we have done everything that could be done to avert the storm which is now coming on. We have petitioned; we have remonstrated; we have supplicated; we have prostrated ourselves before the tyrannical hands of the ministry and parliament. Our petitions have been slighted; our remonstrances have produced additional violence and insult; our supplications have been disregarded; and we have been spurned, with contempt, from the foot of the throne. In vain, after these things, may we indulge the fond hope of peace and reconciliation. There is no longer any room for hope. If we wish to be free—if we mean to preserve inviolate those inestimable privileges for which we have been so long contending—if we mean not basely to abandon the noble struggle in which we have been so long engaged, and which we have pledged ourselves never to abandon until the glorious object of our contest shall be obtained, we must fight! I repeat it, sir, we must fight! An appeal to arms and to the God of Hosts is all that is left us!

They tell us, sir, that we are weak; unable to cope with so formidable an adversary. But when shall we be stronger? Will it be the next week, or the next year? Will it be when we are totally disarmed, and when a British guard shall be stationed in every house? Shall we gather strength by irresolution and inaction? Shall we acquire the means of effectual resistance by lying supinely on our backs, and hugging the delusive phantom of hope, until our enemies shall have bound us hand and foot? Sir, we are not weak, if we make a proper use of the means which the God of nature hath placed in our power. Three millions of people, armed in the holy cause of liberty, and in such a country as that which we possess, are invincible by any force which our enemy can send against us. Besides, sir, we shall not fight our battles alone. There is a just God who presides over the destinies of nations; and who will raise friends to fight our battles for us. The battle, sir, is not to the strong alone; it is to the vigilant, the active, the brave. Besides, sir, we have no election. If we were base enough to desire it, it is now too late to retire from the contest. There is no retreat but in submission and slavery! Our chains are forged! Their clanking may be heard on the plains of Boston! The war is inevitable—and let it come! I repeat it, sir, let it come!

It is in vain, sir, to extenuate the matter. Gentlemen may cry peace, peace—but there is no peace. The war is actually begun! The next gale that sweeps from the North will bring to our ears the clash of resounding arms! Our brethren are already in the field! Why stand we here idle? What is it that gentlemen wish? What would they have? Is life so dear, or peace so sweet, as to be purchased at the price of chains and slavery? Forbid it, Almighty God! I know not what course others may take; but as for me, give me liberty, or give me death!

Source: C. M. Depew, ed., *The Library of Oratory* (New York, 1902), 3: 30.

For Further Reading:

Richard Beeman, *Patrick Henry* (New York: McGraw-Hill, 1974).
Robert Middlekauff, *The Glorious Cause* (New York: Oxford University Press, 1982).
Gordon Wood, *The Radicalism of the American Revolution* (New York: Knopf, 1992).

11. Thomas Paine, Excerpt from *Common Sense* (1776)

1776   Thomas Paine writes *Common Sense*; Continental
         Congress adopts Declaration of Independence
1777   British take Philadelphia
1781   Cornwallis surrenders at Yorktown
1783   Treaty of Paris signed

Probably the most succinct and forceful Revolutionary pamphlet was Thomas Paine's Common Sense. *Written in January 1776, it helped push the colonists into open rebellion. Remarkably, Paine, who was a printer by trade and a radical by vocation, managed to capture and articulate the patriot's cause in spite of the fact that he was only a recent émigré to North America. He had not lived through the Stamp Act riots (see document 9) or the boycott of British goods produced by the Townsend Acts. Nor had he been in the colonies to hear the outcry over the Boston Massacre. Yet, probably more*

"Pulling Down the Statue of George III by the Sons of Freedom, at the Bowling Green, New York City, 1776." Engraving by John McRae, 1859 (Library of Congress).

than any other radical pamphleteer, Paine was able to grasp the colonists'
anger and sense of injustice.

Paine's work was forceful, to an extent, because it offered straightforward
reasons for rebelling, from the notion that it was silly for an island to rule
a continent to the claim that the king of England had no legitimate claim to
North America. Common Sense *was powerful, as well, because of its plain,*
simple style. Paine did not cloud his work with tens of references to classical
authors and modern philosophers, relying instead primarily on The Bible
to bolster his case.

Common Sense *was an immediate best seller. Within three months about*
120,000 copies were sold. Within a year close to a half-million copies had
been bought, and hundreds of thousands of other Americans borrowed
someone else's copy or had it read to them. Ironically, Paine's influence was
relatively short-lived. While he played an important role in Pennsylvania
politics during the Revolution, he did not become a national leader. And
after the Revolution he went to live in France, where he wrote another
seminal revolutionary document, The Rights of Man. *Later in life he moved*
back to the United States, where he lived in poverty and obscurity until his
death in 1819.

Introduction

Perhaps the sentiments contained in the following pages, are not *yet*
sufficiently fashionable to procure them general Favor; a long Habit of not
thinking a Thing *wrong*, gives it a superficial appearance of being *right*, and
raises at first a formidable outcry in defence of Custom. But the Tumult
soon subsides. Time makes more Converts than Reason.

As a long and violent abuse of power is generally the means of calling the
right of it in question, (and in matters too which might never have been
thought of, had not the sufferers been aggravated into the inquiry,) and as
the King of England hath undertaken in his *own right*, to support the Parliament in what he calls *Theirs*, and as the good People of this Country are
grievously oppressed by the Combination, they have an undoubted privilege
to enquire into the Pretensions of both, and equally to reject the Usurpation
of *either*.

In the following Sheets, the Author hath studiously avoided every thing
which is personal among ourselves. Compliments as well as censure to individuals make no part thereof. The wise and the worthy need not the
triumph of a Pamphlet; and those whose sentiments are injudicious or unfriendly will cease of themselves, unless too much pains is bestowed upon
their conversions.

The cause of America is in a great measure the cause of all mankind. Many
circumstances have, and will arise, which are not local, but universal, and
through which the principles of all lovers of mankind are affected, and in

the event of which their affections are interested. The laying a country desolate with fire and sword, declaring war against the natural rights of all mankind, and extirpating the defenders thereof from the face of the earth, is the concern of every man to whom nature hath given the power of feeling; of which class, regardless of party censure, is

THE AUTHOR.

Thoughts on the Present State of American Affairs

In the following pages I offer nothing more than simple facts, plain arguments, and common sense: and have no other preliminaries to settle with the reader, than that he will divest himself of prejudice and prepossession, and suffer his reason and his feelings to determine for themselves: that he will put on, or rather that he will not put off, the true character of a man, and generously enlarge his views beyond the present day.

Volumes have been written on the subject of the struggle between England and America. Men of all ranks have embarked in the controversy, from different motives, and with various designs; but all have been ineffectual, and the period of debate is closed. Arms as the last resource decide the contest; the appeal was the choice of the King, and the Continent has accepted the challenge.

It hath been reported of the late Mr. Pelham (who tho' an able minister was not without his faults) that on his being attacked in the House of Commons on the score that his measures were only of a temporary kind, replied, *"they will last my time."* Should a thought so fatal and unmanly possess the Colonies in the present contest, the name of ancestors will be remembered by future generations with detestation.

The Sun never shined on a cause of greater worth. 'Tis not the affair of a City, a County, a Province, or a Kingdom; but of a Continent—of at least one eighth part of the habitable Globe. 'Tis not the concern of a day, a year, or an age; posterity are virtually involved in the contest, and will be more or less affected even to the end of time, by the proceedings now. Now is the seed-time of Continental union, faith and honour. The least fracture now will be like a name engraved with the point of a pin on the tender rind of a young oak; the wound would enlarge with the tree, and posterity read it in full grown characters.

By referring the matter from argument to arms, a new æra for politics is struck—a new method of thinking hath arisen. All plans, proposals, &c. prior to the nineteenth of April, *i.e.* to the commencement of hostilities, are like the almanacks of the last year; which tho' proper then, are superceded and useless now. Whatever was advanced by the advocates on either side of the question then, terminated in one and the same point, viz. a union with Great Britain; the only difference between the parties was the method of effecting it; the one proposing force, the other friendship; but it hath so far happened that the first hath failed, and the second hath withdrawn her influence.

As much hath been said of the advantages of reconciliation, which, like an agreeable dream, hath passed away and left us as we were, it is but right that we should examine the contrary side of the argument, and enquire into some of the many material injuries which these Colonies sustain, and always will sustain, by being connected with and dependent on Great-Britain. To examine that connection and dependence, on the principles of nature and common sense, to see what we have to trust to, if separated, and what we are to expect, if dependant.

I have heard it asserted by some, that as America has flourished under her former connection with Great-Britain, the same connection is necessary towards her future happiness, and will always have the same effect. Nothing can be more fallacious than this kind of argument. We may as well assert that because a child has thrived upon milk, that it is never to have meat, or that the first twenty years of our lives is to become a precedent for the next twenty. But even this is admitting more than is true; for I answer roundly, that America would have flourished as much, and probably much more, had no European power taken any notice of her. The commerce by which she hath enriched herself are the necessaries of life, and will always have a market while eating is the custom of Europe.

But she has protected us, say some. That she hath engrossed us is true, and defended the Continent at our expense as well as her own, is admitted; and she would have defended Turkey from the same motive, *viz.* for the sake of trade and dominion.

Alas! we have been long led away by ancient prejudices and made large sacrifices to superstition. We have boasted the protection of Great Britain, without considering, that her motive was *interest* not *attachment*; and that she did not protect us from *our enemies* on *our account*; but from *her enemies* on *her own account*, from those who had no quarrel with us on any *other account*, and who will always be our enemies on the *same account*. Let Britain waive her pretensions to the Continent, or the Continent throw off the dependance, and we should be at peace with France and Spain, were they at war with Britain. The miseries of Hanover's last war ought to warn us against connections.

It hath lately been asserted in parliament, that the Colonies have no relation to each other but through the Parent Country, *i.e.* that Pennsylvania and the Jerseys, and so on for the rest, are sister Colonies by the way of England; this is certainly a very roundabout way of proving relationship, but it is the nearest and only true way of proving enmity (or enemyship, if I may so call it.) France and Spain never were, nor perhaps ever will be, our enemies as *Americans*, but as our being the *subjects of Great Britain*.

But Britain is the parent country, say some. Then the more shame upon her conduct. Even brutes do not devour their young, nor savages make war upon their families; Wherefore, the assertion, if true, turns to her reproach; but it happens not to be true, or only partly so, and the phrase *parent* or *mother country* hath been jesuitically adopted by the King and his parasites, with a low papistical design of gaining an unfair bias on the credulous weakness of our minds. Europe, and not England, is the parent country of America. This new World hath been the asylum for the persecuted lovers of civil and religious liberty from *every part* of Europe. Hither have they fled, not from the tender embraces of the mother, but from the cruelty of the monster; and it is so far true of England, that the same tyranny which drove the first emigrants from home, pursues their descendants still.

In this extensive quarter of the globe, we forget the narrow limits of three hundred and sixty miles (the extent of England) and carry our friendship on a larger scale, we claim brotherhood with every European Christian, and triumph in the generosity of the sentiment.

It is pleasant to observe by what regular gradations we surmount the force of local prejudices, as we enlarge our acquaintance with the World. A man born in any town in England divided into parishes, will naturally associate most with his fellow parishioners (because their interests in many cases will be common) and distinguish him by the name of *neighbour*; if he meet him but a few miles from home, he drops the narrow idea of a street, and salutes him by the name of *townsman*; if he travel out of the county and meet him in any other, he forgets the minor divisions of street and town, and calls him *countryman, i.e. countyman:* but if in their foreign excursions they should associate in France, or any other part of *Europe*, their local remembrance would be enlarged into that of *Englishmen*. And by a just parity of reasoning, all Europeans meeting in America, or any other quarter of the globe, are *countrymen;* for England, Holland, Germany, or Sweden, when compared with the whole, stand in the same places on the larger scale, which the divisions of street, town, and county do on the smaller ones; Distinctions too limited for Continental minds. Not one third of the inhabitants, even of this province are of English descent. Wherefore, I reprobate the phrase of Parent or Mother Country applied to England only, as being false, selfish, narrow and ungenerous.

But, admitting that we were all of English descent, what does it amount to? Nothing. Britain, being now an open enemy, extinguishes every other name and title: and to say that reconciliation is our duty, is truly farcical. The first king of England, of the present line (William the Conqueror) was a Frenchman, and half the peers of England are descendants from the same country; wherefore, by the same method of reasoning, England ought to be governed by France.

Much hath been said of the united strength of Britain and the Colonies, that in conjunction they might bid defiance to the world: But this is mere presumption; the fate of war is uncertain, neither do the expressions mean any thing; for this continent would never suffer itself to be drained of inhabitants, to support the British arms in either Asia, Africa, or Europe.

Besides, what have we to do with setting the world at defiance? Our plan is commerce, and that, well attended to, will secure us the peace and friendship of all Europe; because it is the interest of all Europe to have America a free port. Her trade will always be a protection, and her barrenness of gold and silver secure her from invaders.

I challenge the warmest advocate for reconciliation to show a single advantage that this continent can reap by being connected with Great Britain. I repeat the challenge; not a single advantage is derived. Our corn will fetch its price in any market in Europe, and our imported goods must be paid for by them where we will.

But the injuries and disadvantages which we sustain by that connection, are without number; and our duty to mankind at large, as well as to ourselves, instruct us to renounce the alliance: because, any submission to, or dependance on, Great Britain, tends directly to involve this Continent in European wars and quarrels, and set us at variance with nations who would otherwise seek our friendship, and against whom we have neither anger nor complaint. As Europe is our market for trade, we ought to form no partial connection with any part of it. It is the true interest of America to steer clear of European contentions, which she never can do, while, by her dependance on Britain, she is made the makeweight in the scale of British politics.

Europe is too thickly planted with Kingdoms to be long at peace, and whenever a war breaks out between England and any foreign power, the trade of America goes to ruin, *because of her connection with Britain.* The next war may not turn out like the last, and should it not, the advocates for reconciliation now will be wishing for separation then, because neutrality in that case would be a safer convoy than a man of war. Everything that is right or reasonable pleads for separation. The blood of the slain, the weeping voice of nature cries. 'TIS TIME TO PART. Even the distance at which the Almighty hath placed England and America is a strong and natural proof that the authority of the one over the other, was never the design of Heaven. The time likewise at which the Continent was discovered, adds weight to the argument, and the manner in which it was peopled, encreases the force of it. The Reformation was preceded by the discovery of America: As if the Almighty graciously meant to open a sanctuary to the persecuted in future years, when home should afford neither friendship nor safety.

The authority of Great Britain over this continent, is a form of government, which sooner or later must have an end: And a serious mind can draw no true pleasure by looking forward, under the painful and positive conviction that what he calls "the present constitution" is merely temporary. As parents, we can have no joy, knowing that this government is not sufficiently lasting to ensure any thing which we may bequeath to posterity: And by a plain method of argument, as we are running the next generation into debt, we ought to do the work of it, otherwise we use them meanly and pitifully. In order to discover the line of our duty rightly, we should take our children in our hand, and fix our station a few years farther into life; that eminence will present a prospect which a few present fears and prejudices conceal from our sight.

Though I would carefully avoid giving unnecessary offence, yet I am inclined to believe, that all those who espouse the doctrine of reconciliation, may be included within the following descriptions.

Interested men, who are not to be trusted, weak men who *cannot* see, prejudiced men who will not see, and a certain set of moderate men who think better of the European world than it deserves; and this last class, by an ill-judged deliberation, will be the cause of more calamities to this Continent than all the other three.

It is the good fortune of many to live distant from the scene of present sorrow; the evil is not sufficiently brought to their doors to make them feel the precariousness with which all American property is possessed. But let our imaginations transport us a few moments to Boston; that seat of wretchedness will teach us wisdom, and instruct us for ever to renounce a power in whom we can have no trust. The inhabitants of that unfortunate city who but a few months ago were in ease and affluence, have now no other alternative than to stay and starve, or turn out to beg. Endangered by the fire of their friends if they continue within the city, and plundered by the soldiery if they leave it, in their present situation they are prisoners without the hope of redemption, and in a general attack for their relief they would be exposed to the fury of both armies.

Men of passive tempers look somewhat lightly over the offences of Great Britain, and, still hoping for the best, are apt to call out, *Come, come, we shall be friends again for all this.* But examine the passions and feelings of mankind: bring the doctrine of reconciliation to the touchstone of nature, and then tell me whether you can hereafter love, honour, and faithfully serve the power that hath carried fire and sword into your land? If you cannot do all these, then are you only deceiving yourselves, and by your delay bringing ruin upon posterity. Your future connection with Britain, whom you can neither love nor honour, will be forced and unnatural, and being formed only on the plan of present convenience, will in a little time fall into a relapse more wretched than the first. But if you say, you can still pass the violations over, then I ask, hath your house been burnt? Hath your property been destroyed before your face? Are your wife and children destitute of a bed to lie on, or bread to live on? Have you lost a parent or a child by their hands, and yourself the ruined and wretched survivor? If you have not, then you are not a judge of those who have. But if you have, and can still shake hands with the murderers, then are you unworthy the name of husband, father, friend, or lover, and whatever may be your rank or title in life, you have the heart of a coward, and the spirit of a sycophant.

This is not inflaming or exaggerating matters, but trying them by those feelings and affections which nature justifies, and without which we should be incapable of discharging the social duties of life, or enjoying the felicities of it. I mean not to exhibit horror for the purpose of provoking revenge, but to awaken us from fatal and unmanly slumbers, that we may pursue determinately some fixed object. 'Tis not in the power of Britain or of Europe to conquer America, if she doth not conquer herself by delay and timidity. The present winter is worth an age if rightly employed, but if lost or neglected the whole Continent will partake of the misfortune; and there is no punishment which that man doth not deserve, be he who, or what, or where he will, that may be the means of sacrificing a season so precious and useful.

'Tis repugnant to reason, to the universal order of things, to all examples from former ages, to suppose that this Continent can long remain subject to any external power. The most sanguine in Britain doth not think so. The utmost stretch of human wisdom cannot, at this time, compass a plan, short of separation, which can promise the continent even a year's security. Reconciliation is *now* a fallacious dream. Nature hath deserted the connection, and art cannot supply her place. For, as Milton wisely expresses, "never can true reconcilement grow where wounds of deadly hate have pierced so deep."

A government of our own is our natural right: and when a man seriously reflects on the precariousness of human affairs, he will become convinced, that it is infinitely wiser and safer, to form a constitution of our own in a cool deliberate manner, while we have it in our power, than to trust such an interesting event to time and chance. If we omit it now, some Massanello may hereafter arise, who, laying hold of popular disquietudes, may collect together the desperate and the discontented, and by assuming to themselves the powers of government, finally sweep away the liberties of the Continent like a deluge. Should the government of America return again into the hands of Britain, the tottering situation of things will be a temptation for some desperate adventurer to try his fortune; and in such a case, what relief can Britain give? Ere she could hear the news, the fatal business might be done; and ourselves suffering like the wretched Britons under the oppression of the Conqueror. Ye that oppose independance now, ye know not what ye do: ye are opening a door to eternal tyranny, by keeping vacant the seat of government. There are thousands and tens of thousands, who would think it glorious to expel from the Continent, that barbarous and hellish power, which hath stirred up the Indians and the Negroes to destroy us; the cruelty hath a double guilt, it is dealing brutally by us, and treacherously by them.

To talk of friendship with those in whom our reason forbids us to have faith, and our affections wounded thro' a thousand pores instruct us to detest, is madness and folly. Every day wears out the little remains of kindred between us and them; and can there be any reason to hope, that as the relationship expires, the affection will encrease, or that we shall agree better when we have ten times more and greater concerns to quarrel over than ever?

Ye that tell us of harmony and reconciliation, can ye restore to us the time that is past? Can ye give to prostitution its former innocence? neither can ye reconcile Britain and America. The last cord now is broken, the people of England are presenting addresses against us. There are injuries which nature cannot forgive; she would cease to be nature if she did. As well can the lover forgive the ravisher of his mistress, as the Continent forgive the murders of Britain. The Almighty hath implanted in us these unextinguishable feelings for good and wise purposes. They are the Guardians of his Image in our hearts. They distinguish us from the herd of common animals. The social compact would dissolve, and justice be extirpated from the earth, or have only a casual existence were we callous to the touches of affection. The robber and the murderer would often escape unpunished, did not the injuries which our tempers sustain, provoke us into justice.

O! ye that love mankind! Ye that dare oppose not only the tyranny but the tyrant, stand forth! Every spot of the old world is overrun with oppression. Freedom hath been hunted round the Globe. Asia and Africa have long expelled her. Europe regards her like a stranger, and England hath given her warning to depart. O! receive the fugitive, and prepare in time an asylum for mankind.

Source: Thomas Paine, *Common Sense* (Philadelphia, 1776).

For Further Reading:

Eric Foner, *Tom Paine and Revolutionary America* (New York: Oxford University Press, 1976).

Alfred Young, ed., *The American Revolution* (Dekalb: Northern Illinois University Press, 1976).

12. Abigail Adams, "Letter to John Adams" (1776)

1776   Abigail Adams calls for equality
1792   Mary Wollstonecraft, *Vindication of the Rights of Women*

Patrick Henry, Thomas Paine, Thomas Jefferson, and other American revolutionaries protested with vehemence against British usurpations of their rights. They demanded full citizenship and asserted that British authorities had no right to make laws and regulations that affected Americans without the consent of the governed. Yet, none of them challenged the supremacy of men over women. None of them saw that the logic of the colonies' rebellion against the Mother Country could be adapted by women to demand greater sexual equality.

Some might feel that this is a ridiculous point since the notion of sexual equality is a modern belief. However, Abigail Smith Adams, the wife of John Adams, a leading revolutionary and second President of the United States, did broach this very argument. Indeed, Abigail Adams, who was also the mother of John Quincy Adams, sixth President of the United States, can be considered the first American feminist and the mother of the women's rights movement.

In a letter to her husband written during the American Revolution, Abigail adopted the logic of the rebellion against Britain into the sphere of relations between the sexes. She warned her husband that women would protest against laws that they had no part in making. She also made note of the hypocrisy of southern planters who espoused a theory of natural rights— that all men were created equal—while they maintained large holdings of slaves.

It should not be surmised that Abigail's thoughts set her against her husband. On the contrary, during long periods of their marriage, when John was absent because of business or politics, Abigail dutifully raised the children, ran the family farm, and managed household affairs. As First Lady, she set the standard that other First Ladies attempted to follow, entertaining guests on a limited budget and advising her husband on political matters, without pay.

Braintree, March 31, 1776

I wish you would ever write me a Letter half as long as I write you; and tell me if you may where your Fleet are gone? What sort of Defence Virginia can make against our common Enemy? Whether it is so situated as to make an able Defence? Are not the Gentery Lords and the common people vassals, are they not like the uncivilized Natives Brittain represents us to be? I hope their Riffel Men who have shewen themselves very savage and even Blood thirsty; are not a specimen of the Generality of the people.

I am willing to allow the Colony great merit for having produced a Washington but they have been shamefully duped by a Dunmore.

I have sometimes been ready to think that the passion for Liberty cannot be Eaquelly Strong in the Breasts of those who have been accustomed to deprive their fellow Creatures of theirs. Of this I am certain that it is not founded upon that generous and christian principal of doing to others as we would that others should do unto us.

Do not you want to see Boston; I am fearfull of the small pox, or I should have been in before this time. I got Mr. Crane to go to our House and see what state it was in. I find it has been occupied by one of the Doctors of a Regiment, very dirty, but no other damage has been done to it. The few things which were left in it are all gone. Crane has the key which he never delivered up. I have wrote to him for it and am determined to get it cleand as soon as possible and shut it up. I look upon it a new acquisition of property, a property which one month ago I did not value at a single Shilling, and could with pleasure have seen it in flames.

The Town in General is left in a better state than we expected, more oweing to a percipitate flight than any Regard to the inhabitants, tho some individuals discovered a sense of honour and justice and have left the rent of the Houses in which they were, for the owners and the furniture unhurt, or if damaged sufficient to make it good.

Others have committed abominable Ravages. The Mansion House of your President is safe and the furniture unhurt whilst both the House and Furniture of the Solisiter General have fallen a prey to their own merciless party. Surely the very Fiends feel a Reverential awe for Virtue and patriotism, whilst they Detest the paricide and traitor.

I feel very differently at the approach of spring to what I did a month ago. We knew not then whether we could plant or sow with safety, whether when we had toild we could reap the fruits of our own industery, whether we could rest in our own Cottages, or whether we should not be driven from the sea coasts to seek shelter in the wilderness, but now we feel as if we might sit under our own vine and eat the good of the land.

I feel a gaieti de Coar to which before I was a stranger. I think the Sun looks brighter, the Birds sing more melodiously, and Nature puts on a more chearfull countanance. We feel a temporary peace, and the poor fugitives are returning to their deserted habitations.

Tho we felicitate ourselves, we sympathize with those who are trembling least the Lot of Boston should be theirs. But they cannot be in similar circumstances unless pusilanimity and cowardise should take possession of them. They have time and warning given them to see the Evil and shun it.—I long to hear that you have declared an independancy—and by the way in the new Code of Laws which I suppose it will be necessary for you to make I desire you would Remember the Ladies, and be more generous and favourable to them than your ancestors. Do not put such unlimited power into the hands of the Husbands. Remember all Men would be tyrants if they could. If perticuliar care and attention is not paid to the Laidies we are determined to foment a Rebelion, and will not hold ourselves bound by any Laws in which we have no voice, or Representation.

That your Sex are Naturally Tyrannical is a Truth so thoroughly established as to admit of no dispute, but such of you as wish to be happy willingly give up the harsh title of Master for the more tender and endearing one of Friend. Why then, not put it out of the power of the vicious and the Lawless to use us with cruelty and indignity with impunity. Men of Sense in all Ages abhor those customs which treat us only as the vassals of your Sex. Regard us then as Beings placed by providence under your protection and in immitation of the Supreem Being make use of that power only for our happiness.

Source: Charles F. Adams, ed., *Familiar Letters of John Adams and His Wife Abigail Adams, During the Revolution* (New York, 1876).

For Further Reading:

Charles Akers, *Abigail Adams* (Boston: Little, Brown, 1980).
Linda G. DePauw, *Founding Mothers* (Boston: Houghton Mifflin, 1975).
Mary Beth Norton, *Liberty's Daughters* (Boston: Little, Brown, 1980).

13. Phillis Wheatley, "To His Excellency General Washington" (1776)

1767   Wheatley has first poem published
1770   Elegy of George Whitfield published
1773   Wheatley manumitted; book of her poems published
1774   Wheatley writes antislavery letters to old tutor
1784   Wheatley dies; buried in unknown grave

Phillis Wheatley's life and works defied the logic of slavery. At age six or seven she was shipped to America from Africa and sold to the Wheatley family of Boston. In 1767, when she was thirteen or fourteen, her first poem was published. Three years later she gained fame through the publication of a poem in memory of the famous Great Awakening minister, George Whitfield. Indeed, Wheatley's genius as a poet was so contrary to the perception of Africans as inferior, that when a book of her poems was published in 1773, it had to be accompanied by a preface written by Boston's leading citizens, including John Hancock. He testified that the poetry was actually hers.

Three years before the Revolution, Phillis Wheatley was manumitted (freed). Over the next three years, as America moved toward declaring its independence, she asserted her political views more openly than she had in the past. In addition to writing odes to famous religious figures, she penned several subtle and sarcastic antislavery letters to her old tutor. When war

The just man shall be in eternal remembrance

The First Poetical Writer of the Race, 1776.

Engraving of Phillis Wheatley (National Archives).

broke out, she wrote one of her most famous poems, "To His Excellency George Washington." The poem did not criticize the institution of slavery, but it did praise the cause for which Washington was fighting. Washington thanked Wheatley for the poem and sent a copy of it to Thomas Paine for publication in his Pennsylvania Magazine.

The remainder of Wheatley's life was not glorious. In 1778 she married John Peters, a free black man. She bore three children, all of whom died in childhood. He had difficulty attaining employment, and she could not get a lengthy book of her poems published. She died at the young age of thirty in 1784.

SIR.

I Have taken the freedom to address your Excellency in the enclosed poem, and entreat your acceptance, though I am not insensible of its inaccuracies. Your being appointed by the Grand Continental Congress to be General-issimo of the armies of North America, together with the fame of your virtues, excite sensations not easy to suppress. Your generosity, therefore, I presume, will pardon the attempt. Wishing your Excellency all possible success in the great cause you are so generously engaged in. I am,
Your Excellency's most obedient humble servant,
PHILLIS WHEATLEY.

Providence, Oct. 26, 1775.
His Excellency Gen. Washington.

> Celestial choir! enthron'd in realms of light,
>   Columbia's scenes of glorious toils I write.
> While freedom's cause her anxious breast alarms,
> She flashes dreadful in refulgent arms.
> See mother earth her offspring's fate bemoan,
> And nations gaze at scenes before unknown!
> See the bright beams of heaven's revolving light
> Involved in sorrows and the veil of night!
>   The goddess comes, she moves divinely fair,
> Olive and laurel binds her golden hair:
> Wherever shines this native of the skies,
> Unnumber'd charms and recent graces rise.
>   Muse! bow propitious while my pen relates
> How pour her armies through a thousand gates,
> As when Eolus heaven's fair face deforms,
> Enwrapp'd in tempest and a night of storms;
> Astonish'd ocean feels the wild uproar,
> The refluent surges beat the sounding shore;
> Or thick as leaves in Autumn's golden reign,
> Such, and so many, moves the warrior's train.
> In bright array they seek the work of war,
> Where high unfurl'd the ensign waves in air.
> Shall I to Washington their praise recite?
> Enough thou know'st them in the fields of fight.
> Thee, first in peace and honours,—we demand
> The grace and glory of thy martial band.
> Fam'd for thy valour, for thy virtues more,

Hear every tongue thy guardian aid implore!
   One century scarce perform'd its destined round,
When Gallic powers Columbia's fury found;
And so may you, whoever dares disgrace
The land of freedom's heaven-defended race!
Fix'd are the eyes of nations on the scales,
For in their hopes Columbia's arm prevails.
Anon Britannia droops the pensive head,
While round increase the rising hills of dead.
Ah! cruel blindness to Columbia's state!
Lament thy thirst of boundless power too late.
   Proceed, great chief, with virtue on thy side,
Thy ev'ry action let the goddess guide.
A crown, a mansion, and a throne that shine,
With gold unfading, WASHINGTON! be thine.

Source: Phillis Wheatley, *Poems on Various Subjects, Religious and Moral* (London, 1786).

For Further Reading:

Ira Berlin and Ronald Hoffman, eds., *Slavery and Freedom in the Age of the American Revolution* (Charlottesville: University Press of Virginia, 1983).

Benjamin Quarles, *The Negro in the American Revolution* (Chapel Hill: University of North Carolina Press, 1961).

PART II
THE EARLY REPUBLIC

14. James Madison, Excerpt from "Federalist Paper No. 10" (1787)

1781   Articles of Confederation ratified
1786–87   Shays' Rebellion
1787   Constitutional Convention (Philadelphia)
1788   Constitution ratified

The Federalist Papers *were a series of eighty-five essays written by Alexander Hamilton, John Jay, and James Madison. They were written with the immediate goal of persuading the citizens of New York to ratify the U.S. Constitution, which had been drafted the summer before in Philadelphia. More broadly, the* Federalist Papers *explained the Constitution, the theory behind it, and some of its particularities. For example, "Federalist Paper No. 10," written by James Madison, a protegee of Thomas Jefferson, dealt with the issue of factionalism, one of the primary concerns of the founders of the Republic. Historically, political theorists had argued that party strife and factionalism posed a deadly threat to republican governments. Indeed, one of the main arguments in favor of a monarchy or a strong central government was that it could overcome factions. Madison, in "Federalist Paper No. 10," countered this argument, contending that the size of the American nation as well as its plethora of interest groups would actually serve to keep the nation together. Since America was so vast and had so many factions, Madison reasoned, no single faction or section could become powerful enough to dominate the whole or could maintain power for long. Hence, rather than spelling the demise of a republican form of government, factionalism, in the American context, was a good thing; it would bolster the checks and balances of the Constitution itself.*

In part because of the arguments of the Federalists, New Yorkers decided to ratify the Constitution. It had already become the law of the land, but the addition of New York strengthened the new nation. Just as importantly, scholars and jurists still use the Federalist Papers *as the primary source for interpreting the Constitution. Since Madison is considered the author of the Constitution itself, his essays are considered especially important.*

Among the numerous advantages promised by a well-constructed Union, none deserves to be more accurately developed than its tendency to break and control the violence of faction. The friend of popular governments never finds himself so much alarmed for their character and fate as when he contemplates their propensity to this dangerous vice. He will not fail, therefore, to set a due value on any plan which, without violating the principles to which he is attached, provides a proper cure for it. . . .

By a faction I understand a number of citizens, whether amounting to a majority or minority of the whole, who are united and actuated by some common impulse of passion, or of interest, adverse to the rights of other citizens, or to the permanent and aggregate interests of the community.

There are two methods of curing the mischiefs of faction: the one, by removing its causes; the other, by controlling its effects.

There are again two methods of removing the causes of faction: the one, by destroying the liberty which is essential to its existence; the other, by giving to every citizen the same opinions, the same passions, and the same interests.

It could never be more truly said than of the first remedy that it was worse than the disease. Liberty is to faction what air is to fire, an aliment without which it instantly expires. But it could not be a less folly to abolish liberty, which is essential to political life, because it nourishes faction than it would be to wish the annihilation of air, which is essential to animal life, because it imparts to fire its destructive agency.

The second expedient is as impracticable as the first would be unwise. As long as the reason of man continues fallible, and he is at liberty to exercise it, different opinions will be formed. As long as the connection subsists between his reason and his self-love, his opinions and his passions will have a reciprocal influence on each other; and the former will be objects to which the latter will attach themselves. The diversity in the faculties of men, from which the rights of property originate, is not less an insuperable obstacle to a uniformity of interests. The protection of these faculties is the first object of government. From the protection of different and unequal faculties of acquiring property, the possession of different degrees and kinds of property immediately results; and from the influence of these on the sentiments and views of the respective proprietors ensues a division of the society into different interests and parties.

The latent causes of faction are thus sown in the nature of man; and we see them everywhere brought into different degrees of activity, according to the different circumstances of civil society. A zeal for different opinions concerning religion, concerning government, and many other points, as well of speculation as of practice; an attachment to different leaders ambitiously contending for pre-eminence and power; or to persons of other descriptions whose fortunes have been interesting to the human passions, have, in turn, divided mankind into parties, inflamed them with mutual animosity, and rendered them much more disposed to vex and oppress each other than to co-operate for their common good. So strong is this propensity of mankind to fall into mutual animosities that where no substantial occasion presents itself the most frivolous and fanciful distinctions have been sufficient to kindle their unfriendly passions and excite their most violent conflicts. But the most common and durable source of factions has been the various and unequal distribution of property. Those who hold and those who are without property have ever formed distinct interests in society. Those who are creditors, and those who are debtors, fall under a like discrimination. A landed interest, a manufacturing interest, a mercantile interest, a moneyed interest, with many lesser interests, grow up of necessity in civilized nations, and divide them into different classes, actuated by different sentiments and views. . . .

. . . Shall domestic manufacturers be encouraged, and in what degree, by restrictions on foreign manufacturers? are questions which would be differently decided by the landed and the manufacturing classes, and probably by neither with a sole regard to justice and the public good. The apportionment of taxes on the various descriptions of property is an act which seems to require the most exact impartiality; yet there is, perhaps, no legislative act in which greater opportunity and temptation are given to a predominant party to trample on the rules of justice. Every shilling with which they overburden the inferior number is a shilling saved to their own pockets.

It is in vain to say that enlightened statesmen will be able to adjust these clashing interests and render them all subservient to the public good. Enlightened statesmen will not always be at the helm. Nor, in many cases, can such an adjustment be made at all without taking into view indirect and remote considerations, which will rarely prevail over the immediate interest which one party may find in disregarding the rights of another or the good of the whole.

The inference to which we are brought is that the *causes* of faction cannot be removed and that relief is only to be sought in the means of controlling its *effects*.

If a faction consists of less than a majority, relief is supplied by the republican principle, which enables the majority to defeat its sinister views by regular vote. It may clog the administration, it may convulse the society; but it will be unable to execute and mask its violence under the forms of the Constitution. When a majority is included in a faction, the form of popular government, on the other hand, enables it to sacrifice to its ruling passion or interest both the public good and the rights of other citizens. To secure the public good and private rights against the danger of such a faction, and at the same time to preserve the spirit and the form of popular government, is then the great object to which our inquiries are directed. . . .

By what means is this object attainable? Evidently by one of two only. Either the existence of the same passion or interest in a majority at the same time must be prevented, or the majority, having such coexistent passion or interest, must be rendered, by their number and local situation, unable to concert and carry into effect schemes of oppression. . . .

. . . [A] pure democracy, by which I mean a society consisting of a small number of citizens, who assemble and administer the government in person, can admit of no cure for the mischiefs of faction. A common passion or interest will, in almost every case, be felt by a majority of the whole; a communication and concert results from the form of government itself; and there is nothing to check the inducements to sacrifice the weaker party or an obnoxious individual. Hence it is that such democracies have ever been spectacles of turbulence and contention; have ever been found incompatible with personal security or the rights of property; and have in general been as short in their lives as they have been violent in their deaths. . . .

A republic, by which I mean a government in which the scheme of representation takes place, opens a different prospect and promises the cure for which we are seeking. Let us examine the points in which it varies from pure democracy, and we shall comprehend both the nature of the cure and the efficacy which it must derive from the Union.

The two great points of difference between a democracy and a republic are: first, the delegation of the government, in the latter, to a small number of citizens elected by the rest; secondly, the greater number of citizens and greater sphere of country over which the latter may be extended.

The effect of the first difference is, on the one hand, to refine and enlarge the public views by passing them through the medium of a chosen body of citizens, whose wisdom may best discern the true interest of their country and whose patriotism and love of justice will be least likely to sacrifice it to temporary or partial considerations. Under such a regulation it may well happen that the public voice, pronounced by the representatives of the people, will be more consonant to the public good than if pronounced by the people themselves, convened for the purpose. On the other hand, the effect may be inverted. Men of factious tempers, of local prejudices, or of sinister designs, may, by intrigue, by corruption, or by other means, first obtain the suffrages, and then betray the interests of the people. . . .

In the first place it is to be remarked that however small the republic may be the representatives must be raised to a certain number in order to guard against the cabals of a few; and that however large it may be they must be limited to a certain number in order to guard against the confusion of a multitude. . . .

In the next place, as each representative will be chosen by a greater number of citizens in the large than in the small republic, it will be more difficult for unworthy candidates to practise with success the vicious arts by which elections are too often carried; and the suffrages of the people being more free, will be more likely to center on men who possess the most attractive merit and the most diffusive and established characters. . . .

The other point of difference is the greater number of citizens and extent of territory which may be brought within the compass of republican than of democratic government; and it is this circumstance principally which renders factious combinations less to be dreaded in the former than in the latter. The smaller the society, the fewer probably will be the distinct parties and interests composing it; the fewer the distinct parties and interests, the more frequently will a majority be found of the same party; and the smaller the number of individuals composing a majority, and the smaller the compass within which they are placed, the more easily will they concert and execute their plans of oppression. Extend the sphere and you take in a greater variety of parties and interests. . . .

The influence of factious leaders may kindle a flame within their particular States but will be unable to spread a general conflagration through the other States. A religious sect may degenerate into a political faction in a part of the Confederacy; but the variety of sects dispersed over the entire face of it must secure the national councils against any danger from that source. A rage for paper money, for an abolition of debts, for an equal division of property, or for any other improper or wicked project, will be less apt to pervade the whole body of the Union than a particular member of it, in the same proportion as such a malady is more likely to taint a particular county or district than an entire State.

In the extent and proper structure of the Union, therefore, we behold a republican remedy for the diseases most incident to republican government.

Source: *The Federalist* (New York, 1901), pp. 44–52.

For Further Reading:

Jackson Turner Main, *The Antifederalists* (Chapel Hill: University of North Carolina Press, 1961).
Forrest McDonald, *E Pluribus Unum* (Boston: Houghton Mifflin, 1965).
Gordon Wood, *The Creation of the American Republic* (Chapel Hill: University of North Carolina Press, 1969).

15. Alexander Hamilton, Excerpt from "Report on Manufacturing" (1791)

1775   Alexander Hamilton joins Continental Army
1786   Hamilton calls for Constitutional Convention in
         Philadelphia
1788–89   Hamilton takes part in Constitutional Convention
         and debate over ratification
1790–91   Hamilton issues "four reports"

Alexander Hamilton was born in 1757 in the West Indies, the illegitimate son of a Scottish aristocrat. His early years were spent in poverty and he

*was orphaned at age thirteen. His luck took a turn for the better in 1772
when he went to live with his relatives in New York. A year later he enrolled
at King's College (Columbia University), where he authored several well-
known revolutionary pamphlets. When the Revolution broke out, Hamilton
joined the Continental Army, becoming General George Washington's aide-
de-camp and, in a sense, the son he never had. After the Revolution Hamilton
continued to play a seminal role in the nation's affairs. He was responsible
for the gathering of delegates in Philadelphia in 1787. Along with Madison
and Jay he wrote the* Federalist Papers *(see document 14). And in 1789 he
became President Washington's Secretary of the Treasury.*

*Hamilton disliked the loose confederation of states under the Articles of
Confederation, the law of the land from 1781 to 1788. In its place he en-
visioned a strong federal or national government. When Washington requested him to develop a domestic agenda for the new nation, Hamilton
turned this vision into a reality. More precisely, Hamilton issued "four
reports," with specific policy recommendations. The first three reports dealt
with the assumption of outstanding war debt, the creation of a national
bank, and the procurement of revenues through federal taxes. Though
strongly opposed by Thomas Jefferson, Washington's Secretary of State, all
three were ultimately enacted by Congress.*

*Hamilton's fourth report, "On Manufacturing," called for the promotion
of industry by the federal government through a system of tariffs, internal
improvements, and government incentives and regulations. It did not become
law, not only because it was opposed by most agrarian interests but also
because it was ahead of its time for the merchant elite who supported Hamilton's other programs. Nonetheless, his policy recommendations gained popularity in the nineteenth century and his vision of a strong federal
government became a mainstay of many progressives.*

It is now proper to proceed a step further, and to enumerate the
principal circumstances, from which it may be inferred that manufacturing
establishments not only occasion a position augmentation of the produce and
revenue of the society, but that they contribute essentially to rendering
them greater than they could possibly be without such establishments. These
circumstances are:

1. The division of labor.

2. An extension of the use of machinery.

3. Additional employment to classes of the community not ordinarily
   engaged in the business.

4. The promoting of emigration from foreign countries.

5. The furnishing greater scope for the diversity of talents and dispositions, which discriminate men from each other.

6. The affording a more ample and various field for enterprise.

7. The creating, in some instances, a new, and securing, in all, a more certain and steady demand for the surplus produce of the soil.

Each of these circumstances has a considerable influence upon the total mass of industrious effort in a community; together, they add to it a degree of energy and effect which is not easily conceived. . . .

1. As to the Division of Labor

It has justly been observed, that there is scarcely any thing of greater moment in the economy of a nation than the proper division of labor. The separation of occupations causes each to be carried to a much greater perfection than it could possibly acquire if they were blended. This arises principally from three circumstances:

1st. The greater skill and dexterity naturally resulting from a constant and undivided application to a single object. It is evident that these properties must increase in proportion to the separation and simplification of objects, and the steadiness of the attention devoted to each; and must be less in proportion to the complication of objects, and the number among which the attention is distracted.

2nd. The economy of time, by avoiding the loss of it, incident to a frequent transition from operation to another of a different nature. This depends on various circumstances; the transition itself, the orderly disposition of the implements, machines, and materials employed in the operation to be relinquished, the preparatory steps to the commencement of a new one, the interruption of the impulse which the mind of the workman acquires from being engaged in a particular operation, the distractions, hesitations, and reluctances which attend the passage from one kind of business to another.

3rd. An extension of the use of machinery. A man occupied on a single object will have it more in his power, and will be more naturally led to exert his imagination, in devising methods to facilitate and abridge labor, than if he were perplexed by a variety of independent and dissimilar operations. Besides this, the fabrication of machines, in numerous instances, becoming itself a distinct trade, the artist who follows it has all the advantages which have been enumerated, for improvement in his particular art; and, in both ways, the invention and application of machinery are extended.

And from these causes united, the mere separation of the occupation of the cultivator from that of the artificer has the effect of augmenting the productive powers of labor, and with them, the total mass of the produce or revenue of a country. In this single view of the subject, therefore, the

utility of artificers or manufacturers, towards promoting an increase of productive industry, is apparent.

2. As to an Extension of the Use of Machinery, A Point Which, Though Partly Anticipated, Requires to Be Placed in One or Two Additional Lights

The employment of machinery forms an item of great importance in the
general mass of national industry. It is an artificial force brought in aid of
the natural force of man; and, to all the purposes of labor, is an increase of
hands, an accession of strength, unencumbered too by the expense of maintaining the laborer. . . .

The cotton mill, invented in England, within the last twenty years, is a
signal illustration of the general proposition which has been just advanced.
In consequence of it, all the different processes for spinning cotton are
performed by means of machines, which are put in motion by water, and
attended chiefly by women and children—and by a smaller number of persons, in the whole, than are requisite in the ordinary mode of spinning. And
it is an advantage of great moment, that the operations of this mill continue
with convenience during the night as well as through the day. The prodigious
effect of such a machine is easily conceived. To this invention is to be
attributed, essentially, the immense progress, which has been so suddenly
made in Great Britain, in the various fabrics of cotton.

3. As to the Additional Employment of Classes of the Community Not Originally Engaged in the Particular Business

This is not among the least valuable of the means by which manufacturing
institutions contribute to augment the general stock of industry and production. In places where those institutions prevail, besides the persons
regularly engaged in them, they afford occasional and extra employment to
industrious individuals and families, who are willing to devote the leisure
resulting from the intermissions of their ordinary pursuits to collateral labours, as a resource for multiplying their acquisitions or their enjoyments.
The husbandman himself experiences a new source of profit and support
from the increased industry of his wife and daughters, invited and stimulated
by the demands of the neighboring manufactories.

Besides this advantage of occasional employment to classes having different
occupations, there is another, of a nature allied to it, and of a similar tendency. This is the employment of persons who would otherwise be idle, and
in many cases a burthen on the community, either from the bias of temper,
habit, infirmity of body, or some other cause, indisposing or disqualifying
them for the toils of the country. It is worthy of particular remark that, in

general, women and children are rendered more useful, and the latter more early useful by manufacturing establishments, than they would otherwise be. Of the number of persons employed in the cotton manufactories of Great Britain, it is computed that four sevenths nearly are women and children, of whom the greatest proportion are children, and many of them of a very tender age. . . .

4. As to the Promoting of Emigration from Foreign Countries

Men reluctantly quit one course of occupation and livelihood for another, unless invited to it by very apparent and proximate advantages. Many who would go from one country to another, if they had a prospect of continuing with more benefit the callings to which they have been educated, will often not be tempted to change their situation by the hope of doing better in some other way. Manufacturers who, listening to the powerful invitations of a better price for their fabrics, or their labor, of greater cheapness of provisions and raw materials, of an exemption from the chief part of the taxes, burthens and restraints, which they endure in the Old World, of greater personal independence and consequence, under the operation of a more equal government, and of what is far more precious than mere religious toleration, a perfect equality of religious privileges, would probably flock from Europe to the United States to pursue their own trades or professions, if they were once made sensible of the advantages they would enjoy, and were inspired with an assurance of encouragement and employment, will with difficulty, be induced to transplant themselves, with a view to becoming cultivators of Land.

If it be true, then, that it is in the interest of the United States to open every possible avenue to immigration from abroad, it affords a weighty argument for the encouragement of manufactures; which, for the reasons just assigned, will have the strongest tendency to multiply the inducements to it. . . .

5. As to the Furnishing Greater Scope for the Diversity of Talents and Dispositions, Which Discriminate Men from Each Other

This is a much more powerful means of augmenting the fund of national industry, than may at first sight appear. It is a just observation, that minds of the strongest and most active powers for their proper objects, fall below mediocrity, and labor without effect, if confined to uncongenial pursuits. And it is thence to be inferred, that the results of human exertion may be immensely increased by diversifying its objects. When all the different kinds of industry obtain in a community, each individual can find his proper element, and can call into activity the whole vigor of his nature. And the community is benefited by the services of its respective members, in the manner in which each can serve it with most effect.

If there be any thing in a remark often to be met with, namely, that there is, in the genius of the people of this country, a peculiar aptitude for mechanic improvements, it would operate as a forcible reason for giving opportunities to the exercise of that species of talent, by the propagation of manufactures.

6. As to the Affording a More Ample and Various Field for Enterprise

... To cherish and stimulate the activity of the human mind, by multiplying the objects of enterprise, is not among the least considerable of the expedients by which the wealth of a nation may be promoted. Even things in themselves not positively advantageous sometimes become so, by their tendency to provoke exertion. Every new scene which is opened to the busy nature of man to rouse and exert itself, is the addition of a new energy to the general stock of effort.

The spirit of enterprise, useful and prolific as it is, must necessarily be contracted or expanded, in proportion to the simplicity or variety of the occupations and productions which are to be found in a society. It must be less in a nation of mere cultivators, than in a nation of cultivators and merchants; less in a nation of cultivators and merchants, than in a nation of cultivators, artificers and merchants.

7. As to the Creating, in Some Instances, a New, and Securing in All, a More Certain and Steady Demand for the Surplus Produce of the Soil

This is among the most important of the circumstances which have been indicated. It is a principal means by which the establishment of manufactures contributes to an augmentation of the produce or revenue of a country, and has an immediate and direct relation to the prosperity of agriculture.

It is evident that the exertions of the husbandman will be steady or fluctuating, vigorous or feeble, in proportion to the steadiness or fluctuation, adequateness or inadequateness, of the markets on which he must depend for the vent [selling] of the surplus which may be produced by his labor; and that such surplus, in the ordinary course of things, will be greater or less in the same proportion.

For the purpose of this vent, a domestic market is greatly to be preferred to a foreign one; because it is, in the nature of things, far more to be relied upon.

Source: Henry Cabot Lodge, ed., *The Works of Alexander Hamilton* (New York, 1904), 4: 70–198.

For Further Reading:

Forrest McDonald, *Alexander Hamilton* (New York: Norton, 1979).
John C. Miller, *The Federalist Era, 1789–1801* (New York: Harper & Row, 1960).

16. George Washington, Excerpt from "Farewell Address" (1796)

1775	Washington appointed Commander of Continental Army
1787	Washington serves as chair of Constitutional Convention
1788	Washington elected first President
1792	Washington elected to second term
1796	Washington's "Farewell Address"

For nearly half a century George Washington, a Virginia planter and politician, played an extraordinary role in American affairs. During the French-Indian War he was one of the colonies' top commanders. As a member of the Virginia House of Burgess and later the Continental Congress he promoted the cause of the Revolution. In May 1775 he was unanimously selected to command the Continental Army. In 1788 he was unanimously elected as the new nation's first President.

As President, Washington largely delegated authority to his top cabinet members, Hamilton and Jefferson. When frontier farmers challenged the government's tax on whiskey, Washington donned his old army gear and led nearly 13,000 troops into western Pennsylvania to put down the rebellion. While disagreements between Hamilton and Jefferson over the nature and role of the federal government were sharp, generally Washington himself stood above public criticism.

Shortly after deciding not to seek a third term, which set a precedent that others followed for nearly 150 years, Washington delivered his "Farewell Address." The speech examined several issues: America's role in international affairs, political parties, and sectionalism. Washington cautioned against having permanent alliances or foreign enemies. He warned against the formation of political parties and sectional strife. He did not, however, express concern over the possible source of the latter, namely slavery. Indeed, as a planter, as chair of the Constitutional Convention, and as President, Washington displayed his willingness to live with this undemocratic institution. This was his and the young nation's most serious flaw and would prove much more threatening to the nation than party factionalism or foreign affairs.

George Washington Takes the Oath. Drawn by H. A. Ogden (Library of Congress).

The period for a new election of a citizen to administer the executive government of the United States being not far distant, and the time actually arrived when your thoughts must be employed in designating the person who is to be clothed with that important trust, it appears to me proper, especially as it may conduce to a more distinct expression of the public voice, that I should now apprise you of the resolution I have formed to decline being considered among the number of those out of whom a choice is to be made. . . .

The unity of government which constitutes you one people is also now dear to you. It is justly so, for it is a main pillar in the edifice of your real independence, the support of your tranquillity at home, your peace abroad, of your safety, of your prosperity, of that very liberty which you so highly prize. But as it is easy to foresee that from different causes and from different quarters much pains will be taken, many artifices employed, to weaken in your minds the conviction of this truth, as this is the point in your political fortress against which the batteries of internal and external enemies will be most constantly and actively (though often covertly and insidiously) directed, it is of infinite moment that you should properly estimate the immense value of your national union to your collective and individual happiness; that you should cherish a cordial, habitual, and immovable attachment to it; accustoming yourselves to think and speak of it as of the palladium of your political safety and prosperity; watching for its preservation with jealous anxiety; discountenancing whatever may suggest even a suspicion that it can in any event be abandoned, and indignantly frowning upon the first dawning of every attempt to alienate any portion of our country from the rest or to enfeeble the sacred ties which now link together the various parts.

For this you have every inducement of sympathy and interest. Citizens by birth or choice of a common country, that country has a right to concentrate your affections. The name of American, which belongs to you in your national capacity, must always exalt the just pride of patriotism more than any appellation derived from local discriminations. With slight shades of difference, you have the same religion, manners, habits, and political principles. You have in a common cause fought and triumphed together. The independence and liberty you possess are the work of joint councils and joint efforts, of common dangers, sufferings, and successes. . . .

In contemplating the causes which may disturb our union it occurs as matter of serious concern that any ground should have been furnished for characterizing parties by *geographical* discriminations—*Northern* and *Southern, Atlantic* and *Western*—whence designing men may endeavor to excite a belief that there is a real difference of local interests and views. One of the expedients of party to acquire influence within particular districts is to misrepresent the opinions and aims of other districts. You can not shield yourselves too much against the jealousies and heartburnings which spring from these misrepresentations; they tend to render alien to each other those who ought to be bound together by fraternal affection. . . .

To the efficacy and permanency of your union a government for the whole is indispensable. No alliances, however strict, between the parts can be an adequate substitute. They must inevitably experience the infractions and interruptions which all alliances in all times have experienced. Sensible of this momentous truth, you have improved upon your first essay by the adoption of a Constitution of government better calculated than your former for an intimate union and for the efficacious management of your common concerns. This government, the offspring of our own choice, uninfluenced and unawed, adopted upon full investigation and mature deliberation, completely free in its principles, in the distribution of its powers, uniting security with energy, and containing within itself a provision for its own amendment, has a just claim to your confidence and your support. Respect for its authority, compliance with its laws, acquiescence in its measures, are duties enjoined by the fundamental maxims of true liberty. The basis of our political systems is the right of the people to make and to alter their constitutions of government. But the constitution which at any time exists till changed by an explicit and authentic act of the whole people is sacredly obligatory upon all. The very idea of the power and the right of the people to establish government presupposes the duty of every individual to obey the established government. . . .

Toward the preservation of your government and the permanency of your present happy state, it is requisite not only that you steadily discountenance irregular oppositions to its acknowledged authority, but also that you resist with care the spirit of innovation upon its principles, however specious the pretexts. One method of assault may be to effect in the forms of the Constitution alterations which will impair the energy of the system, and thus to undermine what can not be directly overthrown. In all the changes to which you may be invited remember that time and habit are at least as necessary to fix the true character of governments as of other human institutions; that experience is the surest standard by which to test the real tendency of the existing constitution of a country; that facility in changes upon the credit of mere hypothesis and opinion exposes to perpetual change, from the endless variety of hypothesis and opinion; and remember especially that for the efficient management of your common interests in a country so extensive as ours a government of as much vigor as is consistent with the perfect security of liberty is indispensable. . . .

I have already intimated to you the danger of parties in the state, with particular reference to the founding of them on geographical discriminations. Let me now take a more comprehensive view, and warn you in the most solemn manner against the baneful effects of the spirit of party generally.

This spirit, unfortunately, is inseparable from our nature, having its root in the strongest passions of the human mind. It exists under different shapes in all governments, more or less stifled, controlled, or repressed; but in those of the popular form it is seen in its greatest rankness and is truly their worst enemy. . . .

It serves always to distract the public councils and enfeeble the public administration. It agitates the community with illfounded jealousies and false alarms; kindles the animosity of one part against another; foments occasionally riot and insurrection. It opens the door to foreign influence and corruption, which find a facilitated access to the government itself through the channels of party passion. Thus the policy and the will of one country are subjected to the policy and will of another. . . .

Of all the dispositions and habits which lead to political prosperity, religion and morality are indispensable supports. In vain would that man claim the tribute of patriotism who should labor to subvert these great pillars of human happiness—these firmest props of the duties of men and citizens. The mere politician, equally with the pious man, ought to respect and to cherish them. A volume could not trace all their connections with private and public felicity. Let it simply be asked, Where is the security for property, for reputation, for life, if the sense of religious obligation *desert* the oaths which are the instruments of investigation in courts of justice? And let us with caution indulge the supposition that morality can be maintained without religion. Whatever may be conceded to the influence of refined education on minds of peculiar structure, reason and experience both forbid us to expect that national morality can prevail in exclusion of religious principle.

It is substantially true that virtue or morality is a necessary spring of popular government. The rule indeed extends with more or less force to every species of free government. Who that is a sincere friend to it can look with indifference upon attempts to shake the foundation of the fabric? Promote, then, as an object of primary importance, institutions for the general diffusion of knowledge. In proportion as the structure of a government gives force to public opinion, it is essential that public opinion should be enlightened.

As a very important source of strength and security, cherish public credit. One method of preserving it is to use it as sparingly as possible, avoiding occasions of expense by cultivating peace, but remembering also that timely disbursements to prepare for danger frequently prevent much greater disbursements to repel it; avoiding likewise the accumulation of debt, not only by shunning occasions of expense, but by vigorous exertions in time of peace to discharge the debts which unavoidable wars have occasioned, not ungenerously throwing upon prosperity the burthen which we ourselves ought to bear. . . .

Against the insidious wiles of foreign influence (I conjure you to believe me, fellow-citizens) the jealousy of a free people ought to be *constantly* awake, since history and experience prove that foreign influence is one of the most baneful foes of republican government. But that jealousy, to be useful, must be impartial, else it becomes the instrument of the very influence to be avoided, instead of a defense against it. Excessive partiality for one foreign nation and excessive dislike of another cause those whom that actuate to see danger only on one side, and serve to veil and even second the arts of influence on the other. Real patriots who may resist the intrigues of the favorite are liable to become suspected and odious, while its tools and dupes usurp the applause and confidence of the people to surrender their interests.

The great rule of conduct for us in regard to foreign nations is, in extending our commercial relations to have with them as little *political* connection as possible. So far as we have already formed engagements let them be fulfilled with perfect good faith. Here let us stop.

Europe has a set of primary interests which to us have none or a very remote relation. Hence she must be engaged in frequent controversies, the causes of which are essentially foreign to our concerns. Hence, therefore, it must be unwise in us to implicate ourselves to artificial ties in the ordinary vicissitudes of her politics or the ordinary combinations and collisions of her friendships or enmities.

Our detached and distant situation invites and enables us to pursue a different course. If we remain one people, under an efficient government, the period is not far off when we may defy material injury from external annoyance; when we may take such an attitude as will cause the neutrality we may at any time resolve upon to be scrupulously respected; when belligerent nations, under the impossibility of making acquisitions upon us, will not lightly hazard the giving us provocation; when we may choose peace or war, as our interest, guided by justice, shall counsel.

Why forego the advantages of so peculiar a situation? Why quit our own to stand upon foreign ground? Why, by interweaving our destiny with that of any part of Europe, entangle our peace and prosperity in the toils of European ambition, rivalship, interest, humor, or caprice? . . .

Though in reviewing the incidents of my administration I am unconscious of intentional error, I am nevertheless too sensible of my defects not to think it probable that I may have committed many errors. Whatever they may be, I fervently beseech the Almighty to avert or mitigate the evils to which they may tend. I shall also carry with me the hope that my country will never cease to view them with indulgence, and that, after forty-five years of my life dedicated to its service with an upright zeal, the faults of incompetent abilities will be consigned to oblivion, as myself must soon be to the mansions of rest.

Relying on its kindness in this as in other things, and actuated by that fervent love toward it which is so natural to a man who views in it the native soil of himself and his progenitors for several generations, I anticipate with pleasing expectation that retreat in which I promise myself to realize without alloy the sweet enjoyment of partaking in the midst of my fellow-citizens the benign influence of good laws under a free government—the ever-favorite object of my heart, and the happy reward, as I trust, of our mutual cares, labors, and dangers.

Source: James D. Richardson, ed., *Messages and Papers of the Presidents* (Washington, D.C., 1897), 1:223–24.

For Further Reading:

John R. Alden, *George Washington* (Baton Rouge: Louisiana State University Press, 1984).

James T. Flexner, *Washington* (Boston: Little, Brown, 1972).

17. Thomas Jefferson, "First Inaugural Address" (1801)

1796 John Adams elected President
1798 Alien and Sedition Acts
1800 Jefferson defeats Adams for the presidency
1801 Jefferson inaugurated

Thomas Jefferson termed his election as President "the revolution of 1800." Considering that John Adams had been his prerevolutionary colleague and carried on a lengthy and friendly correspondence with him in their senior years, this claim, on first glance, doesn't make sense. Yet the early years of the Republic, especially after Washington's retirement, produced deep conflicts among the body politic. On one side stood the Federalists, devotees of Alexander Hamilton's vision of the federal government as a strong and active body. On the other side stood the Democratic-Republicans, followers of Thomas Jefferson and his goal of a small and restrained nation state. Differences over foreign affairs, fueled by the French Revolution, and battles over the limits of dissent and freedom of the press, culminating with the Alien and Sedition Acts, which limited freedom of speech and the rights of the foreign-born, exacerbated tensions. Ironically, when the election of 1800 was thrown into the House of Representatives, it was up to the House, led by Alexander Hamilton, to grant Jefferson the victory. (Because of a fluke in the way in which the Electoral College's votes were counted, Jefferson and his running mate, Aaron Burr, tied for first. After the election the election laws were changed so that the electors could distinguish between their votes for President and Vice-President.)

Jefferson's first act as President was his delivery of the "Inaugural Ad-

dress." In it he emphasized those things that the Hamiltonians and Jeffer-
sonians held in common, their faith in a republican form of government and
the individual freedoms embodied in the Bill of Rights. Though the two
parties continued to feud, the willingness of the Federalists to hand power
to the Democratic-Republicans without a fight, suggested that Jefferson cor-
rectly identified those ideals that Americans shared.

Called upon to undertake the duties of the first executive office of
our country, I avail myself of the presence of that portion of my fellow-
citizens which is here assembled to express my grateful thanks for the favor
with which they have been pleased to look toward me, to declare a sincere
consciousness that the task is above my talents, and that I approach it with
those anxious and awful presentiments which the greatness of the charge
and the weakness of my powers so justly inspire. A rising nation, spread
over a wide and fruitful land, traversing all the seas with the rich productions
of their industry, engaged in commerce with nations who feel power and
forget right, advancing rapidly to destinies beyond the reach of mortal eyes—
when I contemplate these transcendent objects, and see the honor, the
happiness, and the hopes of this beloved country committed to the issue
and the auspices of this day, I shrink from the contemplation, and humble
myself before the magnitude of the undertaking. Utterly, indeed, should I
despair did not the presence of many whom I here see remind me that in
the other high authorities provided by our Constitution I shall find resources
of wisdom, of virtue, and of zeal on which to rely under all difficulties. To
you, then, gentlemen, who are charged with the sovereign functions of
legislation, and to those associated with you, I look with encouragement for
that guidance and support which may enable us to steer with safety the
vessel in which we are all embarked amidst the conflicting elements of a
troubled world.

During the contest of opinion through which we have passed the animation
of discussions and of exertions has sometimes worn an aspect which might
impose on strangers unused to think freely and to speak and to write what
they think; but this being now decided by the voice of the nation, announced
according to the rules of the Constitution, all will, of course, arrange themselves under the will of the law, and unite in common efforts for the common
good. All, too, will bear in mind this sacred principle, that though the will
of the majority is in all cases to prevail, that will to be rightful must be
reasonable; that the minority possess their equal rights, which equal law
must protect, and to violate would be oppression. Let us, then, fellow-
citizens, unite with one heart and one mind. Let us restore to social intercourse that harmony and affection without which liberty and even life itself
are but dreary things. And let us reflect that, having banished from our land

that religious intolerance under which mankind so long bled and suffered, we have yet gained little if we countenance a political intolerance as despotic, as wicked, and capable of as bitter and bloody persecutions. During the throes and convulsions of the ancient world, during the agonizing spasms of infuriated man, seeking through blood and slaughter his long-lost liberty, it was not wonderful that the agitation of the billows should reach even this distant and peaceful shore; that this should be more felt and feared by some and less by others, and should divide opinions as to measures of safety. But every difference of opinion is not a difference of principle. We have called by different names brethren of the same principle. We are all Republicans, we are all Federalists. If there be any among us who would wish to dissolve this Union or to change its republican form, let them stand undisturbed as monuments of the safety with which error of opinion may be tolerated where reason is left free to combat it. I know, indeed, that some honest men fear that a republican government can not be strong, that this Government is not strong enough; but would the honest patriot, in the full tide of successful experiment, abandon a government which has so far kept us free and firm on the theoretic and visionary fear that this Government, the world's best hope, may by possibility want energy to preserve itself? I trust not. I believe this, on the contrary, the strongest Government on earth. I believe it the only one where every man, at the call of the law, would fly to the standard of the law, and would meet invasions of the public order as his own personal concern. Sometimes it is said that man can not be trusted with government of himself. Can he, then, be trusted with the government of others? Or have we found angels in the forms of kings to govern him? Let history answer this question.

Let us, then, with courage and confidence pursue our own Federal and Republican principles, our attachment to union and representative government. Kindly separated by nature and a wide ocean from the exterminating havoc of one quarter of the globe; too high-minded to endure the degradations of the others; possessing a chosen country, with room enough for our descendants to the thousandth and thousandth generation; entertaining a due sense of our own faculties, to the acquisitions of our own industry, to honor and confidence from our fellow-citizens, resulting not from birth, but from our actions and their sense of them; enlightened by a benign religion, professed, indeed, and practiced in various forms, yet all of them inculcating honesty, truth, temperance, gratitude, and the love of man; acknowledging and adoring an overruling Providence, which by all its dispensations proves that it delights in the happiness of man here and his greater happiness hereafter—with all these blessings, what more is necessary to make us a happy and prosperous people? Still one thing more, fellow-citizens—a wise and frugal Government, which shall restrain men from injuring one another, shall leave them otherwise free to regulate their own pursuits of industry and improvement, and shall not take from the mouth of labor the bread it has earned. This is the sum of good government, and this is necessary to close the circle of our felicities.

About to enter, fellow-citizens, on the exercise of duties which comprehend everything dear and valuable to you, it is proper you should understand what I deem the essential principles of our Government, and consequently those which ought to shape its Administration. I will compress them within the narrowest compass they will bear, stating the general principle, but not all its limitations. Equal and exact justice to all men, of whatever state or persuasion, religious or political; peace, commerce, and honest friendship with all nations, entangling alliances with none; the support of the State governments in all their rights, as the most competent administrations for our domestic concerns and the surest bulwarks against antirepublican tendencies; the preservation of the General Government in its whole constitutional vigor, as the sheet anchor of our peace at home and safety abroad; a jealous care of the right of election by the people—a mild and safe corrective of abuses which are lopped by the sword of revolution where peaceable remedies are unprovided; absolute acquiescence in the decisions of the majority, the vital principle of republics, from which is no appeal but to force, the vital principle and immediate parent of despotism; a well-disciplined militia, our best reliance in peace and for the first moments of war, till regulars may relieve them; the supremacy of the civil over the military authority; economy in the public expense, that labor may be lightly burthened; the honest payment of our debts and sacred preservation of the public faith; encouragement of agriculture, and of commerce as its handmaid; the diffusion of information and arraignment of all abuses at the bar of the public reason; freedom of religion; freedom of the press, and freedom of person under the protection of the habeas corpus, and trial by juries impartially selected. These principles form the bright constellation which has gone before us and guided our steps through an age of revolution and reformation. The wisdom of our sages and blood of our heroes have been devoted to their attainment. They should be the creed of our political faith, the text of civic instruction, the touchstone by which to try the services of those we trust; and should we wander from them in moments of error or of alarm, let us hasten to retrace our steps and to regain the road which alone leads to peace, liberty, and safety.

I repair, then, fellow-citizens, to the post you have assigned me. With experience enough in subordinate offices to have seen the difficulties of this the greatest of all, I have learnt to expect that it will rarely fall to the lot of imperfect man to retire from this station with the reputation and the favor which bring him into it. Without pretentions to that high confidence you reposed in our first and greatest revolutionary character, whose preeminent services had entitled him to the first place in his country's love and destined for him the fairest page in the volume of faithful history, I ask so much confidence only as may give firmness and effect to the legal administration of your affairs. I shall often go wrong through defect of judgment. When right, I shall often be thought wrong by those whose positions will not command a view of the whole ground. I ask your indulgence for my own errors, which will never be intentional, and your support against the errors of others, who may condemn what they would not if seen in all its parts. The approbation implied by your suffrage is a great consolation to me for the past, and my future solicitude will be to retain the good opinion of those who have bestowed it in advance, to conciliate that of others by doing them all the good in my power, and to be instrumental to the happiness and freedom of all.

Relying, then, on the patronage of your good will, I advance with obedience to the work, ready to retire from it whenever you become sensible how much better choice it is in your power to make. And may that infinite Power which rules the destinies of the universe lead our councils to what is best, and give them a favorable issue for your peace and prosperity.

Source: James D. Richardson, ed., *Messages and Papers of the Presidents* (Washington, D.C., 1897), 1:309–12.

For Further Reading:

Lance Banning, *The Jeffersonian Persuasion* (Ithaca, N.Y.: Cornell University Press, 1978).
Dumas Malone, *Jefferson and His Times*, 6 vols. (Boston: Little, Brown, 1948–81).
Merrill Peterson, *Thomas Jefferson and the New Nation* (New York: Oxford University Press, 1970).

18. *Marbury v. Madison*, "Opinion by John Marshall" (1803)

1801   Judiciary Act; Midnight Appointments; John Marshall
        appointed Chief Justice of Supreme Court
1803   *Marbury v. Madison*
1804   House impeaches Judges Pickering and Chase
1819   *McCullock v. Maryland*

Although the Federalists ceded power to the Jeffersonians in 1801, they sought both before and after Jefferson's inauguration to maintain a strong federal government. Since they did not control either the executive or the legislative branch, their main means for promoting their vision lay with the judicial branch. Shortly before leaving office, the Federalist-controlled Con-

gress passed the Judiciary Act, which enabled President John Adams to expand the power of the federal courts and appoint a number of new Federalists to the bench, including John Marshall. After assuming power, the Jeffersonians sought to undo these actions. The House of Representatives impeached Federal District Judge John Pickering and Supreme Court Justice Samuel Chase, both fervid opponents of the Jeffersonians, and the Senate convicted Pickering, although he had not committed any crimes.

Out of the dispute between the two parties arose one of the most famous court cases in U.S. history, Marbury v. Madison. The facts of the case pale in comparison to the reasoning of John Marshall, who delivered the opinion of the Court. Marshall, a Virginian like Jefferson, sought to mold the judicial branch into an equal of the other two branches of government. At the time it was not so. In his opinion, he argued that the Supreme Court had the authority to interpret the Constitution, or more precisely it held the right of judicial review. In other words, he contended that the Court could act as a powerful check on the two elected branches of government.

Although the Court did not actually strike down a law in Marbury and ruled in favor of the Jefferson administration, with its decision it clearly increased its own power and promoted the Hamiltonian vision of a stronger central government. In subsequent years the Supreme Court under Marshall's leadership upheld the supremacy of federal laws over states' rights and increased the prestige of the Court. While some considered these developments a threat to the Republic, today most would argue that a strong Court is crucial to the health of democracy.

The question whether an act repugnant to the constitution can become the law of the land is a question deeply interesting to the United States; but, happily not of an intricacy proportioned to its interest. It seems only necessary to recognize certain principles supposed to have been long and well established, to decide it.

That the people have an original right to establish for their future government such principles as, in their opinion, shall most conduce to their own happiness, is the basis on which the whole American fabric has been erected. The exercise of this original right is a very great exertion, nor can it nor ought it to be frequently repeated. The principles therefore so established are deemed fundamental. And as the authority from which they proceed is supreme and can seldom act, they are designed to be permanent.

This original and supreme will organizes the government, and assigns to different departments their respective powers. It may either stop here or establish certain limits not to be transcended by those departments.

The government of the United States is of the latter description. The powers of the legislature are defined and limited; and that those limits may not be mistaken or forgotten, the constitution is written. To what purpose are powers limited, and to what purpose is that limitation committed to writing, if these limits may, at any time, be passed by those intended to be restrained? The distinction between a government with limited and unlimited powers is abolished if those limits do not confine the persons on whom they are imposed and if acts prohibited and acts allowed are of equal obligation. It is a proposition too plain to be contested, that the constitution controls any legislative act repugnant to it, or, that the legislature may alter the constitution by an ordinary act.

Between these alternatives there is no middle ground. The constitution is either a superior paramount law, unchangeable by ordinary means, or it is on a level with ordinary legislative acts, and, like other acts, is alterable when the legislature shall please to alter it.

If the former part of the alternative be true, then a legislative act contrary to the constitution is not law; if the latter part be true, then written constitutions are absurd attempts, on the part of the people, to limit a power in its own nature illimitable.

Certainly all those who have framed written constitutions contemplate them as forming the fundamental and paramount law of the nation, and consequently the theory of every such government must be that an act of the legislature repugnant to the constitution is void.

This theory is essentially attached to a written constitution, and is consequently to be considered, by this court, as one of the fundamental principles of our society. It is not, therefore, to be lost sight of in the further consideration of this subject.

If an act of the legislature repugnant to the constitution is void, does it, notwithstanding its invalidity, bind the courts and oblige them to give it effect? Or, in other words, though it be not law, does it constitute a rule as operative as if it was a law? This would be to overthrow in fact what was established in theory, and would seem, at first view, an absurdity too gross to be insisted on. It shall, however, receive a more attentive consideration.

It is emphatically the province and duty of the judicial department to say what the law is. Those who apply the rule to particular cases must of necessity expound and interpret that rule. If two laws conflict with each other, the courts must decide on the operation of each.

So if a law be in opposition to the constitution; if both the law and the constitution apply to a particular case, so that the court must either decide that case conformably to the law, disregarding the constitution, or conformably to the constitution, disregarding the law, the court must determine which of these conflicting rules governs the case. This is of the very essence of judicial duty.

If, then, the courts are to regard the constitution, and the constitution is superior to any ordinary act of the legislature, the constitution, and not such ordinary act, must govern the case to which they both apply.

Those, then, who controvert the principle that the constitution is to be considered in court as a paramount law, are reduced to the necessity of maintaining that courts must close their eyes on the constitution and see only the law.

This doctrine would subvert the very foundation of all written constitutions. It would declare that an act which, according to the principles and theory of our government, is entirely void, is yet, in practice, completely obligatory. It would declare that if the legislature shall do what is expressly forbidden, such act, notwithstanding the express prohibition, is in reality effectual. It would be giving to the legislature a practical and real omnipotence with the same breath which professes to restrict their powers within narrow limits. It is prescribing limits and declaring that those limits may be passed at pleasure.

That it thus reduces to nothing what we have deemed the greatest improvement on political institutions, a written constitution, would of itself be sufficient, in America, where written constitutions have been viewed with so much reverence, for rejecting the construction. But the peculiar expressions of the constitution of the United States furnish additional arguments in favor of its rejection.

The judicial power of the United States is extended to all cases arising under the constitution.

Could it be the intention of those who gave this power to say that in using it the constitution should not be looked into? That a case arising under the constitution should be decided without examining the instrument under which it arises?

This is too extravagant to be maintained.

In some cases, then, the constitution must be looked into by the judges. And if they can open it at all, what part of it are they forbidden to read or to obey?

There are many other parts of the constitution which serve to illustrate this subject.

It is declared that "no tax or duty shall be laid on articles exported from any state." Suppose a duty on the export of cotton, of tobacco, or of flour, and a suit instituted to recover it, ought judgment to be rendered in such a case? Ought the judges to close their eyes on the constitution, and only see the law?

The constitution declares "that no bill of attainder of *ex post facto* law shall be passed." If, however, such a bill should be passed, and a person should be prosecuted under it, must the court condemn to death those victims whom the constitution endeavors to preserve?

"No person," says the constitution, "shall be convicted of treason unless on the testimony of two witnesses to the same overt act, or on confession in open court."

Here the language of the constitution is addressed especially to the courts. It prescribes, directly for them, a rule of evidence not to be departed from.

If the legislature should change that rule, and declare one witness, or a confession out of court, sufficient for conviction, must the constitutional principle yield to the legislative act?

From these, and many other selections which might be made, it is apparent that the framers of the constitution contemplated that instrument as a rule for the government of *courts*, as well as of the legislature. Why otherwise does it direct the judges to take an oath to support it? This oath certainly applies in an especial manner to their conduct in their official character. How immoral to impose it on them if they were to be used as the instruments, and the knowing instruments, for violating what they swear to support!

The oath of office, too, imposed by the legislature, is completely demonstrative of the legislative opinion on this subject. It is in these words: "I do solemnly swear that I will administer justice without respect to persons, and do equal right to the poor and to the rich; and that I will faithfully and impartially discharge all the duties incumbent on me as ——, according to the best of my abilities and understanding, agreeably to *the constitution* and laws of the United States." Why does a judge swear to discharge his duties agreeably to the constitution of the United States, if that constitution forms no rule for his government—if it is closed upon him, and cannot be inspected by him?

If such be the real state of things, this is worse than solemn mockery. To prescribe, or to take this oath, becomes equally a crime.

It is also not entirely unworthy of observation, that in declaring what shall be the *supreme* law of the land, the constitution itself is first mentioned, and not the laws of the United States generally, but those only which shall be made in *pursuance* of the constitution, have that rank.

Thus, the particular phraseology of the constitution of the United States confirms and strengthens the principle, supposed to be essential to all written constitutions, that a law repugnant to the constitution is void, and that courts, as well as other departments, are bound by that instrument.

Source: *Marbury v. Madison*, I Cranch, 137 (1803).

For Further Reading:

Leonard Baker, *John Marshall* (New York: Macmillan, 1974).

Morton J. Horwitz, *The Transformation of American Law* (New York: Oxford University Press, 1977).

19. Meriwether Lewis, Excerpt from "Report to Thomas Jefferson" (1806)

1803   Louisiana Purchase
1804   Lewis and Clark set out from St. Louis
1805   President Jefferson receives Lewis' first report
1805–1806   Zebulon Pike explores passage to Far West

In 1803 the United States purchased the Louisiana Territory, stretching from the Mississippi River to the Rocky Mountains, from France for a mere $15 million. By doing so, Jefferson nearly doubled the size of the nation and promoted his vision of America as a decentralized agrarian republic populated by a large class of yeoman farmers. Jefferson also gained tremendous popular backing for the action, winning all but one Electoral College vote in the ensuing presidential election.

Shortly after the deal was finalized, Jefferson commissioned Meriwether Lewis, his one-time personal secretary, and William Clark, a veteran of the frontier, to lead an expedition to explore the Pacific Northwest. This adventure had both commercial and scientific goals. It sought to improve America's understanding of the terrain and vegetation and to uncover goods and routes for trade.

In the spring of 1804, Lewis and Clark and their "corps of discovery," consisting of about fifty men and a few women, including Sacajawea, a Shoshone Indian, and Toussaint Charbonneau, a French Canadian trapper, as guides and interpreters, set out from St. Louis. For over a year the group trekked westward, braving the harsh cold and inadequate supplies. Aided by various Indian tribes, they crossed the Rocky Mountains, rafted down the Columbia River into the Oregon Territory, and finally made the shores of the Pacific Ocean.

Not until the fall of 1805 did Jefferson receive their first report, in the form of a letter from Meriwether Lewis. Circulated in public, the report whetted America's appetite for further western exploration and commercial endeavors. For example, no sooner had Lewis and Clark returned than Zebulon Pike set out in search of a water route to the Far West. Although he never found this, his "discovery" of mineral wealth in the Spanish Southwest intensified America's determination to expand.

It is with pleasure that I announce to you the safe arrival of myself and party at 12 o'clock today at this place with our papers and baggage. In obedience to your orders we have penetrated the continent of North America

"Captain Lewis and Clark holding Council with the Indians." Engraving in Patrick Gass, A Journal of Lewis and Clark (1810) (Library of Congress).

to the Pacific Ocean, and sufficiently explored the interior of the country to affirm with confidence that we have discovered the most practicable route which does exist across the continent by means of the navigable branches of the Missouri and Columbia Rivers. . . .

We view this passage across the continent as affording immense advantages to the fur trade, but fear that the advantages which it offers as a communication for the productions of the East Indies to the United States and thence to Europe will never be found equal on an extensive scale to that by way of the Cape of Good Hope; still we believe that many articles not bulky, brittle nor of a very perishable nature may be conveyed to the United States by this route with more facility and at less expense than by that at present practiced.

The Missouri and all its branches from the Cheyenne upwards abound more in beaver and common otter, than any other streams on earth, particularly that proportion of them lying within the Rocky Mountains. The furs of all this immense tract of country including such as may be collected on the upper portion of the River St. Peters, Red River, and the Assinniboin with the immense country watered by the Columbia, may be conveyed to the mouth of the Columbia by the 1st of August in each year and from thence be shipped to, and arrive in Canton [China] earlier than the furs at present shipped from Montreal annually arrive in London. The British N. West Company of Canada were they permitted by the United States might also convey their furs collected in the Athabaske, on the Saskashawan, and south and west of Lake Winnipic by that route within the period before mentioned.

The productions of nine-tenths of the most valuable fur country of America could be conveyed by the route proposed to the East Indies.

In the infancy of the trade across the continent, or during the period that the trading establishments shall be confined to the Missouri and its branches, the men employed in this trade will be compelled to convey the furs collected in that quarter as low on the Columbia as tide water [near the ocean], in which case they could not return to the falls of the Missouri until about the 1st of October, which would be so late in the season that there would be considerable danger of the river being obstructed by ice before they could reach this place and consequently that the commodities brought from the East Indies would be detained until the following spring; but this difficulty will at once vanish when establishments are also made on the Columbia, and a sufficient number of men employed at them to convey annually the productions of the East Indies to the upper establishment on the Kooskooske, and there exchange them with the men of the Missouri for their furs in the beginning of July. By this means the furs not only of the Missouri but those also of the Columbia may be shipped to the East Indies by the season before mentioned, and the commodities of the East Indies arrive at St. Louis or the mouth of the Ohio by the last of September in each year.

Although the Columbia does not as much as the Missouri abound in beaver and otter, yet it is by no means despicable in this respect, and would furnish a valuable fur trade distinct from any other consideration in addition to the otter and beaver which it could furnish. There might be collected considerable quantities of the skins of three species of bear affording a great variety of colours and of superior delicacy, those also of the tiger cat, several species of fox, martin and several others of an inferior class of furs, besides the valuable sea otter of the coast.

If the government will only aid, even in a very limited manner, the enterprise of her citizens I am fully convinced that we shall shortly derive the benefits of a most lucrative trade from this source, and that in the course of ten or twelve years a tour across the continent by the route mentioned will be undertaken by individuals with as little concern as a voyage across the Atlantic is at present.

The British N. West Company of Canada has for several years carried on a partial trade with the Minnetares, Ahwayhaways and Mandans on the Missouri from their establishments on the Assinniboin at the entrance of Mouse River; at present I have good reason for believing that they intend shortly to form an establishment near those nations with a view to engross the fur trade of the Missouri. The known enterprise and resources of this company, latterly strengthened by an union with their powerful rival the X. Y. Company, renders them formidable in that distant part of the continent to all other traders; and in my opinion if we are to regard the trade of the Missouri as an object of importance to the United States, the strides of this company towards the Missouri cannot be too vigilantly watched nor too firmly and speedily opposed by our government. The embarrassments under which the navigation of the Missouri at present labours from the unfriendly dispositions of the Kancez, the several bands of Tetons, Assinniboins, and those tribes that resort to the British establishments on the Saskashawan is also a subject which requires the earliest attention of our government. As I shall shortly be with you I have deemed it unnecessary here to detail the several ideas which have presented themselves to my mind on those subjects, more especially when I consider that a thorough knowledge of the geography of the country is absolutely necessary to their being understood, and leisure has not yet permitted us to make but one general map of the country which I am unwilling to risk by the mail. . . .

I have brought with me several skins of the sea otter, two skins of the native sheep of America, five skins and skeletons complete of the Bighorn or mountain ram, and a skin of the mule deer besides the skins of several other quadrapeds and birds native of the countries through which we have passed. I have also preserved a pretty extensive collection of plants, and collected nine other vocabularies [of Indian tribes].

I have prevailed on the great chief of the Mandan nation to accompany me to Washington; he is now with my friend and colleague Capt. Clark at this place, in good health and spirits, and very anxious to proceed. . . .

The route by which I purpose traveling from hence to Washington is by way of Cahokia, Vincennes, Louisville, Ky., the Crab Orchard, Abington, Fincastle, Stanton and Charlottesville. Any letters directed to me at Louisville ten days after the receipt of this will most probably meet me at that place. I am very anxious to learn the state of my friends in Albemarle, particularly whether my mother is yet living. I am with every sentiment of esteem your Obt. and very Humble servant.

Source: Reuben Gold Thwaites, ed., *Original Journals of the Lewis and Clark Expedition* (New York, 1904), 7:334–37.

For Further Reading:

Alexander DeConde, *The Affair of Louisiana* (New York: Scribner's, 1976).

Meriwether Lewis and William Clark, *The History of the Expedition Under the Command of Lewis and Clark* (New York: Dover, 1965).

Marshall Smelser, *The Democratic Republic, 1801–1815* (New York: Harper & Row, 1968).

20. Jacob Henry, "Speech on Freedom of Religion" (1809)

1809   Jacob Henry's right to serve in legislature challenged
1835   North Carolina amends constitution

In 1808 Jacob Henry was elected to the state legislature of North Carolina by the citizens of Carteret County. A year later he was reelected. But at the opening session of the new legislature his right to take a seat was challenged by a fellow legislator on the grounds that Henry, who was Jewish, did not meet North Carolina's state constitutional requirement that "no person, who shall deny the being of God or the Truth of the protestant religion . . . shall be capable of holding office."

This challenge disturbed many Americans. Henry himself, in the following speech, defended his right to serve. He argued that North Carolina's own constitution and Declaration of Rights, both adopted in 1776, included sections that contradicted the prohibition on non-Protestants' serving in the legislature. Fortunately for Henry, the legislature agreed and overruled the challenge. However, not until 1835 did the state amend its constitution so as to formally strike the religious restriction. And even then the language of the amended constitution was ambiguous.

During the same period other states maintained restrictions on religious minorities. For example, the Congregational Church remained the established or state church in Massachusetts until 1833. Narrow interpretations of Maryland laws kept Jews from practicing as attorneys until 1826. Indeed, it was not until 1961 that the Supreme Court ruled that restrictions on atheists and religious minorities violated the Bill of Rights' prohibition against infringing on one's freedom of belief.

This said, it should be repeated that Henry's speech convinced his fellows to grant him his seat in the legislature and that his Protestant constituents reelected him in spite of the constitutional restriction against Jews. Moreover, Henry's address was considered an overnight classic. It was reprinted in some of the earliest collections of American speeches, side by side with Patrick Henry's "Give Me Liberty or Give Me Death" and George Washington's "Farewell Address."

I certainly, Mr. Speaker, know not the design of the Declaration of Rights made by the people of this State in the year 1776, if it was not to consecrate certain great and fundamental rights and principles which even the Constitution cannot impair; for the 44th section of the latter instrument declares that the Declaration of Rights ought never to be violated, on any pretence whatever; if there is any apparent difference between the two instruments, they ought, if possible, to be reconciled; but if there is a final repugnance between them, the Declaration of Rights must be considered paramount; for I believe it is to the Constitution, as the Constitution is to law; it controls and directs it absolutely and conclusively. If, then, a belief in the Protestant religion is required by the Constitution, to qualify a man for a seat in this house, and such qualification is dispensed with by the Declaration of Rights, the provision of the Constitution must be altogether inoperative; as the language of the Bill of Rights is, "that all men have a natural and inalienable right to worship ALMIGHTY GOD according to the dictates of their own consciences." It is undoubtedly a natural right, and when it is declared to be an inalienable one by the people in their sovereign and original capacity, any attempt to alienate either by the Constitution or by law, must be vain and fruitless.

It is difficult to conceive how such a provision crept into the Constitution, unless it is from the difficulty the human mind feels in suddenly emancipating itself from fetters by which it has long been enchained: and how adverse it is to the feelings and manners of the people of the present day every gentleman may satisfy himself by glancing at the religious belief of the persons who fill the various offices in this State: there are Presbyterians, Lutherans, Calvinists, Mennonists, Baptists, Trinitarians, and Unitarians. But, as far as my observation extends, there are fewer Protestants, in the strict sense of the word, used by the Constitution, than of any other persuasion; for I suppose that they meant by it, the Protestant religion as established by the law in England. For other persuasions we see houses of worship in almost every part of the State, but very few of the Protestant; so few, that indeed I fear that the people of this State would for some time remain unrepresented in this House, if that clause of the Constitution is supposed to be in force. So far from believing in the Thirty-nine Articles, I will venture to assert that a majority of the people never have read them.

If a man should hold religious principles incompatible with the freedom and safety of the State, I do not hesitate to pronounce that he should be excluded from the public councils of the same; and I trust if I know myself, no one would be more ready to aid and assist than myself. But I should really be at a loss to specify any known religious principles which are thus dangerous. It is surely a question between a man and his Maker, and requires more than human attributes to pronounce which of the numerous sects prevailing in the world is most acceptable to the Deity. If a man fulfills the duties of that religion, which his education or his conscience has pointed to him as the true one, no person, I hold, in this our land of liberty, has a right to arraign him at the bar of any inquisition: and the day, I trust, has long passed, when principles merely speculative were propagated by force; when the sincere and pious were made victims, and the light-minded bribed into hypocrites.

The purest homage man could render to the Almighty was the sacrifice of his passions and the performance of his duties. That the ruler of the universe would receive with equal benignity the various offerings of man's adoration, if they proceeded from the heart. Governments only concern the actions and conduct of man, and not his speculative notions. Who among us feels himself so exalted above his fellows as to have a right to dictate to them any mode of belief? Will you bind the conscience in chains, and fasten conviction upon the mind in spite of the conclusions of reason and of those ties and habitudes which are blended with every pulsation of the heart? Are you prepared to plunge at once from the sublime heights of moral legislation into the dark and gloomy caverns of superstitious ignorance? Will you drive from your shores and from the shelter of your constitution, all who do not lay their oblations on the same altar, observe the same ritual, and subscribe to the same dogmas? If so, which, among the various sects into which we are divided, shall be the favored one?

I should insult the understanding of this House to suppose it possible that they could ever assent to such absurdities; for all know that persecution in all its shapes and modifications, is contrary to the genius of our government and the spirit of our laws, and that it can never produce any other effect than to render men hypocrites or martyrs.

When Charles V, Emperor of Germany, tired of the cares of government, resigned his crown to his son, he retired to a monastery, where he amused the evening of his life in regulating the movements of watches, endeavoring to make a number keep the same time; but, not being able to make any two go exactly alike, it led him to reflect upon the folly and crimes he had committed, in attempting the impossibility of making men think alike!

Nothing is more easily demonstrated than that the conduct alone is the subject of human laws, and that man ought to suffer civil disqualification for what he does, and not for what he thinks. The mind can receive laws only from Him, of whose Divine essence it is a portion; He alone can punish disobedience; for who else can know its movements, or estimate their merits? The religion I profess, inculcates every duty which men owes to his fellow men; it enjoins upon its votaries the practice of every virtue, and the detestation of every vice; it teaches them to hope for the favor of heaven exactly in proportion as their lives have been directed by just, honorable, and beneficent maxims. This, then, gentlemen, is my creed, it was impressed upon my infant mind; it has been the director of my youth, the monitor of my manhood, and will, I trust, be the consolation of my old age. At any rate, Mr. Speaker, I am sure that you cannot see anything in this Religion, to deprive me of my seat in this house. So far as relates to my life and conduct, the examination of these I submit with cheerfulness to your candid and liberal construction. What may be the religion of him who made this objection against me, or whether he has any religion or not I am unable to say. I have never considered it my duty to pry into the belief of other members of this house. If their actions are upright and conduct just, the rest is for their own consideration, not for mine. I do not seek to make converts to my faith, whatever it may be esteemed in the eyes of my officious friend, nor do I exclude any one from my esteem or friendship, because he and I differ in that respect. The same charity, therefore, it is not unreasonable to expect, will be extended to myself, because in all things that relate to the State and to the duties of civil life, I am bound by the same obligations with my fellow-citizens, nor does any man subscribe more sincerely than myself to the maxim, "whatever ye would that men should do unto you do ye so even unto them, for such is the law and the prophets."

Source: John H. Wheeler, *Historical Sketches of North Carolina from 1584 to 1851* (Philadelphia, 1851), 2:74–76.

For Further Reading:

Joseph Blau, *Cornerstones of Religious Freedom in America* (New York: Harper & Row, 1964).
Leonard Levy, *The Establishment Clause* (New York: Macmillan, 1986).

21. Andrew Jackson, Excerpt from "Address to Congress: The Majority Is to Govern" (1829)

1807–30   Property requirements for voting removed; universal
                 manhood suffrage established
1824   House of Representatives chooses John Quincy Adams
                 President
1828   Jackson easily defeats J. Q. Adams for presidency
1832   Jackson vetoes bill rechartering National Bank of the
                 United States; Jackson easily reelected

Although "no taxation without representation" was one of the rallying cries of the American Revolution (see document 9), suffrage remained limited during the early years of the Republic. The House of Representatives was the only branch of the federal government directly elected by the people, and women, blacks, and Native Americans, as well as white males who did not own property, did not enjoy the right to vote. This began to change

Caricature of Andrew Jackson (Library of Congress).

shortly before the War of 1812 and by the mid-1830s universal (white) manhood suffrage was the rule.

Nonetheless, as became evident with the election of 1824, the will of the people was not always followed. The presidential campaign of that year pitted four candidates against one another, all of them officially Democratic-Republicans. None of them won a majority, although Andrew Jackson, one of the heroes of the War of 1812, easily outpolled John Quincy Adams and his other two rivals. Lacking a majority, however, the House of Representatives selected Adams over Andrew Jackson.

Following the election, Jackson helped form the Democratic Party. And in 1828, with the aid of the party, he easily defeated John Q. Adams. In his State of the Union address, which was also his first speech to Congress, Jackson lectured the legislators on the principle of majority rule and the dangers of elitism. He presented himself as one of the people, or the great commoner. Whether or not this was actually the case, the very fact that he sought to portray himself as a self-made man depicted the degree to which political deference or elitism had declined.

FELLOW CITIZENS OF THE SENATE, AND
HOUSE OF REPRESENTATIVES:

It affords me pleasure to tender my friendly greetings to you on the occasion of your assembling at the Seat of Government, to enter upon the important duties to which you have been called by the voice of our coun-trymen. The task devolves on me, under a provision of the Constitution, to present to you, as the Federal Legislature of twenty-four sovereign States, and twelve millions of happy people, a view of our affairs; and to propose such measures as, in the discharge of my official functions, have suggested themselves as necessary to promote the objects of our Union.

In communicating with you for the first time, it is, to me, a source of unfeigned satisfaction, calling for mutual gratulation and devout thanks to a benign Providence, that we are at peace with all mankind; and that our country exhibits the most cheering evidence of general welfare and pro-gressive improvement. Turning our eyes to other nations, our great desire is to see our brethren of the human race secured in the blessings enjoyed by ourselves, and advancing in knowledge, in freedom, and in social happiness.

Our foreign relations, although in their general character pacific and friendly, present subjects of difference between us and other Powers, of deep interest, as well to the country at large as to many of our citizens. To effect an adjustment of these shall continue to be the object of my earnest endeavors; and notwithstanding the difficulties of the task, I do not allow myself to apprehend unfavorable results. Blessed as our country is with every thing which constitutes national strength, she is fully adequate to the maintenance of all her interests. In discharging the responsible trust confided to the Executive in this respect, it is my settled purpose to ask nothing that is not clearly right, and to submit to nothing that is wrong; and I flatter myself, that, supported by the other branches of the Government, and by the intelligence and patriotism of the People, we shall be able, under the protection of Providence, to cause all our just rights to be respected. . . .

I consider it one of the most urgent of my duties to bring to your attention the propriety of amending that part of our Constitution which relates to the election of President and Vice President. Our system of government was, by its framers, deemed an experiment; and they, therefore, consistently provided a mode of remedying its defects.

To the People belongs the right of electing their Chief Magistrate: it was never designed that their choice should, in any case, be defeated, either by the intervention of electoral colleges, or by the agency confided, under certain contingencies, to the House of Representatives. Experience proves, that, in proportion as agents to execute the will of the People are multiplied, there is danger of their wishes being frustrated. Some may be unfaithful: all are liable to err. So far, therefore, as the People can, with convenience, speak, it is safer for them to express their own will.

The number of aspirants to the Presidency, and the diversity of the in-terests which may influence their claims, leave little reason to expect a choice in the first instance: and, in that event, the election must devolve on the

House of Representatives, where, it is obvious, the will of the People may not be always ascertained; or, if ascertained, may not be regarded. From the mode of voting by States, the choice is to be made by twenty-four votes; and it may often occur, that one of these will be controlled by an individual representative. Honors and offices are at the disposal of the successful candidate. Repeated ballotings may make it apparent that a single individual holds the cast in his hand. May he not be tempted to name his reward? But even without corruption—supposing the probity of the Representative to be proof against the powerful motives by which it may be assailed—the will of the People is still constantly liable to be misrepresented. One may err from ignorance of the wishes of his constituents; another, from a conviction that it is his duty to be governed by his own judgment of the fitness of the candidates: finally, although all were inflexibly honest—all accurately informed of the wishes of their constituents—yet, under the present mode of election, a minority may often elect the President; and when this happens, it may reasonably be expected that efforts will be made on the part of the majority to rectify this injurious operation of their institutions. But although no evil of this character should result from such a perversion of the first principle of our system—*that the majority is to govern*—it must be very certain that a President elected by a minority cannot enjoy the confidence necessary to the successful discharge of his duties.

In this, as in all other matters of public concern, policy requires that as few impediments as possible should exist to the free operation of the public will. Let us, then, endeavor so to amend our system, that the office of Chief Magistrate may not be conferred upon any citizen but in pursuance of a fair expression of the will of the majority.

I would therefore recommend such an amendment of the Constitution as may remove all intermediate agency in the election of President and Vice President. The mode may be so regulated as to preserve to each State its present relative weight in the election; and a failure in the first attempt may be provided for, by confining the second to a choice between the two highest candidates. In connexion with such an amendment, it would seem advisable to limit the service of the Chief Magistrate to a single term, of either four or six years. If, however, it should not be adopted, it is worthy of consideration whether a provision disqualifying for office the Representatives in Congress on whom such an election may have devolved, would not be proper.

While members of Congress can be constitutionally appointed to offices of trust and profit, it will be the practice, even under the most conscientious adherence to duty, to select them for such stations as they are believed to be better qualified to fill than other citizens; but the purity of our Government would doubtless be promoted, by their exclusion from all appointments in the gift of the President in whose election they may have been officially concerned. The nature of the judicial office, and the necessity of securing in the Cabinet and in diplomatic stations of the highest rank, the best talents and political experience, should, perhaps, except these from the exclusion.

There are perhaps few men who can for any great length of time enjoy office and power, without being more or less under the influence of feelings unfavorable to the faithful discharge of their public duties. Their integrity may be proof against improper considerations immediately addressed to themselves; but they are apt to acquire a habit of looking with indifference upon the public interests, and of tolerating conduct from which an unpractised man would revolt. Office is considered as a species of property; and Government, rather as a means of promoting individual interests, than as an instrument created solely for the service of the People. Corruption in some, and, in others, a perversion of correct feelings and principles, divert Government from its legitimate ends, and make it an engine for the support of the few at the expense of the many. The duties of all public officers are, or, at least, admit of being made, so plain and simple, that men of intelligence may readily qualify themselves for their performance; and I cannot but believe that more is lost by the long continuance of men in office, than is generally to be gained by their experience. I submit therefore to your consideration, whether the efficiency of the Government would not be promoted, and official industry and integrity better secured, by a general extension of the law which limits appointments to four years.

In a country where offices are created solely for the benefit of the People, no one man has any more intrinsic right to official station than another. Offices were not established to give support to particular men, at the public expense. No individual wrong is therefore done by removal, since neither appointment to, nor continuance in, office, is matter of right. The incumbent became an officer with a view to public benefits; and when these require his removal, they are not to be sacrificed to private interests. It is the People, and they alone, who have a right to complain, when a bad officer is substituted for a good one. He who is removed has the same means of obtaining a living, that are enjoyed by the millions who never held office. The proposed limitation would destroy the idea of property, now so generally connected with official station; and although individual distress may be sometimes produced, it would, by promoting that rotation which constitutes a leading principle in the republican creed, give healthful action to the system.

Source: James D. Richardson, ed., *Messages and Papers of the Presidents* (Washington, D.C., 1897), 2:442–62.

For Further Reading:

Edward Pessen, *Jacksonian America* (Homewood, Ill.: Dorsey Press, 1969).
John William Ward, *Andrew Jackson* (New York: Oxford University Press, 1955).
Chilton Williamson, *American Suffrage* (Princeton, N.J.: Princeton University Press, 1960).

22. "Appeal of the Cherokee Nation" (1830)

1830   Indian Removal Act
1831   *Cherokee Nation v. Georgia*
1831–38   Trail of Tears

While Andrew Jackson presented himself as the representative of the people, as the defender of democracy and opponent of privilege, his definition of the people was colored by racial convention. In no way did he represent the interests of the American Indians. In fact, he owed much of his fame to the role he played in defeating the Indians of the Southwest. And as President he was responsible for their removal from the region.

Jackson's promotion of white interests over the rights of American Indians became clear during the Cherokee Indian affair in the state of Georgia. More than any other tribe, the Cherokees displayed a willingness to assimilate to Western ways. They adopted laws modeled after the Constitution and American penal codes. They converted to Christianity and secured deeds to the land. Some even owned African-American slaves. Nonetheless, when they refused to sell their land, white Georgians with the aid of the state seized their property and forced them to move westward.

Rather than going on the warpath to reclaim their land, the Cherokees went to the courts. In a suit that ultimately wound its way to the U.S. Supreme Court, the Cherokees demanded that the government protect their rights. Remarkably, in Cherokee Nation v. Georgia (1831) the Supreme Court ruled in their favor. Responding to their appeal, Justice John Marshall argued that the state of Georgia was violating the Cherokees' property rights by evicting them. President Jackson responded to this ruling by challenging the Court to enforce its decision. Jackson also sent the army to Georgia to drive the Cherokees out. The Court proved powerless to enforce its ruling and there was little public outcry against President Jackson's action.

Subsequently, the Cherokees and other tribes of the Southwest were forced to trek westward on the "Trail of Tears," to the other side of the Mississippi River. Jackson assured them that there they could live in peace forever. Before they arrived, however, nearly one-third of them died. Moreover, Jackson's promise of peaceful coexistence proved short-lived.

W̲e are aware that some persons suppose it will be for our advantage to remove beyond the Mississippi. We think otherwise. Our people universally think otherwise. Thinking that it would be fatal to their interests, they have almost to a man sent their memorial to Congress, deprecating the necessity of a removal. This question was distinctly before their minds when they signed their memorial. Not an adult person can be found, who has not an opinion on the subject; and if the people were to understand distinctly, that they could be protected against the laws of the neighboring States, there is probably not an adult person in the nation, who would think it best to remove; though possibly a few might emigrate individually. There are doubtless many who would flee to an unknown country, however beset with dangers, privations and sufferings, rather than be sentenced to spend six years in a Georgia prison for advising one of their neighbors not to betray his country. And there are others who could not think of living as outlaws in their native land, exposed to numberless vexations, and excluded from being parties or witnesses in a court of justice. It is incredible that Georgia should ever have enacted the oppressive laws to which reference is here made, unless she had supposed that something extremely terrific in its character was necessary, in order to make the Cherokees willing to remove. We are not willing to remove; and if we could be brought to this extremity, it would be, not by argument; not because our judgment was satisfied; not because our condition will be improved—but only because we cannot endure to be deprived of our national and individual rights, and subjected to a process of intolerable oppression.

We wish to remain on the land of our fathers. We have a perfect and original right to claim this, without interruption or molestation. The treaties with us, and laws of the United States made in pursuance of treaties, guaranty our residence, and our privileges, and secure us against intruders. Our only request is, that these treaties may be fulfilled, and these laws executed.

But if we are compelled to leave our country, we see nothing but ruin before us. The country west of the Arkansas territory is unknown to us. From what we can learn of it, we have no prepossessions in its favor. All the inviting parts of it, as we believe, are preoccupied by various Indian nations, to which it has been assigned. They would regard us as intruders, and look upon us with an evil eye. The far greater part of that region is, beyond all controversy, badly supplied with wood and water; and no Indian tribe can live as agriculturists without these articles. All our neighbors, in case of our removal, though crowded into our near vicinity, would speak a language totally different from ours, and practice different customs. The original possessors of that region are now wandering savages, lurking for prey in the neighborhood. They have always been at war, and would be easily tempted to turn their arms against peaceful emigrants. Were the country to which we are urged much better than it is represented to be, and were it free from the objections which we have made to it, still it is not the land of our birth, nor of our affections. It contains neither the scenes of our childhood, nor the graves of our fathers.

Source: E. C. Tracy, *Memoir of the Life of Jerimiah Evarts* (Boston, 1845), pp. 149–58.

For Further Reading:

Michael D. Green, *The Politics of Indian Removal* (Lincoln: University of Nebraska
    Press, 1982).
Gloria Jahoda, *Trail of Tears* (New York: Holt, Rinehart and Winston, 1975).
Michael Rogin, *Fathers and Children* (New York: Vintage, 1975).

PART III
ANTE-BELLUM REFORM

23. Frances Wright, Excerpt from "The Meaning of Patriotism in America" (1828)

1820–60 Ante-bellum Reform
1825 "New Harmony" established
1829 Wright and Owens publish *Free Enquirer*

From the 1820s through the 1850s a wave of reform swept across America. This reform impulse was a response, in part, to the enormous changes that were taking place in the country, from rapid population growth and geographic expansion to urbanization and industrialization. One reformer was Frances Wright. A native of Scotland, Wright emigrated to America in 1818. Seven years later she formed a utopian community in Tennessee, consisting of ex-slaves and whites. When this venture collapsed, she moved to Robert Dale Owens' better-known utopian community, New Harmony, in upstate New York. Together they founded the Free Enquirer, *a radical newspaper devoted to various causes.*

Wright's "The Meaning of Patriotism," which she delivered during a Fourth of July celebration (she was probably the first woman ever invited to deliver the keynote address at a July 4 ceremony), depicted her interest in human rights and the community of man. Like other reformers, she was disturbed by narrow nationalistic and individualistic definitions of patriotism. She objected to ethnic, racial, and sexual discrimination. And she favored the democratization of American society in the fullest sense of the term.

Dating, as we justly may, a new era in the history of man from the Fourth of July, 1776, it would be well—that is, it would be useful—if on each anniversary we examined the progress made by our species in just knowledge and just practice. Each Fourth of July would then stand as a tidemark in the flood of time by which to ascertain the advance of the human intellect, by which to note the rise and fall of each successive error, the discovery of each important truth, the gradual melioration in our public institutions, social arrangements, and, above all, in our moral feelings and mental views. . . .

In continental Europe, of late years, the words patriotism and patriot have been used in a more enlarged sense than it is usual here to attribute to them, or than is attached to them in Great Britain. Since the political struggles of France, Italy, Spain, and Greece, the word patriotism has been employed, throughout continental Europe, to express a love of the public good; a preference for the interests of the many to thosej of the few, a desire for the emancipation of the human race from the thrall of despotism, religious and civil: in short, patriotism there is used rather to express the interest felt in the human race in general than that felt for any country, or inhabitants of a country, in particular. And patriot, in like manner, is employed to signify a lover of human liberty and human improvement rather than a mere lover of the country in which he lives, or the tribe to which he belongs. Used in this sense, patriotism is a virtue, and a patriot a virtuous man. With such an interpretation, a patriot is a useful member of society, capable of enlarging all minds and bettering all hearts with which he comes in contact: a useful member of the human family capable of establishing fundamental principles and of merging his own interests, those of his associates, and those of his nation in the interests of the human race. Laurels and statues are vain things, and mischievous as they are childish; but could we imagine them of use, on such a patriot alone could they be with any reason bestowed. . . .

If such a patriotism as we have last considered should seem likely to obtain in any country, it should be certainly in this. In this which is truly the home of all nations and in the veins of whose citizens flows the blood of every people on the globe. Patriotism, in the exclusive meaning, is surely not made for America. Mischievous everywhere, it were here both mischievous and absurd. The very origin of the people is opposed to it. The institutions, in their principle, militate against it. The day we are celebrating protests against it. It is for Americans, more especially, to nourish a nobler sentiment; one more consistent with their origin, and more conducive to their future improvement. It is for them more especially to know why they love their country; and to *feel* that they love it, not because it *is* their country, but because it is the palladium of human liberty—the favored scene of human improvement. It is for them, more especially, to examine their institutions; and to *feel* that they honor them because they are based on just principles. It is for them, more especially, to examine their institutions, because they have the means of improving them; to examine their laws, because at will they can alter them. It is for them to lay aside luxury whose wealth is in industry; idle parade whose strength is in knowldge; ambitious distinctions whose principle is equality. It is for them not to rest, satisfied with words, who can seize upon things; and to remember that equality means, not the mere equality of political rights, however valuable, but equality of instruction and equality in virtue; and that liberty means, not the mere voting at elections, but the free and fearless exercise of the mental faculties and that self-possession which springs out of well-reasoned opinions and consistent practice. It is for them to honor principles rather than men—to commemorate events rather than days; when they rejoice, to know for what they rejoice, and to rejoice only for what has brought and what brings peace and happiness to men. The event we commemorate this day has procured much of both, and shall procure in the onward course of human improvement more than we can now conceive of. For this—for the good obtained and yet in store for our race—let us rejoice! But let us rejoice as men, not as children—as human beings rather than as Americans—as reasoning beings, not as ignorants. So shall we rejoice to good purpose and in good feeling; so shall we improve the victory once on this day achieved, until all mankind hold with us the Jubilee of Independence.

Source: Frances Wright, *Course of Popular Lectures* (London, 1934).

For Further Reading:

Celia Morris Eckhardt, *Frances Wright, Rebel in America* (Cambridge, Mass.: Harvard University Press, 1984).

John L. Thomas, "Romantic Reform in America," *American Quarterly* 17, 4 (Winter 1965): 656–81.

Ronald G. Walters, *American Reformers, 1815–60* (New York: Hill & Wang, 1978).

24. Horace Mann, Excerpt from "Report of the Massachusetts Board of Education" (1848)

1837   Horace Mann becomes Secretary of Massachusetts
        Board of Education
1843   Mann travels to Europe
1848   Mann writes twelfth and final report to school board;
        elected to Congress

One reform movement that had a lasting impact on American society was in the field of education. In 1800 public schools existed only in New England, and they were inadequate. By 1860 nearly every state provided some public education and the curriculum had been vastly improved. The individual most responsible for this change was Horace Mann.

Born in a poor rural section of Massachusetts, Mann had firsthand experience with cruel and ill-prepared teachers and with inadequate school facilities. Fortunately, Mann also had an itinerant schoolmaster who encouraged him to pursue his education and who prepared him for higher education. After earning his college degree from Brown University with honors, Mann studied law, established a profitable private practice, and then moved into politics.

First as a leader of the Massachusetts State Senate and then as secretary of the State Board of Education, Mann gained a reputation as an advocate

of universal public education. He worked tirelessly to make education avail-
able to all citizens. After traveling to Europe to study its educational systems,
he initiated curriculum changes and mandatory educational requirements.
In particular he fought for the inclusion of courses that conferred applied
skills and emphasized secular rather than religious matters. In his "Report"
Mann emphasized that a good education was a prerequisite to the success
of an individual and to society. Mann also argued that education was the
great equalizer that would make possible the ideals of the Declaration of
Independence.

In an era in which the vast majority of Americans still earned a living by
working with their hands, most as farmers, Mann was clearly ahead of his
time. His advocacy of education as a precondition for a productive citizenry
and as a key to equal opportunity did not represent the views of the majority.
But in time, his view would become part of the American credo.

Now, it is the especial province and function of the statesman and
the lawgiver—of all those, indeed, whose influence moulds or modifies public opinion—to study out the eternal principles which conduce to the
strength, wisdom, and righteousness of a community; to search for these
principles as for hidden riches; to strive for them as one would strive for his
life; and then to form public institutions in accordance with them. And he
is not worthy to be called a statesman, he is not worthy to be a lawgiver or
leader among men, who, either through the weakness of his head or the
selfishness of his heart, is incapable of marshalling in his mind the great
ideas of knowledge, justice, temperance, and obedience to the laws of God,—
on which foundation alone the structure of human welfare can be erected;
who is not capable of organizing these ideas into a system, and then of
putting that system into operation, as a mechanic does a machine. This only
is true statesmanship. . . .

Without undervaluing any other human agency, it may be safely affirmed
that the common school, improved and energized as it can easily be, may
become the most effective and benignant of all the forces of civilization. Two
reasons sustain this position. In the first place, there is a universality in its
operation, which can be affirmed of no other institution whatever. If administered in the spirit of justice and conciliation, all the rising generation
may be brought within the circle of its reformatory and elevating influences.
And, in the second place, the materials upon which it operates are so pliant
and ductile as to be susceptible of assuming a greater variety of forms than
any other earthly work of the Creator. The inflexibility and ruggedness of
the oak, when compared with the lithe sapling or the tender germ, are but
feeble emblems to typify the docility of childhood when contrasted with the
obduracy and intractableness of man. It is these inherent advantages of the
common school, which, in our own State, have produced results so striking,

from a system so imperfect, and an administration so feeble. In teaching the
blind and the deaf and dumb, in kindling the latent spark of intelligence
that lurks in an idiot's mind, and in the more holy work of reforming abandoned and outcast children, education has proved what it can do by glorious
experiments. These wonders it has done in its infancy, and with the lights
of a limited experience; but when its faculties shall be fully developed, when
it shall be trained to wield its mighty energies for the protection of society
against the giant vices which now invade and torment it,—against intemperance, avarice, war, slavery, bigotry, the woes of want, and the wickedness
of waste,—then there will not be a height to which these enemies of the
race can escape which it will not scale, nor a Titan among them all whom
it will not slay.

I proceed, then, in endeavoring to show how the true business of the
schoolroom connects itself, and becomes identical, with the great interests
of society. The former is the infant, immature state of those interests; the
latter their developed, adult state. As "the child is father to the man," so
may the training of the schoolroom expand into the institutions and fortunes
of the State. . . .

Political Education

The necessity of general intelligence,—that is, of education (for I use the
terms as substantially synonymous, because general intelligence can never
exist without general education, and general education will be sure to produce general intelligence),—the necessity of general intelligence under a
republican form of government, like most other very important truths, has
become a very trite one. It is so trite, indeed, as to have lost much of its
force by its familiarity. Almost all the champions of education seize upon
this argument first of all, because it is so simple as to be understood by the
ignorant, and so strong as to convince the sceptical. Nothing would be easier
than to follow in the train of so many writers, and to demonstrate by logic,
by history, and by the nature of the case, that a republican form of government, without intelligence in the people, must be, on a vast scale, what a
mad-house, without superintendent or keepers, would be on a small one,—
the despotism of a few succeeded by universal anarchy, and anarchy by
despotism, with no change but from bad to worse. . . .

However elevated the moral character of a constituency may be, however
well informed in matters of general science or history, yet they must, if
citizens of a republic, understand something of the true nature and functions
of the government under which they live. That any one, who is to participate
in the government of a country when he becomes a man, should receive no
instruction respecting the nature and functions of the government he is
afterwards to administer, is a political solecism. In all nations, hardly excepting the most rude and barbarous, the future sovereign receives some

training which is supposed to fit him for the exercise of the powers and duties of his anticipated station. Where, by force of law, the government devolves upon the heir while yet in a state of legal infancy, some regency, or other substitute, is appointed to act in his stead until his arrival at mature age; and, in the mean time, he is subjected to such a course of study and discipline as will tend to prepare him, according to the political theory of the time and the place, to assume the reins of authority at the appointed age. If in England, or in the most enlightened European monarchies, it would be a proof of restored barbarism to permit the future sovereign to grow up without any knowledge of his duties,—and who can doubt that it would be such a proof?—then, surely, it would be not less a proof of restored or of never-removed barbarism amongst us to empower any individual to use the elective franchise without preparing him for so momentous a trust. Hence the Constitution of the United States, and of our own State, should be made a study in our public schools. The partition of the powers of government into the three co-ordinate branches—legislative, judicial, and executive,—with the duties appropriately devolving upon each; the mode of electing or of appointing all officers, with the reasons on which it was founded; and, especially, the duty of every citizen, in a government of laws, to appeal to the courts for redress in all cases of alleged wrong, instead of undertaking to vindicate his own rights by his own arm; and, in a government where the people are the acknowledged sources of power, the duty of changing laws and rulers by an appeal to the ballot, and not by rebellion,—should be taught to all the children until they are fully understood.

Moral education is a primal necessity of social existence. The unrestrained passions of men are not only homicidal, but suicidal; and a community without a conscience would soon extinguish itself. Even with a natural conscience, how often has evil triumphed over good! From the beginning of time, wrong has followed right, as the shadow the substance. . . .

But to all doubters, disbelievers, or despairers in human progress, it may still be said, there is one experiment which has never yet been tried. It is an experiment, which, even before its inception, offers the highest authority for its ultimate success. Its formula is intelligible to all; and it is as legible as though written in starry letters on an azure sky. It is expressed in these few and simple words: *"Train up a child in the way he should go; and, when he is old, he will not depart from it."* This declaration is positive. If the conditions are complied with, it makes no provision for a failure. Though pertaining to morals, yet, if the terms of the direction are observed, there is no more reason to doubt the result than there would be in an optical or a chemical experiment.

Source: Mary Mann, ed., *Life and Works of Horace Mann* (Boston, 1868).

For Further Reading:

Lawrence A. Cremin, *American Education: The National Experience* (New York: Harper & Row, 1980).

Carl F. Kaestle, *Pillars of the Republic* (New York: Hill & Wang, 1983).
Michael B. Katz, *The Irony of Early School Reform* (Cambridge, Mass.: Harvard University Press, 1968).

25. Orestes Brownson, Excerpt from "The Laboring Classes" (1840)

1814   Lowell System founded
1817   New York Stock Exchange formed
1825   Erie Canal completed
1827   Philadelphia Workingmen's Party organized
1828   Baltimore & Ohio Railroad, first run
1834   First strike at Lowell mills
1837–43   Economic depression

Following the War of 1812, America began to industrialize. Textile mills appeared, especially in New England, where factories were operated largely by young female workers who lived in company housing (known as the Lowell system). Transportation was revolutionized with the building of new turnpikes, canals, and then railroads. Power-driven machines became more prominent in many lines of work, such as printing and shoe making. And by the 1840s masses of immigrants, most prominently from Ireland and Germany, poured into the United States to meet America's seemingly insatiable demand for cheap unskilled labor.

A byproduct of industrialization was economic inequality. Especially in urban areas a permanent wage working class emerged. Disparities between the wealthy and the poor became greater and many middle-class reformers expressed their concern about this development. One reformer who was especially concerned about the "labor problem," as some termed it, was Orestes Brownson. In "The Laboring Classes," Brownson railed at those aspects of industrial America that he felt threatened its ideals. Like Frances Wright (see document 23) he sought to topple privilege. And more so than many of his fellow reformers, Brownson insisted that economic equality was the foundation of political and social equality.

No one can observe the signs of the times with much care, without perceiving that a crisis as to the relation of wealth and labor is approaching. It is useless to shut our eyes to the fact, and like the ostrich fancy ourselves secure because we have so concealed our heads that we see not the danger.

We or our children will have to meet this crisis. The old war between the King and the Barons is well nigh ended, and so is that between the Barons and the Merchants and Manufacturers,—landed capital and commercial capital. The business man has become the peer of my Lord. And now commences the new struggle between the operative and his employer, between wealth and labor. Every day does this struggle extend further and wax stronger and fiercer; what or when the end will be God only knows. . . .

. . . All over the world this fact stares us in the face, the workingman is poor and depressed, while a large portion of the non-workingmen, in the sense we now use the term, are wealthy. It may be laid down as a general rule, with but few exceptions, that men are rewarded in an inverse ratio to the amount of actual service they perform. Under every government on earth the largest salaries are annexed to those offices, which demand of their incumbents the least amount of actual labor either mental or manual. And this is in perfect harmony with the whole system of repartition of the fruits of industry, which obtain in every department of society. Now here is the system which prevails, and here is its result. The whole class of simple laborers are poor, and in general unable to procure anything beyond the bare necessaries of life. . . .

Now, what is the prospect of those who fall under the operations of this system? We ask, is there a reasonable chance that any considerable portion of the present generation of laborers, shall ever become owners of a sufficient portion of the funds of production, to be able to sustain themselves by laboring on their own capital, that is, as independent laborers? We need not ask this question, for everybody knows there is not. Well, is the condition of a laborer at wages the best that the great mass of the working people ought to be able to aspire to? Is it a condition,—nay can it be made a condition,—with which a man should be satisfied; in which he should be contented to live and die? . . .

Now the great work for this age and the coming, is to raise up the laborer, and to realize in our own social arrangements and in the actual condition of all men, that equality between man and man, which God has established between the rights of one and those of another. In other words, our business is to emancipate the proletaries, as the past has emancipated the slaves. This is our work. There must be no class of our fellow men doomed to toil through life as mere workmen at wages. If wages are tolerated it must be, in the case of the individual operative, only under such conditions that by the time he is of a proper age to settle in life, he shall have accumulated enough to be an independent laborer on his own capital,—on his own farm or in his own shop. Here is our work. How is it to be done? . . .

The truth is, the evil we have pointed out is not merely individual in its character. It is not, in the case of any single individual, of any one man's procuring, nor can the efforts of any one man, directed solely to his own moral and religious perfection, do aught to remove it. What is purely individual in its nature, efforts of individuals to perfect themselves, may remove. But the evil we speak of is inherent in all our social arrangements, and cannot be cured without a radical change of those arrangements. Could we convert all men to Christianity in both theory and practice, as held by the most enlightened sect of Christians among us, the evils of the social state would remain untouched. Continue our present system of trade, and all its present evil consequences will follow, whether it be carried on by your best men or your worst. Put your best men, your wisest, most moral, and most religious men, at the head of your paper money banks, and the evils of the present banking system will remain scarcely diminished. The only way to get rid of its evils is to change the system, not its managers. The evils of slavery do not result from the personal characters of slave masters. They are inseparable from the system, let who will be masters. Make all your rich men good Christians, and you have lessened not the evils of existing inequality in wealth. The mischievous effects of this inequality do not result from the personal character of either rich or poor, but from itself, and they will continue, just so long as there are rich men and poor men in the same community. You must abolish the system or accept its consequences. No man can serve both God and Mammon. If you will serve the devil, you must look to the devil for your wages; we know no other way.

Source: Orestes Brownson, "The Laboring Classes," *The Boston Quarterly Review*, July 1840, pp. 358–95.

For Further Reading:

Edward Pessen, *The Most Uncommon Jacksonians* (Albany: State University of New York Press, 1967).
Arthur M. Schlesinger, *Orestes Brownson* (New York: Octagon Books, 1963).

26. Ralph Waldo Emerson, Excerpt from "An American Scholar" (1837)

1826 American Lyceum founded
1837 Emerson delivers "An American Scholar" at Harvard University
1841 Emerson publishes first collection of essays
1840s Heyday of transcendentalism

Ralph Waldo Emerson, leader of the transcendentalists, a loosely collected group of New England writers who espoused a faith in individual liberation, dissent, and nonconformity, was one of the most influential intellectuals in American history. A prominent member of the lyceum (a speaker's circuit and an early form of adult education, popular in the Northeast and West in the second quarter of the nineteenth century), he gained fame and a following through his speeches and essays. One of his most important speeches was delivered as the Phi Beta Kappa address at Harvard College, his alma matter, in August 1837. Entitled "An American Scholar," the address focused on the issue of America's cultural and intellectual identity and needs. Rather than disdaining America's lack of an artistic and literary tradition, Emerson implored his audience and other intellectuals to create their own, one that would be uniquely democratic and American.

Oliver Wendell Holmes, one of America's first famous writers, who heard the address, later wrote that it was "our intellectual declaration of independence." Nathaniel Hawthorne and Herman Melville had a similar response, and they, along with writers who read Emerson's other works, were inspired to try to create a cultural tradition fitting for a democratic society.

Mr. President and Gentlemen:

I greet you on the recommencement of our literary year. Our anniversary is one of hope, and, perhaps, not enough of labor. We do not meet for games of strength or skill, for the recitation of histories, tragedies, and odes, like the ancient Greeks; for parliaments of love and poesy, like the Troubadours; nor for the advancement of science, like our contemporaries in the British and European capitals. Thus far, our holiday has been simply a friendly sign of the survival of the love of letters amongst a people too busy to give to letters any more. As such it is precious as the sign of an indestructible instinct. Perhaps the time is already come when it ought to be, and will be, something else; when the sluggard intellect of this continent will look from under its iron lids and fill the postponed expectation of the world with something better than the exertions of mechanical skill. Our day of dependence, our long apprenticeship to the learning of other lands, draws to a close. The millions that around us are rushing into life, cannot always be fed on the sere remains of foreign harvests. Events, actions arise, that must be sung, that will sing themselves. Who can doubt that poetry will revive and lead in a new age, as the star in the constellation Harp, which now flames in our zenith, astronomers announce, shall one day be the pole-star for a thousand years?

In this hope I accept the topic which not only usage but the nature of our association seem to prescribe to this day,—the *American Scholar*. Year by year we come up hither to read one more chapter of his biography. Let us inquire what light new days and events have thrown on his character and his hopes.

It is one of those fables which out of an unknown antiquity convey an unlooked-for wisdom, that the gods, in the beginning, divided Man into men, that he might be more helpful to himself; just as the hand was divided into fingers, the better to answer its end.

The old fable covers a doctrine ever new and sublime; that there is One Man,—present to all particular men only partially, or through one faculty; and that you must take the whole society to find the whole man. Man is not a farmer, or a professor, or an engineer, but he is all. Man is priest, and scholar, and statesman, and producer, and soldier. In the *divided* or social state these functions are parcelled out to individuals, each of whom aims to do his stint of the joint work, whilst each other performs his. The fable implies that the individual, to possess himself, must sometimes return from his own labor to embrace all the other laborers. But, unfortunately, this original unit, this fountain of power, has been so distributed to multitudes, has been so minutely subdivided and peddled out, that it is spilled into drops, and cannot be gathered. The state of society is one in which the members have suffered amputation from the trunk, and strut about so many walking monsters,—a good finger, a neck, a stomach, an elbow, but never a man.

Man is thus metamorphosed into a thing, into many things. The planter, who is Man sent out into the field to gather food, is seldom cheered by any idea of the true dignity of his ministry. He sees his bushel and his cart, and nothing beyond, and sinks into the farmer, instead of Man on the farm. The tradesman scarcely ever gives an ideal worth to his work, but is ridden by the routine of his craft, and the soul is subject to dollars. The priest becomes a form; the attorney a statute-book; the mechanic a machine; the sailor a rope of the ship.

In this distribution of functions the scholar is the delegated intellect. In the right state he is *Man Thinking*. In the degenerate state, when the victim of society, he tends to become a mere thinker, or still worse, the parrot of other men's thinking.

In this view of him, as Man Thinking, the theory of his office is contained. Him Nature solicits with all her placid, all her monitory pictures; him the past instructs; him the future invites. Is not indeed every man a student, and do not all things exist for the student's behoof? And, finally, is not the true scholar the only true master? But the old oracle said, "All things have two handles: beware of the wrong one." In life, too often, the scholar errs with mankind and forfeits his privilege. Let us see him in his school, and consider him in reference to the main influences he receives.

I. The first in time and the first in importance of the influences upon the mind is that of nature. Every day, the sun; and, after sunset, Night and her stars. Ever the winds blow; ever the grass grows. Every day, men and women, conversing—beholding and beholden. The scholar is he of all men whom this spectacle most engages. He must settle its value in his mind. What is nature to him? There is never a beginning, there is never an end, to the inexplicable continuity of this web of God, but always circular power returning into itself. Therein it resembles his own spirit, whose beginning, whose ending, he never can find,—so entire, so boundless. Far too as her splendors shine, system on system shooting like rays, upward, downward, without centre, without circumference,—in the mass and in the particle, Nature hastens to render account of herself to the mind. . . .

II. The next great influence into the spirit of the scholar is the mind of the Past,—in whatever form, whether of literature, of art, of institutions, that mind is inscribed. Books are the best type of the influence of the past, and perhaps we shall get at the truth,—learn the amount of this influence more conveniently,—by considering their value alone. . . .

III. There goes in the world a notion that the scholar should be a recluse, a valetudinarian,—as unfit for any handiwork or public labor as a penknife for an axe. The so-called "practical men" sneer at speculative men, as if, because they speculate or *see*, they could do nothing. I have heard it said that the clergy,—who are always, more universally than any other class, the scholars of their day,—are addressed as women; that the rough, spontaneous conversation of men they do not hear, but only a mincing and diluted speech. They are often virtually disfranchised; and indeed there are advocates for their celibacy. As far as this is true of the studious classes, it is not just and wise. Action is with the scholar subordinate, but it is essential. Without it he is not yet man. Without it thought can never ripen into truth. . . .

I read with some joy of the auspicious signs of the coming days, as they glimmer already through poetry and art, through philosophy and science, through church and state.

One of these signs is the fact that the same movement which effected the elevation of what was called the lowest class in the state, assumed in literature a very marked and as benign an aspect. Instead of the sublime and beautiful, the near, the low, the common, was explored and poetized. That which had been negligently trodden under foot by those who were harnessing and provisioning themselves for long journeys into far countries, is suddenly found to be richer than all foreign parts. The literature of the poor, the feelings of the child, the philosophy of the street, the meaning of household life, are the topics of the time. It is a great stride. It is a sign—is it not?— of new vigor when the extremities are made active, when currents of warm life run into the hands and the feet. I ask not for the great, the remote, the romantic; what is doing in Italy or Arabia; what is Greek art, or Provençal minstrelsy; I embrace the common, I explore and sit at the feet of the familiar, the low. Give me insight into to-day, and you may have the antique and future worlds. What would we really know the meaning of? The meal in the firkin; the milk in the pan; the ballad in the street; the news of the boat; the glance of the eye; the form and the gait of the body;—show me the ultimate reason of these matters; show me the sublime presence of the highest spiritual cause lurking, as always it does lurk, in these suburbs and extremities of nature; let me see every trifle bristling with the polarity that ranges it instantly on an eternal law; and the shop, the plough, and the ledger referred to the like cause by which light undulates and poets sing;— and the world lies no longer a dull miscellany and lumber-room, but has form and order; there is no trifle, there is no puzzle, but one design unites and animates the farthest pinnacle and the lowest trench. . . .

Another sign of our times, also marked by an analogous political movement, is the new importance given to the single person. Every thing that tends to insulate the individual,—to surround him with barriers of natural respect, so that each man shall feel the world is his, and man shall treat with man as a sovereign state with a sovereign state,—tends to true union as well as greatness. "I learned," said the melancholy Pestalozzi, "that no man in God's wide earth is either willing or able to help any other man." Help must come from the bosom alone. The scholar is that man who must take up into himself all the ability of the time, all the contributions of the past, all the hopes of the future. He must be an university of knowledges. If there be one lesson more than another which should pierce his ear, it is, The world is nothing, the man is all; in yourself is the law of all nature, and you know not yet how a globule of sap ascends; in yourself slumbers the whole of Reason; it is for you to know all; it is for you to dare all. Mr. President and Gentlemen, this confidence in the unsearched might of man belongs, by all motives, by all prophecy, by all preparation, to the American Scholar. We have listened too long to the courtly muses of Europe. The spirit of the American freeman is already suspected to be timid, imitative, tame. Public and private avarice make the air we breathe thick and fat. The scholar is decent, indolent, complaisant. See already the tragic consequence. The mind of this country, taught to aim at low objects, eats upon itself. There is no work for any but the decorous and the complaisant. Young men of the fairest promise, who begin life upon our shores, inflated by the mountain winds, shined upon by all the stars of God, find the earth below not in unison with these, but are hindered from action by the disgust which the principles on which business is managed inspire, and turn drudges, or die of disgust, some of them suicides. What is the remedy? They did not yet see, and thousands of young men as hopeful now crowding to the barriers for the career do not yet see, that if the single man plant himself indomitably on his instincts, and there abide, the huge world will come round to him. Patience,—patience; with the shades of all the good and great for company; and for solace the perspective of your own infinite life; and for work the study and the communication of principles, the making those instincts prevalent, the conversion of the world. Is it not the chief disgrace in the world, not to be an unit;—not to be reckoned one character;—not to yield that peculiar fruit which each man was created to bear, but to be reckoned in the gross, in the hundred, or the thousand, of the party, the section, to which we belong; and our opinion predicted geographically, as the north, or the south? Not so, brothers and friends—please God, ours shall not be so. We will walk on our own feet; we will work with our own hands; we will speak our own minds. The study of letters shall be no longer a name for pity, for doubt, and for sensual indulgence. The dread of man and the love of man shall be a wall of defence and a wreath of joy around all. A nation of men will for the first time exist, because each believes himself inspired by the Divine Soul which also inspires all men.

Source: Ralph Waldo Emerson, *Essays and English Traits* (New York, 1909).

For Further Reading:

Carl Bode, *The American Lyceum* (New York: Oxford University Press, 1968).
Mary Cayton, *Emerson's Emergence: Self and Society in the Transformation of New England* (Chapel Hill: University of North Carolina Press, 1989).
Perry Miller, *The Transcendentalists* (Cambridge, Mass.: Harvard University Press, 1950).
Larzer Ziff, *Literary Democracy* (New York: Viking Press, 1957).

27. Henry David Thoreau, Excerpt from "Resistance to Civil Government" (1848)

1837   Thoreau graduates from Harvard College
1841–43   Thoreau goes to live with Emerson and family
1845–47   Thoreau moves to one-room hut at Walden Pond
1849   "On Civil Disobedience" or "Resistance to Civil Government" published
1854   *Walden* published

One writer who was influenced by Ralph Waldo Emerson was Henry David Thoreau. A student at Harvard when Emerson delivered his "American Scholar" address (see document 26), Thoreau took the transcendentalist's ideal of individual liberation to its logical extreme. In 1845 he built a log cabin in the woods at the edge of Walden Pond, in Concord, Massachusetts. There, for two years, he lived a hermit's life of total self-reliance, meditated, and wrote. The result was Walden, Or Life in the Woods, *in which Thoreau described his attempt to escape the artificiality of modern materialistic society.*

While at Walden, Thoreau refused to pay his taxes to the federal government. He intended to protest against slavery and the Mexican-American war. He explained this action in a speech entitled "Resistance to Civil Government," subsequently published as "On Civil Disobedience." Thoreau con-

tended that individuals had the right, if not the obligation, to abide by their own conscience, to obey their moral principles. If society's laws contradicted one's moral sensibilities, one should follow one's conscience. Put another way, people should refuse to obey unjust lays, although they should be prepared to suffer the consequence for doing so—Thoreau was sentenced to a brief stay in jail for refusing to pay his taxes.

A century after writing Walden, *Thoreau became a model to many young rebels. Many civil rights activists, including Martin Luther King, Jr. (see document 85), followed his example, advocating nonviolent direct action or civil disobedience. Others duplicated Thoreau's retreat to nature, either by moving to communes or by championing the counterculture.*

I heartily accept the motto,—"That government is best which governs least"; and I should like to see it acted up to more rapidly and systematically. Carried out, it finally amounts to this, which also I believe,—"That government is best which governs not at all"; and when men are prepared for it, that will be the kind of government which they will have. Government is at best but an expedient; but most governments are usually, and all governments are sometimes, inexpedient. The objections which have been brought against a standing army, and they are many and weighty, and deserve to prevail, may also at last be brought against a standing government. The standing army is only an arm of the standing government. The government itself, which is only the mode which the people have chosen to execute their will, is equally liable to be abused and perverted before the people can act through it. Witness the present Mexican war, the work of comparatively a few individuals using the standing government as their tool; for, in the outset, the people would not have consented to this measure.

This American government,—what is it but a tradition, though a recent one, endeavoring to transmit itself unimpaired to posterity, but each instant losing some of its integrity? It has not the vitality and force of a single living man; for a single man can bend it to his will. It is a sort of wooden gun to the people themselves; and, if ever they should use it in earnest as a real one against each other, it will surely split. But it is not the less necessary for this; for the people must have some complicated machinery or other, and hear its din, to satisfy that idea of government which they have. Governments show thus how successfully men can be imposed on, even impose on themselves, for their own advantage. It is excellent, we must all allow; yet this government never of itself furthered any enterprise, but by the alacrity with which it got out of its way. *It* does not keep the country free. *It* does not settle the West. *It* does not educate. The character inherent in the American people has done all that has been accomplished; and it would have done somewhat more, if the government had not sometimes got in its way. For government is an expedient by which men would fain succeed in letting one another alone; and, as has been said, when it is most expedient, the governed are most let alone by it. Trade and commerce, if they were not made of India rubber, would never manage to bounce over the obstacles which legislators are continually putting in their way; and, if one were to judge these men wholly by the effects of their actions, and not partly by their intentions, they would deserve to be classed and punished with those mischievous persons who put obstructions on the railroads. . . .

The mass of men serve the State thus, not as men mainly, but as machines, with their bodies. They are the standing army, and the militia, jailers, constables, *posse comitatus*, &c. In most cases there is no free exercise whatever of the judgment or of the moral sense; but they put themselves on a level with wood and earth and stones, and wooden men can perhaps be manufactured that will serve the purpose as well. Such command no more respect than men of straw, or a lump of dirt. They have the same sort of worth only as horses and dogs. Yet such as these even are commonly esteemed good citizens. Others, as most legislators, politicians, lawyers, ministers, and officeholders, serve the State chiefly with their heads; and, as they rarely make any moral distinctions, they are as likely to serve the devil, without intending it, as God. A very few, as heroes, patriots, martyrs, reformers in the great sense, and *men*, serve the State with their consciences also, and so necessarily resist it for the most part; and they are commonly treated by it as enemies. . . .

All men recognize the right of revolution; that is, the right to refuse allegiance to and to resist the government, when its tyranny or its inefficiency are great and unendurable. But almost all say that such is not the case now. But such was the case, they think, in the Revolution of '75. If one were to tell me that this was a bad government because it taxed certain foreign commodities brought to its ports, it is most probable that I should not make an ado about it, for I can do without them: all machines have their friction; and possibly this does enough good to counterbalance the evil. At any rate, it is a great evil to make a stir about it. But when the friction comes to have its machine, and oppression and robbery are organized, I say, let us not have such a machine any longer. In other words, when a sixth of the population of a nation which has undertaken to be the refuge of liberty are slaves, and a whole country is unjustly overrun and conquered by a foreign army, and subjected to military law, I think that it is not too soon for honest men to rebel and revolutionize. What makes this duty the more urgent is the fact, that the country so overrun is not our own, but ours is the invading army.

Paley, a common authority with many on moral questions, in his chapter on the "Duty of Submission to Civil Government," resolves all civil obligation into expediency; and he proceeds to say, "that so long as the interest of the whole society requires it, that is, so long as the established government cannot be resisted or changed without public inconveniency, it is the will of God that the established government be obeyed, and no longer." . . . "This principle being admitted, the justice of every particular case of resistance is reduced to a computation of the quantity of the danger and grievance on the one side, and of the probability and expense of redressing it on the other." Of this, he says, every man shall judge for himself. But Paley appears never to have contemplated those cases to which the rule of expediency does not apply, in which a people, as well as an individual, must do justice, cost what it may. If I have unjustly wrested a plank from a drowning man, I must restore it to him though I drown myself. This, according to Paley, would be inconvenient. But he that would save his life, in such a case, shall lose it. This people must cease to hold slaves, and to make war on Mexico, though it cost them their existence as a people. . . .

All voting is a sort of gaming, like chequers or backgammon, with a slight moral tinge to it, a playing with right and wrong, with moral questions; and betting naturally accompanies it. The character of the voters is not staked. I cast my vote, perchance, as I think right; but I am not vitally concerned that that right should prevail. I am willing to leave it to the majority. Its obligation, therefore, never exceeds that of expediency. Even voting *for the right* is *doing* nothing for it. It is only expressing to men feebly your desire that it should prevail. A wise man will not leave the right to the mercy of chance, nor wish it to prevail through the power of the majority. There is but little virtue in the action of masses of men. When the majority shall at length vote for the abolition of slavery, it will be because they are indifferent to slavery, or because there is but little slavery left to be abolished by their vote. *They* will then be the only slaves. Only *his* vote can hasten the abolition of slavery who asserts his own freedom by his vote. . . .

Unjust laws exist: shall we be content to obey them, or shall we endeavor to amend them, and obey them until we have succeeded, or shall we transgress them at once? Men generally, under such a government as this, think that they ought to wait until they have persuaded the majority to alter them. They think that, if they should resist, the remedy would be worse than the evil. But it is the fault of the government itself that the remedy *is* worse than the evil. *It* makes it worse. Why is it not more apt to anticipate and provide for reform? Why does it not cherish its wise minority? Why does it cry and resist before it is hurt? Why does it not encourage its citizens to be on the alert to point out its faults, and *do* better than it would have them? Why does it always crucify Christ, and excommunicate Copernicus and Luther, and pronounce Washington and Franklin rebels?

One would think, that a deliberate and practical denial of its authority was the only offence never contemplated by government; else, why has it not assigned its definite, its suitable and proportionate penalty? If a man who has no property refuses but once to earn nine shillings for the State, he is put in prison for a period unlimited by any law that I know, and determined only by the discretion of those who placed him there; but if he should steal ninety times nine shillings from the State, he is soon permitted to go at large again.

If the injustice is part of the necessary friction of the machine of government, let it go, let it go: perchance it will wear smooth,—certainly the machine will wear out. If the injustice has a spring, or a pulley, or a rope, or a crank, exclusively for itself, then perhaps you may consider whether the remedy will not be worse than the evil; but if it is of such a nature that it requires you to be the agent of injustice to another, then, I say, break the law. Let your life be a counter friction to stop the machine. What I have to do is to see, at any rate, that I do not lend myself to the wrong which I condemn.

As for adopting the ways which the State has provided for remedying the evil, I know not of such ways. They take too much time, and a man's life will be gone. I have other affairs to attend to. I came into this world, not chiefly to make this a good place to live in, but to live in it, be it good or bad. A man has not every thing to do, but something; and because he cannot do *every thing*, it is not necessary that he should do *something* wrong. It is not my business to be petitioning the governor or the legislature any more than it is theirs to petition me; and, if they should not hear my petition, what should I do then? But in this case the State has provided no way: its very Constitution is the evil. This may seem to be harsh and stubborn and unconciliatory; but it is to treat with the utmost kindness and consideration the only spirit that can appreciate or deserves it. So is all change for the better, like birth and death which convulse the body.

I do not hesitate to say, that those who call themselves abolitionists should at once effectually withdraw their support, both in person and property, from the government of Massachusetts, and not wait till they constitute a majority of one, before they suffer the right to prevail through them. I think that it is enough if they have God on their side, without waiting for that other one. Moreover, any man more right than his neighbors, constitutes a majority of one already.

I meet this American government, or its representative the State government, directly, and face to face, once a year, no more, in the person of its tax-gatherer; this is the only mode in which a man situated as I am necessarily meets it; and it then says distinctly, Recognize me; and the simplest, the most effectual, and, in the present posture of affairs, the indispensablest mode of treating with it on this head, of expressing your little satisfaction with and love for it, is to deny it then. My civil neighbor, the tax-gatherer, is the very man I have to deal with,—for it is, after all, with men and not with parchment that I quarrel,—and he has voluntarily chosen to be an agent of the government. How shall he ever know well what he is and does as an officer of the government, or as a man, until he is obliged to consider whether he shall treat me, his neighbor, for whom he has respect, as a neighbor and well-disposed man, or as a maniac and disturber of the peace, and see if he can get over this obstruction to his neighborliness without a ruder and more impetuous thought or speech corresponding with his action? I know this well, that if one thousand, if one hundred, if ten men whom I could name,—if ten *honest* men only,—aye, if *one* HONEST man, in this State of Massachusetts, *ceasing to hold slaves*, were actually to withdraw from this co-partnership, and be locked up in the country jail therefor, it would be the abolition of slavery in America. For it matters not how small the beginning may seem to be; what is once well done is done for ever. But we love better to talk about it: that we say is our mission. Reform keeps many scores of newspapers in its service, but not one man. . . .

Under a government which imprisons any unjustly, the true place for a just man is also a prison. The proper place to-day, the only place which Massachusetts has provided for her freer and less desponding spirits, is in her prisons, to be put out and locked out of the State by her own act, as they have already put themselves out by their principles. It is there that the fugitive slave, and the Mexican prisoner on parole, and the Indian come to plead the wrongs of his race, should find them; on that separate, but more free and honorable ground, where the State places those who are not *with* her but *against* her,—the only house in a slave-state in which a free man can abide with honor. If any think that their influence would be lost there, and their voices no longer afflict the ear of the State, that they would not be as an enemy within its walls, they do not know by how much truth is stronger than error, nor how much more eloquently and effectively he can combat injustice who has experienced a little in his own person. Cast your whole vote, not a strip of paper merely, but your whole influence. A majority is powerless while it conforms to the majority; it is not even a minority then; but it is irresistible when it clogs by its whole weight. If the alternative is to keep all just men in prison, or give up war and slavery, the State will not hesitate which to choose. If a thousand men were not to pay their tax-bills this year, that would not be a violent and bloody measure, as it would be to pay them, and enable the State to commit violence and shed innocent blood. This is, in fact, the definition of a peaceable revolution, if any such is possible. If the tax-gatherer, or any other public officer, asks me, as one has done, "But what shall I do?" my answer is, "If you really wish to do any thing, resign your office." When the subject has refused allegiance, and the officer has resigned his office, then the revolution is accomplished. But even suppose blood should flow. Is there not a sort of blood shed when the conscience is wounded? Through this wound a man's real manhood and immortality flow out, and he bleeds to an everlasting death. I see this blood flowing now. . . .

I have paid no poll-tax for six years. I was put into a jail once on this account, for one night; and, as I stood considering the walls of solid stone, two or three feet thick, the door of wood and iron, a foot thick, and the iron grating which strained the light, I could not help being struck with the foolishness of that institution which treated me as if I were mere flesh and blood and bones, to be locked up. I wondered that it should have concluded at length that this was the best use it could put me to, and had never thought to avail itself of my services in some way. I saw that, if there was a wall of stone between me and my townsmen, there was a still more difficult one to climb or break through, before they could get to be as free as I was. I did not for a moment feel confined, and the walls seemed a great waste of stone and mortar. I felt as if I alone of all my townsmen had paid my tax. They plainly did not know how to treat me, but behaved like persons who are underbred. In every threat and in every compliment there was a blunder; for they thought that my chief desire was to stand the other side of that stone wall. I could not but smile to see how industriously they locked the door on my meditations, which followed them out again without let or hinderance, and *they* were really all that was dangerous. As they could not reach me, they had resolved to punish my body; just as boys, if they cannot come at some person against whom they have a spite, will abuse his dog. I saw that the State was half-witted, that it was timid as a lone woman with her silver spoons, and that it did not know its friends from its foes, and I lost all my remaining respect for it, and pitied it.

Thus the State never intentionally confronts a man's sense, intellectual or moral, but only his body, his senses. It is not armed with superior wit or honesty, but with superior physical strength. I was not born to be forced. I will breathe after my own fashion. Let us see who is the strongest. What force has a multitude? They only can force me who obey a higher law than I. They force me to become like themselves. I do not hear of *men* being *forced* to live this way or that by masses of men. What sort of life were that to live? When I meet a government which says to me, "Your money or your life," why should I be in haste to give it my money? It may be in a great strait, and not know what to do: I cannot help that. It must help itself; do as I do. It is not worth the while to snivel about it. I am not responsible for the successful working of the machinery of society. I am not the son of the engineer. I perceive that, when an acorn and a chestnut fall side by side, the one does not remain inert to make way for the other, but both obey their own laws, and spring and grow and flourish as best they can, till one, perchance, overshadows and destroys the other. If a plant cannot live according to its nature, it dies; and so a man.

Source: *The Writings of Henry David Thoreau* (Boston, 1863), 10:131–70.

For Further Reading:

Staughton Lynd, *Intellectual Origins of American Radicalism* (New York: Pantheon Books, 1968).
Richard Schneider, *Henry David Thoreau* (Boston: Twayne, 1987).

28. Excerpt from *The Liberator* (1831)

1831   Nat Turner's Rebellion; *The Liberator* founded
1832   American Antislavery Society established
1837   Elijah Lovejoy lynched, Alton, Illinois
1840–44   Liberal Party runs candidates for office

Of all the reform movements of the ante-bellum period, the most important was the abolitionist or antislavery movement. While antislavery organizations had existed for over fifty years, one can trace the origins of the abolitionists to the publication of The Liberator, *William Lloyd Garrison's radical paper, in 1831 and to the formation of the American Antislavery Society, also headed by Garrison. The latter sponsored public lectures, distributed reams of antislavery literature and pressured the government to adopt antislavery legislation.* The Liberator, *as its masthead declared, lambasted slavery as an immoral institution and demanded its immediate death.*

Initially the abolitionists were not well received. Some were run out of town. Other had bounties put on their heads. Elijah Lovejoy, the descendant of a long line of ministers and an abolitionist, was in fact murdered by a mob in Alton, Illinois. Garrison was jailed for seven weeks for libeling a slave merchant. Yet the abolitionists persevered, and by the 1840s their voice had become a force in American politics. Men and women associated with all sorts of reform movements joined the antislavery crusade. In turn, many abolitionists advocated sexual, religious, economic, and other forms of equality.

I n the month of August, I issued proposals for publishing *The Liberator* in Washington city; but the enterprise, though hailed in different sections of the country, was palsied by public indifference. Since that time, the removal of the *Genius of Universal Emancipation* to the Seat of Government has rendered less imperious the establishment of a similar periodical in that quarter.

During my recent tour for the purpose of exciting the minds of the people by a series of discourses on the subject of slavery, every place that I visited gave fresh evidence of the fact, that a greater revolution in public sentiment was to be effected in the free states—*and particularly in New-England*—than at the south. I found contempt more bitter, opposition more active, detraction more relentless, prejudice more stubborn, and apathy more frozen, than among the slave owners themselves. Of course, there were individual exceptions to the contrary. This state of things afflicted, but did not dishearten me. I determined, at every hazard, to lift up the standard of emancipation in the eyes of the nation, *within sight of Bunker Hill and in the birth place of liberty.* That standard is now unfurled; and long may it float, unhurt by the spoliations of time or the missiles of a desperate foe— yea, till every chain be broken, and every bondman set free! Let southern oppressors tremble—let their secret abettors tremble—let their northern apologists tremble—let all the enemies of the persecuted blacks tremble.

I deem the publication of my original Prospectus unnecessary, as it has obtained a wide circulation. The principles therein inculcated will be steadily pursued in this paper, excepting that I shall not array myself as the political partisan of any man. In defending the great cause of human rights, I wish to derive the assistance of all religions and of all parties.

Assenting to the "self-evident truth" maintained in the American Declaration of Independence, "that all men are created equal, and endowed by their Creator with certain inalienable rights—among which are life, liberty and the pursuit of happiness," I shall strenuously contend for the immediate enfranchisement of our slave population. In Park-street Church, on the Fourth of July, 1829, in an address on slavery, I unreflectingly assented to the popular but pernicious doctrine of *gradual* abolition. I seize this opportunity to make a full and unequivocal recantation, and thus publicly to ask pardon of my God, of my country, and of my brethren the poor slaves, for having uttered a sentiment so full of timidity, injustice and absurdity. A similar recantation, from my pen, was published in the *Genius of Universal Emancipation* at Baltimore, in September, 1829. My conscience is now satisfied.

I am aware that many object to the severity of my language; but is there not cause for severity? I *will be* as harsh as truth, and as uncompromising as justice. On this subject, I do not wish to think, or speak, or write, with moderation. No! no! Tell a man whose house is on fire, to give a moderate alarm; tell him to moderately rescue his wife from the hands of the ravisher; tell the mother to gradually extricate her babe from the fire into which it has fallen;—but urge me not to use moderation in a cause like the present. I am in earnest—I will not equivocate—I will not excuse—I will not retreat a single inch—AND I WILL BE HEARD. The apathy of the people is enough to make every statue leap from its pedestal, and to hasten the resurrection of the dead.

It is pretended, that I am retarding the cause of emancipation, by the coarseness of my invective, and the precipitancy of my measures. *The charge is not true.* On this question my influence,—humble as it is,—is felt at this moment to a considerable extent, and shall be felt in coming years—not perniciously, but beneficially—not as a curse, but as a blessing; and posterity will bear testimony that I was right. I desire to thank God, that he enables me to disregard "the fear of man which bringeth a snare," and to speak his truth in its simplicity and power.

And here I close with this fresh dedication:

"Oppression! I have seen thee, face to face,
And met thy cruel eye and cloudy brow;
But thy soul-withering glance I fear not now—
For dread to prouder feelings doth give place
Of deep abhorrence! Scorning the disgrace
Of slavish knees that at thy footstool bow,
I also kneel—but with far other bow
Do hail thee and thy herd of hirelings base:—
I swear, while life-blood warms my throbbing veins,
Still to oppose and thwart, with heart and hand,
Thy brutalizing sway—'till Afric's chains
Are burst, and Freedom rules the rescued land,—
Trampling Oppression and his iron rod:
*Such is the vow I take—*so HELP ME GOD!"

Source: *The Liberator* 1 (1), January 1, 1831.

For Further Reading:

Louis Filler, *The Crusade Against Slavery* (New York: Harper & Row, 1960).
John L. Thomas, *The Liberator: William Lloyd Garrison* (Boston: Little, Brown, 1963).
Ronald G. Walters, *The Antislavery Appeal* (Baltimore: Johns Hopkins University Press, 1976).

29. Frederick Douglass, Excerpt from the *Narrative of the Life of Frederick Douglass* (1845)

1817   Douglass born in Talbot County, Maryland
1838   Douglass escapes from slavery
1841   Douglass joins antislavery lecture circuit
1845   Douglass' *Narrative* published
1847   Douglass founds the *North Star*

While most abolitionists were white, the antislavery movement benefited tremendously from its recruitment of free black men and women, most fa-

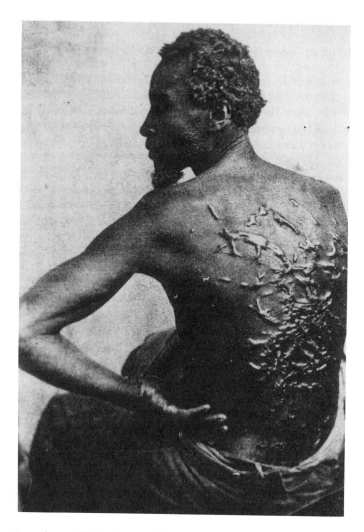

Scars from a Whipping on a Slave's Back, 1863 (National Archives).

mously Sojourner Truth, Harriet Tubman, and Frederick Douglass. They provided the antislavery crusade with an authoritative voice. Speaking from experience, they could testify to the cruelty and immorality of slavery.

Douglass' most notable exposé of slavery was his autobiography, entitled the Narrative of the Life of Frederick Douglass. *It bore vivid witness to his life as a slave, from his relatively calm childhood with the Aulds to his encounter with the brutal slave-breaker, Mr. Covey. Initially published with a preface by William Lloyd Garrison, it created a stir, not simply because of its detail and its moving story, but also for the beauty of its style, which defied the characterization of blacks as ignorant and stupid.*

Douglass also spread his antislavery message in lectures and through antislavery newspapers, including his own Rochester North Star, which first appeared in 1847, nine years after his escape. During the Civil War Douglass met with President Lincoln, imploring him to emancipate the slaves and to enlist the freedmen into the military. After the Civil War Douglass remained the most prominent black spokesman in America, insisting on full citizenship rights for his people.

I left Master Thomas's house, and went to live with Mr. Covey, on the 1st of January, 1833. I was now, for the first time in my life, a field hand. In my new employment, I found myself even more awkward than a country boy appeared to be in a large city. I had been at my new home but one week before Mr. Covey gave me a very severe whipping, cutting my back, causing the blood to run, and raising ridges on my flesh as large as my little finger. The details of this affair are as follows: Mr. Covey sent me, very early in the morning of one of our coldest days in the month of January, to the woods, to get a load of wood. He gave me a team of unbroken oxen. He told me which was the in-hand ox, and which the off-hand one. He then tied the end of a large rope around the horns of the in-hand ox, and gave me the other end of it, and told me, if the oxen started to run, that I must hold on upon the rope. I had never driven oxen before, and of course I was very awkward. I, however, succeeded in getting to the edge of the woods with little difficulty; but I had got a very few rods into the woods, when the oxen took fright, and started full tilt, carrying the cart against trees, and over stumps, in the most frightful manner. I expected every moment that my brains would be dashed out against the trees. After running thus for a considerable distance, they finally upset the cart, dashing it with great force against a tree, and threw themselves into a dense thicket. How I escaped death, I do not know. There I was, entirely alone, in a thick wood, in a place new to me. My cart was upset and shattered, my oxen were entangled among the young trees, and there was none to help me. After a long spell of effort, I succeeded in getting my cart righted, my oxen disentangled, and again yoked to the cart. I now proceeded with my team to the place where I had, the day before, been chopping wood, and loaded my cart pretty heavily, thinking in this way to tame my oxen. I then proceeded on my way home. I had now consumed one half of the day. I got out of the woods safely, and now felt out of danger. I stopped my oxen to open the woods gate; and just as I did so, before I could get hold of my ox-rope, the oxen again started, rushed through the gate, catching it between the wheel and the body of the cart, tearing it to pieces, and coming within a few inches of crushing me against the gate-post. Thus twice, in one short day, I escaped death by the merest chance. On my return, I told Mr. Covey what had happened, and how it happened. He ordered me to return to the woods again immediately.

I did so, and he followed on after me. Just as I got into the woods, he came up and told me to stop my cart, and that he would teach me how to trifle away my time, and break gates. He then went to a large gum-tree, and with his axe cut three large switches, and, after trimming them up neatly with his pocket-knife, he ordered me to take off my clothes. I made him no answer, but stood with my clothes on. He repeated his order. I still made him no answer, nor did I move to strip myself. Upon this he rushed at me with the fierceness of a tiger, tore off my clothes, and lashed me till he had worn out his switches, cutting me so savagely as to leave the marks visible for a long time after. This whipping was the first of a number just like it, and for similar offences.

I lived with Mr. Covey one year. During the first six months, of that year, scarce a week passed without his whipping me. I was seldom free from a sore back. My awkwardness was almost always his excuse for whipping me. We were worked fully up to the point of endurance. Long before day we were up, our horses fed, and by the first approach of day we were off to the field with our hoes and ploughing teams. Mr. Covey gave us enough to eat, but scarce time to eat it. We were often less than five minutes taking our meals. We were often in the field from the first approach of day till its last lingering ray had left us; and at saving-fodder time, midnight often caught us in the field binding blades.

Covey would be out with us. The way he used to stand it, was this. He would spend the most of his afternoons in bed. He would then come out fresh in the evening, ready to urge us on with his words, example, and frequently with the whip. Mr. Covey was one of the few slaveholders who could and did work with his hands. He was a hard-working man. He knew by himself just what a man or a boy could do. There was no deceiving him. His work went on in his absence almost as well as in his presence; and he had the faculty of making us feel that he was ever present with us. This he did by surprising us. He seldom approached the spot where we were at work openly, if he could do it secretly. He always aimed at taking us by surprise. Such was his cunning, that we used to call him, among ourselves, "the snake." When we were at work in the cornfield, he would sometimes crawl on his hands and knees to avoid detection, and all at once he would rise nearly in our midst, and scream out, "Ha, ha! Come, come! Dash on, dash on!" This being his mode of attack, it was never safe to stop a single minute. His comings were like a thief in the night. He appeared to us as being ever at hand. He was under every tree, behind every stump, in every bush, and at every window, on the plantation. He would sometimes mount his horse, as if bound to St. Michael's, a distance of seven miles, and in half an hour afterwards you would see him coiled up in the corner of the wood-fence, watching every motion of the slaves. He would, for this purpose, leave his horse tied up in the woods. Again, he would sometimes walk up to us, and give us orders as though he was upon the point of starting on a long journey, turn his back upon us, and make as though he was going to the house to get ready; and, before he would get half way thither, he would turn short and crawl into a fence-corner, or behind some tree, and there watch us till the going down of the sun.

Mr. Covey's *forte* consisted in his power to deceive. His life was devoted to planning and perpetrating the grossest deceptions. Every thing he possessed in the shape of learning or religion, he made conform to his disposition to deceive. He seemed to think himself equal to deceiving the Almighty. He would make a short prayer in the morning, and a long prayer at night; and, strange as it may seem, few men would at times appear more devotional than he. The exercises of his family devotions were always commenced with singing; and, as he was a very poor singer himself, the duty of raising the hymn generally came upon me. He would read his hymn, and nod at me to commence. I would at times do so; at others, I would not. My noncompliance would almost always produce much confusion. To show himself independent of me, he would start and stagger through with his hymn in the most discordant manner. In this state of mind, he prayed with more than ordinary spirit. Poor man! such was his disposition, and success at deceiving, I do verily believe that he sometimes deceived himself into the solemn belief, that he was a sincere worshipper of the most high God; and this, too, at a time when he may be said to have been guilty of compelling his woman slave to commit the sin of adultery. The facts in the case are these: Mr. Covey was a poor man; he was just commencing in life; he was only able to buy one slave; and, shocking as is the fact, he bought her, as he said, for a *breeder*. This woman was named Caroline. Mr. Covey bought her from Mr. Thomas Lowe, about six miles from St. Michael's. She was a large, able-bodied woman, about twenty years old. She had already given birth to one child, which proved her to be just what he wanted. After buying her, he hired a married man of Mr. Samuel Harrison, to live with him one year; and him he used to fasten up with her every night! The result was, that, at the end of the year, the miserable woman gave birth to twins. At this result Mr. Covey seemed to be highly pleased, both with the man and the wretched woman. Such was his joy, and that of his wife, that nothing they could do for Caroline during her confinement was too good, or too hard, to be done. The children were regarded as being quite an addition to his wealth.

If at any one time of my life more than another, I was made to drink the bitterest dregs of slavery, that time was during the first six months of my stay with Mr. Covey. We were worked in all weathers. It was never too hot or too cold; it could never rain, blow, hail, or snow, too hard for us to work in the field. Work, work, work, was scarcely more the order of the day than of the night. The longest days were too short for him, and the shortest nights too long for him. I was somewhat unmanageable when I first went there, but a few months of this discipline tamed me. Mr. Covey succeeded in breaking me. I was broken in body, soul, and spirit. My natural elasticity was crushed, my intellect languished, the disposition to read departed, the cheerful spark that lingered about my eye died; the dark night of slavery closed in upon me; and behold a man transformed into a brute! . . .

I have already intimated that my condition was much worse, during the first six months of my stay at Mr. Covey's, than in the last six. The circumstances leading to the change in Mr. Covey's course toward me form an epoch in my humble history. You have seen how a man was made a slave; you shall see how a slave was made a man. On one of the hottest days of the month of August, 1833, Bill Smith, William Hughes, a slave named Eli, and myself, were engaged in fanning wheat. Hughes was clearing the fanned wheat from before the fan, Eli was turning, Smith was feeding, and I was carrying wheat to the fan. The work was simple, requiring strength rather than intellect; yet, to one entirely unused to such work, it came very hard. About three o'clock of that day, I broke down; my strength failed me; I was seized with a violent aching of the head, attended with extreme dizziness; I trembled in every limb. Finding what was coming, I nerved myself up, feeling it would never do to stop work. I stood as long as I could stagger to the hopper with grain. When I could stand no longer, I fell, and felt as if held down by an immense weight. The fan of course stopped; every one had his own work to do; and no one could do the work of the other, and have his own go on at the same time.

Mr. Covey was at the house, about one hundred yards from the treading-yard where we were fanning. On hearing the fan stop, he left immediately, and came to the spot where we were. He hastily inquired what the matter was. Bill answered that I was sick, and there was no one to bring wheat to the fan. I had by this time crawled away under the side of the post and rail-fence by which the yard was enclosed, hoping to find relief by getting out of the sun. He then asked where I was. He was told by one of the hands. He came to the spot, and, after looking at me awhile, asked me what was the matter. I told him as well as I could, for I scarce had strength to speak. He then gave me a savage kick in the side, and told me to get up. I tried to do so, but fell back in the attempt. He gave me another kick, and again told me to rise. I again tried, and succeeded in gaining my feet; but, stooping to get the tub with which I was feeding the fan, I again staggered and fell. While down in this situation, Mr. Covey took up the hickory slat with which Hughes had been striking off the half-bushel measure, and with it gave me a heavy blow upon the head, making a large wound, and the blood ran freely; and with this again told me to get up. I made no effort to comply, having now made up my mind to let him do his worst. In a short time after receiving this blow, my head grew better. Mr. Covey had now left me to my fate. At this moment I resolved, for the first time, to go to my master, enter a complaint, and ask his protection. In order to [do] this, I must that afternoon walk seven miles; and this, under the circumstances, was truly a severe undertaking. I was exceedingly feeble; made so as much by the kicks and blows which I received, as by the severe fit of sickness to which I had been subjected. I, however, watched my chance, while Covey was looking in an opposite direction, and started for St. Michael's. I succeeded in getting a considerable distance on my way to the woods, when Covey discovered me, and called after me to come back, threatening what he would do if I did not come. I disregarded both his calls and his threats, and made my way to the woods as fast as my feeble state would allow; and thinking I might be over-hauled by him if I kept the road, I walked through the woods, keeping far enough from the road to avoid detection, and near enough to prevent losing my way. I had not gone far before my little strength again failed me. I could go no farther. I fell down, and lay for a considerable time. The blood was yet oozing from the wound on my head. For a time I thought I should bleed to death; and think now that I should have done so, but that the blood so matted my hair as to stop the wound. After lying there about three quarters of an hour, I nerved myself up again, and started on my way, through bogs and briers, barefooted and bareheaded, tearing my feet sometimes at nearly every step; and after a journey of about seven miles, occupying some five hours to perform it, I arrived at master's store. I then presented an appearance enough to affect any but a heart of iron. From the crown of my head to my feet, I was covered with blood. My hair was all clotted with dust and blood; my shirt was stiff with blood. My legs and feet were torn in sundry places with briers and thorns, and were also covered with blood. I suppose I looked like a man who had escaped a den of wild beasts, and barely escaped them. In this state I appeared before my master, humbly entreating him to interpose his authority for my protection. I told him all the circumstances as well as I could, and it seemed, as I spoke, at times to affect him. He would then walk the floor, and seek to justify Covey by saying he expected I deserved it. He asked me what I wanted. I told him, to let me get a new home; that as sure as I lived with Mr. Covey again, I should live with but to die with him; that Covey would surely kill me; he was in a fair way for it. Master Thomas ridiculed the idea that there was any danger of Mr. Covey's killing me, and said that he knew Mr. Covey; that he was a good man, and that he could not think of taking me from him; that, should he do so, he would lose the whole year's wages; that I belonged to Mr. Covey for one year, and that I must go back to him, come what might; and that I must not trouble him with any more stories, or that he would himself *get hold of me.* After threatening me thus, he gave me a very large dose of salts, telling me that I might remain in St. Michael's that night, (it being quite late,) but that I must be off back to Mr. Covey's early in the morning; and that if I did not, he would *get hold of me,* which meant that he would whip me. I remained all night, and, according to his orders, I started off to Covey's in the morning, (Saturday morning,) wearied in body and broken in spirit. I got no supper that night, or breakfast that morning. I reached

Covey's about nine o'clock; and just as I was getting over the fence that divided Mrs. Kemp's fields from ours, out ran Covey with his cowskin, to give me another whipping. Before he could reach me, I succeeded in getting to the cornfield; and as the corn was very high, it afforded me the means of hiding. He seemed very angry, and searched for me a long time. My behavior was altogether unaccountable. He finally gave up the chase, thinking, I suppose, that I must come home for something to eat; he would give himself no further trouble in looking for me. . . . Upon entering the yard gate, out came Mr. Covey on his way to meeting. He spoke to me very kindly, bade me drive the pigs from a lot near by, and passed on towards the church. . . . All went well till Monday morning. . . . Long before daylight, I was called to go and rub, curry, and feed, the horses. I obeyed, and was glad to obey. But whilst thus engaged, whilst in the act of throwing down some blades from the loft, Mr. Covey entered the stable with a long rope; and just as I was half out of the loft, he caught hold of my legs, and was about tying me. As soon as I found what he was up to, I gave a sudden spring, and as I did so, he holding to my legs, I was brought sprawling on the stable floor. Mr. Covey seemed now to think he had me, and could do what he pleased; but at this moment—from whence came the spirit I don't know—I resolved to fight; and, suiting my action to the resolution, I seized Covey hard by the throat; and as I did so, I rose. He held on to me, and I to him. My resistance was so entirely unexpected, that Covey seemed taken all aback. He trembled like a leaf. This gave me assurance, and I held him uneasy, causing the blood to run where I touched him with the ends of my fingers. Mr. Covey soon called out to Hughes for help. Hughes came, and, while Covey held me, attempted to tie my right hand. While he was in the act of doing so, I watched my chance, and gave him a heavy kick close under the ribs. This kick fairly sickened Hughes, so that he left me in the hands of Mr. Covey. This kick had the effect of not only weakening Hughes, but Covey also. When he saw Hughes bending over with pain, his courage quailed. He asked me if I meant to persist in my resistance. I told him I did, come what might; that he had used me like a brute for six months, and that I was determined to be used so no longer. With that, he strove to drag me to a stick that was lying just out of the stable door. He meant to knock me down. But just as he was leaning over to get the stick, I seized him with both hands by his collar, and brought him by a sudden snatch to the ground. By this time, Bill came. Covey called upon him for assistance. Bill wanted to know what he could do. Covey said, "Take hold of him, take hold of him!" Bill said his master hired him out to work, and not to help to whip me; so he left Covey and myself to fight our own battle out. We were at it for nearly two hours. Covey at length let me go, puffing and blowing at a great rate, saying that if I had not resisted, he would not have whipped me half so much. The truth was, that he had not whipped me at all. I considered him as getting entirely the worst end of the bargain; for he had drawn no blood from me, but I had from him. The whole six months afterwards, that I spend with Mr. Covey, he never laid the weight of his finger upon me in anger. He would occasionally say, he didn't want to get hold of me again. "No," thought I, "you need not; for you will come off worse than you did before."

This battle with Mr. Covey was the turning-point in my career as a slave. It rekindled the few expiring embers of freedom, and revived within me a sense of my own manhood. It recalled the departed self-confidence, and inspired me again with a determination to be free. The gratification afforded by the triumph was a full compensation for whatever else might follow, even death itself. He only can understand the deep satisfaction which I experienced, who has himself repelled by force the bloody arm of slavery. I felt as I never felt before. It was a glorious resurrection, from the tomb of slavery, to the heaven of freedom. My long-crushed spirit rose, cowardice departed, bold defiance took its place; and I now resolved that, however long I might remain a slave in form, the day had passed forever when I could be a slave in fact. I did not hesitate to let it be known of me, that the white man who expected to succeed in whipping, must also succeed in killing me. . . .

My term of actual service to Mr. Edward Covey ended on Christmas day, 1833. The days between Christmas and New Year's day are allowed as holidays; and, accordingly, we were not required to perform any labor, more than to feed and take care of the stock. This time we regarded as our own, by the grace of our masters; and we therefore used or abused it nearly as we pleased. Those of us who had families at a distance, were generally allowed to spend the whole six days in their society. This time, however, was spent in various ways. The staid, sober, thinking and industrious ones of our number would employ themselves in making corn-brooms, mats, horse-collars, and baskets; and another class of us would spend the time in hunting opossums, hares, and coons. But by far the larger part engaged in such sports and merriments as playing ball, wrestling, running foot-races, fiddling, dancing, and drinking whisky; and this latter mode of spending the time was by far the most agreeable to the feelings of our masters. A slave who would work during the holidays was considered by our masters as scarcely deserving them. He was regarded as one who rejected the favor of his master. It was deemed a disgrace not to get drunk at Christmas; and he was regarded as lazy indeed, who had not provided himself with the necessary means, during the year, to get whisky enough to last him through Christmas.

From what I know of the effect of these holidays upon the slave, I believe them to be among the most effective means in the hands of the slaveholder in keeping down the spirit of insurrection. Were the slaveholders at once to abandon this practice, I have not the slightest doubt it would lead to an immediate insurrection among the slaves. These holidays serve as conductors, or safety-valves, to carry off the rebellious spirit of enslaved humanity. But for these, the slave would be forced up to the wildest desperation; and woe betide the slaveholder, the day he ventures to remove or hinder the operation of those conductors! I warn him that, in such an event, a spirit will go forth in their midst, more to be dreaded than the most appalling earthquake.

The holidays are part and parcel of the gross fraud, wrong, and inhumanity of slavery. They are professedly a custom established by the benevolence of the slaveholders; but I undertake to say, it is the result of selfishness, and one of the grossest frauds committed upon the down-trodden slave. They do not give the slaves this time because they would not like to have their work during its continuance, but because they know it would be unsafe to deprive them of it. This will be seen by the fact, that the slaveholders like to have their slaves spend those days just in such a manner as to make them as glad of their ending as of their beginning. Their object seems to be, to disgust their slaves with freedom, by plunging them into the lowest depths of dissipation. For instance, the slaveholders not only like to see the slave drink of his own accord, but will adopt various plans to make him drunk. One plan is, to make bets on their slaves, as to who can drink the most whisky without getting drunk; and in this way they succeed in getting whole multitudes to drink to excess. Thus, when the slave asks for virtuous freedom, the cunning slaveholder, knowing his ignorance, cheats him with a dose of vicious dissipation, artfully labelled with the name of liberty. The most of us used to drink it down, and the result was just what might be supposed: many of us were led to think that there was little to choose between liberty and slavery. We felt, and very properly too, that we had almost as well be slaves to man as to rum. So, when the holidays ended, we staggered up from the filth of our wallowing, took a long breath, and marched to the field,—feeling, upon the whole, rather glad to go, from what our master had deceived us into a belief was freedom, back to the arms of slavery.

Source: Frederick Douglass, *Narrative of the Life of Frederick Douglass, an American Slave* (Boston, 1845).

For Further Reading:

William S. McFeely, *Frederick Douglass* (New York: Norton, 1991).
Benjamin Quarles, *Black Abolitionists* (New York: Oxford University Press, 1969).

30. Angelina Grimké, Excerpt from "Human Rights Not Founded on Sex" (1837)

1829   Angelina Grimké moves to Philadelphia

1835   Angelina Grimké, "An Appeal to the Christian Woman of the South"

1836   Sarah Grimké, "An Epistle to the Clergy of Southern States"

1836–38   Angelina Grimké censured for speaking before mixed audience of men and women

1837–38   Grimké sisters turn attention to women's rights, publishing "Letters on the Equality of the Sexes"

1838   Angelina Grimké marries Theodore Dwight Weld, leading abolitionist

Although women were initially not welcome as full participants in the abolitionist movement, they soon became some of its most important participants. They served on executive committees, wrote abolitionist tracts and novels, and delivered biting antislavery speeches. In part because they encountered discrimination within the antislavery ranks, and because their involvement in the fight to eradicate racial inequality led them to perceive other forms of inequality, many female abolitionists became advocates for women's rights.

Two leading opponents of racial and sexual inequality were the Grimké sisters, Angelina and Sarah. Both were raised on a South Carolina plantation and received a "proper" southern education. Their religious fervor, however, led them to question the peculiar institution of slavery. When they spoke out, they were compelled to flee north. Upon arriving in New England, these two converts to Quakerism joined the antislavery movement. To their chagrin, many male abolitionists were no more receptive to them than southern planters had been—not because they opposed slavery but because they were opposed to women speaking out, period. One abolitionist minister stated that women should not lecture men, they should obey them.

The Grimké sisters were not to be deterred. Not only did they continue to speak out against slavery; they won the admiration of many men in the process and began to condemn all forms of discrimination. As Angelina's "Human Rights Not Founded on Sex" demonstrated, the Grimké sisters felt that all individuals, black and white, male and female, deserved the same rights. The essay originally appeared in a letter that Angelina wrote to

Catherine Beecher, the sister of the famous abolitionist novelist Harriet Beecher Stowe. Catherine, who remained unconvinced by Angelina's cry for sexual equality, made the letter public.

Dear Friend—The investigation of the rights of the slave has led me to a better understanding of my own. I have found the Anti-Slavery cause to be the high school of morals in our land—the school in which *human rights* are more fully investigated, and better understood and taught, than in any other. Here a great fundamental principle is uplifted and illuminated, and from this central light, rays innumerable stream all around. Human beings have *rights*, because they are *moral* beings: the rights of *all* men grow out of their moral nature; and as all men have the same moral nature, they have essentially the same rights. These rights may be wrested from the slave, but they cannot be alienated: his title to himself is as perfect *now*, as is that of Lyman Beecher: it is stamped on his moral being, and is, like it, imperishable. Now if rights are founded in the nature of our moral being, then the *mere circumstance of sex* does not give to man higher rights and responsibilities, than to woman. To suppose that it does, would be to deny the self-evident truth, that the "physical constitution is the mere instrument of the moral nature." To suppose that it does, would be to break up utterly the relations, of the two natures, and to reverse their functions, exalting the animal nature into a monarch, and humbling the moral into a slave; making the former a proprietor, and the latter its property. When human beings are regarded as *moral* beings, *sex*, instead of being enthroned upon the summit, administering upon rights and responsibilities, sinks into insignificance and nothingness. My doctrine then is, that whatever it is morally right for man to do, it is morally right for women to do. Our duties originate, not from difference of sex, but from the diversity of our relations in life, the various gifts and talents committed to our care, and the different eras in which we live.

This regulation of duty by the mere circumstance of sex, rather than by the fundamental principle of moral being, has led to all that multifarious train of evils flowing out of the anti-christian doctrine of masculine and feminine virtues. By this doctrine, man has been converted into the warrior, and clothed with sternness, and those other kindred qualities, which in common estimation belong to his character as a *man*; whilst woman has been taught to lean upon an arm of flesh, to sit as a doll arrayed in "gold, and pearls, and costly array," to be admired for her personal charms, and caressed and humored like a spoiled child, or converted into a mere drudge to suit the convenience of her lord and master. Thus have all the diversified relations of life been filled with "confusion and every evil work." This principle has given to man a charter for the exercise of tyranny and selfishness, pride and arrogance, lust and brutal violence. It has robbed woman of essential rights, the right to think and speak and act on all great moral questions, just as men think and speak and act; the right to share their responsibilities, perils and toils; the right to fulfil the great end of her being, as a moral, intellectual and immortal creature, and of glorifying God in her body and her spirit which are His. Hitherto, instead of being a help mate to man, in the highest, noblest sense of the term, as a companion, a co-worker, an equal; she has been a mere appendage of his being, an instrument of his convenience and pleasure, the pretty toy with which he wiled away his leisure moments, or the pet animal whom he humored into playfulness and submission. Woman, instead of being regarded as the equal of man, has uniformly been looked down upon as his inferior, a mere gift to fill up the measure of his happiness. In "the poetry of romantic gallantry," it is true, she has been called "the last *best gift* of God to man;" but I believe I speak forth the words of truth and soberness when I affirm, that woman never was given to man. She was created, like him, in the image of God, and crowned with glory and honor; created only a little lower than the angels—not, as is almost universally assumed, a little lower than man; on her brow, as well as on his, was placed the "diadem of beauty," and in her hands the sceptre of universal dominion. Genesis 1: 27, 28. "The last *best gift* of God to man!" Where is the scripture warrant for this "rhetorical flourish, this splendid absurdity?" Let us examine the account of her creation. "And the rib which the Lord God had taken from man, made he a woman, and brought her unto the man." Not as a gift—for Adam immediately recognized her *as a part of himself*—("this is now bone of my bone, and flesh of my flesh")—a companion and equal, not one hair's breadth beneath him in the majesty and glory of her moral being; not placed under his authority as a *subject*, but by his side, on the same platform of human rights, under the government of God only. This idea of woman's being "the last best gift of God to man," however pretty it may sound to the ears of those who love to discourse upon "the poetry of romantic gallantry, and the generous promptings of chivalry," has nevertheless been the means of sinking her from an *end* into a mere *means*—of turning her into an *appendage* to man, instead of recognizing her as *a part of man*—of destroying her individuality, and rights, and responsibilities, and merging her moral being in that of man. Instead of *Jehovah* being *her* king, *her* lawgiver, and *her* judge, she has been taken out of the exalted scale of existence in which He placed her, and subjected to the despotic control of man.

I have often been amused at the vain efforts made to define the rights and responsibilities of immortal beings as *men* and *women*. No one has yet found out just *where* the line of separation between them should be drawn, and for this simple reason, that no one knows just how far below man woman is, whether she be a head shorter in her moral responsibilities, or head and shoulders, or the full length of his noble stature, below him, i.e., under his feet. Confusion, uncertainty, and great inconsistencies, must exist on this point, so long as woman is regarded in the least degree inferior to man; but place her where her Maker placed her, on the same high level of human rights with man, side by side with him, and difficulties vanish, the mountains of perplexity flow down at the pressence of this grand equalizing principle. Measure her rights and duties by the unerring standard of *moral being*, not by the false weights and measures of a mere circumstance of her human existence, and then the truth will be self-evident, that whatever it is *morally* right for a man to do, it is *morally* right for a woman to do. I recognize no rights but *human* rights—I know nothing of men's rights and women's rights; for in Christ Jesus, there is neither male nor female. It is my solemn conviction, that, until this principle of equality is recognised and embodied in practice, the church can do nothing effectual for the permanent reformation of the world. Woman was the first transgressor, and the first victim of power. In all heathen nations, she has been the slave of man, and Christian nations have never acknowledged her rights. Nay more, no Christian denomination or Society has ever acknowledged them on the broad basis of humanity. I know that in some denominations, she is permitted to preach the gospel; not from a conviction of her rights, nor upon the ground of her equality as a *human being*, but of her equality in spiritual gifts—for we find that woman, even in these Societies, is allowed no voice in framing the Discipline by which she is to be governed. Now, I believe it is woman's right to have a voice in all the laws and regulations by which she is to be *governed*, whether in Church or State; and that the present arrangements of society, on these points, are *a violation of human rights, a rank usurpation of power*, a violent seizure and confiscation of what is sacredly and inalienably hers—thus inflicting upon woman outrageous wrongs, working mischief incalculable in the social circle, and in its influence on the world producing only evil, and that continually. *If* Ecclesiastical and Civil governments are ordained of God, *then* I contend that woman has just as much right to sit in solemn counsel in Conventions, Conferences, Associations and General Assemblies, as man—just as much right to sit upon the throne of England, or in the Presidential chair of the United States.

Source: Angelina Grimké, "Letter XII," *Letters to Catherine F. Beecher* (Boston, 1838).

For Further Reading:

Blanche Glassman Hersh, *The Slave of Sex* (Urbana: University of Illinois Press, 1978).

Gerda Lerner, *The Grimké Sisters from South Carolina* (Boston: Houghton Mifflin, 1967).

31. "Seneca Falls Declaration and Resolutions" (1848)

1833   Lucretia Mott helps found Female Anti-Slavery Society
1840   Mott and Elizabeth Cady Stanton excluded from World
       Anti-Slavery convention, London, England
1848   Seneca Falls Convention
1850   Mott publishes *Discourse on Women*
1851   Stanton and Susan B. Anthony begin collaboration
       leading to formation of National Woman Suffrage
       Association (1869)

The subordination of women within the antislavery movement, as well as the general spirit of perfectionism propounded by many reformers, led more and more women to join the fight for sexual equality. Lucretia Mott and Elizabeth Cady Stanton, two early female abolitionists, turned their attention to the issue of women's rights in the 1840s. And in 1848, over two hundred men and women gathered in Seneca Falls, New York, for the first women's rights convention in American history.

The highlight of the convention was the adoption of the "Declaration of Sentiments" and a set of resolutions. Drafted by Stanton, the manifesto was modeled after the Declaration of Independence. It asserted that women enjoyed the same inalienable natural rights as men and deserved equal treatment. Ironically, the delegates considered the resolution calling for the vote too radical and did not pass it until after Frederick Douglass and Stanton made impassioned pleas in its favor.

After Seneca Falls, Mott, Stanton, and Susan B. Anthony helped forge the earliest women's rights organization, the National Woman Suffrage Association. However, the impact of the women's rights movement was not as great as the antislavery movement. The Equal Rights Amendment, which was modeled after the resolutions passed by the Seneca Falls delegates, failed to gain passage, and after the Civil War many abolitionists and women's rights advocates split into warring factions.

When, in the course of human events, it becomes necessary for one portion of the family of man to assume among the people of the earth a position different from that which they have hitherto occupied, but one to which the laws of nature and of nature's God entitle them, a decent respect to the opinions of mankind requires that they should declare the causes that impel them to such a course.

We hold these truths to be self-evident: that all men and women are created equal; that they are endowed by their Creator with certain inalienable rights; that among these are life, liberty, and the pursuit of happiness; that to secure these rights governments are instituted, deriving their just powers from the consent of the governed. Whenever any form of government becomes destructive of these ends, it is the right of those who suffer from it to refuse allegiance to it, and to insist upon the institution of a new government, laying its foundations on such principles, and organizing its powers in such form, as to them shall seem most likely to effect their safety and happiness. Prudence, indeed, will dictate that governments long established should not be changed for light and transient causes; and accordingly all experience hath shown that mankind are more disposed to suffer, while evils are sufferable, than to right themselves by abolishing the forms to which they were accustomed. But when a long train of abuses and usurpations, pursuing invariably the same object evinces a design to reduce them under absolute despotism, it is their duty to throw off such government, and to provide new guards for their future security. Such has been the patient sufferance of the women under this government, and such is now the necessity which constrains them to demand the equal station to which they are entitled.

The history of mankind is a history of repeated injuries and usurpations on the part of man toward woman, having in direct object the establishment of an absolute tyranny over her. To prove this, let facts be submitted to a candid world.

He has never permitted her to exercise her inalienable right to the elective franchise.

He has compelled her to submit to laws, in the formation of which she had no voice.

He has withheld from her rights which are given to the most ignorant and degraded men—both natives and foreigners.

Having deprived her of this first right of a citizen, the elective franchise, thereby leaving her without representation in the halls of legislation, he has opposed her on all sides.

He has made her, if married, in the eye of the law, civilly dead.

He has taken from her all right in property, even to the wages she earns.

He has made her, morally, an irresponsible being, as she can commit many crimes with impunity, provided they be done in the presence of her husband. In the covenant of marriage, she is compelled to promise obedience to her husband, he becoming, to all intents and purposes, her master—the law giving him power to deprive her of her liberty, and to administer chastisement.

He has so framed the laws of divorce, as to what shall be the proper causes, and in case of separation, to whom the guardianship of the children shall be given, as to be wholly regardless of the happiness of women—the law, in all cases, going upon a false supposition of the supremacy of man, and giving all power into his hands.

After depriving her of all rights as a married woman, if single, and the owner of property, he has taxed her to support a government which recognizes her only when her property can be made profitable to it.

He has monopolized nearly all the profitable employments, and from those she is permitted to follow, she receives but a scanty remuneration. He closes against her all the avenues to wealth and distinction which he considers most honorable to himself. As a teacher of theology, medicine, or law, she is not known.

He has denied her the facilities for obtaining a thorough education, all colleges being closed against her.

He allows her in Church, as well as State, but a subordinate position, claiming Apostolic authority for her exclusion from the ministry, and, with some exceptions, from any public participation in the affairs of the Church.

He has created a false public sentiment by giving to the world a different code of morals for men and women, by which moral delinquencies which exclude women from society, are not only tolerated, but deemed of little account in man.

He has usurped the prerogative of Jehovah himself, claiming it as his right to assign for her a sphere of action, when that belongs to her conscience and to her God.

He has endeavored, in every way that he could, to destroy her confidence in her own powers, to lessen her self-respect, and to make her willing to lead a dependent and abject life.

Now, in view of this entire disfranchisement of one-half the people of this country, their social and religious degradation—in view of the unjust laws above mentioned, and because women do not feel themselves aggrieved, oppressed, and fradulently deprived of their most sacred rights, we insist that they have immediate admission to all the rights and privileges which belong to them as citizens of the United States.

In entering upon the great work before us, we anticipate no small amount of misconception, misrepresentation, and ridicule; but we shall use every instrumentality within our power to effect our object. We shall employ agents, circulate tracts, petition the State and National legislatures, and endeavor to enlist the pulpit and the press in our behalf. We hope this Convention will be followed by a series of Conventions embracing every part of the country.

Resolutions

WHEREAS, The great precept of nature is conceded to be, that "man shall pursue his own true and substantial happiness." Blackstone in his Commentaries remarks, that this law of Nature being coequal with mankind, and dictated by God himself, is of course superior in obligation to any other. It is binding over all the globe, in all countries and at all times; no human laws are of any validity if contrary to this, and such of them as are valid, derive all their force, and all their validity, and all their authority, mediately and immediately, from this original; therefore,

Resolved, That such laws as conflict, in any way, with the true and substantial happiness of woman, are contrary to the great precept of nature and of no validity, for this is "superior in obligation to any other."

Resolved, That all laws which prevent woman from occupying such a station in society as her conscience shall dictate, or which place her in a position inferior to that of man, are contrary to the great precept of nature, and therefore of no force or authority.

Resolved, That woman is man's equal—was intended to be so by the Creator, and the highest good of the race demands that she should be recognized as such.

Resolved, That the women of this country ought to be enlightened in regard to the laws under which they live, that they may no longer publish their degradation by declaring themselves satisfied with their present position, nor their ignorance, by asserting that they have all the rights they want.

Resolved, That inasmuch as man, while claiming for himself intellectual superiority, does accord to woman moral superiority, it is pre-eminently his duty to encourage her to speak and teach, as she has an opportunity, in all religious assemblies.

Resolved, That the same amount of virtue, delicacy, and refinement of behavior that is required of woman in the social state, should also be required of man, and the same transgressions should be visited with equal severity on both man and woman.

Resolved, That the objection of indelicacy and impropriety, which is so often brought against woman when she addresses a public audience, comes with a very ill-grace from those who encourage, by their attendance, her appearance on the stage, in the concert, or in feats of the circus.

Resolved, That woman has too long rested satisfied in the circumscribed limits which corrupt customs and a perverted application of the Scriptures have marked out for her, and that it is time she should move in the enlarged sphere which her great Creator has assigned her.

Resolved, That it is the duty of the women of this country to secure to themselves their sacred right to the elective franchise.

Resolved, That the equality of human rights results necessarily from the fact of the identity of the race in capabilities and responsibilities.

Resolved, therefore, That, being invested by the Creator with the same capabilities, and the same consciousness of responsibility for their exercise, it is demonstrably the right and duty of woman, equally with man, to promote every righteous cause by every righteous means; and especially in regard to the great subjects of morals and religion, it is self-evidently her right to participate with her brother in teaching them, both in private and in public, by writing and by speaking, by any instrumentalities proper to be used, and in any assemblies proper to be held; and this being a self-evident truth growing out of the divinely implanted principles of human nature, any custom or authority adverse to it, whether modern or wearing the hoary sanction of antiquity, is to be regarded as a self-evident falsehood, and at war with mankind.

Source: Susan B. Anthony, Elizabeth Cady Stanton, and Matilda Joslyn Gage, eds., *History of Woman Suffrage* (Rochester, 1889), 1:75–80.

For Further Reading:

Lois Banner, *Elizabeth Cady Stanton* (Boston: Little, Brown, 1980).
Elisabeth Griffith, *In Her Own Right* (New York: Oxford University Press, 1984).

32. Harriet Beecher Stowe, Excerpt from *Uncle Tom's Cabin* (1852)

1811   Harriet Beecher born in Litchfield, Connecticut
1832   Beecher family moves to Cincinnati, Ohio
1836   Harriet marries Calvin Ellis Stowe, professor at Lane
        Seminary
1851   *Uncle Tom's Cabin* released in serial form
1852   *Uncle Tom's Cabin* published in book form
1853   *The Key to Uncle Tom's Cabin* published

Harriet Beecher Stowe, the daughter of Lyman Beecher, a prominent Congregational minister, grew up with a deep moral and religious dislike of slavery. In 1832 she moved with her family to Cincinnati, Ohio, where she gained a firsthand view of the "peculiar institution," which flourished in Kentucky, just on the other side of the Ohio River. While in Cincinnati she also came into contact with fugitive slaves.

Uncle Tom's Cabin, Stowe's greatest novel, was first published in 1851 in serialized form in the National Era, *an antislavery paper. A year later the story was published in its entirety, in book form, and became an overnight best seller. By mid-1853 over one million copies had been sold. Subsequently it was adapted to the stage, where hundreds of thousands more Americans watched the story of Tom and Eliza unfold before their eyes.*

The work had a tremendous impact on the public. On meeting her, in the

"Eliza Crosses the Ohio on the Floating Ice" (Scene from *Uncle Tom's Cabin*). Woodcut from drawing by George Cruikshank (Library of Congress).

1860s, President Lincoln reportedly remarked: "So this is the little woman who wrote the book that made the great war." Ralph Waldo Emerson, Frederick Douglass, and other abolitionists praised the novel and testified to its accuracy. Southerners, in contrast, attacked Stowe in print and in public. She defended herself with the publication of The Key to Uncle Tom's Cabin, *a collection of slave narratives.*

Chapter 5 of the novel relates a key turning point in the history of two of the novel's key characters. In it, Eliza and Tom decide that they must run away. Note the title of the chapter, which emphasizes the abolitionist point that slaves were treated as pieces of property, not as human beings.

Showing the Feelings of Living Property on Changing Owners

Mr. and Mrs. Shelby had retired to their apartment for the night. He was lounging in a large easy-chair, looking over some letters that had come in the afternoon mail, and she was standing before her mirror, brushing out the complicated braids and curls in which Eliza had arranged her hair; for, noticing her pale cheeks and haggard eyes, she had excused her attendance that night, and ordered her to bed. The employment, naturally enough, suggested her conversation with the girl in the morning; and, in turning to her husband, she said, carelessly,

"By the by, Arthur, who was that low-bred fellow that you lugged in to our dinner-table to-day?"

"Haley is his name," said Shelby, turning himself rather uneasily in his chair, and continuing with his eyes fixed on a letter.

"Haley! Who is he, and what may be his business here, pray?"

"Well, he's a man that I transacted some business with, last time I was at Natchez," said Mr. Shelby.

"And he presumed on it to make himself quite at home, and call and dine here, ay?"

"Why, I invited him; I had some accounts with him," said Shelby.

"Is he a negro-trader?" said Mrs. Shelby, noticing a certain embarrassment in her husband's manner.

"Why, my dear, what put that into your head?" said Shelby, looking up.

"Nothing,—only Eliza came in here, after dinner, in a great worry, crying and taking on, and said you were talking with a trader, and that she heard him make an offer for her boy—the ridiculous little goose!"

"She did, hey?" said Mr. Shelby, returning to his paper, which he seemed for a few moments quite intent upon, not perceiving that he was holding it bottom upwards.

"It will have to come out," said he, mentally; "as well now as ever."

"I told Eliza," said Mrs. Shelby, as she continued brushing her hair, "that she was a little fool for her pains, and that you never had anything to do with that sort of persons. Of course, I knew you never meant to sell any of our people,—least of all, to such a fellow."

"Well, Emily," said her husband, "so I have always felt and said; but the fact is that my business lies so that I cannot get on without. I shall have to sell some of my hands."

"To that creature? Impossible! Mr. Shelby, you cannot be serious."

"I'm sorry to say that I am," said Mr. Shelby. "I've agreed to sell Tom."

"What! our Tom?—that good, faithful creature!—been your faithful servant from a boy! O, Mr. Shelby!—and you have promised him his freedom, too,—you and I have spoken to him a hundred times of it. Well, I can believe anything now,—I can believe *now* that you could sell little Harry, poor Eliza's only child!" said Mrs. Shelby, in a tone between grief and indignation.

"Well, since you must know all, it is so. I have agreed to sell Tom and Harry both; and I don't know why I am to be rated, as if I were a monster, for doing what every one does every day."

"But why, of all others, choose these?" said Mrs. Shelby. "Why sell them, of all on the place, if you must sell at all?"

"Because they will bring the highest sum of any,—that's why. I could choose another, if you say so. The fellow made me a high bid on Eliza, if that would suit you any better," said Mr. Shelby.

"The wretch!" said Mrs. Shelby, vehemently.

"Well, I didn't listen to it, a moment,—out of regard to your feelings, I wouldn't;—so give me some credit."

"My dear," said Mrs. Shelby, recollecting herself, "forgive me. I have been hasty. I was surprised, and entirely unprepared for this;—but surely you will allow me to intercede for these poor creatures. Tom is a noble-hearted, faithful fellow, if he is black. I do believe, Mr. Shelby, that if he were put to it, he would lay down his life for you."

"I know it,—I dare say;—but what's the use of all this?—I can't help myself."

"Why not make a pecuniary sacrifice? I'm willing to bear my part of the inconvenience. O, Mr. Shelby, I have tried—tried most faithfully, as a Christian woman should—to do my duty to these poor, simple, dependent creatures. I have cared for them, instructed them, watched over them, and known all their little cares and joys, for years; and how can I ever hold up my head again among them, if, for the sake of a little paltry gain, we sell such a faithful, excellent, confiding creature as poor Tom, and tear from him in a moment all we have taught him to love and value? I have taught them the duties of the family, of parent and child, and husband and wife; and how can I bear to have this open acknowledgment that we care for no tie, no duty, no relation, however sacred, compared with money? I have talked with Eliza about her boy—her duty to him as a Christian mother, to watch over him, pray for him, and bring him up in a Christian way; and now what can I say, if you tear him away, and sell him, soul and body, to a profane, unprincipled man, just to save a little money? I have told her that one soul is worth more than all the money in the world; and how will she believe me when she sees us turn round and sell her child?—sell him, perhaps, to certain ruin of body and soul!"

"I'm sorry you feel so about it, Emily,—indeed I am," said Mr. Shelby; "and I respect your feelings, too, though I don't pretend to share them to their full extent; but I tell you now, solemnly, it's of no use—I can't help myself. I didn't mean to tell you this, Emily; but, in plain words, there is no choice between selling these two and selling everything. Either they must go, or *all* must. Haley has come into possession of a mortgage, which, if I don't clear off with him directly, will take everything before it. I've raked, and scraped, and borrowed, and all but begged,—and the price of these two was needed to make up the balance, and I had to give them up. Haley fancied the child; he agreed to settle the matter that way, and no other. I was in his power, and *had* to do it. If you feel so to have them sold, would it be any better to have *all* sold?"

Mrs. Shelby stood like one stricken. Finally, turning to her toilet, she rested her face in her hands, and gave a sort of groan.

"This is God's curse on slavery!—a bitter, bitter, most accursed thing!— a curse to the master and a curse to the slave! I was a fool to think I could make anything good out of such a deadly evil. It is a sin to hold a slave under laws like ours,—I always felt it was,—I always thought so when I was a girl,—I thought so still more after I joined the church; but I thought I could gild it over,—I thought, by kindness, and care, and instruction, I could make the condition of mine better than freedom—fool that I was!"

"Why, wife, you are getting to be an abolitionist, quite."

"Abolitionist! if they knew all I know about slavery, they *might* talk! We don't need them to tell us; you know I never thought that slavery was right— never felt willing to own slaves."

"Well, therein you differ from many wise and pious men," said Mr. Shelby. "You remember Mr. B.'s sermon, the other Sunday?"

"I don't want to hear such sermons; I never wish to hear Mr. B. in our church again. Ministers can't help the evil, perhaps,—can't cure it, any more than we can,—but defend it!—it always went against my common sense. And I think you didn't think much of that sermon, either."

"Well," said Shelby, "I must say these ministers sometimes carry matters further than we poor sinners would exactly dare to do. We men of the world must wink pretty hard at various things, and get used to a deal that isn't the exact thing. But we don't quite fancy, when women and ministers come out broad and square, and go beyond us in matters of either modesty or morals, that's a fact. But now, my dear, I trust you see the necessity of the thing, and you see that I have done the very best that circumstances would allow."

"O yes, yes!" said Mrs. Shelby, hurriedly and abstractedly fingering her gold watch,—"I haven't any jewelry of any amount," she added, thoughtfully; "but would not this watch do something?—it was an expensive one, when it was bought. If I could only at least save Eliza's child, I would sacrifice anything I have."

"I'm sorry, very sorry, Emily," said Mr. Shelby, "I'm sorry this takes hold of you so; but it will do no good. The fact is, Emily, the thing's done; the bills of sale are already signed, and in Haley's hands; and you must be thankful it is no worse. That man has had it in his power to ruin us all,— and now he is fairly off. If you knew the man as I do, you'd think that we had had a narrow escape."

"Is he so hard, then?"

"Why, not a cruel man, exactly, but a man of leather,—a man alive to nothing but trade and profit,—cool, and unhesitating, and unrelenting, as death and the grave. He'd sell his own mother at a good per centage—not wishing the old woman any harm, either."

"And this wretch owns that good, faithful Tom, and Eliza's child!"

"Well, my dear, the fact is that this goes rather hard with me; it's a thing I hate to think of. Haley wants to drive matters, and take possession to-morrow. I'm going to get out my horse bright and early, and be off. I can't see Tom, that's a fact; and you had better arrange a drive somewhere, and carry Eliza off. Let the thing be done when she is out of sight."

"No, no," said Mrs. Shelby; "I'll be in no sense accomplice or help in this cruel business. I'll go and see poor old Tom, God help him, in his distress! They shall see, at any rate, that their mistress can feel for and with them. As to Eliza, I dare not think about it. The Lord forgive us! What have we done, that this cruel necessity should come on us?"

There was one listener to this conversation whom Mr. and Mrs. Shelby little suspected.

Communicating with their apartment was a large closet, opening by a door into the outer passage. When Mrs. Shelby had dismissed Eliza for the night, her feverish and excited mind had suggested the idea of this closet; and she had hidden herself there, and, with her ear pressed close against the crack of the door, had lost not a word of the conversation.

When the voices died into silence, she rose and crept stealthily away. Pale, shivering, with rigid features and compressed lips, she looked an entirely altered being from the soft and timid creature she had been hitherto. She moved cautiously along the entry, paused one moment at her mistress' door, and raised her hands in mute appeal to Heaven, and then turned and glided into her own room. It was a quiet, neat apartment, on the same floor with her mistress. There was the pleasant sunny window, where she had often sat singing at her sewing; there a little case of books, and various little fancy articles, ranged by them, the gifts of Christmas holidays; there was her simple wardrobe in the closet and in the drawers:—here was, in short, her home; and, on the whole, a happy one it had been to her. But there, on the bed, lay her slumbering boy, his long curls falling negligently around his unconscious face, his rosy mouth half open, his little fat hands thrown out over the bed-clothes, and a smile spread like a sunbeam over his whole face.

"Poor boy! poor fellow!" said Eliza; "they have sold you! but your mother will save you yet!"

No tear dropped over that pillow; in such straits as these, the heart has no tears to give,—it drops only blood, bleeding itself away in silence. She took a piece of paper and pencil, and wrote, hastily,

"O, Missis! dear Missis! don't think me ungrateful,—don't think hard of me, any way,—I heard all you and master said to-night. I am going to try to save my boy—you will not blame me! God bless and reward you for all your kindness!"

Hastily folding and directing this, she went to a drawer and made up a little package of clothing for her boy, which she tied with a handkerchief firmly round her waist; and, so fond is a mother's remembrance, that, even in the terrors of that hour, she did not forget to put in the little package one or two of his favorite toys, reserving a gayly painted parrot to amuse him, when she should be called on to awaken him. It was some trouble to arouse the little sleeper; but, after some effort, he sat up, and was playing with his bird, while his mother was putting on her bonnet and shawl.

"Where are you going, mother?" said he, as she drew near the bed, with his little coat and cap.

His mother drew near, and looked so earnestly into his eyes, that he at once divined that something unusual was the matter.

"Hush, Harry," she said; "musn't speak loud, or they will hear us. A wicked man was coming to take little Harry away from his mother, and carry him 'way off in the dark; but mother won't let him—she's going to put on her little boy's cap and coat, and run off with him, so the ugly man can't catch him."

Saying these words, she had tied and buttoned on the child's simple outfit, and, taking him in her arms, she whispered to him to be very still; and, opening a door in her room which led into the outer verandah, she glided noiselessly out.

It was a sparkling, frosty, star-light night, and the mother wrapped the shawl close round her child, as, perfectly quiet with vague terror, he clung round her neck.

Old Bruno, a great Newfoundland, who slept at the end of the porch, rose, with a low growl, as she came near. She gently spoke his name, and the animal, an old pet and playmate of hers, instantly, wagging his tail, prepared to follow her, though apparently revolving much, in his simple dog's head, what such an indiscreet midnight promenade might mean. Some dim ideas of imprudence or impropriety in the measure seemed to embarrass him considerably; for he often stopped, as Eliza glided forward, and looked wistfully, first at her and then at the house, and then, as if reassured by reflection, he pattered along after her again. A few minutes brought them to the window of Uncle Tom's cottage, and Eliza, stopping, tapped lightly on the window-pane.

The prayer-meeting at Uncle Tom's had, in the order of hymn-singing, been protracted to a very late hour; and, as Uncle Tom had indulged himself in a few lengthy solos afterwards, the consequence was, that, although it was now between twelve and one o'clock, he and his worthy helpmeet were not yet asleep.

"Good Lord! what's that?" said Aunt Chloe, starting up and hastily drawing the curtain. "My sakes alive, if it an't Lizy! Get on your clothes, old man, quick!—there's old Bruno, too, a pawin' round; what on airth! I'm gwine to open the door."

And, suiting the action to the word, the door flew open, and the light of the tallow candle, which Tom had hastily lighted, fell on the haggard face and dark, wild eyes of the fugitive.

"Lord bless you!—I'm skeered to look at ye, Lizy! Are ye tuck sick, or what's come over ye?"

"I'm running away—Uncle Tom and Aunt Chloe—carrying off my child— Master sold him!"

"Sold him?" echoed both, lifting up their hands in dismay.

"Yes, sold him!" said Eliza, firmly; "I crept into the closet by Mistress' door to-night, and I heard Master tell Missis that he had sold my Harry, and you, Uncle Tom, both, to a trader; and that he was going off this morning on his horse, and that the man was to take possession to-day."

Tom had stood, during this speech, with his hands raised, and his eyes dilated, like a man in a dream. Slowly and gradually, as its meaning came over him, he collapsed, rather than seated himself, on his old chair, and sunk his head down upon his knees.

"The good Lord have pity on us!" said Aunt Chloe. "O! it don't seem as if it was true! What has he done, that Mas'r should sell *him*?"

"He hasn't done anything,—it isn't for that. Master don't want to sell; and Missis—she's always good. I heard her plead and beg for us; but he told her 't was no use; that he was in this man's debt, and that this man had got the power over him; and that if he didn't pay him off clear, it would end in his having to sell the place and all the people, and move off. Yes, I heard him say there was no choice between selling these two and selling all, the man was driving him so hard. Master said he was sorry; but oh, Missis—you ought to have heard her talk! If she an't a Christian and an angel, there never was one. I 'm a wicked girl to leave her so; but, then, I can't help it. She said, herself, one soul was worth more than the world; and this boy has a soul, and if I let him be carried off, who knows what'll become of it? It must be right: but, if it an't right, the Lord forgive me, for I can't help doing it!"

"Well, old man!" said Aunt Chloe, "why don't you go, too? Will you wait to be toted down river, where they kill niggers with hard work and starving? I'd a heap rather die than go there, any day! There's time for ye,—be off with Lizy,—you've got a pass to come and go any time. Come, bustle up, and I'll get your things together."

Tom slowly raised his head, and looked sorrowfully but quietly around, and said,

"No, no—I an't going. Let Eliza go—it's her right! I wouldn't be the one to say no—'t an't in *natur* for her to stay; but you heard what she said! If I must be sold, or all the people on the place, and everything go to rack, why, let me be sold. I s'pose I can b'ar it as well as any on 'em," he added, while something like a sob and a sigh shook his broad, rough chest convulsively. "Mas'r always found me on the spot—he always will. I never have broke trust, nor used my pass no ways contrary to my word, and I never will. It's better for me alone to go, than to break up the place and sell all. Mas'r an't to blame, Chloe, and he'll take care of you and the poor—"

Here he turned to the rough trundle-bed full of little woolly heads, and broke fairly down. He leaned over the back of the chair, and covered his face with his large hands. Sobs, heavy, hoarse and loud, shook the chair, and great tears fell through his fingers on the floor: just such tears, sir, as you dropped into the coffin where lay your first-born son; such tears, woman, as you shed when you heard the cries of your dying babe. For, sir, he was a man,—and you are but another man. And, woman, though dressed in silk and jewels, you are but a woman, and, in life's great straits and mighty griefs, ye feel but one sorrow!

"And now," said Eliza, as she stood in the door, "I saw my husband only this afternoon, and I little knew then what was to come. They have pushed him to the very last standing-place, and he told me, to-day, that he was going to run away. Do try, if you can, to get word to him. Tell him how I went, and why I went; and tell him I'm going to try and find Canada. You must give my love to him, and tell him, if I never see him again,"—she turned away, and stood with her back to them for a moment, and then added, in a husky voice, "tell him to be as good as he can, and try and meet me in the kingdom of heaven."

"Call Bruno in there," she added. "Shut the door on him, poor beast! He mustn't go with me!"

A few last words and tears, a few simple adieus and blessings, and, clasping her wondering and affrighted child in her arms, she glided noiselessly away.

Source: Harriet Beecher Stowe, *Uncle Tom's Cabin, or, Life Among the Lowly* (Cleveland, Ohio, 1852), chap. 5.

For Further Reading:

Thomas F. Gossett, *Uncle Tom's Cabin and American Culture* (Dallas: Southern Methodist University Press, 1985).

David Potter, *The Impending Crisis, 1848–1860* (New York: Harper & Row, 1976).

33. John Brown, "Last Statement to the Court" (1859)

1854   Kansas-Nebraska Act
1855–56   Bleeding Kansas
1857   *Dred Scott v. Sanford*
1859   John Brown's Raid on Harper's Ferry Armory

John Brown was a fanatical abolitionist who dedicated much of his adult life to overthrowing slavery. A deeply religious man, he agreed with William Lloyd Garrison, America's most prominent abolitionist, that slavery was immoral and that the entire nation was stained by its perpetuation (see document 28). In 1855 Brown and five of his sons moved to Kansas to keep the territory free from slaves. The Kansas-Nebraska Act had opened up the territory to slaves. Once there he became part of the fight between antislavery and proslavery advocates, known as Bleeding Kansas. On one gruesome occasion, he took part in the murder of several of his opponents.

After this incident, Brown moved back to New England, largely to win support for his grand plan for abolishing slavery. This plan took as its core the idea that a small group of white abolitionists could catalyze a massive slave rebellion. In 1859 Brown put his plan into motion, moving to Virginia, where he established himself and several of his sons on a small farm and then prepared an invasion of the armory at Harper's Ferry. But soon after Brown and his small army successfully captured the armory, his plans went awry as federal troops, commanded by Colonel Robert E. Lee, easily retook the armory and captured Brown. Brown was then tried and convicted of treason, murder, and fomenting insurrection, all capital crimes.

After being sentenced to hang, Brown delivered his "Last Statement." While many considered him crazy, this speech suggested otherwise. Indeed his behavior during and after the trial along with the speech turned him into a martyr for many northerners. For example, Henry Wadsworth Longfellow remarked that the day of Brown's death would henceforth stand as "a great day in our history; the date of a new revolution." On the same day, all across the North, churchbells were rung and Brown was commemorated as a great hero.

I have, may it please the Court, a few words to say.

In the first place, I deny everything but what I have all along admitted: of a design on my part to free slaves. I intended certainly to have made a clean thing of that matter, as I did last winter, when I went into Missouri

Last Days of John Brown (Library of Congress).

and there took slaves without the snapping of a gun on either side, moving them through the country, and finally leaving them in Canada. I designed to have done the same thing again on a larger scale. That was all I intended. I never did intend murder, or treason, or the destruction of property, or to exercise or incite slaves to rebellion, or to make insurrection.

I have another objection, and that is that it is unjust that I should suffer such a penalty. Had I interfered in the manner which I admit, and which I admit has been fairly proved—for I admire the truthfulness and candor of the greater portion of the witnesses who have testified in this case—Had I so interfered in behalf of the rich, the powerful, the intelligent, the so-called great, or in behalf of any of their friends, either father, mother, brother, sister, wife or children, or any of that class, and suffered and sacrificed what I have in this interference, it would have been all right. Every man in this Court would have deemed it an act worthy of reward rather than punishment.

This Court acknowledges, too, as I suppose, the validity of the law of God. I see a book kissed, which I suppose to be the Bible, or at least the New Testament, which teaches me that all things whatsoever I would that men should do to me, I should do even so to them. It teaches me, further, to remember them that are in bonds as bound with them. I endeavored to act up to that instruction. I say I am yet too young to understand that God is any respecter of persons. I believe that to have interfered as I have done, as I have always freely admitted I have done, in behalf of His despised poor, I did no wrong, but right. Now, if it is deemed necessary that I should forfeit my life for the furtherance of the ends of justice, and mingle my blood further with the blood of my children and with the blood of millions in this slave country whose rights are disregarded by wicked, cruel, and unjust enactments, I say, let it be done.

Let me say one word further. I feel entirely satisfied with the treatment I have received on my trial. Considering all the circumstances, it has been more generous than I expected. But I feel no consciousness of guilt. I have stated from the first what was my intention, and what was not. I never had any design against the liberty of any person, nor any disposition to commit treason or incite slaves to rebel or make any general insurrection. I never encouraged any man to do so, but always discouraged any idea of that kind.

Let me say, also, in regard to the statements made by some of those who were connected with me, I hear it has been stated by some of them that I have induced them to join me. But the contrary is true. I do not say this to injure them, but as regretting their weakness. Not one but joined me of his own accord, and the greater part at their own expense. A number of them I never saw, and never had a word of conversation with, till the day they came to me, and that was for the purpose I have stated.

Now, I have done.

Source: *The Life and Execution of Captain John Brown, Known as "Old Brown of Ossawatomie"* (New York, 1859).

For Further Reading:

Aileen S. Kraditor, *Means and Ends in American Abolitionism* (New York: Pantheon Books, 1969).
Stephen Oates, *To Purge This Land with Blood* (New York: Harper & Row, 1970).
Benjamin Quarles, *Allies for Freedom* (New York: Oxford University Press, 1974).

34. Carl Schurz, Excerpt from "True Americanism" (1859)

1845   Potato famine begins in Ireland
1847–57   Peak years of immigration from Ireland and
          Germany
1830–60   Rise of nativism in United States
1853–56   Appearance of American or Know-Nothing Party

Jacob Henry's "Speech on Freedom of Religion" (see document 20) revealed that discrimination against religious minorities was prevalent during the early years of the Republic. But during those years the number of ethnic or religious minorities remained relatively small and thus ethnic prejudice never reached a fever pitch. In contrast, during the decades preceding the Civil War a massive wave of immigrants, most from Ireland and Germany, came to America and prejudice or nativism reached a new height. Even though the immigrants were vital to the industrial and economic expansion of the nation, many "natives" attacked them as foes of the Republic. Some joined nativist groups, culminating with the birth of the American or Know-Nothing Party in the 1850s. Others merely pressured the Whigs and Democrats to pass anti-immigrant legislation, such as laws lengthening the time it took to become a citizen.

In "True Americanism," Carl Schurz, a German-born immigrant to America and a leader of the newly formed Republican Party, attacked nativism, in general, and a proposal before the Massachusetts state legislature restricting the rights of the foreign born, in particular. Ironically, Schurz shared some of the native born's prejudices toward Irish Catholics, although, as becomes clear in his speech, ultimately he felt that democracy rested on the principle of inclusion and tolerance, not exclusion and self-righteousness. To an extent one can argue that Schurz's views predominated, as the restrictive piece of legislation before the Massachusetts legislature did not pass and, more importantly, the Know-Nothing Party disappeared and the more inclusive Republican Party flourished.

A few days ago I stood on the cupola of your Statehouse and overlooked for the first time this venerable city and the country surrounding it. Then the streets and hills and waters around me began to teem with the life of historical recollections, recollections dear to all mankind, and a feeling of pride arose in my heart, and I said to myself, I, too, am an American citizen. There was Bunker Hill; there Charlestown, Lexington, and Dorchester Heights not far off; there the harbor into which the British tea was sunk; there the place where the old liberty tree stood; there John Hancock's house; there Benjamin Franklin's birthplace. And now I stand in this grand old hall, which so often resounded with the noblest appeals that ever thrilled American hearts, and where I am almost afraid to hear the echo of my own feeble voice. Oh, sir, no man that loves liberty, wherever he may have first seen the light of day, can fail on this sacred spot to pay his tribute to Americanism. And here, with all these glorious memories crowding upon my heart, I will offer mine. I, born in a foreign land, pay my tribute to Americanism? Yes, for to me the word "Americanism," *true* "Americanism," comprehends the noblest ideas which ever swelled a human heart with noble pride. . . .

I say all this, not as though I indulged in the presumptuous delusion that my personal feelings and experience would be of any interest to you but in order to show you what America is to the thousands of thinking men in the Old World who, disappointed in their fondest hopes and depressed by the saddest experience, cling with their last remnant of confidence in human nature to the last spot on earth where man is free to follow the road to attainable perfection, and where, unbiased by the disastrous influence of traditional notions, customs, and institutions, he acts on his own responsibility. They ask themselves: Was it but a wild delusion when we thought that man has the faculty to be free and to govern himself? Have we been fighting, were we ready to die for a mere phantom, for a mere product of a morbid imagination? This question downtrodden humanity cries out into the world, and from this country it expects an answer.

As its advocate I speak to you. I will speak of Americanism as the great representative of the reformatory age, as the great champion of the dignity of human nature, as the great repository of the last hopes of suffering mankind. I will speak of the ideal mission of this country and of this people. . . .

. . . The youthful elements which constitute people of the New World cannot submit to rules which are not of their own making; they must throw off the fetters which bind them to an old, decrepit order of things. They resolve to enter the great family of nations as an independent member. And in the colony of free humanity, whose mother country is the world, they establish *the republic of equal rights, where the title of manhood is the title to citizenship.* My friends, if I had a thousand tongues and a voice strong as the thunder of heaven, they would not be sufficient to impress upon your minds forcibly enough the greatness of this idea, the overshadowing glory of this result. This was the dream of the truest friends of man from the beginning; for this the noblest blood of martyrs has been shed; for this has mankind waded through seas of blood and tears. There it is now; there it stands, the noble fabric in all the splendor of reality.

They speak of the greatness of the Roman Republic! Oh, sir, if I could call the proudest of Romans from his grave, I would take him by the hand

and say to him, Look at this picture, and at this! The greatness of thy Roman Republic consisted in its despotic rule over the world; the greatness of the American Republic consists in the secured right of man to govern himself. The dignity of the Roman citizen consisted in his exclusive privileges; the dignity of the American citizen consists in his holding the natural rights of his neighbor just as sacred as his own. The Roman Republic recognized and protected the *rights of the citizen,* at the same time disregarding and leaving unprotected the *rights of man*; Roman citizenship was founded upon monopoly, not upon the claims of human nature. What the citizen of Rome claimed for himself, he did not respect in others; his own greatness was his only object; his own liberty, as he regarded it, gave him the privilege to oppress his fellow beings. His democracy, instead of elevating mankind to his own level, trampled the rights of man into the dust. The security of the Roman Republic, therefore, consisted in the power of the sword; the security of the American Republic rests in the equality of human rights! The Roman Republic perished by the sword; the American Republic will stand as long as the equality of human rights remains inviolate. Which of the two republics is the greater—the republic of the Roman or the republic of *man*?

Sir, I wish the words of the Declaration of Independence, "that all men are created free and equal, and are endowed with certain inalienable rights," were inscribed upon every gatepost within the limits of this republic. From this principle the revolutionary fathers derived their claim to independence; upon this they founded the institutions of this country; and the whole structure was to be the living incarnation of this idea. This principle contains the program of our political existence. It is the most progressive and at the same time the most conservative one; the most progressive, for it takes even the lowliest members of the human family out of their degradation and inspires them with the elevating consciousness of equal human dignity; the most conservative, for it makes a common cause of individual rights. From the equality of rights springs identity of our highest interests; you cannot subvert your neighbor's rights without striking a dangerous blow at your own. And when the rights of one cannot be infringed without finding a ready defense in all others who defend their own rights in defending his, then and only then are the rights of all safe against the usurpations of governmental authority.

This general identity of interests is the only thing that can guarantee the stability of democratic institutions. Equality of rights, embodied in general self-government, is the great moral element of true democracy; it is the only reliable safety valve in the machinery of modern society. There is the solid foundation of our system of government; there is our mission; there is our greatness; there is our safety; there and nowhere else! This is true Americanism and to this I pay the tribute of my devotion.

Shall I point out to you the consequences of a deviation from this principle? Look at the slave states. There is a class of men who are deprived of their natural rights. But this is not the only deplorable feature of that peculiar organization of society. Equally deplorable is it that there is another class of men who keep the former in subjection. That there are slaves is bad; but almost worse is it that there are masters. Are not the masters freemen? No, sir! Where is their liberty of the press? Where is their liberty of speech? Where is the man among them who dares to advocate openly principles not in strict accordance with the ruling system? They speak of a republican form of government, they speak of democracy; but the despotic spirit of slavery and mastership combined pervades their whole political life like a liquid poison. They do not dare to be free lest the spirit of liberty become contagious. The system of slavery has enslaved them all, master as well as slave. What is the cause of all this? It is that you cannot deny one class of society the full measure of their natural rights without imposing restraints upon your own liberty. If you want to be free, there is but one way—it is to guarantee an equally full measure of liberty to all your neighbors. There is no other.

True, there are difficulties connected with an organization of society founded upon the basis of equal rights. Nobody denies it. A large number of those who come to you from foreign lands are not as capable of taking part in the administration of government as the man who was fortunate enough to drink the milk of liberty in his cradle. And certain religious denominations do, perhaps, nourish principles which are hardly in accordance with the doctrines of true democracy. There is a conglomeration on this continent of heterogeneous elements; there is a warfare of clashing interest and unruly aspirations; and, with all this, our democratic system gives rights to the ignorant and power to the inexperienced. And the billows of passion will lash the sides of the ship, and the storm of party warfare will bend its masts, and the pusillanimous will cry out—"Master, master, we perish!" But the genius of true democracy will arise from his slumber and rebuke the winds and the raging of the water, and say unto them—"Where is your faith?" Aye, where is the faith that led the fathers of this republic to invite the weary and burdened of all nations to the enjoyment of equal rights? Where is that broad and generous confidence in the efficiency of true democratic institutions? Has the present generation forgotten that true democracy bears in itself the remedy for all the difficulties that may grow out of it?

It is an old dodge of the advocates of despotism throughout the world that the people who are not experienced in self-government are not fit for the exercise of self-government and must first be educated under the rule of a superior authority. But at the same time the advocates of despotism will never offer them an opportunity to acquire experience in self-government lest they suddenly become fit for its independent exercise. To this treacherous sophistry the fathers of this republic opposed the noble doctrine that liberty is the best school for liberty, and that self-government cannot be learned but by practising it. This, sir, is a truly American idea; this is true Americanism; and to this I pay the tribute of my devotion.

Source: *Speeches, Correspondence and Political Papers of Carl Schurz*, ed. Frederick Bancroft (New York, 1913), 1:48–72.

For Further Reading:

Ray Allen Billington, *The Protestant Crusade* (New York: Macmillan, 1938).

Hasia R. Diner, *Erin's Daughters in America* (Baltimore: Johns Hopkins University Press, 1983).

Oscar Handlin, *Boston's Immigrants*, rev. ed. (Cambridge, Mass.: Harvard University Press, 1979).

35. Anonymous, "Vote Yourself a Farm" (ca. 1846)

1840   George Henry Evans spells out "safety-valve" theory
1844   Evans founds National Reform Association, which takes as its motto "Vote Yourself a Farm"
1848   Free Soil Party formed
1854   Republican Party formed
1862   Homestead Act passed

Ever since the first colonists arrived in America, the availability of land had been part of the attraction of America. English and other European immigrants came to North America, in part, because they could own their own property. Thomas Jefferson predicated the success of the Republic on the growth of a large class of yeoman or self-sufficient and independent farmers. Andrew Jackson's removal of the Indians from the Southwest represented a fulfillment of the unwritten pledge that land would be made available to the common (white) man. Even the antislavery society expanded its appeal by pledging to keep the West free from slavery and open to purchase by the average (white) citizen.

The following piece was originally circulated by the National Reform Association, an organization founded by George Henry Evans, a one-time leader of various workingmen parties. Land reform or the opening up of public lands was seen as one of the primary solutions to the development of a permanent class of wage workers. Evans argued that the ability to buy land in the West kept wages high and provided an outlet to discontented workers. Both the Free Soil and the Republican parties adopted this view in their platforms in one form or another. And in 1862, in the midst of the

Civil War, Congress passed and Lincoln signed into law the Homestead Act of 1862, which made land in the West available for a small filing fee, as long as the purchaser agreed to reside on and improve (work) the land. Whether the western lands actually served as a safety valve is still a matter of great historical debate, although few can challenge the claim that many working-men and women and even more reformers perceived land reform as one of the keys to maintaining a democratic life in America.

Are you an American citizen? Then you are a joint owner of the public lands. Why not take enough of your property to provide yourself a home? Why not vote yourself a farm?

Remember Poor Richard's saying: "Now I have a sheep and a cow, every-one bids me 'good morrow.' " If a man have a house and a home of his own, though it be a thousand miles off, he is well received in other people's houses; while the homeless wretch is turned away. The bare right to a farm, though you should never go near it, would save you from many an insult. Therefore, vote yourself a farm.

Are you a party follower? Then you have long enough employed your vote to benefit scheming office seekers; use it for once to benefit yourself. Vote yourself a farm.

Are you tired of slavery, of drudging for others, of poverty and its attendant miseries? Then, vote yourself a farm.

Are you endowed with reason? Then you must know that your right to life hereby includes the right to a place to live in, the right to a home. Assert this right so long denied mankind by feudal robbers and their attorneys. Vote yourself a farm.

Are you a believer in the Scriptures: Then assert that the land is the Lord's because He made it. Resist then the blasphemers who exact money for His word even as you would resist them should they claim to be worshiped for His holiness. Emancipate the poor from the necessity of encouraging such blasphemy. Vote the freedom of the public lands.

Are you a man? Then assert the sacred rights of man, especially your right to stand upon God's earth and to till it for your own profit. Vote yourself a farm.

Would you free your country and the sons of toil everywhere from the heartless irresponsible mastery of the aristocracy of avarice? Would you disarm this aristocracy of its chief weapon, the fearful power of banishment from God's earth? Then join with your neighbors to form a true American party, having for its guidance the principles of the American Revolution, and whose chief measures shall be: (1) to limit the quantity of land that any one man may henceforth monopolize or inherit; and (2) to make the public lands free to actual settlers only, each having the right to sell his improve-ments to any man not possessed of other land. These great measures, once carried, wealth would become a changed social element; it would then consist of the accumulated products of human labor instead of a hoggish monopoly of the products of God's labor; and the antagonism of capital and labor would forever cease.

Capital could no longer grasp the largest share of the laborer's earnings as a reward for not doing him all the injury the laws of the feudal aristocracy authorize, viz., the denial of all stock to work upon and all place to live in. To derive any profit from the laborer, it must first give him work; for it could no longer wax fat by levying a dead tax upon his existence. The hoary iniquities of Norman land pirates would cease to pass current as American law. Capital, with its power for good undiminished, would lose the power to oppress; and a new era would dawn upon the earth and rejoice the souls of a thousand generations. Therefore, forget not to vote yourself a farm.

Source: John R. Commons et al., *A Documentary History of American Industrial Society* (Cleveland, Ohio, 1910), 7:305-307.

For Further Reading:

Eric Foner, *Free Soil, Free Labor, Free Men* (New York: Oxford University Press, 1970).
Henry Nash Smith, *Virgin Land* (New York: Vintage Books, 1950).

PART IV

THE CIVIL WAR AND RECONSTRUCTION

36. Abraham Lincoln, "The Emancipation Proclamation" (1863)

1860   Lincoln elected President; South Carolina secedes
1861   Six more southern states secede; Lincoln inaugurated; Battle of Fort Sumter, Civil War begins; four more southern states secede
1862   Battle of Antietam; Lincoln issues Preliminary Emancipation Proclamation
1863   (January 1) Lincoln signs Emancipation Proclamation
1865   Civil War ends; Thirteenth Amendment ratified

By the time Lincoln was inaugurated as the sixteenth President of the United States, seven southern slave states had already left the Union. They did so not because the new President had promised to abolish slavery. Time and time again, Lincoln had declared that he had no plans to "interfere with the institution of slavery in the states where it exists." Indeed, during the first two years of the Civil War no slaves were freed by Lincoln.

In the summer of 1862, however, Lincoln's views toward slavery began to shift. Abolitionists pressured him to make the war into something greater than a fight to preserve the Union. Lincoln himself began to feel that he might only be able to win the war by freeing the slaves. Such an act could easily cause havoc in the South and add to the number of troops the Union could muster in the field.

In June 1862 Lincoln drafted the Emancipation Proclamation, which announced his intention to free the slaves in rebel territories. However, he waited until after the Union had won a victory on the battlefield in Antietam in September to issue the proclamation. And even then the Emancipation Proclamation did not take effect until January 1863, and it freed slaves only in the rebel states. If the rebel states agreed to rejoin the Union, they could retain their slaves—but none of them did. The proclamation also left the status of slaves in the nonrebel states unchanged. Therefore, since only slaves in rebel areas were deemed free, in actuality the Emancipation Proclamation did not immediately free anyone.

This said, as the Union Army marched through the South, millions of slaves were freed. Moreover, the proclamation placed the nation on record in opposition to slavery. Perhaps in honor of this, after the Civil War, African Americans regularly commemorated January 1, the date on which the Emancipation Proclamation became effective, as a great day in their history.

Abraham Lincoln Signing Emancipation Proclamation. Oil Painting by Francis Bicknell Carpenter (Library of Congress).

W hereas on the 22d day of September, A.D. 1862, a proclamation was issued by the President of the United States, containing among other things, the following, to wit:

"That on the 1st day of January, A.D. 1863, all persons held as slaves within any State or designated part of a State the people whereof shall then be in rebellion against the United States shall be then, thenceforward, and forever free; and the executive government of the United States, including the military and naval authority thereof, will recognize and maintain the freedom of such persons and will do no act or acts to repress such persons, or any of them, in any efforts they may make for their actual freedom.

"That the executive will on the 1st day of January aforesaid, by procla-mation, designate the States and parts of States, if any, in which the people thereof, respectively, shall then be in rebellion against the United States; and the fact that any State or the people thereof shall on that day be in good faith represented in the Congress of the United States by members chosen thereto at elections wherein a majority of the qualified voters of such States shall have participated shall, in the absence of strong countervailing testi-mony, be deemed conclusive evidence that such State and the people thereof are not then in rebellion against the United States."

Now, therefore, I, Abraham Lincoln, President of the United States, by virtue of the power in me vested as Commander-in-Chief of the Army and Navy of the United States in time of actual armed rebellion against the authority and government of the United States, and as a fit and necessary war measure for suppressing said rebellion, do, on this 1st day of January, A.D. 1863, and in accordance with my purpose so to do, publicly proclaimed for the full period of one hundred days from the first day above mentioned, order and designate as the States and parts of States wherein the people thereof, respectively, are this day in rebellion against the United States the following, to wit:

Arkansas, Texas, Louisiana (except the parishes of St. Bernard, Plaque-mines, Jefferson, St. John, St. Charles, St. James, Ascension, Assumption, Terrebonne, Lafourche, St. Mary, St. Martin, and Orleans, including the city of New Orleans), Mississippi, Alabama, Florida, Georgia, South Caro-lina, North Carolina, and Virginia (except the forty-eight counties designated as West Virginia, and also the counties of Berkeley, Accomac, Northhamp-ton, Elizabeth City, York, Princess Anne, and Norfolk, including the cities of Norfolk and Portsmouth), and which expected parts are for the present left precisely as if this proclamation were not issued.

And by virtue of the power and for the purpose aforesaid, I do order and declare that all persons held as slaves within said designated States and parts of States are, and henceforward shall be, free; and that the Executive Gov-ernment of the United States, including the military and naval authorities thereof, will recognize and maintain the freedom of said persons.

And I hereby enjoin upon the people so declared to be free to abstain from all violence, unless in necessary self-defense; and I recommend to them that, in all cases when allowed, they labor faithfully for reasonable wages.

And I further declare and make known that such persons of suitable condition will be received into the armed service of the United States to garrison forts, positions, stations, and other places, and to man vessels of all sorts in said service.

And upon this act, sincerely believed to be an act of justice, warranted by the Constitution upon military necessity, I invoke the considerate judgment of mankind and the gracious favor of Almighty God.

Source: *U.S. Statutes at Large* (Boston, 1869), 12:1268–69.

For Further Reading:

LaWanda Cox, *Lincoln and Black Freedom* (Columbia: University of South Carolina Press, 1981).
Leon Litwack, *Been in the Storm So Long* (New York: Knopf, 1979).

37. Abraham Lincoln, "Gettysburg Address" (November 19, 1863)

1863   (July 1-3) Battle of Gettysburg; (November 19) Lincoln delivers Gettysburg Address

Six months, to the day, after Lincoln signed the Emancipation Proclamation (see document 36), the pivotal battle of the Civil War began in Gettysburg, Pennsylvania. By the time it ended on July 3, the two sides had suffered over 43,000 casualties.

Gettysburg was a defining moment in the nation's history, and in mid-November 1863 President Lincoln sought to make sense of the event. At a ceremony in Gettysburg to dedicate the cemetery where so many of his countrymen lay buried, he delivered his greatest speech, one that Carl Sandburg later hailed as one of America's great poems. In the "Gettysburg Address," Lincoln asserted that the soldiers had not died in vain. They sacrificed their lives, Lincoln stated, not just to preserve the Union but for the idea or principles for which the Union stood, rule "of the people." They had died, in essence, for the cause of democracy.

Although one of the best-known documents in American history, the "Gettysburg Address" has been shrouded in myth and half-truths almost since its delivery. One commonly heard myth is that Lincoln wrote the address on the back of an envelope while traveling by train to Gettysburg from

President Abraham Lincoln, 1863. Meserve #59 (Library of Congress).

Washington. Another popular myth is that the speech received little attention at the time. In fact, while Lincoln may have edited the address en route to Gettysburg or at the home of Judge Wills, where he slept the night before the ceremony, he drafted the speech with care while still in Washington. Furthermore, he based his comments on thoughts that he had had for some time regarding the meaning of the war. Finally, while awareness of the significance and beauty of the address grew with time, many of Lincoln's contemporaries recognized it immediately as a classic. Harper's Weekly, for example, observed that "It was as simple and felicitous and earnest a word as was ever spoken." And Secretary of War Edward Stanton commented that "it will be remembered as long as anyone's speeches are remembered."

Fourscore and seven years ago our fathers brought forth, on this continent, a new nation, conceived in Liberty, and dedicated to the proposition that all men are created equal.

Now we are engaged in a great civil war, testing whether that nation, or any nation so conceived, and so dedicated, can long endure. We are met on a great battlefield of that war. We have come to dedicate a portion of that field, as a final resting-place for those who here gave their lives, that that nation might live. It is altogether fitting and proper that we should do this.

But, in a larger sense, we can not dedicate—we can not consecrate—we can not hallow—this ground. The brave men, living and dead, who struggled here, have consecrated it far above our poor power to add or detract. The world will little note, nor long remember what we say here, but it can never forget what they did here. It is for us the living, rather, to be dedicated here to the unfinished work which they who fought here have thus far so nobly advanced. It is rather for us to be here dedicated to the great task remaining before us—that from these honored dead we take increased devotion to that cause for which they here gave the last full measure of devotion—that we here highly resolve that these dead shall not have died in vain—that this nation, under God, shall have a new birth of freedom—and that government of the people, by the people, for the people, shall not perish from the earth.

Source: Arthur Brooks Lapsley, ed., *The Writings of Abraham Lincoln*, federal ed. (New York, 1905), 7:20.

For Further Reading:

James McPherson, *Battle Cry of Freedom* (New York: Oxford University Press, 1988).
James G. Randall, *Mr. Lincoln* (New York: Dodd, Mead, 1957).
Garry Wills, *Lincoln at Gettysburg* (New York: Simon & Schuster, 1992).

38. Abraham Lincoln, "Second Inaugural Address" (1865)

1865   (March 4) Lincoln inaugurated for second time; (April 9) Lee surrenders to Grant at Appomattox; (April 14) Lincoln assassinated; Vice-President Andrew Johnson sworn in as new President

By the date of Abraham Lincoln's second inauguration, the Union's victory in the Civil War was assured. General William T. Sherman's troops were

completing their destructive march through the Deep South. General Grant's forces were overwhelming Lee's Army of the Potomac. Confederate forces in the West, commanded by General Hood, had been defeated. Hence Lincoln saw the goal of the "Second Inaugural Address" as one of reviewing the causes of the Civil War and looking at the forthcoming reconstruction of the nation. The inaugural, although the shortest ever delivered, is also one of the most memorable, containing the immortal words "with malice toward none."

A little over a month after he delivered the address, Lincoln lay dead from an assassin's bullet. He joined over 600,000 other Americans who had been sent to their graves by the sectional rivalry over slavery. Five days before Lincoln's assassination, General Lee had surrendered to General Grant at the Court House in Appomattox, Virginia. Grant had treated Lee in the spirit invoked by Lincoln. He allowed the general and his troops to depart honorably from the battlefield. Neither Lee nor most of the other Confederate leaders were ever charged with a crime or imprisoned for their treasonous behavior. Indeed, under Johnson's reconstruction plan, all southerners had to do to regain their citizenship rights was to swear their loyalty to the United States.

FELLOW COUNTRYMEN:

At this second appearing to take the oath of the presidential office, there is less occasion for an extended address than there was at the first. Then a statement, somewhat in detail, of a course to be pursued, seemed fitting and proper. Now, at the expiration of four years, during which public declarations have been constantly called forth on every point and phase of the great contest which still absorbs the attention, and engrosses the energies of the nation, little that is new could be presented. The progress of our arms, upon which all else chiefly depends, is as well known to the public as to myself; and it is, I trust, reasonably satisfactory and encouraging to all. With high hope for the future, no prediction in regard to it is ventured.

On the occasion corresponding to this four years ago, all thoughts were anxiously directed to an impending civil-war. All dreaded it—all sought to avert it. While the inaugural address was being delivered from this place, devoted altogether to *saving* the Union without war, insurgent agents were in the city seeking to *destroy* it without war—seeking to dissolve the Union, and divide effects, by negotiation. Both parties deprecated war; but one of them would *make* war rather than let the nation survive; and the other would *accept* war rather than let it perish. And the war came.

One eighth of the whole population were colored slaves, not distributed generally over the Union, but localized in the Southern part of it. These slaves constituted a peculiar and powerful interest. All knew that this interest was, somehow, the cause of the war. To strengthen, perpetuate, and extend this interest was the object for which the insurgents would rend the Union, even by war; while the government claimed no right to do more than to restrict the territorial enlargement of it. Neither party expected for the war, the magnitude, or the duration, which it has already attained. Neither anticipated that the *cause* of the conflict might cease with, or even before, the conflict itself should cease. Each looked for an easier triumph, and a result less fundamental and astounding. Both read the same Bible, and pray to the same God; and each invokes His aid against the other. It may seem strange that any men should dare to ask a just God's assistance in wringing their bread from the sweat of other men's faces; but let us judge not that we be not judged. The prayers of both could not be answered; that of neither has been answered fully. The Almighty has His own purposes. "Woe unto the world because of offences! for it must needs be that offences come; but woe to that man by whom the offence cometh!" If we shall suppose that American Slavery is one of those offences which, in the providence of God, must needs come, but which, having continued through His appointed time, He now wills to remove, and that He gives to both North and South, this terrible war, as the woe due to those by whom the offence came, shall we discern therein any departure from those divine attributes which the believers in a Living God always ascribe to Him? Fondly do we hope—fervently do we pray—that this mighty scourge of war may speedily pass away. Yet, if God wills that it continue, until all the wealth piled by the bond-man's two hundred and fifty years of unrequited toil shall be sunk, and until every drop of blood drawn with the lash, shall be paid by another drawn with the sword, as was said three thousand years ago, so still it must be said "the judgments of the Lord, are true and righteous altogether."

With malice toward none; with charity for all; with firmness in the right, as God gives us to see the right, let us strive on to finish the work we are in; to bind up the nation's wounds; to care for him who shall have borne the battle, and for his widow, and his orphan—to do all which may achieve and cherish a just, and a lasting peace, among ourselves, and with all nations.

Source: James D. Richardson, ed., *Messages and Papers of the Presidents* (Washington, D.C., 1899), 6:276.

For Further Reading:

Richard N. Current, *The Lincoln Nobody Knows* (New York: Scribner's, 1958).
David Donald, *Lincoln Reconsidered*, 2d ed. (New York: Knopf, 1956).
Edmund Wilson, *Patriotic Gore* (New York: Oxford University Press, 1962).

39. Martin R. Delany, Excerpt from "Advice to Ex-Slaves" (1865)

1865   Freedmen's Bureau established; southern states
        readmitted to Union by President Andrew Johnson
1865–66   Southern states pass Black Codes
1866–67   Civil Rights and Military Reconstruction Acts
        enacted
1868   Fourteenth Amendment ratified
1870   Fifteenth Amendment ratified

Martin R. Delany came from a long line of African chieftains. Although his royal grandfathers had been captured in war, sold into slavery, and shipped to America, they instilled in their children and in Martin himself pride in their heritage. Delany, who was raised as a free black in Virginia, educated at Harvard, and commissioned as an officer in the Union Army during the Civil War, was both a leading abolitionist before the conflict and a prominent political spokesman afterward. He is also considered the father of black nationalism in the United States.

Delany delivered "Advice to Ex-Slaves" to a gathering of recently freed slaves at St. Helena's Island, South Carolina. In it Delany asserted that freedmen and women needed to demand and fight for their freedom and equality. Along the same lines, Delany warned against trusting either southern whites or northern liberals. Indeed, to ensure their own freedom, Delany suggested that blacks had to be willing to defend their rights. This included using armed force if necessary.

Given the conditions of the time, Delany's suggestions were quite pragmatic. Most southerners showed that they had no intention of treating the former slaves as equals. Southern states enacted "black codes," which restricted the rights of African Americans, and individual southerners joined the Ku Klux Klan, which set out to maintain white supremacy through terror. The federal government, led by Radical Republicans, sought to overcome these codes through the passage of the Fourteenth and Fifteenth Amendments, which granted the freedmen civil rights and the vote. And it sought to break the Klan through the Military Reconstruction Act, which placed the South under federal control. On the other hand, the Radical Republicans in Congress refused to provide freedmen with economic security by granting them land. Moreover, most northerners were unprepared for Delany's assertiveness. They tended to see themselves as the guarantors of freedom and liberty and expected the freedmen to passively thank them for their aid and

"Patience on a Monument, 1868." Woodcut after Thomas Nast in *Harper's Weekly*, October 10, 1868, p. 648 (Library of Congress).

protection. Many of them continued to see blacks as inferiors, as men and women in need of the help of white superiors.

It was only a War policy of the Government, to declare the slaves of the South free, knowing that the whole power of the South, laid in the possession of the Slaves. But I want you to understand, that we would not have become free, had we not armed ourselves and fought out our independence.

. . . People say that you are too lazy to work, that you have no intelligence to get on for yourselves, without being guided and driven to the work by overseers. I say it is a lie, and a blasphemous lie, and I will prove it to be so.

I am going to tell you now, *what* you are worth. As you know Christopher Columbus landed here in 1492. They came here only for the purpose to dig gold, gather precious pearls, diamonds and all sorts of jewels, only for the proud Aristocracy of the White Spaniards and Portuguese, to adorn their persons, to have brooches for their breasts, earrings for their ears, Bracelets for their ankles and rings for their limbs and fingers. They found here (red men) Indians whom they obliged to dig and work and slave for them—but they found out that they died away too fast and cannot stand the work. In course of time they had taken some blacks (Africans) along with them and put *them* to work—they could stand it—and yet the Whites say they are superior to our race, though they could not stand it. (At the present day in some of the Eastern parts of Spain, the Spaniard there [having been once conquered by the black race] have black eyes, black hair, black complexion. They have Negroe blood in them!!) The work was so profitable which those poor blacks did, that in the year 1502 Charles the V. gave permission to import into America yearly 4,000 blacks. The profit of these sales was so immense, that afterwards even the Virgin Queen of England and James the II. took part in the Slave trade and were accumulating great wealth for the Treasury of the Government. And so you *always* have been the means of riches.

I tell you I have been all over Africa . . . and I tell you (as I told to the Geographical Faculty in London) that those people there, are a well-driving class of cultivators, and I never saw or heard of one of our brethern there to travel without taking seeds with him as much as he can carry and to sow it wherever he goes to, or to exchange it with his brethern.

So you ought further to know, that all the spices, cotton, rice and coffee has only been brought over by *you*, from the land of our brethern.

Your masters who lived in opulence, kept you to hard work by some contemptible being called overseer—who chastised and beat you whenever he pleased—while your master lived in some Northern town or in Europe to squander away the wealth only you acquired for him. He never earned a single Dollar in his life. You men and women, every one of you around me, made thousands and thousands of dollars for your master. Only you were the means for your masters to lead the idle and inglorious life, and to give his children the education, which he denied to you, for fear you may awake to conscience. If I look around me, I tell you all the houses on this Island and in Beaufort, they are all familiar to my eye, they are the same structures which I have met with in Africa. They have all been made by the Negroes, you can see it by such exteriors.

I tell you they (white man) cannot teach you anything, and they could not make them because they have not the brain to do it. (*after a pause*) At least I mean the Southern people; Oh the Yankees they are smart. Now tell me from all you have heard from me, are you not worth anything? Are you those men whom they think, God only created as a curse and for a slave? Whom they do not consider their equals? As I said before the Yankees are smart; there are good ones and bad ones. The good ones, if they are good they are very good, if they are bad, they are very bad. But the worst and most contemptible, and even worse than even your masters were, are those Yankees, who hired themselves as *overseers*.

Believe not in these School teachers, Emissaries, Ministers, and agents, because they never tell you the truth, and I particularly warn you against those Cotton Agents, who come honey mouthed unto you, their only intent being to make profit by your inexperience.

If there is a man who comes to you, who will meddle with your affairs, send him to one of your more enlightened brothers, who shall ask him who he is, what business he seeks with you, etc.

Believe none but those Agents who are sent out by Government, to enlighten and guide you. I am an officer in the service of the U.S. Government, and ordered to aid Gen'l Saxton, who has been only lately appointed Asst Comr for South Carolina. So is Gen'l Wild Asst Comr for Georgia.

When Chief Justice Chase was down here to speak to you, some of those malicious and abominable New York papers derived from it that he only seeks to be elected by you as President. I have no such ambition, I let them have for a President a white or a black one. I don't care who it be—it may be who has a mind to. I shall not be intimidated whether by threats or imprisonment, and no power will keep me from telling you the truth. So I expressed myself even at Charleston, the hotbed of those scoundrels, your old masters, without fear or reluctance.

So I will come to the main purpose for which I have come to see you. As before the whole South depended upon you, now the *whole country* will depend upon you. I give you an advice how to get along. Get up a community and get all the lands you can—if you cannot get any singly.

Grow as much vegetables, etc, as you want for your families; on the other part of the land you cultivate Rice and Cotton. Now for instance 1. Acre will grow a crop of Cotton of $90—now a land with 10 Acres will bring $900 every year: if you cannot get the land all yourself,—the community can, and so you can divide the profit. There is Tobacco for instance (Virginia is the great place for Tobacco). There are whole squares at Dublin and Liverpool named after some place of Tobacco notoriety, so you see of what enormous value your labor was to the benefits of your masters. Now you understand that I want you to be the producers of this country. It is the wish of the Government for you to be so. We will send friends to you, who will further instruct you how to come to the end of our wishes. You see that by so adhering to our views, you will become a wealthy and powerful population.

Now I look around me and notice a man, barefooted, covered with rags and dirt. Now I ask, what is that man doing, for whom is he working. I hear that he works for that and that farmer for 30 cents a day. I tell you that must not be. That would be cursed slavery over again. I will not have it, the Government will not have it, and the Government shall hear about it. I will tell the Government. I tell you slavery is over, and shall never return again. We have now 200,000 of our men well drilled in arms and used to War fare and I tell you it is with you and them that slavery shall not come back again, if you are determined it will not return again.

Source: Philip S. Foner, ed., *Voice of Black America* (New York, 1972) 1:320–23.

For Further Reading:

W.E.B. Du Bois, *Black Reconstruction in America, 1860–1880* (New York: Russell & Russell, 1935).

Eric Foner, *Reconstruction* (New York: Haper & Row, 1988).

Leon Litwack, *Been in the Storm So Long* (New York: Knopf, 1979).

Joel Williamson, *After Slavery* (Chapel Hill: University of North Carolina Press, 1965).

40. Sojourner Truth, Excerpt from "When Woman Gets Her Rights Man Will Be Right" (1867)

1797   Sojourner Truth (Isabella) born
1827   Truth escapes from slavery
1843   Changes name to Sojourner Truth
1851   Truth delivers famous "Ain't I a Woman" address
1864   Truth meets with President Lincoln
1869   National Woman Suffrage Association founded

Born a slave named Isabella in Ulster County, New York, Sojourner Truth escaped to freedom just before the enactment of the New York State Eman-

cipation Act of 1827. Shortly thereafter, she went to live in New York City with an evangelist sect and then at the utopian community "Zion Hill," in upstate New York. In 1843, claiming that she had heard God's voice, she changed her name to Sojourner Truth and set out on the road as an itinerant preacher dedicated to speaking "the truth."

During this stage of her life she joined the abolitionist crusade and became associated with the budding women's rights movement. Her book The Narrative of Sojourner Truth, *published in 1850 with a preface written by William Lloyd Garrison (a second edition contained a preface written by Harriet Beecher Stowe), won her widespread recognition. A speech she delivered in Akron, Ohio, in 1851, in which she declared, "Ain't I a Woman," earned her a place as a leading opponent of sexual inequality and discrimination.*

Following the Civil War she remained a prominent activist, pushing for the passage of the Thirteenth, Fourteenth, and Fifteenth Amendments. However, she found that many leaders of the women's rights movement felt betrayed by male abolitionists who refused to fight for women's suffrage. Truth, as is evident in her speech "When Woman Gets Her Rights Man Will Be Right," which she delivered to the First Annual Meeting of the American Equal Rights Association, insisted that one had to fight for both racial and sexual equality. She refused to side with one faction or the other. Yet her position left her in the minority.

My friends, I am rejoiced that you are glad, but I don't know how you will feel when I get through. I come from another field—the country of the slave. They have got their rights—so much good luck. Now what is to be done about it? I feel that I have got as much responsibility as anybody else. I have as good rights as anybody. There is a great stir about colored men getting their rights, but not a word about the colored women; and if colored men get their rights, and not colored women get theirs, there will be a bad time about it. So I am for keeping the thing going while things are stirring; because if we wait till it is still, it will take a great while to get it going again. White women are a great deal smarter, and know more than colored women, while colored women do not know scarcely anything. They go out washing, which is about as high as a colored woman gets, and their men go about idle, strutting up and down; and when the women come home, they ask for their money and take it all, and then scold because there is no food. I want you to consider on that, chil'n. I want women to have their rights. In the courts women have no right, no voice; nobody speaks for them. I wish woman to have her voice there among the pettifoggers. If it is not a fit place for women, it is unfit for men to be there. I am above eighty years old; it is about time for me to be going. But I suppose I am kept here because something remains for me to do; I suppose I am yet to help break the chain.

I have done a great deal of work—as much as a man, but did not get so much pay. I used to work in the field and bind grain, keeping up with the cradler; but men never doing no more, got twice as much pay. So with the German women. They work in the field and do as much work, but do not get the pay. We do as much, we eat as much, we want as much. I suppose I am about the only colored woman that goes about to speak for the rights of the colored woman, I want to keep the thing stirring, now that the ice is broken. What we want is a little money. You men know that you get as much again as women when you write, or for what you do. When we get our rights, we shall not have to come to you for money, for then we shall have money enough of our own. It is a good consolation to know that when we have got this we shall not be coming to you any more. You have been having our right so long, that you think, like a slaveholder, that you own us. I know that it is hard for one who has held the reins for so long to give up; it cuts like a knife. It will feel all better when it closes up again. I have been in Washington about three years, seeing about those colored people. Now colored men have a right to vote; and what I want is to have colored women have the right to vote. There ought to be equal rights more than ever, since colored people have got their freedom. . . .

I know that it is hard for men to give up entirely. They must run in the old track. I was amused how men speak up for one another. They cannot bear that a woman should say anything about the man, but they will stand here and take up the time in man's cause. But we are going, tremble or no tremble. Men are trying to help us. I know that all—the spirit they have got; and they cannot help us much until some of the spirit is taken out of them that belongs among the women. Men have got their rights, and women has not got their rights. That is the trouble. When woman gets her rights man will be right. How beautiful that will be. Then it will be peace on earth and good will to men. But it cannot be until it be right. . . . It will come. . . . Yes, it will come quickly. It must come. And now when the waters is troubled, and now is the time to step into the pool. There is a great deal now with the minds, and now is the time to start forth. . . . The great fight was to keep the rights of the poor colored people. That made a great battle. And now I hope that this will be the last battle that will be in the world. Let us finish up so that there be no more fighting. I have faith in God and there is truth in humanity. Be strong women! Blush not! Tremble not! I want you to keep a good faith and good courage. And I am going round after I get my business settled and get more equality. People in the North, I am going round to lecture on human rights. I will shake every place I go to.

Source: *National Anti-Slavery Standard*, June 1, 1867.

For Further Reading:

Jacqueline Bernard, *Journey Toward Freedom* (New York: The Feminist Press, 1990).
Ellen Du Bois, *Feminism and Suffrage* (Ithaca, N.Y.: Cornell University Press, 1978).

41. Frederick Douglass, Excerpt from "Address on the Anniversary of the Emancipation of Slaves in the District of Columbia" (1888)

1876   Presidential election between Hayes and Tilden ends in deadlock
1877   Compromise of 1877: Hayes becomes President; removes troops from South, signaling end of Reconstruction
1896   In *Plessy v. Ferguson* Supreme Court upholds Jim Crow laws

Twenty-five years after the enactment of the Emancipation Proclamation (see document 36), Frederick Douglass, a former slave and a reknowned abolitionist, visited the Deep South to examine the conditions of America's exslaves. He was appalled by what he saw. In 1877 Rutherford B. Hayes had become President through a backroom deal. Following a close election, in which the votes of several states remained in doubt after election day, Hayes promised to remove federal troops from the South in exchange for the presidency. Hayes' Democratic opponents agreed to this deal provided that Republicans in Congress would curtail legislative efforts to protect blacks in southern states. The fact that Congress had previously refused to redistribute land during Reconstruction, to provide the freedman with economic independence, combined with the white South's open disregard for the Fourteenth and Fifteenth Amendments, which followed Hayes' election, placed the freedman at the mercy of southern interests. Indeed, in his "Address on the Anniversary of the Emancipation of Slaves in the District of Columbia," which many thought would be a celebration of the Emancipation Proclamation, Douglass delivered some of his most biting and critical words ever. He termed the proclamation a "fraud" and lambasted the federal government for refusing to uphold the principles of the Declaration of Independence and the Constitution of the United States.

Douglass' remarks received little attention at the time. The Republican Party had retreated from its advocacy of racial equality under the law. Even leading black figures, such as Booker T. Washington, were retreating from the assertive approach practiced by Douglass, Delany (see document 39), and other black abolitionists. Moreover, less than a decade after his address, the Supreme Court in Plessy v. Ferguson, *legitimized the dismantling of*

Frederick Douglass, ca. 1870 (National Archives).

Reconstruction by declaring that the Fourteenth Amendment did not prohibit racial segregation. Yet, as Douglass observed, the issue of color would not go away.

Friends and fellow citizens: it has been my privilege to assist in several anniversary celebrations of the abolition of slavery in the District of Columbia, but I remember no occasion of this kind when I felt a deeper solicitude for the future welfare of our emancipated people than now.

The chief cause of anxiety is not in the condition of the colored people of the District of Columbia, though there is much that is wrong and unsatisfactory here, but the deplorable condition of the Negro in the Southern states. At no time since the abolition of slavery has there been more cause for alarm on this account than at this juncture in our history.

I have recently been in two of the Southern states—South Carolina and Georgia—and my impression from what I saw, heard and learned there is not favorable to my hopes for the race. I know this is a sad message to bring you on this twenty-sixth anniversary of freedom in the District of Columbia, but I know, too, that I have a duty to perform and that duty is to tell the truth, the whole truth, and nothing but the truth, and I should be unworthy to stand here, unworthy of the confidence of the colored people of this country, if I should from any considerations of policy withhold any fact or feature of the condition of the freedmen which the people of this country ought to know.

The temptation on anniversary occasions like this is to prophesy smooth things, to be joyful and glad, to indulge in the illusions of hope—to bring glad tidings on our tongues, and words of peace reveal. But while I know it is always easier to be the bearer of glad tidings than sad ones, while I know that hope is a powerful motive to exertion and high endeavor, while I know that people generally would rather look upon the bright side of their condition than to know the worst; there comes a time when it is best that the worst should be made known, and in my judgment that time, in respect to the condition of the colored people of the South, is now. There are times when neither hope nor fear should be allowed to control our speech. Cry aloud and spare not, is the word of wisdom as well as of Scripture. "Ye shall know the truth, and the truth shall make you free," applies to the body not less than the soul, to this world not less than the world to come. Outside the truth there is no solid foundation for any of us, and I assume that you who have invited me to speak, and you who have come to hear me speak, expect me to speak the truth as I understand the truth.

The truth at which we should get on this occasion respects the precise relation subsisting between the white and colored people of the South, or, in other words, between the colored people people and the old master class of the South. We have need to know this and to take it to heart.

It is well said that "a people may lose its liberty in a day and not miss it in half a century," and that "the price of liberty is eternal vigilance." In my judgment, with my knowledge of what has already taken place in the South, these wise and wide-awake sentiments were never more apt and timely than now.

I have assisted in fighting one battle for the abolition of slavery, and the American people have shed their blood in defense of the Union and the Constitution, and neither I nor they should wish to fight this battle over again; and in order that we may not, we should look the facts in the face today and, if possible, nip the evil in the bud.

I have no taste for the role of an alarmist. If my wishes could be allowed to dictate my speech I would tell you something quite the reverse of what

I now intend. I would tell you that everything is lovely with the Negro in the South; I would tell you that the rights of the Negro are respected, and that he has no wrongs to redress; I would tell you that he is honestly paid for his labor; that he is secure in his liberty; that he is tried by a jury of his peers when accused of crime; that he is no longer subject to lynch law; that he has freedom of speech; that the gates of knowledge are open to him; that he goes to the ballot box unmolested; that his vote is duly counted and given its proper weight in determining result; I would tell you that he is making splendid progress in the acquisition of knowledge, wealth and influence; I would tell you that his bitterest enemies have become his warmest friends; that the desire to make him a slave no longer exists anywhere in the South; that the Democratic party is a better friend to him than the Republican party, and that each party is competing with the other to see which can do the most to make his liberty a blessing to himself and to the country and the world. But in telling you all this I should be telling you what is absolutely false, and what you know to be false, and the only thing which would save such a story from being a lie would be its utter inability to deceive.

What is the condition of the Negro at the South at this moment? Let us look at it both in the light of facts and in the light of reason. To understand it we must consult nature as well as circumstances, the past as well as the present. No fact is more obvious than the fact that there is a perpetual tendency of power to encroach upon weakness, and of the crafty to take advantage of the simple. This is as natural as for smoke to ascend or water to run down. The love of power is one of the strongest traits in the Anglo-Saxon race. This love of power common to the white race has been nursed and strengthened at the South by slavery: accustomed during two hundred years to the unlimited possession and exercise of irresponsible power, the love of it has become stronger by habit. To assume that this feeling of pride and power has died out and disappeared from the South is to assume a miracle. Any man who tells you that it has died out or has ceased to be exercised and made effective, tells you that which is untrue and in the nature of things could not be true. Not only is the love of power there, but a talent for its exercise has been fully developed. This talent makes the old master class of the South not only the masters of the Negro, but the masters of Congress and, if not checked, will make them the masters of the nation.

It was something more than an empty boast in the old times, when it was said that one slave master was equal to three Northern men. Though this did not turn out to be true on the battlefield, it does seem to be true in the councils of the nation. In sight of all the nation these ambitious men of the South have dared to take possession of the government which they, with broad blades and bloody hands, sought to destroy; in sight of all the nation they have disregarded and trampled upon the Constitution, and organized parties on sectional lines. From the ramparts of the Solid South, with their 153 electoral votes in the Electoral College, they have dared to defy the nation to put a Republican in the Presidential chair for the next four years, as they once threatened the nation with civil war if it elected Abraham Lincoln. With this grip on the Presidential chair, with the House of Representatives in their hands, with the Supreme Court deciding every question in favor of the states, as against the powers of the federal government, denying to the government the right to protect the elective franchise of its own citizens, they may well feel themselves masters, not only of their former slaves, but of the whole situation. With these facts before us, tell me not that the Negro is safe in the possession of his liberty. Tell me not that power will not assert itself. Tell me not that they who despise the Constitution they have sworn to support will respect the rights of the Negro, whom they already despise. Tell me not that men who thus break faith with God will be scrupulous in keeping faith with the poor Negro laborer of the South. Tell me not that a people who have lived by the sweat of other men's faces, and thought themselves Christian gentlemen while doing it, will feel themselves bound by principles of justice to their former victims in their weakness. Such a pretense in face of facts is shameful, shocking and sickening. Yet there are men at the North who believe all this.

Well may it be said that Americans have no memories. We look over the House of Representatives and see the Solid South enthroned there. We listen with calmness to eulogies of the South and of the traitors, and forget Andersonville. We look over the Senate and see the Senator from South Carolina, and we forget Hamburg. We see Robert Smalls cheated out of his seat in Congress, and forget the *Planter*, and the service rendered by the colored troops in the late war for the Union.

Well, the nation may forget; it may shut its eyes to the past and frown upon any who may do otherwise, but the colored people of this country are bound to keep fresh a memory of the past till justice shall be done them in the present. When this shall be done we shall as readily as any other part of our respected citizens plead for an act of oblivion.

We are often confronted of late in the press and on the platform with the discouraging statement that the problem of the Negro as a free man and a citizen is not yet solved; that since his emancipation he has disappointed the best hopes of his friends and fulfilled the worst predictions of his enemies, and that he has shown himself unfit for the position assigned him by the mistaken statesmanship of the nation. It is said that physically, morally, socially and religiously he is in a condition vastly more deplorable than was his condition as a slave; that he has not proved himself so good a master to himself as his old master was to him; that he is gradually, but surely, sinking below the point of industry, good manners and civilization to which he attained in a state of slavery; that his industry is fitful; that his economy is wasteful; that his honesty is deceitful; that his morals are impure; that his domestic life is beastly; that his religion is fetichism, and his worship is simply emotional; and that, in a word, he is falling into a state of barbarism.

Such is the distressing description of the emancipated Negro as drawn by his enemies and as it is found reported in the journals of the South. Unhappily, however, it is a description not confined to the South. It has gone forth to the North. It has crossed the ocean; I met with it in Europe. And it has gone as far as the wings of the press and the power of speech can carry it. There is no measuring the injury inflicted upon the Negro by it. It cools our friends, heats our enemies, and turns away from us much of the sympathy and aid which we need and deserve to receive at the hands of our fellow men.

But now comes the question, Is this description of the emancipated Negro true? In answer to this question I must say, Yes and no. It is not true in all its lines and specifications and to the full extent of the ground it covers, but it certainly is true in many of its important features, and there is no race under heaven of which the same would not be equally true with the same antecedents and the same treatment which the Negro is receiving at the hands of this nation and the old master class, to which the Negro is still a subject.

I admit that the Negro, and especially the plantation Negro, the tiller of the soil, has made little progress from barbarism to civilization, and that he is in a deplorable condition since his emancipation. That he is worse off, in many respects, than when he was a slave, I am compelled to admit, but I contend that the fault is not his, but that of his heartless accusers. He is the victim of a cunningly devised swindle, one which paralyzes his energies, suppresses his ambition, and blasts all his hopes; and though he is nominally free he is actually a slave. I here and now denounce his so-called emancipation as a stupendous fraud—a fraud upon him, a fraud upon the world. It was not so meant by Abraham Lincoln; it was not so meant by the Republican party; but whether so meant or not, it is practically a lie, keeping the word of promise to the ear and breaking it to the heart.

Do you ask me why the Negro of the plantation has made so little progress, why his cupboard is empty, why he flutters in rags, why his children run naked, and why his wife hides herself behind the hut when a stranger is passing? I will tell you. It is because he is systematically and universally cheated out of his hard earnings. The same class that once extorted his labor under the lash now gets his labor by a mean, sneaking, and fraudulent device. That device is a trucking system which never permits him to see or to save a dollar of his hard earnings. He struggles and struggles, but, like a man in a morass, the more he struggles the deeper he sinks. The highest wages paid him is eight dollars a month, and this he receives only in orders on the store, which, in many cases, is owned by his employer. The scrip has purchasing power on that one store, and that one only. A blind man can see that the laborer is by this arrangement bound hand and foot, and is completely in the power of his employer. He can charge the poor fellow what he pleases and give what kind of goods he pleases, and he does both. His victim cannot go to another store and buy, and this the storekeeper knows. The only security the wretched Negro has under this arrangement is the conscience of the storekeeper—a conscience educated in the school of slavery, where the idea prevailed in theory and practice that the Negro had no rights which white men were bound to respect, an arrangement in which everything in the way of food or clothing, whether tainted meat or damaged cloth, is deemed good enough for the Negro. For these he is often made to pay a double price.

But this is not all, or the worst result of the system. It puts it out of the power of the Negro to save anything of what he earns. If a man gets an honest dollar for his day's work, he has a motive for laying it by and saving it for future emergency. It will be as good for use in the future and perhaps better a year hence than now, but this miserable scrip has in no sense the quality of a dollar. It is only good at one store and for a limited period. Thus the man who has it is tempted to get rid of it as soon as possible. It may be out of date before he knows it, or the storekeeper may move away and it may be left worthless on his hands.

But this is not the only evil involved in this satanic arrangement. It promotes dishonesty. The Negro sees himself paid but limited wages—far too limited to support himself and family, and that in worthless scrip—and he is tempted to fight the devil with fire. Finding himself systematically robbed he goes to stealing and as a result finds his liberty—such as it is—taken from him, and himself put to work for a master in a chain gang, and he comes out, if he ever gets out, a ruined man.

Every Northern man who visits the old master class, the landowners and landlords of the South, is told by the old slaveholders with a great show of virtue that they are glad that they are rid of slavery and would not have the slave system back if they could; that they are better off than they ever were before, and much more of the same tenor. Thus Northern men come home duped and go on a mission of duping others by telling the same pleasing story.

There are very good reasons why these people would not have slavery back if they could—reasons far more creditable to their cunning than to their conscience. With slavery they had some care and responsibility for the physical well-being of their slaves. Now they have as firm a grip on the freedman's labor as when he was a slave and without any burden of caring for his children or himself. The whole arrangement is stamped with fraud and is supported by hypocrisy, and I here and now, on this Emancipation Day: denounce it as a villainous swindle, and invoke the press, the pulpit and the lawmaker to assist in exposing it and blotting it out forever.

Source: *Washington National Republican*, April 17, 1888.

For Further Reading:

William Gillette, *Retreat from Reconstruction, 1869–1879* (Baton Rouge: Louisiana State University Press, 1979).

Roger L. Ransom and Richard Sutch, *One Kind of Freedom* (New York: Cambridge University Press, 1977).

Joel Williamson, *The Crucible of Race* (New York: Oxford University Press, 1984).

C. Vann Woodward, *The Strange Career of Jim Crow*, rev. ed. (New York: Oxford University Press, 1957).

PART V
WESTWARD AND INDUSTRIAL EXPANSION

42. Chief Joseph, "We Will Fight No More, Forever" (1877)

1867   New Indian policy adopted: Indians to be placed on
        reservations
1875–76   Sioux Wars; Little Big Horn
1877   Nez Percé defeated

When the Civil War ended, 250,000 to 300,000 American Indians lived west of the Mississippi River. There they hunted, farmed, and carried on their daily lives relatively free and unfettered by western or white ways. Perceptions of the Great Plains as uninhabitable, as well as government policies that guaranteed the American Indians their liberty in the western territories, led many to believe that the two cultures could peacefully coexist for many years. But several developments, from the discovery of gold and silver to the building of the transcontinental railroad, unleashed a mass wave of migration by white settlers to the West, which produced a wave of wars with the Indians. As General Philip Sheridan observed, "We took away their country and their means of support, broke up their mode of living, their habits of life, introduced disease and decay among them, and it was for this and against this that they made war. Could anyone expect less?"

One war involved the Nez Percé. They had lived in peace in the Pacific Northwest for years, having even aided Lewis and Clark during their journey (see document 19). As of 1870 they even claimed never to have killed a white man. But the rapid influx of settlers into the Walla Walla Valley combined with unfair enforcement of existing treaties led to conflict. For nearly three months in 1877, the Nez Percé fought against superior forces commanded by General O. O. Howard, the former head of the Freedmen's Bureau. After winning some surprise victories, the Nez Percé fled toward the Canadian border, peacefully interacting with white sightseers in Yellowstone. But then Howard caught the Nez Percé in Montana, only thirty miles from the Canadian border. Upon his capture Chief Joseph delivered a brief though eloquent speech on why the Indians felt they could fight no more. Afterward, the remaining Nez Percé settled on Indian reservations in the Dakotas.

Tell General Howard I know his heart. What he told me before, I have it in my heart. I am tired of fighting. Our chiefs are killed. Looking Glass is dead. Toohoolhoolzote is dead. The old men are all dead. It is the young men who say, "Yes" or "No." He who led the young men is dead. It is cold, and we have no blankets. The little children are freezing to death.

Chief Joseph of the Nez Percé (Library of Congress).

My people, some of them, have run away to the hills, and have no blankets, no food. No one knows where they are—perhaps freezing to death. I want to have time to look for my children, and see how many of them I can find. Maybe I shall find them among the dead. Hear me, my chiefs! I am tired. My heart is sick and sad. From where the sun now stands I will fight no more forever.

Source: *Harper's Weekly*, November 17, 1877.

For Further Reading:

Ralph Andrist, *The Long Death* (New York: Macmillan, 1964).
Alvin Josephy, *The Nez Percé Indians and the Opening of the Northwest* (New Haven, Conn.: Yale University Press, 1965).
Robert M. Utley, *The Last Days of the Sioux Nation* (New Haven, Conn.: Yale University Press, 1964).

43. Helen Hunt Jackson, Excerpt from A Century of Dishonor (1881)

1881 A Century of Dishonor published
1887 Dawes Severalty Act
1890 Ghost Dance and massacre at Wounded Knee

Through most of American history whites rarely questioned their westward march and the defeat of the Indians. While a few voiced their disapproval of the brutality of some military commanders and frontiersmen, almost no-body questioned the logic of expansion: that white settlement and subjugation of the Indians represented the progress of civilization. Indeed, it was not until after the Indians had been removed to reservations that a more sym-pathetic view emerged.

In 1881 Helen Hunt Jackson, the daughter of a New England professor and the wife of a western financier, wrote A Century of Dishonor, a critique of America's treatment of the American Indians, and the reservation system in particular. She sent a copy of her book to every member of Congress. The book also became a best seller. Largely as a result of Jackson's book, in 1887 the federal government enacted the Dawes Severalty Act. It offered Indians the opportunity to become full citizens of the United States if they agreed to reject their Indian culture, take ownership of a plot of land on the reservation, and turn themselves into family farmers.

The Dawes Act failed miserably. Most Indians did not want to assimilate. Moreover, they were not granted parcels of land in the healthy and fertile fields of their ancestors. Rather they were offered plots on the desolate reservations of Nevada and the Dakotas. The failure of the Dawes Act became evident in 1890 with the massacre at Wounded Knee. This slaughter of about two hundred Sioux men, women, and children by federal troops took place following a renaissance of traditional Indian culture, namely the Ghost Dance. When the federal government ordered the Sioux to cease practicing this ritual of music, dance, and meditation, the Sioux retreated into the Black Hills of the Dakotas. Rather than leave them alone, federal troops followed them to Wounded Knee, where, following a gunshot of unknown origins, they fired on them with gatling guns and repeating rifles.

The winter of 1877 and summer of 1878 were terrible seasons for the Cheyennes. Their fall hunt had proved unsuccessful. Indians from other reservations had hunted the ground over before them, and driven the buffalo off; and the Cheyennes made their way home again in straggling parties, destitute and hungry. Their agent reports that the result of this hunt has clearly proved that "in the future the Indian must rely on tilling the ground as the principal means of support; and if this conviction can be firmly established, the greatest obstacle to advancement in agriculture will be overcome. With the buffalo gone, and their pony herds being constantly decimated by the inroads of horse-thieves, they must soon adopt, in all its varieties, the way of the white man."

The ration allowed to these Indians is reported as being "reduced and insufficient," and the small sums they have been able to earn by selling buffalo-hides are said to have been "of material assistance" to them in "supplementing" this ration. But in this year there have been sold only $657 worth of skins by the Cheyennes and Arapahoes together. In 1876 they sold $17,600 worth. Here is a falling off enough to cause very great suffering in a little community of five thousand people. But this was only the beginning of their troubles. The summer proved one of unusual heat. Extreme heat, chills and fever, and "a reduced and insufficient ration," all combined, resulted in an amount of sickness heart-rending to read of. "It is no exaggerated estimate," says the agent, "to place the number of sick people on the reservation at two thousand. Many deaths occurred which might have been obviated had there been a proper supply of anti-malarial remedies at hand. Hundreds applying for treatment have been refused medicine."

The Northern Cheyennes grew more and more restless and unhappy. "In council and elsewhere they profess an intense desire to be sent North, where they say they will settle down as the others have done," says the report; adding, with an obtuseness which is inexplicable, that "no difference has been made in the treatment of the Indians," but that the "compliance" of these Northern Cheyennes has been "of an entirely different nature from that of the other Indians," and that it may be "necessary in the future to compel what so far we have been unable to effect by kindness and appeal to their better natures."

If it is "an appeal to men's better natures" to remove them by force from a healthful Northern climate, which they love and thrive in, to a malarial Southern one, where they are struck down by chills and fever—refuse them medicine which can combat chills and fever, and finally starve them—there indeed, might be said to have been most forcible appeals made to the "better natures" of these Northern Cheyennes. What might have been predicted followed.

Early in the autumn, after this terrible summer, a band of some three hundred of these Northern Cheyennes took the desperate step of running off and attempting to make their way back to Dakota. They were pursued, fought desperately, but were finally overpowered, and surrendered. They surrendered, however, only on the condition that they should be taken to Dakota. They were unanimous in declaring that they would rather die than go back to the Indian Territory. This was nothing more, in fact, than saying that they would rather die by bullets than of chills and fever and starvation.

These Indians were taken to Fort Robinson, Nebraska. Here they were confined as prisoners of war, and held subject to the orders of the Department of the Interior. The department was informed of the Indians' determination never to be taken back alive to Indian Territory. The army officers in charge reiterated these statements, and implored the department to permit them to remain at the North; but it was of no avail. Orders came— explicit, repeated, finally stern—insisting on the return of these Indians to their agency. The commanding officer at Fort Robinson has been censured severely for the course he pursued in his effort to carry out those orders. It is difficult to see what else he could have done, except to have resigned his post. He could not take three hundred Indians by sheer brute force and carry them hundreds of miles, especially when they were so desperate that they had broken up the iron stoves in their quarters, and wrought and twisted them into weapons with which to resist. He thought perhaps he could starve them into submission. He stopped the issue of food; he also stopped the issue of fuel to them. It was midwinter; the mercury froze in that month at Fort Robinson. At the end of two days he asked the Indians to let their women and children come out that he might feed them. Not a woman would come out. On the night of the fourth day—or, according to some accounts, the sixth—these starving, freezing Indians broke prison, overpowered the guards, and fled, carrying their women and children with them. They held the pursuing troops at bay for several days; finally made a last stand in a deep ravine, and were shot down—men, women, and children together. Out of the whole band there were left alive some fifty women and children and seven men, who, having been confined in another part of the fort, had not had the good fortune to share in this outbreak and meet their death in the ravine. These, with their wives and children, were sent to Fort Leavenworth to be put in prison; the men to be tried for murders committed in their skirmishes in Kansas on their way to the north. Red Cloud, a Sioux chief, came to Fort Robinson immediately after this massacre and entreated to be allowed to take the Cheyenne widows and orphans into his tribe to be cared for. The Government, therefore, kindly permitted twenty-two Cheyenne widows and thirty-two Cheyenne children—many of them orphans—to be received into the band of the Ogallalla Sioux.

An attempt was made by the Commissioner of Indian Affairs, in his Report for 1879, to show by tables and figures that these Indians were not starving at the time of their flight from Indian Territory. The attempt only redounded to his own disgrace; it being proved, by the testimony given by a former clerk of the Indian Bureau before the Senate committee appointed to investigate the case of the Northern Cheyennes, that the commissioner had been guilty of absolute dishonesty in his estimates, and that the quantity of beef actually issued to the Cheyenne Agency was hundreds of pounds less than he had reported it, and that the Indians were actually, as they had claimed, "starving."

The testimony given before this committee by some of the Cheyenne prisoners themselves is heart-rending. One must have a callous heart who can read it unmoved.

When asked by Senator [John T.] Morgan [of Alabama], "Did you ever really suffer from hunger?" one of the chiefs replied. "We were always hungry; we never had enough. When they that were sick once in awhile felt as though they could eat something, we had nothing to give them."

"Did you not go out on the plains sometimes and hunt buffalo, with the consent of the agent?"

"We went out on a buffalo-hunt, and nearly starved while out; we could not find any buffalo hardly; we could hardly get back with our ponies; we had to kill a good many of our ponies to eat, to save ourselves from starving."

"How many children got sick and died?"

"Between the fall of 1877 and 1878 we lost fifty children. A great many of our finest young men died, as well as many women."

"Old Crow," a chief who served faithfully as Indian scout and ally under General [George] Crook [commander of Far Western troops since 1868] for years, said: "I did not feel like doing anything for awhile, because I had no heart. I did not want to be in this country. I was all the time wanting to get back to the better country where I was born, and where my children are buried, and where my mother and sister yet live. So I have laid in my lodge most of the time with nothing to think about but that, and the affair up north at Fort Robinson, and my relatives and friends who were killed there. But now I feel as though, if I had a wagon and a horse or two, and some land, I would try to work. If I had something, so that I could do something, I might not think so much about these other things. As it is now, I feel as though I would just as soon be asleep with the rest."

The wife of one of the chiefs confined at Fort Leavenworth testified before the committee as follows: "The main thing I complained of was that we didn't get enough to eat; my children nearly starved to death; then sickness came, and there was nothing good for them to eat; for a long time the most they had to eat was corn-meal and salt. Three or four children died every day for awhile, and that frightened us."

When asked if there were anything she would like to say to the committee, the poor woman replied: "I wish you would do what you can to get my husband released. I am very poor here, and do not know what is to become of me. If he were released he would come down here, and we would live together quietly, and do no harm to anybody, and make no trouble. But I should never get over my desire to get back north; I should always want to get back where my children were born, and died, and were buried. That country is better than this in every respect. There is plenty of good, cool water there—pure water—while here the water is not good. It is not hot there, nor so sickly. Are you going where my husband is? Can you tell when he is likely to be released?"...

It is stated also that there was not sufficient clothing to furnish each Indian with a warm suit of clothing, "as promised by the treaty," and that, "by reference to official correspondence, the fact is established that the Cheyennes and Arapahoes are judged as having no legal rights to any lands, having forfeited their treaty reservation by a failure to settle thereon," and their "present reservation not having been, as yet, confirmed by Congress. Inasmuch as the Indians fully understood, and were assured that this reservation was given to them in lieu of their treaty reservation, and have commenced farming in the belief that there was no uncertainty about the matter it is but common justice that definite action be had at an early day, securing to them what is their right."

It would seem that there could be found nowhere in the melancholy record of the experiences of our Indians a more glaring instance of confused multiplication of injustices than this. The Cheyennes were pursued and slain for venturing to leave this very reservation, which, it appears, is not their reservation at all, and they have no legal right to it. Are there any words to fitly characterize such treatment as this from a great, powerful, rich nation, to a handful of helpless people?

Source: Helen Hunt Jackson, *A Century of Dishonor* (New York: Harper & Brothers, 1881), pp. 92–102.

For Further Reading:

Alexander Dee Brown, *Bury My Heart at Wounded Knee* (New York: Holt, Rinehart and Winston, 1970).
Frederick E. Hoxie, *A Final Promise* (Lincoln: University of Nebraska Press, 1989).

44. Walt Whitman, Excerpt from "Democratic Vistas" (1871)

1847   Walt Whitman begins work on *Leaves of Grass*
1855   First edition of *Leaves of Grass* published
1871   *Democratic Vistas* published

The poet Walt Whitman was born and raised in Long Island, New York. After five years of common schooling he got his first job as an office clerk and then as a printer. In the 1830s and 1840s he worked for and edited

Walt Whitman, ca. 1866. Photograph by Mathew Brady (National Archives).

various newspapers, most associated with the Democratic Party. Then in 1847 he quit his newspaper job, went to live with his parents in Brooklyn, New York, and set to work on his great poetic work, Leaves of Grass.

First released on July 4, 1855, Leaves of Grass represented a revolutionary break with the literary canon. Its main theme was Whitman's reflections on democracy, based on personal experience rather than readings of the classics. It was written in free verse, not traditional poetic style. Though it sold few copies in its first edition, it soon captured the attention of some of America's leading intellectuals, including Emerson and Thoreau (see documents 26 and 27). In part, they saw Whitman's work as a response to their

*call for a truly democratic, American cultural tradition. In time most literary
critics have agreed.*

*Following the Civil War Whitman dwelled further on the theme of de-
mocracy and added new pieces to* Leaves of Grass. *At the same time he
wrote two essays, "Democracy" and "Personalism," which, in 1871, were
joined under the title* Democratic Vistas. *In these essays, Whitman championed the cause of the common man. He also bemoaned America's crass
materialism and the growth of the business culture, which he felt was corrupting and threatening democracy. Indeed, Whitman warned that unless
America concerned itself with creating a democratic culture, its broader
experiment in democracy would be jeopardized.*

I say that democracy can never prove itself beyond cavil, until it
founds and luxuriantly grows its own forms of art, poems, schools, theology,
displacing all that exists, or that has been produced anywhere in the past,
under opposite influences. It is curious to me that while so many voices,
pens, minds, in the press, lecture rooms, in our Congress, etc., are discussing
intellectual topics, pecuniary dangers, legislative problems, the suffrage,
tariff and labor questions, and the various business and benevolent needs
of America, with propositions, remedies, often worth deep attention, there
is one need, a hiatus the profoundest, that no eye seems to perceive, no
voice to state. Our fundamental want today in the United States, with closest,
amplest reference to present conditions, and to the future, is of a class, and
the clear idea of a class, of native authors, literatuses, far different, far higher
in grade, than any yet known, sacerdotal, modern, fit to cope with our
occasions, lands, permeating the whole mass of American mentality, taste,
belief, breathing into it a new breath of life, giving it decision, affecting
politics far more than the popular superficial suffrage, with results inside
and underneath the elections of Presidents or Congresses—radiating, be-
getting appropriate teachers, schools, manners, and, as its grandest result,
accomplishing (what neither the schools nor the churches and their clergy
have hitherto accomplish'd, and without which this nation will no more stand,
permanently, soundly, than a house will stand without a sub-stratum), a
religious and moral character beneath the political and productive and intellectual bases of the States. For know you not, dear, earnest reader, that
the people of our land may all read and write, and may all possess the right
to vote—and yet the main things may be entirely lacking?—(and this to
suggest them).

View'd, today, from a point of view sufficiently over-arching, the problem
of humanity all over the civilized world is social and religious, and is to be
finally met and treated by literature. The priest departs, the divine literatus
comes. Never was anything more wanted than, today, and here in the States,
the poet of the modern is wanted, or the great literatus of the modern. At

all times, perhaps, the central point in any nation, and that whence it is
itself really sway'd the most, and whence it sways others, is its national
literature, especially its archetypal poems. Above all previous lands, a great
original literature is surely to become the justification and reliance (in some
respects the sole reliance of American democracy).

Few are aware how the great literature penetrates all, gives hue to all,
shapes aggregates and individuals, and, after subtle ways, with irresistible
power, constructs, sustains, demolishes at will. Why tower, in reminiscence,
above all the nations of the earth, two special lands, petty in themselves,
yet inexpressibly gigantic, beautiful, columnar? Immortal Judah lives, and
Greece immortal lives, in a couple of poems. . . .

I say we had best look our times and lands searchingly in the face, like a
physician diagnosing some deep disease. Never was there, perhaps, more
hollowness at heart than at present, and here in the United States. Genuine
belief seems to have left us. The underlying principles of the States are not
honestly believ'd in (for all this hectic glow, and these melodramatic scream-
ings), nor is humanity itself believ'd in. What penetrating eye does not
everywhere see through the mask? The spectacle is appalling. We live in
an atmosphere of hypocrisy throughout. The men believe not in the women,
nor the women in the men. A scornful superciliousness rules in literature.
The aim of all the *littérateurs* is to find something to make fun of. A lot of
churches, sects, etc., the most dismal phantasms I know, usurp the name
of religion. Conversation is a mass of badinage. From deceit in the spirit,
the mother of all false deeds, the offspring is already incalculable. An acute
and candid person, in the revenue department in Washington, who is led
by the course of his employment to regularly visit the cities, north, south,
and west, to investigate frauds, has talked much with me about his discoveries. The depravity of the business classes of our country is not less than
has been supposed, but infinitely greater. The official services of America,
national, state, and municipal, in all their branches and departments, except
the judiciary, are saturated in corruption, bribery, falsehood, maladminis-
tration; and the judiciary is tainted. The great cities reek with respectable
as much as non-respectable robbery and scoundrelism. In fashionable life,
flippancy, tepid amours, weak infidelism, small aims, or no aims at all, only
to kill time. In business (this all-devouring modern word, business), the one
sole object is, by any means, pecuniary gain. The magician's serpent in the
fable ate up all the other serpents, and moneymaking is our magician's
serpent, remaining today sole master of the field. The best class we show,
is but a mob of fashionably dress'd speculators and vulgarians. True, indeed,
behind this fantastic farce, enacted on the visible stage of society, solid things
and stupendous labors are to be discover'd, existing crudely and going on
in the background, to advance and tell themselves in time. Yet the truths
are none the less terrible. I say that our New World democracy, however
great a success in uplifting the masses out of their sloughs, in materialistic

development, products, and in a certain highly deceptive superficial popular intellectuality, is, so far, an almost complete failure in its social aspects, and in really grand religious, moral, literary, and aesthetic results. In vain do we march with unprecedented strides to empire so colossal, outvying the antique, beyond Alexander's, beyond the proudest sway of Rome. In vain have we annex'd Texas, California, Alaska, and reach north for Canada and south for Cuba. It is as if we were somehow being endow'd with a vast and more and more thoroughly appointed body, and then left with little or no soul. . . .

I submit, therefore, that the fruition of democracy, on aught like a grand scale, resides altogether in the future. As, under any profound and comprehensive view of the gorgeous-composite feudal world, we see in it, through the long ages and cycles of ages, the results of a deep, integral, human and divine principle, or fountain, from which issued laws, ecclesia, manners, institutes, costumes, personalities, poems (hitherto unequal'd), faithfully partaking of their source, and indeed only arising either to betoken it, or to furnish parts of that varied-flowing display, whose center was one and absolute—so, long ages hence, shall the due historian or critic make at least an equal retrospect, an equal history for the democratic principle. It too must be adorn'd, credited with its results—then, when it, with imperial power, through amplest time, has dominated mankind—has been the source and test of all the moral, æsthetic, social, political, and religious expressions and institutes of the civilized world—has begotten them in spirit and in form, and has carried them to its own unprecedented heights—has had (it is possible) monastics and ascetics, more numerous, more devout than the monks and priests of all previous creeds—has sway'd the ages with a breadth and rectitude tallying Nature's own—has fashion'd, systematized, and triumphantly finish'd and carried out, in its own interest, and with unparallel'd success, a new earth and a new man.

Thus we presume to write, as it were, upon things that exist not, and travel by maps yet unmade, and a blank. But the throes of birth are upon us; and we have something of this advantage in seasons of strong formations, doubts, suspense—for then the afflatus of such themes haply may fall upon us, more or less; and then, hot from surrounding war and revolution, our speech, though without polish'd coherence, and a failure by the standard called criticism, comes forth, real at least as the lightnings.

And maybe we, these days, have, too, our own reward—(for there are yet some, in all lands, worthy to be so encouraged). Though not for us the joy of entering at the last the conquered city—not ours the chance ever to see with our own eyes the peerless power and splendid *éclat* of the democratic principle, arriv'd at meridian, filling the world with effulgence and majesty far beyond those of past history's kings, or all dynastic sway—there is yet, to whoever is eligible among us, the prophetic vision, the joy of being toss'd in the brave turmoil of these times—the promulgation and the path, obedient, lowly reverent to the voice, the gesture of the god, or holy ghost, which others see not, hear not—with the proud consciousness that amid whatever clouds, seductions, or heart-wearying postponements, we have never deserted, never despair'd, never abandon'd the faith. . . .

Assuming Democracy to be at present in its embryo condition, and that the only large and satisfactory justification of it resides in the future, mainly through the copious production of perfect characters among the people, and through the advent of a sane and pervading religiousness, it is with regard to the atmosphere and spaciousness fit for such characters, and of certain nutriment and cartoon-draftings proper for them, and indicating them for New World purposes, that I continue the present statement—an exploration, as of new ground, wherein, like other primitive surveyors, I must do the best I can, leaving it to those who come after me to do much better. (The service, in fact, if any, must be to break a sort of first path or track, no matter how rude and ungeometrical.) . . .

America has yet morally and artistically originated nothing. She seems singularly unaware that the models of persons, books, manners, etc., appropriate for former conditions and for European lands, are but exiles and exotics here. No current of her life, as shown on the surfaces of what is authoritatively called her society, accepts or runs into social or æsthetic democracy; but all the currents set squarely against it. Never, in the Old World, was thoroughly upholster'd exterior appearance and show, mental and other, built entirely on the idea of caste, and on the sufficiency of mere outside acquisition—never were glibness, verbal intellect more the test, the emulation—more loftily elevated as head and sample—than they are on the surface of our republican States this day. The writers of a time hint the mottoes of its gods. The word of the modern, say these voices, in the word Culture.

We find ourselves abruptly in close quarters with the enemy. This word Culture, or what it has come to represent, involves, by contrast, our whole theme, and has been, indeed, the spur, urging us to engagement. Certain questions arise. As now taught, accepted and carried out, are not the processes of culture rapidly creating a class of supercilious infidels, who believe in nothing? Shall a man lose himself in countless masses of adjustments, and be so shaped with reference to this, that, and the other, that the simply good and healthy and brave parts of him are reduced and clipp'd away, like the bordering of box in a garden? You can cultivate corn and roses and orchards—but who shall cultivate the mountain peaks, the ocean, and the tumbling gorgeousness of the clouds? Lastly—is the readily given reply that culture only seeks to help, systematize, and put in attitude, the elements of fertility and power, a conclusive reply?

I do not so much object to the name, or word, but I should certainly insist, for the purposes of these States, on a radical change of category, in the distribution of precedence. I should demand a programme of culture, drawn out, not for a single class alone, or for the parlors or lecture rooms, but with an eye to practical life, the west, the workingmen, the facts of farms and jackplanes and engineers, and of the broad range of the women also of the middle and working strata, and with reference to the perfect equality of women, and of a grand and powerful motherhood. I should demand of this programme or theory a scope generous enough to include the widest human area. It must have for its spinal meaning the formation of a typical personality of character, eligible to the uses of the high average of men— and *not* restricted by conditions ineligible to the masses. The best culture will always be that of the manly and courageous instincts, and loving perceptions, and of self-respect—aiming to form, over this continent, an idiocrasy of universalism, which, true child of America, will bring joy to its mother, returning to her in her own spirit, recruiting myriads of offspring, able, natural, perceptive, tolerant, devout believers in her, America, and with some definite instinct why and for what she has arisen, most vast, most formidable of historic births, and is, now and here, with wonderful step, journeying through Time.

The problem, as it seems to me, presented to the New World, is, under permanent law and order, and after preserving cohesion (ensemble-Individuality), at all hazards, to vitalize man's free play of special Personalism, recognizing in it something that calls ever more to be consider'd, fed, and adopted as the substratum for the best that belongs to us (government indeed is for it), including the new æsthetics of our future.

To formulate beyond this present vagueness—to help line and put before us the species, or a specimen of the species, of the democratic ethnology of the future, is a work toward which the genius of our land, with peculiar encouragement, invites her well-wishers. Already certain limnings, more or less grotesque, more or less fading and watery, have appear'd. We too (repressing doubts and qualms) will try our hand.

Attempting, then, however crudely, a basic model or portrait of personality for general use for the manliness of the State (and doubtless that is most useful which is most simple and comprehensive for all, and toned low enough), we should prepare the canvas well beforehand. Parentage must consider itself in advance. (Will the time hasten when fatherhood and motherhood shall become a science—and the noblest science?) To our model, a clear-blooded, strong-fibered physique is indispensable; the questions of food, drink, air, exercise, assimilation, digestion, can never be intermitted. Out of these we descry a well-begotten selfhood—in youth, fresh, ardent, emotional, aspiring, full of adventure; at maturity, brave, perceptive, under control, neither too talkative nor too reticent, neither flippant nor somber; of the bodily figure, the movements easy, the complexion showing the best blood, somewhat flush'd, breast expanded, an erect attitude, a voice whose sound outvies music, eyes of calm and steady gaze, yet capable also of flashing—and a general presence that holds its own in the company of the highest. (For it is native personality, and that alone, that endows a man to stand before presidents or generals, or in any distinguished collection, with *aplomb*—and *not* culture, or any knowledge or intellect whatever.)

Source: *Walt Whitman, Democratic Vistas and Other Papers* (Toronto, 1888).

For Further Reading:

Van Wyck Brooks, *The Times of Melville and Whitman* (New York: Dutton, 1947). Alan Trachtenberg, ed., *Democratic Vistas, 1860–1880* (New York: Braziller, 1970). Edmund Wilson, *Patriotic Gore* (New York: Oxford University Press, 1962).

45. People's Party (Populists), Excerpt from "Omaha Platform" (1892)

1867   Granger Movement founded
1870–90   Farmers' Alliances formed
1892   General James Weaver runs for President

In the decades that followed the Civil War, western farmers transformed what had once been referred to as the Great American Desert into the Breadbasket of the World. Paradoxically, the boom in production produced a decline in their standard of living. By 1890, prices for corn, wheat, cotton, and other farm commodities were about one-half what they were a generation earlier. Simultaneously, many of the farmer's costs, most importantly the cost of money or credit and of transportation, rose. As a result, millions of Americans who had migrated westward and toiled in the hot sun and cold of winter to live the American dream, found their life turning into a nightmare. To make matters worse, farmers found their cultural and political power in decline.

Farmers responded to these worsening conditions by joining together, first with the Granger Movement (an association of farmers dedicated to improving their lot) in the Midwest in the 1860s, and then, more importantly, with the Farmers' Alliances and the populist movement of the 1880s and 1890s. The Alliances encouraged farmers to cooperatively buy and sell goods and products, to reduce costs, and increase the price they got for their crops. The Alliances also pressured the government to enact reforms that addressed unfair transportation costs, a shortage of credit, and inequities and corruption in the political system.

In 1892 the populist movement took a new turn when it came together to form a third or independent political party, the People's or Populist Party.

From all over America, farmers and their supporters joined in Omaha to write a party platform and to nominate a candidate for the presidency. The platform represented their views and goals. Its preamble was written by Ignatius Donnelly, a radical Minnesota newspaper editor. He defended American producers and warned that democracy itself was at stake. The platform also proposed several reforms, from direct election of Senators to an income tax.

Preamble

The conditions which surround us best justify our cooperation; we meet in the midst of a nation brought to the verge of moral, political, and material ruin. Corruption dominates the ballot-box, the Legislatures, the Congress, and touches even the ermine of the bench. The people are demoralized; most of the States have been compelled to isolate the voters at the polling places to prevent universal intimidation and bribery. The newspapers are largely subsidized or muzzled, public opinion silenced, business prostrated, homes covered with mortgages, labor impoverished, and the land concentrating in the hands of capitalists. The urban workmen are denied the right to organize for self-protection, imported pauperized labor beats down their wages, a hireling standing army, unrecognized by our laws, is established to shoot them down, and they are rapidly degenerating into European conditions. The fruits of the toil of millions are boldly stolen to build up colossal fortunes for a few, unprecedented in the history of mankind; and the possessors of these, in turn, despise the Republic and endanger liberty. From the same prolific womb of governmental injustice we breed the two great classes—tramps and millionaires. . . .

Assembled on the anniversary of the birthday of the nation, and filled with the spirit of the grand general and chief who established our independence, we seek to restore the government of the Republic to the hands of the "plain people," with which class it originated. We assert our purposes to be identical with the purposes of the National Constitution; to form a more perfect union and establish justice, insure domestic tranquility, provide for the common defence, promote the general welfare, and secure the blessings of liberty for ourselves and our posterity. . . .

Platform

We declare, therefore—

First.—That the union of the labor forces of the United States this day consummated shall be permanent and perpetual; may its spirit enter into all hearts for the salvation of the Republic and the uplifting of mankind.

Second.—Wealth belongs to him who creates it, and every dollar taken from industry without an equivalent is robbery. "If any will not work, neither shall he eat." The interests of rural and civil labor are the same; their enemies are identical.

Third.—We believe that the time has come when the railroad corporations will either own the people or the people must own the railroads. . . .

FINANCE.—We demand a national currency, safe, sound, and flexible issued by the general government only, a full legal tender for all debts, public and private. . . .

1. We demand free and unlimited coinage of silver and gold at the present legal ratio of 16 to 1.

2. We demand that the amount of circulating medium be speedily increased to not less than $50 per capita.

3. We demand a graduated income tax.

4. We believe that the money of the country should be kept as much as possible in the hands of the people, and hence we demand that all State and national revenues shall be limited to the necessary expenses of the government, economically and honestly administered.

5. We demand that postal savings banks be established by the government for the safe deposit of the earnings of the people and to facilitate exchange.

TRANSPORTATION.—Transportation being a means of exchange and a public necessity, the government should own and operate the railroads in the interest of the people. The telegraph and telephone, like the post-office system, being a necessity for the transmission of news, should be owned and operated by the government in the interest of the people.

LAND.—The land, including all the natural sources of wealth, is the heritage of the people, and should not be monopolized for speculative purposes, and alien ownership of land should be prohibited. All land now held by railroads and other corporations in excess of their actual needs, and all lands now owned by aliens should be reclaimed by the government and held for actual settlers only.

Expression of Sentiments

1. RESOLVED, That we demand a free ballot, and a fair count in all elections, and pledge ourselves to secure it to every legal voter without Federal intervention, through the adoption by the States of the unperverted Australian or secret ballot system.

2. RESOLVED, That the revenue derived from a graduated income tax should be applied to the reduction of the burden of taxation now levied upon the domestic industries of this country.

3. RESOLVED, That we pledge our support to fair and liberal pensions to ex-Union soldiers and sailors.

4. RESOLVED, That we condemn the fallacy of protecting American labor under the present system, which opens our ports to the pauper and criminal classes of the world and crowds out our wage-earners; and we denounce the present ineffective laws against contract labor, and demand the further restriction of undesirable emigration.

5. RESOLVED, That we cordially sympathize with the efforts of organized workingmen to shorten the hours of labor, and demand a rigid enforcement of the existing eight-hour law on Government work, and ask that a penalty clause be added to the said law.

6. RESOLVED, That we regard the maintenance of a large standing army of mercenaries, known as the Pinkerton system, as a menace to our liberties, and we demand its abolition. . . .

7. RESOLVED, That we commend to the favorable consideration of the people and the reform press the legislative system known as the initiative and referendum.

8. RESOLVED, That we favor a constitutional provision limiting the office of President and Vice-President to one term, and providing for the election of Senators of the United States by a direct vote of the people.

9. RESOLVED, That we oppose any subsidy or national aid to any private corporation for any purpose.

Source: Edward McPherson, *A Handbook for Politics for 1892* (Washington, 1892), p. 269.

For Further Reading:

Lawrence Goodwyn, *Democratic Vistas* (New York: Oxford University Press, 1976).
John D. Hicks, *The Populist Revolt* (Minneapolis: University of Minnesota Press, 1931).

46. Thomas Watson, Excerpt from "The Negro Question in the South" (1892)

1890   Tom Watson elected to Congress from Georgia
1896   Tom Watson receives Populists' vice-presidential nomination

While farmers in general were hurt by the decline in prices and rise in costs (see document 45), southern farmers were especially hard hit. White south-

ern farmers were often stuck with deteriorating land and mounds of debt. Black farmers faced an even worse lot. Not surprisingly, southern farmers were among the first to organize Alliances, to form cooperatives and to pressure the government to address their needs. Members of the Texas Alliance, for instance, called for the federal government to establish sub-treasuries, whereby the government would loan money to farmers at a more reasonable cost than available via merchants or eastern bankers. As the southern farmers entered the political fray, however, they had to confront the issue of race. Historically, poor whites and blacks had not cooperated. The former believed that they were superior to the latter, and the planter class had effectively promoted this belief in times when a challenge to it was mounted.

In "The Negro Question in the South," Tom Watson, a southern populist leader and the People's Party's vice-presidential nominee in 1896, addressed the issue of race head on. He urged white farmers to shed their prejudices and to join forces with black farmers. Both groups were already equally poor, Watson declared.

Watson's call for class unity, across racial lines, was not an easy one to make. Whites and blacks who joined together at the polls in 1896 often faced persecution afterward. In fact, following the Populist Party's loss in 1896, Watson himself jettisoned his call for a color-blind society and championed white supremacy. Still, it should be remembered that for a moment Watson and white populists in the South flirted with the notion of forging a color-blind movement. This was democracy in its purist form and vision.

T he key to the new political movement called the People's Party has been that the Democratic farmer was as ready to leave the Democratic ranks as the Republican farmer was to leave the Republican ranks. In exact proportion as the West received the assurance that the South was ready for a new party, it has moved. In exact proportion to the proof we could bring that the West had broken Republican ties, the South has moved. Without a decided break in both sections, neither would move. With that decided break, both moved.

The very same principle governs the race question in the South. The two races can never act together permanently, harmoniously, beneficially, till each race demonstrates to the other a readiness to leave old party affiliations and to form new ones, based upon the profound conviction that, in acting together, both races are seeking new laws which will benefit both. On no other basis under heaven can the "Negro Question" be solved. . . .

This is so obviously true it is no wonder both these unhappy laborers stop to listen. No wonder they begin to realize that no change of law can benefit the white tenant which does not benefit the black one likewise; that no system which now does injustice to one of them can fail to injure both. Their every material interest is identical. The moment this becomes a conviction, mere selfishness, the mere desire to better their conditions, escape onerous taxes, avoid usurious charges, lighten their rents, or change their precarious tenements into smiling, happy homes, will drive these two men together, just as their mutually inflamed prejudices now drive them apart.

Suppose these two men now to have become fully imbued with the idea that their material welfare depends upon the reforms we demand. Then they act together to secure them. Every white reformer finds it to the vital interest of his home, his family, his fortune, to see to it that the vote of the colored reformer is freely cast and fairly counted.

Then what? Every colored voter will be thereafter a subject of industrial education and political teaching.

Concede that in the final event, a colored man will vote where his material interests dictate that he should vote; concede that in the South the accident of color can make no possible difference in the interests of farmers, croppers, and laborers; concede that under full and fair discussion the people can be depended upon to ascertain where their interests lie—and we reach the conclusion that the Southern race question can be solved by the People's Party on the simple proposition that each race will be led by self-interest to support that which benefits it, when so presented that neither is hindered by the bitter party antagonisms of the past.

Let the colored laborer realize that our platform gives him a better guaranty for political independence; for a fair return for his work; a better chance to buy a home and keep it; a better chance to educate his children and see them profitably employed; a better chance to have public life freed from race collisions; a better chance for every citizen to be considered as a *citizen* regardless of color in the making and enforcing of laws,—let all this be fully realized, and the race question in the South will have settled itself through the evolution of a political movement in which both whites and blacks recognize their surest way out of wretchedness into comfort and independence.

The illustration could be made quite as clearly from other planks in the People's Party platform. On questions of land, transportation and finance, especially, the welfare of the two races so clearly depends upon that which benefits either, that intelligent discussion would necessarily lead to just conclusions.

Why should the colored man always be taught that the white man of his neighborhood hates him, while a Northern man, who taxes every rag on his back, loves him? Why should not my tenant come to regard me as his friend rather than the manufacturer who plunders us both? Why should we perpetuate a policy which drives the black man into the arms of the Northern politician? . . .

To the emasculated individual who cries "Negro supremacy!" there is little to be said. His cowardice shows him to be a degeneration from the race which has never yet feared any other race. Existing under such conditions as they now do in this country, there is no earthly chance for Negro domination, unless we are ready to admit that the colored man is our superior in will power, courage, and intellect.

Not being prepared to make any such admission in favor of any race the sun ever shone on, I have no words which can portray my contempt for the white men, Anglo-Saxons, who can knock their knees together, and through their chattering teeth and pale lips admit that they are afraid the Negroes will "dominate us."

The question of social equality does not enter into the calculation at all. That is a thing each citizen decides for himself. No statute ever yet drew the latch of the humblest home—or ever will. Each citizen regulates his own visiting list—and always will.

The conclusion, then, seems to me to be this: the crushing burdens which now oppress both races in the South will cause each to make an effort to cast them off. They will see a similarity of cause and a similarity of remedy. They will recognize that each should help the other in the work of repealing bad laws and enacting good ones. They will become political allies, and neither can injure the other without weakening both. It will be to the interest of both that each should have justice. And on these broad lines of mutual interest, mutual forbearance, and mutual support the present will be made the stepping-stone to future peace and prosperity.

Source: Thomas E. Watson, "The Negro Question in the South," *Arena* 35 (1892): 541–44, 548–50.

For Further Reading:

Steve Hahn, *The Roots of Southern Populism* (New York: Oxford University Press, 1983).

C. Vann Woodward, *Tom Watson, Agrarian Rebel* 2d ed. (Savannah, Ga.: Beehive Press, 1973).

47. William Jennings Bryan, Excerpt from "The Cross of Gold" (1896)

1873   Coinage Act demonetizes silver
1893   Panic of 1893; depression begins
1896   Bryan captures Democratic and Populist nomination; defeated by William McKinley

From 1892 to 1896 the Populist challenge to the two major parties spread (see documents 45 and 46). In 1892 General Weaver, the Populist Party's

William J. Bryan, ca. 1892 (Library of Congress).

presidential candidate, won 8.5 percent of the vote and the Populists elected five senators, ten Congressmen, three governors, and hundreds of lesser local officials. They seemed assured of doing much better in 1896. Before the Populists held their nominating convention, however, the Democrats held their own. There, William Jennings Bryan, a young two-term Congressman from Nebraska, with a populist ring to his voice, stole the show and the nomination. He did so by delivering one of the most memorable addresses in American political history, "The Cross of Gold" speech.

In the speech Bryan championed the cause of the American farmers. They were the backbone of American society, he asserted, and if they fell the entire nation would crumble. Fail to heed their cry, and America would be ruined.

Bryan, who went on to win the Populist nomination as well, faced William McKinley, the hand-picked candidate of Marcus Hanna, an industrial rainmaker, in the general election. The nation had never seen a campaign like it before, as Bryan crisscrossed the nation and Hanna spent millions of dollars to elect McKinley. Over 85 percent of the eligible voters went to the polls, a record turnout. McKinley won, in part because of the size of his campaign treasury chest and the heavy-handed tactics of his supporters. But Bryan also deserved some of the blame. By focusing on free silver, he weakened his appeal among wage workers and undercut the coalition of producers that Donnelly wrote of in the Omaha Platform (see document 45).

The People's Party never again mounted a challenge to the Democrats and Republicans. Yet neither Bryan nor many of the populist ideas disappeared. Many of their proposals were enacted by the progressives and Bryan remained a prominent figure in the Democratic Party through the mid-1920s.

Never before in the history of this country has there been witnessed such a contest as that through which we have just passed. Never before in the history of American politics has a great issue been fought out as this issue has been, by the voters of a great party. On the fourth of March, 1895, a few Democrats, most of them members of Congress, issued an address to the Democrats of the nation, asserting that the money question was the paramount issue of the hour; declaring that a majority of the Democratic party had the right to control the action of the party on this paramount issue; and concluding with the request that the believers in the free coinage of silver in the Democratic party should organize, take charge of, and control the policy of the Democratic party. Three months later, at Memphis, an organization was perfected, and the silver Democrats went forth openly and courageously proclaiming their belief, and declaring that, if successful, they would crystallize into a platform the declaration which they had made. Then began the conflict. With a zeal approaching the zeal which inspired the crusaders who followed Peter the Hermit, our silver Democrats went forth from victory unto victory until they are now assembled, not to discuss, not to debate, but to enter up the judgment already rendered by the plain people of this country. In this contest brother has been arrayed against brother, father against son. The warmest ties of love, acquaintance and association have been disregarded; old leaders have been cast aside when they have refused to give expression to the sentiments of those whom they would lead, and new leaders have sprung up to give direction to this cause of truth. Thus has the contest been waged, and we have assembled here under as binding and solemn instructions as were ever imposed upon representatives of the people. . . .

Ah, my friends, we say not one word against those who live upon the Atlantic coast, but the hardy pioneers who have braved all the dangers of the wilderness, who have made the desert to blossom as the rose—the pioneers away out there (*pointing to the West*), who rear their children near to Nature's heart, where they can mingle their voices with the voices of the birds—out there where they have erected schoolhouses for the education of their young, churches where they praise their Creator, and cemeteries where rest the ashes of their dead—these people, we say, are as deserving of the consideration of our party as any people in this country. It is for these that we speak. We do not come as aggressors. Our war is not a war of conquest; we are fighting in the defense of our homes, our families, and posterity. We have petitioned, and our petitions have been scorned; we have entreated, and our entreaties have been disregarded; we have begged, and they have mocked when our calamity came. We beg no longer; we entreat no more; we petition no more. We defy them.

The gentleman from Wisconsin has said that he fears a Robespierre. My friends, in this land of the free you need not fear that a tyrant will spring up from among the people: What we need is an Andrew Jackson to stand, as Jackson stood, against the encroachments of organized wealth.

They tell us that this platform was made to catch votes. We reply to them that changing conditions make new issues; that the principles upon which Democracy rests are as everlasting as the hills, but that they must be applied to new conditions as they arise. Conditions have arisen, and we are here to meet those conditions. They tell us that the income tax ought not to be brought in here; that it is a new idea. They criticise us for our criticism of the Supreme Court of the United States. My friends, we have not criticised; we have simply called attention to what you already know. If you want criticisms, read the dissenting opinions of the court. There you will find criticisms. They say that we passed an unconstitutional law; we deny it. The income tax law was not unconstitutional when it was passed; it was not unconstitutional when it went before the Supreme Court for the first time; it did not become unconstitutional until one of the judges changed his mind, and we cannot be expected to know when a judge will change his mind. The income tax is just. It simply intends to put the burdens of government justly upon the backs of the people. I am in favor of an income tax. When I find a man who is not willing to bear his share of the burdens of the government which protects him, I find a man who is unworthy to enjoy the blessings of a government like ours.

They say that we are opposing national bank currency; it is true. If you will read what Thomas Benton said, you will find he said that, in searching history, he could find but one parallel to Andrew Jackson; that was Cicero, who destroyed the conspiracy of Cataline and saved Rome. Benton said that Cicero only did for Rome what Jackson did for us when he destroyed the bank conspiracy and saved America. We say in our platform that we believe that the right to coin and issue money is a function of government. We believe it. We believe that it is a part of sovereignty, and can no more with safety be delegated to private individuals than we could afford to delegate to private individuals the power to make penal statutes or levy taxes. Mr. Jefferson, who was once regarded as good Democratic authority, seems to have differed in opinion from the gentleman who has addressed us on the part of the minority. Those who are opposed to this proposition tell us that the issue of paper money is a function of the bank, and that the Government ought to go out of the banking business. I stand with Jefferson rather than with them, and tell them, as he did, that the issue of money is a function of government, and that the banks ought to go out of the governing business.

They complain about the plank which declares against life tenure in office. They have tried to strain it to mean that which it does not mean. What we oppose by that plank is the life tenure which is being built up in Washington, and which excludes from participation in official benefits the humbler members of society.

Let me call your attention to two or three important things. The gentleman from New York says that he will propose an amendment to the platform providing that the proposed change in our monetary system shall not affect contracts already made. Let me remind you that there is no intention of affecting those contracts which according to present laws are made payable in gold; but if he means to say that we cannot change our monetary system without protecting those who have loaned money before the change was made, I desire to ask him where, in law or in morals, he can find justification for not protecting the debtors when the act of 1873 was passed, if he now insists that we must protect the creditors.

He says he will also propose an amendment which will provide for the suspension of free coinage if we fail to maintain the parity within a year. We reply that when we advocate a policy which we believe will be succeessful, we are not compelled to raise a doubt as to our own sincerity by suggesting what we shall do if we fail. I ask him, if he would apply his logic to us, why he does not apply it to himself. He says he wants this country to try to secure an international agreement. Why does he not tell us what he is going to do if he fails to secure an international agreement? There is more reason for him to do that than there is for us to provide against the failure to maintain the parity. Our opponents have tried for twenty years to secure an international agreement, and those are waiting for it most patiently who do not want it at all.

And now, my friends, let me come to the paramount issue. If they ask us why it is that we say more on the money question than we say upon the tariff question, I reply that, if protection has slain its thousands, the gold standard has slain its tens of thousands. If they ask us why we do not embody in our platform all the things that we believe in, we reply that when we have restored the money of the Constitution all other necessary reforms will be possible; but that until this is done there is no other reform that can be accomplished.

Why is it that within three months such a change has come over the country? Three months ago, when it was confidently asserted that those who believe in the gold standard would frame our platform and nominate our candidates, even the advocates of the gold standard did not think that we could elect a president. And they had good reason for their doubt, because there is scarcely a State here today asking for the gold standard which is not in the absolute control of the Republican party. But note the change. Mr. McKinley was nominated at St. Louis upon a platform which declared for the maintenance of the gold standard until it can be changed into bimetallism by international agreement. Mr. McKinley was the most popular man among the Republicans, and three months ago everybody in the Republican party prophesied his election. How is today? Why, the man who was once pleased to think that he looked like Napoleon—that man shudders today when he remembers that he was nominated on the anniversary of the battle of Waterloo. Not only that, but as he listens he can hear with ever-increasing distinctness the sound of the waves as they beat upon the lonely shores of St. Helena.

Why this change? Ah, my friends, is not the reason for the change evident to any one who will look at the matter? No private character, however, pure, no personal popularity, however great, can protect from the avenging wrath of an indignant people a man who will declare that he is in favor of fastening the gold standard upon this country, or who is willing to surrender the right of self-government and place the legislative control of our affairs in the hands of foreign potentates and powers.

We go forth confident that we shall win. Why? Because upon the paramount issue of this campaign there is not a spot of ground upon which the enemy will dare to challenge battle. If they tell us that the gold standard is a good thing, we shall point to their platform and tell them that their platform pledges the party to get rid of the gold standard and substitute bimetallism. If the gold standard is a good thing, why try to get rid of it? I call your attention to the fact that some of the very people who are in this convention today and who tell us that we ought to declare in favor of international bimetallism—thereby declaring that the gold standard is wrong and that the principle of bimetallism is better—these very people four months ago were open and avowed advocates of the gold standard, and were then telling us that we could not legislate two metals together, even with the aid of all the world. If the gold standard is a good thing, we ought to declare in favor of its retention and not in favor of abandoning it; and if the gold standard is a bad thing why should we wait until other nations are willing to help us to let go? Here is the line of battle, and we care not upon which issue they force the fight; we are prepared to meet them on either issue or on both. If they tell us that the gold standard is the standard of civilization, we reply to them that this, the most enlightened of all the nations of the earth, has never declared for a gold standard and that both the great parties this year are declaring against it. If the gold standard is the standard of civilization, why, my friends, should we not have it? If they come to meet us on that issue we can present the history of our nation. More than that; we can tell them that they will search the pages of history in vain to find a single instance where the common people of any land have ever declared themselves in favor of the gold standard. They can find where the holders of fixed investments have declared for a gold standard, but not where the masses have.

Mr. Carlisle said in 1878 that this was a struggle between "the idle holders of idle capital" and "the struggling masses, who produce the wealth and pay the taxes of the country"; and, my friends, the question we are to decide is: Upon which side will the Democratic party fight; upon the side of "the idle holders of idle capital" or upon the side of "the struggling masses"? That is the question which the party must answer first, and then it must be answered by each individual hereafter. The sympathies of the Democratic party, as shown by the platform, are on the side of the struggling masses who have ever been the foundation of the Democratic party. There are two ideas of government. There are those who believe that, if you will only legislate to make the well-to-do prosperous, their prosperity will leak through on those below. The Democratic idea, however, has been that if you legislate to make the masses prosperous, their prosperity will find its way up through every class which rests upon them.

You come to us and tell us that the great cities are in favor of the gold standard; we reply that the great cities rest upon our broad and fertile prairies. Burn down your cities and leave our farms, and your cities will spring up again as if by magic; but destroy our farms and the grass will grow in the streets of every city in the country.

My friends, we declare that this nation is able to legislate for its own people on every question, without waiting for the aid or consent of any other nation on earth; and upon that issue we expect to carry every State in the Union. I shall not slander the inhabitants of the fair State of Massachusetts nor the inhabitants of the State of New York by saying that, when they are confronted with the proposition, they will declare that this nation is not able to attend to its own business. It is the issue of 1776 over again. Our ancestors, when but three millions in number, had the courage to declare their political independence of every other nation; shall we, their descendants, when we have grown to seventy millions, declare that we are less independent than our forefathers? No, my friends, that will never be the verdict of our people. Therefore, we care not upon what lines the battle is fought. If they say bimetallism is good, but that we cannot have it until other nations help us, we reply that, instead of having a gold standard because England has, we will restore bimetallism, and then let Engand have bimetallism because the United States has it. If they dare to come out in the open field and defend the gold standard as a good thing, we will fight them to the uttermost. Having behind us the producing masses of this nation and the world, supported by the commercial interests, the laboring interests, and the toilers everywhere, we will answer their demand for a gold standard by saying to them: You shall not press down upon the brow of labor this crown of thorns, you shall not crucify mankind upon a cross of gold.

Source: William J. Bryan, *The First Battle* (Chicago, 1896), pp. 199–200, 203–206.

For Further Reading:

Robert W. Cherny, *A Righteous Cause* (Boston: Little, Brown, 1985).
Paul Glad, *The Trumpet Soundeth* (Lincoln: University of Nebraska Press, 1964).

48. Emma Lazarus, "The New Colossus" (1883)

1880–1920   Peak years of immigration
1883   Lazarus writes "The New Colossus"
1886   Statue of Liberty dedicated
1903   Lazarus poem placed on a bronze plaque
1945   Poem moved to plaque at main entrance of Statue of
Liberty

From 1880 to 1920 over 18 million European immigrants poured into the United States. Coming at first from Northern and Central Europe and then primarily from Eastern and Southern Europe, they came in search of economic opportunity and political and religious freedom. Most settled along the eastern seaboard or in the Midwest, filling industry's needs for unskilled cheap labor. Once in the United States, the immigrants built vibrant communities, with their own churches, fraternal associations, newspapers, and other reminders of their traditional culture.

In the 1880s, Frédéric-Auguste Bartholdi, a French sculptor, offered to construct a gigantic statue as a symbol of French-American friendship and the ideal of liberty. Paid for with private donations, the Statue of Liberty was unveiled in New York harbor in 1886. At 152 feet tall, it was one of the largest structures in the world and towered over the New York harbor, where many of the immigrants arrived from Europe.

To raise money to pay for the pedestal for the statue, community leaders solicited pieces of art and literature from the artistic community, which they then auctioned off to the public. Among the pieces submitted was the poem "The New Colossus," written by Emma Lazarus, an American citizen of Jewish descent. For years Lazarus' poem received little attention. Her perception of the United States as a refuge for the poor and persecuted did not sit well with much of the American middle class. In fact, nativism, a social and political anti-immigrant movement, was once again on the rise. However, in the 1930s, after mass immigration had stopped, Louis Adamic, a Yugo-

Statue of Liberty. *Frank Leslie's Illustrated Newspaper*, July 2, 1887 (Library of Congress).

slavian-American writer, helped popularize the piece, and at the end of World War II a plaque with the poem's words was placed at the main entrance of the Statue of Liberty, becoming as much a part of the display as Lady Liberty herself.

Not like the brazen giant of Greek fame,
With conquering limbs astride from land to land,
Here at our sea-washed, sunset gates shall stand
A mighty woman with a torch, whose flame
Is the imprisoned lightning, and her name
Mother of Exiles. From her beacon-hand
Glows world-wide welcome; her mild eyes command
The air-bridged harbor that twin cities frame.

"Keep, ancient lands, your storied pomp!" cries she
With silent lips. "Give me your tired, your poor,
Your huddled masses yearning to breathe free,
The wretched refuse of your teeming shore.
Send these, the homeless, tempest-tost to me,
I lift my lamp beside the golden door!"

Source: Emma Lazarus, "The New Colossus." Original manuscript, American Jewish Historical Society, New York.

For Further Reading:

John Higham, *Send These to Me* (New York: Atheneum, 1975).
Heinrich E. Jacob, *The World of Emma Lazarus* (New York: Schocken Books, 1949).
Philip A. M. Taylor, *The Distant Magnet* (New York: Harper & Row, 1971).

49. "Preamble to the Constitution of the Knights of Labor" (1878)

1877   Great Railroad Strike
1879   Knights of Labor elect Terrence Powderly grand master
1881–86   Knights of Labor membership skyrockets
1886   Haymarket Incident
1886–90   Knights of Labor collapses

As the pace of industrialization quickened in the latter half of the nineteenth century, the nature of work and social relations between employers and employees underwent a dramatic change. Mechanization, the subdivision of labor, the building of enormous factories, and the introduction of "scientific management" undercut the importance of skilled labor and created an enormous demand for unskilled operatives. Workers had much more difficulty taking pride in their labor than they had in the past, and they were treated like commodities rather than as equal participants in the community. Poor pay and work conditions made things even worse for millions of wage workers.

Many workers responded to their decline in status and living conditions by joining unions, although extremely anti-union sentiment among employers and much of the middle class made most early unions unstable and unsuccessful. One of the first national unions was the Knights of Labor. Founded as a secret organization right before the Civil War by Philadelphia garment workers, the Knights had fewer than 10,000 members in 1879. Then it decided to shed its secrecy and elected Terrence Powderly, a Catholic machinist from Pennsylvania, as its Grand Master. Under his leadership the membership of the Knights skyrocketed. By 1886 it had about 700,000 members.

The Knights spelled out their general goals in their constitution. They sought to represent all workers, skilled and unskilled, black and white,

Leadership of the Knights of Labor (Library of Congress).

immigrant and native, men and women. They hoped to establish a cooperative commonwealth and abolish the wage system. In general they frowned on strikes as contrary to the goal of cooperation.

Unfortunately for the Knights, a wave of antiradicalism, unleashed by the Haymarket incident (see document 50), combined with the antilabor practices of most employees and the federal government, spelled disaster. By 1900 the Knights had disappeared, their place taken by the American Federation of Labor, a much more pragmatic and less inclusive labor organization.

The recent alarming development and aggression of aggregated wealth, which, unless checked, will invariably lead to the pauperization and hopeless degradation of the toiling masses, render it imperative, if we desire to enjoy the blessings of life, that a check should be placed upon its power and upon unjust accumulation, and a system adopted which will secure to the laborer the fruits of his toil; and as this much-desired object can only be accomplished by the thorough unification of labor, and the united efforts of those who obey the divine injunction that "In the sweat of thy brow shalt thou eat bread," we have formed the ***** with a view of securing the organization and direction, by co-operative effort, of the power of the industrial classes; and we submit to the world the object sought to be accomplished by our organization, calling upon all who believe in securing "the greatest good to the greatest number" to aid and assist us:—

I. To bring within the folds of organization every department of productive industry, making knowledge a standpoint for action, and industrial and moral worth, not wealth, the true standard of individual and national greatness.

II. To secure to the toilers a proper share of the wealth that they create; more of the leisure that rightfully belongs to them; more societary advantages; more of the benefits, privileges, and emoluments of the world; in word, all those rights and privileges necessary to make them capable of enjoying, appreciating, defending, and perpetuating the blessing of good government.

III. To arrive at the true condition of the producing masses in their educational, moral, and financial condition, by demanding from the various governments the establishment of bureaus of Labor Statistics.

IV. The establishment of co-operative institutions, productive and distributive.

V. The reserving of the public lands—the heritage of the people—for the actual settler;—not another acre for railroads or speculators.

VI. The abrogation of all laws that do not bear equally upon capital and labor, the removal of unjust technicalities, delays, and discriminations in the administration of justice, and the adopting of measures providing for the health and safety of those engaged in mining, manufacturing, or building pursuits.

VII. The enactment of laws to compel chartered corporations to pay their employees weekly, in full, for labor performed during the preceding week, in the lawful money of the country.

VIII. The enactment of laws giving mechanics and laborers a first lien on their work for their full wages.

IX. The abolishment of the contract system on national, state, and municipal work.

X. The substitution of arbitration for strikes, whenever and wherever employers and employees are willing to meet on equitable grounds.

XI. The prohibition of the employment of children in workshops, mines, and factories before attaining their fourteenth year.

XII. To abolish the system of letting out by contract the labor of convicts in our prisons and reformatory institutions.

XIII. To secure for both sexes equal pay for equal work.

XIV. The reduction of the hours of labor to eight per day, so that the laborers may have more time for social enjoyment and intellectual improvement, and be enabled to reap the advantages conferred by the labor-saving machinery which their brains have created.

XV. To prevail upon governments to establish a purely national circulating medium, based upon the faith and resources of the nation, and issued directly to the people, without the intervention of any system of banking corporations, which money shall be a legal tender in payment of all debts, public or private.

Source: Terrence Powderly, *Thirty Years of Labor* (Columbus, Ohio, 1890), pp. 243–46.

For Further Reading:

Leon Fink, *Workingmen's Democracy* (Urbana: University of Illinois Press, 1983).
Norman Ware, *The Labor Movement in the United States, 1860–1895* (New York: D. Appleton, 1929).

50. August Spies, Excerpt from an "Address to the Court" (1886)

1886   (May 1) Eight-hour protests begin; (May 3) police attack
        striking workers at McCormick reaper plant in Chicago;
        (May 4) Haymarket bombing
1887   Four Haymarket "anarchists" hanged
1893   Governor John P. Altgeld pardons remaining anarchists

*In the spring of 1886, various workers' organizations joined forces to protest
the deterioration of conditions for wage workers. They concentrated their
energies on winning an eight-hour work day. Chicago, America's great industrial city, served as the venue of the most important demonstrations. The
protest began peacefully on May 1, but on May 3 Chicago police attacked
workers at the gigantic McCormick plant. In response, the organizers called
for a mass rally to be held at Haymarket Square.*

*Initially the rally on May 4 went without incident. Even the mayor at-
tended for a while. But then, toward evening, the police charged the crowd,
even though protest leaders had obtained a permit to be there. As they
attacked, a bomb was thrown. It exploded, killing seven and injuring seventy
more.*

*The bombing produced hysteria in Chicago and the nation. Mass arrests
took place. Newspaper publishers, politicians, and even ministers demanded
revenge. Eight anarchists, who had helped organize the rally and who had
a long history of activity in Chicago, were arrested and brought to trial.
Since the state's chief prosecutor, John Grinnell, could not prove that any
of them had actually thrown the bomb, he charged the eight with conspiracy
to commit murder, arguing that the anarchists' ideas had produced the
bombing.*

*The evidence was purely circumstantial. Nonetheless the eight were con-
victed and sentenced to hang. Following their sentencing the judge allowed
the defendants to speak. One of those to do so was August Spies. Spies
denounced the judge, prosecutor, and John Bonfield, the captain of the police
unit that had attacked the protesters at Haymarket Square. Spies also proclaimed his innocence, adding that the anarchists were the true Americans,
that they were the defenders of freedom of speech and the right to a fair
trial.*

*The defendant's words fell on deaf ears in the courtroom but not outside.
A protest movement demanding clemency mounted. Nonetheless, Spies and
three others were hanged in November 1887. Six years later, however, four*

Haymarket Incident, Chicago, Illinois, May 4, 1886. Drawn by T. de Thulstrup, in *Harper's Weekly*, May 15, 1886 (Library of Congress).

of the defendants (one hanged himself) were pardoned by Illinois Governor
John P. Altgeld, who declared the trial a travesty of justice. Ever since,
workers all over the world have celebrated May Day as the unofficial labor
day.

Your Honor: In addressing this court I speak as the representative
of one class to the representative of another. I will begin with the words
uttered five hundred years ago on a similar occasion, by the Venetian Doge
Faheri, who, addressing the court, said: *"My defense is your accusation; the*
causes of my alleged crime your history!" I have been indicted on a charge
of murder, as an accomplice or accessory. Upon this indictment I have been
convicted. There was no evidence produced by the State to show or even
indicate that I had any knowledge of the man who threw the bomb, or that
I myself had anything to do with the throwing of the missile, unless, of
course, you weigh the testimony of the accomplices of the State's attorney
and Bonfield, the testimony of Thompson and Gilmer, by the price they
were paid for it. If there was no evidence to show that I was legally responsible for the deed, then my conviction and the execution of the sentence
is nothing less than willful, malicious, and deliberate murder, as foul a
murder as may be found in the annals of religious, political, or any other
sort of persecution. There have been many judicial murders committed
where the representatives of the State were acting in good faith, believing
their victims to be guilty of the charge accused of. In this case the representatives of the State cannot shield themselves with a similar excuse. For
they themselves have fabricated most of the testimony which was used as a
pretense to convict us; to convict us by a jury picked out to convict! Before
this court, and before the public, which is supposed to be the State, I charge
the State's attorney and Bonfield with the heinous conspiracy to commit
murder. . . .

No, I repeat, the prosecution has not established our legal guilt, notwithstanding the purchased and perjured testimony of some, and notwithstanding the originality of the proceedings of this trial. And as long as this
has not been done, and you pronounce upon us the sentence of an appointed
vigilance committee, acting as a jury, I say, you, the alleged representatives
and high priests of "law and order," are the real and only law breakers, and
in this case to the extent of murder. It is well that the people know this.
And when I speak of the people I don't mean the few co-conspirators of
Grinnell, the noble politicians who thrive upon the misery of the multitudes.
These drones may constitute the State, they may control the State, they
may have their Grinnells, their Bonfields and other hirelings! No, when I
speak of the people I speak of the great mass of human bees, the working
people, who unfortunately are not yet conscious of the rascalities that are
perpetrated in the "name of the people,"—in their name.

The contemplated murder of eight men, whose only crime is that they have dared to speak the truth, may open the eyes of these suffering millions; may wake them up. Indeed, I have noticed that our conviction has worked miracles in this direction already. The class that clamors for our lives, the good, devout Christians, have attempted in every way, through their newspapers and otherwise, to conceal the true and only issue in this case. By simply designating the defendants as Anarchists, and picturing them as a newly discovered tribe or species of cannibals, and by inventing shocking and horrifying stories of dark conspiracies said to be planned by them— these good Christians zealously sought to keep the naked fact from the working people and other righteous parties, namely: That on the evening of May 4, two hundred armed men, under the command of a notorious ruffian, attacked a meeting of peaceable citizens! With what intention? With the intention of murdering them, or as many of them as they could. I refer to the testimony given by two of our witnesses. The wage workers of this city began to object to being fleeced too much—they began to say some very true things, but they were highly disagreeable to our Patrician class; they put forth—well, some very modest demands. They thought eight hours hard toil a day for scarcely two hours' pay was enough. This "lawless rabble" had to be silenced! The only way to silence them was to frighten them, and murder those whom they looked up to as their leaders. Yes, these "foreign dogs" had to be taught a lesson, so that they might never again interfere with the high-handed exploitation of their benevolent and Christian masters. Bonfield, the man who would bring a blush of shame to the managers of the St. Bartholomew night—Bonfield, the illustrious gentleman with a visage that would have done excellent service to Dore in portraying Dante's fiends of hell—Bonfield was the man best fitted to consummate the conspiracy of the Citizens' Association, of our Patricians. If I had thrown that bomb, or had caused it to be thrown, or had known of it, I would not hesitate a moment to say so. It is true that a number of lives were lost—many were wounded. But hundreds of lives were thereby saved! But for that bomb, there would have been a hundred widows and hundreds of orphans where now there are a few. These facts have been carefully suppressed, and we were accused and convicted of conspiracy by the real conspirators and their agents. This, your honor, is one reason why sentence should not be passed by a court of justice—if that name has any significance at all. . . .

My efforts in behalf of the disinherited and disfranchised millions, my agitation in this direction, the popularization of economic teachings—in short, the education of the wage workers, is declared "a conspiracy against society." The word "society" is here wisely substituted for "the State," as represented by the Patricians of today. It has always been the opinion of the ruling classes that the people must be kept in ignorance, for they lose their servility, their modesty and their obedience to the powers that be, as their intelligence increases. The education of a black slave a quarter of a century ago was a criminal offense. Why? Because the intelligent slave would throw off his shackles at whatever cost. Why is the education of the working people of today looked upon by a certain class as an offense against the State? For the same reason! The State, however, wisely avoided this point in the prosecution of this case. From their testimony one is forced to conclude that we had, in our speeches and publications, preached nothing else but destruction and dynamite. The court has this morning stated that there is no case in history like this. I have noticed, during this trial, that the gentlemen of the legal profession are not well versed in history. In all historical cases of this kind truth had to be perverted by the priests of the established power that was nearing its end.

What have we said in our speeches and publications?

We have interpreted to the people their conditions and relations in society. We have explained to them the different social phenomena and the social laws and circumstances under which they occur. We have, by way of scientific investigation, incontrovertibly proved and brought to their knowledge that the system of wages is the root of the present social iniquities—iniquities so monstrous that they cry to heaven. We have further said that the wage system, as a specific form of social development, would, by the necessity of logic, have to give way to higher forms of civilization; that the wage system must furnish the foundation for a social system of co-operation—that is, Socialism. That whether this or that theory, this or that scheme regarding future arrangements were accepted was not a matter of choice, but one of historical necessity, and that to us the tendency of progress seemed to be Anarchism—that is, a free society without kings or classes—a society of sovereigns in which liberty and economic equality of all would furnish an unshakable equilibrium as a foundation for natural order.

It is not likely that the honorable Bonfield and Grinnell can conceive of a social order not held intact by the policeman's club and pistol, nor of a free society without prisons, gallows, and State's attorneys. In such a society they probably fail to find a place for themselves. And is this the reason why Anarchism is such a "pernicious and damnable doctrine?"

Grinnell has intimated to us that Anarchism was on trial. The theory of Anarchism belongs to the realm of speculative philosophy. There was not a syllable said about Anarchism at the Haymarket meeting. At that meeting the very popular theme of reducing the hours of toil was discussed. But, "Anarchism is on trial!" foams Mr. Grinnell. If that is the case, your honor, very well; you may sentence me, for I am an Anarchist. I believe with Buckle, with Paine, Jefferson, Emerson, and Spencer, and many other great thinkers of this century, that the state of castes and classes—the state where one class dominates over and lives upon the labor of another class, and calls this order—yes, I believe that this barbaric form of social organization, with its legalized plunder and murder, is doomed to die, and make room for a free society, voluntary association, or universal brotherhood, if you like. You may pronounce the sentence upon me, honorable judge, but let the world know that in A.D. 1886, in the State of Illinois, eight men were sentenced to death, because they believed in a better future; because they had not lost their faith in the ultimate victory of liberty and justice! . . .

"We have preached dynamite!" Yes, we have predicted from the lessons history teaches, that the ruling classes of today would no more listen to the voice of reason than their predecessors; that they would attempt by brute force to stay the wheels of progress. Is it a lie, or was it the truth we told? Are not the large industries of this once free country already conducted under the surveillance of the police, the detectives, the military and the sheriffs—and is this return to militancy not developing from day to day? American sovereigns—think of it—working like galley convicts under military guards! We have predicted this, and predict that soon these conditions will grow unbearable. What then? The mandate of the feudal lords of our time is slavery, starvation, and death! This has been their program for years. We have said to the toilers, that science had penetrated the mystery of nature—that from Jove's head once more has sprung a Minerva—dynamite! If this declaration is synonymous with murder, why not charge those with the crime to whom we owe the invention? . . .

The position generally taken in this case is that we are morally responsible for the police riot on May 4. Four or five years ago I sat in this very court room as a witness. The workingmen had been trying to obtain redress in a lawful manner. They had voted and, among others, had elected their aldermanic candidate from the fourteenth ward. But the street car company did not like the man. And two of the three election judges of one precinct, knowing this, took the ballot box to their home and "corrected" the election returns, so as to cheat the constituents of the elected candidate of their rightful representative and give the representation to the benevolent street car monopoly. The workingmen spent $1,500 in the prosecution of the perpetrators of this crime. The proof against them was so overwhelming that they confessed to having falsified the returns and forged the official documents. Judge Gardner, who was presiding in this court, acquitted them, stating that "that act had apparently not been prompted by criminal intent." I will make no comment. But when we approach the field of moral responsibility, it has an immense scope! Every man who has in the past assisted in thwarting the efforts of those seeking reform is responsible for the existence of the revolutionists in this city today! . . .

. . . Accompany me to the quarters of the wealth creators in this city. Go with me to the half-starved miners of the Hocking Valley. Look at the pariahs in the Monongahela Valley, and many other mining districts in this country, or pass along the railroads of that great and most orderly and law-abiding citizen, Jay Gould. And then tell me whether this order has in it any moral principle for which it should be preserved. I say that the preservation of such an order is criminal—is murderous. It means the preservation of the systematic destruction of children and women in factories. It means the preservation of enforced idleness of large armies of men, and their degradation. It means the preservation of intemperance, and sexual as well as intellectual prostitution. It means the preservation of misery, want and servility on the one hand, and the dangerous accumulation of spoils, idleness, voluptuousness and tyranny on the other. It means the preservation of vice in every form. And last but not least, it means the preservation of the class struggle, of strikes, riots and bloodshed. That is your "order," gentlemen. Yes, and it is worthy of you to be the champions of such an order. You are eminently fitted for that role. You have my compliments! . . .

Grinnell spoke of Victor Hugo. I need not repeat what he said, but will answer him in the language of one of our German philosophers: "Our bourgeoisie erect monuments in honor of the memory of the classics. If they had read them they would burn them!" Why, amongst the articles read here from the *Arbeiter-Zeitung*, put in evidence by the State, by which they intend to convince the jury of the dangerous character of the accused Anarchists, is an extract from Goethe's Faust,

"Es erben sich Gesetz und Rechte,
Wie eine ew'ge Krankheit fort," etc.

(Laws and class privileges are transmitted like an hereditary disease.) And Mr. Ingham in his speech told the Christian jurors that our comrades, the Paris Communists, had in 1871, dethroned God, the Almighty, and had put up in His place a low prostitute. The effect was marvelous! The good Christians were shocked. I wish your honor would inform the learned gentlemen that the episode related occurred in Paris nearly a century ago, and that the sacrilegious perpetrators were the co-temporaries of the founders of this Republic—and among them was Thomas Paine. Nor was the woman a prostitute, but a good *citoyenne de Paris*, who served on that occasion simply as an allegory of the goddess of reason. . . .

A few weeks before I was arrested and charged with the crime for which I have been convicted, I was invited by the clergyman of the Congregational Church to lecture upon the subject of Socialism, and debate with them. This took place at the Grand Pacific Hotel. And so that it cannot be said that after I have been arrested, after I have been indicted, and after I have been convicted, I have put together some principles to justify my action, I will read what I said then—

Capt. Black: Give the date of the paper.

Mr. Spies: January 9, 1886.

Capt. Black: What paper, the *Alarm?*

Mr. Spies: The *Alarm*. When I was asked upon that occasion what Socialism was, I said this:

"Socialism is simply a resume of the phenomena of the social life of the past and present traced to their fundamental causes, and brought into logical connection with one another. It rests upon the established fact that the economic conditions and institutions of a people from the ground work of all their social conditions, of their ideas—aye, even of their religion, and further, that all changes of economic conditions, every step in advance, arise from the struggles between the dominating and dominated class in different ages. You, gentlemen, cannot place yourselves at this standpoint of speculative science; your profession demands that you occupy the opposite position; not that which professes acquaintance with things as they actually exist, but which presumes a thorough understanding of matters which to ordinary mortals are entirely incomprehensible. It is for this reason that you cannot become Socialists. (*Cries of 'Oh! oh!'*) Lest you should be unable to exactly grasp my meaning, however, I will now state the matter a little more plainly. It cannot be unknown to you that in the course of this century there have appeared an infinite number of inventions and discoveries, which have brought about great, aye, astonishing changes in the production of the necessities and comforts of life. The work of machines has, to a great extent, replaced that of men. . . .

"Machinery involves a great accumulation of power, and always a greater division of labor in consequence. . . .

"Our large factories and mines, and the machinery of exchange and transportation, apart from every other consideration, have become too vast for private control. Individuals can no longer monopolize them.

"Everywhere, wherever we cast our eyes, we find forced upon our attention the unnatural and injurious effects of unregulated private production. We see how one man, or a number of men, have not only brought into the embrace of their private ownership a few inventions in technical lines, but have also confiscated for their exclusive advantage all natural powers, such as water, steam, and electricity. Every fresh invention, every discovery belongs to them. The world exists for them only. That they destroy their fellow beings right and left they little care. That, by their machinery, they even work the bodies of little children into gold pieces, they hold to be an especially good work and a genuine Christian act. They murder, as we have said, little children and women by hard labor, while they let strong men go hungry for lack of work.

"People ask themselves how such things are possible, and the answer is that the competitive system is the cause of it. The thought of a co-operative, social, rational, and well regulated system of management irresistibly impresses the observer. The advantages of such a system are of such a convincing kind, so patent to observation—and where could there be any other way out of it? According to physical laws a body always moves itself, consciously or unconsciously, along the line of least resistance. So does society as a whole. The path of co-operative labor and distribution is leveled by the concentration of the means of labor under the private capitalistic system. We are already moving right in that track. We cannot retreat even if we would. The force of circumstances drives us on to Socialism. . . ."

Now, if we cannot be directly implicated with this affair, connected with the throwing of the bomb, where is the law that says, these men shall be picked out to suffer? Show me that law if you have it! If the position of the court is correct, then half of the population of this city ought to be hanged, because they are responsible the same as we are for that act on May 4. And if half of the population of Chicago is not hanged, then show me the law that says, "eight men shall be picked out and hanged as scapegoats!" You have no good law. Your decision, your verdict, our conviction is nothing but an arbitrary will of this lawless court. It is true there is no precedent in jurisprudence in this case! It is true we have called upon the people to arm themselves. It is true that we told them time and again that the great day of change was coming. It was not our desire to have bloodshed. We are not beasts. We would not be Socialists if we were beasts. It is because of our sensitiveness that we have gone into this movement for the emancipation of the oppressed and suffering. It is true we have called upon the people to arm and prepare for the stormy times before us.

This seems to be the ground upon which the verdict is to be sustained. "But when a long train of abuses and usurpations pursuing invariably the same object evinces a design to reduce the people under absolute despotism, it is their right, it is their duty to throw off such government and provide new guards for their future safety." This is a quotation from the Declaration of Independence. Have we broken any laws by showing to the people how these abuses, that have occurred for the last twenty years, are invariably pursuing one object, viz: to establish an oligarchy in this country so strong and powerful and monstrous as never before has existed in any country? I can well understand why that man Grinnell did not urge upon the grand jury to charge us with treason. I can well understand it. You cannot try and convict a man for treason who has upheld the constitution against those who trample it under their feet. It would not have been as easy a job to do that, Mr. Grinnell, as to charge these men with murder.

Now, these are my ideas. They constitute a part of myself. I cannot divest myself of them, nor would I, if I could. And if you think that you can crush out these ideas that are gaining ground more and more every day; if you think you can crush them out by sending us to the gallows; if you would once more have people suffer the penalty of death because they have dared to tell the truth—and I defy you to show us where we have told a lie—I say, if death is the penalty for proclaiming the truth, then I will proudly and defiantly pay the costly price! Call your hangman! Truth crucified in Socrates, in Christ, in Giordano Bruno, in Huss, in Galileo, still lives—they and others whose number is legion have preceded us on this path. We are ready to follow!

Source: Lucy Eldine (Gonzalez) Parsons, *Famous Speeches of the Eight Chicago Anarchists in Court . . .* , 2d ed. (Chicago, 1910), pp. 11–24.

For Further Reading:

Paul Avrich, *The Haymarket Tragedy* (Princeton, N.J.: Princeton University Press, 1984).
Bruce C. Nelson, *Beyond the Martyrs* (New Brunswick, N.J.: Rutgers University Press, 1989).

51. Samuel Gompers, Excerpts from "What Does the Working Man Want?" (1890)

1886   American Federation of Labor (AFL) founded
1886–1924   Samuel Gompers leads AFL with exception of one
         year

Out of the ashes of the Knights of Labor and the Haymarket incident (see documents 49 and 50) emerged the American Federation of Labor (AFL). First formed in 1881 as the Federation of Organized Trades and Labor Unions and then recharted as the AFL in 1886, it is the largest and oldest labor federation in the world.

The AFL had more pragmatic goals than the Knights of Labor. It has been called a "bread and butter" union, meaning that it seeks better wages and conditions, not the overthrow of the wage system and the creation of cooperative commonwealths. Headed by Samuel Gompers, a Dutch-born cigar-maker, from 1886 until Gompers' death in 1924 (with the exception of one year), the AFL grew at a steady pace, from about 150,000 members in 1886 to over 1.5 million in 1904 and over 3 million by the end of World War I.

In "What Does the Working Man Want?" Gompers described the AFL's basic goals to workers in Louisville, Kentucky. At the time of this address, 1890, Gompers frowned on political activism, especially the idea of working toward a labor party. Later in life he altered his views about politics, arguing that the labor federation needed to reward its friends and punish its enemies. This shift took place, in part, because the Supreme Court ruled against the use of secondary boycotts as an unlawful restriction of trade.

My friends, we have met here today to celebrate the idea that has prompted thousands of working-people of Louisville and New Albany to parade the streets of y[our city]; that prompts the toilers of Chicago to turn out by their fifty or hundred thousand of men; that prompts the vast army of wage-workers in New York to demonstrate their enthusiasm and appreciation of the importance of this idea; that prompts the toilers of England, Ireland, Germany, France, Italy, Spain, and Austria to defy the manifestos of the autocrats of the world and say that on May the first, 1890, the wage-workers of the world will lay down their tools in sympathy with the wage-workers of America, to establish a principle of limitations of hours of labor to eight hours for sleep [*applause*], eight hours for work, and eight hours for what we will. [*Applause.*]

It has been charged time and again that were we to have more hours of leisure we would merely devote it to debauchery, to the cultivation of vicious habits—in other words, that we would get drunk. I desire to say this in answer to that charge: As a rule, there are two classes in society who get drunk. One is the class who has no work to do in consequence of too much money; the other class, who also has no work to do, because it can't get any, and gets drunk on its face. [*Laughter.*] I maintain that that class in our social life that exhibits the greatest degree of sobriety is that class who are able, by a fair number of hours of day's work to earn fair wages—not overworked. The man who works twelve, fourteen, and sixteen hours a day requires some artificial stimulant to restore the life ground out of him in the drudgery of the day. [*Applause.*] . . .

We ought to be able to discuss this question on a higher ground, and I am pleased to say that the movement in which we are engaged will stimulate us to it. They tell us that the eight-hour movement can not be enforced, for the reason that it must check industrial and commercial progress. I say that the history of this country, in its industrial and commercial relations, shows the reverse. I say that is the plane on which this question ought to be discussed—that is the social question. As long as they make this question an economic one, I am willing to discuss it with them. I would retrace every step I have taken to advance this movement did it mean industrial and commercial stagnation. But it does not mean that. It means greater prosperity; it means a greater degree of progress for the whole people; it means more advancement and intelligence, and a nobler race of people. . . .

They say they can't afford it. Is that true? Let us see for one moment. If a reduction in the hours of labor causes industrial and commercial ruination, it would naturally follow increased hours of labor would increase the prosperity, commercial and industrial. If that were true, England and America ought to be at the tail end, and China at the head of civilization. [*Applause.*]

Is it not a fact that we find laborers in England and the United States, where the hours are eight, nine and ten hours a day—do we not find that the employers and laborers are more successful? Don't we find them selling articles cheaper? We do not need to trust the modern moralist to tell us those things. In all industries where the hours of labor are long, there you will find the least development of the power of invention. Where the hours of labor are long, men are cheap, and where men are cheap there is no necessity for invention. How can you expect a man to work ten or twelve or fourteen hours at his calling and then devote any time to the invention of a machine or discovery of a new principle or force? If he be so fortunate as to be able to read a paper he will fall asleep before he has read through the second or third line. [*Laughter.*]

Why, when you reduce the hours of labor, say an hour a day, just think what it means. Suppose men who work ten hours a day had the time lessened to nine, or men who work nine hours a day have it reduced to eight hours; what does it mean? It means millions of golden hours and opportunities for thought. Some men might say you will go to sleep. Well, some men might sleep sixteen hours a day; the ordinary man might try that, but he would soon find he could not do it long. He would have to do something. He would probably go to the theater one night, to a concert another night, but he could not do that every night. He would probably become interested in some study and the hours that have been taken from manual labor are devoted to mental labor, and the mental labor of one hour will produce for him more wealth than the physical labor of a dozen hours. [*Applause.*]

I maintain that this is a true proposition—that men under the short-hour system not only have opportunity to improve themselves, but to make a greater degree of prosperity for their employers. Why, my friends, how is it in China, how is it in Spain, how is it in India and Russia, how is it in Italy? Cast your eye throughout the universe and observe the industry that forces nature to yield up its fruits to man's necessities, and you will find that where the hours of labor are the shortest the progress of invention in machinery and the prosperity of the people are the greatest. It is the greatest impediment to progress to hire men cheaply. Wherever men are cheap, there you find the least degree of progress. It has only been under the great influence of our great republic, where our people have exhibited their great senses, that we can move forward, upward and onward, and are watched with interest in our movements of progress and reform. . . .

The man who works the long hours has no necessities except the barest to keep body and soul together, so he can work. He goes to sleep and dreams of work; he rises in the morning to go to work; he takes his frugal lunch to work; he comes home again to throw himself down on a miserable apology for a bed so that he can get that little rest that he may be able to go to work again. He is nothing but a veritable machine. He lives to work instead of working to live. [*Loud applause.*]

My friends, the only thing the working people need besides the necessities of life, is time. Time. Time with which our lives begin; time with which our lives close; time to cultivate the better nature within us; time to brighten our homes. Time, which brings us from the lowest condition up to the highest civilization; time, so that we can raise men to a higher plane.

My friends, you will find that it has been ascertained that there is more than a million of our brothers and sisters—able-bodied men and women—

on the streets, and on the highways and byways of our country willing to work but who cannot find it. You know that it is the theory of our government that we can work or cease to work at will. It is only a theory. You know that it is only a theory and not a fact. It is true that we can cease to work when we want to, but I deny that we can work when we will, so long as there are a million idle men and women tramping the streets of our cities, searching for work. The theory that we can work or cease to work when we will is a delusion and a snare. It is a lie.

What we want to consider is, first, to make our employment more secure, and, secondly, to make wages more permanent, and, thirdly, to give these poor people a chance to work. The laborer has been regarded as a mere producing machine . . . but back of labor is the soul of man and honesty of purpose and aspiration. Now you can not, as the political economists and college professors, say that labor is a commodity to be bought and sold. I say we are American citizens with the heritage of all the great men who have stood before us; men who have sacrificed all in the cause except honor. Our enemies would like to see this movement thrust into hades, they would like to see it in a warmer climate [*laughter*], but I say to you that this labor movement has come to stay. [*Loud applause.*] Like Banquo's ghost, it will not down. [*Applause.*] I say the labor movement is a fixed fact. It has grown out of the necessities of the people, and, although some may desire to see it fail, still the labor movement will be found to have a strong lodgment in the hearts of the people, and we will go on until success has been achieved.

We want eight hours and nothing less. We have been accused of being selfish, and it has been said that we will want more; that last year we got an advance of ten cents and now we want more. We do want more. You will find that a man generally wants more. Go and ask a tramp what he wants, and if he doesn't want a drink he will want a good, square meal. You ask a workingman, who is getting two dollars a day, and he will say that he wants ten cents more. Ask a man who gets five dollars a day and he will want fifty cents more. The man who receives five thousand dollars a year wants six thousand dollars a year, and the man who owns eight or nine hundred thousand dollars will want a hundred thousand dollars more to make it a million, while the man who has his millions will want every thing he can lay his hands on and then raise his voice against the poor devil who wants ten cents more a day. We live in the latter part of the Nineteenth century. In the age of electricity and steam that has produced wealth a hundred fold, we insist that it has been brought about by the intelligence and energy of the workingmen, and while we find that it is now easier to produce it is harder to live. We do want more, and when it becomes more, we shall still want more. [*Applause.*] And we shall never cease to demand more until we have received the results of our labor.

Source: *Louisville Courier Journal*, May 2, 1890.

For Further Reading:

Stuart B. Kaufman, *Samuel Gompers and the Origins of the American Federation of Labor* (Westport, Conn.: Greenwood Press, 1973).
Philip Taft, *The A.F. of L. in the Time of Gompers* (New York: Harper & Row, 1957).

52. Henry George, Excerpt from *Progress and Poverty* (1879)

1879   Henry George's *Progress and Poverty* published
1886   Henry George runs for mayor of New York City
1888   Edward Bellamy's *Looking Backward* published
1894   Henry D. Lloyd's *Wealth Against Commonwealth* published

In the latter part of the nineteenth century a number of intellectuals joined labor unionists and populists in voicing their protest against the inequities of wealth and power in the United States. These "romantic reformers," as some have called them, wrote a number of best-selling works of nonfiction and fiction, most notably Progress and Poverty, Looking Backward, *and* Wealth Against Commonwealth. *In* Progress and Poverty, *Henry George presented one of the most appealing solutions to the problem of poverty. His travels to the West convinced him that westward and industrial expansion had its disadvantages. The flood of migrants into the West and America's cities created a perfect setting for speculators, or the rich. They hiked rents or resold property to the newcomers at enormous windfall profits without having to improve their properties. To make matters worse, the newcomers had to pay a larger and larger share of their income to find shelter, thus increasing poverty in the country. To counter this undemocratic trend, George proposed levying a "single tax" on property, with the goal of giving back to the people the value that their demand, not anyone's work, added to the land.*

George's analysis and his proposed remedies made him famous and a hero to many workingmen and women. In 1886 he ran for mayor of New York City and nearly won. In fact, he received more votes than Theodore Roosevelt, the future President of the United States. Moreover, "land and labor clubs," dedicated to promoting George's reform, sprung up all across the country and the British Isles. Edward Bellamy's Looking Backward *led to a similar response. In 1897 George ran for mayor of New York City again. He died in the midst of the campaign.*

Addie Laird, 12 years old, Spinner in Cotton Mill, North Pownal, Vermont, February 9, 1910. Photograph by Lewis Hine (National Archives).

The Persistence of Poverty Amid Advancing Wealth

The great problem, of which these recurring seasons of industrial depression are but peculiar manifestations, is now, I think, fully solved, and the social phenomena which all over the civilized world appall the philanthropist and perplex the statesman, which hang with clouds the future of the most advanced races, and suggest doubts of the reality and ultimate goal of what we have fondly called progress, are now explained.

The reason why, in spite of the increase of productive power, wages constantly tend to a minimum which will give but a bare living, is that, with increase in productive power, rent tends to even greater increase, thus producing a constant tendency to the forcing down of wages.

In every direction, the direct tendency of advancing civilization is to increase the power of human labor to satisfy human desires—to extirpate poverty, and to banish want and the fear of want. All the things in which progress consists, all the conditions which progressive communities are striving for, have for their direct and natural result the improvement of the material (and consequently the intellectual and moral) condition of all within their influence. The growth of population, the increase and extension of exchanges, the discoveries of science, the march of invention, the spread of education, the improvement of government, and the amelioration of manners, considered as material forces, have all a direct tendency to increase the productive power of labor—not of some labor, but of all labor; not in some departments of industry, but in all departments of industry; for the law of the production of wealth in society is the law of "each for all, and all for each."

But labor cannot reap the benefits which advancing civilization thus brings, because they are intercepted. Land being necessary to labor, and being reduced to private ownership, every increase in the productive power of labor but increases rent—the price that labor must pay for the opportunity to utilize its powers; and thus all the advantages gained by the march of progress go to the owners of land, and wages do not increase. Wages cannot increase; for the greater the earnings of labor the greater the price that labor must pay out of its earnings for the opportunity to make any earnings at all. The mere laborer has thus no more interest in the general advance of productive power than the Cuban slave has in advance in the price of sugar. And just as an advance in the price of sugar may make the condition of the slave worse, by inducing the master to drive him harder, so may the condition of the free laborer be positively, as well as relatively, changed for the worse by the increase in the productive power of his labor. For, begotten of the continuous advance of rents, arises a speculative tendency which discounts the effect of future improvements by a still further advance of rent, and thus tends, where this has not occurred from the normal advance of rent, to drive wages down to the slave point—the point at which the laborer can just live.

And thus robbed of all the benefits of the increase in productive power, labor is exposed to certain effects of advancing civilization which, without the advantages that naturally accompany them, are positive evils, and of themselves tend to reduce the free laborer to the helpless and degraded condition of the slave.

For all the improvements which add to productive power as civilization advances, consist in, or necessitate, a still further subdivision of labor, and the efficiency of the whole body of laborers is increased at the expense of the independence of the constituents. The individual laborer acquires knowledge of, and skill in, but an infinitesimal part of the varied processes which are required to supply even the commonest wants. The aggregate produce of the labor of a savage tribe is small, but each member is capable of an independent life. He can build his own habitation, hew out or stitch together his own canoe, make his own clothing, manufacture his own weapons, snares, tools and ornaments. He has all the knowledge of nature possessed by his tribe—knows what vegetable productions are fit for food, and where they may be found; knows the habits and resorts of beasts, birds, fishes, and insects; can pilot himself by the sun or the stars, by the turning of blossoms or the mosses on the trees; is, in short, capable of supplying all his wants. He may be cut off from his fellows and still live; and thus possesses an independent power which makes him a free contracting party in his relations to the community of which he is a member.

Compare with this savage the laborer in the lowest ranks of civilized society, whose life is spent in producing but one thing, or oftener but the infinitesimal part of one thing, out of the multiplicity of things that constitute the wealth of society and go to supply even the most primitive wants; who not only cannot make even the tools required for his work, but often works with tools that he does not own, and can never hope to own. Compelled to even closer and more continuous labor than the savage, and gaining by it no more than the savage gets—the mere necessaries of life—he loses the independence of the savage. He is not only unable to apply his own powers to the direct satisfaction of his own wants, but, without the concurrence of many others, he is unable to apply them indirectly to the satisfaction of his wants. He is a mere link in an enormous chain of producers and consumers, helpless to separate himself, and helpless to move, except as they move. The worse his position in society, the more dependent is he on society; the more utterly unable does he become to do anything for himself. The very power of exerting his labor for the satisfaction of his wants passes from his own control, and may be taken away or restored by the actions of others, or by general causes over which he has no more influence than he has over the motions of the solar system. . . .

What constitutes the rightful basis of property? What is it that enables a man to justly say of a thing, "It is mine!" From what springs the sentiment which acknowledges his exclusive right as against all the world? Is it not, primarily, the right of a man to himself, to the use of his own powers, to the enjoyment of the fruits of his own exertions? Is it not this individual right, which springs from and is testified to by the natural facts of individual organization—the fact that each particular pair of hands obey a particular brain and are related to a particular stomach; the fact that each man is a definite, coherent, independent whole—which alone justifies individual ownership? As a man belongs to himself, so his labor when put in concrete form belongs to him.

And for this reason, that which a man makes or produces is his own, as against all the world—to enjoy or to destroy, to use, to exchange, or to give. No one else can rightfully claim it, and his exclusive right to it involves no wrong to any one else. Thus there is to everything produced by human exertion a clear and indisputable title to exclusive possession and enjoyment, which is perfectly consistent with justice, as it descends from the original producer, in whom it vested by natural law. The pen with which I am writing is justly mine. No other human being can rightfully lay claim to it, for in me is the title of the producers who made it. It has become mine, because transferred to me by the stationer, to whom it was transferred by the importer, who obtained the exclusive right to it by transfer from the manufacturer, in whom, by the same process of purchase, vested the rights of those who dug the material from the ground and shaped it into a pen. Thus, my exclusive right of ownership in the pen springs from the natural right of the individual to the use of his own faculties. . . .

There is no escape from this position. To affirm that a man can rightfully claim exclusive ownership in his own labor when embodied in material things, is to deny that any one can rightfully claim exclusive ownership in land. To affirm the rightfulness of property in land, is to affirm a claim which has no warrant in nature, as against a claim founded in the organization of man and the laws of the material universe.

What most prevents the realization of the injustice of private property in land is the habit of including all the things that are made the subject of ownership in one category, as property, or, if any distinction is made, drawing the line, according to the unphilosophical distinction of the lawyers, between personal property and real estate, or things movable and things immovable. The real and natural distinction is between things which are the produce of labor and things which are the gratuitous offerings of nature; or, to adopt the terms of political economy, between wealth and land.

These two classes of things are in essence and relations widely different, and to class them together as property is to confuse all thought when we come to consider the justice or the injustice, the right or the wrong of property.

A house and the lot on which it stands are alike property, as being the subject of ownership, and are alike classed by the lawyers as real estate. Yet in nature and relations they differ widely. The one is produced by human labor, and belongs to the class in political economy styled wealth. The other is a part of nature, and belongs to the class in political economy styled land.

The essential character of the one class of things is that they embody labor, are brought into being by human exertion, their existence or non-existence, their increase or diminution, depending on man. The essential character of the other class of things is that they do not embody labor, and exist irrespective of human exertion and irrespective of man; they are the field or environment in which man finds himself; the storehouse from which his needs must be supplied, the raw material upon which, and the forces with which alone his labor can act.

The moment this distinction is realized, that moment is it seen that the sanction which natural justice gives to one species of property is denied to the other; that the rightfulness which attaches to individual property in the produce of labor implies the wrongfulness of individual property in land; that, whereas the recognition of the one places all men upon equal terms, securing to each the due reward of his labor, the recognition of the other is the denial of the equal rights of men, permitting those who do not labor to take the natural reward of those who do.

Whatever may be said for the institution of private property in land, it is therefore plain that it cannot be defended on the score of justice.

The equal right of all men to the use of land is as clear as their equal right to breathe the air—it is a right proclaimed by the fact of their existence. For we cannot suppose that some men have a right to be in this world and others no right.

If we are all here by the equal permission of the Creator, we are all here with an equal title to the enjoyment of his bounty—with an equal right to the use of all that nature so impartially offers. This is a right which is natural and inalienable; it is a right which vests in every human being as he enters the world, and which during his continuance in the world can be limited only by the equal rights of others. There is in nature no such thing as a fee simple in land. There is on earth no power which can rightfully make a grant of exclusive ownership in land. If all existing men were to unite to grant away their equal rights, they could not grant away the right of those who follow them. For what are we but tenants for a day? Have we made the earth, that we should determine the rights of those who after us shall tenant it in their turn? The Almighty, who created the earth for man and man for the earth, has entailed it upon all the generations of the children of men by a decree written upon the constitution of all things—a decree which no human action can bar and no prescription determine. Let the parchments be ever so many, or possession ever so long, natural justice can recognize no right in one man to the possession and enjoyment of land that is not equally the right of all his fellows. . . .

What is necessary for the use of land is not its private ownership, but the security of improvements. It is not necessary to say to a man, "this land is yours," in order to induce him to cultivate or improve it. It is only necessary to say to him, "whatever your labor or capital produces on this land shall be yours." Give a man security that he may reap, and he will sow; assure him of the possession of the house he wants to build, and he will build it. These are the natural rewards of labor. It is for the sake of the reaping that men sow; it is for the sake of possessing houses that men build. The ownership of land has nothing to do with it.

It was for the sake of obtaining this security, that in the beginning of the feudal period so many of the smaller landholders surrendered the ownership of their lands to a military chieftain, receiving back the use of them in fief or trust, and kneeling bareheaded before the lord, with their hands between his hands, swore to serve him with life, and limb, and worldly honor. Similar instances of the giving up of ownership in land for the sake of security in its enjoyment are to be seen in Turkey, where a peculiar exemption from taxation and extortion attaches to *vakouf*, or church lands, and where it is a common thing for a land owner to sell his land to a mosque for a nominal price, with the understanding that he may remain as tenant upon it at a fixed rent. . . .

I do not propose either to purchase or to confiscate private property in land. The first would be unjust; the second, needless. Let the individuals who now hold it still retain, if they want to, possession of what they are pleased to call *their* land. Let them continue to call it *their* land. Let them buy and sell, and bequeath and devise it. We may safely leave them the shell, if we take the kernel. *It is not necessary to confiscate land; it is only necessary to confiscate rent.*

Nor to take rent for public uses is it necessary that the State should bother with the letting of lands, and assume the chances of the favoritism, collusion, and corruption this might involve. It is not necessary that any new machinery should be created. The machinery already exists. Instead of extending it, all we have to do is to simplify and reduce it. By leaving to land owners a percentage of rent which would probably be much less than the cost and loss involved in attempting to rent lands through State agency, and by making use of this existing machinery, we may, without jar or shock, assert the common right to land by taking rent for public uses.

We already take some rent in taxation. We have only to make some changes in our modes of taxation to take it all.

What I, therefore, propose, as the simple yet sovereign remedy, which will raise wages, increase the earnings of capital, extirpate pauperism, abolish poverty, give remunerative employment to whoever wishes it, afford free scope to human powers, lessen crime, elevate morals, and taste, and intelligence, purify government and carry civilization to yet nobler hights, is—*to appropriate rent by taxation.*

In this way, the State may become the universal landlord without calling herself so, and without assuming a single new function. In form, the ownership of land would remain just as now. No owner of land need be dispossessed, and no restriction need be placed upon the amount of land any one could hold. For, rent being taken by the State in taxes, land, no matter in whose name it stood, or in what parcels it was held, would be really common property, and every member of the community would participate in the advantages of its ownership.

Now, insomuch as the taxation of rent, or land values, must necessarily be increased just as we abolish other taxes, we may put the proposition into practical form by proposing—

To Abolish All Taxation Save That upon Land Values....

Experience has taught me (for I have been for some years endeavoring to popularize this proposition) that wherever the idea of concentrating all taxation upon land values finds lodgment sufficient to induce consideration, it invariably makes way, but that there are few of the classes most to be benefitted by it, who at first, or even for a long time afterwards, see its full significance and power. It is difficult for workingmen to get over the idea that there is a real antagonism between capital and labor. It is difficult for small farmers and homestead owners to get over the idea that to put all taxes on the value of land would be to unduly tax them. It is difficult for both classes to get over the idea that to exempt capital from taxation would be to make the rich richer, and the poor poorer. These ideas spring from confused thought. But behind ignorance and prejudice there is a powerful interest, which has hitherto dominated literature, education, and opinion. A great wrong always dies hard, and the great wrong which in every civilized country condemns the masses of men to poverty and want, will not die without a bitter struggle.

Source: Henry George, *Progress and Poverty* (New York, 1887).

For Further Reading:

Samuel P. Hays, *The Response to Industrialism* (Chicago: University of Chicago Press, 1957).

John L. Thomas, *Alternative America* (Cambridge, Mass.: Belknap Press, 1983).

53. Selections from "The IWW Little Red Songbook" (ca. 1914)

1905   Industrial Workers of the World (IWW) formed
1908–16   IWW "fight for free speech" in the West
1912   Lawrence, Massachusetts, "Bread and Roses" strike
1913   Paterson, New Jersey, strike

In 1905 an assortment of militant trade unionists, socialists, and radicals gathered in Chicago to establish the Industrial Workers of the World (IWW),

"The Workers of the World Unite." Lithograph by Rockwell Kent (Library of Congress).

a union dedicated to organizing all workers and overthrowing capitalism. Among the IWW's founders were Eugene Debs, the Socialist Party's leader; Lucy Parsons, the widow of one of the Haymarket eight; and William (Big Bill) Haywood of the Western Federation of Miners. While the IWW grew slowly, it gained much notoriety and eventually a substantial membership, in part because of its militancy and willingness to fight for the downtrodden. For example, from 1906 through 1916, the IWW set out to organize lumberjacks, migrant farm workers, merchant seamen, and other western wage workers. Organizers would set out with a "Little Red Song Book" and union cards for western towns like Spokane, Washington, and Fresno, California, and after arriving they stood on soap boxes and addressed crowds of workingmen about the injustices of the wage system. Quite often they would be thrown in jail. In turn, the IWW argued that it, not the town's authorities, believed in freedom of speech, and that the latter were tools of the owners of industry who cared only about profits and power, not democracy.

One tool that the IWW used to reach workers was music. Organizers and members would sing songs that outlined the workers' plight, written by Joe Hill, Ralph Chaplin, and other working-class minstrels. These songs raised the spirits of rank and file workers in a number of IWW led strikes. They also provided a link to a small but vibrant radical artistic community centered in New York City's Greenwich Village.

PREAMBLE
as adopted by the 1905 I.W.W. Convention

The working class and the employing class have nothing in common. There can be no peace so long as hunger and want are found among millions of working people and the few, who make up the employing class, have all the good things of life.

Between these two classes a struggle must go on until all the toilers come together on the political, as well as on the industrial field, and take and hold that which they produce by their labor, through an economic organization of the working class without affiliation with any political party.

The rapid gathering of wealth and the centering of the management of industries into fewer and fewer hands make the trades unions unable to cope with the ever-growing power of the employing class, because the trades unions foster a state of things which allows one set of workers to be pitted against another set of workers in the same industry, thereby helping defeat one another in wage wars. The trades unions aid the employing class to mislead the workers into the belief that the working class have interests in common with their employers.

These sad conditions can be changed and the interests of the working class upheld only by an organization formed in such a way that all its members in any one industry, or in all industries, if necessary, cease work whenever a strike or lockout is on in any department thereof, thus making an injury to one an injury to all.

SOLIDARITY FOREVER!
By Ralph Chaplin
(Tune: "John Brown's Body")

When the Union's inspiration through the workers' blood shall
    run,

There can be no power greater anywhere beneath the sun.
Yet what force on earth is weaker than the feeble strength of
   one?
But the Union makes us strong.

Chorus:

   Solidarity forever!
   Solidarity forever!
   Solidarity forever!
   For the Union makes us strong.

Is there aught we hold in common with the greedy parasite
Who would lash us into serfdom and would crush us with his
   might?
Is there anything left for us but to organize and fight?
For the Union makes us strong.

It is we who plowed the prairies; built the cities where they
   trade;
Dug the mines and built the workshops; endless miles of
   railroad laid.
Now we stand, outcast and starving, 'mid the wonders we have
   made;
But the Union makes us strong.

All the world that's owned by idle drones, is ours and ours
   alone.
We have laid the wide foundations; built it skyward stone by
   stone.
It is ours, not to slave in, but to master and to own,
While the Union makes us strong.

They have taken untold millions that they never toiled to earn.
But without our brain and muscle not a single wheel can turn.
We can break their haughty power; gain our freedom when we
   learn
That the Union makes us strong.

In our hands is placed a power greater than their hoarded
   gold;
Greater than the might of armies, magnified a thousand-fold.
We can bring to birth the new world from the ashes of the
   old,
For the Union makes us strong.

THE PREACHER AND THE SLAVE
By Joe Hill
(*Tune: "Sweet Bye and Bye"*)

Long-haired preachers come out every night,
Try to tell you what's wrong and what's right;
But when asked how 'bout something to eat
They will answer with voices so sweet:

Chorus:

You will eat, bye and bye,
In that glorious land above the sky;
Work and pray, live on hay,
You'll get pie in the sky when you die.

The starvation army they play,
They sing and they clap and they pray.
Till they get all your coin on the drum,
Then they tell you when you are on the bum:

Chorus:

You will eat, bye and bye,
In that glorious land above the sky;
Work and pray, live on hay,
You'll get pie in the sky when you die.

Holy Rollers and jumpers come out,
They holler, they jump and they shout.
Give your money to Jesus they say,
He will cure all diseases today.

If you fight hard for children and wife—
Try to get something good in this life—
You're a sinner and bad man, they tell,
When you die you will sure go to hell.

Workingmen of all countries unite,
Side by side we for freedom will fight:
When the world and its wealth we have gained
To the grafters we'll sing this refrain:

Last Chorus:

You will eat, bye and bye.
When you've learned how to cook and to fry;

Chop some wood, 'twill do you good,
And you'll eat in the sweet bye and bye.

THE REBEL GIRL
(*Words and Music by Joe Hill*)

There are women of many descriptions
In this queer world, as every one knows,
Some are living in beautiful mansions,
And are wearing the finest of clothes.
There are blue-blooded queens and princesses,
Who have charms made of diamonds and pearl;
But the only and Thoroughbred Lady
Is the Rebel Girl.

     Chorus

That's the Rebel Girl. That's the Rebel Girl.
To the working class she's a precious pearl.
She brings courage, pride and joy
To the Fighting Rebel Boy.
We've had girls before
But we need some more
In the Industrial Workers of the World,
For it's great to fight for freedom
With a Rebel Girl.

Yes, her hands may be harden'd from labor
And her dress may not be very fine;
But a heart in her bosom is beating
That is true to her class and her kind.
And the grafters in terror are trembling
When her spite and defiance she'll hurl.
For the only and Thoroughbred Lady
Is the Rebel Girl.

Source: *Little Red Songbook*, 34th ed. (Chicago, 1973).

For Further Reading:

Melvyn Dubofsky, *We Shall Be All*, 2d ed. (Urbana: University of Illinois Press, 1988).

Wayne Hampton, *Guerrilla Minstrels* (Knoxville: University of Tennessee Press, 1986).

William D. Heywood, *The Autobiography of William D. Heywood* (New York: International Publishers, 1929).

PART VI
THE PROGRESSIVE ERA

54. Upton Sinclair, Excerpt from *The Jungle* (1906)

1903   Ida Tarbell writes muckraking history of Standard Oil
1904   Lincoln Steffens' *Shame of the Cities* published
1906   Upton Sinclair's *The Jungle* published; Pure Food and
        Drug Act and Meat Inspection Act enacted

In the early 1900s, Upton Sinclair went to live in Chicago to study life and labor in and around the famous packinghouses. From what he saw "back of the yards," inside the gigantic meat packing factories and from his general sense of the impact of industrialism, he wrote The Jungle. *Along with* Uncle Tom's Cabin *(see document 32) it ranks as one of the great pieces of fiction, in terms of political and social impact. Like the works of Henry George (see document 52), Edward Bellamy, and Henry Lloyd,* The Jungle *examined the inequities of wealth and power in America. But its detail and sensitivity to the plight of the immigrant worker, along with the fact that it was initially published in serialized form, lent it greater weight. It has come to symbolize muckraking, a form of journalism and writing that predominated at the turn of the century. Like other muckraking works, such as Lincoln Steffens'* Shame of the Cities, *it had an immediate political impact. The* Jungle's *passages on the production of meat turned President Teddy Roosevelt's stomach and resulted in the passage of the Pure Food and Drug Act and the Meat Inspection Act.*

Unlike many of the muckrakers, Sinclair was a socialist and he favored fundamental changes, not simply reforms. Indeed, The Jungle *ended with an endorsement of socialism. Yet this part of the novel did not strike as responsive a chord with the public as did his exposé of the meat-packing industry.*

In 1934, in the midst of the Great Depression, Sinclair ran for governor of California on an independent-socialist ticket. Although he lost, the campaign was a memorable one, with some historians considering it one of the most hard-fought in American history.

Now Antanas Rudkus was the meekest man that God ever put on earth, and so Jurgis found it a striking confirmation of what the men all said, that his father had been at work only two days before he came home as bitter as any of them, and cursing Durham's with all the power of his soul. For they had set him to cleaning out the traps; and the family sat round and listened in wonder while he told them what that meant. It seemed that he was working in the room where the men prepared the beef for canning, and the beef had lain in vats full of chemicals, and men with great forks speared it out and dumped it into trucks, to be taken to the cooking room. When they had speared out all they could reach, they emptied the vat on the floor, and then with shovels scraped off the balance and dumped it into the truck. This floor was filthy, yet they set Antanas with his mop slopping the "pickle" into a hole that connected with a sink, where it was caught and used over again forever; and if that was not enough, there was a trap in the pipe, where all the scraps of meat and odds and ends of refuse were caught, and every few days it was the old man's task to clean these out, and shovel their contents into one of the trucks with the rest of the meat!

This was the experience of Antanas; and then there came also Jonas and Marija with tales to tell. Marija was working for one of the independent packers, and was quite beside herself and outrageous with triumph over the sums of money she was making as a painter of cans. But one day she walked home with a pale-faced little woman who worked opposite to her, Jadvyga Marcinkus by name, and Jadvyga told her how she, Marija, had chanced to get her job. She had taken the place of an Irish woman who had been working in that factory ever since anyone could remember, for over fifteen years, so she declared. Mary Dennis was her name, and a long time ago she had been seduced, and had a little boy; he was a cripple, and an epileptic, but still he was all that she had in the world to love, and they had lived in a little room alone somewhere back of Halsted Street, where the Irish were. Mary had had consumption, and all day long you might hear her coughing as she worked; of late she had been going all to pieces, and when Marija came, the "forelady" had suddenly decided to turn her off. The forelady had to come up to a certain standard herself, and could not stop for sick people, Jadvyga explained. The fact that Mary had been there so long had not made any difference to her—it was doubtful if she even knew that, for both the forelady and the superintendent were new people, having only been there two or three years themselves. Jadvyga did not know what had become of the poor creature; she would have gone to see her, but had been sick herself. She had pains in her back all the time, Jadvyga explained, and feared that she had womb trouble. It was not fit work for a woman, handling fourteen-pound cans all day.

It was a striking circumstance that Jonas, too, had gotten his job by the misfortune of some other person. Jonas pushed a truck loaded with hams from the smoke rooms on to an elevator, and thence to the packing rooms. The trucks were all of iron, and heavy, and they put about threescore hams on each of them, a load of more than a quarter of a ton. On the uneven floor it was a task for a man to start one of these trucks, unless he was a giant; and when it was once started he naturally tried his best to keep it going. There was always the boss prowling about, and if there was a second's delay he would fall to cursing; Lithuanians and Slovaks and such, who could not understand what was said to them, the bosses were wont to kick about the place like so many dogs. Therefore these trucks went for the most part on the run; and the predecessor of Jonas had been jammed against the wall by one and crushed in a horrible and nameless manner.

All of these were sinister incidents; but they were trifles compared to what Jurgis saw with his own eyes before long. One curious thing he had noticed, the very first day, in his profession of shoveler of guts; which was the sharp trick of the floor bosses whenever there chanced to come a "slunk" calf. Any man who knows anything about butchering knows that the flesh of a cow that is about to calve, or has just calved, is not fit for food. A good many of these came every day to the packing houses—and, of course, if they had chosen, it would have been an easy matter for the packers to keep them till they were fit for food. But for the saving of time and fodder, it was the law that cows of that sort came along with the others, and whoever noticed it would tell the boss, and the boss would start up a conversation with the government inspector, and the two would stroll away. So, in a trice the carcass of the cow would be cleaned out, and the entrails would have vanished; it was Jurgis' task to slide them into the trap, calves and all, and on the floor below they took out these "slunk" calves, and butchered them for meat, and used even the skins of them.

One day a man slipped and hurt his leg; and that afternoon, when the last of the cattle had been disposed of, and the men were leaving, Jurgis was ordered to remain and do some special work which this injured man had usually done. It was late, almost dark, and the government inspectors had all gone, and there were only a dozen or two of men on the floor. That day they had killed about four thousand cattle, and these cattle had come in freight trains from far states, and some of them had got hurt. There were some with broken legs, and some with gored sides; there were some that had died, from what cause no one could say; and they were all to be disposed of, here in the darkness and silence. "Downers," the men called them; and the packing house had a special elevator upon which they were raised to the killing beds, where the gang proceeded to handle them, with an air of businesslike nonchalance which said plainer than any words that it was a matter of everyday routine. It took a couple of hours to get them out of the way, and in the end Jurgis saw them go into the chilling rooms with the rest of the meat, being carefully scattered here and there so that they could not be identified. When he came home that night he was in a very somber mood, having begun to see at last how those might be right who had laughed at him for his faith in America. . . .

Jurgis heard of these things little by little, in the gossip of those who were obliged to perpetrate them. It seemed as if every time you met a person from a new department, you heard of new swindles and new crimes. There was, for instance, a Lithuanian who was a cattle butcher for the plant where Marija had worked, which killed meat for canning only; and to hear this man describe the animals which came to his place would have been worthwhile for a Dante or a Zola. It seemed that they must have agencies all over the country, to hunt out old and crippled and diseased cattle to be canned. There were cattle which had been fed on "whiskey malt," the refuse of the breweries, and had become what the men called "steerly"—which means covered with boils. It was a nasty job killing these, for when you plunged your knife into them they would burst and splash foul-smelling stuff into your face; and when a man's sleeves were smeared with blood, and his hands steeped in it, how was he ever to wipe his face, or to clear his eyes so that he could see? It was stuff such as this that made the "embalmed beef" that had killed several times as many United States soldiers as all the bullets of the Spaniards; only the army beef, besides, was not fresh canned, it was old stuff that had been lying for years in the cellars.

Then one Sunday evening, Jurgis sat puffing his pipe by the kitchen stove, and talking with an old fellow whom Jonas had introduced, and who worked in the canning-rooms at Durham's; and so Jurgis learned a few things about the great and only Durham canned goods, which had become a national institution. They were regular alchemists at Durham's; they advertised a mushroom-catsup, and the men who made it did not know what a mushroom looked like. They advertised "potted chicken"—and it was like the boarding-house soup of the comic papers, through which a chicken had walked with rubbers on. Perhaps they had a secret process for making chickens chemi-cally—who knows? said Jurgis's friend; the things that went into the mixture were tripe, and the fat of pork, and beef suet, and hearts of beef, and finally the waste ends of veal, when they had any. They put these up in several grades, and sold them at several prices; but the contents of the cans all came out of the same hopper. And then there was "potted game" and "potted grouse," "potted ham," and "deviled ham"—de-vyled, as the men called it. "De-vyled" ham was made out of the waste ends of smoked beef that were too small to be sliced by the machines; and also tripe, dyed with chemicals so that it would not show white, and trimmings of hams and corned beef, and potatoes, skins and all, and finally the hard cartilaginous gullets of beef, after the tongues had been cut out. All this ingenious mixture was ground up and flavored with spices to make it taste like something. Anybody who could invent a new imitation had been sure of a fortune from old Durham, said Jurgis's informant, but it was hard to think of anything new in a place where so many sharp wits had been at work for so long; where men welcomed tuberculosis in the cattle they were feeding, because it made them fatten more quickly; and where they bought up all the old rancid butter left over in the grocery stores of a continent, and "oxidized" it by a forced-air process, to take away the odor, rechurned it with skim milk, and sold it in bricks in the cities! Up to a year or two ago it had been the custom to kill horses in the yards—ostensibly for fertilizer; but after long agitation the newspapers had been able to make the public realize that the horses were being canned.

Now it was against the law to kill horses in Packingtown, and the law was really complied with—for the present, at any rate. Any day, however, one might see sharp-horned and shaggy-haired creatures running with the sheep—and yet what a job you would have to get the public to believe that a good part of what it buys for lamb and mutton is really goat's flesh!

There was another interesting set of statistics that a person might have gathered in Packingtown—those of the various afflictions of the workers. When Jurgis had first inspected the packing plants with Szedvilas, he had marveled while he listened to the tale of all the things that were made out of the carcasses of animals, and of all the lesser industries that were maintained there; now he found that each one of these lesser industries was a separate little inferno, in its way as horrible as the killing-beds, the source and fountain of them all. The workers in each of them had their own peculiar diseases. And the wandering visitor peering down through the damp and the steam, and as old Durham's architects had not built the killing room for the convenience of the hoisters, at every few feet they would have to stoop under a beam, say four feet above the one they ran on, which got them into the habit of stooping, so that in a few years they would be walking like chimpanzees. Worst of any, however, were the fertilizer men, and those who served in the cooking rooms. These people could not be shown to the visitor—for the odor of a fertilizer man would scare any ordinary visitor at a hundred yards, and as for the other men, who worked in tank rooms full of steam, and in some of which there were open vats near the level of the floor, their peculiar trouble was that they fell into the vats; and when they were fished out, there was never enough of them left to be worth exhibiting— sometimes they would be overlooked for days, till all but the bones of them had gone out to the world as Durham's Pure Leaf Lard! . . .

With one member trimming beef in a cannery, and another working in a sausage factory, the family had a first-hand knowledge of the great majority of Packingtown swindles. For it was the custom, as they found, whenever meat was so spoiled that it could not be used for anything else, either to can it or else to chop it up into sausage. With what had been told them by Jonas, who had worked in the pickle rooms, they could now study the whole of the spoiled-meat industry on the inside, and read a new and grim meaning into that old Packingtown jest—that they use everything of the pig except the squeal.

Jonas had told them how the meat that was taken out of pickle would often be found sour, and how they would rub it up with soda to take away the smell, and sell it to be eaten on free-lunch counters; also of all the miracles of chemistry which they performed, giving to any sort of meat, fresh or salted, whole or chopped, any color and any flavor and any odor they chose. In the pickling of hams they had an ingenious apparatus, by which they saved time and increased the capacity of the plant—a machine consisting of a hollow needle attached to a pump; by plunging this needle into the meat and working with his foot a man could fill a ham with pickle in a few seconds. And yet, in spite of this, there would be hams found spoiled, some of them with an odor so bad that a man could hardly bear to be in the room with them. To pump into these the packers had a second and much stronger pickle which destroyed the odor—a process known to the workers as "giving them thirty per cent." Also, after the hams had been smoked, there would be found some that had gone to the bad. Formerly these had been sold as "Number Three Grade," but later on some ingenious person had hit upon a new device, and now they would extract the bone, about which the bad part generally lay, and insert in the hole a white-hot iron. After this invention there was no longer Number One, Two, and Three Grade—there was only Number One Grade. The packers were always originating such schemes—they had what they called "boneless hams," which were all the odds and ends of pork stuffed into casings; and "California hams," which were the shoulders, with big knuckle joints, and nearly all the meat cut out; and fancy "skinned hams," which were made of the oldest hogs, whose skins were so heavy and coarse that no one would buy them—that is, until they had been cooked and chopped fine and labelled "head cheese"!

It was only when the whole ham was spoiled that it came into the department of Elzbieta. Cut up by the two-thousand-revolutions-a-minute flyers, and mixed with half a ton of other meat, no odor that ever was in a ham could make any difference. There was never the least attention paid to what was cut up for sausage; there would come all the way back from Europe old sausage that had been rejected, and that was mouldy and white—it would be dosed with borax and glycerine, and dumped into the hoppers, and made over again for home consumption. There would be meat that had tumbled out on the floor, in the dirt and sawdust, where the workers had tramped and spit uncounted billions of consumption germs. There would be meat stored in great piles in rooms; and the water from leaky roofs would drip over it, and thousands of rats would race about on it. It was too dark in these storage places to see well, but a man could run his hand over these piles of meat and sweep off handfuls of the dried dung of rats. These rats were nuisances, and the packers would put poisoned bread out for them, they would die, and then rats, bread, and meat would go into the hoppers together. This is no fairy story and no joke; the meat would be shovelled into carts, and the man who did the shoveling would not trouble to lift out a rat even when he saw one—there were things that went into the sausage in comparison with which a poisoned rat was a tidbit. There was no place for the men to wash their hands before they ate their dinner, and so they made a practice of washing them in the water that was to be ladled into the sausage. There were the butt-ends of smoked meat, and the scraps of corned beef, and all the odds and ends of the waste of the plants, that would be dumped into old barrels in the cellar and left there. Under the system of rigid economy which the packers enforced, there were some jobs that it only paid to do once in a long time, and among these was the cleaning out of the waste barrels. Every spring they did it; and in the barrels would be dirt and rust and old nails and stale water—and cart load after cart load of it would be taken up and dumped into the hoppers with fresh meat, and sent out to the public's breakfast. Some of it they would make into "smoked" sausage—but as the smoking took time, and was therefore expensive, they would call upon their chemistry department, and preserve it with borax and color it with gelatine to make it brown. All of their sausage came out of the same bowl, but when they came to wrap it they would stamp some of it "special," and for this they would charge two cents more a pound.

Source: Upton Sinclair, *The Jungle* (New York, 1906).

For Further Reading:

James Barrett, *Work and Community in the Jungle* (Urbana: University of Illinois Press, 1987).
Louis Filler, *Crusaders for American Liberalism* (New York: Harcourt Brace, 1938).
Richard Hofstadter, *The Age of Reform* (New York: Knopf, 1955).
Louise Carroll Wade, *Chicago's Pride: The Stockyards, Parkington, and Environs in the Nineteenth Century* (Urbana: University of Illinois Press, 1987).

55. Louis Brandeis, Excerpt from "Competition" (1913)

1890 Sherman Antitrust Act
1911 Standard Oil and American Tobacco cases
1916 Louis Brandeis appointed to Supreme Court

By the beginning of the twentieth century huge firms, from Standard Oil to U.S. Steel, dominated the industrial landscape. Not only did they enjoy monopoly positions in the marketplace, they accrued tremendous political power from their economic largess. Even moderate and conservative figures, beginning to sense the dangers inherent in these monopolies, called for some type of governmental reform. In 1890 the Sherman Antitrust Act was enacted, but it went largely unenforced until the progressive era. Then Presidents Roosevelt, Taft, and Wilson pushed through a number of antitrust suits, breaking up Standard Oil, American Tobacco, and several other monopolies.

One individual who devoted much time and attention to the problem of monopolies and the threat they posed to democracy was Louis Brandeis. He was a liberal attorney, an adviser to President Wilson, a leading legal scholar, and ultimately a Supreme Court justice. As a lawyer and a judge he argued in favor of considering empirical data about social matters as well as legal precedent in determining the merits of a case. Along with Oliver Wendell Holmes, Jr. he steered the court in a new direction, toward a more relativist interpretation of the Constitution.

In "Competition," which he wrote before he was appointed to the Supreme Court, Brandeis argued in favor of aggressive federal action to combat monopolies. Like Wilson, who appointed him, Brandeis believed that the nation needed "a body of laws which will look after the men who are on the make, rather than men who are already made" (Wilson's words). Brandeis and Wilson felt that small businessmen constituted the backbone of democratic society and that their demise would prove perilous to the nation.

P‌ractically all Americans agree there is a trust problem; but upon every matter relating to the problem there is the greatest diversity of opinion. . . .

Some men who believe in competition think we have adequate governmental machinery now to secure competition, and all that is necessary is to enforce the Sherman law as it stands. Other men who believe in competition think we lack governmental machinery necessary to secure and maintain it, and that appropriate machinery should be devised and adopted for regulating competition. Likewise, some men who believe that private monopoly should be permissible think that the public will be best served if we simply repeal the Sherman law and let business take care of itself. Other men who believe in private monopoly think that we should devise and introduce new governmental machinery by which monopoly would be regulated. . . .

In saying that the New Party stands for monopoly I do not mean that it wants to introduce monopoly generally in private industry, but merely that it accepts private monopoly as permissible, and the trusts as in themselves unobjectionable, requiring only that they be "good." It is prepared to protect existing trusts from dismemberment, if only they will be "good" hereafter, thus leaving them in the possession of the huge profits obtained through violations of law. But once we treat monopoly as permissible, we have given away the whole case of competition, for monopoly is the path of least effort in business, and is sure to be pursued, if opened.

On the other hand those who stand for competition do not advocate what has been frequently described as "unrestricted" or "destructive" competition. They demand a regulated competition or, if one may adopt the phrase, competition which is "good."

Regulation is essential to the preservation of competition and to its best development just as regulation is necessary to the preservation and development of civil or political liberty. To preserve civil and political liberty to the many we have found it necessary to restrict the liberty of the few.

Unlicensed liberty leads necessarily to despotism or oligarchy. Those who are stronger must to some extent be curbed. We curb the physically strong in order to protect those physically weaker. . . .

The right of competition must be similarly limited; for excesses of competition lead to monopoly just as excesses of liberty have led to despotism. It is another case where the extremes meet.

What are those excesses of competition which should be prevented because they lead to monopoly? The answer to that question should be sought— not in theorizing, but in the abundant experiences of the last twenty-five years, during which the trusts have been developed. We have but to study the facts and ascertain:

"How did monopoly, wherever it obtained foothold, acquire its position?"

And we can, in the first place, give the comprehensive answer, which should relieve the doubts and fears of many: no monopoly in private industry in America has yet been attained by efficiency alone. No business has been so superior to its competitors in the processes of manufacture or of distribution as to enable it to control the market solely by reason of its superiority. There is nothing in our industrial history to indicate that there is any need whatever to limit the natural growth of a business in order to preserve competition. We may emphatically declare: "Give fair play to efficiency."

One has heard of late the phrases: "You can't make people compete by law." "Artificial competition is undesirable." These are truisms, but their implication is false. Believers in competition make no suggestion that traders be compelled to compete. They ask merely that no trader should be allowed to kill competition. Competition consists in trying to do things better than someone else; that is, making or selling a better article, or the same article at a lesser cost, or otherwise giving better service. It is not competition to resort to methods of the prize ring, and simply "knock the other man out." That is killing a competitor. . . .

Earnest argument is constantly made in support of monopoly by pointing to the wastefulness of competition. Undoubtedly competition involves some waste. What human activity does not? The wastes of democracy are among the greatest obvious wastes, but we have compensations in democracy which far outweigh that waste and make it more efficient than absolutism. So it is with competition. Incentive and development which are incident to the former system of business result in so much achievement that the accompanying waste is relatively insignificant. The margin between that which men naturally do and which they can do is so great that a system which urges men on to action, enterprise, and initiative is preferable in spite of the wastes that necessarily attend that process. I say, "necessarily" because there have been and are today wastes incidental to competition that are unnecessary. Those are the wastes which attend that competition which do not develop, but kill. Those wastes the law can and should eliminate. It may do so by regulating competition. . . .

But the efficiency of monopolies, even if established, would not justify their existence unless the community should reap benefit from the efficiency; experience teaches us that whenever trusts have developed efficiency, their fruits have been absorbed almost wholly by the trusts themselves. From such efficiency as they have developed the community has gained substantially nothing. . . .

Diagnosis shows monopoly to be an artificial, not a natural, product. Competition, therefore, may be preserved by preventing that course of conduct by which in the past monopolies have been established. If we had in the past undertaken by appropriate legal and administrative machinery to prevent our financiers and others from carrying out agreements to form monopolies; if we had seriously attempted to prevent those methods of destructive or unfair competition, as are manifest in "cut-throat competition"—discrimination against customers who will not deal exclusively with the combination; if we had made any persistent, intelligent effort to stop advantages gained by railroad discrimination, espionage, or the practice of establishing "fake independents," or to stop those who have secured control of essential raw material from denying business rivals access to it—few of the trusts, of which we now complain, would have come into existence, or would, at all events, have acquired power to control the market. We made no serious attempt to stop monopoly—certainly no intelligent attempt; partly because we lacked knowledge, partly because we lacked desire; for we had a sneaking feeling that perhaps, after all, a private monopoly might be a good thing, and we had no adequate governmental machinery to employ for this purpose. But in the past twenty-two years we have acquired much experience with trusts. We know their ways. We have learned what the defects in the existing machinery are; and if we will but remedy those defects by appropriate legal and administrative machinery—somewhat on the lines proposed in the La Follette–Stanley and Newlands bills—and supplement the prohibition of monopoly by the regulation of competition, we shall be able, not only to preserve the competition we now enjoy, but gradually regain the free soil upon which private monopoly has encroached, and we may be assured that, despite all industrial changes, the day for industrial liberty has not yet passed.

Source: Louis Brandeis, "Competition," *American Legal News* 44 (January 1913): 5–14.

For Further Reading:

Arthur S. Link and Richard McCormick, *Progressivism* (Arlington Heights, Va.: Harlan Davidson, 1983).

Melvin I. Urofsky, *Louis Brandeis and the Progressive Tradition* (Boston: Little, Brown, 1985).

56. Herbert Croly, Excerpt from *The Promise of American Life* (1909)

1909   *The Promise of American Life* published
1912   Teddy Roosevelt advocates "new nationalism"
1913   Federal Reserve Act

Brandeis' neo-Jeffersonian vision of America (see document 55) was not the only progressive response to the problems of modern American society. In The Promise of American Life *and* Progressive Democracy, *Herbert Croly presented a neo-Hamiltonian alternative. Whereas Brandeis sought to bolster competition and thus the small businessman, Croly more readily accepted the advantages inherent in big business, such as efficiency in size, while simultaneously calling for a stronger national government to counter the disadvantages. A key to Croly's thought was the notion of a public good or national will that he felt was threatened by business largess. He contended that the nation could overcome this threat by encouraging a civic-minded elite to play an active role in public life.*

Although not as widely read as The Jungle *(see document 54), Croly's works had a considerable influence, especially on Teddy Roosevelt. During the 1912 campaign, running as the Progressive candidate for President, Roosevelt called for a "new nationalism," which in its tone and details mirrored Croly's views. Even though Roosevelt lost the election, President Wilson enacted several acts that put Croly's ideas into play, such as the Federal Reserve Act, which established federal regulations of the banking industry.*

What Is the Promise of American Life?

The average American is nothing if not patriotic. "The Americans are filled," says Mr. Emil Reich in his "Success among the Nations," "with such an implicit and absolute confidence in their Union and in their future success that any remark other than laudatory is inacceptable to the majority of them. We have had many opportunities of hearing public speakers in America cast doubts upon the very existence of God and of Providence, question the historic nature or veracity of the whole fabric of Christianity; but never has it been our fortune to catch the slightest whisper of doubt, the slightest want of faith, in the chief God of America—unlimited belief in the future of America." Mr. Reich's method of emphasis may not be very happy, but the substance of what he says is true. The faith of Americans in their own country is religious, if not in its intensity, at any rate in its almost absolute and universal authority. It pervades the air we breathe. As children we hear it asserted or implied in the conversation of our elders. Every new stage of our educational training provides some additional testimony on its behalf. Newspapers and novelists, orators and playwrights, even if they are little else, are at least loyal preachers of the Truth. The skeptic is not controverted; he is overlooked. It constitutes the kind of faith which is the implication, rather than the object, of thought, and consciously or unconsciously it enters largely into our personal lives as a formative influence. We may distrust and dislike much that is done in the name of our country by our fellow-countrymen; but our country itself, its democratic system, and its prosperous future are above suspicion. . . .

The higher American patriotism . . . combines loyalty to historical tradition and precedent with the imaginative projection of an ideal national Promise. The Land of Democracy has always appealed to its more enthusiastic children chiefly as a land of wonderful and more than national possibilities. "Neither race nor tradition," says Professor Hugo Münsterberg in his volume on "The Americans," "nor the actual past, binds the American to his countrymen, but rather the future which together they are building." This vision of a better future is not, perhaps, as unclouded for the present generation of Americans as it was for certain former generations; but in spite of a more friendly acquaintance with all sorts of obstacles and pitfalls, our country is still figured in the imagination of its citizens as the Land of Promise. They still believe that somehow and sometime something better will happen to good Americans than has happened to men in any other country; and this belief, vague, innocent, and uninformed though it be, is the expression of an essential constituent in our national ideal. The past should mean less to a European than it does to an American, and the future should mean more. To be sure, American life cannot with impunity be wrenched violently from its moorings any more than the life of a European country can; but our American past, compared to that of any European country, has a character all its own. Its peculiarity consists, not merely in its brevity, but in the fact that from the beginning it has been informed by an idea. From the beginning Americans have been anticipating and projecting a better future. From the beginning the Land of Democracy has been figured as the Land of Promise. Thus the American's loyalty to the national tradition rather affirms than denies the imaginative projection of a better future. An America which was not the Land of Promise, which was not informed by a prophetic outlook and a more or less constructive ideal, would not be the America bequeathed to us by our forefathers. In cherishing the Promise of a better national future the American is fulfilling rather than imperiling the substance of the national tradition. . . .

The great majority of Americans would expect a book written about "The

Promise of American Life" to contain chiefly a fanciful description of the glorious American future—a sort of Utopia up-to-date, situated in the land of Good-Enough, and flying the Stars and Stripes. They might admit in words that the achievement of this glorious future implied certain responsibilities, but they would not regard the admission either as startling or novel. Such responsibilities were met by our predecessors; they will be met by our followers. Inasmuch as it is the honorable American past which prophesies on behalf of the better American future, our national responsibility consists fundamentally in remaining true to traditional ways of behavior, standards, and ideals. What we Americans have to do in order to fulfill our national Promise is to keep up the good work—to continue resolutely and cheerfully along the appointed path.

The reader who expects this book to contain a collection of patriotic prophecies will be disappointed. I am not a prophet in any sense of the word, and I entertain an active and intense dislike of the foregoing mixture of optimism, fatalism, and conservatism. To conceive the better American future as a consummation which will take care of itself—as the necessary result of our customary conditions, institutions, and ideas—persistence in such a conception is admirably designed to deprive American life of any promise at all. The better future which Americans propose to build is nothing if not an idea which must in certain essential respects emancipate them from their past. American history contains much matter for pride and congratulation, and much matter for regret and humiliation. On the whole, it is a past of which the loyal American has no reason to feel ashamed, chiefly because it has throughout been made better than it was by the vision of a better future; and the American of to-day and to-morrow must remain true to that traditional vision. He must be prepared to sacrifice to that traditional vision even the traditional American ways of realizing it. Such a sacrifice is, I believe, coming to be demanded; and unless it is made, American life will gradually cease to have any specific Promise. . . .

No doubt Americans have in some measure always conceived their national future as an ideal to be fulfilled. Their anticipations have been uplifting as well as confident and vainglorious. They have been prophesying not merely a safe and triumphant, but also a better, future. The ideal demand for some sort of individual and social amelioration has always accompanied even their vainest flights of patriotic prophecy. They may never have sufficiently realized that this better future, just in so far as it is better, will have to be planned and constructed rather than fulfilled of its own momentum; but at any rate, in seeking to disentangle and emphasize the ideal implications of the American national Promise, I am not wholly false to the accepted American tradition. Even if Americans have neglected these ideal implications, even if they have conceived the better future as containing chiefly a larger portion of familiar benefits, the ideal demand, nevertheless, has always been palpably present; and if it can be established as the dominant aspect of the American tradition, that tradition may be transformed, but it will not be violated.

Furthermore, much as we may dislike the American disposition to take the fulfillment of our national Promise for granted, the fact that such a disposition exists in its present volume and vigor demands respectful consideration. It has its roots in the salient conditions of American life, and in the actual experience of the American people. The national Promise, as it is popularly understood, has in a way been fulfilling itself. If the underlying conditions were to remain much as they have been, the prevalent mixture of optimism, fatalism, and conservatism might retain a formidable measure of justification; and the changes which are taking place in the underlying conditions and in the scope of American national experience afford the most reasonable expectation that this state of mind will undergo a radical alteration. It is new conditions which are forcing Americans to choose between the conception of their national Promise as a process and an ideal. Before, however, the nature of these novel conditions and their significance can be considered, we must examine with more care the relation between the earlier American economic and social conditions and the ideas and institutions associated with them. Only by a better understanding of the popular tradition, only by an analysis of its merits and its difficulties, can we reach a more consistent and edifying conception of the Promise of American life. . . .

How the Promise Is to Be Realized

In the preceding section I have been seeking to render justice to the actual achievements of the American nation. A work of manifest individual and social value has been wrought; and this work, not only explains the expectant popular outlook towards the future, but it partially determines the character as distinguished from the continued fulfillment of the American national Promise. The better future, whatever else it may bring, must bring at any rate a continuation of the good things of the past. The drama of its fulfillment must find an appropriate setting in the familiar American social and economic scenery. No matter how remote the end may be, no matter what unfamiliar sacrifices may eventually be required on its behalf, the substance of the existing achievement must constitute a veritable beginning, because on no other condition can the attribution of a peculiar Promise to American life find a specific warrant. On no other condition would our national Promise constitute more than an admirable but irrelevant moral and social aspiration.

The moral and social aspiration proper to American life is, of course, the aspiration vaguely described by the word democratic; and the actual achievement of the American nation points towards an adequate and fruitful definition of the democratic ideal. Americans are usually satisfied by a most inadequate verbal description of democracy, but their national achievement implies one which is much more comprehensive and formative. In order to be true to their past, the increasing comfort and economic independence of an ever increasing proportion of the population must be secured, and it must be secured by a combination of individual effort and proper political organization. Above all, however, this economic and political system must be made to secure results of moral and social value. It is the seeking of such results which converts democracy from a political system into a constructive social ideal; and the more the ideal significance of the American national Promise is asserted and emphasized, the greater will become the importance of securing these moral and social benefits.

The fault in the vision of our national future possessed by the ordinary American does not consist in the expectation of some continuity of achievement. It consists rather in the expectation that the familiar benefits will continue to accumulate automatically. In his mind the ideal Promise is identified with the processes and conditions which hitherto have very much simplified its fulfillment, and he fails sufficiently to realize that the conditions and processes are one thing and the ideal Promise quite another. Moreover, these underlying social and economic conditions are themselves changing, in such wise that hereafter the ideal Promise, instead of being automatically fulfilled, may well be automatically stifled. For two generations and more the American people were, from the economic point of view, most happily situated. They were able, in a sense, to slide down hill into the valley of fulfillment. Economic conditions were such that, given a fair start, they could scarcely avoid reaching a desirable goal. But such is no longer the case. Economic conditions have been profoundly modified, and American political and social problems have been modified with them. The Promise of American life must depend less than it did upon the virgin wilderness and the Atlantic Ocean, for the virgin wilderness has disappeared, and the Atlantic Ocean has become merely a big channel. The same results can no longer be achieved by the same easy methods. Ugly obstacles have jumped into view, and ugly obstacles are peculiarly dangerous to a person who is sliding down hill. The man who is clambering up hill is in a much better position to evade or overcome them. Americans will possess a safer as well as a worthier vision of their national Promise as soon as they give it a house on a hill-top rather than in a valley. . . .

. . . The automatic fulfillment of the American national Promise is to be abandoned, if at all, precisely because the traditional American confidence in individual freedom has resulted in a morally and socially undesirable distribution of wealth.

In making the concluding statement of the last paragraph I am venturing, of course, upon very debatable ground. Neither can I attempt in this immediate connection to offer any justification for the statement which might or should be sufficient to satisfy a stubborn skeptic. I must be content for the present with the bare assertion that the prevailing abuses and sins, which have made reform necessary, are all of them associated with the prodigious concentration of wealth, and of the power exercised by wealth, in the hands of a few men. I am far from believing that this concentration of economic power is wholly an undesirable thing, and I am also far from believing that the men in whose hands this power is concentrated deserve, on the whole, any exceptional moral reprobation for the manner in which it has been used. In certain respects they have served their country well, and in almost every respect their moral or immoral standards are those of the great majority of their fellow-countrymen. But it is none the less true that the political corruption, the unwise economic organization, and the legal support afforded to certain economic privileges are all under existing conditions due to the malevolent social influence of individual and incorporated American wealth; and it is equally true that these abuses, and the excessive "money power" with which they are associated, have originated in the peculiar freedom which the American tradition and organization have granted to the individual. Up to a certain point that freedom has been and still is beneficial. Beyond that point it is not merely harmful; it is by way of being fatal. Efficient regulation there must be; and it must be regulation which will strike, not at the symptoms of the evil, but at its roots. The existing concentration of wealth and financial power in the hands of a few irresponsible men is the inevitable outcome of the chaotic individualism of our political and economic organization, while at the same time it is inimical to democracy, because it tends to erect political abuses and social inequalities into a system. The inference which follows may be disagreeable, but it is not to be escaped. In becoming responsible for the subordination of the individual to the demand of a dominant and constructive national purpose, the American state will in effect be making itself responsible for a morally and socially desirable distribution of wealth.

Source: Herbert Croly, *The Promise of American Life* (New York, 1909).

For Further Reading:

Charles Forcey, *The Crossroads of Liberalism* (New York: Oxford University Press, 1961).

George F. Mowry, *Theodore Roosevelt and the Progressive Movement* (Madison: University of Wisconsin Press, 1946).

David Noble, *The Paradox of Progressive Thought* (Minneapolis: University of Minnesota Press, 1958).

57. Theodore Roosevelt, Excerpt from "The Natural Resources of the Nation" (1913)

1902   National Reclamation (Newlands) Act
1907   Roosevelt adds twenty-one forest reserves
1909   First National Conservation Commission meets;
          Ballinger-Pinchot Affair

One of Teddy Roosevelt's more lasting legacies and a prime example of his willingness to use the federal government to counter the excesses of big business came in the field of conservation. While President he added over 40 million acres of land to the national forests, via the National Reclamation or Newlands Act, and established sixteen national monuments and fifty-three wildlife refuges. One of the main reasons he chose to run for the presidency in 1912, against his own hand-selected successor, William Howard Taft, was that he felt Taft's record on conservation was deplorable. The firing of Gifford Pinchot, a prominent conservationist and the chief forester in the United States, by the Secretary of Interior, Richard Ballinger, in particular, upset Roosevelt.

Roosevelt spelled out some of his feelings and actions on conservation in this excerpt from his Autobiography, *written after he lost the 1912 election. In it, Roosevelt clearly lambasted the practices of the past, namely the unregulated use of the nation's resources. He also criticized private interests and public officials who blocked his attempts to implement a new policy for the use of the land, water, and forests.*

This said, Teddy Roosevelt's conservation was not identical to preservation and differed in many ways from the more recent drive to protect the environment. True, Roosevelt was a great lover of the outdoors. True, he helped promote the national parks. Yet Roosevelt promoted conservation because in the long run he thought it benefited business. Gifford Pinchot, one of his top advisers in the area of conservation, had helped convince him that unregulated use of the forests and public lands would reap short-term windfall profits but damage the forest and farm industries in the long run. Hence Pinchot and Roosevelt enacted legislation that compelled private firms to plan their use of America's natural resources, and at the same time sought to convince corporations that such behavior was in their own self-interest. For example, federal regulations required the forestry industry to replant trees and to establish means for containing forest fires.

Theodore Roosevelt with John Muir at Yosemite National Park (Library of Congress).

When Governor of New York . . . I had been in consultation with Gifford Pinchot and F. H. Newell, and had shaped my recommendations about forestry largely in accordance with their suggestions. Like other men who had thought about the national future at all, I had been growing more and more concerned over the destruction of the forests.

While I had lived in the West I had come to realize the vital need of irrigation to the country, and I had been both amused and irritated by the attitude of Eastern men who obtained from Congress grants of National money to develop harbors and yet fought the use of the Nation's power to develop the irrigation work of the West. . . .

. . . Gifford Pinchot is the man to whom the nation owes most for what has been accomplished as regards the preservation of the natural resources of our country. He led, and indeed during its most vital period embodied, the fight for the preservation through use of our forests. He played one of the leading parts in the effort to make the National Government the chief instrument in developing the irrigation of the arid West. He was the foremost leader in the great struggle to coördinate all our social and governmental forces in the effort to secure the adoption of a rational and farseeing policy for securing the conservation of all our national resources. He was already in the Government service as head of the Forestry Bureau when I became President; he continued throughout my term, not only as head of the Forest service, but as the moving and directing spirit in most of the conservation work, and as counsellor and assistant on most of the other work connected with the internal affairs of the country. Taking into account the varied nature of the work he did, its vital importance to the nation and the fact that as regards much of it he was practically breaking new ground, and taking into account also his tireless energy and activity, his fearlessness, his complete disinterestedness, his single-minded devotion to the interests of the plain people, and his extraordinary efficiency, I believe it is but just to say that among the many, many public officials who under my administration rendered literally invaluable service to the people of the United States, he, on the whole, stood first. A few months after I left the Presidency he was removed from office by President Taft.

The first work I took up when I became President was the work of reclamation. . . .

The idea that our natural resources were inexhaustible still obtained, and there was as yet no real knowledge of their extent and condition. The relation of the conservation of natural resources to the problems of National welfare and National efficiency had not yet dawned on the public mind. The reclamation of arid public lands in the West was still a matter for private enterprise alone; and our magnificent river system, with its superb possibilities for public usefulness, was dealt with by the National Government not as a unit, but as a disconnected series of pork-barrel problems, whose only real interest was in their effect on the reëlection or defeat of a Congressman here and there—a theory which, I regret to say, still obtains.

The place of the farmer in the National economy was still regarded solely as that of a grower of food to be eaten by others, while the human needs and interests of himself and his wife and children still remained wholly outside the recognition of the Government.

All the forests which belonged to the United States were held and administered in one Department, and all the foresters in Government employ were in another Department. Forests and foresters had nothing whatever to do with each other. The National Forests in the West (then called forest reserves) were wholly inadequate in area to meet the purposes for which they were created, while the need for forest protection in the East had not yet begun to enter the public mind.

Such was the condition of things when Newell and Pinchot called on me. I was a warm believer in reclamation and in forestry, and, after listening to my two guests, I asked them to prepare material on the subject for me to use in my first message to Congress, of December 3, 1901. This message laid the foundation for the development of irrigation and forestry during the next seven and one-half years. It set forth the new attitude toward the natural resources in the words: "The Forest and water problems are perhaps the most vital internal problems of the United States." . . .

The men upon whom the responsibility of handling some sixty million acres of National Forest lands was thus thrown were ready for the work, both in the office and in the field, because they had been preparing for it for more than five years. Without delay they proceeded, under the leadership of Pinchot, to apply to the new work the principles they had already formulated. One of these was to open all the resources of the National Forests to regulated use. Another was that of putting every part of the land to that use in which it would best serve the public. Following this principle, the Act of June 11, 1906, was drawn, and its passage was secured from Congress. This law throws open to settlement all land in the National Forests that is found, on examination, to be chiefly valuable for agriculture. Hitherto all such land had been closed to the settler.

The principles thus formulated and applied may be summed up in the statement that the rights of the public to the natural resources outweigh private rights, and must be given its first consideration. Until that time, in dealing with the National Forests, and the public lands generally, private rights had almost uniformly been allowed to overbalance public rights. The change we made was right, and was vitally necessary; but, of course, it created bitter opposition from private interests.

One of the principles whose application was the source of much hostility was this: It is better for the Government to help a poor man to make a living for his family than to help a rich man make more profit for his company. This principle was too sound to be fought openly. It is the kind of principle to which politicians delight to pay unctuous homage in words. But we translated the words into deeds; and when they found that this was the case, many rich men, especially sheep owners, were stirred to hostility, and they used the Congressmen they controlled to assault us—getting most aid from certain demagogues, who were equally glad improperly to denounce rich men in public and improperly to serve them in private. The Forest Service established and enforced regulations which favored the settler as against the large stock owner; required that necessary reductions in the stock grazed on any National Forest should bear first on the big man, before the few head of the small man, upon which the living of his family depended, were reduced; and made grazing in the National Forests a help, instead of a hindrance, to permanent settlement. As a result, the small settlers and their families became, on the whole, the best friends the Forest Service has; although in places their ignorance was played on by demagogues to influence them against the policy that was primarily for their own interest.

Another principle which led to the bitterest antagonism of all was this— whoever (except a bona-fide settler) takes public property for private profit should pay for what he gets. . . .

Like the rest of the Commissions described in this chapter, the Country Life Commission cost the Government not one cent, but laid before the President and the country a mass of information so accurate and so vitally important as to disturb the serenity of the advocates of things as they are; and therefore it incurred the bitter opposition of the reactionaries. The report of the Country Life Commission was transmitted to Congress by me on February 9, 1909. In the accompanying message I asked for $25,000 to print and circulate the report and to prepare for publication the immense amount of valuable material collected by the Commission but still unpublished. The reply made by Congress was not only a refusal to appropriate the money, but a positive prohibition against continuing the work. The Tawney amendment to the Sundry Civil bill forbade the President to appoint any further Commissions unless specifically authorized by Congress to do so. Had this prohibition been enacted earlier *and complied with*, it would have prevented the appointment of the six Roosevelt Commissions. But I would not have complied with it. Mr. Tawney, one of the most efficient representatives of the cause of special privilege as against public interest to be found in the House, was later, in conjunction with Senator Hale and others, able to induce my successor to accept their view. As what was almost my last official act, I replied to Congress that if I did not believe the Tawney amendment to be unconstitutional I would veto the Sundry Civil bill which contained it, and that if I were remaining in office I would refuse to obey it. The memorandum ran in part: "The chief object of this provision, however, is to prevent the Executive repeating what it has done within the last year in connection with the Conservation Commission and the Country Life Commission. It is for the people of the country to decide whether or not they believe in the work done by the Conservation Commission and by the Country Life Commission. . . .

"If they believe in improving our waterways, in preventing the waste of soil, in preserving the forests, in thrifty use of the mineral resources of the country for the nation as a whole rather than merely for private monopolies, in working for the betterment of the condition of the men and women who live on the farms, then they will unstintedly condemn the action of every man who is in any way responsible for inserting this provision, and will support those members of the legislative branch who opposed its adoption.

I would not sign the bill at all if I thought the provision entirely effective. But the Congress cannot prevent the President from seeking advice. Any future President can do as I have done, and ask disinterested men who desire to serve the people to give this service free to the people through these commissions."

Source: Theodore Roosevelt, *An Autobiography* (New York, 1913), pp. 428–31; 437–38; 454–57.

For Further Reading:

Samuel P. Hays, *Conservation and the Gospel of Efficiency* (Cambridge, Mass.: Harvard University Press, 1959).

George Mowry, *Theodore Roosevelt and the Progressive Movement* (Madison: University of Wisconsin Press, 1946).

58. Carrie Chapman Catt, Excerpt from an "Address to National American Woman Suffrage Association" (1902)

1890   National American Woman Suffrage Association (NAWSA) formed

1900   Carrie Chapman Catt elected president of NAWSA

1916   National Women's Party established

1919–20   Nineteenth Amendment passed by Congress and ratified by states

Women played a prominent role in public affairs during the progressive era. As members of the National Consumers League and various other voluntary associations, they lobbied federal and state governments to enact laws that protected consumers, children, and workers. Emphasizing their traditional role as nurturers of the young, they promoted reforms aimed at improving education and public health and hygiene. Starting with the establishment of Hull House by Jane Addams, they opened and operated hundreds of settlement houses that served the needs of the urban poor. They took the lead in pushing for Prohibition and other moral reforms. And they fought for and won the vote.

The struggle for the vote had been a long one, dating back at least to the Seneca Falls convention of 1848 (see document 31). It received a boost during the progressive era when American suffragettes followed the example of their English sisters and adopted militant tactics. They held parades, rallies,

"Suffragists Parade Along Fifth Avenue, New York." *New York Times*, part 1, p. 1, May 11, 1913 (Library of Congress).

and even picketed in front of the White House. The suffrage movement also benefited from the development of a new argument for granting women the vote. Rather than claiming that women deserved the vote because they were equal to men, as did the Seneca Falls declaration, suffragettes contended that they should be granted the vote because of their differences, namely, their more moral and sensitive nature. In turn, some suffragettes claimed, women would elect more moral politicians.

Born in 1859, Carrie Chapman Catt, head of the NAWSA, which resulted from a merger of the National Woman Suffrage Association and the American Woman Suffrage Association, fought tirelessly for the vote for much of her adult life. In her 1902 presidential address, she exhibited her militant side. At other times she was much more pragmatic. For example, during World War I, she refused to condemn suffragettes who supported America's entrance into the war, despite her own opposition to it, because she felt such criticism would undercut the final push for gaining passage of the Nineteenth Amendment.

The question of woman suffrage is a very simple one. The plea is dignified, calm and logical. Yet, great as is the victory over conservatism which is represented in the accomplishment of man suffrage, infinitely greater will be the attainment of woman suffrage. Man suffrage exists through the surrender of many a stronghold of ancient thought, deemed impregnable, yet these obstacles were the veriest Don Quixote windmills compared with the opposition which has stood arrayed against woman suffrage.

Woman suffrage must meet precisely the same objections which have been urged against man suffrage, but in addition, it must combat sex-prejudice, the oldest, the most unreasoning, the most stubborn of all human idiosyncrasies. What *is* prejudice? An opinion, which is not based upon reason; a judgment, without having heard the argument; a feeling, without being able to trace from whence it came. And sex-prejudice is a pre-judgment against the rights, liberties and opportunities of women. A belief, without proof, in the incapacity of women to do that which they have never done. Sex-prejudice has been the chief hindrance in the rapid advance of the woman's rights movement to its present status, and it is still a stupendous obstacle to be overcome.

In the United States, at least, we need no longer argue woman's intellectual, moral and physical qualification for the ballot with the intelligent. The Reason of the best of our citizens has long been convinced. The justice of the argument has been admitted, but sex-prejudice is far from conquered.

When a great church official exclaims petulantly, that if women are no more modest in their demands men may be obliged to take to drowning female infants again; when a renowned United States Senator declares no human being can find an answer to the arguments for woman suffrage, but with all the force of his position and influence he will oppose it; when a popular woman novelist speaks of the advocates of the movement as the "shrieking sisterhood;" when a prominent politician says "to argue against woman suffrage is to repudiate the Declaration of Independence," yet he hopes it may never come, the question flies entirely outside the domain of reason, and retreats within the realm of sex-prejudice, where neither logic nor common sense can dislodge it. . . .

Four chief causes led to the subjection of women, each the logical deduction from the theory that men were the units of the race—obedience, ignorance, the denial of personal liberty, and the denial of right to property and wages. These forces united in cultivating a spirit of egotism and tyranny in men and weak dependence in women. . . . In fastening these disabilities upon women, the world acted logically when reasoning from the premise that man is the race and woman his dependent. The perpetual tutelage and subjection robbed women of all freedom of thought and action, and all incentive for growth, and they logically became the inane weaklings the world would have them, and their condition strengthened the universal belief in their incapacity. This world taught woman nothing skillful and then said her work was valueless. It permitted her no opinions and said she did not know how to think. It forbade her to speak in public, and said the sex had no orators. It denied her the schools, and said the sex had no genius. It robbed her of every vestige of responsibility, and then called her weak. It taught her that every pleasure must come as a favor from men, and when to gain it she decked herself in paint and fine feathers, as she had been taught to do, it called her vain.

This was the woman enshrined in literature. She was immortalized in song and story. Chivalry paid her fantastic compliments. As Diderot said: "when woman is the theme, the pen must be dipped in the rainbow, and the pages must be dried with a butterfly's wing." Surrounded by a halo of this kind of mysticism woman was encouraged to believe herself adored. This woman who was pretty, coquettish, affectionate, obedient, self effacive [sic], now gentle and meek, now furious and emotional, always ignorant, weak and silly, became the ideal woman of the world.

When at last the New Woman came, bearing the torch of truth, and with calm dignity asked a share in the world's education, opportunities and duties, it is no wonder these untrained weaklings should have shrunk away in horror. . . . Nor was it any wonder that man should arise to defend the woman of the past, whom he had learned to love and cherish. Her very weakness and dependence were dear to him and he loved to think of her as the tender clinging vine, while he was the strong and sturdy oak. He had worshiped her ideal through the age of chivalry as though she were a goddess, but he had governed her as though she were an idiot. Without the slightest comprehension of the inconsistency of his position, he believed this relation to be in accordance with God's command. . . .

The whole aim of the woman movement has been to destroy the idea that obedience is necessary to women; to train women to such self-respect that they would not grant obedience and to train men to such comprehension of equity they would not exact it. . . . As John Stuart Mill said in speaking of the conditions which preceded the enfranchisement of men: "The noble has been gradually going down on the social ladder and the commoner has been gradually going up. Every half century has brought them nearer to each other"; so we may say, for the past hundred years, man as the dominant power in the world has been going down the ladder and woman has been climbing up. Every decade has brought them nearer together. The opposition to the enfranchisement of women is the last defense of the old theory that obedience is necessary for women, because man alone is the creator of the race.

The whole effort of the woman movement has been to destroy obedience of woman in the home. That end has been very generally attained, and the average civilized woman enjoys the right of individual liberty in the home of her father, her husband, and her son. The individual woman no longer obeys the individual man. She enjoys self-government in the home and in society. The question now is, shall all women as a body obey all men as a body? Shall the woman who enjoys the right of self-government in every other department of life be permitted the right of self-government in the State? It is no more right for all men to govern all women than it was for one man to govern one woman. It is no more right for men to govern women than it was for one man to govern other men.

Source: Diane Ravitch, ed., *The American Reader* (New York, 1990).

For Further Reading:

Eleanor Flexner, *Century of Struggle* (Cambridge, Mass.: Belknap Press, 1959).
Aileen S. Kraditor, *The Ideas of the Women's Suffrage Movement, 1890–1920* (New York: Norton, 1981).

59. Charlotte Perkins Gilman, Excerpt from *Women and Economics* (1898)

1898   *Women and Economics* published
1899   "The Yellow Wallpaper" published
1903   *The Home* published
1916   Gilman helps found National Women's Party
1923   *His Religion and Hers* published

Charlotte Perkins Gilman, a socialist, feminist, and a prolific writer, went well beyond the suffragettes in her advocacy of sexual equality. While the

National American Woman Suffrage Association focused on the vote (see document 58), Gilman explored the broader goal of gaining full equality politically, culturally, and, most important, economically. Indeed, Gilman called herself a feminist so as to distinguish herself from the suffragettes, who had a much more narrow agenda.

Gilman's insight into the impact of economics on sexual inequality can be seen through an examination of one of her earliest publications, Women and Economics. *In it she asserted that except for one example in the animal Kingdom—the female hornbill—only female homo sapiens depended entirely on the male of their species for sustenance. The impact of such dependency, Gilman contended, was enormous, affecting everything from marital relations to a woman's psychological and emotional development. Gilman made much the same argument in her fictional pieces, most famously in "The Yellow Wallpaper," a semiautobiographical short story about a woman who goes insane because of the restrictions placed on her life.*

Although Gilman often criticized the suffragettes for their timidity, and they often distanced themselves from her, it has been argued that her radical feminism helped the suffragettes win the vote. She made them look like moderates, or more respectable, to the middle class. In time, moreover, some of the suffragettes and many of their descendants would take up the themes broached by Gilman. In the 1960s, for instance, many feminists looked back on Gilman as the founder of their cause. They were inspired by her essays on economics, family, social relations, and history.

W e are the only animal species in which the female depends on the male for food, the only animal species in which the sex-relation is also an economic relation. With us an entire sex lives in a relation of economic dependence upon the other sex, and the economic relation is combined with the sex-relation. The economic status of the human female is relative to the sex-relation.

It is commonly assumed that this condition also obtains among other animals, but such is not the case. There are many birds among which, during the nesting season, the male helps the female feed the young, and partially feeds her; and, with certain of the higher carnivora, the male helps the female feed the young, and partially feeds her. In no case does she depend on him absolutely, even during this season, save in that of the hornbill, where the female, sitting on her nest in a hollow tree, is walled in with clay by the male, so that only her beak projects; and then he feeds her while the eggs are developing. But even the female hornbill does not expect to be fed at any other time. The female bee and ant are economically dependent, but not on the male. The workers are females, too, specialized to economic functions solely. And with the carnivora, if the young are to lose one parent, it might far better be the father: the mother is quite competent to take care of them herself. With many species, as in the case of the common cat, she not only feeds herself and her young, but has to defend the young against the male as well. In no case is the female throughout her life supported by the male.

In the human species the condition is permanent and general, though there are exceptions, and though the present century is witnessing the beginnings of a great change in this respect. We have not been accustomed to face this fact beyond our loose generalization that it was "natural," and that other animals did so, too.

To many this view will not seem clear at first; and the case of working peasant women or females of savage tribes, and the general household industry of women, will be instanced against it. Some careful and honest discrimination is needed to make plain to ourselves the essential facts of the relation, even in these cases. The horse, in his free natural condition, is economically independent. He gets his living by his own exertions, irrespective of any other creature. The horse, in his present condition of slavery, is economically dependent. He gets his living at the hands of his master; and his exertions, though strenuous, bear no direct relation to his living. In fact, the horses who are the best fed and cared for and the horses who are the hardest worked are quite different animals. The horse works, it is true; but what he gets to eat depends on the power and will of his master. His living comes through another. He is economically dependent. So with the hard-worked savage or peasant women. Their labor is the property of another: they work under another will; and what they receive depends not on their labor, but on the power and will of another. They are economically dependent. This is true of the human female both individually and collectively.

In studying the economic position of the sexes collectively, the difference is most marked. As a social animal, the economic status of man rests on the combined and exchanged services of vast numbers of progressively specialized individuals. The economic progress of the race, its maintenance at any period, its continued advance, involve the collective activities of all the trades, crafts, arts, manufactures, inventions, discoveries, and all the civil and military institutions that go to maintain them. The economic status of any race at any time, with its involved effect on all the constituent individuals, depends on their world-wide labors and their free exchange. Economic progress, however, is almost exclusively masculine. Such economic processes as women have been allowed to exercise are of the earliest and most primitive kind. Were men to perform no economic services save such as are still performed by women, our racial status in economics would be reduced to most painful limitations.

To take from any community its male workers would paralyze it economically to a far greater degree than to remove its female workers. The labor now performed by the women could be performed by the men, requiring only the setting back of many advanced workers into earlier forms of industry; but the labor now performed by the men could not be performed by the women without generations of effort and adaptation. Men can cook, clean, and sew as well as women; but the making and managing of the great engines of modern industry, the threading of earth and sea in our vast systems of transportation, the handling of our elaborate machinery of trade, commerce, government—these things could not be done so well by women in their present degree of economic development.

This is not owing to lack of the essential human faculties necessary to such achievements, nor to any inherent disability of sex, but to the present condition of woman, forbidding the development of this degree of economic ability. The male human being is thousands of years in advance of the female in economic status. . . .

Studied individually, the facts are even more plainly visible, more open and familiar. From the day laborer to the millionnaire, the wife's worn dress or flashing jewels, her low roof or her lordly one, her weary feet or her rich equipage—these speak of the economic ability of the husband. The comfort, the luxury, the necessities of life itself, which the woman receives, are obtained by the husband, and given her by him. And, when the woman, left alone with no man to "support" her, tries to meet her own economic necessities, the difficulties which confront her prove conclusively what the general economic status of the woman is. None can deny these patent facts— that the economic status of women generally depends upon that of men generally, and that the economic status of women individually depends upon that of men individually, those men to whom they are related. But we are instantly confronted by the commonly received opinion that, although it must be admitted that men make and distribute the wealth of the world, yet women earn their share of it as wives. This assumes either that the husband is in the position of employer and the wife as employee, or that marriage is a "partnership," and the wife an equal factor with the husband in producing wealth. . . .

Women consume economic goods. What economic product do they give in exchange for what they consume? The claim that marriage is a partnership, in which the two persons married produce wealth which neither of them, separately, could produce, will not bear examination. A man happy and comfortable can produce more than one unhappy and uncomfortable, but this is as true of a father or son as of a husband. To take from a man any of the conditions which make him happy and strong is to cripple his industry, generally speaking. But those relatives who make him happy are not therefore his business partners, and entitled to share his income.

Grateful return for happiness conferred is not the method of exchange in a partnership. The comfort a man takes with his wife is not in the nature of a business partnership, nor are her frugality and industry. A housekeeper, in her place, might be as frugal, as industrious, but would not therefore be a partner. Man and wife are partners truly in their mutual obligation to their children—their common love, duty, and service. But a manufacturer who marries, or a doctor, or a lawyer, does not take a partner in his business, when he takes a partner in parenthood, unless his wife is also a manufacturer, a doctor, or a lawyer. In his business, she cannot even advise wisely without training and experience. To love her husband, the composer, does not enable her to compose; and the loss of a man's wife, though it may break his heart, does not cripple his business, unless his mind is affected by grief. She is in no sense a business partner, unless she contributes capital or experience or labor, as a man would in like relation. Most men would hesitate very seriously before entering a business partnership with any woman, wife or not.

If the wife is not, then, truly a business partner, in what way does she earn from her husband the food, clothing, and shelter she receives at his hands? By house service, it will be instantly replied. This is the general misty idea upon the subject—that women earn all they get, and more, by house service. Here we come to a very practical and definite economic ground. Although not producers of wealth, women serve in the final processes of preparation and distribution. Their labor in the household has a genuine economic value.

For a certain percentage of persons to serve other persons, in order that the ones so served may produce more, is a contribution not to be overlooked. The labor of women in the house, certainly, enables men to produce more wealth than they otherwise could; and in this way women are economic factors in society. But so are horses. The labor of horses enables men to produce more wealth than they otherwise could. The horse is an economic factor in society. But the horse is not economically independent, nor is the woman. If a man plus a valet can perform more useful service than he could minus a valet, then the valet is performing useful service. But, if the valet is the property of the man, is obliged to perform this service, and is not paid for it, he is not economically independent.

The labor which the wife performs in the household is given as part of her functional duty, not as employment. The wife of the poor man, who works hard in a small house, doing all the work for the family, or the wife of the rich man, who wisely and gracefully manages a large house and administers its functions, each is entitled to fair pay for services rendered.

To take this ground and hold it honestly, wives, as earners through domestic service, are entitled to the wages of cooks, housemaids, nursemaids, seamstresses, or housekeepers, and to no more. This would of course reduce the spending money of the wives of the rich, and put it out of the power of the poor man to "support" a wife at all. . . .

But the salient fact in this discussion is that, whatever the economic value of the domestic industry of women is, they do not get it. The women who do the most work get the least money, and the women who have the most money do the least work. Their labor is neither given nor taken as a factor in economic exchange. . . . We are told that the duties and services of the mother entitle her to support.

If this is so, if motherhood is an exchangeable commodity given by women in payment for clothes and food, then we must of course find some relation between the quantity or quality of the motherhood and the quantity and quality of the pay. This being true, then the women who are not mothers have no economic status at all; and the economic status of those who are must be shown to be relative to their motherhood. This is obviously absurd. The childless wife has as much money as the mother of many—more; for the children of the latter consume what would otherwise be hers; and the inefficient mother is no less provided for than the efficient one. Visibly, and upon the face of it, women are not maintained in economic prosperity proportioned to their motherhood. Motherhood bears no relation to their economic status. . . . Are we willing to consider motherhood as a business, a form of commercial exchange? Are the cares and duties of the mother, her travail and her love, commodities to be exchanged for bread?

It is revolting so to consider them; and, if we dare face our own thoughts, and force them to their logical conclusion, we shall see that nothing could be more repugnant to human feeling, or more socially and individually injurious, than to make motherhood a trade. Driven off these alleged grounds of women's economic independence; shown that women, as a class, neither produce nor distribute wealth; that women, as individuals, labor mainly as house servants, are not paid as such, and would not be satisfied with such an economic status if they were so paid; that wives are not business partners or co-producers of wealth with their husbands, unless they actually practise the same profession; that they are not salaried as mothers, and that it would be unspeakably degrading if they were—what remains to those who deny that women are supported by men? This (and a most amusing position it is)—that the function of maternity unfits a woman for economic production, and, therefore, it is right that she should be supported by her husband. . . .

. . . Because of her maternal duties, the human female is said to be unable to get her own living. As the maternal duties of other females do not unfit them for getting their own living and also the livings of their young, it would seem that the human maternal duties require the segregation of the entire energies of the mother to the service of the child during her entire adult life, or so large a proportion of them that no enough remains to devote to the individual interests of the mother.

Such a condition, did it exist, would of course excuse and justify the pitiful dependence of the human female, and her support by the male. As the queen bee, modified entirely to maternity, is supported, not by the male, to be sure, but by her co-workers, the "old maids," the barren working bees, who labor so patiently and lovingly in their branch of the maternal duties of the hive, so would the human female, modified entirely to maternity, become unfit for any other exertion, and a helpless dependant.

Is this the condition of human motherhood? Does the human mother, by her motherhood, thereby lose control of brain and body, lose power and skill and desire for any other work? Do we see before us the human race, with all its females segregated entirely to the uses of motherhood, conse-crated, set apart, specially developed, spending every power of their nature on the service of their children?

We do not. We see the human mother worked far harder than a mare, laboring her life long in the service, not of her children only, but of men; husbands, brothers, fathers, whatever male relatives she has; for mother and sister also; for the church a little, if she is allowed; for society, if she is able; for charity and education and reform—working in many ways that are not the ways of motherhood.

It is not motherhood that keeps the housewife on her feet from dawn till dark; it is house service, not child service. Women work longer and harder than most men, and not solely in maternal duties. . . .

In spite of her supposed segregation to maternal duties, the human female, the world over, works at extra-maternal duties for hours enough to provide her with an independent living, and then is denied independence on the ground that motherhood prevents her working! . . .

. . . A human female, healthy, sound, has twenty-five years of life before she is a mother, and should have twenty-five years more after the period of such maternal service as is expected of her has been given. . . .

. . . The women whose splendid extravagance dazzles the world, whose economic goods are the greatest, are often neither houseworkers nor moth-ers, but simply the women who hold most power over the men who have the most money. The female of genus homo is economically dependent on the male. He is her food supply.

Source: Charlotte Perkins Gilman, *Women and Economics* (Boston, 1898), pp. 5–22.

For Further Reading:

Mary Jo Buhle, *Women and American Socialism* (Urbana: University of Illinois Press, 1981).

Nancy Cott, *The Grounding of Modern Feminism* (New Haven, Conn.: Yale Uni-versity Press, 1988).

Mary Hill, *Charlotte Perkins Gilman* (Philadelphia: Temple University Press, 1980).

60. Margaret Sanger, Excerpt from *My Fight for Birth Control* (1931)

1914 Margaret Sanger coins term "birth control"; indicted for publishing "obscene" literature
1916 Sanger jailed for opening first birth control clinic
1921 Sanger founds American Birth Control League
1923 Sanger opens Birth Control Clinical Research Bureau
1942 Planned Parenthood founded

When Margaret Sanger, a mother of three children and a nurse in New York City, first advocated using birth control as a means to ameliorate the conditions of America's immigrant poor, she was attacked as a dangerous radical. Middle-class America and government authorities saw her distribution of information on contraception as a threat to the family and traditional values. In 1914 Sanger was indicted for publishing material on contraception in her journal The Woman Rebel, *on the grounds that the material was obscene—it actually described contraception. Two years later she was arrested for opening the first birth control clinic in Brooklyn, New York, and forced to flee the nation.*

In time, however, more and more people, especially middle-class youths, came to see her as a hero, as a great fighter for freedom and independence. In the late 1920s she was a favorite speaker on the college lecture circuit. They agreed with her that "no woman can call herself free who does not own and control her own body."

In her autobiography, My Fight for Birth Control, *she described the roots of her crusade. The absence of birth control, Sanger wrote, resulted in thousands of unnecessary deaths and terrible sorrow and pain. The wise and scientific use of birth control, she argued, would improve the lives of millions of Americans and free women to enjoy greater personal fulfillment. Not until the 1960s, however, did the Supreme Court guarantee a consenting adult the right to use contraception.*

Awakening and Revolt

Early in the year 1912 I came to a sudden realization that my work as a nurse and my activities in social service were entirely palliative and consequently futile and useless to relieve the misery I saw all about me. . . .

It is among the mothers here that the most difficult problems arise—the

Margaret Sanger at the Birth Control Trial (Library of Congress).

outcasts of society with theft, filth, perjury, cruelty, brutality oozing from beneath.

Ignorance and neglect go on day by day; children born to breathe but a few hours and pass out of life; pregnant women toiling early and late to give food to four or five children, always hungry; boarders taken into homes where there is not sufficient room for the family; little girls eight and ten years of age sleeping in the same room with dirty, foul smelling, loathsome men; women whose weary, pregnant, shapless bodies refuse to accommodate themselves to the husbands' desires find husbands looking with lustful eyes upon other women, sometimes upon their own little daughters, six and seven years of age.

In this atmosphere abortions and birth become the main theme of conversation. On Saturday nights I have seen groups of fifty to one hundred women going into questionable offices well known in the community for cheap abortions. I asked several women what took place there, and they all gave the same reply: a quick examination, a probe inserted into the uterus and turned a few times to disturb the fertilized ovum, and then the woman was sent home. Usually the flow began the next day and often continued four or five weeks. Sometimes an ambulance carried the victim to the hospital for a curetage, and if she returned home at all she was looked upon as a lucky woman.

This state of things became a nightmare with me. There seemed no sense to it all, no reason for such waste of mother life, no right to exhaust women's vitality and to throw them on the scrap-heap before the age of thirty-five.

Everywhere I looked, misery and fear stalked—men fearful of losing their jobs, women fearful that even worse conditions might come upon them. The menace of another pregnancy hung like a sword over the head of every poor woman I came in contact with that year. The question which met me was always the same: What can I do to keep from it? or, What can I do to get out of this? Sometimes they talked among themselves bitterly.

"It's the rich that know the tricks," they'd say, "while we have all the kids." Then, if the women were Roman Catholics, they talked about "Yankee tricks," and asked me if I knew what the Protestants did to keep their families down. When I said that I didn't believe that the rich knew much more than they did I was laughed at and suspected of holding back information for money. They would nudge each other and say something about paying me before I left the case if I would reveal the "secret." . . .

I heard over and over again of their desperate efforts at bringing themselves "around"—drinking various herb-teas, taking drops of turpentine on sugar, steaming over a chamber of boiling coffee or of turpentine water, rolling down stairs, and finally inserting slippery-elm sticks, or knitting needles, or shoe hooks into the uterus. I used to shudder with horror as I heard the details and, worse yet, learned of the conditions *behind the reason* for such desperate actions.

. . . Each time I returned it was to hear that Mrs. Cohen had been carried to a hospital but had never come back, that Mrs. Kelly had sent the children to a neighbor's and had put her head into the gas oven to end her misery. Many of the women had consulted midwives, social workers and doctors at the dispensary and asked a way to limit their families, but they were denied this help, sometimes indignantly or gruffly, sometimes jokingly; but always knowledge was denied them. Life for them had but one choice: either to abandon themselves to incessant childbearing, or to terminate their pregnancies through abortions. Is it any wonder they resigned themselves hopelessly, as the Jewish and Italian mothers, or fell into drunkenness, as the Irish and Scotch? The latter were often beaten by husbands, as well as by their sons and daughters. They were driven and cowed, and only as beasts of burden were allowed to exist. . . .

They claimed my thoughts night and day. One by one these women, with their worried, sad, pensive and ageing faces would marshal themselves before me in my dreams, sometimes appealingly, sometimes accusingly. I could not escape from the facts of their misery, neither was I able to see the way out of their problems and their troubles. . . .

Finally the thing began to shape itself, to become accumulative during the three weeks I spent in the home of a desperately sick woman living on Grand Street, a lower section of New York's East Side.

Mrs. Sacks was only twenty-eight years old; her husband, an unskilled worker, thirty-two. Three children, aged five, three and one, were none too strong nor sturdy, and it took all the earnings of the father and the ingenuity of the mother to keep them clean, provide them with air and proper food, and give them a chance to grow into decent manhood and womanhood.

Both parents were devoted to these children and to each other. The woman had become pregnant and had taken various drugs and purgatives, as advised by her neighbors. Then, in desperation, she had used some instrument lent to her by a friend. She was found prostrate on the floor amidst the crying children when her husband returned from work. Neighbors advised against the ambulance, and a friendly doctor was called. The husband would not hear of her going to a hospital, and as a little money had been saved in the bank a nurse was called and the battle for that precious life began.

. . . The three-room apartment was turned into a hospital for the dying patient. Never had I worked so fast, so concentratedly as I did to keep alive that little mother. . . .

. . . July's sultry days and nights were melted into a torpid inferno. Day after day, night after night, I slept only in brief snatches, ever too anxious about the condition of that feeble heart bravely carrying on, to stay long from the bedside of the patient. With but one toilet for the building and that on the floor below, everything had to be carried down for disposal, while ice, food and other necessities had to be carried three flights up. It was one of those old airshaft buildings of which there were several thousands then standing in New York City.

At the end of two weeks recovery was in sight, and at the end of three weeks I was preparing to leave the fragile patient to take up the ordinary duties of her life, including those of wifehood and motherhood. . . .

But as the hour for my departure came nearer, her anxiety increased, and finally with trembling voice she said: "Another baby will finish me, I suppose."

"It's too early to talk about that," I said, and resolved that I would turn the question over to the doctor for his advice. When he came I said: "Mrs. Sacks is worried about having another baby."

"She well might be," replied the doctor, and then he stood before her and said: "Any more such capers, young woman, and there will be no need to call me."

"Yes, yes—I know, Doctor," said the patient with trembling voice, "but," and she hesitated as if it took all of her courage to say it, "*what* can I do to prevent getting that way again?"

"Oh ho!" laughed the doctor good naturedly, "You want your cake while you eat it too, do you? Well, it can't be done." Then, familiarly slapping her on the back and picking up his hat and bag to depart, he said: "I'll tell you the only sure thing to do. Tell Jake to sleep on the roof!"

With those words he closed the door and went down the stairs, leaving us both petrified and stunned.

Tears sprang to my eyes, and a lump came in my throat as I looked at that face before me. It was stamped with sheer horror. I thought for a moment she might have gone insane, but she conquered her feelings, whatever they may have been, and turning to me in desperation said: "He can't understand, can he?—he's a man after all—but you do, don't you? You're a woman and you'll tell me the secret and I'll never tell it to a soul."

She clasped her hands as if in prayer, she leaned over and looked straight into my eyes and beseechingly implored me to tell her something—something *I really did not know*. . . .

I had to turn away from that imploring face. I could not answer her then. I quieted her as best I could. She saw that I was moved by the tears in my eyes. I promised that I would come back in a few days and tell her what she wanted to know. The few simple means of limiting the family like *coitus interruptus* or the condom were laughed at by the neighboring women when told these were the means used by men in the well-to-do families. That was not believed, and I knew such an answer would be swept aside as useless were I to tell her this at such a time. . . .

The intelligent reasoning of the young mother—how to *prevent* getting that way again—how sensible, how just she had been—yes, I promised myself I'd go back and have a long talk with her and tell her more, and perhaps she would not laugh but would believe that those methods were all that were really known.

But time flew past, and weeks rolled into months. . . . I was about to retire one night three months later when the telephone rang and an agitated man's voice begged me to come at once to help his wife who was sick again. It was the husband of Mrs. Sacks, and I intuitively knew before I left the telephone that it was almost useless to go.

. . . I arrived a few minutes after the doctor, the same one who had given her such noble advice. The woman was dying. She was unconscious. She died within ten minutes after my arrival. It was the same result, the same story told a thousand times before—death from abortion. She had become pregnant, had used drugs, had then consulted a five-dollar professional abortionist, and death followed.

The doctor shook his head as he rose from listening for the heart beat. . . . The gentle woman, the devoted mother, the loving wife had passed on leaving behind her a frantic husband, helpless in his loneliness, bewildered in his helplessness as he paced up and down the room, hands clenching his head, moaning "My God! My God! My God!"

The Revolution came—but not as it has been pictured nor as history relates that revolutions have come. . . .

After I left that desolate house I walked and walked and walked; for hours and hours I kept on, bag in hand, thinking, regretting, dreading to stop; fearful of my conscience, dreading to face my own accusing soul. At three in the morning I arrived home still clutching a heavy load the weight of which I was quite unconscious.

. . . As I stood at the window and looked out, the miseries and problems of that sleeping city arose before me in a clear vision like a panorama: crowded homes, too many children; babies dying in infancy; mothers overworked; baby nurseries; children neglected and hungry—mothers so nervously wrought they could not give the little things the comfort nor care they needed; mothers half sick most of their lives—"always ailing, never failing"; women made into drudges; children working in cellars; children aged six and seven pushed into the labor market to help earn a living; another baby on the way; still another; yet another; a baby born dead—great relief; an older child dies—sorrow, but nevertheless relief—insurance helps; a mother's death—children scattered into institutions; the father, desperate, drunken; he slinks away to become an outcast in a society which has trapped him.

. . . There was only one thing to be done: call out, start the alarm, set the heather on fire! Awaken the womanhood of America to free the motherhood of the world! I released from my almost paralyzed hand the nursing bag which unconsciously I had clutched, threw it across the room, tore the uniform from my body, flung it into a corner, and renounced all palliative work forever.

I would never go back again to nurse women's ailing bodies while their miseries were as vast as the stars. I was now finished with superficial cures, with doctors and nurses and social workers who were brought face to face with this overwhelming truth of women's needs and yet turned to pass on the other side. They must be made to see these facts. I resolved that women should have knowledge of contraception. They have every right to know about their own bodies. I would strike out—I would scream from the housetops. I would tell the world what was going on in the lives of these poor women. I *would* be heard. No matter what it should cost. *I would be heard.*

Source: Margaret Sanger, *My Fight for Birth Control* (New York, 1931), chap. 3.

For Further Reading:

Ellen Chesler, *Woman of Valor* (New York: Simon & Schuster, 1992).

Linda Gordon, *Woman's Body, Woman's Rights* (New York: Grossman, 1976).

David Kennedy, *Birth Control in America* (New Haven, Conn.: Yale University Press, 1970).

61. W.E.B. Du Bois, Excerpt from *The Souls of Black Folk* (1903)

1895   Booker T. Washington, "Atlanta Exposition Address"
1903   W.E.B. Du Bois, *The Souls of Black Folk*
1906   Atlanta race riot
1905   Niagara Movement founded
1909   NAACP established

In general, the progressive era was not one of progress for African Americans. Segregation became more entrenched, with even the nation's capital adopting "Jim Crow" laws (separation of the races in public facilities). Most African Americans still lived in the South, working as sharecroppers, trapped in a vicious cycle of debt, illiteracy, and poverty. The period was marked by deadly race riots, such as one in Atlanta in 1906 in which tens of black men and women were killed by white mobs, and an increase in lynchings. To make matters worse, American intellectuals developed pseudo-scientific theories that "proved" that African Americans were biologically inferior. They also claimed that Reconstruction was the most tragic era in American history, because Radical Republicans had attempted the impossible by treating blacks as if they were equal. This viewpoint was popularized by the blockbuster movie Birth of a Nation, *which President Wilson, a professional historian by trade, hailed. The movie ended with the Ku Klux Klan saving democracy.*

W.E.B. Du Bois, a Harvard-trained black scholar and political activist, refused to accept these views or Booker T. Washington's strategy of accommodation. In his famous "Atlanta Exposition Address," Washington, a former slave and the founder of Tuskegee Institute, argued that blacks needed to quit blaming whites for their problems. Many whites found Washington's prescription for improving race relations soothing. Even President Roosevelt invited him to the White House.

Du Bois, however, found Washington's counsel appalling. Like Frederick Douglass (see document 41), Du Bois demanded full equality as an African American's birthright. He refused to moderate his tone so as to appease whites, either in his writings or his political activism. In The Souls of Black Folk, *one of his earliest writings, Du Bois presented a straightforward critique of Booker T. Washington. Several years later, Du Bois helped found the Niagara Movement, the immediate predecessor of the National Association for the Advancement of Colored People (NAACP), the most prominent civil rights organization of the twentieth century, of which Du Bois served as a leader for over three decades.*

Easily the most striking thing in the history of the American Negro since 1876 is the ascendancy of Mr. Booker T. Washington. It began at the time when war memories and ideals were rapidly passing; a day of astonishing commercial development was dawning; a sense of doubt and hesitation overtook the freedmen's sons—then it was that his leading began. Mr. Washington came, with a simple definite programme, at the psychological moment when the nation was a little ashamed of having bestowed so much sentiment on Negroes, and was concentrating its energies on Dollars. His programme of industrial education, conciliation of the South, and submission and silence as to civil and political rights, was not wholly original; the Free Negroes from 1830 up to war-time had striven to build industrial schools, and the American Missionary Association had from the first taught various trades; and Price and others had sought a way of honorable alliance with the best of the Southerners. But Mr. Washington first indissolubly linked these things; he put enthusiasm, unlimited energy, and perfect faith into this programme, and changed it from a by-path into a veritable Way of Life. And the tale of the methods by which he did this is a fascinating study of human life.

It startled the nation to hear a Negro advocating such a programme after many decades of bitter complaint; it startled and won the applause of the South, it interested and won the admiration of the North; and after a confused murmur of protest, it silenced if it did not convert the Negroes themselves.

To gain the sympathy and cooperation of the various elements comprising the white South was Mr. Washington's first task; and this, at the time Tuskegee was founded, seemed, for a black man, well-nigh impossible. And yet ten years later it was done in the word spoken at Atlanta: "In all things purely social we can be as separate as the five fingers, and yet one as the hand in all things essential to mutual progress." This "Atlanta Compromise" is by all odds the most notable thing in Mr. Washington's career. The South interpreted it in different ways: the radicals received it as a complete surrender of the demand for civil and political equality; the conservatives, as a generously conceived working basis for mutual understanding. So both approved it, and to-day its author is certainly the most distinguished Southerner since Jefferson Davis, and the one with the largest personal following.

Next to this achievement comes Mr. Washington's work in gaining place and consideration in the North. Others less shrewd and tactful had formerly essayed to sit on these two stools and had fallen between them; but as Mr. Washington knew the heart of the South from birth and training, so by singular insight he intuitively grasped the spirit of the age which was dominating the North. And so thoroughly did he learn the speech and thought of triumphant commercialism, and the ideals of material prosperity, that the picture of a lone black boy poring over a French grammar amid the weeds and dirt of a neglected home soon seemed to him the acme of absurdities. One wonders what Socrates and St. Francis of Assisi would say to this.

And yet this very singleness of vision and thorough oneness with his age is a mark of the successful man. It is as though Nature must needs make men narrow in order to give them force. So Mr. Washington's cult has gained unquestioning followers, his work has wonderfully prospered, his friends are legion, and his enemies are confounded. To-day he stands as the one recognized spokesman of his ten million fellows, and one of the most notable figures in a nation of seventy millions. One hesitates, therefore, to criticise a life which, beginning with so little, has done so much. And yet the time is come when one may speak in all sincerity and utter courtesy of the mistakes and shortcomings of Mr. Washington's career, as well as of his triumphs, without being thought captious or envious, and without forgetting that it is easier to do ill than well in the world. . . .

Mr. Washington represents in Negro thought the old attitude of adjustment and submission; but adjustment at such a peculiar time as to make his programme unique. This is an age of unusual economic development, and Mr. Washington's programme naturally takes an economic cast, becoming a gospel of Work and Money to such an extent as apparently almost completely to overshadow the higher aims of life. Moreover, this is an age when the more advanced races are coming in closer contact with the less developed races, and the race-feeling is therefore intensified; and Mr. Washington's programme practically accepts the alleged inferiority of the Negro races. Again, in our own land, the reaction from the sentiment of war time has given impetus to race-prejudice against Negroes, and Mr. Washington withdraws many of the high demands of Negroes as men and American citizens. In other periods of intensified prejudice all the Negro's tendency to self-assertion has been called forth; at this period a policy of submission is advocated. In the history of nearly all other races and peoples the doctrine preached at such crises has been that manly self-respect is worth more than lands and houses, and that a people who voluntarily surrender such respect, or cease striving for it, are not worth civilizing.

In answer to this, it has been claimed that the Negro can survive only through submission. Mr. Washington distinctly asks that black people give up, at least for the present, three things—

First, political power.

Second, insistence on civil rights,

Third, higher education of Negro youth—and concentrate all their energies on industrial education, the accumulation of wealth, and the conciliation of the South. This policy has been courageously and insistently advocated for over fifteen years, and has been triumphant for perhaps ten years. As a result of this tender of the palm-branch, what has been the return? In these years there have occurred:

1. The disfranchisement of the Negro.

2. The legal creation of a distinct status of civil inferiority for the Negro.

3. The steady withdrawal of aid from institutions for the higher training of the Negro.

These movements are not, to be sure, direct results of Mr. Washington's teachings; but his propaganda has, without a shadow of doubt, helped their speedier accomplishment. The question then comes: Is it possible, and probable, that nine millions of men can make effective progress in economic lines if they are deprived of political rights, made a servile caste, and allowed only the most meagre chance for developing their exceptional men? If history and reason give any distinct answer to these questions, it is an emphatic *No*. And Mr. Washington thus faces the triple paradox of his career:

1. He is striving nobly to make Negro artisans business men and property-owners; but it is utterly impossible, under modern competitive methods, for workingmen and property-owners to defend their rights and exist without the right of suffrage.

2. He insists on thrift and self-respect, but at the same time counsels a silent submission to civic inferiority such as is bound to sap the manhood of any race in the long run.

3. He advocates common-school and industrial training, and depreciates institutions of higher learning; but neither the Negro common-schools, nor Tuskegee itself, could remain open a day were it not for teachers trained in Negro colleges, or trained by their graduates.

This triple paradox in Mr. Washington's position is the object of criticism by two classes of colored Americans. One class is spiritually descended from Toussaint the Savior, through Gabriel, Vesey, and Turner, and they represent the attitude of revolt and revenge; they hate the white South blindly and distrust the white race generally, and so far as they agree on definite action, think that the Negro's only hope lies in emigration beyond the borders of the United States. And yet, by the irony of fate, nothing has more effectually made this programme seem hopeless than the recent course of the United States toward weaker and darker peoples in the West Indies, Hawaii, and the Philippines—for where in the world may we go and be safe from lying and brute force?

The other class of Negroes who cannot agree with Mr. Washington has hitherto said little aloud. They deprecate the sight of scattered counsels, of internal disagreement; and especially they dislike making their just criticism of a useful and earnest man an excuse for a general discharge of venom from small-minded opponents. Nevertheless, the questions involved are so fundamental and serious that it is difficult to see how men like the Grimkes, Kelly Miller, J. W. E. Bowen, and other representatives of this group, can much longer be silent. Such men feel in conscience bound to ask of this nation three things:

1. The right to vote.
2. Civic equality.
3. The education of youth according to ability.

They acknowledge Mr. Washington's invaluable service in counselling patience and courtesy in such demands; they do not ask that ignorant black men vote when ignorant whites are debarred, or that any reasonable restrictions in the suffrage should not be applied; they know that the low social level of the mass of the race is responsible for much discrimination against it, but they also know, and the nation knows, that relentless color-prejudice is more often a cause than a result of the Negro's degradation; they seek the abatement of this relic of barbarism, and not its systematic encouragement and pampering by all agencies of social power from the Associated Press to the Church of Christ. They advocate, with Mr. Washington, a broad system of Negro common schools supplemented by thorough industrial training; but they are surprised that a man of Mr. Washington's insight cannot see that no such educational system ever has rested or can rest on any other basis than that of the well-equipped college and university, and they insist that there is a demand for a few such institutions throughout the South to train the best of the Negro youth as teachers, professional men, and leaders.

This group of men honor Mr. Washington for his attitude of conciliation toward the white South; they accept the "Atlanta Compromise" in its broadest interpretation; they recognize, with him, many signs of promise, many men of high purpose and fair judgment, in this section; they know that no easy task has been laid upon a region already tottering under heavy burdens. But, nevertheless, they insist that the way to truth and right lies in straightforward honesty, not in indiscriminate flattery. . . .

The black men of America have a duty to perform, a duty stern and delicate—a forward movement to oppose a part of the work of their greatest leader. So far as Mr. Washington preaches Thrift, Patience, and Industrial Training for the masses, we must hold up his hands and strive with him, rejoicing in his honors and glorying in the strength of this Joshua called of God and of man to lead the headless host. But so far as Mr. Washington apologizes for injustice, North or South, does not rightly value the privilege and duty of voting, belittles the emasculating effects of caste distinctions, and opposes the higher training and ambition of our brighter minds—so far as he, the South, or the Nation, does this—we must unceasingly and firmly oppose them. By every civilized and peaceful method we must strive for the rights which the world accords to men, clinging unwaveringly to those great words which the sons of the Fathers would fain forget: "We hold these truths to be self-evident: That all men are created equal; that they are endowed by their Creator with certain unalienable rights; that among these are life, liberty, and the pursuit of happiness."

Source: W.E.B. Du Bois, *The Souls of Black Folk* (Chicago, 1903).

For Further Reading:

Charles Kellogg, *NAACP, Vol. 1* (Baltimore: Johns Hopkins University Press, 1967).
Augustine Meier, *Negro Thought in America, 1880–1915* (Ann Arbor: University of Michigan Press, 1963).
Elliot M. Rudwick, *W.E.B. Du Bois* (New York: Atheneum, 1969).

62. William Jennings Bryan, "America's Mission" (1899)

1898   Spanish-American War
1899   Debate over treaty
1900–1901   Philippines insurrection
1913–15   Bryan serves as Wilson's Secretary of State

In 1898, two years after William Jennings Bryan lost the presidential election to William McKinley, the United States declared war on Spain. Bryan, who was still a relatively young man, enlisted in support of the war, which was aimed largely at liberating Cuba from Spanish rule, at least in the public's eye. After the war ended, however, Bryan joined forces with those who opposed the treaty with Spain, in part because it granted the United States control over the Philippines and other former Spanish colonies. Indeed, Bryan became the leader of the "anti-imperialist" forces, first with the treaty fight and then during the early twentieth century as President Theodore Roosevelt found one reason after another to intervene abroad.

Bryan's primary foe was Senator Albert Beveridge, who argued that American rule in the Philippines would benefit both the United States and the natives. Beveridge even contended that God had chosen the United States to spread its way of life to the heathen and undemocratic people of the world. Bryan sharply disagreed with this position, arguing that imperialism was both un-American and anti-Christian. To take command of the Philippines without the consent of the natives contradicted the fundamental principles on which the United States was founded.

Although Bryan lost the treaty fight, in 1913 he became Woodrow Wilson's Secretary of State. While a cabinet member, he fostered international peace, via mediation of disputes. When war erupted in Europe in 1914, he wholeheartedly supported President Wilson's call for neutrality. In 1915, however, he resigned his post because he felt that Wilson and other cabinet members were aiding the British while cloaking themselves in the banner of peace.

When the advocates of imperialism find it impossible to reconcile a colonial policy with the principles of our government or with the canons of morality; when they are unable to defend it upon the ground of religious duty or pecuniary profit, they fall back in helpless despair upon the assertion that it is destiny. "Suppose it does violate the constitution," they say; "suppose it does break all the commandments; suppose it does entail upon the nation an incalculable expenditure of blood and money; it is destiny and we must submit."

The people have not voted for imperialism; no national convention has declared for it; no Congress has passed upon it. To whom, then, has the future been revealed? Whence this voice of authority? We can all prophesy, but our prophesies are merely guesses, colored by our hopes and our surroundings. Man's opinion of what is to be is half wish and half environment. Avarice paints destiny with a dollar mark before it, militarism equips it with a sword.

He is the best prophet who, recognizing the omnipotence of truth, comprehends most clearly the great forces which are working out the progress, not of one party, not of one nation, but of the human race.

History is replete with predictions which once wore the hue of destiny, but which failed of fulfillment because those who uttered them saw too small an arc of the circle of events. When Pharaoh pursued the fleeing Israelites to the edge of the Red Sea he was confident that their bondage would be renewed and that they would again make bricks without straw, but destiny was not revealed until Moses and his followers reached the farther shore dry shod and the waves rolled over the horses and chariots of the Egyptians. When Belshazzar, on the last night of his reign, led his thousand lords into the Babylonian banquet hall and sat down to a table glittering with vessels of silver and gold he felt sure of his kingdom for many years to come, but destiny was not revealed until the hand wrote upon the wall those awe-inspiring words, "Mene, Mene, Tekel Upharsin." When Abderrahman swept northward with his conquering hosts his imagination saw the Crescent triumphant throughout the world, but destiny was not revealed until Charles Martel raised the cross above the battlefield of Tours and saved Europe from the sword of Mohammedanism. When Napoleon emerged victorious from Marengo, from Ulm and from Austerlitz he thought himself the child of destiny, but destiny was not revealed until Blucher's forces joined the army of Wellington and the vanquished Corsican began his melancholy march toward St. Helena. When the redcoats of George the Third routed the New Englanders at Lexington and Bunker Hill there arose before the British sovereign visions of colonies taxed without representation and drained of their wealth by foreign-made laws, but destiny was not revealed until the surrender of Cornwallis completed the work begun at Independence Hall and ushered into existence a government deriving its just powers from the consent of the governed.

We have reached another crisis. The ancient doctrine of imperialism, banished from our land more than a century ago, has recrossed the Atlantic and challenged democracy to mortal combat upon American soil.

Whether the Spanish war shall be known in history as a war for liberty or as a war of conquest; whether the principles of self-government shall be strengthened or abandoned; whether this nation shall remain a homogeneous republic or become a heterogeneous empire—these questions must be answered by the American people—when they speak, and not until then, will destiny be revealed.

Destiny is not a matter of chance, it is a matter of choice; it is not a thing to be waited for, it is a thing to be achieved.

No one can see the end from the beginning, but every one can make his course an honorable one from beginning to end, by adhering to the right under all circumstances. Whether a man steals much or little may depend upon his opportunities, but whether he steals at all depends upon his own volition.

So with our nation. If we embark upon a career of conquest no one can tell how many islands we may be able to seize, or how many races we may be able to subjugate; neither can any one estimate the cost, immediate and remote, to the nation's purse and to the nation's character, but whether we shall enter upon such a career is a question which the people have a right to decide for themselves.

Unexpected events may retard or advance the nation's growth, but the nation's purpose determines its destiny.

What is the nation's purpose?

The main purpose of the founders of our government was to secure for themselves and for posterity the blessings of liberty, and that purpose has been faithfully followed up to this time. Our statesmen have opposed each other upon economic questions, but they have agreed in defending self-government as the controlling national idea. They have quarreled among themselves over tariff and finance, but they have been united in their opposition to an entangling alliance with any European power.

Under this policy our nation has grown in numbers and in strength. Under this policy its beneficent influence has encircled the globe. Under this policy the taxpayers have been spared the burden and the menace of a large military establishment and the young men have been taught the arts of peace rather than the science of war. On each returning Fourth of July our people have met to celebrate the signing of the Declaration of Independence; their hearts have renewed their vows to free institutions and their voices have praised the forefathers whose wisdom and courage and patriotism made it possible for each succeeding generation to repeat the words,

"My country, 'tis of thee,
Sweet land of liberty,
    Of thee I sing."

This sentiment was well-nigh universal until a year ago. It was to this sentiment that the Cuban insurgents appealed; it was this sentiment that impelled our people to enter into the war with Spain. Have the people so changed within a few short months that they are now willing to apologize for the War of the Revolution and force upon the Filipinos the same system of government against which the colonists protested with fire and sword?

The hour of temptation has come, but temptations do not destroy, they merely test the strength of individuals and nations; they are stumbling blocks or stepping-stones; they lead to infamy or fame, according to the use made of them.

Benedict Arnold and Ethan Allen served together in the Continental army and both were offered British gold. Arnold yielded to the temptation and made his name a synonym for treason; Allen resisted and lives in the affections of his countrymen.

Our nation is tempted to depart from its "standard of morality" and adopt a policy of "criminal aggression." But, will it yield?

If I mistake not the sentiment of the American people they will spurn the bribe of imperialism, and, by resisting temptation, win such a victory as has not been won since the battle of Yorktown. Let it be written of the United States: Behold a republic that took up arms to aid a neighboring people, struggling to be free; a republic that, in the progress of the war, helped distant races whose wrongs were not in contemplation when hostilities began; a republic that, when peace was restored, turned a deaf ear to the clamorous voice of greed and to those borne down by the weight of a foreign yoke, spoke the welcome words, Stand up; be free—let this be the record made on history's page and the silent example of this republic, true to its principles in the hour of trial, will do more to extend the area of self-government and civilization than could be done by all the wars of conquest that we could wage in a generation.

The forcible annexation of the Philippine Islands is not necessary to make the United States a world power. For over ten decades our nation has been a world power. During its brief existence it has exerted upon the human race an influence more potent for good than all the other nations of the earth combined, and it has exerted that influence without the use of sword or Gatling gun. Mexico and the republics of Central and South America testify to the benign influence of our institutions, while Europe and Asia give evidence of the working of the leaven of self-government. In the growth of democracy we observe the triumphant march of an idea—an idea that would be weighted down rather than aided by the armor and weapons proffered by imperialism.

Much has been said of late about Anglo-Saxon civilization. Far be it from me to detract from the service rendered to the world by the sturdy race whose language we speak. The union of the Angle and the Saxon formed a new and valuable type, but the process of race evolution was not completed when the Angle and the Saxon met. A still later type has appeared which is superior to any which has existed heretofore; and with this new type will come a higher civilization than any which has preceded it. Great has been the Greek, the Latin, the Slav, the Celt, the Teuton and the Anglo-Saxon, but greater than any of these is the American, in whom are blended the virtues of them all.

Civil and religious liberty, universal education and the right to participate, directly or through representatives chosen by himself, in all the affairs of government—these give to the American citizen an opportunity and an inspiration which can be found nowhere else.

Standing upon the vantage ground already gained the American people can aspire to a grander destiny than has opened before any other race.

Anglo-Saxon civilization has taught the individual to protect his own rights, American civilization will teach him to respect the rights of others.

Anglo-Saxon civilization has taught the individual to take care of himself, American civilization, proclaiming the equality of all before the law, will teach him that his own highest good requires the observance of the commandment: "Thou shalt love thy neighbor as thyself."

Anglo-Saxon civilization has, by force of arms, applied the art of government to other races for the benefit of Anglo-Saxons; American civilization will, by the influence of example, excite in other races a desire for self-government and a determination to secure it.

Anglo-Saxon civilization has carried its flag to every clime and defended it with forts and garrisons. American civilization will imprint its flag upon the hearts of all who long for freedom.

To American civilization, all hail!

"Time's noblest offspring is the last!"

Source: William J. Bryan, "Address at Washington Day Banquet," Washington, D.C., February 22, 1899, reprinted in William J. Bryan, *Bryan on Imperialism* (New York: Ayer, 1970), pp. 20–24.

For Further Reading:

Robert W. Cherny, *A Righteous Cause* (Boston: Little, Brown, 1985).
E. Berkeley Tompkins, *Anti-Imperialism in the United States* (Philadelphia: Temple University Press, 1970).

63. Woodrow Wilson, Excerpt from "War Message" (1917)

1914 World War I breaks out in Europe; Wilson declares American neutrality
1915 *Lusitania* is sunk; Wilson demands that Germany abandon submarine warfare
1916 Wilson campaigns for reelection on peace platform, defeats Charles Evans Hughes
1917 Wilson delivers war message; Congress declares war
1918 Armistice signed
1919 Wilson negotiates Treaty of Versailles; Senate refuses to ratify

When Woodrow Wilson became President of the United States in 1912, he promised a new era of freedom at home and abroad. Even after sending troops to Mexico in 1914, Wilson claimed he was devoted to a policy of peace and democracy. Like William Jennings Bryan (see document 62), he reacted to the outbreak of war in Europe in 1914 with disgust and declared a policy of American neutrality. And during his campaign for reelection in 1916, Wilson highlighted his record of having kept the nation out of war.

Nonetheless, in the spring of 1917, shortly after being inaugurated for the second time, Wilson called a special session of Congress to request a declaration of war on Germany. While historians still debate the reasons for Wilson's decision, his war message made clear that he sought to cast American involvement in a highly idealistic light. "The world must be made safe for democracy," he told Congress. This war would be fought so as to "end all wars."

Of course Wilson never achieved these goals. At the war's end the victorious European powers demanded reparations from Germany, virtually ensuring a future war, and refused to relinquish their colonies, making a mockery of Wilson's claim that the war was fought to expand democracy. Even the United States Senate refused to ratify the treaty that Wilson brought back from Versailles, to a large degree because it frowned on the idea of joining the League of Nations. Still, it is worth reading Wilson's call for war. It illustrates the American belief in itself as an exceptional place, as a nation of peace and goodwill.

I have called the Congress into extraordinary session because there are serious, very serious choices of policy to be made, and made immediately,

President Woodrow Wilson Addresses Joint Session of Congress, February 26, 1916 (Library of Congress).

which it was neither right nor constitutionally permissible that I should assume the responsibility of making.

On the third of February last I officially laid before you the extraordinary announcement of the Imperial German Government that on and after the first day of February it was its purpose to put aside all restraints of law or of humanity and use its submarines to sink every vessel that sought to approach either the ports of Great Britain and Ireland or the western coasts of Europe or any of the ports controlled by the enemies of Germany within the Mediterranean. . . .

I was for a little while unable to believe that such things would in fact be done by any government that had hitherto subscribed to the humane practices of civilized nations. International law had its origin in the attempt to set up some law which would be respected and observed upon the seas, where no nation had right of dominion and where lay the free highways of the world. . . . This minimum of right the German Government has swept aside under the plea of retaliation and necessity and because it had no weapons which it could use at sea except these which it is impossible to employ as it is employing them without throwing to the winds all scruples of humanity or of respect for all understandings that were supposed to underlie the intercourse of the world. I am not now thinking of the loss of property involved, immense and serious as that is, but only of the wanton and wholesale destruction of the lives of non-combatants, men, women, and children, engaged in pursuits which have always, even in the darkest periods of modern history, been deemed innocent and legitimate. Property can be paid for; the lives of peaceful and innocent people cannot be. The present German submarine warfare against commerce is a warfare against mankind.

It is a war against all nations. American ships have been sunk, American lives taken, in ways which it has stirred us very deeply to learn of, but the ships and people of other neutral and friendly nations have been sunk and overwhelmed in the waters in the same way. There has been no discrimination. The challenge is to all mankind. Each nation must decide for itself how it will meet it. The choice we make for ourselves must be made with a moderation of counsel and a temperateness of judgement befitting our character and our motives as a nation. We must put excited feeling away. Our motive will not be revenge or the victorious assertion of the physical might of the nation, but only the vindication of right, of human right, of which we are only a single champion. . . .

With a profound sense of the solemn and even tragical character of the step I am taking and of the grave responsibilities which it involves, but in unhesitating obedience to what I deem my constitutional duty, I advise that the Congress declare the recent course of the Imperial German Government to be in fact nothing less than war against the government and people of the United States; that it formally accept the status of belligerent which has thus been thrust upon it; and that it take immediate steps not only to put the country in a more thorough state of defense but also to exert all its power and employ all its resources to bring the Government of the German Empire to terms and end the war. . . .

We have no quarrel with the German people. We have no feeling towards them but one of sympathy and friendship. It was not upon their impulse that their government acted in entering this war. It was not with their previous knowledge or approval. It was a war determined upon as wars used to be determined upon in the old, unhappy days when peoples were nowhere consulted by their rulers and wars were provoked and waged in the interest of dynasties or of little groups of ambitious men who were accustomed to use their fellow men as pawns and tools. . . .

We are accepting this challenge of hostile purpose because we know that in such a Government, following such methods, we can never have a friend; and that in the presence of its organized power, always lying in wait to accomplish we know not what purpose, there can be no assured security for the democratic Governments of the world. We are now about to accept gauge of battle with this natural foe to liberty and shall, if necessary, spend the whole force of the nation to check and nullify its pretensions and its power. We are glad, now that we see the facts with no veil of false pretense about them, to fight thus for the ultimate peace of the world and for the liberation of its peoples, the German peoples included: for the rights of nations great and small and the privilege of men everywhere to choose their way of life and of obedience. The world must be made safe for democracy. Its peace must be planted upon the tested foundations of political liberty. We have no selfish ends to serve. We desire no conquest, no dominion. We seek no indemnities for ourselves, no material compensation for the sacrifices we shall freely make. We are but one of the champions of the rights of mankind. We shall be satisfied when those rights have been made as secure as the faith and the freedom of nations can make them. . . .

It will be all the easier for us to conduct ourselves as belligerents in a high spirit of right and fairness because we act without animus, not in enmity towards a people or with the desire to bring any injury or disadvantage upon them, but only in armed opposition to an irresponsible government which has thrown aside all considerations of humanity and of right and is running amuck. We are, let me say again, the sincere friends of the German people, and shall desire nothing so much as the early reestablishment of intimate relations of mutual advantage between us—however hard it may be for them, for the time being, to believe that this is spoken from our hearts. We have borne with their present Government through all these bitter months be-cause of that friendship—exercising a patience and forbearance which would otherwise have been impossible. We shall, happily, still have an opportunity to prove that friendship in our daily attitude and actions towards the millions of men and women of German birth and native sympathy who live amongst us and share our life, and we shall be proud to prove it towards all who are in fact loyal to their neighbors and to the Government in the hour of test. They are, most of them, as true and loyal Americans as if they had never known any other fealty of allegiance. They will be prompt to stand with us in rebuking and restraining the few who may be of a different mind and purpose. If there should be disloyalty, it will be dealt with with a firm hand of stern repression; but, if it lifts its head at all, it will lift it only here and there and without countenance except from a lawless and malignant few.

It is a distressing and oppressive duty, Gentlemen of the Congress, which I have performed in thus addressing you. There are, it may be, many months of fiery trial and sacrifice ahead of us. It is a fearful thing to lead this great peaceful people into war, into the most terrible and disastrous of all wars, civilization itself seeming to be in the balance. But the right is more precious than peace, and we shall fight for the things which we have always carried nearest our hearts—for democracy, for the right of those who submit to authority to have a voice in their own Governments, for the rights and liberties of small nations, for a universal dominion of right by such a concert of free peoples as shall bring peace and safety to all nations and make the world itself at last free. To such a task we can dedicate our lives and our fortunes, everything that we have, with the pride of those who know that the day has come when America is privileged to spend her blood and her might for the principles that gave her birth and happiness and the peace which she has treasured. God helping her, she can do no other.

Source: *New York Times*, April 3, 1917.

For Further Reading:

Thomas Bailey, *Woodrow Wilson and the Great Betrayal* (Chicago: Quadrangle, 1945).

Robert Ferrell, *Woodrow Wilson and World War I* (New York: Harper & Row, 1985).

N. Gordon Levin, Jr., *Woodrow Wilson and World Politics* (New York: Oxford, 1968).

64. Oliver Wendell Holmes, Excerpt from "Dissenting Opinion in *Abrams v. United States*" (1919)

1917 Espionage Act
1918 Sedition Act
1919 *Schenck v. United States*; *Abrams v. United States*
1920 American Civil Liberties Union (ACLU) founded

Fearing that dissent would endanger America's ability to mobilize for war, President Woodrow Wilson and Congress enacted the Espionage Act of 1917, which allowed the Postmaster General to deny the use of the mails to any material that he considered dangerous to the prosecution of the war. A year later Congress and Wilson went even further, passing the Sedition Act of 1918, which outlawed antiwar speech. Among those to be prosecuted for breaking this law was Socialist leader Eugene Debs.

The right of the government to limit freedom of expression in wartime became a matter of much debate, especially within the legal community. The Supreme Court unanimously upheld the Espionage Act in Schenck v. U.S. *But a number of leading academics criticized its reasoning, including Zechariah Chafee of Harvard University. While Chafee felt that some limitation was constitutional, he argued that the breadth of the Espionage and Sedition Acts and the government's prosecution of both laws were unwarranted.*

Perhaps influenced by Chafee's argument, Supreme Court Justice Oliver Wendell Holmes, Jr., wrote a dissenting opinion in the Abrams *case, in which the defendant, Jacob Abrams, challenged the constitutionality of the Sedition Act. Holmes' opinion is considered by many one of the most important in American history. In it he criticizes the majority's ruling in favor of the Sedition Act, arguing that except in cases where free speech presents a "clear and present danger" to the nation, it is unconstitutional to restrict it. In time Holmes' standard became that of the majority of the court. And many, including the founders of the American Civil Liberties Union, such as Roger Baldwin, who had been arrested and jailed for defending those who broke this law, contended that Holmes' standard itself was too narrow, that speech, in and of itself, could not be considered a criminal activity, only behavior could.*

H olmes, J., dissenting. This indictment is found wholly upon the publication of two leaflets which I shall describe in a moment. The first count charges a conspiracy pending the war with Germany to publish abusive language about the form of government of the United States, laying the preparation and publishing of the first leaflet as overt acts. The second count charges a conspiracy pending the war to publish language intended to bring the form of government into contempt, laying the preparation and publishing of the two leaflets as overt acts. The third count alleges a conspiracy to encourage resistance to the United States in the same war and to attempt to effectuate the purpose by publishing the same leaflets. The fourth count lays a conspiracy to incite curtailment of production of things necessary to the prosecution of the war and to attempt to accomplish it by publishing the second leaflet to which I have referred. . . .

No argument seems to me necessary to show that these pronunciamentos in no way attack the form of government of the United States, or that they do not support either of the first two counts. What little I have to say about the third count may be postponed until I have considered the fourth. With regard to that it seems too plain to be denied that the suggestion to workers in the ammunition factories that they are producing bullets to murder their dearest, and the further advocacy of a general strike, both in the second leaflet, do urge curtailment of production of things necessary to the prosecution of the war within the meaning of the Act of May 16, 1918, c. 75, 40

Stat. 553, amending part 3 of the earlier Act of 1917. But to make the conduct criminal that statute requires that it should be "with intent by such curtailment to cripple or hinder the United States in the prosecution of the war." It seems to me that no such intent is proved.

I am aware of course that the word intent as vaguely used in ordinary legal discussion means no more than knowledge at the time of the act that the consequences said to be intended will ensue. Even less than that will satisfy the general principle of civil and criminal liability. A man may have to pay damages, may be sent to prison, at common law might be hanged, if at the time of his act he knew facts from which common experience showed that the consequences would follow, whether he individually could foresee them or not. But, when words are used exactly, a deed is not done with intent to produce a consequence unless that consequence is the aim of the deed. It may be obvious, and obvious to the actor, that the consequence will follow, and he may be liable for it even if he regrets it, but he does not do the act with intent to produce it unless the aim to produce it is the proximate motive of the specific act, although there may be some deeper motive behind. . . .

I do not see how anyone can find the intent required by the statute in any of the defendants' words. The second leaflet is the only one that affords even a foundation for the charge, and there, without invoking the hatred of German militarism expressed in the former one, it is evident from the beginning to the end that the only object of the paper is to help Russia and stop American intervention there against the popular government—not to impede the United States in the war that it was carrying on. To say that two phrases taken literally might import a suggestion of conduct that would have interference with the war as an indirect and probably undesired effect seems to me by no means enough to show an attempt to produce that effect. . . .

In this case sentences of twenty years imprisonment have been imposed for the publishing of two leaflets that I believe the defendants had as much right to publish as the Government has to publish the Constitution of the United States now vainly invoked by them. Even if I am technically wrong and enough can be squeezed from these poor and puny anonymities to turn the color of legal litmus paper; I will add, even if what I think the necessary intent were shown; the most nominal punishment seems to me all that possibly could be inflicted, unless the defendants are to be made to suffer not for what the indictment alleges but for the creed that they avow—a creed that I believe to be the creed of ignorance and immaturity when honestly held, as I see no reason to doubt that it was held here, but which, although made the subject of examination at the trial, no one has a right even to consider in dealing with the charges before the Court.

Persecution for the expression of opinions seems to me perfectly logical. If you have no doubt of your premises or your power and want a certain result with all your heart you naturally express your wishes in law and sweep away all opposition. To allow opposition by speech seems to indicate that you think the speech impotent, as when a man says that he has squared the circle, or that you do not care whole-heartedly for the result, or that you doubt either your power or your premises. But when men have realized that time has upset many fighting faiths, they may come to believe even more than they believe the very foundations of their own conduct that the ultimate good desired is better reached by free trade in ideas—that the best test of truth is the power of the thought to get itself accepted in the competition of the market, and that truth is the only ground upon which their wishes safely can be carried out. That at any rate is the theory of our Constitution. It is an experiment, as all life is an experiment. Every year if not every day we have to wager our salvation upon some prophecy based upon imperfect knowledge. While that experiment is part of our system I think that we should be eternally vigilant against attempts to check the expression of opinions that we loathe and believe to be fraught with death, unless they so imminently threaten immediate interference with the lawful and pressing purposes of the law that an immediate check is required to save the country. I wholly disagree with the argument of the Government that the First Amendment left the common law as to seditious libel in force. History seems to me against the notion. I had conceived that the United States through many years had shown its repentence for the Sedition Act of 1798, by repaying fines that it imposed. Only the emergency that makes it immediately dangerous to leave the correction of evil counsels to time warrants making any exception to the sweeping command, "Congress shall make no law . . . abridging the freedom of speech." Of course I am speaking only of expressions of opinion and exhortations, which were all that were uttered here, but I regret that I cannot put into more impressive words my belief that in their conviction upon this indictment the defendants were deprived of their rights under the Constitution of the United States.

Mr. Justice Brandeis concurs with the foregoing opinion.

Source: *Abrams v. United States*, 250 U.S. 616 (1919).

For Further Reading:

Liva Baker, *The Justice from Beacon Hill* (New York: Harper Collins, 1991).
Zechariah Chafee, Jr., *Free Speech in the United States* (Cambridge, Mass.: Harvard University Press, 1941).
David Kennedy, *Over Here* (New York: Oxford University Press, 1980).

65. Randolph Bourne, Excerpt from "Trans-National America" (1916)

1916   John Dewey publishes *Democracy and Education*
1918   Randolph Bourne writes "War and the Intellectuals"

Suppression of free speech (see document 64) was not the only antidemocratic aspect of World War I. The war unleashed a red scare, anti-union drives, race riots, a new wave of nativism, and a general cultural intolerance of nonconformity, not to mention the draft, strict government regulation of the economy, and Prohibition. Perhaps because he foresaw the drift toward intolerance and "100 percent Americanism," Randolph Bourne, a brilliant essayist and opponent of the war, wrote "Trans-National America" in 1916. Like Carl Schurz (see document 34), Bourne held an inclusive, pluralist, or multicultural definition of Americanism or patriotism. While many expressed horror at the ethnic and economic divisions that the war brought to the fore, Bourne celebrated American diversity. Indeed, while at a later date it became quite common to declare: "We are all foreign-born or the descendants of foreign-born," Bourne was one of the first to emphasize this aspect of American history.

In addition to writing this penetrating article, Bourne penned several seminal antiwar essays. His "War and the Intellectuals" stands as a classic indictment of the intellectuals of his era who accepted Wilson's claim that war was justifiable since it was being fought for idealistic ends. Bourne insisted that it was impossible to separate ends and means and that the war would not produce a virtuous result. Likewise, his incomplete "The State" remains one of the best studies on the power and dangers of the modern government.

Bourne had been a student of John Dewey, the most famous American philosopher of the first third of the twentieth century. Dewey's philosophy of pragmatism as presented in Dewey's most famous book, Democracy in Education, *symbolized the American faith in experimentation. Yet, during the war, Bourne aimed his sharp pen at Dewey for supporting the war. In a sense, Bourne was the twentieth century's version of Henry David Thoreau (see document 27). Both criticized the state and their mentors with an intellectual honesty unusual even among social critics. Bourne's untimely death in 1918, at the age of thirty-six, deprived the nation of a valuable social critic.*

No reverberatory effect of the great war has caused American public opinion more solicitude than the failure of the "melting-pot." The discovery of diverse nationalistic feelings among our great alien population has come to most people as an intense shock. It has brought out the unpleasant inconsistencies of our traditional beliefs. We have had to watch hard-hearted old Brahmins virtuously indignant at the spectacle of the immigrant refusing to be melted, while they jeer at patriots like Mary Antin who write about "our forefathers." We have had to listen to publicists who express themselves as stunned by the evidence of vigorous nationalistic and cultural movements in this country among Germans, Scandinavians, Bohemians, and Poles, while in the same breath they insist that the alien shall be forcibly assimilated to that Anglo-Saxon tradition which they unquestioningly label "American."

As the unpleasant truth has come upon us that assimilation in this country was proceeding on lines very different from those we had marked out for it, we found ourselves inclined to blame those who were thwarting our prophecies. The truth became culpable. We blamed the war, we blamed the Germans. And then we discovered with a moral shock that these movements had been making great headway before the war even began. We found that the tendency, reprehensible and paradoxical as it might be, has been for the national clusters of immigrants, as they became more and more firmly established and more and more prosperous, to cultivate more and more assiduously the literatures and cultural traditions of their homelands. Assimilation, in other words, instead of washing out the memories of Europe, made them more and more intensely real. Just as these clusters became more and more objectively American, did they become more and more German or Scandinavian or Bohemian or Polish.

To face the fact that our aliens are already strong enough to take a share in the direction of their own destiny, and that the strong cultural movements represented by the foreign press, schools, and colonies are a challenge to our facile attempts, is not, however, to admit the failure of Americanization. It is not to fear the failure of democracy. It is rather to urge us to an investigation of what Americanism may rightly mean. It is to ask ourselves whether our ideal has been broad or narrow—whether perhaps the time has not come to assert a higher ideal than the "melting-pot." Surely we cannot be certain of our spiritual democracy when, claiming to melt the nations within us to a comprehension of our free and democratic institutions, we fly into panic at the first sign of their own will and tendency. We act as if we wanted Americanization to take place only on our own terms, and not by the consent of the governed. All our elaborate machinery of settlement and school and union, of social and political naturalization, however, will move with friction just in so far as it neglects to take into account this strong and virile insistence that America shall be what the immigrant will have a hand in making it, and not what a ruling class, descendant of those British stocks which were the first permanent immigrants, decide that America shall be made. This is the condition which confronts us, and which demands a clear and general readjustment of our attitude and our ideal. . . .

I

We are all foreign-born or the descendants of foreign-born, and if distinctions are to be made between us they should rightly be on some other ground than indigenousness. The early colonists came over with motives no less colonial than the later. They did not come to be assimilated in an American melting-pot. They did not come to adopt the culture of the American Indian. They had not the smallest intention of "giving themselves without reservation" to the new country. They came to get freedom to live as they wanted to. They came to escape from the stifling air and chaos of the old world; they came to make their fortune in a new land. They invented no new social framework. Rather they brought over bodily the old ways to which they had been accustomed. Tightly concentrated on a hostile frontier, they were conservative beyond belief. Their pioneer daring was reserved for the objective conquest of material resources. In their folkways, in their social and political institutions, they were, like every colonial people, slavishly imitative of the mother-country. So that, in spite of the "Revolution," our whole legal and political system remained more English than the English, petrified and unchanging, while in England law developed to meet the needs of the changing times.

It is just this English-American conservatism that has been our chief obstacle to social advance. We have needed the new peoples—the order of the German and Scandinavian, the turbulence of the Slav and Hun—to save us from our own stagnation. I do not mean that the illiterate Slav is now the equal of the New Englander of pure descent. He is raw material to be educated, not into a New Englander, but into a socialized American along such lines as those thirty nationalities are being educated in the amazing schools of Gary. I do not believe that this process is to be one of decades of evolution. The spectacle of Japan's sudden jump from mediævalism to post-modernism should have destroyed that superstition. We are not dealing with individuals who are to "evolve." We are dealing with their children, who, with that education we are about to have, will start level with all of us. Let us cease to think of ideals like democracy as magical qualities inherent in certain peoples. Let us speak, not of inferior races, but of inferior civilizations. We are all to educate and to be educated. These peoples in America are in a common enterprise. It is not what we are now that concerns us, but what this plastic next generation may become in the light of a new cosmopolitan ideal.

We are not dealing with static factors, but with fluid and dynamic generations. To contrast the older and the newer immigrants and see the one

class as democratically motivated by love of liberty, and the other by mere
money-getting, is not to illuminate the future. To think of earlier nationalities
as culturally assimilated to America, while we picture the later as a sodden
and resistive mass, makes only for bitterness and misunderstanding. There
may be a difference between these earlier and these later stocks, but it lies
neither in motive for coming nor in strength of cultural allegiance to the
homeland. The truth is that no more tenacious cultural allegiance to the
mother country has been shown by any alien nation than by the ruling class
of Anglo-Saxon descendants in these American States. English snobberies,
English religion, English literary styles, English literary reverences and
canons, English ethics, English superiorities, have been the cultural food
that we have drunk in from our mothers' breasts. . . . The unpopular and
dreaded German-American of the present day is a beginning amateur in
comparison with those foolish Anglophiles of Boston and New York and
Philadelphia whose reversion to cultural type sees uncritically in England's
cause the cause of Civilization, and, under the guise of ethical independence
of thought, carries along European traditions which are no more "American"
than the German categories themselves. . . .

The non-English American can scarcely be blamed if he sometimes thinks
of the Anglo-Saxon predominance in America as little more than a predominance of priority. The Anglo-Saxon was merely the first immigrant, the first
to found a colony. He has never really ceased to be the descendant of
immigrants, nor has he ever succeeded in transforming that colony into a
real nation, with a tenacious, richly woven fabric of native culture. Colonials
from the other nations have come and settled down beside him. They found
no definite native culture which should startle them out of their colonialism,
and consequently they looked back to their mother-country, as the earlier
Anglo-Saxon immigrant was looking back to his. What has been offered the
newcomer has been the chance to learn English, to become a citizen, to
salute the flag. And those elements of our ruling classes who are responsible
for the public schools, the settlements, all the organizations for amelioration
in the cities, have every reason to be proud of the care and labor which they
have devoted to absorbing the immigrant. His opportunities the immigrant
has taken to gladly, with almost a pathetic eagerness to make his way in the
new land without friction or disturbance. The common language has made
not only for the necessary communication, but for all the amenities of life.

If freedom means the right to do pretty much as one pleases, so long as
one does not interfere with others, the immigrant has found freedom, and
the ruling element has been singularly liberal in its treatment of the invading
hordes. But if freedom means a democratic coöperation in determining the
ideals and purposes and industrial and social institutions of a country, then
the immigrant has not been free, and the Anglo-Saxon element is guilty of
just what every dominant race is guilty of in every European country: the
imposition of its own culture upon the minority peoples. The fact that this

imposition has been so mild and, indeed, semi-conscious does not alter its quality. And the war has brought out just the degree to which that purpose of "Americanizing," that is, "Anglo-Saxonizing," the immigrant has failed.

For the Anglo-Saxon now in his bitterness to turn upon the other peoples, talk about their "arrogance," scold them for not being melted in a pot which never existed, is to betray the unconscious purpose which lay at the bottom of his heart. It betrays too the possession of a racial jealousy similar to that of which he is now accusing the so-called "hyphenates." Let the Anglo-Saxon be proud enough of the heroic toil and heroic sacrifices which moulded the nation. But let him ask himself, if he had had to depend on the English descendants, where he would have been living to-day. To those of us who see in the exploitation of unskilled labor the strident red *leit-motif* of our civilization, the settling of the country presents a great social drama as the waves of immigration broke over it.

Let the Anglo-Saxon ask himself where he would have been if these races had not come? Let those who feel the inferiority of the non-Anglo-Saxon immigrant contemplate that region of the States which has remained the most distinctively "American," the South. Let him ask himself whether he would really like to see the foreign hordes Americanized into such an Americanization. Let him ask himself how superior this native civilization is to the great "alien" states of Wisconsin and Minnesota, where Scandinavians, Poles, and Germans have self-consciously labored to preserve their traditional culture, while being outwardly and satisfactorily American. Let him ask himself how much more wisdom, intelligence, industry and social leadership has come out of these alien states than out of all the truly American ones. The South, in fact, while this vast Northern development has gone on, still remains an English colony, stagnant and complacent, having progressed culturally scarcely beyond the early Victorian era. It is culturally sterile because it has had no advantage of cross-fertilization like the Northern states. What has happened in states such as Wisconsin and Minnesota is that strong foreign cultures have struck root in a new and fertile soil. America has meant liberation, and German and Scandinavian political ideas and social energies have expanded to a new potency. The process has not been at all the fancied "assimilation" of the Scandinavian or Teuton. Rather has it been a process of their assimilation of us—I speak as an Anglo-Saxon. The foreign cultures have not been melted down or run together, made into some homogeneous Americanism, but have remained distinct but coöperating to the greater glory and benefit, not only of themselves but of all the native "Americanism" around them.

What we emphatically do not want is that these distinctive qualities should be washed out into a tasteless, colorless fluid of uniformity. Already we have far too much of this insipidity—masses of people who are cultural half-breeds, neither assimilated Anglo-Saxons nor nationals of another culture. Each national colony in this country seems to retain in its foreign press, its vernacular literature, its schools, its intellectual and patriotic leaders, a central cultural nucleus. From this nucleus the colony extends out by imperceptible gradations to a fringe where national characteristics are all but lost. Our cities are filled with these half-breeds who retain their foreign names but have lost the foreign savor. This does not mean that they have actually been changed into New Englanders or Middle Westerners. It does not mean that they have been really Americanized. It means that, letting slip from them whatever native culture they had, they have substituted for it only the most rudimentary American—the American culture of the cheap newspaper, the "movies," the popular song, the ubiquitous automobile. The unthinking who survey this class call them assimilated, Americanized. The great American public school has done its work. With these people our institutions are safe. We may thrill with dread at the aggressive hyphenate, but this tame flabbiness is accepted as Americanization. The same moulders of opinion whose ideal is to melt the different races into Anglo-Saxon gold hail this poor product -as the satisfying result of their alchemy.

Yet a truer cultural sense would have told us that it is not the self-conscious cultural nuclei that sap at our American life, but these fringes. It is not the Jew who sticks proudly to the faith of his fathers and boasts of that venerable culture of his who is dangerous to America, but the Jew who has lost the Jewish fire and become a mere elementary, grasping animal. It is not the Bohemian who supports the Bohemian schools in Chicago whose influence is sinister, but the Bohemian who has made money and has got into ward politics. Just so surely as we tend to disintegrate these nuclei of nationalistic culture do we tend to create hordes of men and women without a spiritual country, cultural outlaws, without taste, without standards but those of the mob. We sentence them to live on the most rudimentary planes of American life. The influences at the centre of the nuclei are centripetal. They make for the intelligence and the social values which mean an enhancement of life. And just because the foreign-born retains this expressiveness is he likely to be a better citizen of the American community. The influences at the fringe, however, are centrifugal, anarchical. They make for detached fragments of peoples. Those who came to find liberty achieve only license. They become the flotsam and jetsam of American life, the downward undertow of our civilization with its leering cheapness and falseness of taste and spiritual outlook, the absence of mind and sincere feeling which we see in our slovenly towns, our vapid moving pictures, our popular novels, and in the vacuous faces of the crowds on the city street. . . .

The war has shown us that . . . no intense nationalism of the European plan can be ours. But do we not begin to see a new and more adventurous ideal? Do we not see how the national colonies in America, deriving power from the deep cultural heart of Europe and yet living here in mutual toleration, freed from the age-long tangles of races, creeds, and dynasties, may work out a federated ideal? America is transplanted Europe, but a Europe that has not been disintegrated and scattered in the transplanting as in some Dispersion. Its colonies live here inextricably mingled, yet not homogeneous. They merge but they do not fuse.

America is a unique sociological fabric, and it bespeaks poverty of imagination not to be thrilled at the incalculable potentialities of so novel a union of men. To seek no other goal than the weary old nationalism—belligerent, exclusive, inbreeding, the poison of which we are witnessing now in Europe—is to make patriotism a hollow sham, and to declare that, in spite of our boastings, America must ever be a follower and not a leader of nations.

Source: Randolph Bourne, "Trans-National America," *Atlantic* 118 (July 1916): 86–97.

For Further Reading:

Edward Abrahams, *The Lyrical Left* (Charlottesville: University Press of Virginia, 1986).
Bruce Clayton, *Forgotten Prophet* (Baton Rouge: Louisiana State University Press, 1984).

PART VII
MODERNIZING AMERICA

66. Al Smith, Excerpt from "Campaign Address" (1928)

1921 First Quota Bill
1924 Second Quota Bill—National Origins Act
1925 Ku Klux Klan membership peaks
1927 Sacco and Vanzetti executed
1928 Democrats nominate Al Smith for presidency; Herbert Hoover wins

Bourne's call for pluralism (see document 65) could not thwart the rise of nativism that followed World War I. The Ku Klux Klan, dead since the end of Reconstruction, was reborn, reaching a peak membership of about 5 million in 1925. This time the KKK was as much an anti-Catholic and anti-immigrant group as it was antiblack. Fearing "racial suicide," the United States passed laws that restricted the entrance of European immigration for the first time in its history. The laws were crafted with strict quotas, so as to diminish the number of newcomers from Southern and Eastern Europe. In a trial that many considered representative of the nation's anti-immigrant fervor, two Italian-Americans, Nicola Sacco and Bartolomeo Vanzetti, were convicted and sentenced to death for murder, based on very flimsy evidence.

By the end of the 1920s, however, immigrant Americans were breaking through this intolerance. A year after Sacco and Vanzetti were hanged, the Democratic Party nominated Al Smith as their candidate for the presidency. He was the first Roman Catholic American to receive the presidential nomination of a major party. On several occasions during the campaign, he responded to charges that he was un-American or subservient to the Pope. In the following campaign address, which he delivered to a hostile, Protestant, Bible-belt crowd in Oklahoma City, Smith stood up for the rights of all Americans, regardless of their ethnic and religious heritage. He proclaimed that voters should judge a candidate on his merits, not his background. Even though he lost the election, the fact that he was nominated and that his campaign broached the subject of Americanism resulted in a more tolerant, open, and democratic society.

I feel that I owe it to the Democratic Party to talk out plainly. If I had listened to the counselors that advised political expediency I would probably keep quiet, but I'm not by nature a quiet man.

I never keep anything to myself. I talk it out. And I feel I owe it, not only to the party, but I sincerely believe that I owe it to the country itself to drag this un-American propaganda out into the open. Because this country, to my way of thinking, cannot be successful if it ever divides on sectarian lines.

If there are any considerable number of our people that are going to listen to appeals to their passion and to their prejudice, if bigotry and intolerance and their sister vices are going to succeed, it is dangerous for the future life of the Republic, and the best way to kill anything un-American is to drag it out into the open; because anything un-American cannot live in the sunlight. . . .

Now there is another lie, or series of lies, being carefully put out around the country, and it is surprising to find the number of people who seem to believe it. I would have refrained from talking about this if it were not for the avalanche of letters that have poured into the National Committee, and have poured into my own office in the Executive Department at Albany, asking for the facts.

And that is the lie that has been spread around that since I have been Governor of the State of New York nobody has even been appointed to office but Catholics. . . .

The cabinet of the Governorship is made up of fourteen men. Three of them are Catholics, ten of them are Protestants, and one of them is a Jew.

Outside of the cabinet members, the Governor appoints two boards and commissions under the cabinet, twenty-six people. Twelve of them are Protestants.

Aside from that, various other State officials, making up boards and commissions, were appointed by the Governor, making a total of 157 appointments, of which 35 were Catholics, 106 were Protestants, 12 were Jewish, and four we were unable to find out about. . . .

Now just another word and I am going to finish. Here [a circular] is the meanest thing that I have seen in the whole campaign. This is the product of the lowest and most cunning mind that could train itself to do something mean or dirty.

This was sent to me by a member of the Masonic Order, a personal friend of mine. It purports to be a circular sent out under Catholic auspices to Catholic voters, and tells how "we have control in New York; stick together and we'll get control of the country."

And designedly, it said to the roster of the Masonic Order in my State, because so many members of that order are friends of mine and have been voting for me for the last ten years, "Stand together."

Source: *New York Times*, September 21, 1928.

For Further Reading:

Oscar Handlin, *Al Smith and His America* (Boston: Little, Brown, 1958).

John Higham, *Strangers in the Land* (New Brunswick, N.J.: Rutgers University Press, 1955).

William Leuchtenburg, *The Perils of Prosperity* (Chicago: University of Chicago Press, 1958).

67. Clarence Darrow, Excerpt from "Defense of John Scopes" (1924)

1924   Scopes trial

Another development related to the general intolerance of the 1920s (see documents 764, 65, and 66) was the renaissance in religious fundamentalism. Especially strong in rural areas, where rapid changes in America's culture, economy, and social make-up seemed most alien, fundamentalism offered its adherents a simple, absolute answer to their many questions or concerns about modern life. Fundamentalists posited that the Bible should be interpreted literally and that it was absolutely valid. To an extent, the growth of fundamentalism revealed that people could shed many of their old ways, but that they retained a need for some absolutes, for an unshakable base.

Yet this faith in a literal interpretation of the Bible placed the fundamentalists at odds with many modern developments, and to a certain extent with the principle of freedom of expression. This conflict came to a head in 1924 with the infamous "Monkey" or Scopes trial in Dayton, Tennessee. The state of Tennessee tried John Scopes, a high school biology teacher and a native of the town, with breaking the state's prohibition against teaching evolution in the classroom, a law inspired by the fundamentalists' literal interpretation of the book of Genesis and the story of creation.

The case gained special attention because it pitted William Jennings Bryan (see document 62), as one of the prosecutors, against Clarence Darrow, Scopes' chief defense attorney. For years Bryan and Darrow had been friends and political colleagues. Both were anti-imperialists and Darrow, one of the nation's most famous criminal defense attorneys, had supported Bryan in his bids for the presidency. But religious fundamentalism and its restrictions on freedom of expression drove a wedge between the two.

Scopes was initially convicted in the case. However, a higher court later overturned his conviction on a technicality. The case broke the momentum of the fundamentalists, as only a few more states enacted laws that restricted the teaching of evolution and they were eventually repealed or overturned by the courts. The debate over teaching evolution in the schools remains a controversial one.

This case we have to argue is a case at law, and hard as it is for me to bring my mind to conceive it, almost impossible as it is to put my mind back into the sixteenth century, I am going to argue it as if it was serious, and as if it was a death struggle between two civilizations.

We have been informed that the legislature has the right to prescribe the course of study in the public schools. Within reason, they no doubt have. They could not prescribe a course of study, I am inclined to think, under your constitution, which omitted arithmetic and geography and writing. Neither, under the rest of the constitution, if it shall remain in force in the state, could they prescribe it if the course of study was only to teach religion; because several hundred years ago, when our people believed in freedom, and when no men felt so sure of their own sophistry that they were willing to send a man to jail who did not believe them, the people of Tennessee adopted a constitution, and they made it broad and plain, and said that the people of Tennessee should always enjoy religious freedom in its broadest terms. So I assume that no legislature could fix a course of study which violated that. . . .

I remember, long ago, Mr. Bancroft wrote this sentence, which is true: "That it is all right to preserve freedom in constitutions, but when the spirit of freedom has fled from the hearts of the people, then its matter is easily sacrificed under law." And so it is, unless there is left enough of the spirit of freedom in the state of Tennessee, and in the United States, there is not a single line of any constitution that can withstand bigotry and ignorance when it seeks to destroy the rights of the individual; and bigotry and ignorance are ever active. Here, we find today, as brazen and as bold an attempt to destroy learning as was ever made in the Middle Ages, and the only difference is we have not provided that they shall be burned at the stake, but there is time for that, Your Honor. We have to approach these things gradually.

Now, let us see what we claim with reference to this law. If this proceeding both in form and substance, can prevail in this court, then, Your Honor, no law—no matter how foolish, wicked, ambiguous, or ancient—but can come back to Tennessee. All the guarantees go for nothing. All of the past has gone, will be forgotten—if this can succeed. . . .

. . . Does this statute state what you shall teach and what you shall not? Oh, no! Oh, no! Not at all. Does it say you cannot teach the earth is round because Genesis says it is flat? No. Does it say you cannot teach that the earth is millions of ages old, because the account in Genesis makes it less than six thousand years old? Oh, no. It doesn't state that. If it did you could understand it. It says you shan't teach any theory of the origin of man that is contrary to the divine theory contained in the Bible.

Now let us pass up the word "divine"! No legislature is strong enough in any state in the Union to characterize and pick any book as being divine. Let us take it as it is. What is the Bible? Your Honor, I have read it myself. I might read it more or more wisely. Others may understand it better. Others may think they understand it better when they do not. But in a general way I know what it is. I know there are millions of people in the world who look on it as being a divine book, and I have not the slightest objection to it. I know there are millions of people in the world who derive consolation in their times of trouble and solace in times of distress from the Bible. I would be pretty near the last one in the world to do anything or take any action to take it away. I feel just exactly the same toward the religious creed of every human being who lives. If anybody finds anything in this life that brings them consolation and health and happiness I think they ought to have it, whatever they get. I haven't any fault to find with them at all. But what is it?

The Bible is not one book. The Bible is made up of 66 books written over a period of about 1,000 years, some of them very early and some of them comparatively late. It is a book primarily of religion and morals. It is not a book of science. Never was and was never meant to be. Under it there is nothing prescribed that would tell you how to build a railroad or a steamboat or to make anything that would advance civilization. It is not a textbook or a text on chemistry. It is not big enough to be. It is not a book on geology; they knew nothing about geology. It is not a book on biology; they knew nothing about it. It is not a work on evolution; that is a mystery. It is not a work on astronomy. The man who looked out at the universe and studied the heavens had no thought but that the earth was the center of the universe. But we know better than that. We know that the sun is the center of the solar system. And that there are an infinity of other systems around about us. They thought the sun went around the earth and gave us light and gave us night. We know better. We know the earth turns on its axis to produce days and nights. They thought the earth was created 4,004 years before the Christian Era. We know better. I doubt if there is a person in Tennessee who does not know better. They told it the best they knew. And while suns may change all you may learn of chemistry, geometry and mathematics, there are no doubt certain primitive, elemental instincts in the organs of man that remain the same. He finds out what he can and yearns to know more and supplements his knowledge with hope and faith.

That is the province of religion and I haven't the slightest fault to find with it. . . . If Mr. Scopes is to be indicted and prosecuted because he taught a wrong theory of the origin of life, why not tell him what he must teach? Why not say that you must teach that man was made of the dust; and still stranger, not directly from the dust, without taking any chances on it, whatever, that Eve was made out of Adam's rib? You will know what I am talking about.

Now my client must be familiar with the whole book, and must know all about all of these warring sects of Christians and know which of them is right and which wrong, in order that he will not commit crime. Nothing was heard of all that until the fundamentalists got into Tennessee. I trust that when they prosecute their wildly made charge upon the intelligence of some other sect they may modify this mistake and state in simple language what was the account contained in the Bible that could not be taught. So, unless other sects have something to do with it, we must know just what we are charged with doing. This statute, I say, Your Honor, is indefinite and uncertain. No man could obey it, no court could enforce it and it is bad for indefiniteness and uncertainty. . . .

Let us look at this act, Your Honor. Here is a law which makes it a crime to teach any theory of the origin of man excepting that contained in the divine account, which we find in the Bible. All right. Now that act applies to what? Teachers in the public schools. Now I have seen somewhere a statement of Mr. Bryan's that the fellow that made the pay check had a right to regulate the teachers. All right, let us see. I do not question the right of the legislature to fix the courses of study, but the state of Tennessee has no right under the police power of the State to carve out a law which applies to schoolteachers, a law which is a criminal statute and nothing else; which makes no effort to prescribe the school law or course of study. It says that John Smith who teaches evolution is a criminal if he teaches it in the public schools. There is no question about this act; there is no question where it belongs; there is no question of its origin. Nobody would claim that the act could be passed for a minute excepting that teaching evolution was in the nature of a criminal act; that it smacked of policemen and criminals and jails and grand juries; that it was in the nature of something that was criminal and, therefore, the State should forbid it.

It cannot stand a minute in this court on any theory than that it is a criminal act, simply because they say it contravenes the teaching of Moses without telling us what those teachings are. Now, if this is the subject of a criminal act, then it cannot make a criminal out of a teacher in the public schools and leave a man free to teach it in a private school. It cannot make it criminal for a teacher in the public schools to teach evolution, and for the same man to stand among the hustings and teach it. It cannot make it a criminal act for this teacher to teach evolution and permit books upon evolution to be sold in every store in the state of Tennessee and to permit the newspapers from foreign cities to bring into your peaceful community the horrible utterances of evolution. Oh, no, nothing like that. If the state of Tennessee has any force in this day of fundamentalism, in this day when religious bigotry and hatred is being kindled all over our land, see what can be done?

Now, Your Honor, there is an old saying that nits make lice. I don't know whether you know what it makes possible down here in Tennessee. I know, I was raised in Ohio. It is a good idea to clear the nits, safer and easier.

To strangle puppies is good when they grow up into mad dogs, maybe. I will tell you what is going to happen, and I do not pretend to be a prophet, but I do not need to be a prophet to know. Your Honor knows the fires that have been lighted in America to kindle religious bigotry and hate. You can take judicial notice of them if you cannot of anything else. You know that there is no suspicion which possesses the minds of men like bigotry and ignorance and hatred.

If today you can take a thing like evolution and make it a crime to teach it in the public school, tomorrow you can make it a crime to teach it in the private school, and the next year you can make it a crime to teach it from the hustings or in the church. At the next session you may ban books and the newspapers. Soon you may set Catholic against Protestant and Protestant against Protestant, and try to foist your own religion upon the minds of men. If you can do one you can do the other. Ignorance and fanaticism is ever busy and needs feeding. Always it is feeding and gloating for more. Today it is the public-school teachers, tomorrow the private. The next day the preachers and the lecturers, the magazines, the books, the newspapers. After a while, Your Honor, it is the setting of man against man and creed against creed until, with flying banners and beating drums, we are marching backward to the glorious ages of the sixteenth century when bigots lighted fagots to burn the men who dared to bring any intelligence and enlightenment and culture to the human mind.

Source: Clarence Darrow, *Attorney for the Damned*, ed. Arthur Weinberg (New York, 1957), pp. 176–88.

For Further Reading:

Ray Ginger, *Six Days or Forever?* (New York: Oxford University Press, 1958).
Lawrence W. Levine, *Defender of the Faith* (New York: Oxford University Press, 1965).
Irving Stone, *Clarence Darrow for the Defense* (Garden City, N.Y.: Doubleday, 1941).

68. Langston Hughes, "I, Too" (1925)

1920–30 Harlem Renaissance
1921 "Shuffle Along"
1925 Alain Locke, *The New Negro*
1926 Langston Hughes, *The Weary Blues*

While intolerance was one of the themes of the 1920s, the decade was also one of artistic and cultural growth and intellectual and youth rebellion.

Some historians have dubbed the period the "Jazz Age." This was especially so in certain enclaves of the population. College youths displayed an intolerance for traditional values and mores on a scale unseen before in American history. They flouted Prohibition and danced the Charleston, Black Bottom, and other daring rages. The cultural rebellion of young middle-class women was especially pronounced, as they bobbed their hair, shortened their skirts, smoked, drank, and challenged traditional sexual taboos.

For urban African Americans the 1920s was less a decade of cultural rebellion than one of assertion and discovery. Like college youths, African American art came of age, but unlike the youth rebellion this was no passing fad. In Harlem, in particular, African Americans displayed a newfound pride in their art forms and gained widespread respect. New Yorkers, who had always taken pride in their culture, flocked uptown to Harlem's nightclubs to hear the likes of Duke Ellington and Eubie Blake. Black performers such as Paul Robeson and Bill Robinson gained fame downtown. And black writers and poets came into their own.

One of the most famous black poets was Langston Hughes. His poem "I, Too" emblemized the new assertiveness of black artists. It appeared first in The New Negro, *Alain Locke's journal of African American art and literature, and then in* The Weary Blues, *Hughes' first full book of poetry.*

I, too, sing America.
I am the darker brother.
They send me to eat in the kitchen
When company comes,
But I laugh,
And eat well,
And grow strong.

Tomorrow,
I'll be at the table
When company comes.
Nobody'll dare
Say to me,
"Eat in the kitchen,"
Then.

Besides,
They'll see how beautiful I am
And be ashamed—

I, too, am America.

Source: Langston Hughes, *The Weary Blues* (New York, 1926).

For Further Reading:

Paula Fass, *The Damned and the Beautiful* (New York: Oxford University Press, 1975).

Nathan Huggins, *Harlem Renaissance* (New York: Oxford University Press, 1971).

Arnold Rampersad, *The Life of Langston Hughes*, 2 vols. (New York: Oxford University Press, 1986–88).

69. Henry Ford, Excerpt from *My Life and Work* (1922)

1908   Ford designs Model T
1911   Ford builds assembly plant in Highland Park, Michigan
1914   Ford establishes $5-a-day wage
1925   Ford Motor Company produces nearly one car every
        ten seconds

Except for a brief recession immediately following World War I, the 1920s were years of economic prosperity. The Gross National Product climbed steadily. Per capita income and real wages grew. New amenities, from radios to washing machines, appeared in the homes of millions of Americans. Clearly the automobile industry was one of the main engines of economic growth, and Henry Ford and his Model T became the symbol of America's industrial prowess and middle-class prosperity.

Before Ford opened his assembly plant in Highland Park, Michigan, in 1911, automobiles were a luxury item. Only a couple of thousand were produced each year, and the average worker never would have dreamed of owning one. By 1929 one out of every five families owned a car and there were a total of 26 million on the roads, as compared to about 300,000 years earlier. Ford intentionally sold his cars at a reasonable price, about $300, and he provided thousands of reasonably well-paying jobs—Ford started paying $5 a day in 1914, well above the average rate for an industrial worker. Moreover, the automobile boom generated jobs in tens of other sectors of the economy, from steel production and road construction to sales and advertising. Put another way, by paying decent wages, producing cars at a reasonable price, and generating a demand for goods and commodities, he was turning America into a land of the middle class, rather than one of rich and poor, reinforcing or strengthening rather than undercutting it. Indeed, this is exactly the image that Ford portrayed of himself in his 1922 autobiography.

Henry Ford and His First Car, n.d. (Library of Congress).

But when the Great Depression struck, Ford's promise of high wages disappeared rapidly. No matter how low the cost of his cars, people still could not afford them, in part because the great wealth of the 1920s had never been well distributed. Ford, who had always adamantly opposed unions, grew bitter with those who challenged his power and paternalism. And his workers grew angry with him.

I will build a motor car for the great multitude. It will be large enough for the family but small enough for the individual to run and care for. It will be constructed of the best materials, by the best men to be hired, after the simplest designs that modern engineering can devise. But it will be so low in price that no man making a good salary will be unable to own one—and enjoy with his family the blessing of hours of pleasure in God's great open spaces.

This announcement was received not without pleasure. The general comment was:

"If Ford does that he will be out of business in six months."

The impression was that a good car could not be built at a low price, and that, anyhow, there was no use in building a low-priced car because only wealthy people were in the market for cars. The 1908–1909 sales of more than ten thousand cars had convinced me that we needed a new factory. We already had a big modern factory—the Piquette Street plant. It was as good as, perhaps a little better than, any automobile factory in the country. But I did not see how it was going to care for the sales and production that were inevitable. So I bought sixty acres at Highland Park, which was then considered away out in the country from Detroit. The amount of ground bought and the plans for a bigger factory than the world has ever seen were opposed. The question was already being asked:

"How soon will Ford blow up?"

Nobody knows how many thousand times it has been asked since. It is asked only because of the failure to grasp that a principle rather than an individual is at work, and the principle is so simple that it seems mysterious.

For 1909–1910, in order to pay for the new land and buildings, I slightly raised the prices. This is perfectly justifiable and results in a benefit, not an injury, to the purchaser. I did exactly the same thing a few years ago—or rather, in that case I did not lower the price as is my annual custom, in order to build the River Rouge plant. The extra money might in each case have been had by borrowing, but then we should have had a continuing charge upon the business and all subsequent cars would have had to bear this charge. The price of all the models was increased $100, with the exception of the roadster, which was increased only $75 and of the landaulet and town car, which were increased $150 and $200 respectively. We sold 18,664 cars, and then for 1910–1911, with the new facilities, I cut the touring car from $950 to $780 and we sold 34,528 cars. That is the beginning of the steady reduction in the price of the cars in the face of ever-increasing cost of materials and ever-higher wages.

Contrast the year 1908 with the year 1911. The factory space increased from 2.65 to 32 acres. The average number of employees from 1,908 to 4,110, and the cars built from a little over six thousand to nearly thirty-five thousand. You will note that men were not employed in proportion to the output.

We were, almost overnight it seems, in great production. How did all this come about?

Simply through the application of an inevitable principle. By the application of intelligently directed power and machinery. In a little dark shop on a side street an old man had laboured for years making axe handles. Out of seasoned hickory he fashioned them, with the help of a draw shave, a chisel, and a supply of sandpaper. Carefully was each handle weighed and balanced. No two of them were alike. The curve must exactly fit the hand and must conform to the grain of the wood. From dawn until dark the old man laboured. His average product was eight handles a week, for which he received a dollar and a half each. And often some of these were unsaleable—because the balance was not true.

To-day you can buy a better axe handle, made by machinery, for a few cents. And you need not worry about the balance. They are all alike—and every one is perfect. Modern methods applied in a big way have not only brought the cost of axe handles down to a fraction of their former cost—but they have immensely improved the product.

It was the application of these same methods to the making of the Ford car that at the very start lowered the price and heightened the quality. We just developed an idea. The nucleus of a business may be an idea. That is, an inventor or a thoughtful workman works out a new and better way to serve some established human need; the idea commends itself, and people want to avail themselves of it. In this way a single individual may prove, through his idea or discovery, the nucleus of a business. But the creation of the body and bulk of that business is shared by everyone who has anything to do with it. No manufacturer can say: "I built this business"—if he has required the help of thousands of men in building it. It is a joint production. Everyone employed in it has contributed something to it. By working and producing they make it possible for the purchasing world to keep coming to that business for the type of service it provides, and thus they help establish a custom, a trade, a habit which supplies them with a livelihood. That is the way our company grew and just how I shall start explaining in the next chapter. . . .

There is nothing to running a business by custom—to saying: "I pay the going rate of wages."

The same man would not so easily say: "I have nothing better or cheaper to sell than any one has." No manufacturer in his right mind would contend that buying only the cheapest materials is the way to make certain of manufacturing the best article. Then why do we hear so much talk about the "liquidation of labour" and the benefits that will flow to the country from cutting wages—which means only the cutting of buying power and the curtailing of the home market? What good is industry if it be so unskillfully managed as not to return a living to everyone concerned? No question is more important than that of wages—most of the people of the country live on wages. The scale of their living—the rate of their wages—determines the prosperity of the country.

Throughout all the Ford industries we now have a minimum wage of six dollars a day; we used to have a minimum of five dollars; before that we paid whatever it was necessary to pay. It would be bad morals to go back to the old market rate of paying—but also it would be the worst sort of bad business.

First get at the relationships. It is not usual to speak of an employee as a partner, and yet what else is he? Whenever a man finds the management of a business too much for his own time or strength, he calls in assistants to share the management with him. Why, then, if a man finds the production part of a business too much for his own two hands should he deny the title of "partner" to those who come in and help him produce? Every business that employs more than one man is a kind of partnership. The moment a man calls for assistance in his business—even though the assistant be but a boy—that moment he has taken a partner. He may himself be sole owner of the resources of the business and sole director of its operations, but only while he remains sole manager and sole producer can he claim complete independence. No man is independent as long as he has to depend on another man to help him. It is a reciprocal relation—the boss is the partner of his worker, the worker is partner of his boss. And such being the case, it is useless for one group or the other to assume that it is the one indispensable unit. Both are indispensable. The one can become unduly assertive only at the expense of the other—and eventually at its own expense as well. It is utterly foolish for Capital or for Labour to think of themselves as groups. They are partners. When they pull and haul against each other—they simply injure the organization in which they are partners and from which both draw support.

It ought to be the employer's ambition, as leader, to pay better wages than any similar line of business, and it ought to be the workman's ambition to make this possible. Of course there are men in all shops who seem to believe that if they do their best, it will be only for the employer's benefit— and not at all for their own. It is a pity that such a feeling should exist. But it does exist and perhaps it has some justification. If an employer urges men to do their best, and the men learn after a while that their best does not bring any reward, then they naturally drop back into "getting by." But if they see the fruits of hard work in their pay envelope—proof that harder work means higher pay—then also they begin to learn that they are a part of the business, and that its success depends on them and their success depends on it.

"What ought the employer to pay?"—"What ought the employee to receive?" These are but minor questions. The basic question is "What can the business stand?" Certainly no business can stand outgo that exceeds its income. When you pump water out of a well at a faster rate than the water flows in, the well goes dry. And when the well runs dry, those who depend on it go thirsty. And if, perchance, they imagine they can pump one well dry and then jump to some other well, it is only a matter of time when all the wells will be dry. There is now a widespread demand for more justly divided rewards, but it must be recognized that there are limits to rewards. The business itself sets the limits. You cannot distribute $150,000 out of a business that brings in only $100,000. The business limits the wages, but does anything limit the business? The business limits itself by following bad precedents.

If men, instead of saying "the employer ought to do thus-and-so," would say, "the business ought to be so stimulated and managed that it can do thus-and-so," they would get somewhere. Because only the business can pay wages. Certainly the employer cannot, unless the business warrants. But if that business does warrant higher wages and the employer refuses, what is to be done? As a rule a business means the livelihood of too many men, to be tampered with. It is criminal to assassinate a business to which large numbers of men have given their labours and to which they have learned to look as their field of usefulness and their source of livelihood. Killing the business by a strike or a lockout does not help. The employer can gain nothing by looking over the employees and asking himself, "How little can I get them to take?" Nor the employee by glaring back and asking, "How much can I force him to give?" Eventually both will have to turn to the business and ask, "How can this industry be made safe and profitable, so that it will be able to provide a sure and comfortable living for all of us?"

But by no means all employers or all employees will think straight. The habit of acting shortsightedly is a hard one to break. What can be done? Nothing. No rules or laws will effect the changes. But enlightened self-interest will. It takes a little while for enlightenment to spread. But spread it must, for the concern in which both employer and employees work to the same end of service is bound to forge ahead in business.

What do we mean by high wages, anyway?

We mean a higher wage than was paid ten months or ten years ago. We do not mean a higher wage than ought to be paid. Our high wages of to-day may be low wages ten years from now.

If it is right for the manager of a business to try to make it pay larger dividends, it is quite as right that he should try to make it pay higher wages. But it is not the manager of the business who pays the high wages. Of course, if he can and will not, then the blame is on him. But he alone can never make high wages possible. High wages cannot be paid unless the workmen earn them. Their labour is the productive factor. It is not the only productive factor—poor management can waste labour and material and nullify the efforts of labour. Labour can nullify the results of good management. But in a partnership of skilled management and honest labour, it is the workman who makes high wages possible. He invests his energy and skill, and if he makes an honest, wholehearted investment, high wages ought to be his reward. Not only has he earned them, but he has had a big part in creating them.

Source: Henry Ford, *My Life and Work* (Garden City, N.Y., 1922), pp. 73–76, 116–17.

For Further Reading:

James J. Flink, *The Car Culture* (Cambridge, Mass.: MIT Press, 1975).
Robert Lacey, *Ford, the Men and the Machine* (Boston: Little, Brown, 1986).
George Soule, *Prosperity Decade* (Armonk, N.Y.: M. E. Sharp, 1975).

70. Oscar Ameringer, "Testimony on Unemployment" (1932)

1929   Stock Market crash
1932–33   "The Cruelest Year"

In 1929 the New York Stock Market crashed, ushering in the worst depression in the nation's history. Unemployment skyrocketed, to above 25 percent in 1932–33, and remained above 15 percent through most of the 1930s. Industrial production and personal income declined precipitously, while hopelessness, bread lines, and bank failures rose to unprecedented heights. Among those who were particularly hard hit by the Depression were American farmers. In addition to low prices, farmers on the plains faced great dust storms. Fertile fields were turned into wastelands, farmers into scavengers.

Though most individuals initially blamed themselves for their plight, in time they cried out against the nation's political leadership and the wealthy. The following testimony by Oscar Ameringer, a newspaper editor from Oklahoma City, to a congressional subcommittee on labor, provides a sense of the nation's mood during its "cruelest year," 1932–33.

Ameringer was not alone in describing the mood of the people in such bleak terms. Novelists such as John Steinbeck painted a similar picture in their Depression-era works. So, too, did photographers like Dorothea Lange. Still, these same intellectuals remained somewhat optimistic about the nation's prospects. They felt this way, in part, because of their faith in the basic goodness of the average man or the folk they trusted to overcome adversity. This view marked a shift from the 1920s, when intellectuals felt divorced from the people and lost faith in the common man as the basis for democracy.

During the last three months I have visited, as I have said, some twenty states of this wonderfully rich and beautiful country. Here are some of the things I heard and saw:

In the state of Washington I was told that the forest fires raging in that region all summer and fall were caused by unemployed timber workers and bankrupt farmers in an endeavor to earn a few honest dollars as firefighters. The last thing I saw on the night I left Seattle was numbers of women searching for scraps of food in the refuse piles of the principal market of that city. A number of Montana citizens told me of thousands of bushels of wheat left in the fields uncut on account of its low price that hardly paid for the

"Children in a Democracy." Photograph by Dorothea Lange, November 1940 (National Archives).

harvesting. In Oregon I saw thousands of bushels of apples rotting in the orchards. Only absolute[ly] flawless apples were still salable, at from 40 to 50 cents a box containing 200 apples. At the same time, there are millions of children who, on account of the poverty of their parents, will not eat one apple this winter.

While I was in Oregon the Portland *Oregonian* bemoaned the fact that thousands of ewes were killed by the sheep raisers because they did not bring enough in the market to pay the freight on them. And while Oregon sheep raisers fed mutton to the buzzards, I saw men picking for meat scraps in the garbage cans in the cities of New York and Chicago. I talked to one man in a restaurant in Chicago. He told me of his experience in raising sheep. He said that he had killed 3,000 sheep this fall and thrown them down the canyon, because it cost $1.10 to ship a sheep, and then he would get less than a dollar for it. He said he could not afford to feed the sheep, and he would not let them starve, so he just cut their throats and threw them down the canyon.

The roads of the West and Southwest teem with hungry hitchhikers. The camp fires of the homeless are seen along every railroad track. I saw men, women, and children walking over the hard roads. Most of them were tenant farmers who had lost their all in the late slump in wheat and cotton. Between Clarksville and Russellville, Ark., I picked up a family. The woman was hugging a dead chicken under a ragged coat. When I asked her where she had procured the fowl, first she told me she had found it dead in the road, and then added in grim humor, "They promised me a chicken in the pot, and now I got mine."

In Oklahoma, Texas, Arkansas, and Louisiana I saw untold bales of cotton rotting in the fields because the cotton pickers could not keep body and soul together on 35 cents paid for picking 100 pounds. . . .

As a result of this appalling overproduction on the one side and the staggering underconsumption on the other side, 70 per cent of the farmers of Oklahoma were unable to pay the interests on their mortgages. Last week one of the largest and oldest mortgage companies in that state went into the hands of the receiver. In that and other states we have now the interesting spectacle of farmers losing their farms by foreclosure and mortgage companies losing their recouped holdings by tax sales.

The farmers are being pauperized by the poverty of industrial populations, and the industrial populations are being pauperized by the poverty of the farmers. Neither has the money to buy the product of the other, hence we have overproduction and underconsumption at the same time and in the same country.

I have not come here to stir you in a recital of the necessity for relief for our suffering fellow citizens. However, unless something is done for them and done soon, you will have a revolution on hand. And when that revolution comes it will not come from Moscow, it will not be made by the poor Communists whom our police are heading up regularly and efficiently. When the revolution comes it will bear the label "Laid in the U.S.A." and its chief promoters will be the people of American stock. . . .

Some time ago a cowman came into my office in Oklahoma City. He was one of these double-fisted gentlemen, with the gallon hat and all. He said, "You do not know me from Adam's ox."

I said, "No; I do not believe I know you." . . .

He said, "I came to this country without a cent, but, knowing my onions, and by tending strictly to business, I finally accumulated two sections of land and a fine herd of white-faced Hereford cattle. I was independent."

I remarked that anybody could do that if he worked hard and did not gamble and used good management.

He said, "After the war, cattle began to drop, and I was feeding them corn, and by the time I got them to Chicago the price of cattle, considering the price of corn I had fed them, was not enough to even pay my expenses. I could not pay anything."

Continuing, he said, "I mortgaged my two sections of land, and to-day I am cleaned out; by God, I am not going to stand for it."

I asked him what he was going to do about it, and he said, "We have got to have a revolution here like they had in Russia and clean them up."

I finally asked him, "Who is going to make the revolution?"

He said, "I just want to tell you I am going to be one of them, and I am going to do my share in it."

I asked what his share was and he said, "I will capture a certain fort. I know I can get in with twenty of my boys," meaning his cowboys, "because I know the inside and outside of it, and I [will] capture that with my men."

I rejoined, "Then what?"

He said, "We will have 400 machine guns, so many batteries of artillery, tractors, and munitions and rifles, and everything else needed to supply a pretty good army."

Then I asked, "What then?"

He said, "If there are enough fellows with guts in this country to do like us, we will march eastward and we will cut the East off. We will cut the East off from the West. We have got the granaries; we have the hogs, the cattle, the corn; the East has nothing but mortgages on our places. We will show them what we can do."

That man may be very foolish, and I think he is, but he is in dead earnest; he is a hard-shelled Baptist and a hard-shelled Democrat, not a Socialist or a Communist, but just a plain American cattleman whose ancestors went from Carolina to Tennessee, then to Arkansas, and then to Oklahoma. I have heard much of this talk from serious-minded prosperous men of other days.

As you know, talk is always a mental preparation for action. Nothing is done until people talk and talk and talk it, and they finally get the notion that they will do it.

I do not say we are going to have a revolution on hand within the next year or two, perhaps never. I hope we may not have such; but the danger is here. That is the feeling of our people—as reflected in the letters I have read. I have met these people virtually every day all over the country. There is a feeling among the masses generally that something is radically wrong. They are despairing of political action. They say the only thing you do in Washington is to take money from the pockets of the poor and put it into the pockets of the rich. They say that this Government is a conspiracy against the common people to enrich the already rich. I hear such remarks every day.

I never pass a hitchhiker without inviting him in and talking to him. Bankers even are talking about that. They are talking in irrational tones. You have more Bolshevism among the bankers to-day than the hod carriers, I think. It is a terrible situation, and I think something should be done and done immediately.

Source: *Unemployment in the United States. Hearings before a subcommittee of the Committee on Labor, House of Representatives, Seventy-Second Congress, First Session* (1932), pp. 98–101.

For Further Reading:

Caroline Bird, *The Invisible Scar* (New York: Longman, 1966).
Richard H. Pells, *Radical Visions and American Dreams* (New York: Harper & Row, 1973).
Donald Worster, *Dust Bowl* (New York: Oxford University Press, 1979).

71. Franklin Delano Roosevelt, Excerpt from "First Inaugural Address" (1933)

1920   Democratic Party nominates Franklin Roosevelt for vice-presidency
1921   Roosevelt contracts polio
1928   Roosevelt elected governor of New York
1932   Roosevelt elected President, defeating Herbert Hoover
1933   First hundred days

Franklin Delano Roosevelt came from a distinguished upstate New York family, made more famous by his distant cousin Teddy Roosevelt. Franklin grew up in comfort, attended the right schools, and then enjoyed a meteoric rise in his chosen career of politics. Then, after receiving the Democratic Party's nomination for the vice-presidency, in 1920, as James Cox's running mate, tragedy struck. In the summer of 1921, while vacationing he contracted polio. He never regained full use of his legs.

Yet Roosevelt refused to let the disease cripple his life. In the late 1920s he made a remarkable political comeback, becoming governor of New York in 1928 and then winning the Democratic Party's presidential nomination in 1932. Campaigning on the promise to bring America a New Deal, FDR easily defeated Herbert Hoover and then, while the nation sank deeper and deeper into economic despair, awaited his March inauguration and what he called his "rendezvous with destiny."

FDR's inaugural address was one of the most memorable ever delivered. In it the new President sought to restore the nation's confidence in itself and its leadership, uttering the famous words "The only thing we have to fear is fear itself." Then FDR assured the public that he would act, adopting extraordinary powers if necessary, to combat the economic disaster. In the first hundred days of his presidency he enacted tens of significant pieces of legislation, ranging from the Emergency Banking Bill to massive federal relief appropriations. Nothing like it had ever been seen before. His willingness to act, combined with his ability to communicate, endeared him to the American people.

Inauguration of Franklin Delano Roosevelt, March 4, 1933 (Library of Congress).

This is a day of national consecration, and I am certain that my fellow-Americans expect that on my induction into the Presidency I will address them with a candor and a decision which the present situation of our nation impels. This is pre-eminently the time to speak the truth, the whole truth, frankly and boldly. Nor need we shrink from honestly facing conditions in our country today. This great nation will endure as it has endured, will revive and will prosper.

So first of all let me assert my firm belief that the only thing we have to fear is fear itself—nameless, unreasoning, unjustified terror which paralyzes needed efforts to convert retreat into advance. In every dark hour of our national life a leadership of frankness and vigor has met with that understanding and support of the people themselves which is essential to victory. I am convinced that you will again give that support to leadership in these critical days.

In such a spirit on my part and on yours we face our common difficulties. They concern, thank God, only material things. Values have shrunken to fantastic levels; taxes have risen; our ability to pay has fallen; government of all kinds is faced by serious curtailment of income; the means of exchange are frozen in the currents of trade; the withered leaves of industrial enterprise lie on every side; farmers find no markets for their produce; the savings of many years in thousands of families are gone.

More important, a host of unemployed citizens face the grim problem of existence, and an equally great number toil with little return. Only a foolish optimist can deny the dark realities of the moment.

Yet our distress comes from no failure of substance. We are stricken by no plague of locusts. Compared with the perils which our forefathers conquered because they believed and were not afraid, we have still much to be thankful for. Nature still offers her bounty and human efforts have multiplied it. Plenty is at our doorstep, but a generous use of it languishes in the very sight of the supply. Primarily, this is because the rulers of the exchange of mankind's goods have failed through their own stubbornness and their own incompetence, have admitted their failure and abdicated. Practices of the unscrupulous money changers stand indicted in the court of public opinion, rejected by the hearts and minds of men.

True, they have tried, but their efforts have been cast in the pattern of an outworn tradition. Faced by failure of credit, they have proposed only the lending of more money. Stripped of the lure of profit by which to induce our people to follow their false leadership, they have resorted to exhortations, pleading tearfully for restored confidence. They know only the rules of a generation of self-seekers. They have no vision, and when there is no vision the people perish.

The money changers have fled from their high seats in the temple of our civilization. We may now restore that temple to the ancient truths. The measure of the restoration lies in the extent to which we apply social values more noble than mere monetary profit.

Happiness lies not in the mere possession of money; it lies in the joy of achievement, in the thrill of creative effort. The joy and moral stimulation of work no longer must be forgotten in the mad chase of evanescent profits. These dark days will be worth all they cost us if they teach us that our true destiny is not to be ministered unto but to minister to ourselves and to our fellow-men.

Recognition of the falsity of material wealth as the standard of success goes hand in hand with the abandonment of the false belief that public office and high political position are to be valued only by the standards of pride of place and personal profit; and there must be an end to a conduct in banking and in business which too often has given to a sacred trust the likeness of callous and selfish wrongdoing. Small wonder that confidence languishes, for it thrives only on honesty, on honor, on the sacredness of obligations, on faithful protection, on unselfish performance. Without them it cannot live.

Restoration calls, however, not for changes in ethics alone. This nation asks for action, and action now.

Our greatest primary task is to put people to work. This is no unsolvable problem if we face it wisely and courageously. It can be accomplished in part by direct recruiting by the Government itself, treating the task as we would treat the emergency of war, but at the same time, through this employment, accomplishing greatly needed projects to stimulate and reorganize the use of our natural resources.

Hand in hand with this, we must frankly recognize the overbalance of population in our industrial centers and, by engaging on a national scale in the redistribution, endeavor to provide a better use of the land for those best fitted for the land. The task can be helped by definite efforts to raise the values of agricultural products and with this the power to purchase the output of our cities. It can be helped by preventing realistically the tragedy of the growing loss, through foreclosure, of our small homes and our farms. It can be helped by insistence that the Federal, State and local governments act forthwith on the demand that their cost be drastically reduced. It can be helped by the unifying of relief activities which today are often scattered, uneconomical and unequal. It can be helped by national planning for a supervision of all forms of transportation and of communications and other utilities which have a definitely public character. There are many ways in which it can be helped, but it can never be helped merely by talking about it. We must act, and act quickly. . . .

. . . This I propose to offer, pledging that the larger purposes will bind upon us all as a sacred obligation with a unity of duty hitherto evoked only in the time of armed strife.

With this pledge taken, I assume unhesitatingly the leadership of this great army of our people, dedicated to a disciplined attack upon our common problems.

Action in this image and to this end is feasible under the form of government which we have inherited from our ancestors. Our Constitution is so simple and practical that it is possible always to meet extraordinary needs by changes in emphasis and arrangement without loss of essential form. That is why our constitutional system has proved itself the most superbly enduring political mechanism the modern world has produced. It has met every stress of vast expansion of territory, of foreign wars, of bitter internal strife, of world relations.

It is to be hoped that the normal balance of executive and legislative authority may be wholly adequate to meet the unprecedented task before us. But it may be that an unprecedented demand and need for undelayed action may call for temporary departure from that normal balance of public procedure.

I am prepared under my constitutional duty to recommend the measures that a stricken nation in the midst of a stricken world may require. These measures, or such other measures as the Congress may build out of its experience and wisdom, I shall seek, within my constitutional authority, to bring to speedy adoption.

But in the event that the Congress shall fail to take one of these two courses, and in the event that the national emergency is still critical, I shall not evade the clear course of duty that will then confront me. I shall ask the Congress for the one remaining instrument to meet the crisis—broad Executive power to wage a war against the emergency as great as the power that would be given me if we were in fact invaded by a foreign foe.

For the trust reposed in me I will return the courage and the devotion that befit the time. I can do no less.

Source: *New York Times*, March 5, 1933.

For Further Reading:

William Leuchtenburg, *Franklin D. Roosevelt and the New Deal, 1932–1940* (New York: Harper & Row, 1963).

Arthur Schlesinger, Jr., *The Age of Roosevelt*, 3 vols. (Boston: Houghton Mifflin, 1957–60).

72. Frances Perkins, Excerpt from "Radio Address on Social Security" (1935)

1933   Frances Perkins appointed Secretary of Labor
1935   Social Security Act; Works Progress Administration
1938   Fair Labor Standards Act

The New Deal entailed the passage of tens of laws or programs aimed at providing relief, recovery, and reform. The Works Progress Administration or WPA, created in 1935 to supplant earlier New Deal relief measures, provided work to over 8 million Americans. The Agricultural Adjustment Act or AAA addressed the problem of overproduction by farmers. The Banking and Securities Exchange Acts sought to bolster America's financial system.

The single piece of New Deal legislation that has had the most lasting

Migrant Mother, Nipomo, Calif., 1936. Photograph by Dorothea Lange (Library of Congress).

impact was the Social Security Act. Although not an emergency measure, without the Great Depression it is not likely that it would have been enacted. Yet President Roosevelt used the economic crisis as an opportunity to push what was a long-sought progressive reform through Congress. Nearly sixty years later Social Security still stands as the most important source of income for the elderly and insurance for the disabled. Furthermore, the creation of Social Security symbolized the federal government's recognition that it has a responsibility to provide at least a modicum of security to all its citizens. Indeed, even though the original Social Security Act was quite limited— million were not covered, the benefits were small, and there was no health insurance—it showed that henceforth the federal government would pay heed to the words of the preamble of the Constitution, to provide for the welfare of its people.

Franklin Roosevelt's Secretary of Labor, Frances Perkins, the first woman cabinet member in American history, played a crucial role in getting the Social Security Act enacted. A longtime social reformer and associate of Roosevelt, she fought for about a quarter of a century for some form of governmental protection against the dangers of work and the fragility of old age. In addition to Social Security she helped push through the Fair Labor Standards Act, which prohibited child labor and established minimum wages and working conditions. She also wrote one of the first and best insider accounts of the New Deal.

P eople who work for a living in the United States of America can join with all other good citizens on this forty-eighth anniversary of Labor Day in satisfaction that the Congress has passed the Social Security Act. This act establishes unemployment insurance as a substitute for haphazard methods of assistance in periods when men and women willing and able to work are without jobs. It provides for old-age pensions which mark great progress over the measures upon which we have hitherto depended in caring for those who have been unable to provide for the years when they no longer can work. It also provides security for dependent and crippled children, mothers, the indigent disabled and the blind.

Old people who are in need, unemployables, children, mothers and the sightless, will find systematic regular provisions for needs. The Act limits the Federal aid to not more than $15 per month for the individual, provided the State in which he resides appropriates a like amount. There is nothing to prevent a State from contributing more than $15 per month in special cases and there is no requirement to allow as much as $15 from either State or Federal funds when a particular case has some personal provision and needs less than the total allowed.

Following essentially the same procedure, the Act as passed provides for Federal assistance to the States in caring for the blind, a contribution by the States of up to $15 a month to be matched in turn by a like contribution by the Federal Government. The Act also contains provision for assistance to the States in providing payments to dependent children under sixteen years of age. There also is provision in the Act for cooperation with medical and health organizations charged with rehabilitation of physically handicapped children. The necessity for adequate service in the fields of public and maternal health and child welfare calls for the extension of these services to meet individual community needs.

Consider for a moment those portions of the Act which, while they will not be effective this present year, yet will exert a profound and far-reaching effect upon millions of citizens. I refer to the provision for a system of old-age benefits supported by the contributions of employer and employees, and to the section which sets up the initial machinery for unemployment insurance.

Old-age benefits in the form of monthly payments are to be paid to individuals who have worked and contributed to the insurance fund in direct proportion to the total wages earned by such individuals in the course of their employment subsequent to 1936. The minimum monthly payment is to be $10, the maximum $85. These payments will begin in the year 1942 and will be to those who have worked and contributed. . . .

Federal legislation was framed in the thought that the attack upon the problems of insecurity should be a cooperative venture participated in by both the Federal and State Governments, preserving the benefits of local administration and national leadership. It was thought unwise to have the Federal Government decide all questions of policy and dictate completely what the States should do. Only very necessary minimum standards are included in the Federal measure leaving wide latitude to the States. . . .

The social security measure looks primarily to the future and is only a part of the administration's plan to promote sound and stable economic life. We cannot think of it as disassociated from the Government's program to save the homes, the farms, the businesses and banks of the Nation, and especially must we consider it a companion measure to the Works Relief Act which does undertake to provide immediate increase in employment and corresponding stimulation to private industry by purchase of supplies.

While it is not anticipated as a complete remedy for the abnormal conditions confronting us at the present time, it is designed to afford protection for the individual against future major economic vicissitudes. . . .

Our social security program will be a vital force working against the recurrence of severe depressions in the future. We can, as the principle of sustained purchasing power in hard times makes itself felt in every shop, store and mill, grow old without being haunted by the spectre of a poverty-ridden old age or of being a burden on our children. . . .

The passage of this act with so few dissenting votes and with so much intelligent public support is deeply significant of the progress which the American people have made in thought in the social field and awareness of methods of using cooperation through government to overcome social hazards against which the individual alone is inadequate.

Source: *Vital Speeches*, Vol. I, No. 25, (September 9, 1935), p. 792.

For Further Reading:

Paul Conkin, *The New Deal*, 2d ed. (Arlington Heights, Va.: Harlan Davidson, 1975).
Roy Lubove, *The Struggle for Social Security* (Cambridge, Mass.: Harvard University Press, 1968).
Frances Perkins, *The Roosevelt I Knew* (New York: Viking, 1946).

73. Huey Long, Excerpt from "Every Man a King" (1934)

1928   Huey Long elected governor of Louisiana
1932   Long elected to U.S. Senate
1932–35   Long promotes "Share Our Wealth Plan"
1935   Long assassinated

Although he was elected President an unprecedented four times, Franklin D. Roosevelt had his share of critics and rivals. On the right, the American Liberty League accused FDR of taking the nation down the road of socialism. On the left, socialists and communists chastised the President for his timidity, especially when it came to the civil rights of African Americans. But FDR's most significant critic was neither a right-wing conservative nor a socialist, he was Huey P. Long.

Nicknamed the "Kingfish" after a character on the famous "Amos 'n Andy" radio program, Long built up a powerful political machine in Louisiana as governor from 1928 to 1932. Then as a Senator he won a national following by calling for an implementation of his "Share Our Wealth Plan." While the details of this program varied, its message was clear. Long considered the maldistribution of wealth to be the nation's primary problem, and he proposed ending the Depression through a program of high taxes on the wealthy and a guaranteed income or dignity for all—thus the slogan "Every Man a King." Long spelled out his program in a series of addresses to Congress, including one entitled "Every Man a King."

Although Long cast himself as a buffoon, he was a very intelligent and ruthless politician. By unofficially allying himself with Father Charles Coughlin, the so-called radio priest, who demanded monetary reform and railed at the financial elite, Long put himself in a position to challenge Roosevelt in 1936 or at least in 1940. FDR responded to Long's threat by stealing some of his thunder via the Wealth Tax and Social Security Acts. But most political pundits believe that if Long had not been assassinated in 1935 (by the son of a state employee who had lost his job because of his opposition to Long's programs in the state of Louisiana), he would have won a significant number of votes as an independent candidate in 1936 and perhaps even defeated FDR in 1940.

I contend, my friends, that we have no difficult problem to solve in America, and that is the view of nearly everyone with whom I have discussed

Photograph by Dorothea Lange (National Archives).

the matter here in Washington and elsewhere throughout the United States—that we have no very difficult problem to solve.

It is not the difficulty of the problem which we have; it is the fact that the rich people of this country—and by rich people I mean the superrich—will not allow us to solve the problems, or rather the one little problem that is afflicting this country, because in order to cure all of our woes it is necessary to scale down the big fortunes, that we may scatter the wealth to be shared by all of the people. . . .

How many of you remember the first thing that the Declaration of Independence said? It said, "We hold these truths to be self-evident, that there are certain inalienable rights for the people, and among them are life, liberty, and the pursuit of happiness"; and it said, further, "We hold the view that all men are created equal."

Now, what did they mean by that? Did they mean, my friends, to say that all men were created equal and that that meant that any one man was born to inherit $10 billion and that another child was to be born to inherit nothing?

Did that mean, my friends, that someone would come into this world without having had an opportunity, of course, to have hit one lick of work, should be born with more than it and all of its children and children's children could ever dispose of, but that another one would have to be born into a life of starvation?

That was not the meaning of the Declaration of Independence when it said that all men are created equal or "That we hold that all men are created equal."

Nor was it the meaning of the Declaration of Independence when it said that they held that there were certain rights that were inalienable—the right of life, liberty, and the pursuit of happiness.

Is that right of life, my friends, when the young children of this country are being reared into a sphere which is more owned by 12 men than it is by 120 million people?

Is that, my friends, giving them a fair shake of the dice or anything like the inalienable right of life, liberty, and the pursuit of happiness, or anything resembling the fact that all people are created equal; when we have today in America thousands and hundreds of thousands and millions of children on the verge of starvation in a land that is overflowing with too much to eat and too much to wear?

I do not think you will contend that, and I do not think for a moment that they will contend it. . . .

We have in America today more wealth, more goods, more food, more clothing, more houses than we have ever had. We have everything in abundance here.

We have the farm problem, my friends, because we have too much cotton, because we have too much wheat, and have too much corn, and too much potatoes.

We have a home-loan problem because we have too many houses, and yet nobody can buy them and live in them.

We have trouble, my friends, in the country, because we have too much money owing, the greatest indebtedness that has ever been given to civilization, where it has been shown that we are incapable of distributing the actual things that are here, because the people have not money enough to supply themselves with them, and because the greed of a few men is such that they think it is necessary that they own everything, and their pleasure consists in the starvation of the masses, and in their possessing things they cannot use, and their children cannot use, but who bask in the splendor of sunlight and wealth, casting darkness and despair and impressing it on every-one else. . . .

Now, my friends, if you were off on an island where there were 100 lunches, you could not let one man eat up the hundred lunches, or take the hundred lunches and not let anybody else eat any of them. If you did, there would not be anything else for the balance of the people to consume.

So, we have in America today, my friends, a condition by which about 10 men dominate the means of activity in at least 85 percent of the activities that you own. They either own directly everything or they have got some kind of mortgage on it, with a very small percentage to be excepted. They own the banks, they own the steel mills, they own the railroads, they own the bonds, they own the mortgages, they own the stores, and they have chained the country from one end to the other until there is not any kind of business that a small, independent man could go into today and make a living, and there is not any kind of business that an independent man can go into and make any money to buy an automobile with; and they have finally and gradually and steadily eliminated everybody from the fields in which there is a living to be made, and still they have got little enough sense to think they ought to be able to get more business out of it anyway.

If you reduce a man to the point where he is starving to death and bleeding and dying, how do you expect that man to get hold of any money to spend with you? It is not possible.

Then, ladies and gentlemen, how do you expect people to live, when the wherewith cannot be had by the people? . . .

Both of these men, Mr. Hoover and Mr. Roosevelt, came out and said there had to be a decentralization of wealth, but neither one of them did anything about it. But, nevertheless, they recognized the principle. The fact that neither one of them ever did anything about it is their own problem that I am not undertaking to criticize; but had Mr. Hoover carried out what he says ought to be done, he would be retiring from the President's office, very probably, three years from now, instead of one year ago; and had Mr. Roosevelt proceeded along the lines that he stated were necessary for the decentralization of wealth, he would have gone, my friends, a long way already, and within a few months he would have probably reached a solution of all of the problems that afflict this country today.

But I wish to warn you now that nothing that has been done up to this date has taken one dime away from these big-fortune holders; they own just as much as they did, and probably a little bit more; they hold just as many of the debts of the common people as they ever held, and probably a little bit more; and unless we, my friends, are going to give the people of this country a fair shake of the dice, by which they will all get something out of the funds of this land, there is not a chance on the topside of this God's eternal earth by which we can rescue this country and rescue the people of this country.

It is necessary to save the Government of the country, but is much more necessary to save the people of America. We love this country. We love this Government. It is a religion, I say. It is a kind of religion people have read of when women, in the name of religion, would take their infant babes and throw them into the burning flame, where they would be instantly devoured by the all-consuming fire, in days gone by; and there probably are some people of the world even today, who, in the name of religion, throw their own babes to destruction; but in the name of our good Government people today are seeing their own children hungry, tired, half-naked, lifting their tear-dimmed eyes into the sad faces of their fathers and mothers, who cannot give them food and clothing they both needed, and which is necessary to sustain them, and that goes on day after day, and night after night, when day gets into darkness and blackness, knowing those children would arise in the morning without being fed, and probably go to bed at night without being fed.

Yet in the name of our Government, and all alone, those people undertake and strive as hard as they can to keep a good government alive, and how long they can stand that no one knows. If I were in their place tonight, the place where millions are, I hope that I would have what I might say—I cannot give you the word to express the kind of fortitude they have; that is the word—I hope that I might have the fortitude to praise and honor my Government that had allowed me here in this land, where there is too much to eat and too much to wear, to starve in order that a handful of men can have so much more than they can ever eat or they can ever wear.

Now, we have organized a society, and we call it share-our-wealth society, a society with the motto "Every man a king."

Every man a king, so there would be no such thing as a man or woman who did not have the necessities of life, who would not be dependent upon the whims and caprices and ipsi dixit of the financial martyrs for a living. What do we propose by this society? We propose to limit the wealth of big men in the country. There is an average of $15,000 in wealth to every family in America. That is right here today.

We do not propose to divide it up equally. We do not propose a division of wealth, but we propose to limit poverty that we will allow to be inflicted upon any man's family. We will not say we are going to try to guarantee any equality, or $15,000 to families. No; but we do say that one third of the average is low enough for any one family to hold, that there should be a guaranty of a family wealth of around $5,000; enough for a home, an automobile, a radio, and the ordinary conveniences, and the opportunity to educate their children; a fair share of the income of this land thereafter to that family so there will be no such thing as merely the select to have those things, and so there will be no such thing as a family living in poverty and distress.

We have to limit fortunes. Our present plan is that we will allow no one man to own more than $50 million. We think that with that limit we will be able to carry out the balance of the program. It may be necessary that we limit it to less than $50 million. It may be necessary, in working out of the plans, that no man's fortune would be more than $10 million or $15 million. But be that as it may, it will still be more than any one man, or any one man and his children and their children, will be able to spend in their lifetimes; and it is not necessary or reasonable to have wealth piled up beyond that point where we cannot prevent poverty among the masses.

Another thing we propose is [an] old-age pension of $30 a month for everyone that is 60 years old. Now, we do not give this pension to a man making $1,000 a year, and we do not give it to him if he has $10,000 in property, but outside of that we do.

We will limit hours of work. There is not any necessity of having over-production. . . .

We will not have any trouble taking care of the agricultural situation. All you have to do is balance your production with your consumption. You simply have to abandon a particular crop that you have too much of, and all you have to do is store the surplus for the next year, and the Government will take it over. . . .

Those are the things we propose to do. "Every man a king." Every man to eat when there is something to eat; all to wear something when there is something to wear. That makes us all a sovereign. . . .

Get together in your community tonight or tomorrow and organize one of our share-our-wealth societies. If you do not understand it, write me and let me send you the platform; let me give you the proof of it.

This is Huey P. Long talking, United States Senator, Washington, D.C. Write me and let me send you the data on this proposition. Enroll with us. Let us make known to the people what we are going to do. I will send you a button, if I have got enough of them left. We have got a little button that some of our friends designed, with our message around the rim of the button, and in the center "Every man a king." Many thousands of them are meeting through the United States, and every day we are getting hundreds and hundreds of letters. Share-our-wealth societies are now being organized, and people have it within their power to relieve themselves from this terrible situation.

Look at what the Mayo brothers announced this week, these greatest scientists of all the world today, who are entitled to have more money than all the Morgans and the Rockefellers, or anyone else, and yet the Mayos turn back their big fortunes to be used for treating the sick, and said they did not want to lay up fortunes in this earth, but wanted to turn them back where they would do some good; but the other big capitalists are not willing to do that, are not willing to do what these men, 10 times more worthy, have already done, and it is going to take a law to require them to do it.

Source: *Congressional Record*, 73rd Cong., 2d Sess., p. 3450.

For Further Reading:

Alan Brinkley, *Voices of Protest* (New York: Knopf, 1982).
T. Harry Williams, *Huey Long* (New York: Knopf, 1969).

74. John L. Lewis, Excerpt from "Guests at Labor's Table" (1937)

1933–34 Militant strikes in San Francisco, Minneapolis,
         Toledo
1935   Wagner Act enacted; Committee of Industrial
         Organizations (CIO) formed
1936–37 CIO splits with American Federation of Labor
         (AFL); CIO organizes steel, auto, and other mass
         industries

The Great Depression hit factory workers hard, with unemployment running around 50 percent in many industrial communities. At first workers tended to blame themselves for their troubles. But as the 1930s progressed, they joined together and turned their anger on their employers. Indeed, from San Francisco to Minneapolis, workers displayed a newfound militancy.

The passage of the Wagner Act in 1935 (which granted unions the right to bargain collectively and outlawed certain anti-union tactics) and the birth of the CIO, first as a committee within the AFL and then as a separate labor federation, added to labor's militancy. Workers were further aided by the able leadership of John L. Lewis, president of the United Mineworkers and head of the CIO. Then, beginning in December 1936, autoworkers staged a sitdown strike against General Motors. After three long months off the job, they won union recognition from the largest employer in the world, which, in turn, inspired thousands of other workers to stage a sitdown. The strike also convinced the U.S. Steel Corporation, one of the biggest corporations in America and one of the oldest union foes, to sign a contract with the United Steel Workers to avoid a strike.

Yet so-called Little Steel, the name given to several of the smaller non-union steel companies, remained committed to fending off labor's surge. They hired strikebreakers and goons to defeat the labor movement, culminating with a clash near Republic Steel's south Chicago mill, known as the Memorial Day Massacre, in which ten men and women were shot to death and many more were wounded. After the massacre, John L. Lewis lashed out at Little Steel in a public radio address. Part of his speech dealt with

Ford Workers Battle with Police, March 1932 (National Archives).

the company's claim that unions were undemocratic and un-American. On the contrary, Lewis proclaimed, workers simply wanted a more democratic workplace and decent wages and conditions. It was employers who used undemocratic means to maintain un-American conditions.

Out of the agony and travail of economic America the Committee for Industrial Organization was born. To millions of Americans, exploited without stint by corporate industry and socially debased beyond the understanding of the fortunate, its coming was as welcome as the dawn to the night watcher. To a lesser group of Americans, infinitely more fortunately situated, blessed with larger quantities of the world's goods and insolent in their assumption of privilege, its coming was heralded as a harbinger of ill, sinister of purpose, of unclean methods and non-virtuous objectives.

But the Committee for Industrial Organization is here. It is now and henceforth a definite instrumentality, destined greatly to influence the lives of our people and the internal and external course of the Republic.

This is true only because the purpose and objectives of the Committee for Industrial Organization find economic, social, political and moral justification in the hearts of the millions who are its members and the millions more who support it. The organization and constant onward sweep of this movement exemplifies the resentment of the many toward the selfishness, greed and the neglect of the few. The workers of the nation were tired of waiting for corporate industry to right their economic wrongs, to alleviate their social agony and to grant them their political rights. Despairing of fair treatment, they resolved to do something for themselves. They, therefore, have organized a new labor movement, conceived within the principles of the national bill of rights and committed to the proposition that the workers are free to assemble in their own forums, voice their own grievances, declare their own hopes and contract on even terms with modern industry for the sale of their only material possession—their labor. . . .

Labor does not seek industrial strife. It wants peace, but a peace with justice. In the long struggle for labor's rights it has been patient and forbearing. Sabotage and destructive syndicalism have had no part in the American labor movement. Workers have kept faith in American institutions. Most of the conflicts which have occurred have been when labor's right to live has been challenged and denied. If there is to be peace in our industrial life let the employer recognize his obligation to his employees—at least to the degree set forth in existing statutes. Ordinary problems affecting wages, hours and working conditions, in most instances, will quickly respond to negotiation in the council room.

The United States Chamber of Commerce, the National Association of Manufacturers and similar groups representing industry and financial interests, are rendering a disservice to the American people in their attempts to frustrate the organization of labor and in their refusal to accept collective bargaining as one of our economic institutions. These groups are encouraging a systematic organization of vigilante groups to fight unionization under the sham pretext of local interests. They equip these vigilantes with tin hats, wooden clubs, gas masks and lethal weapons and train them in the arts of brutality and oppression. They bring in snoops, finks, hatchet gangs and Chowderhead Cohens to infest their plants and disturb the communities. Fascist organizations have been launched and financed under the shabby pretext that the C.I.O. movement is communistic. The real breeders of discontent and alien doctrines of government and philosophies subversive of good citizenship are such as these who take the law into their own hands. No tin hat brigade of goose-stepping vigilantes or bibble-babbling mob of blackguarding and corporation-paid scoundrels will prevent the onward march of labor, or divert its purpose to play its natural and rational part in the development of the economic, political and social life of our nation. . . .

Do those who have hatched this foolish cry of communism in the C.I.O. fear the increased influence of labor in our democracy? Do they fear its influence will be cast on the side of shorter hours, a better system of distributed employment, better homes for the underprivileged, social security for the aged, a fairer distribution of the national income?

Certainly the workers that are being organized want a voice in the determination of these objectives of social justice.

Certainly labor wants a fairer share in the national income. Assuredly labor wants a larger participation in increased productive efficiency. Obviously the population is entitled to participate in the fruits of the genius of our men of achievement in the field of the material sciences. Labor has suffered just as our farm population has suffered from a viciously unequal distribution of the national income. In the exploitation of both classes of workers has been the source of panic and depression, and upon the economic welfare of both rests the best assurance of a sound and permanent prosperity. . . .

Under the banner of the Committee for Industrial Organization, American labor is on the march. Its objectives today are those it had in the beginning: to strive for the unionization of our unorganized millions of workers and for the acceptance of collective bargaining as a recognized American institution. It seeks peace with the industrial world. It seeks cooperation and mutuality of effort with the agricultural population. It would avoid strikes. It would have its rights determined under the law by the peaceful negotiations and contract relationships that are supposed to characterize American commercial life. Until an aroused public opinion demands that employers accept that rule, labor has no recourse but to surrender its rights or struggle for their realization with its own economic power. . . .

I repeat that labor seeks peace and guarantees its own loyalty, but the voice of labor, insistent upon its rights, should not be annoying to the ears of justice or offensive to the conscience of the American people.

Source: *Vital Speeches*, Vol. III, No. 23 (September 15, 1937), pp. 731–33.

For Further Reading:

Irving Bernstein, *Turbulent Years* (Boston: Houghton Mifflin, 1970).
Melvyn Dubofsky and Warren Van Tine, *John L. Lewis* (New York: Quadrangle, 1977).

75. Woody Guthrie, "This Land Is Your Land" (1944)

For over a century, American intellectuals, from Ralph Waldo Emerson to Walt Whitman (see documents 26 and 44), called on artists to create a truly democratic and American culture. In the 1930s, some intellectual historians have argued, such a culture emerged. Writers such as John Steinbeck and James Farrell, photographers and artists such as Walker Evans, Dorothea Lange, and Thomas Hart Benson, film makers like Frank Capra, and songwriters like Woody Guthrie celebrated the common folk. In spite of the devastating impact of the Depression, these artists maintained faith in the common man's ability to overcome adversity and to regenerate America.

Guthrie, born Woodrow Wilson Guthrie in 1912, in Okemah, Oklahoma, especially reflected the burst of cultural nationalism or folk art of the Depression years. He wrote thousands of songs, generally based on well-known folk tunes. Many became anthems of the labor movement or elegies to the migrant worker, such as "Union Maid" and "Roll On, Columbia."

Ironically, Guthrie originally wrote "This Land Is Your Land" in a fit of anger and cynicism in 1940, as a parody of Irving Berlin's "God Bless America," which Guthrie felt ignored the reality of life in the Depression. By the time Guthrie recorded "This Land Is Your Land" in 1944, however, he was not in as cynical a mood. And in the post–World War II period, millions of children sang it in an uplifting manner.

This land is your land . . .
this land is my land
from California
to the New York island
From the Redwood forest
to the Gulf Stream waters
This land was made for you and me.

As I was walking that ribbon of highway
I saw above me that endless skyway

I saw below me that golden valley
This land was made for you and me.

I've roamed and rambled
and I've followed my footsteps
to the sparkling sands of
her diamond deserts
and all around me
a voice was sounding
This land was made for you and me.

When the sun came shining
and I was strolling
And the wheat fields waving
and the dustclouds rolling
As the fog was lifting
a voice was chanting
This land was made for you and me.

Source: Landon Gerald Dowdy, *Journey to Freedom: A Casebook with Music* (Chicago, 1969), p. 75.

For Further Reading:

Richard Pells, *Radical Visions and American Dreams* (New York: Harper & Row, 1973).
Warren Sussman, "The Thirties," in *The Development of American Culture*, ed. Stanley Coben and Lorman Rather, 2d ed. (New York: St. Martin's Press, 1970).
Woody Guthrie, *Bound for Glory* (New York: E. P. Dutton, 1969).

PART VIII
WORLD WAR II AND THE COLD WAR

76. Franklin Delano Roosevelt, "War Message" (1941)

1935–37   Neutrality Acts
1937   Japan invades China
1938   Germany occupies Sudetenland, Czechoslovakia, and Austria
1939   Germany invades Poland; Britain and France declare war on Germany
1940   United States slaps oil embargo on Japan; Lend Lease; Atlantic Charter
1941   (December 7) Japan attacks Pearl Harbor; Roosevelt issues his "War Message"

While the United States adopted a relatively isolationist position toward Germany in the years following World War I, it practiced a more hard-line position toward the Japanese. When Japan started to expand in the Far East in search of resources and markets, Roosevelt's Secretary of State, Cordell Hull, demanded that it desist. Following Japan's invasion of Southeast Asia, the United States went one step farther, placing an oil embargo on Japan. Still, Japan's surprise attack on Pearl Harbor shocked Americans. And despite some claims to the contrary, there is no good evidence that President Roosevelt knew of the attack in advance and allowed or encouraged the Japanese to demolish much of the Pacific fleet.

Unlike President Wilson, who cast America's entrance into World War I as a great moral crusade, FDR framed his call for war on the basis of lost lives and national security. This is not to suggest that the United States fought World War II without any principles. In the summer of 1940 FDR had presented the "Atlantic Charter," which like Wilson's "Fourteen Points" championed the right of self-determination. Furthermore, the fact that Hitler was one of the foes, and that the Japanese had conquered China and much of Southeast Asia, made it easier for the American people to believe that World War II was a "good" war, than was the case with World War I.

Yesterday, December 7, 1941—a date which will live in infamy—the United States of America was suddenly and deliberately attacked by naval and air forces of the Empire of Japan.

The United States was at peace with that nation and, at the solicitation of Japan, was still in conversation with its Government and its Emperor looking toward the maintenance of peace in the Pacific. Indeed, one hour

U.S.S. *Shaw* Exploding During Japanese Raid on Pearl Harbor, December 7, 1941 (National Archives).

after Japanese air squadrons had commenced bombing in Oahu, the Japanese Ambassador to the United States and his colleague delivered to the Secretary of State a formal reply to a recent American message. While this reply stated that it seemed useless to continue the existing diplomatic negotiations, it contained no threat or hint of war or armed attack.

It will be recorded that the distance of Hawaii from Japan makes it obvious that the attack was deliberately planned many days or even weeks ago. During the intervening time the Japanese Government has deliberately sought to deceive the United States by false statements and expressions of hope for continued peace.

The attack yesterday on the Hawaiian Islands has caused severe damage to American naval and military forces. Very many American lives have been lost. In addition American ships have been reported torpedoed on the high seas between San Francisco and Honolulu.

Yesterday the Japanese Government also launched an attack against Malaya. Last night Japanese forces attacked Hong Kong. Last night Japanese forces attacked Guam. Last night Japanese forces attacked the Philippine Islands. Last night the Japanese attacked Wake Island. This morning the Japanese attacked Midway Island.

Japan has, therefore, undertaken a surprise offensive extending throughout the Pacific area. The facts of yesterday speak for themselves. The people of the United States have already formed their opinions and well understand the implications to the very life and safety of our nation.

As Commander-in-Chief of the Army and Navy, I have directed that all measures be taken for our defense.

Always will we remember the character of the onslaught against us.

No matter how long it may take us to overcome this premeditated invasion, the American people in their righteous might will win through to absolute victory.

I believe I interpret the will of the Congress and of the people when I assert that we will not only defend ourselves to the uttermost but will make very certain that this form of treachery shall never endanger us again.

Hostilities exist. There is no blinking at the fact that our people, our territory and our interests are in grave danger.

With confidence in our armed forces—with the unbounded determination of our people—we will gain the inevitable triumph—so help us God.

I ask that the Congress declare that since the unprovoked and dastardly attack by Japan on Sunday, December seventh, a state of war has existed between the United States and the Japanese Empire.

Source: *New York Times*, December 9, 1941.

For Further Reading:

Robert Dallek, *Franklin D. Roosevelt and American Foreign Policy* (New York: Oxford University Press, 1979).

Charles Neu, *The Troubled Encounter* (New York: Wiley, 1975).
Gordon Prange, *At Dawn We Slept* (New York: McGraw-Hill, 1981).

77. Franklin Delano Roosevelt, "Economic Bill of Rights" (1944)

1942   Office of Price Control fixes prices
1944   Congress passes GI Bill of Rights (Serviceman's
        Readjustment Act)

Although most American men and women lived far away from the battlefront, they too had to sacrifice during World War II. Goods were rationed; housing and services were in short supply. Work hours were long, with much mandatory overtime, and though pay was better than in the past, it often did not keep up with inflation. While reports from the war front were generally good, many Americans had to endure the news of deaths in the family or among close friends. Not surprisingly, despite the fact that the cause was a good one, morale sagged, especially as the war dragged on.

With the end of the war still apparently far away, President Roosevelt delivered one of the most important speeches of his career. In it he sought to lift morale and to address the broader issue of the economic responsibilities of the government. By proclaiming the existence of an Economic Bill of Rights, FDR sought to reward the nation for its sacrifices. He also lent weight to a view that had once been considered quite radical, that the state had the duty to protect and preserve a decent standard of living as much as it had the obligation to ensure civil and political rights.

For a nation that had just experienced the Great Depression and was in the midst of a World War, FDR's words struck a very responsive chord. Even though his "Economic Bill of Rights" did not become part of the Constitution, Congress enacted the GI Bill of Rights, which after the war provided millions of servicemen with education and medical benefits and small business and home loans. This aid helped stimulate the economy and ensured that millions of other Americans would enjoy a middle-class life.

If ever there was a time to subordinate individual or group selfishness to the national good, that time is now. Disunity at home—bickerings, self-seeking partisanship, stoppages of work, inflation, business as usual, politics as usual, luxury as usual—these are the influences which can undermine the morale of the brave men ready to die at the front for us here.

Those who are doing most of the complaining are not deliberately striving to sabotage the national war effort. They are laboring under the delusion that the time is past when we must make prodigious sacrifices—that the war is already won and we can begin to slacken off. But the dangerous folly of that point of view can be measured by the distance that separates our troops from their ultimate objectives in Berlin and Tokyo—and by the sum of all the perils that lie along the way.

Let us remember the lessons of 1918. In the summer of that year the tide turned in favor of the Allies. But this Government did not relax. In fact, our national effort was stepped up. In August, 1918, the draft age limits were broadened from 21–31 to 18–45. The President called for "force to the utmost," and his call was heeded. And in November, only three months later, Germany surrendered.

That is the way to fight and win a war—all out—and not with half-an-eye on the battlefronts abroad and the other eye-and-a-half on personal, selfish, or political interests here at home.

Therefore, in order to concentrate all our energies and resources on winning the war, and to maintain a fair and stable economy at home, I recommend that the Congress adopt:

1. A realistic tax law—which will tax all unreasonable profits, both individual and corporate, and reduce the ultimate cost of the war to our sons and daughters. The tax bill now under consideration by the Congress does not begin to meet this test.

2. A continuation of the law for the renegotiation of war contracts—which will prevent exorbitant profits and assure fair prices to the Government. For two long years I have pleaded with the Congress to take undue profits out of the war.

3. A cost of food law—which will enable the Government (a) to place a reasonable floor under the prices the farmer may expect for his production, and (b) to place a ceiling on the prices a consumer will have to pay for the food he buys. This should apply to necessities only; and will require public funds to carry out. It will cost in appropriations about 1 per cent of the present annual cost of the war.

4. Early enactment of the stabilization statute of October, 1942. This expires June 30, 1944, and if it is not extended well in advance the country might just as well expect price chaos by summer. We cannot have stabilization by wishful thinking. We must take positive action to maintain the integrity of the American dollar.

5. A national service law—which, for the duration of the war, will prevent strikes, and with certain appropriate exceptions, will make available for war production or for any other essential services every able-bodied adult in the nation.

These five measures together form a just and equitable whole. I would not recommend a national service law unless the other laws were passed to keep down the cost of living, to share equitably the burdens of taxation, to hold the stabilization line, and to prevent undue profits.

The Federal Government already has the basic power to draft capital and property of all kinds for war purposes on a basis of just compensation.

As you know, I have for three years hesitated to recommend a national service act. Today, however, I am convinced of its necessity. Although I believe that we and our Allies can win the war without such a measure, I am certain that nothing less than total mobilization of all our resources of manpower and capital will guarantee an earlier victory, and reduce the toll of suffering and sorrow and blood.

I have received a joint recommendation for this law from the heads of the War Department, the Navy Department, and the Maritime Commission. These are the men who bear responsibility for the procurement of the necessary arms and equipment, and for the successful prosecution of the war in the field. They say:

When the very life of the nation is in peril the responsibility for service is common to all men and women. In such a time there can be no discrimination between the men and women who are assigned by the Government to its defense at the battle front and the men and women assigned to produce the vital materials essential to successful military operations. A prompt enactment of a national service law would be merely an expression of the universality of this responsibility.

It is our duty now to begin to lay plans and determine the strategy for the winning of a lasting peace and the establishment of an American standard of living higher than ever before known. We cannot be content, no matter how high the general standard of living may be, if some fraction of our people—whether it be one-third or one-fifth or one-tenth—is ill-fed, ill-clothed, ill-housed, and insecure.

This Republic had its beginning, and grew to its present strength, under the protection of certain inalienable political rights—among them the right of free speech, free press, free worship, trial by jury, freedom from unreasonable searches and seizures. They were our rights to life and liberty.

As our nation has grown in size and stature, however—as our industrial economy expanded—these political rights proved inadequate to assure us equality in the pursuit of happiness.

We have come to a clear realization of the fact that true individual freedom cannot exist without economic security and independence. "Necessitous men are not free men." People who are hungry and out of a job are the stuff of which dictatorships are made.

In our day these economic truths have become accepted as self-evident. We have accepted, so to speak, a second Bill of Rights under which a new basis of security and prosperity can be established for all, reguardless of station, race or creed.

Among these are:

The right to a useful and remunerative job in the industries or shops or farms or mines of the nation;

The right to earn enough to provide adequate food and clothing and recreation;

The right of every farmer to raise and sell his products at a return which will give him and his family a decent living;

The right of every business man, large and small, to trade in an atmosphere of freedom from unfair competition and domination by monopolies at home or abroad;

The right of every family to a decent home;

The right to adequate medical care and the opportunity to achieve and enjoy good health;

The right to adequate protection from the economic fears of old age, sickness, accident and unemployment;

The right to a good education.

All of these rights spell security. And after this war is won we must be prepared to move forward, in the implementation of these rights, to new goals of human happiness and well-being.

America's own rightful place in the world depends in large part upon how fully these and similar rights have been carried into practice for our citizens. For unless there is security here at home there cannot be lasting peace in the world.

Source: *New York Times*, January 12, 1944.

For Further Reading:

James Blum, *V Was for Victory* (New York: Harcourt Brace Jovanovich, 1976).
James MacGregor Burns, *Roosevelt: The Soldier of Freedom* (New York: Harcourt Brace Jovanovich, 1970).
Richard Polenberg, *War and Society* (Philadelphia: Lippincott, 1972).

78. Judge Learned Hand, Excerpt from "The Spirit of Liberty" (1944)

1941   Office of Censorship established
1942   Office of War Information formed

Unlike World War I, World War II generally did not generate intolerance and persecution, with the exception of the internment of Japanese-Americans (see documents 64, 65, and 79). For example, in World War II war dissenters and pacifists were not rounded up, deported, or arrested under wartime sedition laws. On the contrary, many were allowed to choose some form of alternative service and treated with respect. Moreover, even though the government produced propaganda, information flowed much more freely than during World War I.

Shortly before Japan attacked Pearl Harbor, President Roosevelt proclaimed that the United States stood for "four freedoms": the freedom of speech and expression, freedom of religion, freedom from want, and freedom from fear of foreign expansion. Three years later, Judge Learned Hand, one of the nation's most respected jurists, pondered the same theme in a speech delivered to a large crowd at an "I Am an American Day," in New York City's Central Park. Tolerance, Hand asserted, was the cornerstone of liberty. Before the Battle of Dunbar in 1650, when English forces under the command of Oliver Cromwell defeated the Scots, Hand noted, Cromwell declared: "I beseech ye in the bowels of Christ, think that ye may be mistaken." Put another way, act with respect for another's views and err on the side of tolerance and nonconformity. While such a view did not stop Hand from devoting himself to the war, it tempered his righteousness and lent an air of humility to the war effort.

We have gathered here to affirm a faith, a faith in a common purpose, a common conviction, a common devotion. Some of us have chosen America as the land of our adoption; the rest have come from those who did the same. For this reason we have some right to consider ourselves a picked group, a group of those who had the courage to break from the past and brave the dangers and the loneliness of a strange land. What was the object that nerved us, or those who went before us, to this choice? We sought liberty; freedom from oppression, freedom from want, freedom to be ourselves. This we then sought; this we now believe that we are by way of winning. What do we mean when we say that first of all we seek liberty? I often wonder whether we do not rest our hopes too much upon constitutions, upon laws and upon courts. These are false hopes; believe me, these are false hopes. Liberty lies in the hearts of men and women; when it dies there, no constitution, no law, no court can save it; no constitution, no law, no court can even do much to help it. While it lies there it needs no constitution, no law, no court to save it. And what is this liberty which must lie in the hearts of men and women? It is not the ruthless, the unbridled will; it is not freedom to do as one likes. That is the denial of liberty, and leads straight to its overthrow. A society in which men recognize no check upon their freedom soon becomes a society where freedom is the possession of only a savage few; as we have learned to our sorrow.

What this is the spirit of liberty? I cannot define it; I can only tell you my own faith. The spirit of liberty is the spirit which is not too sure that it is right; the spirit of liberty is the spirit which seeks to understand the minds of other men and women; the spirit of liberty is the spirit which weighs their interests alongside its own without bias; the spirit of liberty remembers that not even a sparrow falls to earth unheeded; the spirit of liberty is the spirit of Him who, near two thousand years ago, taught mankind that lesson it has never learned, but has never quite forgotten; that there may be a kingdom where the least shall be heard and considered side by side with the greatest. And now in that spirit, that spirit of an America which has never been, and which may never be; nay, which never will be except as the conscience and courage of Americans create it; yet in the spirit of that America which lies hidden in some form in the aspirations of us all; in the spirit of that America for which our young men are at this moment fighting and dying; in that spirit of liberty and of America I ask you to rise and with me pledge our faith in the glorious destiny of our beloved country.

Source: Learned Hand, *The Spirit of Liberty, Paper and Addresses of Learned Hand*, ed. Irving Dillard (New York: Knopf, 1952).

For Further Reading:

Cynthia Eller, *Conscientious Objectors and the Second World War* (New York: Praeger, 1991).
Allan M. Winkler, *The Politics of Propaganda* (New Haven, Conn.: Yale University Press, 1978).

79. *Korematsu v. United States*, Excerpt from Dissenting Opinions by Justices Frank Murphy and Robert H. Jackson (1944)

1942 Relocation and Enemies Act establishes internment camps
1944 *Korematsu v. United States*
1988 Reparations for Japanese-American Internees

While the general mood of World War II was one of tolerance, there was one glaring exception, namely, the internment of Japanese-Americans. Most of those who were forced to leave their homes and to live in desolate con-centration camps were American citizens. The rest were permanent resi-dents. None of those interned were accused, tried, or convicted of committing a crime. Rather the Japanese-American treatment was based on their alleged

Internment of Japanese Americans (National Archives).

*potential threat and on the claim that public hysteria required the govern-
ment to relocate them for their own safety. True, the attack on Pearl Harbor
inflamed public fears about Japanese espionage. But if there had not already
been a long history of anti-Asian sentiment on the west coast and if Japanese-
Americans had not been racially distinct from the white majority, it is doubtful that they would have been interned.*

In Korematsu v. United States *the Supreme Court upheld the policy of
placing Japanese-Americans in camps. Indeed, Justices Hugo Black and Felix
Frankfurter justified the order to relocate them on the grounds that the
Constitution granted the federal government broad powers during wartime,
including the power to "wage war successfully," in Frankfurter's words. Yet
no one ever established in a court of law that those interned threatened*

*America's war capabilities, and Justices Murphy and Jackson issued sharp
dissents in the case. Moreover, they both condemned the criteria used to
intern Japanese-Americans, namely race.*

*Forty years after the Relocation Act was issued, a special government
commission argued that the United States had committed a "grave injustice"
by establishing internment camps for Japanese-Americans. In 1988, President Ronald Reagan signed into law a congressional act that granted the
surviving internees some financial compensation. On signing the measure
he declared that it was time to "right a grave wrong."*

Mr. Justice Murphy, dissenting.

It must be conceded that the military and naval situation in the spring of
1942 was such as to generate a very real fear of invasion of the Pacific Coast,
accompanied by fears of sabotage and espionage in that area. The military
command was therefore justified in adopting all reasonable means necessary
to combat these dangers. In adjudging the military action taken in light of
the then apparent dangers, we must not erect too high or too meticulous
standards; it is necessary only that the action have some reasonable relation
to the removal of the dangers of invasion, sabotage, and espionage. But the
exclusion, either temporarily or permanently, of all persons with Japanese
blood in their veins has no such reasonable relation. And that relation is
lacking because the exclusion order necessarily must rely for its reasonableness upon the assumption that *all* persons of Japanese ancestry may have a
dangerous tendency to commit sabotage and espionage and to aid our Japanese enemy in other ways. It is difficult to believe that reason, logic, or
experience could be marshaled in support of such an assumption.

That this forced exclusion was the result in good measure of this erroneous
assumption of racial guilt rather than bona fide military necessity is evidenced
by the Commanding General's Final Report on the evacuation from the
Pacific Coast area. In it he refers to all individuals of Japanese descent as
"subversive," as belonging to "an enemy race" whose "racial strains are
undiluted," and as constituting "over 112,000 potential enemies . . . at large
today" along the Pacific Coast. In support of this blanket condemnation of
all persons of Japanese descent, however, no reliable evidence is cited to
show that such individuals were generally disloyal, or had generally so conducted themselves in this area as to constitute a special menace to defense
installations or war industries, or had otherwise by their behavior furnished
reasonable ground for their exclusion as a group.

Justification for the exclusion is sought, instead, mainly upon questionable
racial and sociological grounds not ordinarily within the realm of expert
military judgment, supplemented by certain semi-military conclusions
drawn from an unwarranted use of circumstantial evidence. Individuals of
Japanese ancestry are condemned because they are said to be "a large,

unassimilated, tightly knit racial group, bound to an enemy nation by strong ties of race, culture, custom and religion." They are claimed to be given to "emperor-worshiping ceremonies" and to "dual citizenship." Japanese language schools and allegedly pro-Japanese organizations are cited as evidence of possible group disloyalty, together with facts as to certain persons being educated and residing at length in Japan. It is intimated that many of these individuals deliberately resided "adjacent to strategic points," thus enabling them "to carry into execution a tremendous program of sabotage on a mass scale should any considerable number of them have been inclined to do so."

The need for protective custody is also asserted. The report refers without identity to "numerous incidents of violence" as well as to other admittedly unverified or cumulative incidents. From this, plus certain other events not shown to have been connected with the Japanese Americans, it is concluded that the "situation was fraught with danger to the Japanese population itself" and that the general public "was ready to take matters into its own hands." Finally, it is intimated, though not directly charged or proved, that persons of Japanese ancestry were responsible for three minor isolated shellings and bombings of the Pacific Coast area, as well as for unidentified radio transmissions and night signaling.

The main reasons relied upon by those responsible for the forced evacuation, therefore, do not prove a reasonable relation between the group characteristics of Japanese Americans and the dangers of invasion, sabotage, and espionage. The reasons appear, instead, to be largely an accumulation of much of the misinformation, half-truths, and insinuations that for years have been directed against Japanese Americans by people with racial and economic prejudices—the same people who have been among the foremost advocates of the evacuation. A military judgment based upon such racial and sociological considerations is not entitled to the great weight ordinarily given the judgments based upon strictly military considerations. Especially is this so when every charge relative to race, religion, culture, geographical location, and legal and economic status has been substantially discredited by independent studies made by experts in these matters.

The military necessity which is essential to the validity of the evacuation order thus resolves itself into a few intimations that certain individuals actively aided the enemy, from which it is inferred that the entire group of Japanese Americans could not be trusted to be or remain loyal to the United States. . . .

No adequate reason is given for the failure to treat these Japanese Americans on an individual basis by holding investigations and hearings to separate the loyal from the disloyal, as was done in the case of persons of German and Italian ancestry. See House Report No. 2124 (77th Cong., 2d Sess.) 247–52. It is asserted merely that the loyalties of this group "were unknown and time was of the essence." Yet nearly four months elapsed after Pearl Harbor before the first exclusion order was issued;

nearly eight months went by until the last order was issued; and the last of these "subversive" persons was not actually removed until almost eleven months had elapsed. Leisure and deliberation seem to have been more of the essence than speed. And the fact that conditions were not such as to warrant a declaration of martial law adds strength to the belief that the factors of time and military necessity were not as urgent as they have been represented to be.

Moreover, there was no adequate proof that the Federal Bureau of Investigation and the military and naval intelligence services did not have the espionage and sabotage situation well in hand during this long period. Nor is there any denial of the fact that not one person of Japanese ancestry was accused or convicted of espionage or sabotage after Pearl Harbor while they were still free, a fact which is some evidence of the loyalty of the vast majority of these individuals and of the effectiveness of the established methods of combatting these evils. It seems incredible that under these circumstances it would have been impossible to hold loyalty hearings for the mere 112,000 persons involved—or at least for the 70,000 American citizens—especially when a large part of this number represented children and elderly men and women. Any inconvenience that may have accompanied an attempt to conform to procedural due process cannot be said to justify violations of constitutional rights of individuals.

I dissent, therefore, from this legalization of racism. Racial discrimination in any form and in any degree has no justifiable part whatever in our democratic way of life. It is unattractive in any setting but it is utterly revolting among a free people who have embraced the principles set forth in the Constitution of the United States. All residents of this nation are kin in some way by blood or culture to a foreign land. Yet they are primarily and necessarily a part of the new and distinct civilization of the United States. They must accordingly be treated at all times as the heirs of the American experiment and as entitled to all the rights and freedoms guaranteed by the Constitution.

Mr. Justice Jackson, dissenting.

Korematsu was born on our soil, of parents born in Japan. The Constitution makes him a citizen of the United States by nativity and a citizen of California by residence. No claim is made that he is not loyal to this country. There is no suggestion that apart from the matter involved here he is not law-abiding and well disposed. Korematsu, however, has been convicted of an act not commonly a crime. It consists merely of being present in the state whereof he is a citizen, near the place where he was born, and where all his life he has lived.

Even more unusual is the series of military orders which made this conduct a crime. They forbid such a one to remain, and they also forbid him to leave.

They were so drawn that the only way Korematsu could avoid violation was to give himself up to the military authority. This meant submission to custody, examination, and transportation out of the territory, to be followed by indeterminate confinement in detention camps.

A citizen's presence in the locality, however, was made a crime only if his parents were of Japanese birth. Had Korematsu been one of four—the others being, say, a German alien enemy, an Italian alien enemy, and a citizen of American-born ancestors convicted of treason but out on parole—only Korematsu's presence would have violated the order. The difference between their innocence and his crime would result, not from anything he did, said, or thought different than they but only in that he was born of different racial stock.

Now, if any fundamental assumption underlies our system, it is that guilt is personal and not inheritable. Even if all of one's antecedents had been convicted of treason, the Constitution forbids its penalties to be visited upon him, for it provides that "no attainder of treason shall work corruption of blood or forfeiture except during the life of the person attainted." But here is an attempt to make an otherwise innocent act a crime merely because this prisoner is the son of parents as to whom he had no choice and belongs to a race from which there is no way to resign. If Congress in peacetime legislation should enact such a criminal law, I should suppose this Court would refuse to enforce it.

But the "law" which this prisoner is convicted of disregarding is not found in an act of Congress but in a military order. Neither the act of Congress nor the executive order of the President, nor both together, would afford a basis for this conviction. It rests on the orders of General DeWitt. And it is said that if the military commander had reasonable military grounds for promulgating the orders, they are constitutional and become law, and the Court is required to enforce them. There are several reasons why I cannot subscribe to this doctrine.

It would be impracticable and dangerous idealism to expect or insist that each specific military command in an area of probable operations will conform to conventional tests of constitutionality. When an area is so beset that it must be put under military control at all, the paramount consideration is that its measures be successful rather than legal. The armed services must protect a society, not merely its Constitution. The very essence of the military job is to marshal physical force, to remove every obstacle to its effectiveness, to give it every strategic advantage. Defense measures will not, and often should not, be held within the limits that bind civil authority in peace. No court can require such a commander in such circumstances to act as a reasonable man; he may be unreasonably cautious and exacting. Perhaps he should be. But a commander in temporarily focusing the life of a community on defense is carrying out a military program; he is not making law in the sense the courts know the term. He issues orders, and they may have a certain authority as military commands, although they may be very bad as constitutional law.

But if we cannot confine military expedients by the Constitution, neither would I distort the Constitution to approve all that the military may deem expedient. That is what the Court appears to be doing, whether consciously or not. I cannot say, from any evidence before me, that the orders of General DeWitt were not reasonably expedient military precautions, nor could I say that they were. But even if they were permissible military procedures, I deny that it follows that they are constitutional. If, as the Court holds, it does follow, then we may as well say that any military order will be constitutional and have done with it. . . .

A military order, however unconstitutional, is not apt to last longer than the military emergency. Even during that period a succeeding commander may revoke it all. But once a judicial opinion rationalizes such an order to show that it conforms to the Constitution, or rather rationalizes the Constitution to show that the Constitution sanctions such an order, the Court for all time has validated the principle of racial discrimination in criminal procedure and of transplanting American citizens. The principle then lies about like a loaded weapon ready for the hand of any authority that can bring forward a plausible claim of an urgent need. Every repetition imbeds that principle more deeply in our law and thinking and expands it to new purposes. All who observe the work of courts are familiar with what Judge Cardozo described as "the tendency of a principle to expand itself to the limit of its logic." A military commander may overstep the bounds of constitutionality and it is an incident. But if we review and approve, that passing incident becomes the doctrine of the Constitution. There it has a generative power of its own, and all that it creates will be in its own image. Nothing better illustrates this danger than does the Court's opinion in this case. . . .

I should hold that a civil court cannot be made to enforce an order which violates constitutional limitations even if it is a reasonable exercise of military authority. The courts can exercise only the judicial power, can apply only law, and must abide by the Constitution, or they cease to be civil courts and become instruments of military policy.

Source: *Korematsu v. United States*, 323 U.S. 214 (1944).

For Further Reading:

Roger Daniels, *Concentration Camps USA* (New York: Holt, Rinehart and Winston, 1981).

Peter Irons, *Justice at War* (New York: Oxford University Press, 1983).

Michi Weglyn, *Years of Infamy* (New York: William Morrow, 1976).

80. A. Philip Randolph, Excerpt from "Keynote Address to the March on Washington Movement" (1942)

1940–45   700,000 blacks migrate out of South
1941   A. Philip Randolph calls for March on Washington;
       FDR issues Executive Order 8802
1942   Congress of Racial Equality (CORE) established,
       protests against segregation
1943   Race riots in Detroit and elsewhere

World War II had an enormous impact on African Americans and race relations in general in the United States. Before the war began, most blacks still lived in the rural South, working as sharecroppers. Most could not vote and they enjoyed few citizenship rights. The segregation of the military and of the Red Cross's blood supply depicted the persistence of racial inequality.

Yet the war unleashed a wave of change. Lured by jobs in the defense industry, over 700,000 blacks left the South. Nearly one million served in the military. Both of these developments lent blacks a newfound determination to win equality and provided some of the resources for doing so, from better-paying jobs to the vote. Wartime propaganda, which railed at Nazi racism and touted America as the land of the free, bolstered the hopes and aspirations of African Americans.

In 1941 A. Philip Randolph, president of the Brotherhood of Sleeping Car Porters and a longtime black leader, announced plans to stage a mass March on Washington, D.C., to demand equal treatment in the military. Rather than face the prospect of hundreds of thousands of civil rights protesters in Washington, D.C., just as he was trying to unite the country behind the war, President Roosevelt issued Executive Order 8802, which desegregated the defense industries and created the Fair Employment Practices Commission (FEPC). In exchange, Randolph agreed to cancel the March. But as Randolph made clear in his "Keynote Address to the March on Washington Movement," he remained committed to using the war for gaining full equality. Although he was initially unsuccessful in these efforts, he did help establish a base for launching the post–World War II civil rights movement.

Fellow Marchers and delegates to the Policy Conference of the March on Washington Movement and Friends:
We have met at an hour when the sinister shadows of war are lengthening

and becoming more threatening. As one of the sections of the oppressed darker races, and representing a part of the exploited millions of the workers of the world, we are deeply concerned that the totalitarian legions of Hitler, Hirohito, and Mussolini do not batter the last bastions of democracy. We know that our fate is tied with the fate of the democratic way of life. And so, out of the depth of our hearts, a cry goes up for the triumph of the United Nations. But we would not be honest with ourselves were we to stop with a call for a victory of arms alone. We know this is not enough. We fight that the democratic faiths, values, heritages and ideals may prevail.

Unless this war sounds the death knell to the old Anglo-American empire systems, the hapless story of which is one of exploitation for the profit and power of monopoly capitalist economy, it will have been fought in vain. Our aim then must not only be to defeat nazism, fascism, and militarism on the battlefield but to win the peace, for democracy, for freedom and the Brotherhood of Man without regard to his pigmentation, land of his birth or the God of his fathers. . . .

Thus our feet are set in the path toward equality—economic, political and social and racial. . . . Equality is the heart and essence of democracy, freedom and justice. Without equality of opportunity in industry, in labor unions, schools and colleges, government, politics and before the law, without equality in social relations and in all phases of human endeavor, the Negro is certain to be consigned to an inferior status. There must be no dual standards of justice, no dual rights privileges, duties or responsibilities of citizenship. No dual forms of freedom. . . .

Our nearer goals include the abolition of discrimination, segregation, and jim-crow in the Government, the Army, Navy, Air Corps, U.S. Marine . . . and defense industries; the elimination of discrimination in hotels, restaurants, on public transportation conveyances, in educational, recreational, cultural, and amusement and entertainment places such as theaters, beaches and so forth.

We want the full works of citizenship with no reservations. We will accept nothing less.

But goals must be achieved. They are not secured because it is just and right that they be possessed by Negro or white people. Slavery was not abolished because it was bad and unjust. It was abolished because men fought, bled and died on the battlefield. . . . They must win them and to win them they must fight, sacrifice, suffer, go to jail and, if need be, die for them. These rights will not be given. They must be taken.

Democracy was fought for and taken from political royalists—the kings. Industrial democracy, the rights of the workers to organize and designate the representative of their own choosing to bargain collectively is being won and taken from the economic royalists—big business. . . .

As to the composition of our movement. Our policy is that it be all-Negro, and pro-Negro but not anti-white, or anti-semitic or anti-labor, or anti-

Catholic. The reason for this policy is that all oppressed people must assume the responsibility and take the initiative to free themselves. . . .

This does not mean . . . that our movement should not call for the collaboration of Jews, Catholics, Trade unions and white liberals. . . . No, not at all. . . .

The essential value of an all-Negro movement such as the March on Washington is that it helps to create faith by Negroes in Negroes. It develops a sense of self-reliance with Negroes depending on Negroes in vital matters. It helps to break down the slave psychology and inferiority-complex in Negroes which comes and is nourished with Negroes relying on white people for direction and support. . . .

Now, let us be unafraid. We are fighting for big stakes. Our stakes are liberty, justice, and democracy. Every Negro should hang his head in shame who fails to do his part now for freedom. This is the hour of the Negro. It is the hour of the common man. May we rise to the challenge to struggle for our rights. Come what will or may, let us not falter.

Source: A. Philip Randolph, "Keynote Address to the March on Washington Movement," September 26, 1942.

For Further Reading:

Jervis Anderson, *A. Philip Randolph* (New York: Harcourt Brace Jovanovich, 1976).
Neil A. Wynn, *The Afro-American and the Second World War* (New York: Holmes & Meier, 1976).

81. Henry Steele Commager, Excerpts from "Who Is Loyal to America?" (1947)

1945   House Committee on Un-American Activities (HUAC) receives permanent status
1947   President Harry Truman establishes Federal Loyalty Program; Taft-Hartley Act passed over Truman's veto
1948   Smith Act trials

The onset of the Cold War brought with it a new wave of intolerance. Concern over internal subversion and Soviet espionage, prompted the nation to embark on a new red hunt. While President Truman does not deserve the title of the initiator of the red scare, he was a key participant. In 1947 he established a Federal Loyalty program, whereby the federal government was empowered to investigate the background of all its employees. By the time the 1950s were over, an individual could not apply for the simplest of government jobs without swearing that they were not members of a group committed to overthrowing the government. At the same time Congress passed the Taft-Hartley Act, over Truman's veto, which was the first of many laws that restricted the rights of communists, in this instance communist labor officials. A year later, in the midst of a hard-fought political campaign, Truman challenged the loyalty of former Vice-President Henry Wallace, who was running for president on a third-party ticket. Truman's actions legitimized the use of anti-communism in the political arena. On top of this came the Smith Act trials, in which eleven top U.S. Communist Party officials were charged, tried, and convicted of violating the Smith or Alien Registration Act, passed in 1940 to guard against the advocacy of violent overthrow of the government. This was all numerous opportunistic politicians needed to unleash a series of irresponsible hearings and reports on the threat of communism at home.

In the face of the new red scare, many liberals retreated from their defense of civil liberties. They were unwilling to risk their own security or positions to protect the freedom of expression and association of communists or alleged communists. Hubert Humphrey, for example, the most famous liberal of the postwar era, sponsored the Communist Control Act, which required that communists register with the federal government. John F. Kennedy supported this legislation and was one of the few Senators not to censure fellow Irish-American Senator Joe McCarthy for his abusive behavior in pursuit of "un-Americans" in the mid-1950s.

Henry Steele Commager, a renowned historian and a noncommunist, was an early critic of the red scare and the liberal retreat from a defense of civil liberties. In "Who Is Loyal to America?" he not only criticized the misrepresentations made by many anticommunists, he challenged the validity of the notion of disloyalty or un-American activity, short of actual treason, in the first place (see document 82).

On May 6 a Russian-born girl, Mrs. Shura Lewis, gave a talk to the students of the Western High School of Washington, D.C. She talked about Russia—its school system, its public health program, the position of women, of the aged, of the workers, the farmers, and the professional classes—and compared, superficially and uncritically, some American and Russian social institutions. The most careful examination of the speech—happily reprinted for us in the *Congressional Record*—does not disclose a single disparagement of anything American unless it is a quasi-humorous reference to the cost of having a baby and of dental treatment in this country. Mrs. Lewis said nothing that had not been said a thousand times, in speeches, in newspapers, magazines, and books. She said nothing that any normal person could find objectionable.

Her speech, however; created a sensation. A few students walked out on it. Others improvised placards proclaiming their devotion to Americanism. Indignant mothers telephoned their protests. Newspapers took a strong stand against the outrage. Congress, rarely concerned for the political or economic welfare of the citizens of the capital city, reacted sharply when its intellectual welfare was at stake. Congressmen Rankin and Dirksen thundered and lightened; the District of Columbia Committee went into a huddle; there were demands for housecleaning in the whole school system, which was obviously shot through and through with Communism.

All this might be ignored, for we have learned not to expect either intelligence or understanding of Americanism from this element in our Congress. More ominous was the reaction of the educators entrusted with the high responsibility of guiding and guarding the intellectual welfare of our boys and girls. Did they stand up for intellectual freedom? Did they insist that high-school children had the right and the duty to learn about other countries? Did they protest that students were to be trusted to use intelligence and common sense? Did they affirm that the Americanism of their students was staunch enough to resist propaganda? Did they perform even the elementary task, expected of educators above all, of analyzing the much-criticized speech?

Not at all. The District Superintendent of Schools, Dr. Hobart Corning, hastened to agree with the animadversions of Representatives Rankin and Dirksen. The whole thing was, he confessed, "a very unfortunate occurrence," and had "shocked the whole school system." What Mrs. Lewis said, he added gratuitously, was "repugnant to all who are working with youth in the Washington schools," and "the entire affair contrary to the philosophy of education under which we operate." Mr. Danowsky, the hapless principal of the Western High School, was "the most shocked and regretful of all." The District of Columbia Committee would be happy to know that though he was innocent in the matter, he had been properly reprimanded!

It is the reaction of the educators that makes this episode more than a tempest in a teapot. We expect hysteria from Mr. Rankin and some newspapers; we are shocked when we see educators, timid before criticism and confused about first principles, betray their trust. And we wonder what can be that "philosophy of education" which believes that young people can be trained to the duties of citizenship by wrapping their minds in cotton-wool.

Merely by talking about Russia Mrs. Lewis was thought to be attacking Americanism. It is indicative of the seriousness of the situation that during this same week the House found it necessary to take time out from the discussion of the labor bill, the tax bill, the International Trade Organization, and the world famine, to meet assaults upon Americanism from a new quarter. This time it was the artists who were undermining the American system, and members of the House spent some hours passing around reproductions of the paintings which the State Department had sent abroad as part of its program for advertising American culture. . . .

. . . Increasingly Congress is concerned with the eradication of disloyalty and the defense of Americanism, and scarcely a day passes that some congressman does not treat us to exhortations and admonitions, impassioned appeals and eloquent declamations, . . . And scarcely a day passes that the outlines of the new loyalty and the new Americanism are not etched more sharply in public policy.

And this is what is significant—the emergence of new patterns of Americanism and of loyalty, patterns radically different from those which have long been traditional. It is not only the Congress that is busy designing the new patterns. They are outlined in President Truman's recent disloyalty order; in similar orders formulated by the New York City Council and by state and local authorities throughout the country; in the programs of the D.A.R., the American Legion, and similar patriotic organizations; in the editorials of the Hearst and the McCormick-Patterson papers; and in an elaborate series of advertisements sponsored by large corporations and business organizations. In the making is a revival of the red hysteria of the early 1920's, one of the shabbiest chapters in the history of American democracy; and more than a revival, for the new crusade is designed not merely to frustrate Communism but to formulate a positive definition of Americanism, and a positive concept of loyalty.

What is the new loyalty? It is, above all, conformity. It is the uncritical and unquestioning acceptance of America as it is—the political institutions, the social relationships, the economic practices. It rejects inquiry into the race question or socialized medicine, or public housing, or into the wisdom or validity of our foreign policy. It regards as particularly heinous any challenge to what is called "the system of private enterprise," identifying that system with Americanism. It abandons evolution, repudiates the once popular concept of progress, and regards America as a finished product, perfect and complete.

It is, it must be added, easily satisfied. For it wants not intellectual conviction nor spiritual conquest, but mere outward conformity. In matters of loyalty it takes the word for the deed, the gesture for the principle. It is content with the flag salute, and does not pause to consider the warning of our Supreme Court that "a person gets from a symbol the meaning he puts into it, and what is one man's comfort and inspiration is another's jest and scorn." It is satisfied with membership in respectable organizations and, as it assumes that every member of a liberal organization is a Communist, concludes that every member of a conservative one is a true American. It has not yet learned that not everyone who saith Lord, Lord, shall enter into the kingdom of Heaven. It is designed neither to discover real disloyalty nor to foster true loyalty.

II

What is wrong with this new concept of loyalty? What, fundamentally, is wrong with the pusillanimous retreat of the Washington educators, the barbarous antics of Washington legislators, the hysterical outbursts of the D.A.R., the gross and vulgar appeals of business corporations? It is not merely that these things are offensive. It is rather that they are wrong—morally, socially, and politically.

The concept of loyalty as conformity is a false one. It is narrow and restrictive, denies freedom of thought and of conscience, and is irremediably stained by private and selfish considerations. "Enlightened loyalty," wrote Josiah Royce, who made loyalty the very core of his philosophy,

> means harm to no man's loyalty. It is at war only with disloyalty, and its warfare, unless necessity constrains, is only a spiritual warfare. It does not foster class hatreds; it knows of nothing reasonable about race prejudices; and it regards all races of men as one in their need of loyalty. It ignores mutual misunderstandings. It loves its own wherever upon earth its own, namely loyalty itself, is to be found.

Justice, charity, wisdom, spirituality, he added, were all definable in terms of loyalty, and we may properly ask which of these qualities our contemporary champions of loyalty display.

Above all, loyalty must be to something larger than oneself, untainted by private purposes or selfish ends. But what are we to say of the attempts by the NAM and by individual corporations to identify loyalty with the system of private enterprise? Is it not as if officeholders should attempt to identify loyalty with their own party, their own political careers? Do not those corporations which pay for full-page advertisements associating Americanism with the competitive system expect, ultimately, to profit from that association? Do not those organizations that deplore, in the name of patriotism, the extension of government operation of hydro-electric power expect to profit from their campaign? . . .

There is, it should be added, a further danger in the willful identification of Americanism with a particular body of economic practices. Many learned economists predict for the near future an economic crash similar to that of 1929. If Americanism is equated with competitive capitalism, what happens to it if competitive capitalism comes a cropper? If loyalty and private enterprise are inextricably associated, what is to preserve loyalty if private enterprise fails? Those who associate Americanism with a particular program of economic practices have a grave responsibility, for if their program should fail, they expose Americanism itself to disrepute. . . .

True loyalty may require, in fact, what appears to the naïve to be disloyalty. It may require hostility to certain provisions of the Constitution itself, and historians have not concluded that those who subscribed to the "Higher Law" were lacking in patriotism. We should not forget that our tradition is one of protest and revolt, and it is stultifying to celebrate the rebels of the past—Jefferson and Paine, Emerson and Thoreau—while we silence the rebels of the present. "We are a rebellious nation," said Theodore Parker, known in his day as the Great American Preacher, and went on:

> Our whole history is treason; our blood was attainted before we were born; our creeds are infidelity to the mother church; our constitution, treason to our fatherland. What of that? Though all the governors in the world bid us commit treason against man, and set the example, let us never submit.

Those who would impose upon us a new concept of loyalty not only assume that this is possible, but have the presumption to believe that they are competent to write the definition. We are reminded of Whitman's defiance of the "never-ending audacity of elected persons." Who are those who would set the standards of loyalty? They are Rankins and Bilbos, officials of the D.A.R. and the Legion and the NAM, Hearsts and McCormicks. May we not say of Rankin's harangues on loyalty what Emerson said of Webster at the time of the Seventh of March speech: "The word honor in the mouth of Mr. Webster is like the word love in the mouth of a whore."

What do men know of loyalty who make a mockery of the Declaration of Independence and the Bill of Rights, whose energies are dedicated to stirring up race and class hatreds, who would straitjacket the American spirit? What indeed do they know of America—the America of Sam Adams and Tom Paine, of Jackson's defiance of the Court and Lincoln's celebration of labor, of Thoreau's essay on Civil Disobedience and Emerson's championship of John Brown, of the America of the Fourierists and the Come-Outers, of cranks and fanatics, of socialists and anarchists? Who among American heroes could meet their tests, who would be cleared by their committees? Not Washington, who was a rebel. Not Jefferson, who wrote that all men are created equal and whose motto was "rebellion to tyrants is obedience to God." Not Garrison, who publicly burned the Constitution; or Wendell Philips, who spoke for the underprivileged everywhere and counted himself a philosophical anarchist; not Seward of the Higher Law or Sumner of racial equality. Not Lincoln, who admonished us to have malice toward none, charity for all; or Wilson, who warned that our flag was "a flag of liberty of opinion as well as of political liberty"; or Justice Holmes, who said that our Constitution is an experiment and that while that experiment is being made "we should be eternally vigilant against attempts to check the expression of opinions that we loathe and believe to be fraught with death."

III

There are further and more practical objections against the imposition of fixed concepts of loyalty or tests of disloyalty. The effort is itself a confession of fear, a declaration of insolvency. Those who are sure of themselves do not need reassurance, and those who have confidence in the strength and the virtue of America do not need to fear either criticism or competition. The effort is bound to miscarry. It will not apprehend those who are really disloyal, it will not even frighten them; it will affect only those who can be labeled "radical." It is sobering to recall that though the Japanese relocation program, carried through at such incalculable cost in misery and tragedy, was justified to us on the ground that the Japanese were potentially disloyal, the record does not disclose a single case of Japanese disloyalty or sabotage during the whole war. . . .

Finally, disloyalty tests are not only futile in application, they are pernicious in their consequences. They distract attention from activities that are really disloyal, and silence criticism inspired by true loyalty. That there are disloyal elements in America will not be denied, but there is no reason to suppose that any of the tests now formulated will ever be applied to them. It is relevant to remember that when Rankin was asked why his Committee did not investigate the Ku Klux Klan he replied that the Klan was not un-American, it was American!

Who are those who are really disloyal? Those who inflame racial hatreds, who sow religious and class dissensions. Those who subvert the Constitution by violating the freedom of the ballot box. Those who make a mockery of majority rule by the use of the filibuster. Those who impair democracy by denying equal educational facilities. Those who frustrate justice by lynch law or by making a farce of jury trials. Those who deny freedom of speech and of the press and of assembly. Those who press for special favors against the interest of the commonwealth. Those who regard public office as a source of private gain. Those who would exalt the military over the civil. Those who for selfish and private purposes stir up national antagonisms and expose the world to the ruin of war.

Will the House Committee on Un-American Activities interfere with the activities of these? Will Mr. Truman's disloyalty proclamation reach these? Will the current campaigns for Americanism convert these? If past experience is any guide, they will not. What they will do, if they are successful, is to silence criticism, stamp out dissent—or drive it underground. But if our democracy is to flourish it must have criticism, if our government is to function it must have dissent. Only totalitarian governments insist upon conformity and they—as we know—do so at their peril. Without criticism abuses will go unrebuked; without dissent our dynamic system will become static. The American people have a stake in the maintenance of the most thorough-going inquisition into American institutions. They have a stake in nonconformity, for they know that the American genius is nonconformist. They have a stake in experimentation of the most radical character, for they know that only those who prove all things can hold fast that which is good.

Source: Henry Steele Commager, "Who Is Loyal to America?," *Harper's*, September 1947, p. 193.

For Further Reading:

David Caute, *The Great Fear* (New York: Simon & Schuster, 1978).

Robert Griffith and Athan Theoharris, eds., *The Specter* (New York: New Viewpoints, 1974).

Mary Sperling McAuliffe, *Crisis on the Left* (Amherst: University of Massachusetts Press, 1978).

82. Edward R. Murrow, Excerpt from "TV Comment on Joseph McCarthy" (1954)

1949–50   Alger Hiss hearings and trial
1950   Rosenbergs' trial
1950–54   Joseph McCarthy's heyday
1954   Army-McCarthy Hearings
1955   McCarthy censured by Senate

From 1949 through 1954 America experienced a red scare, comparable to the Salem witchcraft hysteria of 1692 (see document 5). Beginning with a series of sensational congressional investigations and trials, most notably those of former New Dealer Alger Hiss and of Julius and Ethel Rosenberg, who were accused of providing the Soviet Union with secret information about the atomic bomb, Americans became obsessed with fear of communism at home and the threat of internal subversion. Opportunistic and demagogic politicians worsened the situation, especially Joseph McCarthy.

Prior to 1950, McCarthy had been one of the lesser-known figures in Washington, D.C. Then, in February 1950, following a meeting with several advisers who suggested that he needed an issue to improve his political standing, McCarthy stunned the world with his claim that he had a long list of 205 communists in the State Department. Even though his charges never resulted in the criminal conviction of a single State Department employee, he dominated the national scene by issuing one new charge after another. The fact that most of McCarthy's fellow Republicans refused to

"Pay Dirt," Cartoon by Fitzpatrick. *St. Louis Post-Dispatch*, September 1952 (Library of Congress).

challenge him, except to suggest that his methods were wrong, enhanced his power. Another reason McCarthy was able to scare the nation was that the press, by and large, either fostered his attacks or did not mount a significant challenge to him.

This began to change in 1953 when President Eisenhower assumed office. Henceforth, McCarthy was something of a liability to the Republican Party. McCarthy's investigations into subversion within the military hurt him, as it further turned Eisenhower, a former five-star general, against McCarthy and soured the public on McCarthy's methods.

One of the keys to McCarthy's decline came in 1954 when Edward R. Murrow, the dean of television news and a famous World War II radio correspondent, challenged McCarthy on his "See It Now" program. Murrow's commentary ended with a sharp barb that prodded other Americans to speak up. In addition to representing a key moment in the history of

McCarthyism, Murrow's remarks displayed the growing importance of a new technology in America—television.

No one familiar with the history of this country can deny that congressional committees are useful. It is necessary to investigate before legislating. But the line between investigation and persecuting is a very fine one, and the junior senator from Wisconsin has stepped over it repeatedly. His primary achievement has been in confusing the public mind as between the internal and the external threat of Communism. We must not confuse dissent with disloyalty. We must remember always that accusation is not proof and that conviction depends upon evidence and due process of law. We will not walk in fear, one of another. We will not be driven by fear into an age of unreason if we dig deep in our history and our doctrine and remember that we are not descended from fearful men, not from men who feared to write, to speak, to associate and to defend causes which were for the moment unpopular.

This is no time for men who oppose Senator McCarthy's methods to keep silent, *or* for those who approve. We can deny our heritage and our history, but we cannot escape responsibility for the result. As a nation we have come into our full inheritance at a tender age. We proclaim ourselves, as indeed we are, the defenders of freedom—what's left of it—but we cannot defend freedom abroad by deserting it at home. The actions of the junior senator from Wisconsin have caused alarm and dismay amongst our allies abroad and given considerable comfort to our enemies. And whose fault is that? Not really his; he didn't create this situation of fear, he merely exploited it and rather successfully. Cassius was right. "The fault, dear Brutus, is not in our stars but in ourselves."

Source: Edward Bliss, Jr., ed., *In Search of Light: The Broadcasts of Edward R. Murrow, 1938–1961* (New York, 1967), p. 247.

For Further Reading:

Robert Griffith, *The Politics of Fear* (Lexington: University Press of Kentucky, 1970).
David M. Oshinsky, *A Conspiracy So Immense* (New York: Free Press, 1983).
Thomas C. Reeves, *The Life and Times of Joe McCarthy* (New York: Stein and Day, 1982).

PART IX
RECENT AMERICA

83. President's Committee on Civil Rights, Excerpt from "To Secure These Rights" (1947)

1945–46   Wave of postwar lynchings
1947   "To Secure These Rights"
1948   Southern Dixiecrats bolt from Democratic Party

No single issue was more important to the course of democracy in the post–World War II years than civil rights. During the war African Americans had made great strides and their expectations had been raised. The migration of hundreds of thousands of blacks out of the rural South, alone, had shaken traditional race relations (see document 80). Yet African Americans were still far from being equal citizens and many conservative Americans, especially in the South, were dedicated to maintaining white supremacy.

The brutal lynching of several black World War II veterans awoke some Americans from their stupor. President Harry S. Truman responded to a series of mob attacks by southern whites on black army veterans by appointing a Presidential Committee on Civil Rights to investigate race relations and to make recommendations based on its study. Concerns over how racial incidents were effecting America's image abroad and the United States' ability to conduct the Cold War prodded the commission and the President to take an honest look at the subject.

In 1947, the committee issued its report, entitled "To Secure These Rights." The report delineated the basic rights and principles of a democratic society and then, in detail, described the many ways in which African Americans were denied these rights. Not only was the commission the first of its kind, but its charges stood as the strongest official condemnation of racial inequality since at least Reconstruction.

Shortly after the commission report appeared, President Truman requested that Congress implement its recommendations. Truman himself, acting as commander-in-chief, desegregated the armed forces. Most of the recommendations, however, would not be implemented for another fifteen years.

The Time Is Now

Twice before in American history the nation has found it necessary to review the state of its civil rights. The first time was during the 15 years between 1776 and 1791, from the drafting of the Declaration of Indepen-

dence through the Articles of Confederation experiment to the writing of
the Constitution and the Bill of Rights. It was then that the distinctively
American heritage was finally distilled from earlier views of liberty. The
second time was when the Union was temporarily sundered over the question
of whether it could exist "half-slave" and "half-free."

It is our profound conviction that we have come to a time for a third re-
examination of the situation, and a sustained drive ahead. Our reasons for
believing this are those of conscience, of self-interest, and of survival in a
threatening world. Or to put it another way, we have a moral reason, an
economic reason, and an international reason for believing that the time for
action is now.

The Moral Reason

We have considered the American heritage of freedom at some length.
We need no further justification for a broad and immediate program than
the need to reaffirm our faith in the traditional American morality. The
pervasive gap between our aims and what we actually do is creating a kind
of moral dry rot which eats away at the emotional and rational bases of
democratic beliefs. There are times when the difference between what we
preach about civil rights and what we practice is shockingly illustrated by
individual outrages. There are times when the whole structure of our ide-
ology is made ridiculous by individual instances. And there are certain continuing, quiet, omnipresent practices which do irreparable damage to our
beliefs.

As examples of "moral erosion" there are the consequences of suffrage
limitations in the South. The fact that Negroes and many whites have not
been allowed to vote in some states has actually sapped the morality underlying universal suffrage. Many men in public and private life do not
believe that those who have been kept from voting are capable of self rule.
They finally convince themselves that disfranchised people do not really
have the right to vote.

Wartime segregation in the armed forces is another instance of how a
social pattern may wreak moral havoc. Practically all white officers and
enlisted men in all branches of service saw Negro military personnel performing only the most menial functions. They saw Negroes recruited for the
common defense treated as men apart and distinct from themselves. As a
result, men who might otherwise have maintained the equalitarian morality
of their forebears were given reason to look down on their fellow citizens.
This has been sharply illustrated by the Army study discussed previously,
in which white servicemen expressed great surprise at the excellent performance of Negroes who joined them in the firing line. Even now, very few
people know of the successful experiment with integrated combat units. Yet

it is important in explaining why some Negro troops did not do well; it is proof that equal treatment can produce equal performance.

It is impossible to decide who suffers the greatest moral damage from our civil rights transgressions, because all of us are hurt. That is certainly true of those who are victimized. Their belief in the basic truth of the American promise is undermined. But they do have the realization, galling as it sometimes is, of being morally in the right. The damage to those who are responsible for these violations of our moral standards may well be greater. They, too, have been reared to honor the command of "free and equal." And all of us must share in the shame at the growth of hypocrisies like the "automatic" marble champion. All of us must endure the cynicism about democratic values which our failures breed.

The United States can no longer countenance these burdens on its common conscience, these inroads on its moral fiber.

The Economic Reason

One of the principal economic problems facing us and the rest of the world is achieving maximum production and continued prosperity. The loss of a huge, potential market for goods is a direct result of the economic discrimination which is practiced against many of our minority groups. A sort of vicious circle is produced. Discrimination depresses the wages and income of minority groups. As a result, their purchasing power is curtailed and markets are reduced. Reduced markets result in reduced production. This cuts down employment, which of course means lower wages and still fewer job opportunities. Rising fear, prejudice, and insecurity aggravate the very discrimination in employment which sets the vicious circle in motion.

Minority groups are not the sole victims of this economic waste; its impact is inevitably felt by the entire population.

Discrimination imposes a direct cost upon our economy through the wasteful duplication and many facilities and services required by the "separate but equal" policy. That the resources of the South are sorely strained by the burden of a double system of schools and other public services has already been indicated. Segregation is also economically wasteful for private business. Public transportation companies must often provide duplicate facilities to serve majority and minority groups separately. Places of public accommodation and recreation reject business when it comes in the form of unwanted persons. Stores reduce their sales by turning away minority customers. Factories must provide separate locker rooms, pay windows, drinking fountains, and washrooms for the different groups.

Similarly, the rates of disease, crime, and fires are disproportionately great in areas which are economically depressed as compared with wealthier areas. Many of the prominent American American minorities are confined—by economic discrimination, by law, by restrictive covenants, and by social pressure—to the most dilapidated, undesirable locations. Property in these locations yields a smaller return in taxes, which is seldom sufficient to meet the inordinately high cost of public services in depressed areas. The majority pays a high price in taxes for the low status of minorities.

. . . It is not at all surprising that a people relegated to second-class citizenship should behave as second-class citizens. This is true, in varying degrees, of all of our minorities. What we have lost in money, production, invention, citizenship, and leadership as the price for damaged, thwarted personalities—these are beyond estimate.

The United States can no longer afford this heavy drain upon its human wealth, its national competence.

The International Reason

Our position in the postwar world is so vital to the future that our smallest actions have far-reaching effects. We have come to know that our own security in a highly interdependent world is inextricably tied to the security and well-being of all people and all countries. Our foreign policy is designed to make the United States an enormous, positive influence for peace and progress throughout the world. We have tried to let nothing, not even extreme political differences between ourselves and foreign nations, stand in the way of this goal. But our domestic civil rights shortcomings are a serious obstacle.

We cannot escape the fact that our civil rights record has been an issue in world politics. The world's press and radio are full of it. This Committee has seen a multitude of samples. We and our friends have been, and are, stressing our achievements. Those with competing philosophies have stressed—and are shamelessly distorting—our shortcomings. They have not only tried to create hostility toward us among specific nations, races, and religious groups. They have tried to prove our democracy an empty fraud, and our nation a consistent oppressor of underprivileged people. This may seem ludicrous to Americans, but it is sufficiently important to worry our friends.

. . . Our achievements in building and maintaining a state dedicated to the fundamentals of freedom have already served as a guide for those seeking the best road from chaos to liberty and prosperity. But it is not indelibly written that democracy will encompass the world. We are convinced that our way of life—the free way of life—holds a promise of hope for all people. We have what is perhaps the greatest responsibility ever placed upon a people to keep this promise alive. Only still greater achievements will do it.

The United States is not so strong, the final triumph of the democratic ideal is not so inevitable that we can ignore what the world thinks of us or our record.

Source: "To Secure These Rights: The Report of the President's Committee on Civil Rights" (Washington, D.C., 1947).

For Further Reading:

Alonzo L. Hamby, *Beyond the New Deal* (New York: Columbia University Press, 1973).

Donald R. McCoy and Richard T. Reutten, *Quest and Response* (Lawrence: University Press of Kansas, 1973).

84. Brown v. Board of Education of Topeka, Kansas (1954)

1950 *McLaurin v. Oklahoma* and *Sweatt v. Painter*
1954 *Brown v. Board of Education*
1955 "Southern Manifesto"; *Brown II* (enforcement decree)

During the 1930s, the National Association for the Advancement of Colored People (NAACP) mapped out a strategy for challenging "Jim Crow" (laws that segregated blacks and whites) in general and segregation in higher education in particular. Through a series of suits, including McLaurin v. Oklahoma *and* Sweatt v. Painter, *it whittled away the latter. Then, in the early 1950s, the Supreme Court agreed to hear arguments on the broader issue of segregation in public education. After first reviewing evidence on several cases, joined together as* Brown v. Board of Education, *the court ordered attorneys from both sides to submit further information regarding the intent of the framers of the Fourteenth Amendment. Before fully reviewing this material, Chief Justice Frederick M. Vinson died and President Eisenhower nominated Earl Warren, the governor of California, to replace him.*

In arguing the case, the NAACP's lawyers, led by future Supreme Court Justice Thurgood Marshall, contended that segregation itself was discriminatory and violated the Fourteenth Amendment. In earlier cases the NAACP had not requested that the Court overturn Plessy v. Ferguson's *"separate but equal" dictum. In 1896 the Supreme Court had ruled that laws which segregated blacks and whites did not violate the Fourteenth Amendment's prohibition against racial discrimination as long as blacks and whites were treated in an equal manner. In a unanimous decision, written by the new Supreme Court Chief Justice, the Court overruled* Plessy v. Ferguson *in the NAACP's favor.*

Despite the unanimity of the decision, desegregation did not come immediately to American schools. The enforcement of the decision was not spelled out until 1955 with Brown II. *It called for desegregation with "all deliberate speed," which many southerners took to mean never. Southern political leaders, for example, joined together to denounce the decision and to call on southerners to defy the decision in all legal ways possible. Other southerners took much more drastic actions. In 1957 President Eisenhower was compelled to send federal troops into Little Rock, Arkansas, to protect nine black students from unruly mobs attempting to prevent from them entering Central High. In 1958, after being forced to integrate, local authorities determined that they preferred no public education to desegregated education, and closed their schools. Other districts followed suit.*

W arren, C. J. These cases come to us from the States of Kansas, South Carolina, Virginia, and Delaware. They are premised on different facts and different local conditions, but a common legal question justifies their consideration together in this consolidated opinion.

In each of the cases, minors of the Negro race, through their legal representatives, seek the aid of the courts in obtaining admission to the public schools of their community on a nonsegregated basis. In each instance, they have been denied admission to schools attended by white children under laws requiring or permitting segregation according to race. This segregation was alleged to deprive the plaintiffs of the equal protection of the laws under the Fourteenth Amendment. In each of the cases other than the Delaware case, a three-judge federal district court denied relief to the plaintiffs on the so-called "separate but equal" doctrine announced by this Court in *Plessy v. Ferguson*, 163 U.S. 537. Under that doctrine, equality of treatment is accorded when the races are provided substantially equal facilities, even though these facilities be separate. In the Delaware case, the Supreme Court of Delaware adhered to that doctrine, but ordered that the plaintiffs be admitted to the white schools because of their superiority to the Negro schools.

The plaintiffs contend that segregated public schools are not "equal" and cannot be made "equal," and that hence they are deprived of the equal protection of the laws. Because of the obvious importance of the question presented, the Court took jurisdiction. Argument was heard in the 1952

Term, and reargument was heard this Term on certain questions propounded by the Court.

Reargument was largely devoted to the circumstances surrounding the adoption of the Fourteenth Amendment in 1868. It covered exhaustively consideration of the Amendment in Congress, ratification by the states, then existing practices in racial segregation, and the views of proponents and opponents of the Amendment. This discussion and our own investigation convince us that, although these sources cast some light, it is not enough to resolve the problem with which we are faced. At best, they are inconclusive. The most avid proponents of the post-War Amendments undoubtedly intended them to remove all legal distinctions among "all persons born or naturalized in the United States." Their opponents, just as certainly, were antagonistic to both the letter and the spirit of the Amendments and wished them to have the most limited effect. What others in Congress and the state legislatures had in mind cannot be determined with any degree of certainty.

An additional reason for the inconclusive nature of the Amendment's history, with respect to segregated schools, is the status of public education at that time. In the South, the movement toward free common schools, supported by general taxation, had not yet taken hold. Education of white children was largely in the hands of private groups. Education of Negroes was almost nonexistent, and practically all of the race were illiterate. In fact, any education of Negroes was forbidden by law in some states. Today, in contrast, many Negroes have achieved outstanding success in the arts and sciences as well as in the business and professional world. It is true that public education had already advanced further in the North, but the effect of the Amendment on Northern States was generally ignored in the congressional debates. Even in the North, the conditions of public education did not approximate those existing today. The curriculum was usually rudimentary; ungraded schools were common in rural areas; the school term was but three months a year in many states; and compulsory school attendance was virtually unknown. As a consequence, it is not surprising that there should be so little in the history of the Fourteenth Amendment relating to its intended effect on public education.

In the first cases in this Court construing the Fourteenth Amendment, decided shortly after its adoption, the Court interpreted it as proscribing all state-imposed discriminations against the Negro race. The doctrine of "separate but equal" did not make its appearance in this Court until 1896 in the case of *Plessy v. Ferguson*, supra, involving not education but transportation. American courts have since labored with the doctrine for over half a century. In this Court, there have been six cases involving the "separate but equal" doctrine in the field of public education. In *Cumming v. Board of Education of Richmond County*, 175 U.S. 528, and *Gong Lum v. Rice*, 275 U.S. 78, the validity of the doctrine itself was not challenged. In more recent cases, all on the graduate school level, inequality was found in that specific benefits enjoyed by white students were denied to Negro students of the same educational qualifications. *State of Missouri ex rel. Gaines v. Canada*, 305 U.S. 337; *Sipuel v. Board of Regents of University of Oklahoma*, 332 U.S. 631; *Sweatt v. Painter*, 339 U.S. 629; *McLaurin v. Oklahoma State Regents*, 339 U.S. 637. In none of these cases was it necessary to reexamine the doctrine to grant relief to the Negro plaintiff. And in *Sweatt v. Painter*, supra, the Court expressly reserved decision on the question whether *Plessy v. Ferguson* should be held inapplicable to public education.

In the instant cases, that question is directly presented. Here, unlike *Sweatt v. Painter*, there are findings below that the Negro and white schools involved have been equalized, or are being equalized, with respect to buildings, curricula, qualifications and salaries of teachers, and other "tangible" factors. Our decision, therefore, cannot turn on merely a comparison of these tangible factors in the Negro and white schools involved in each of the cases. We must look instead to the effect of segregation itself on public education.

In approaching this problem, we cannot turn the clock back to 1868 when the Amendment was adopted, or even to 1896 when *Plessy v. Ferguson* was written. We must consider public education in the light of its full development and its present place in American life throughout the Nation. Only in this way can it be determined if segregation in public schools deprives these plaintiffs of the equal protection of the laws.

Today, education is perhaps the most important function of state and local governments. Compulsory school attendance laws and the great expenditures for education both demonstrate our recognition of the importance of education to our democratic society. It is required in the performance of our most basic public responsibilities, even service in the armed forces. It is the very foundation of good citizenship. Today it is a principal instrument in awakening the child to cultural values, in preparing him for later professional training, and in helping him to adjust normally to his environment. In these days, it is doubtful that any child may reasonably be expected to succeed in life if he is denied the opportunity of an education. Such an opportunity, where the state has undertaken to provide it, is a right which must be made available to all on equal terms.

We come then to the question presented: Does segregation of children in public schools solely on the basis of race, even though the physical facilities and other "tangible" factors may be equal, deprive the children of the minority group of equal educational opportunities? We believe that it does.

In *Sweatt v. Painter*, supra [339 U.S. 629, 70 S.Ct. 850], in finding that a segregated law school for Negroes could not provide them equal educational opportunities, this Court relied in large part on "those qualities which are incapable of objective measurement but which make for greatness in a law school." In *McLaurin v. Oklahoma State Regents*, supra [339 U.S. 637, 70 S.Ct. 853], the Court, in requiring that a Negro admitted to a white graduate school be treated like all other students, again resorted to intangible considerations: "... his ability to study, to engage in discussions and exchange views with other students, and, in general, to learn his profession." Such considerations apply with added force to children in grade and high schools. To separate them from others of similar age and qualifications solely because of their race generates a feeling of inferiority as to their status in the community that may affect their hearts and minds in a way unlikely ever to be undone. The effect of this separation on their educational opportunities was well stated by a finding in the Kansas case by a court which nevertheless felt compelled to rule against the Negro plaintiffs.

> Segregation of white and colored children in public schools has a detrimental effect upon the colored children. The impact is greater when it has the sanction of the law; for the policy of separating the races is usually interpreted as denoting the inferiority of the Negro group. A sense of inferiority affects the motivation of a child to learn. Segregation with the sanction of law, therefore, has a tendency to retard the educational and mental development of Negro children and to deprive them of some of the benefits they would receive in a racially integrated school system.

Whatever may have been the extent of psychological knowledge at the time of *Plessy v. Ferguson*, this finding is amply supported by modern authority. Any language in *Plessy v. Ferguson* contrary to this finding is rejected.

We conclude that in the field of public education the doctrine of "separate but equal" has no place. Separate educational facilities are inherently unequal. Therefore, we hold that the plaintiffs and others similarly situated for whom the actions have been brought are, by reason of the segregation complained of, deprived of the equal protection of the laws guaranteed by the Fourteenth Amendment. This deposition makes unnecessary any discussion whether such segregation also violates the Due Process Clause of the Fourteenth Amendment.

Because these are class actions, because of the wide applicability of this decision, and because of the great variety of local conditions, the formulation of decrees in these cases presents problems of considerable complexity. On reargument, the consideration of appropriate relief was necessarily subordinated to the primary question—the constitutionality of segregation in public education. We have now announced that such segregation is a denial of the equal protection of the laws. In order that we may have the full assistance of the parties in formulating decrees, the cases will be restored to the docket, and the parties are requested to present further argument. . . . The Attorney General of the United States is again invited to participate. The Attorneys General of the states requiring or permitting segregation in public education

will also be permitted to appear as *amici curiae* upon request to do so by
September 15, 1954, and submission of briefs by October 1, 1954.

It is so ordered.

Source: *Brown v. Board of Education of Topeka, Kansas*, 347 U.S. 483 (1954).

For Further Reading:

Numan V. Bartley, *The Rise of Massive Resistance* (Baton Rouge: Louisiana State
University Press, 1969).

Richard Kluger, *Simple Justice* (New York: Knopf, 1975).

85. Martin Luther King, Jr., Excerpt from "I Have a Dream" (1963)

1955–56   Montgomery, Alabama, bus boycott
1963   Birmingham, Alabama, protests; March on Washington
1964   King awarded Nobel Peace Prize

*From 1955 through 1965, America experienced a second revolution. With
African Americans in the lead, civil rights activists fought to square reality
with the Declaration of Independence and the Constitution. In 1955, Rosa
Parks, a 47-year-old seamstress, helped launch this revolution when she
refused to give up her seat on a public bus to a white man. For over a year,
black Montgomerians, led by Martin Luther King, Jr., boycotted the buses
to win equal treatment and respect from the white community. In the early
1960s the pace of protest picked up, first with a series of sit-ins at Wool-
worth's and other chain stores and then with the Freedom Rides, whereby
activists rode through the South on buses in an integrated manner. In both
cases, college students constituted the army for change and they utilized the
weapon of nonviolent direct action to wage their war.*

*The struggle for racial equality reached a new height in 1963. Mass pro-
tests erupted across the nation, most notably in Birmingham, Alabama,
where Martin Luther King, Jr. and the Southern Christian Leadership Conference pressured the town's leaders to desegregate their facilities, hire
blacks in downtown stores, and grant them full citizenship rights. The protests revealed the raw brutality of white supremacy to the nation, as local
authorities trained water cannon on peaceful demonstrators and allowed
their vicious German shepherd dogs to bite young nonviolent activists. Ultimately, the protests prodded John F. Kennedy to demand congressional
action (see document 87).*

That same summer, over 200,000 men and women, black and white, young and old, representing virtually all of the arms of the civil rights crusade, joined together in Washington, D.C., for the March for Jobs and Freedom. Organized by A. Philip Randolph (see document 80), the march was one of the stellar moments of the movement and was the stage for the delivery of one of the greatest speeches in United States history, Martin Luther King, Jr.'s "I Have a Dream." In it he presented a vision of democracy that has few rivals.

Five score years ago, a great American, in whose symbolic shadow we stand, signed the Emancipation Proclamation. This momentous decree came as a great beacon of light of hope to millions of Negro slaves who had been seared in the flames of withering injustice. It came as a joyous daybreak to end the long night of captivity.

But one hundred years later, we must face the tragic fact that the Negro is still not free. One hundred years later, the life of the Negro is still sadly crippled by the manacles of segregation and the chains of discrimination. One hundred years later, the Negro lives on a lonely island of poverty in the midst of a vast ocean of material prosperity. . . . So we have come here today to dramatize an appalling condition.

In a sense we have come to our nation's Capital to cash a check. When the architects of our republic wrote the magnificent words of the Constitution and the Declaration of Independence, they were signing a promissory note to which every American was to fall heir. This note was a promise that all men would be guaranteed the unalienable rights of life, liberty, and the pursuit of happiness.

It is obvious today that America has defaulted on this promissory note insofar as her citizens of color are concerned. Instead of honoring this sacred obligation, America has given the Negro people a bad check; a check which has come back marked "insufficient funds." But we refuse to believe that the bank of justice is bankrupt. We refuse to believe that there are insufficient funds in the great vaults of opportunity of this nation. So we have come to cash this check. . . .

We have also come to this hallowed spot to remind America of the fierce urgency of now. This is no time to engage in the luxury of cooling off or to take a tranquilizing dose of gradualism. Now is the time to make real the promises of Democracy. Now is the time to rise from the dark and desolate valley of segregation to the sunlit path of racial justice. Now is the time to open the doors of opportunity to all of God's children. Now is the time to lift our nation from the quicksands of racial injustice to the solid rock of brotherhood.

It would be fatal for the nation to overlook the urgency of the moment and to underestimate the determination of the Negro. The sweltering summer of the Negro's legitimate discontent will not pass until there is an invigorating autumn of freedom and equality. 1963 is not an end, but a beginning. Those who hope that the Negro needed to blow off steam and will now be content will have a rude awakening if the Nation returns to business as usual. There will be neither rest nor tranquility in America until the Negro is granted his citizenship rights. The whirlwinds of revolt will continue to shake the foundations of our Nation until the bright day of justice emerges.

But there is something that I must say to my people who stand on the warm threshold which leads into the palace of justice. In the process of gaining our rightful place we must not be guilty of wrongful deeds. Let us not need to satisfy our thirst for freedom by drinking from the cup of bitterness and hatred. We must forever conduct our struggle on the high plane of dignity and discipline. . . . The marvelous new militancy which has engulfed the Negro community must not lead us to distrust white people, for many of our white brothers, as evidenced by their presence here today, have come to realize that their destiny is tied up with our destiny and their freedom is inextricably bound to our freedom. We cannot walk alone. . . .

There are those who are asking the devotees of civil rights, "When will you be satisfied?" We can never be satisfied as long as the Negro is the victim of the unspeakable horrors of police brutality. . . . We cannot be satisfied as long as the Negro's basic mobility is from a smaller ghetto to a larger one. We can never be satisfied as long as a Negro in Mississippi cannot vote and a Negro in New York believes he has nothing for which to vote. No, no we are not satisfied, and we will not be satisfied until justice rolls down like waters and righteousness like a mighty stream.

I am not unmindful that some of you have come here out of great trials and tribulations. Some of you have come fresh from narrow jail cells. Some of you have come from areas where you quest for freedom left you battered by the storms of persecution. You have been the veterans of creative suffering. Continue to work with the faith that unearned suffering is redemptive.

Go back to Mississippi, go back to Alabama, go back to South Carolina, . . . go back to the slums and ghettos of our modern cities, knowing that somehow this situation can and will be changed. Let us not wallow in the valley of despair.

I say to you today, my friends, that in spite of the difficulties and frustrations of the moment I still have a dream. It is a dream deeply rooted in the American dream.

I have a dream that one day this nation will rise up and live out the true meaning of its creed: "We hold these truths to be self-evident; that all men are created equal."

I have a dream that one day on the red hills of Georgia the sons of former slaves and the sons of former slaveowners will be able to sit down together at the table of brotherhood.

I have a dream that one day even the state of Mississippi, a desert state sweltering with the heat of injustice and oppression, will be transformed into an oasis of freedom and justice.

I have a dream that my four children will one day live in a nation where they will not be judged by the color of their skin but by the content of their character.

I have a dream today.

I have a dream that one day the state of Alabama, whose governor's lips are presently dripping with the words of interposition and nullification, will be transformed into a situation where little black boys and black girls will be able to join hands with little white boys and white girls and walk together as sisters and brothers.

I have a dream today.

I have a dream that one day every valley shall be exalted, every hill and mountain shall be made low, the rough places will be made plains, and the crooked places will be made straight, and the glory of the Lord shall be revealed, and all flesh shall see it together.

This is our hope. This is the faith with which I return to the South. With this faith we will be able to hew out of the mountain of despair a stone of hope. With this faith we will be able to transform the jangling discords of our nation into a beautiful symphony of brotherhood. With this faith we will be able to work together, to pray together, to struggle together, to go to jail together, to stand up for freedom together, knowing that we will be free one day.

This will be the day when all God's children will be able to sing with new meaning "My country 'tis of thee, sweet land of liberty, of thee I sing. Land where my fathers died, land of the pilgrim's pride, from every mountainside, let freedom ring."

And if America is to be a great nation this must come to be true. So let freedom ring from the prodigious hilltops of New Hampshire. Let freedom ring from the mighty mountains of New York. Let freedom ring from the heightening Alleghenies of Pennsylvania!

. . . But not only that; let freedom ring from Stone Mountain of Georgia! Let freedom ring from Lookout Mountain, Tennessee! Let freedom ring from every hill and mole hill of Mississippi. From every mountainside, let freedom ring.

When we let freedom ring, when we let it ring from every village and every hamlet, from every state and every city, we will be able to speed up that day when all of God's children, black men and white men, Jews and Gentiles, Protestants and Catholics, will be able to join hands and sing in the words of the old Negro spiritual, "Free at last! Free at last! thank God almighty, we are free at last!"

Source: Martin Luther King, Jr., "I Have a Dream," August 28, 1963.

For Further Reading:

Taylor Branch, *Parting the Waters* (New York: Simon & Schuster, 1988).
David J. Garrow, *Bearing the Cross* (New York: William Morrow, 1986).

86. "We Shall Overcome" (n.d.)

1960   Sit-ins
1961   Freedom Rides
1960–65   Student Nonviolent Coordinating Committee
         (SNCC), Congress of Racial Equality (CORE), and
         independent activists protest across the South

Through most of American history, democracy has come about only through mass resistance to oppression. American revolutionaries gained independence from Britain only after years of armed struggle. Slavery was overthrown only through the courageous efforts of abolitionists, the defiance of slave rebels, and the death of hundreds of thousands of soldiers on the battlefield. Workers gained fair wages through years of strife. Women won the vote only after thousands of them marched in the streets. Similarly, the modern struggle for civil rights witnessed extreme sacrifice and commitment in the face of brutal repression.

A recurrent theme in these fights is the use of song or music to bolster the morale of the activists and to reach out to the uncommitted. The Industrial Workers of the World (IWW), for example, used tunes such as "Rebel Girl" and "The Preacher and the Slave" (see document 53) to recruit and rally workers for a better life. One of the greatest protest songs is "We Shall Overcome." Originally sung by striking tobacco workers in the 1940s, the song was picked up by Highlander Folk School, an untraditional workers' and human rights educational institution, and passed down to civil rights activists in the 1950s. "We Shall Overcome" became the movement's anthem. Activists sang it and many other songs in the streets, while in jail and at mass demonstrations and sit-ins. It portrayed both their commitment to nonviolent struggle and their sense of the long struggle for democracy in America and elsewhere.

We shall overcome
We shall overcome
We shall overcome someday
Oh, deep in my heart

March on Washington for Jobs and Freedom, August 28, 1963 (National Archives).

I do believe
We shall overcome someday!

We'll walk hand in hand, we'll walk hand in hand,
We'll walk hand in hand, some day.
Oh, deep in my heart I do believe,
That we shall overcome some day.

We are not afraid, we are not afraid,
We are not afraid, today.
Oh, deep in my heart I do believe
That we shall overcome some day.

We shall overcome, etc.

(*Additional verses*)

We shall live in peace . . .

The truth will make us free . . .

We shall brothers be . . .

Source: Guy and Candie Carawan, eds., *We Shall Overcome! Songs of the Southern Freedom Movement* (New York, 1963).

For Further Reading:

Clayborne Carson, *In Struggle* (Cambridge, Mass.: Harvard University Press, 1981).
Mary King, *Freedom Song* (New York: William Morrow, 1987).

87. John F. Kennedy, Excerpt from "Address on Civil Rights" (1963)

1960   John F. Kennedy defeats Richard Nixon
1962   University of Mississippi crisis
1963   Birmingham, Alabama, protests; "Address on Civil
       Rights"; JFK assassinated
1964   Lyndon Johnson signs Civil Rights Act of 1964

John F. Kennedy's election to the presidency, his promise to get the nation moving again, and his reputation for political courage and vigor raised the hopes of African Americans. They expected him to take the lead in promoting racial equality. Yet for two years President Kennedy proved timid on civil rights. Not wanting to jeopardize the rest of his domestic and foreign agenda, which depended on southern support, he neither proposed significant civil rights legislation nor spoke to the nation about the problem. Even when faced with crises, like the University of Mississippi's refusal in 1962 to register James Meredith, the first black person to be admitted to the University of Mississippi, President Kennedy tended to equivocate.

Yet the civil rights struggle did not retreat from the streets, and President Kennedy was ultimately forced to act. During the spring of 1963, protests for equality grabbed the nation's headlines, most notably via the demonstrations in Birmingham, Alabama, led by Martin Luther King, Jr. Telegrams and letters poured into the White House expressing disgust with the treatment of blacks in the South. America's image abroad was taking a beating. Hence, on the evening of June 11, 1963, Kennedy went before the people and delivered a nationally televised address on civil rights. The speech stands as one of the most significant addresses by a President on race relations in American history. In it President Kennedy demanded that America live up to its moral principles and its leadership role in the world.

JFK followed his address by proposing significant civil rights legislation. Through the summer and fall months of 1963, however, he was unable to

Debate between presidential candidates John F. Kennedy and Richard Nixon, 1960
(Library of Congress).

push the bill through Congress. And in November 1963 he was assassinated
before the congressional deadlock was broken. Less than a year later, Pres-
ident Lyndon Johnson signed into law the Civil Rights Act of 1964. It was
the most sweeping civil rights measure passed in United States history.

Good evening my fellow citizens. This afternoon, following a series
of threats and defiant statements, the presence of Alabama National Guards-
men was required on the campus of the University of Alabama to carry out
the final and unequivocal order of the United States District Court of the
Northern District of Alabama.

The order called for the admission of two clearly qualified young Alabama
residents who happened to have been born Negro.

That they were admitted peacefully on the campus is due in good measure
to the conduct of the students of the University of Alabama who met their
responsibilities in a constructive way.

I hope that every American, regardless of where he lives, will stop and
examine his conscience about this and other related incidents.

This nation was founded by men of many nations and backgrounds. It was founded on the principle that all men are created equal, and that the rights of every man are diminished when the rights of one man are threatened.

Today we are committed to a worldwide struggle to promote and protect the rights of all who wish to be free. And when Americans are sent to Vietnam or West Berlin we do not ask for whites only.

It ought to be possible, therefore, for American students of any color to attend any public institution they select without having to be backed up by troops. It ought to be possible for American consumers of any color to receive equal service in places of public accommodation, such as hotels and restaurants, and theaters and retail stores without being forced to resort to demonstrations in the street.

And it ought to be possible for American citizens of any color to register and to vote in a free election without interference or fear of reprisal.

It ought to be possible, in short, for every American to enjoy the privileges of being American without regard to his race or his color.

In short, every American ought to have the right to be treated as he would wish to be treated, as one would wish his children to be treated. But this is not the case.

The Negro baby born in America today, regardless of the section or the state in which he is born, has about one-half as much chance of completing high school as a white baby, born in the same place, on the same day . . . twice as much chance of becoming unemployed . . . a life expectancy which is seven years shorter. . . .

This is not a sectional issue. Difficulties over segregation and discrimination exist in almost every city . . . producing . . . a rising tide of discontent that threatens the public safety.

Nor is this a partisan issue. In a time of domestic crisis, men of goodwill and generosity should be able to unite regardless of party or politics.

This is not even a legal or legislative issue alone. It is better to settle these matters in the courts than on the streets, and new laws are needed at every level. But law alone cannot make men see right.

We are confronted primarily with a moral issue. It is as old as the Scriptures and is as clear as the American Constitution. The heart of the question is whether all Americans are to be afforded equal rights and equal opportunities; whether we are going to treat our fellow Americans as we want to be treated.

If an American, because his skin is dark, cannot eat lunch in a restaurant open to the public; if he cannot send his children to the best public school available; if he cannot vote for the public officials who represent him; if, in short, he cannot enjoy the full and free life which all of us want, then who among us would be content to have the color of his skin changed and stand in his place?

Who among us would then be content with the counsels of patience and delay. One hundred years of delay have passed since President Lincoln freed the slaves, yet their heirs, their grandsons, are not fully free. . . .

And this nation, for all its hopes and all its boasts, will not be fully free until all its citizens are free.

We preach freedom around the world, and we mean it. And we cherish our freedom here at home. But are we to say to the world—and more importantly to each other—that this is the land of the free, except for the Negroes. . . .

Now the time has come for this nation to fulfill its promise. The events in Birmingham and elsewhere have so increased the cries for equality that no city or state or legislative body can prudently choose to ignore them.

The fires of frustration and discord are burning in every city, North and South. Where legal remedies are not at hand, redress is sought in the streets in demonstrations, parades and protests, which create tensions and threaten violence—and threaten lives.

We face, therefore, a moral crisis as a country and a people. It cannot be met by repressive police action. It cannot be left to increased demonstrations in the streets. It cannot be quieted by token moves or talk. It is time to act in the Congress, in your state and local legislative body, in all of our daily lives.

It is not enough to pin the blame on others, to say this is a problem of one section of the country or another, or deplore the facts that we face. A great change is at hand, and our task, our obligation is to make that revolution, that change peaceful and constructive for all.

Those who do nothing are inviting shame as well as violence. Those who act boldly are recognizing right as well as reality.

Next week I shall ask the Congress of the United States to act, to make a commitment it has not fully made in this century to the proposition that race has no place in American life or law. . . .

But legislation, I repeat, cannot solve this problem alone. It must be solved in the homes of every American in every community across our country.

In this respect, I want to pay tribute to those citizens, North and South, who've been working in their communities to make life better for all. They are acting not out of a sense of legal duty but out of a sense of human decency. Like our soldiers and sailors in all parts of the world, they are meeting freedom's challenge on the firing line and I salute them for their honor—their courage. . . .

We have a right to expect that the Negro community will be responsible, will uphold the law. But they have a right to expect that the law will be fair, that the Constitution will be color blind, as Justice Harlan said at the turn of the century.

This is what we're talking about. This is a matter which concerns this country and what it stands for, and in meeting it I ask the support of all our citizens.

Source: John F. Kennedy, "Address," June 11, 1963.

For Further Reading:

Carl Brauer, *John F. Kennedy and the Second Reconstruction* (New York: Columbia University Press, 1977).

Hugh Davis Graham, *The Civil Rights Era* (New York: Oxford University Press, 1990).

Harvard Sitkoff, *The Struggle for Black Equality, 1954–1992* (New York: Hill & Wang, 1993).

88. Fannie Lou Hamer, Excerpt from "Testimony Before the Credentials Committee of the Democratic National Convention" (1964)

1964   Mississippi Summer
1968–72   Democratic Party reforms nominating procedure

In the summer of 1964, civil rights forces organized a massive campaign known as Mississippi Summer. Spearheaded by the Student Nonviolent Coordinating Committee (SNCC), it represented a turning point in the civil rights struggle. Nearly one thousand volunteers, many white college students, traveled to Mississippi to organize a grass-roots movement, including the Mississippi Freedom Democratic Party (MFDP). MFDP was a multiracial political party established in part to challenge the state's regular Democratic Party for recognition at the Democratic Party's national convention in Atlantic City. The highlight of this effort was Fannie Lou Hamer's testimony to the Credentials Committee of the Democratic National Convention.

Hamer personified the grass-roots strength of the movement. A sharecropper and mother, her courage was legendary. Her story convinced many delegates of the virtue of the MFDP's case. Unwilling to risk a walkout of southern delegates, however, President Johnson commanded the party's apparatus to offer a "compromise" of two at-large delegates for the MFDP, rather that full representation. Not only did the MFDP reject this token offer, but many of its allies were forever embittered against Lyndon Johnson and white liberals who promoted the "compromise." Within a year the civil rights movement had entered a new phase. Riots had broken out in Watts,

Los Angeles, and spread elsewhere. SNCC and other student groups jetti-soned their commitment to nonviolence and integration.

This said, while Hamer's testimony did not win MFDP recognition in 1964, it did prompt the Democratic Party to reform its methods for selecting delegates and nominating candidates. Four years later a number of MFDP veterans entered another challenge to the regular party from Mississippi, which was still all-white and opposed to civil rights. This time the MFDP won, as the Democratic Party refused to seat the state's regular slate and instead granted recognition to a group made up of MFDP veterans and other reformers. Indeed, the MFDP challenge helped open up the political process to many other groups, so that by 1972 the nominating process was a much more democratic affair.

Mr. Chairman, and the Credentials Committee, my name is Mrs. Fannie Lou Hamer, and I live at 626 East Lafayette Street, Ruleville, Mississippi, Sunflower County, the home of Senator James O. Eastland, and Senator Stennis.

It was the 31st of August in 1962 that 18 of us traveled 26 miles to the county courthouse in Indianola to try to register to try to became first-class citizens. We was met in Indianola by Mississippi men, Highway Patrolmen and they allowed two of us in to take the literacy test at the time. After we had taken the test and started back to Ruleville, we was held up by the City Police and the State Highway Patrolmen and carried back to Indianola where the bus driver was charged that day with driving a bus the wrong color.

After we paid the fine among us, we continued on to Ruleville, and Reverend Jeff Sunny carried me the four miles in the rural area where I had worked as a time-keeper and sharecropper for 18 years. I was met there by my children, who told me the plantation owner was angry because I had gone down to try to register.

After they told me, my husband came, and said the plantation owner was raising cain because I had tried to register and before he quit talking the plantation owner came, and said, "Fannie Lou, do you know—did Pap tell you what I said?" And I said, "Yes sir." He said, "I mean that. . . . If you don't go down and withdraw . . . well—you might have to go because we are not ready for that." . . .

And I addressed him and told him and said, "I didn't try to register for you. I tried to register for myself."

I had to leave that same night.

On the 10th of September, 1962, 16 bullets was fired into the home of Mr. and Mrs. Robert Tucker for me. That same night two girls were shot in Ruleville, Mississippi. Also Mr. Joe McDonald's house was shot in.

And in June, the 9th, 1963, I had attended a voter registration workshop, was returning back to Mississippi. Ten of us was traveling by the Continental

Trailways bus. When we got to Winona, Mississippi, which is Montgomery County, four of the people got off to use the washroom. . . . I stepped off the bus to see what was happening and somebody screamed from the car that four workers was in and said, "Get that one there," and when I went to get in the car, when the man told me I was under arrest, he kicked me.

I was carried to the county jail and put in the holding room. They left some of the people in the booking room and began to place us in cells. I was placed in a cell with a young woman called Miss Euvester Simpson. After I was placed in the cell I began to hear sounds of licks and screams. I could hear the sounds of licks and horrible screams, and I could hear somebody say, "Can you say, yes, sir, nigger?" "Can you say yes, sir?"

And they would say horrible names. She would say. "Yes, I can say yes, sir." . . . They beat her, I don't know how long, and after a while she began to pray and asked God to have Mercy on those people. And it wasn't too long before three white men came to my cell. One of these men was a State Highway Patrolmen and he asked me where I was from, and I told him Ruleville; he said, "We are going to check this."

And they left my cell and it wasn't too long before they came back. He said, "You are from Ruleville all right," and he used a curse word, he said, "We are going to beat you until you wish you was dead."

I was carried out of that cell into another cell where they had two Negro prisoners. The State Highway patrolmen ordered the first Negro to take the blackjack. The first Negro prisoner ordered me, by orders from the State Highway Patrolmen, for me to lay down on a bunk bed on my face, and I laid on my face.

The first Negro began to beat, and I was beat by the first Negro until he was exhausted, and I was holding my hands behind at this time on my left side because I suffered polio when I was six years old. After the first Negro had beat until he was exhausted the state Highway Patrolman ordered the second Negro to take the blackjack. The second Negro began to beat and I began to work my feet, and the State Highway Patrolman ordered the first Negro who had beat to set on my feet to keep me from working my feet. I began to scream and one white man got up and began to beat me in my head and tell me to hush.

One white man—my dress had worked up high, he walked over and pulled my dress down and he pulled my dress back, back up. . . .

All of this on account we want to register, to become first-class citizens, and if the freedom Democratic Party is not seated now, I question America, is this America, the land of the free and the home of the brave where we have to sleep with our telephones off the hooks because our lives be threatened daily because we want to live as decent human beings, in America?

Source: "Testimony of Fannie Lou Hamer Before the Credentials Committee of the Democratic National Convention," August 22, 1964, Atlantic City, New Jersey.

For Further Reading:

Len Holt, *The Summer That Didn't End* (New York: Da Capo Press, 1992).
Doug McAdam, *Freedom Summer* (New York: Oxford University Press, 1988).

89. Albert S. Bigelow, Excerpt from "Why I Am Sailing into the Pacific Bomb-Test Area" (1958)

1950   First hydrogen bomb detonated
1958   Bigelow protests against nuclear weapons testing
1963   United States and Soviets sign nuclear test-ban treaty

When the Cold War began, American statesmen presented the case for "containing" the Soviet Union with moral clarity. President Truman, for example, defended the "Truman Doctrine," whereby the United States granted military aid to Greece and Turkey, on the grounds that they represented freedom and that the line against communist aggression and terror had to be established before it was too late. While a handful of prominent men and women objected to this policy and the reasoning behind it, by and large criticism of American foreign policy was muted throughout the 1950s. For example, few protested America's decision to develop a hydrogen bomb program and those who did were often censured for doing so.

Toward the end of the decade, however, a small core of activists, many of them pacifists, began to challenge America's international role, or at least aspects of it. One to do so was Albert S. Bigelow, a World War II veteran and a convert to Quakerism. In particular, Bigelow aimed his protest at what he saw as the most galling example of the excesses of the Cold War, the atmospheric testing of nuclear weapons. He did so in the tradition of nonviolent direct action as spelled out by Henry David Thoreau (see document 27) and practiced by the civil rights movement. Specifically, he sailed a small boat into the test bomb area sight. He explained his reasons for doing so in an essay that appeared in Liberation, *an independent left-wing journal.*

Bigelow's action had no immediate effect. He was arrested by naval authorities and the testing went on as planned. Yet he did encourage others to protest. By 1963, in fact, thousands of Americans joined together to protest nuclear testing. And shortly before his death, President Kennedy signed a treaty with the Soviet Union that banned atmospheric testing of nuclear weapons.

Atomic Cloud from blast at Bikini Island, July 25, 1946 (National Archives).

$\mathbf{M}$y friend Bill Huntington and I are planning to sail a small vessel westward into the Pacific H-bomb test area. By April we expect to reach nuclear testing grounds at Eniwetok. We will remain there as long as the tests of H-bombs continue. With us will be two other volunteers.

Why? Because it is the way I can say to my government, to the British government, and to the Kremlin: "Stop! Stop this madness before it is too late. For God's sake, turn back!"

How have I come to this conviction? Why do I feel under compulsion, under moral orders, as it were, to do this?

The answer to such questions, at least in part, has to do with my experience as a Naval officer during World War II. The day after Pearl Harbor was attacked, I was at the Navy recruiting offices. I had had a lot of experience in navigating vessels. Life in the Navy would be a glamorous change from the dull mechanism of daily civilian living. My experience assured me of success. All this adventure ahead and the prospect of becoming a hero into the bargain.

I suppose, too, that I had an enormous latent desire to conform, to go along with the rest of my fellows. I was swayed by the age-old psychology of meeting force with force. It did not really occur to me to resist the drag of the institution of war, the pattern of organized violence, which had existed for so many centuries. This psychology prevailed even though I had already reflected on the fantastic wastefulness of war—the German *Bismarck* hunting the British *Hood* and sending it to the bottom of the sea, and the British Navy hunting the *Bismarck* and scuttling it. . . .

Later in World War II, I was Captain of the destroyer escort *Dale W. Peterson*—DE 337—and I was on the bridge as we came into Pearl Harbor from San Francisco when the first news arrived of the explosion of an atomic bomb over Hiroshima. Although I had no way of understanding what an atom bomb was, I was absolutely awestruck, as I suppose all men were for a moment. Intuitively it was then that I realized for the first time that morally war is impossible.

I don't suppose I had the same absolute realization with my whole being, so to speak, of the immorality and "impossibility" of nuclear war until the morning of August 7, 1957. On that day, I sat with a score of friends, before dawn, in the Nevada desert just outside the entrance to the Camp Mercury testing grounds. The day before, eleven of us, in protest against the summer-long tests, had tried to enter the restricted area. We had been arrested as we stepped one after another over the boundary line, and had been carried off to a ghost town which stands at the entrance to Death Valley. There we had been given a speedy trial under the charge of trespassing under the Nevada laws. Sentencing had been suspended for a year, and later in the afternoon we had returned to Camp Mercury to continue the prayer and Conscience Vigil along with others who had remained there during our civil disobedience action. In the early morning of August 7 an experimental bomb was exploded. We sat with our backs to the explosion site. But when the flash came I felt again the utterly impossible horror of this whole business, the same complete realization that nuclear war must go, that I had felt twelve years before on the bridge of U.S.S. *Dale W. Peterson*, off Pearl Harbor.

I think also that deep down somewhere in me, and in men at all times, there is a realization that the pattern of violence meeting violence makes no sense, and that war violates something central in the human heart and that of God, as we Quakers sometimes say. . . .

Then came the experience of having in our home for some months two of the Hiroshima maidens who had been injured and disfigured in the bombing of August 6, 1945. Norman Cousins and other wonderful people brought them to this country for plastic surgery. There were two things about these girls that hit me very hard and forced me to see that I had no choice but to make the commitment to live, as best I could, a life of nonviolence and reconciliation. One was the fact that when they were bombed in 1945 the two girls in our home were nine and thirteen years old. What earthly thing could they have done to give some semblance of what we call justice to the ordeal inflicted upon them and hundreds like them? What possible good could come out of human action—war—which bore such fruits? Is it not utter blasphemy to think that there is anything moral or Christian about such behavior?

The other thing that struck me was that these young women found it difficult to believe that *we*, who were not members of their families, could love *them*. But *they* loved *us*; they harbored no resentment against us or other Americans. How are you going to respond to that kind of attitude? The newly-elected president of the National Council of Churches, Edwin T. Dahlberg, said in his inaugural talk that instead of "massive retaliation" the business of Christians is to practice "massive reconciliation." Well, these Hiroshima girls practiced "massive reconciliation" on us, on me, who had laughed derisively at "Smiling Jack." What response can one make to this other than to give oneself utterly to destroying the evil, war, that dealt so shamefully with them and try to live in the spirit of sensitivity and reconciliation which they displayed?

As I have said, I think there is that in all men that abhors and rejects war and knows that force and violence can bring no good thing to pass. Yet men are bound by old patterns of feeling, thought and action. The organs of public opinion are almost completely shut against us. It seems practically impossible, moreover, for the ordinary person by ordinary means to speak to, and affect the action of, his government. I have had a recent experience of this which has strengthened my conviction that it is only by such acts as sailing a boat to Eniwetok and thus "speaking" to the government right in the testing area that we can expect to be heard.

Tell It to the Policeman

I was asked by the New England office of the American Friends Service Committee to take to the White House 17,411 signatures to a petition to cancel the Pacific tests. Ten thousand signatures had previously been sent in. I realize that even a President in good health cannot see personally everyone who has a message for him. Yet the right of petition exists—in theory—and is held to be a key factor in democratic process. And the President presumably has assistants to see to it that all serious petitions are somehow brought to his attention. For matters of this kind, there is Maxwell Rabb, secretary to the cabinet.

Twenty-seven thousand is quite a few people to have signed a somewhat unusual petition. The A.F.S.C. is widely known and recognized as a highly useful agency. I am known to Maxwell Rabb with whom I worked in Republican politics in Massachusetts. I was a precinct captain for Eisenhower in the 1952 primaries. Yet a couple of days work on the part of the staff of the Friends Committee on National Legislation failed to secure even an assurance that some time on Tuesday, December 31, the day I would be in Washington, Max Rabb would see me to receive the petitions. On that day I made five calls and talked with his secretary. Each time I was assured that she would call me back within ten minutes. Each time the return call failed to come and I tried again. The last time, early in the afternoon, I held on to the telephone for ten minutes, only to be told finally that the office was about to close for the day.

Each time I telephoned, including the last, I was told I could, of course, leave the petitions with the policeman at the gate. This I refused to do. It seems terrible to me that Americans can no longer speak to or be seen by their government. Has it become their master, not their servant? Can it not listen to their humble and reasonable pleas? This experience may in one sense be a small matter but I am sure it is symptomatic—among other things—of a sort of fear on the part of officials to listen to what in their hearts they feel is right but on which they cannot act without breaking with old patterns of thought. At any rate, the experience strengthened in me the conviction that we must, whatever the cost, find ways to make our witness and protest heard.

I Am Going Because . . .

I am going because, as Shakespeare said, "Action is eloquence." Without some such direct action, ordinary citizens lack the power any longer to be seen or heard by their government.

I am going because it is time to do something about peace, not just talk about peace.

I am going because, like all men, in my heart I know that all nuclear explosions are monstrous, evil, unworthy of human beings.

I am going because war is no longer a feudal jousting match; it is an unthinkable catastrophe for all men.

I am going because it is now the little children, and most of all, the as yet unborn who are the front line troops. It is my duty to stand between them and the horrible danger.

I am going because it is cowardly and degrading for me to stand by any longer, to consent, and thus to collaborate in atrocities.

I am going because I cannot say that the end justifies the means. A Quaker, William Penn, said, "A good man cannot sanctify evil means; nor must we ever do evil that good may come of it." A Communist, Miloc Djilas, says, "As soon as means which would ensure the end are shown to be evil, the end will show itself as unrealizable."

I am going because, as Gandhi said, "God sits in the man opposite me; therefore to injure him is to injure God himself."

I am going to witness to the deep inward truth we all know, "Force can subdue, but love gains."

I am going because however mistaken, unrighteous and unrepentant governments may seem, I still believe all men are really good at heart, and that my act will speak to them.

I am going in the hope of helping change the hearts and minds of men in government. If necessary I am willing to give my life to help change a policy of fear, force, and destruction to one of trust, kindness, and help.

I am going in order to say, "Quit this waste, this arms race. Turn instead to a disarmament race. Stop competing for evil, compete for good."

I am going because I have to—if I am to call myself a human being.

When you see something horrible happening your instinct is to do something about it. You can freeze into fearful apathy or you can even talk yourself into saying that it isn't horrible. I can't do that. I have to act. This is too horrible. We know it. Let's all act.

Source: Albert S. Bigelow, "Why I Am Sailing into the Pacific Bomb-Test Area," *Liberation*, February 1958, pp. 4–6.

For Further Reading:

Robert Divine, *Blowing in the Wind* (New York: Oxford University Press, 1978).
Nat Hentoff, *Peace Agitator* (New York: Macmillan, 1963).
Lawrence Wittner, *Rebels Against the War*, rev. ed. (Philadelphia: Temple University Press, 1984).

90. Dwight D. Eisenhower, Excerpt from "Farewell Address" (1961)

1950–53   Korean War
1952–60   Eisenhower presidency
1957   *Sputnik* launched
1960   John F. Kennedy complains about "missile gap"

Through most of its history the United States maintained a small standing army and a relatively small defense industry. While this necessitated rapid military build-ups during times of war, which in turn produced economic dislocation and tensions, some have argued that it served as a bulwark of democracy. In countries with large standing armies, they observe, democracies have fallen prey to military coups d'état. In the United States, however, the only time that a coup was even threatened was immediately following the revolution, and it was quickly thwarted by General George Washington, who convinced his troops to return home.

The Cold War altered this situation. A large standing army and defense industry became the rule rather than the exception. Even after the Korean War ended, the United States maintained a standing army of 2.5 million active soldiers and a defense budget in the tens of millions of dollars. In his "Farewell Address" President Eisenhower considered the impact that the "military-industrial complex" (Eisenhower's words) might have on the United States. He worried that if it was not carefully watched, the military-industrial complex could have an adverse impact on democracy. Coming from a genuine war hero, this warning carried greater weight than if it had come from a life-long civilian.

Nevertheless, in the 1960 campaign, John F. Kennedy criticized the Eisenhower administration for allowing a missile gap to develop between the United States and the Soviet Union. Even though no such gap existed, the public, already alarmed by the Soviet's launching of Sputnik, the first artificial satellite to orbit the earth, supported Kennedy's goal of increasing the size of America's nuclear arsenal. Hence, even before President Johnson escalated the war in Vietnam, the United States had increased its defense spending and the military-industrial complex had grown ever larger.

A vital element in keeping the peace is our military establishment. Our arms must be mighty, ready for instant action, so that no potential aggressor may be tempted to risk his own destruction.

Our military organization today bears little relation to that known by any of my predecessors in peacetime, or indeed by the fighting men of World War II or Korea.

Until the latest of our world conflicts, the United States had no armaments industry. American makers of plowshares could, with time and as required, make swords as well. But now we can no longer risk emergency improvisation of national defense; we have been compelled to create a permanent armaments industry of vast proportions. Added to this, three and a half million men and women are directly engaged in the defense establishment. We annually spend on military security more than the net income of all United States corporations.

This conjunction of an immense military establishment and a large arms industry is new in the American experience. The total influence—economic, political, even spiritual—is felt in every city, every statehouse, every office of the federal government. We recognize the imperative need for this development. Yet we must not fail to comprehend its grave implications. Our toil, resources, and livelihood are all involved; so is the very structure of our society.

In the councils of government, we must guard against the acquisition of unwarranted influence, whether sought or unsought, by the military-industrial complex. The potential for the disastrous rise of misplaced power exists and will persist.

We must never let the weight of this combination endanger our liberties or democratic processes. We should take nothing for granted. Only an alert and knowledgeable citizenry can compel the proper meshing of the huge industrial and military machinery of defense with our peaceful methods and goals, so that security and liberty may prosper together.

Akin to, and largely responsible for the sweeping changes in our industrial-military posture, has been the technological revolution during recent decades.

In this revolution, research has become central; it also becomes more formalized, complex, and costly. A steadily increasing share is conducted for, by, or at the direction of, the federal government. . . .

The prospect of domination of the nation's scholars by federal employment, project allocations, and the power of money is ever present—and is gravely to be regarded.

Yet, in holding scientific research and discovery in respect, as we should, we must also be alert to the equal and opposite danger that public policy could itself become the captive of a scientific-technological elite.

It is the task of statesmanship to mold, to balance, and to integrate these and other forces, new and old, within the principles of our democratic system—ever aiming toward the supreme goals of our free society.

Another factor in maintaining balance involves the element of time. As we peer into society's future, we—you and I, and our government—must avoid the impulse to live only for today, plundering, for our own ease and convenience, the precious resources of tomorrow. We cannot mortgage the material assets of our grandchildren without risking the loss also of their political and spiritual heritage. We want democracy to survive for all generations to come, not to become the insolvent phantom of tomorrow.

Down the long lane of the history yet to be written America knows that this world of ours, ever growing smaller, must avoid becoming a community of dreadful fear and hate, and be, instead, a proud confederation of mutual trust and respect.

Such a confederation must be one of equals. The weakest must come to the conference table with the same confidence as do we, protected as we are by our moral, economic, and military strength. That table, though scarred by many past frustrations, cannot be abandoned for the certain agony of the battlefield.

Disarmament, with mutual honor and confidence, is a continuing imperative. Together we must learn how to compose differences, not with arms, but with intellect and decent purpose. Because this need is so sharp and apparent I confess that I lay down my official responsibilities in this field with a definite sense of disappointment. As one who has witnessed the horror and the lingering sadness of war—as one who knows that another war could utterly destroy this civilization which has been so slowly and painfully built over thousands of years—I wish I could say tonight that a lasting peace is in sight.

Happily, I can say that war has been avoided. Steady progress toward our ultimate goal has been made. But, so much remains to be done. As a private citizen, I shall never cease to do what little I can to help the world advance along that road.

Source: *New York Times*, January 18, 1961.

For Further Reading:

Stephen E. Ambrose, *Eisenhower* (New York: Simon & Schuster, 1990).
Seymour Melman, *The Permanent War Economy*, rev. ed. (New York: Simon & Schuster, 1974).

91. Students for a Democratic Society, Excerpt from "Port Huron Statement" (1962)

1962   SDS issues "Port Huron Statement"
1964   Free Speech Movement at University of California at Berkeley
1965   SDS organizes Antiwar March in Washington, D.C.
1967–70   Student unrest peaks

In his famous inaugural address, John F. Kennedy, the youngest man ever to be elected President, stirred the nation with his call: "Ask not what your country can do for you—ask what you can do for your country." Some "baby boomers" responded to Kennedy's appeal by joining the Peace Corps. Others joined the Marines. Still others filled the ranks of the growing civil rights and peace movements.

One of the most important student organizations of the 1960s was the Students for a Democratic Society, or SDS. In 1962 its members gathered at the United Automobile Workers' retreat in Port Huron, Michigan, to develop a manifesto. The result was the "Port Huron Statement." Largely written by Tom Hayden, a former editor of the University of Michigan's student newspaper, the "Statement" singled out racism and the threat of nuclear war as its generation's paramount concerns. Other problems could be ignored, the manifesto declared, but not these.

By the mid-1960s, SDS would become a household name, recruiting thousands of students to its ranks. Remarkably, just a couple of years before the "Port Huron Statement" was released, social commentators were bemoaning the apathy of students. By the end of the 1960s, student protest would be considered the nation's "number one" problem.

While reading the "Port Huron Statement," consider its similarity to the writings of earlier American reformers. Like those of the era of ante-bellum reform (documents 30 to 35), it exhibited a belief in the perfectibility of man and a highly idealistic conception of democracy. Ironically, toward the end of the 1960s, many student activists adopted the exact opposite stance. Perhaps because they felt betrayed by Kennedy and Johnson, who escalated the Vietnam War and responded timidly to the civil rights movement, they proclaimed that the United States was bankrupt and called for an overthrow of "the system."

We are people of this generation, bred in at least modest comfort, housed now in universities, looking uncomfortably to the world we inherit.

When we were kids the United States was the wealthiest and strongest country in the world; the only one with the atom bomb, the least scarred by modern war, an initiator of the United Nations that we thought would distribute Western influence throughout the world. Freedom and equality for each individual, government of, by, and for the people—these American values we found good, principles by which we could live as men. Many of us began maturing in complacency.

As we grew, however, our comfort was penetrated by events too troubling to dismiss. First, the permeating and victimizing fact of human degradation, symbolized by the Southern struggle against racial bigotry, compelled most of us from silence to activism. Second, the enclosing fact of the Cold War, symbolized by the presence of the Bomb, brought awareness that we ourselves, and our friends, and millions of abstract "others" we knew more directly because of our common peril, might die at any time. We might deliberately ignore, or avoid, or fail to feel all other human problems, but not these two, for these were too immediate and crushing in their impact, too challenging in the demand that we as individuals take the responsibility for encounter and resolution.

While these and other problems either directly oppressed us or rankled our consciences and became our own subjective concern, we began to see complicated and disturbing paradoxes in our surrounding America. The declaration "all men are created equal . . . " rang hollow before the facts of Negro life in the South and the big cities of the North. The proclaimed peaceful intentions of the United States contradicted its economic and military investments in the Cold War status quo.

We witnessed, and continue to witness, other paradoxes. With nuclear energy whole cities can easily be powered, yet the dominant nation-states seem more likely to unleash destruction greater than that incurred in all wars of human history. Although our own technology is destroying old and creating new forms of social organization, men still tolerate meaningless work and idleness. While two-thirds of mankind suffers undernourishment, our own upper classes revel amidst superfluous abundance. Although world population is expected to double in forty years, the nations still tolerate anarchy as a major principle of international conduct and uncontrolled exploitation governs the sapping of the earth's physical resources. Although mankind desperately needs revolutionary leadership, America rests in national stalemate, its goals ambiguous and tradition-bound instead of informed and clear, its democratic system apathetic and manipulated rather than "of, by, and for the people."

Not only did tarnish appear on our image of American virtue, not only did disillusion occur when the hypocrisy of American ideals was discovered, but we began to sense that what we had originally seen as the American Golden Age was actually the decline of an era. The worldwide outbreak of revolution against colonialism and imperialism, the entrenchment of totalitarian states, the menace of war, overpopulation, international disorder, supertechnology—these trends were testing the tenacity of our own commitment to democracy and freedom and our abilities to visualize their application to a world in upheaval.

Our work is guided by the sense that we may be the last generation in the experiment with living. But we are a minority—the vast majority of our people regard the temporary equilibriums of our society and world as eternally functional parts. In this is perhaps the outstanding paradox: we ourselves are imbued with urgency, yet the message of our society is that there is no viable alternative to the present. Beneath the reassuring tones of the politicians, beneath the common opinion that America will "muddle through," beneath the stagnation of those who have closed their minds to the future, is the pervading feeling that there simply are no alternatives, that our times have witnessed the exhaustion not only of Utopias, but of any new departures as well. Feeling the press of complexity upon the emptiness of life, people are fearful of the thought that at any moment things might be thrust out of control. They fear change itself, since change might smash whatever invisible framework seems to hold back chaos for them now. For most Americans, all crusades are suspect, threatening. The fact that each individual sees apathy in his fellows perpetuates the common reluctance to organize for change. The dominant institutions are complex enough to blunt the minds of their potential critics, and entrenched enough to swiftly dissipate or entirely repel the energies of protest and reform, thus limiting human expectancies. Then, too, we are a materially improved society, and by our own improvements we seem to have weakened the case for further change.

Some would have us believe that Americans feel contentment amidst prosperity—but might it not better be called a glaze above deeply felt anxieties about their role in the new world? And if these anxieties produce a developed indifference to human affairs, do they not as well produce a yearning to believe there *is* an alternative to the present, that something *can* be done to change circumstances in the school, the workplaces, the bureaucracies, the government? It is to this latter yearning, at once the spark and engine of change, that we direct our present appeal. The search for truly democratic alternatives to the present, and a commitment to social experimentation with them, is a worthy and fulfilling human enterprise, one which moves us and, we hope, others today. On such a basis do we offer this document of our convictions and analysis: as an effort in understanding and changing the conditions of humanity in the late twentieth century, an effort rooted in the ancient, still unfulfilled conception of man attaining determining influence over his circumstances of life.

Source: Students for a Democratic Society, "Port Huron Statement," SDS Papers, State Historical Society of Wisconsin, Madison, Wisconsin.

For Further Reading:

Todd Gitlin, *The Sixties* (New York: Bantam, 1987).
Jim Miller, *Democracy Is in the Streets* (New York: Simon & Schuster, 1987).
Kirkpatrick Sale, *SDS* (New York: Random House, 1973).

92. J. William Fulbright, Excerpt from "A Sick Society" (1967)

1950   Truman grants aid to French in Indochina
1954–60   Eisenhower deepens American involvement in
          Southeast Asia
1961–63   Kennedy increases troop strength, including Green
          Berets
1964   Gulf of Tonkin Resolution
1965–68   Johnson escalates war in Vietnam
1965–68   Antiwar protests increase

The United States involvement in the war in Vietnam began in 1950 when President Truman granted military aid to the French, who were trying to maintain possession of their colonies in Indochina. For the next eighteen years, Presidents Eisenhower, Kennedy, and Johnson increased America's commitment to defeating Ho Chi Minh, the communist leader of North Vietnam, so that by the end of 1967 over 500,000 American troops were in Vietnam and the United States was launching air strikes greater in number and tonnage than those of World War II. Yet it was not until 1965 that a substantial antiwar movement emerged, and even then it tended to attract fringe groups, not mainstream politicians.

"March Against Death," Washington, D.C., November 13, 1969 (Vietnam War Protestors deposit names of killed soldiers in casket) (Library of Congress).

By the end of 1967, however, the antiwar movement had grown considerably in size and strength. It counted as its members well-known Americans, from Benjamin Spock, the famous and respected baby doctor, to Martin Luther King, Jr. Among the more forceful opponents of the war was J. William Fulbright (Democrat, Ark.), head of the Senate Foreign Relations Committee. His investigations into America's conduct in Vietnam revealed that President Johnson had intentionally misled the people in gaining passage of the Gulf of Tonkin Resolution—the equivalent of the declaration of war. Indeed, in "A Sick Society" and other speeches, Fulbright argued that the Vietnam War was poisoning American society. Martin Luther King, Jr., George McGovern, and many other antiwar statesmen made the same claim.

Standing in the smoke and rubble of Detroit, a Negro veteran said: "I just got back from Vietnam a few months ago, but you know, I think the war is here."

There are in fact two wars going on. One is the war of power politics which our soldiers are fighting in the jungles of southeast Asia. The other is a war for America's soul which is being fought in the streets of Newark and Detroit and in the halls of Congress, in churches and protest meetings and on college campuses, and in the hearts and minds of silent Americans from Maine to Hawaii. I believe that the two wars have something to do with each other, not in the direct, tangibly causal way that bureaucrats require as proof of a connection between two things, but in a subtler, moral and qualitative way that is no less real for being intangible. Each of these wars might well be going on in the absence of the other, but neither, I suspect, standing alone, would seem so hopeless and demoralizing.

The connection between Vietnam and Detroit is in their conflicting and incompatible demands upon traditional American values. The one demands that they be set aside, the other that they be fulfilled. The one demands the acceptance by America of an imperial role in the world, or of what our policy makers like to call the "responsibilities of power," or of what I have called the "arrogance of power." The other demands freedom and social justice at home, an end to poverty, the fulfillment of our flawed democracy, and an effort to create a role for ourselves in the world which is compatible with our traditional values. The question, it should be emphasized, is not whether it is *possible* to engage in traditional power politics abroad and at the same time the perfect democracy at home, but whether it is possible for *us Americans*, with our particular history and national character, to combine morally incompatible roles.

Administration officials tell us that we can indeed afford both Vietnam and the Great Society, and they produce impressive statistics of the gross national product to prove it. The statistics show financial capacity but they do not show moral and psychological capacity. They do not show how a President preoccupied with bombing missions over North and South Vietnam can provide strong and consistent leadership for the renewal of our cities. They do not show how a Congress burdened with war costs and war measures, with emergency briefings and an endless series of dramatic appeals, with anxious constituents and a mounting anxiety of their own, can tend to the workaday business of studying social problems and legislating programs to meet them. Nor do the statistics tell how an anxious and puzzled people, bombarded by press and television with the bad news of American deaths in Vietnam, the "good news" of enemy deaths—and with vividly horrifying pictures to illustrate them–can be expected to support neighborhood anti-poverty projects and national programs for urban renewal, employment and education. . . .

At present much of the world is repelled by America and what America seems to stand for in the world. Both in our foreign affairs and in our domestic life we convey an image of violence; I do not care very much about images as distinguished from the things they reflect, but this image is rooted in reality. Abroad we are engaged in a savage and unsuccessful war against poor people in a small and backward nation. At home—largely because of the neglect from twenty-five years of preoccupation with foreign involvements—our cities are exploding in violent protest against generations of social injustice. America, which only a few years ago seemed to the world to be a model of democracy and social justice, has become a symbol of violence and undisciplined power. . . . By our undisciplined use of physical power we have divested ourselves of a greater power: the power of example. How, for example, can we commend peaceful compromise to the Arabs and the Israelis when we are unwilling to suspend our relentless bombing of North Vietnam? How can we commend democratic social reform to Latin America when Newark, Detroit, and Milwaukee are providing explosive evidence of our own inadequate efforts at democratic social reform? How can we commend the free enterprise system to Asians and Africans when in our own country it has produced vast, chaotic, noisy, dangerous and dirty urban complexes while poisoning the very air and land and water? . . .

While the death toll mounts in Vietnam, it is mounting too in the war at home. During a single week of July 1967, 164 Americans were killed and 1,442 wounded in Vietnam, while 65 Americans were killed and 2,100 were wounded in city riots in the United States. We are truly fighting a two-front war and doing badly in both. Each war feeds on the other and, although the President assures us that we have the resources to win both wars, in fact we are not winning either.

Together the two wars have set in motion a process of deterioration in American society and there is no question that each of the two crises is heightened by the impact of the other. Not only does the Vietnam war divert human and material resources from our festering cites; not only does it foster the conviction on the part of slum Negroes that their country is indifferent to their plight. In addition the war feeds the idea of violence as a way of solving problems. If, as Mr. Rusk tells us, only the rain of bombs can bring Ho Chi Minh to reason, why should not the same principle apply at home? Why should not riots and snipers' bullets bring the white man to an awareness of the Negro's plight when peaceful programs for housing and jobs and training have been more rhetoric than reality? Ugly and shocking thoughts are in the American air and they were forged in the Vietnam crucible. Black power extremists talk of "wars of liberation" in the urban ghettoes of America. . . .

Priorities are reflected in the things we spend money on. Far from being a dry accounting of bookkeepers, a nation's budget is full of moral implications; it tells what a society cares about and what it does not care about; it tells what its values are.

Here are a few statistics on America's values: Since 1946 we have spent over $1,578 billion through our regular national budget. Of this amount over $904 billion, or 57.29 percent of the total, have gone for military power. By contrast, less than $96 billion, or 6.08 percent, were spent on "social functions" including education, health, labor and welfare programs, housing and community development. The Administration's budget for fiscal year 1968 calls for almost $76 billion to be spent on the military and only $15 billion for "social functions."

I would not say that we have shown ourselves to value weapons five or ten times as much as we value domestic social needs, as the figures suggest; certainly much of our military spending has been necessitated by genuine requirements of national security. I think, however, that we have embraced the necessity with excessive enthusiasm, that the Congress has been too willing to provide unlimited sums for the military and not really very reluctant at all to offset these costs to a very small degree by cutting away funds for the poverty program and urban renewal, for rent supplements for the poor and even for a program to help protect slum children from being bitten by rats. . . .

While the country sickens for lack of moral leadership, a most remarkable younger generation has taken up the standard of American idealism. Unlike so many of their elders, they have perceived the fraud and sham in American life and are unequivocally rejecting it. Some, the hippies, have simply withdrawn, and while we may regret the loss of their energies and their sense of decency, we can hardly gainsay their evaluation of the state of society. Others of our youth are sardonic and skeptical, not, I think, because they do not want ideals but because they want the genuine article and will not tolerate fraud. Others—students who wrestle with their consciences about the draft, soldiers who wrestle with their consciences about the war, Peace Corps volunteers who strive to light the spark of human dignity among the poor of India or Brazil, and VISTA volunteers who try to do the same for our own poor in Harlem or Appalachia—are striving to keep alive the traditional values of American democracy.

They are not really radical, these young idealists, no more radical, that is, than Jefferson's idea of freedom, Lincoln's idea of equality, or Wilson's idea of a peaceful community of nations. Some of them, it is true, are taking what many regard as radical action, but they are doing it in defense of traditional values and in protest against the radical departure from those values embodied in the idea of an imperial destiny for America.

The focus of their protest is the war in Vietnam and the measure of their integrity is the fortitude with which they refused to be deceived about it. By striking contrast with the young Germans who accepted the Nazi evil because the values of their society had disintegrated and they had no normal frame of reference, these young Americans are demonstrating the vitality of American values. . . .

It may be that the challenge will succeed, that America will succumb to becoming a traditional empire and will reign for a time over what must surely be a moral if not a physical wasteland, and then, like the great empires of the past, will decline or fall. Or it may be that the effort to create so grotesque an anachronism will go up in flames of nuclear holocaust. But if I had to bet my money on what is going to happen, I would bet on this younger generation—this generation who reject the inhumanity of war in a poor and distant land, who reject the poverty and sham in their own country, this generation who are telling their elders what their elders ought to have known, that the price of empire is America's soul and that price is too high.

Source: *Congressional Record, Senate*, August 9, 1967, pp. 22126–129.

For Further Reading:

George Herring, *America's Longest War* (New York: Wiley, 1979).
Melvin Small, *Johnson, Nixon and the Doves* (New Brunswick, N.J.: Rutgers University Press, 1988).
Nancy Zaroulis and Gerald Sullivan, *Who Spoke Up?* (Garden City, N.Y.: Doubleday, 1984).

93. Lyndon B. Johnson, Excerpt from "The Great Society" (1964)

1964   Johnson signs Civil Rights Act; proposes War on
       Poverty; defeats Barry Goldwater in landslide
1965   Voting Rights Act and Great Society measures enacted
1968   Johnson announces that he will not seek reelection

Even though President Lyndon B. Johnson lacked John F. Kennedy's charisma, he inspired the nation by challenging it to help him create a "Great Society." For example, in a speech delivered to students at the University of Michigan, in the spring of 1964, Johnson presented his broad plans for improving America. Seeing himself as the heir to Franklin D. Roosevelt, Johnson declared that it was time to complete the struggle for economic justice initiated by the New Deal. While FDR had enacted Social Security, LBJ proposed providing medical coverage for the elderly and poor. Whereas the New Deal provided relief to the unemployed, the Great Society would create job-training programs. While one of Roosevelt's favorite programs had been the Civilian Conservation Corps, which brought unemployed urban youth out to the countryside to build trails and fight fires, Johnson created Vista, a domestic version of The Peace Corps, to fight urban blight, and the National Endowment for the Arts and the National Endowment for the Humanities, to uplift minds.

In the 1964 presidential election, President Johnson defeated his conservative opponent, Barry Goldwater, in the biggest landslide in modern American history. In 1965 he quickly enacted one Great Society measure after another. But by 1968 his dream lay in shambles. He was trapped in a quagmire in Vietnam, which was draining valuable resources from his do-

President Lyndon B. Johnson signing Voting Rights Act of 1965 (Library of Congress).

mestic programs and tearing the nation apart. Race riots had swept across the nation. And conservatives and liberals were busy criticizing the Great Society as ill conceived. Still, it is worth reading Johnson's speech, to get a sense of what many Americans briefly saw as the proper role for the federal government in a democracy. Like Franklin D. Roosevelt (see document 77), Johnson felt that the government had the responsibility to provide for and promote the public welfare.

I have come today from the turmoil of your Capital to the tranquility of your campus to speak about the future of your country.

The purpose of protecting the life of our Nation and preserving the liberty of our citizens is to pursue the happiness of our people. Our success in that pursuit is the test of our success as a Nation.

For a century we labored to settle and to subdue a continent. For half a century we called upon unbounded invention and untiring industry to create an order of plenty for all of our people.

The challenge of the next half century is whether we have the wisdom to use that wealth to enrich and elevate our national life, and to advance the quality of our American civilization.

Your imagination, your initiative, and your indignation will determine whether we build a society where progress is the servant of our needs, or a society where old values and new visions are buried under unbridled growth. For in your time we have the opportunity to move not only toward the rich society and the powerful society, but upward to the Great Society.

The Great Society rests on abundance and liberty for all. It demands an end to poverty and racial injustice, to which we are totally committed in our time. But that is just the beginning.

The Great Society is a place where every child can find knowledge to enrich his mind and to enlarge his talents. It is a place where leisure is a welcome chance to build and reflect, not a feared cause of boredom and restlessness. It is a place where the city of man serves not only the needs of the body and the demands of commerce but the desire for beauty and the hunger for community.

It is a place where man can renew contact with nature. It is a place which honors creation for its own sake and for what it adds to the understanding of the race. It is a place where men are more concerned with the quality of their goals than the quantity of their goods.

But most of all, the Great Society is not a safe harbor, a resting place, a final objective, a finished work. It is a challenge constantly renewed, beckoning us toward a destiny where the meaning of our lives matches the marvelous products of our labor.

So I want to talk to you today about three places where we begin to build the Great Society—in our cities, in our countryside, and in our classrooms.

Many of you will live to see the day, perhaps 50 years from now, when there will be 400 million Americans—four-fifths of them in urban areas. In the remainder of this century urban population will double, city land will double, and we will have to build homes, highways, and facilities equal to all those built since this country was first settled. So in the next 40 years we must rebuild the entire urban United States.

Aristotle said: "Men come together in cities in order to live, but they remain together in order to live the good life." It is harder and harder to live the good life in American cities today.

The catalog of ills is long: there is the decay of the centers and the despoiling of the suburbs. There is not enough housing for our people or transportation for our traffic. Open land is vanishing and old landmarks are violated.

Worst of all expansion is eroding the precious and time honored values of community with neighbors and communion with nature. The loss of these values breeds loneliness and boredom and indifference.

Our society will never be great until our cities are great. Today the frontier of imagination and innovation is inside those cities and not beyond their borders.

New experiments are already going on. It will be the task of your generation to make the American city a place where future generations will come, not only to live but to live the good life. . . .

A second place where we begin to build the Great Society is in our countryside. We have always prided ourselves on being not only America the strong and America the free, but America the beautiful. Today that beauty is in danger. The water we drink, the food we eat, the very air that we breathe, are threatened with pollution. Our parks are overcrowded, our seashores overburdened. Green fields and dense forests are disappearing.

A few years ago we were greatly concerned about the "Ugly American." Today we must act to prevent an ugly America.

For once the battle is lost, once our natural splendor is destroyed, it can never be recaptured. And once man can no longer walk with beauty or wonder at nature his spirit will wither and his sustenance be wasted.

A third place to build the Great Society is in the classrooms of America. There your children's lives will be shaped. Our society will not be great until every young mind is set free to scan the farthest reaches of thought and imagination. We are still far from that goal.

Today, 8 million adult Americans, more than the entire population of Michigan, have not finished 5 years of school. Nearly 20 million have not finished 8 years of school. Nearly 54 million—more than one-quarter of all America—have not even finished high school.

Each year more than 100,000 high school graduates, with proved ability, do not enter college because they cannot afford it. And if we cannot educate today's youth, what will we do in 1970 when elementary school enrollment will be 5 million greater than 1960? And high school enrollment will rise by 5 million. College enrollment will increase by more than 3 million.

In many places, classrooms are overcrowded and curricula are outdated. Most of our qualified teachers are underpaid, and many of our paid teachers are unqualified. So we must give every child a place to sit and a teacher to learn from. Poverty must not be a bar to learning, and learning must offer an escape from poverty.

But more classrooms and more teachers are not enough. We must seek an educational system which grows in excellence as it grows in size. This means better training for our teachers. It means preparing youth to enjoy their hours of leisure as well as their hours of labor. It means exploring new techniques of teaching, to find new ways to stimulate the love of learning and the capacity for creation.

These are three of the central issues of the Great Society. While our Government has many programs directed at those issues, I do not pretend that we have the full answer to those problems.

But I do promise this: We are going to assemble the best thought and the broadest knowledge from all over the world to find those answers for America. I intend to establish working groups to prepare a series of White House conferences and meetings—on the cities, on natural beauty, on the quality of education, and on other emerging challenges. And from these meetings and from this inspiration and from these studies we will begin to set our course toward the Great Society.

The solution to these problems does not rest on a massive program in Washington, nor can it rely solely on the strained resources of local authority. They require us to create new concepts of cooperation, a creative federalism, between the National Capital and the leaders of local communities. . . .

For better or for worse, your generation has been appointed by history to deal with those problems and to lead America toward a new age. You have the chance never before afforded to any people in any age. You can help build a society where the demands of morality, and the needs of the spirit, can be realized in the life of the Nation.

So, will you join in the battle to give every citizen the full equality which God enjoins and the law requires, whatever his belief, or race, or the color of his skin?

Will you join in the battle to give every citizen an escape from the crushing weight of poverty?

Will you join in the battle to make it possible for all nations to live in enduring peace—as neighbors and not as mortal enemies?

Will you join in the battle to build the Great Society, to prove that our material progress is only the foundation on which we will build a richer life of mind and spirit?

There are those timid souls who say this battle cannot be won; that we are condemned to a soulless wealth. I do not agree. We have the power to shape the civilization that we want. But we need your will, your labor, your hearts, if we are to build that kind of society.

Those who came to this land sought to build more than just a new country. They sought a new world. So I have come here today to your campus to say that you can make their vision our reality. So let us from this moment begin our work so that in the future men will look back and say: It was then, after a long and weary way, that man turned the exploits of his genius to the full enrichment of his life.

Thank you. Good-bye.

Source: *Public Papers of the Presidents of the United States, Lyndon B. Johnson, 1963–64, I* (Washington, D.C., 1965), pp. 704–5.

For Further Reading:

Doris Kearns Goodwin, *Lyndon Johnson* (New York: Harper & Row, 1976).
Allen Matusow, *The Unravelling of America* (New York: Harper & Row, 1984).

94. Michael Harrington, Excerpt from
The Other America (1963)

1962   *The Other America* published
1964   Economic Opportunity Act
1965   Medicare Act; Appalachian Regional Development Act
1966   Demonstration Cities Act

In 1962 Michael Harrington's The Other America, *a passionate and well-documented study of the persistence of poverty in the United States, was published. Prior to its release, many Americans believed that the United States had either eradicated poverty or was well on its way toward eradicating it. Harrington's book demonstrated that this was not the case. Like Harriet Beecher Stowe's* Uncle Tom's Cabin *and Upton Sinclair's* The Jungle *(see documents 32 and 54), Harrington's work inspired the nation and its political leaders to act. After reading* The Other America *President Kennedy pushed forward his economic growth package. And President Johnson developed the much more grandiose and ambitious "War on Poverty," which included the Economic Opportunity Act of 1964 and the Appalachian Regional Development Act of 1965.*

Like Sinclair, Harrington was a socialist. He spent several years working with Dorothy Day's Catholic Worker movement, among the poor of New York City. He was an associate of some of the earliest student activists of the early 1960s and an adviser to some labor groups. Harrington applauded the development of the War on Poverty. And later in life he harshly criticized President Reagan for his efforts to dismantle federal social programs. His consistent concern for the poor put him at odds with the general political mood of the 1970s and 1980s, when conservatives argued that federal spending and social programs were wasteful and merely perpetuated or encouraged dependency on the welfare state. Ironically, he finally won some admiration from leftists, who during the 1960s had condemned him for his staunch anticommunism and willingness to ally himself with President Johnson.

There is a familiar America. It is celebrated in speeches and advertised on television and in the magazines. It has the highest mass standard of living the world has ever known.

In the 1950's this America worried about itself, yet even its anxieties were products of abundance. The title of a brilliant book was widely misinterpreted, and the familiar America began to call itself "the affluent society."

There was introspection about Madison Avenue and tail fins; there was discussion of the emotional suffering taking place in the suburbs. In all this, there was an implicit assumption that the basic grinding economic problems had been solved in the United States. In this theory the nation's problems were no longer a matter of basic human needs, of food, shelter, and clothing. Now they were seen as qualitative, a question of learning to live decently amid luxury.

While this discussion was carried on, there existed another America. In it dwelt somewhere between 40,000,000 and 50,000,000 citizens of this land. They were poor. They still are.

To be sure, the other America is not impoverished in the same sense as those poor nations where millions cling to hunger as a defense against starvation. This country has escaped such extremes. That does not change the fact that tens of millions of Americans are, at this very moment, maimed in body and spirit, existing at levels beneath those necessary for human decency. If these people are not starving, they are hungry, and sometimes fat with hunger, for that is what cheap foods do. They are without adequate housing and education and medical care. . . .

This book is a description of the world in which these people live; it is about the other America. Here are the unskilled workers, the migrant farm workers, the aged, the minorities, and all the others who live in the economic underworld of American life. . . .

The millions who are poor in the United States tend to become increasingly invisible. Here is a great mass of people, yet it takes an effort of the intellect and will even to see them.

I discovered this personally in a curious way. After I wrote my first article on poverty in America, I had all the statistics down on paper. I had proved to my satisfaction that there were around 50,000,000 poor in this country. Yet, I realized I did not believe my own figures. The poor existed in the Government reports; they were percentages and numbers in long, close columns, but they were not part of my experience. I could prove that the other America existed, but I had never been there.

My response was not accidental. It was typical of what is happening to an entire society, and it reflects profound social changes in this nation. The other America, the America of poverty, is hidden today in a way that it never was before. Its millions are socially invisible to the rest of us. No wonder that so many misinterpreted Galbraith's title and assumed that "the affluent society" meant that everyone had a decent standard of life. The misinterpretation was true as far as the actual day-to-day lives of two-thirds of the nation were concerned. Thus, one must begin a description of the other America by understanding why we do not see it.

There are perennial reasons that make the other America an invisible land.

Poverty is often off the beaten track. It always has been. The ordinary tourist never left the main highway, and today he rides interstate turnpikes. He does not go into the valleys of Pennsylvania where the towns look like movie sets of Wales in the thirties. He does not see the company houses in rows, the rutted roads (the poor always have bad roads whether they live in the city, in towns, or on farms), and everything is black and dirty. And even if he were to pass through such a place by accident, the tourist would not meet the unemployed men in the bar or the women coming home from a runaway sweatshop.

Then, too, beauty and myths are perennial masks of poverty. The traveler comes to the Appalachians in the lovely season. He sees the hills, the streams, the foliage—but not the poor. Or perhaps he looks at a run-down mountain house and, remembering Rousseau rather than seeing with his eyes, decides that "those people" are truly fortunate to be living the way they are and that they are lucky to be exempt from the strains and tensions of the middle class. The only problem is that "those people," the quaint inhabitants of those hills, are undereducated, underprivileged, lack medical care, and are in the process of being forced from the land into a life in the cities, where they are misfits.

These are normal and obvious causes of the invisibility of the poor. They operated a generation ago; they will be functioning a generation hence. It is more important to understand that the very development of American society is creating a new kind of blindness about poverty. The poor are increasingly slipping out of the very experience and consciousness of the nation.

If the middle class never did like ugliness and poverty, it was at least aware of them. "Across the tracks" was not a very long way to go. There were forays into the slums at Christmas time; there were charitable organizations that brought contact with the poor. Occasionally, almost everyone passed through the Negro ghetto or the blocks of tenements, if only to get downtown to work or to entertainment.

Now the American city has been transformed. The poor still inhabit the miserable housing in the central area, but they are increasingly isolated from contact with, or sight of, anybody else. Middle-class women coming in from Suburbia on a rare trip may catch the merest glimpse of the other America on the way to an evening at the theater, but their children are segregated in suburban schools. The business or professional man may drive along the fringes of slums in a car or bus, but it is not an important experience to him. The failures, the unskilled, the disabled, the aged, and the minorities are right there, across the tracks, where they have always been. But hardly anyone else is.

In short, the very development of the American city has removed poverty from the living, emotional experience of millions upon millions of middle-class Americans. Living out in the suburbs, it is easy to assume that ours is, indeed, an affluent society. . . .

It is a blow to reform and the political hopes of the poor that the middle class no longer understands that poverty exists. But, perhaps more important, the poor are losing their links with the great world. If statistics and sociology can measure a feeling as delicate as loneliness (and some of the attempts to do so will be cited later on), the other America is becoming increasingly populated by those who do not belong to anybody or anything. They are no longer participants in an ethnic culture from the old country; they are less and less religious; they do not belong to unions or clubs. They are not seen, and because of that they themselves cannot see. Their horizon has become more and more restricted; they see one another, and that means they see little reason to hope. . . .

There are mighty historical and economic forces that keep the poor down; and there are human beings who help out in this grim business, many of them unwittingly. There are sociological and political reasons why poverty is not seen; and there are misconceptions and prejudices that literally blind the eyes. The latter must be understood if anyone is to make the necessary act of intellect and will so that the poor can be noticed.

Here is the most familiar version of social blindness: "The poor are that way because they are afraid of work. And anyway they all have big cars. If they were like me (or my father or my grandfather), they could pay their own way. But they prefer to live on the dole and cheat the taxpayers."

This theory, usually thought of as a virtuous and moral statement, is one of the means of making it impossible for the poor ever to pay their way. There are, one must assume, citizens of the other America who choose impoverishment out of fear of work (though, writing it down, I really do not believe it). But the real explanation of why the poor are where they are is that they made the mistake of being born to the wrong parents, in the wrong section of the country, in the wrong industry, or in the wrong racial or ethnic group. Once that mistake has been made, they could have been paragons of will and morality, but most of them would never even have had a chance to get out of the other America.

There are two important ways of saying this: The poor are caught in a vicious circle; or, The poor live in a culture of poverty.

In a sense, one might define the contemporary poor in the United States as those who, for reasons beyond their control, cannot help themselves. All the most decisive factors making for opportunity and advance are against them. They are born going downward, and most of them stay down. They are victims whose lives are endlessly blown round and round the other America.

Here is one of the most familiar forms of the vicious circle of poverty. The poor get sick more than anyone else in the society. That is because they live in slums, jammed together under unhygienic conditions; they have inadequate diets, and cannot get decent medical care. When they become sick, they are sick longer than any other group in society. Because they are sick more often and longer than anyone else, they lose wages and work, and find it difficult to hold a steady job. And because of this, they cannot pay for good housing, for a nutritious diet, for doctors. At any given point in the circle, particularly when there is a major illness, their prospect is to move to an even lower level and to begin the cycle, round and round, toward even more suffering. . . .

Throughout, I work on an assumption that cannot be proved by Government figures or even documented by impressions of the other America. It is an ethical proposition, and it can be simply stated: In a nation with a technology that could provide every citizen with a decent life, it is an outrage and a scandal that there should be such social misery. Only if one begins with this assumption is it possible to pierce through the invisibility of 40,000,000 to 50,000,000 human beings and to see the other America. We must perceive passionately, if this blindness is to be lifted from us. A fact can be rationalized and explained away; an indignity cannot.

What shall we tell the American poor, once we have seen them? Shall we say to them that they are better off than the Indian poor, the Italian poor, the Russian poor? That is one answer, but it is heartless. I should put it another way. I want to tell every well-fed and optimistic American that it is intolerable that so many millions should be maimed in body and in spirit when it is not necessary that they should be. My standard of comparison is not how much worse things used to be. It is how much better they could be if only we were stirred. . . .

These, then, are the strangest poor in the history of mankind.

They exist within the most powerful and rich society the world has ever known. Their misery has continued while the majority of the nation talked of itself as being "affluent" and worried about neuroses in the suburbs. In this way tens of millions of human beings became invisible. They dropped out of sight and out of mind; they were without their own political voice.

Yet this need not be. The means are at hand to fulfill the age-old dream: poverty can now be abolished. How long shall we ignore this underdeveloped nation in our midst? How long shall we look the other way while our fellow human beings suffer? How long?

Source: Michael Harrington, *The Other America* (New York, 1962).

For Further Reading:

Richard Cloward and Francis Fox Piven, *Poor People's Movements* (New York: Pantheon, 1977).

Michael Harrington, *The Long Distance Runner* (New York: Holt, 1988).

95. Betty Friedan, Excerpt from *The Feminine Mystique* (1963)

1963   *The Feminine Mystique* published
1964   Title VII of Civil Rights Act enacted, prohibiting sexual discrimination in employment
1966   National Organization for Women founded
1972   Equal Rights Amendment passed by Congress (not ratified by states)

Betty Friedan's The Feminine Mystique *had at least as much impact as Michael Harrington's* The Other America *(see document 94). Friedan articulated the feeling of many middle-class American women in the late 1950s and early 1960s that something was wrong with their lives. Friedan argued that the life of a suburban housewife was not the ideal it was cracked up to be. In fact, for many, it was downright unfulfilling. Like blacks in the South, Friedan observed, women had been relegated to an unequal sphere and forced to accept a limited place or role.*

Friedan's study helped unleash a rebirth of the women's rights movement. Other middle-aged women like Friedan, joined by millions of younger women, many of them veterans of the civil rights struggle, formed new women's groups, from the National Organization of Women, headed by Friedan, to the Boston Women's Health Collective. These organizations addressed issues ranging from discrimination in the workplace to the blatant treatment of women as sexual objects. Women sponsored "consciousness-raising" sessions, lobbied for political reforms, most notably the Equal Rights Amendment, which passed Congress in 1972 but never won ratification, and staged their own individual struggles for equality.

The problem lay buried, unspoken, for many years in the minds of American women. It was a strange stirring, a sense of dissatisfaction, a yearning that women suffered in the middle of the twentieth century in the United States. Each suburban wife struggled with it alone. As she made the beds, shopped for groceries, matched slipcover material, ate peanut butter sandwiches with her children, chauffeured Cub Scouts and Brownies, lay beside her husband at night—she was afraid to ask even of herself the silent question—"Is this all?"

For over fifteen years there was no word of this yearning in the millions of words written about women, for women, in all the columns, books and articles by experts telling women their role was to seek fulfillment as wives

"Sisterhood Is Powerfull" Poster (National Organization of Women).

and mothers. Over and over women heard in voices of tradition and of Freudian sophistication that they could desire no greater destiny than to glory in their own femininity. Experts told them how to catch a man and keep him, how to breastfeed children and handle their toilet training, how to cope with sibling rivalry and adolescent rebellion; how to buy a dishwasher, bake bread, cook gourmet snails, and build a swimming pool with their own hands; how to dress, look, and act more feminine and make marriage more exciting; how to keep their husbands from dying young and their sons from growing into delinquents. They were taught to pity the neurotic, unfeminine, unhappy women who wanted to be poets or physicists or presidents. They learned that truly feminine women do not want careers, higher education, political rights—the independence and the opportunities that the old-fashioned feminists fought for. Some women, in their forties and fifties, still remembered painfully giving up those dreams, but more of the younger women no longer thought about them. A thousand expert voices applauded their femininity, their adjustment, their new maturity. All they had to do was devote their lives from earliest girlhood to finding a husband and bearing children.

By the end of the nineteen-fifties, the average marriage age of women in America dropped to 20, and was still dropping, into the teens. Fourteen million girls were engaged by 17. The proportion of women attending college in comparison with men dropping from 47 per cent in 1920 to 35 per cent in 1958. A century earlier, women had fought for higher education; now girls went to college to get a husband. By the mid-fifties, 60 per cent dropped out of college to marry, or because they were afraid too much education would be a marriage bar. Colleges built dormitories for "married students," but the students were almost always the husbands. A new degree was instituted for the wives—"Ph.T." (Putting Husband Through)....

By the end of the fifties, the United States birthrate was overtaking India's. The birth-control movement, renamed Planned Parenthood, was asked to find a method whereby women who had been advised that a third or fourth baby would be born dead or defective might have it anyhow. Statisticians were especially astounded at the fantastic increase in the number of babies among college women. Where once they had two children, now they had four, five, six. Women who had once wanted careers were now making careers out of having babies. So rejoiced *Life* magazine in a 1956 paean to the movement of American women back to the home.

In a New York hospital, a woman had a nervous breakdown when she found she could not breastfeed her baby. In other hospitals, women dying of cancer refused a drug which research had proved might save their lives: its side effects were said to be unfeminine. "If I have only one life, let me live it as a blonde," a larger-than-life-sized picture of a pretty, vacuous woman proclaimed from newspaper, magazine, and drugstore ads. And across America, three out of every ten women dyed their hair blonde. They ate a chalk called Metrecal, instead of food, to shrink to the size of the thin young models. Department-store buyers reported that American women, since 1939, had become three and four sizes smaller. "Women are out to fit the clothes, instead of vice-versa," one buyer said.

Interior decorators were designing kitchens with mosaic murals and original paintings, for kitchens were once again the center of women's lives. Home sewing became a million-dollar industry. Many women no longer left their homes, except to shop, chauffeur their children, or attend a social engagement with their husbands. Girls were growing up in America without ever having jobs outside the home. In the late fifties, a sociological phenomenon was suddenly remarked: a third of American women now worked, but most were no longer young and very few were pursuing careers. They were married women who held part-time jobs, selling or secretarial, to put their husbands through school, their sons through college, or to help pay the mortgage. Or they were widows supporting families. Fewer and fewer women were entering professional work. The shortages in the nursing, social work, and teaching professions caused crises in almost every American city. Concerned over the Soviet Union's lead in the space race, scientists noted that America's greatest source of unused brain-power was women. But girls would not study physics: it was "unfeminine." A girl refused a science fellowship at Johns Hopkins to take a job in a real-estate office. All she wanted, she said, was what every other American girl wanted—to get married, have four children and live in a nice house in a nice suburb.

The suburban housewife—she was the dream image of the young American women and the envy, it was said, of women all over the world. The American housewife—freed by science and labor-saving appliances from the drudgery, the dangers of childbirth and the illnesses of her grandmother. She was healthy, beautiful, educated, concerned only about her husband, her children, her home. She had found true feminine fulfillment. As a housewife and mother, she was respected as a full and equal partner to man in his world. She was free to choose automobiles, clothes, appliances, supermarkets; she had everything that women ever dreamed of.

In the fifteen years after World War II, this mystique of feminine fulfillment became the cherished and self-perpetuating core of contemporary American culture. Millions of women lived their lives in the image of those pretty pictures of the American suburban housewife, kissing their husbands goodbye in front of the picture window, depositing their stationwagonsful of children at school, and smiling as they ran the new electric waxer over the spotless kitchen floor. They baked their own bread, sewed their own and their children's clothes, kept their new washing machines and dryers running all day. They changed the sheets on the beds twice a week instead of once, took the rug-hooking class in adult education, and pitied their poor frustrated mothers, who had dreamed of having a career. Their only dream was to be perfect wives and mothers; their highest ambition to have five children and a beautiful house, their only fight to get and keep their husbands. They had no thought for the unfeminine problems of the world outside the home; they wanted the men to make the major decisions. They gloried in their role as women, and wrote proudly on the census blank: "Occupation: housewife.". . .

If the woman had a problem in the 1950's and 1960's, she knew that something must be wrong with her marriage, or with herself. Other women were satisfied with their lives, she thought. What kind of a woman was she if she did not feel this mysterious fulfillment waxing the kitchen floor? She was so ashamed to admit her dissatisfaction that she never knew how many other women shared it. . . .

But on an April morning in 1959, I heard a mother of four, having coffee with four other mothers in a suburban development fifteen miles from New York, say in a tone of quiet desperation, "the problem." And the others knew, without words, that she was not talking about a problem with her husband, or her children, or her home. Suddenly they realized they all shared the same problem, the problem that has no name. They began, hesitantly, to talk about it. Later, after they had picked up their children at nursery school and taken them home to nap, two of the women cried, in sheer relief, just to know they were not alone.

Gradually I came to realize that the problem that has no name was shared by countless women in America. As a magazine writer I often interviewed women about problems with their children, or their marriages, or their houses, or their communities. But after a while I began to recognize the telltale signs of this other problem. I saw the same signs in suburban ranch houses and split-levels on Long Island and in New Jersey and Westchester County; in colonial houses in a small Massachusetts town; on patios in Memphis; in surburban and city apartments; in living rooms in the Midwest. Sometimes I sensed the problem, not as a reporter, but as a suburban housewife, for during this time I was also bringing up my own three children in Rockland County, New York. I heard echoes of the problem in college dormitories and semi-private maternity wards, at PTA meetings and luncheons of the League of Women Voters, at suburban cocktail parties, in station wagons waiting for trains, and in snatches of conversation overheard at Schrafft's. The groping words I heard from other women, on quiet afternoons when children were at school or on quiet evenings when husbands worked late, I think I understood first as a woman long before I understood their larger social and psychological implications.

Just what was this problem that has no name? What were the words women used when they tried to express it? Sometimes a woman would say "I feel empty somehow . . . incomplete." Or she would say, "I feel as if I don't exist." Sometimes she blotted out the feeling with a tranquilizer. . . .

It is no longer possible to ignore that voice, to dismiss the desperation of so many American women. This is not what being a woman means, no matter what the experts say. For human suffering there is a reason; perhaps the reason has not been found because the right questions have not been asked, or pressed far enough. I do not accept the answer that there is no problem because American women have luxuries that women in other times and lands never dreamed of; part of the strange newness of the problem is that it cannot be understood in terms of the age-old material problems of man: poverty, sickness, hunger, cold. The women who suffer this problem have a hunger that food cannot fill. It persists in women whose husbands are struggling interns and law clerks, or prosperous doctors and lawyers; in wives of workers and executives who make $5,000 a year or $50,000. It is not caused by lack of material advantages; it may not even be felt by women preoccupied with desperate problems of hunger, poverty or illness. And women who think it will be solved by more money, a bigger house, a second car, moving to a better suburb, often discover it gets worse.

It is no longer possible today to blame the problem on loss of femininity: to say that education and independence and equality with men have made American women unfeminine. I have heard so many women try to deny this dissatisfied voice within themselves because it does not fit the pretty picture of femininity the experts have given them. I think, in fact, that this is the first clue to the mystery: the problem cannot be understood in the generally accepted terms by which scientists have studied women, doctors have treated them, counselors have advised them, and writers have written about them. Women who suffer this problem, in whom this voice is stirring, have lived their whole lives in the pursuit of feminine fulfillment. They are not career women (although career women may have other problems); they are women whose greatest ambition has been marriage and children. For the oldest of these women, these daughters of the American middle class, no other dream was possible. The ones in their forties and fifties who once had other dreams gave them up and threw themselves joyously into life as housewives. For the youngest, the new wives and mothers, this was the only dream. They are the ones who quit high school and college to marry, or marked time in some job in which they had no real interest until they married. These women are very "feminine" in the usual sense, and yet they still suffer the problem. . . .

If I am right, the problem that has no name stirring in the minds of so many American women today is not a matter of loss of femininity or too much education, or the demands of domesticity. It is far more important than anyone recognizes. It is the key to these other new and old problems which have been torturing women and their husbands and children, and puzzling their doctors and educators for years. It may well be the key to our future as a nation and a culture. We can no longer ignore that voice within women that says: "I want something more than my husband and my children and my home."

Source: Betty Friedan, *The Feminine Mystique* (New York, 1963).

For Further Reading:

Sara Evans, *Personal Politics* (New York: Vintage, 1979).

Jo Freeman, *The Politics of Women's Liberation* (New York: McKay, 1979).

Susan M. Hartmann, *From Margin to Mainstream* (Philadelphia: Temple University Press, 1989).

96. Roe v. Wade, Justice Harry Blackmun, Excerpt from "Majority Opinion" (1973)

1954–69   Warren Court
1960   Birth control pill commercially introduced
1973   *Our Bodies, Ourselves* published; *Roe v. Wade*

One aspect of the women's rights movement was greater discussion of sexuality and the breakdown of many traditional sexual taboos. The publication of Our Bodies, Ourselves *by the Boston Women's Health Collective, in 1973, and the broad readership it immediately gained, symbolized both a desire by women to learn more about their own sexuality, and health issues related to it, and a greater openness on society's part to such issues. Indeed, women had traveled a long way from the time when Margaret Sanger was arrested for merely trying to distribute information on birth control (see document 60).*

Central to Our Bodies, Ourselves *was the notion that until women could control their own biological destiny, they could not be free and equal. This concept also received attention in the courts, culminating with the case* Roe v. Wade, *which made it illegal to ban abortion in the early part of a woman's pregnancy. While the case remains one of the most controversial in American history, its decision was built on other cases dealing with sexuality and privacy, including those in which the Supreme Court had struck down state laws prohibiting the distribution of literature on contraception and the use of contraceptives by consenting (married) adults, most notably the* Griswold *case.*

Roe v. Wade *also symbolized the transformation of the Supreme Court from a bulwark of conservatism to an active and liberal branch of government. In the early 1930s the Court had stood in the way of the New Deal. By the mid-1960s, under the leadership of Chief Justice Earl Warren, it recognized the rights of minorities, criminal defendants, and the press. For example, in* Gideon v. Wainwright *the Supreme Court declared that defendants in capital cases had to be provided with adequate counsel.*

Roe v. Wade *itself was not a Warren Court decision. Rather it was made after Warren Burger had replaced Earl Warren as Chief Justice. Since its decision, the Court has continued to change, shifting in a more conservative direction. As a result, the decision in* Roe v. Wade, *which has been one of the Court's most controversial in its history, stands in jeopardy of being overturned.*

We forthwith acknowledge our awareness of the sensitive and emotional nature of the abortion controversy, of the vigorous opposing views, even among physicians, and of the deep and seemingly absolute convictions that the subject inspires. One's philosophy, one's experiences, one's exposure to the raw edges of human existence, one's religious training, one's attitudes toward life and family and their values, and the moral standards one establishes and seeks to observe, are all likely to influence and to color one's thinking and conclusions about abortion.

In addition, population growth, pollution, poverty, and racial overtones tend to complicate and not to simplify the problem.

Our task, of course, is to resolve the issue by constitutional measurement free of emotion and of predilection. We seek earnestly to do this, and, because we do, we have inquired into, and in this opinion place some emphasis upon, medical and medical-legal history and what that history reveals about man's attitudes toward the abortive procedure over the centuries. . . .

Jane Roe, a single woman who was residing in Dallas County, Texas, instituted this federal action in March 1970 against the District Attorney of the county. She sought a declaratory judgment that the Texas criminal abortion statutes were unconstitutional on their face, and an injunction restraining the defendant from enforcing the statutes.

Roe alleged that she was unmarried and pregnant; that she wished to terminate her pregnancy by an abortion "performed by a competent, licensed physician, under safe, clinical conditions"; that she was unable to get a "legal" abortion in Texas because her life did not appear to be threatened by the continuation of her pregnancy; and that she could not afford to travel to another jurisdiction in order to secure a legal abortion under safe conditions. She claimed that the Texas statutes were unconstitutionally vague and that they abridged her right of personal privacy, protected by the First, Fourth, Fifth, Ninth, and Fourteenth Amendments. By an amendment to her complaint Roe purported to sue "on behalf of herself and all other women" similarly situated. . . .

On the merits, the District Court held that the "fundamental right of single women and married persons to choose whether to have children is protected by the Ninth Amendment, through the Fourteenth Amendment," and that the Texas criminal abortion statutes were void on their face because they were both unconstitutionally vague and constituted an overbroad infringement of the plaintiffs' Ninth Amendment rights. . . .

The appellee . . . suggests that Roe's case must now be moot because she and all other members of her class are no longer subject to any 1970 pregnancy.

The usual rule in federal cases is that an actual controversy must exist at stages of appellate or certiorari review, and not simply at the date the action is initiated. . . .

But when, as here, pregnancy is a significant fact in the litigation, the normal 266-day human gestation period is so short that the pregnancy will come to term before the usual appellate process is complete. If that termination makes a case moot, pregnancy litigation seldom will survive much beyond the trial stage, and appellate review will be effectively denied. Our law should not be that rigid. . . .

It perhaps is not generally appreciated that the restrictive criminal abortion laws in effect in a majority of States today are of relatively recent vintage. Those laws, generally proscribing abortion or its attempt at any time during pregnancy except when necessary to preserve the pregnant woman's life, are not of ancient or even of common law origin. Instead, they derive from statutory changes effected, for the most part, in the latter half of the 19th century . . . .

Three reasons have been advanced to explain historically the enactment of criminal abortion laws in the 19th century and to justify their continued existence. . . .

It has been argued occasionally that these laws were the product of a Victorian social concern to discourage illicit sexual conduct. Texas, however, does not advance this justification in the present case, and it appears that no court or commentator has taken the argument seriously. . . .

A second reason is concerned with abortion as a medical procedure. When most criminal abortion laws were first enacted, the procedure was a hazardous one for the woman. This was particularly true prior to the development of antisepsis. . . . Abortion mortality was high. . . . Thus it has been argued that a State's real concern in enacting a criminal abortion law was to protect the pregnant woman, that is, to restrain her from submitting to a procedure that placed her life in serious jeopardy. . . .

The third reason is the State's interest—some phrase it in terms of duty—in protecting prenatal life. . . .

[A]s long as at least *potential* life is involved, the State may assert interests beyond the protection of the pregnant woman alone. . . .

It is with these interests, and the weight to be attached to them, that this case is concerned.

The Constitution does not explicitly mention any right of privacy. In a line of decisions, however, going back perhaps as far as . . . [1891], the Court has recognized that a right of personal privacy, or a guarantee of certain areas or zones of privacy, does exist under the Constitution. . . .

This right of privacy, whether it be founded in the Fourteenth Amendment's concept of personal liberty and restrictions upon state action, as we feel it is, or, as the District Court determined, in the Ninth Amendment's reservation of rights to the people, is broad enough to encompass a woman's decision whether or not to terminate her pregnancy. The detriment that the State would impose upon the pregnant woman by denying this choice altogether is apparent. Specific and direct harm medically diagnosable even in early pregnancy may be involved. Maternity, or additional offspring, may force upon the woman a distressful life and future. Psychological harm may be imminent. Mental and physical health may be taxed by child care. There is also the distress, for all concerned, associated with the unwanted child, and there is the problem of bringing a child into a family already unable, psychologically and otherwise, to care for it. In other cases, as in this one, the additional difficulties and continuing stigma of unwed motherhood may be involved. . . .

On the basis of elements such as these, appellants and some *amici* argue that the woman's right is absolute and that she is entitled to terminate her pregnancy at whatever time, in whatever way, and for whatever reason she alone chooses. With this we do not agree. . . . [A] state may properly assert important interests in safeguarding health, in maintaining medical standards, and in protecting potential life. At some point in pregnancy, these respective interests become sufficiently compelling to sustain regulation of the factors that govern the abortion decision. The privacy right involved, therefore, cannot be said to be absolute. . . .

We therefore conclude that the right of personal privacy includes the abortion decision, but that this right is not unqualified and must be considered against important state interests in regulation. . . .

Where certain "fundamental rights" are involved, the Court has held that regulation limiting these rights may be justified only by a "compelling state interest," . . . and that legislative enactments must be narrowly drawn to express only the legitimate state interests at stake. . . .

. . . The appellee and certain *amici* argue that the fetus is a "person" within the language and meaning of the Fourteenth Amendment. . . .

The Constitution does not define "person" in so many words. . . . All this, together with our observation, . . . that throughout the major portion of the 19th century prevailing legal abortion practices were far freer than they are today, persuades us that the word "person," as used in the Fourteenth Amendment, does not include the unborn. . . .

Texas urges that, apart from the Fourteenth Amendment, life begins at conception and is present throughout pregnancy, and that, therefore, the State has a compelling interest in protecting that life from and after conception. We need not resolve the difficult question of when life begins. When those trained in the respective disciplines of medicine, philosophy, and theology are unable to arrive at any consensus, the judiciary, at this point in the development of man's knowledge, is not in a position to speculate as to the answer.

It should be sufficient to note briefly the wide divergence of thinking on this most sensitive and difficult question. . . .

In areas other than criminal abortion the law has been reluctant to endorse any theory that life, as we recognize it, begins before live birth or to accord legal rights to the unborn except in narrowly defined situations and except when the rights are contingent upon live birth. . . . [T]he unborn have never been recognized in the law as persons in the whole sense.

. . . [T]he State does have an important and legitimate interest in preserving and protecting the health of the pregnant woman, whether she be a resident of the State or a nonresident who seeks medical consultation and treatment there, and that it has still *another* important and legitimate interest in protecting the potentiality of human life. These interests are separate and distinct. Each grows in substantiality as the woman approaches term and, at a point during pregnancy, each becomes "compelling."

With respect to the State's important and legitimate interest in the health of the mother, the "compelling" point, in the light of present medical knowledge, is at approximately the end of the first trimester. This is so because of the now established medical fact, referred to above, that until the end of the first trimester mortality in abortion is less than mortality in normal childbirth. It follows that, from and after this point, a State may regulate the abortion procedure to the extent that the regulation reasonably relates to the preservation and protection of maternal health. . . .

With respect to the State's important and legitimate interest in potential life, the "compelling" point is at viability. This is so because the fetus then presumably has the capability of meaningful life outside the mother's womb. State regulation protective of fetal life after viability thus has both logical and biological justifications. If the State is interested in protecting fetal life after viability, it may go so far as to proscribe abortion during that period except when it is necessary to preserve the life or health of the mother. . . .

To summarize and to repeat:

1. A state criminal abortion statute of the current Texas type, that excepts from criminality only a *life saving* procedure on behalf of the mother, without regard to pregnancy stage and without recognition of the other interests involved, is violative of the Due Process Clause of the Fourteenth Amendment.

(a) For the stage prior to approximately the end of the first trimester, the abortion decision and its effectuation must be left to the medical judgment of the pregnant woman's attending physician.

(b) For the stage subsequent to approximately the end of the first trimester, the State, in promoting its interest in the health of the mother, may, if it chooses, regulate the abortion procedure in ways that are reasonably related to maternal health.

(c) For the stage subsequent to viability the State, in promoting its interest in the potentiality of human life, may, if it chooses, regulate, and even proscribe, abortion except where it is necessary, in appropriate medical judgment, for the preservation of the life or health of the mother. . . .

. . . The decision leaves the State free to place increasing restrictions on abortion as the period of pregnancy lengthens, so long as those restrictions are tailored to the recognized state interests. The decision vindicates the right of the physician to administer medical treatment according to his professional judgment up to the points where important state interests provide compelling justifications for intervention. Up to those points the abortion decision in all its aspects is inherently, and primarily, a medical decision, and basic responsibility for it must rest with the physician. If an individual practitioner abuses the privilege of exercising proper medical judgment, the usual remedies, judicial and intraprofessional, are available. . . .

It is so ordered.

Source: *Roe v. Wade*, 410 U.S. 113 (1973).

For Further Reading:

Marian Faux, *Roe v. Wade* (New York: Macmillan, 1988).
Faye Ginsburg, *Contested Lives* (Berkeley: University of California Press, 1989).

97. Cesar Chavez, "Letter from Delano" (1969)

1965   United Farm Workers formed
1965–73   Grape boycotts
1973   Table grape growers sign contract with United Farm
         Workers (UFW)

For years migrant farm workers had been some of the most exploited men and women in America. John Steinbeck's novel The Grapes of Wrath *(1939) and the film* Harvest of Shame *(1959) had both documented their oppression. Even during the 1960s, a period of prosperity, they suffered from extremely poor pay and work conditions. Moreover, up until 1965, all efforts to organize migrant farm workers, by the Industrial Workers of the World (IWW), Communist Party, and American Federation of Labor–Congress of Industrial Organizations (AFL-CIO), had failed.*

This changed in 1965 with the emergence of the United Farm Workers of America. Led by Cesar Chavez, this union, which won broad support from the student left, civil rights activists, and the AFL-CIO, launched a strike and then a massive national consumer boycott against California's produce growers (most importantly its table grape growers). The boycott galvanized the nation and ultimately won the union a contract.

The United Farm Workers succeeded where others had failed for several reasons. First, they were led by one of their own; Chavez was Mexican-American and so were most of the migrant workers. Second, like the civil rights movement, their nonviolent tactics garnered them broad middle-class support. A corollary of this was their ability to mobilize many clergymen and liberal churches behind their cause, as evidenced by Chavez's "Letter from Delano," which was reprinted by the Christian Century *and the* National Catholic Reporter. *Lastly, the UFW won the support of millions of Americans by casting its struggle, often referred to as "La Causa," as the embodiment of the principles of democracy and its foes as old-fashioned despots.*

Good Friday 1969.

E. L. Barr, Jr., President
California Grape and Tree Fruit League
717 Market St.
San Francisco, California

Dear Mr. Barr:

I am sad to hear about your accusations in the press that our union movement and table grape boycott have been successful because we have used violence and terror tactics. If what you say is true, I have been a failure and should withdraw from the struggle; but you are left with the awesome moral responsibility, before God and man, to come forward with whatever information you have so that corrective action can begin at once. If for any reason you fail to come forth to substantiate your charges, then you must be held responsible for committing violence against us, albeit violence of the tongue. I am convinced that you as a human being did not mean what you said but rather acted hastily under pressure from the public relations firm that has been hired to try to counteract the tremendous moral force of our movement. How many times we ourselves have felt the need to lash out in anger and bitterness.

Today on Good Friday 1969 we remember the life and the sacrifice of Martin Luther King, Jr., who gave himself totally to the nonviolent struggle for peace and justice. In his "Letter from Birmingham Jail" Dr. King describes better than I could our hopes for the strike and boycott: "Injustice must be exposed, with all the tension its exposure creates, to the light of human conscience and the air of national opinion before it can be cured." For our part I admit that we have seized upon every tactic and strategy consistent with the morality of our cause to expose that injustice and thus to heighten the sensitivity of the American conscience so that farm workers will have without bloodshed their own union and the dignity of bargaining with their agribusiness employers. By lying about the nature of our movement, Mr. Barr, you are working against nonviolent social change. Unwittingly perhaps, you may unleash that other force which our union by discipline and deed, censure and education has sought to avoid, that panacean shortcut: that senseless violence which honors no color, class or neighborhood.

You must understand—I must make you understand—that our membership and the hopes and aspirations of the hundreds of thousands of the poor and dispossessed that have been raised on our account are, above all, human beings, no better and no worse than any other cross-section of human society; we are not saints because we are poor, but by the same measure neither are we immoral. We are men and women who have suffered and endured much, and not only because of our abject poverty but because we have been kept poor. The colors of our skins, the languages of our cultural and native origins, the lack of formal education, the exclusion from the democratic process, the numbers of our slain in recent wars—all these burdens generation after generation have sought to demoralize us, to break our human spirit. But God knows that we are not beasts of burden, agricultural implements or rented slaves; we are men. And mark this well, Mr. Barr, we are men locked in a death struggle against man's inhumanity to man in the industry that you represent. And this struggle itself gives meaning to our life and ennobles our dying.

As your industry has experienced, our strikers here in Delano and those who represent us throughout the world are well trained for this struggle. They have been under the gun, they have been kicked and beaten and herded by dogs, they have been cursed and ridiculed, they have been stripped and chained and jailed, they have been sprayed with the poisons used in the vineyards; but they have been taught not to lie down and die nor to flee in shame, but to resist with every ounce of human endurance and spirit. To resist not with retaliation in kind but to overcome with love and compassion, with ingenuity and creativity, with hard work and longer hours, with stamina and patient tenacity, with truth and public appeal, with friends and allies, with mobility and discipline, with politics and law, and with prayer and fasting. They were not trained in a month or even a year; after all, this new harvest season will mark our fourth full year of strike and even now we continue to plan and prepare for the years to come. Time accomplishes for the poor what money does for the rich.

This is not to pretend that we have everywhere been successful enough or that we have not made mistakes. And while we do not belittle or underestimate our adversaries—for they are the rich and the powerful and they possess the land—we are not afraid nor do we cringe from the confrontation. We welcome it! We have planned for it. We know that our cause is just, that history is a story of social revolution, and that the poor shall inherit the land.

Once again, I appeal to you as the representative of your industry and as a man. I ask you to recognize and bargain with our union before the economic pressure of the boycott and strike takes an irrevocable toll; but if not, I ask you to at least sit down with us to discuss the safeguards necessary to keep our historical struggle free of violence. I make this appeal because as one of the leaders of our nonviolent movement, I know and accept my responsibility for preventing, if possible, the destruction of human life and property. For these reasons and knowing of Gandhi's admonition that fasting is the last resort in place of the sword, during a most critical time in our movement last February 1968 I undertook a 25-day fast. I repeat to you the principle enunciated to the membership at the start of the fast: if to build our union required the deliberate taking of life, either the life of a grower or his child, or the life of a farm worker or his child, then I choose not to see the union built.

Mr. Barr, let me be painfully honest with you. You must understand these things. We advocate militant nonviolence as our means for social revolution and to achieve justice for our people, but we are not blind or deaf to the desperate and moody winds of human frustration, impatience and rage that blow among us. Gandhi himself admitted that if his only choice were cowardice or violence, he would choose violence. Men are not angels, and time and tide wait for no man. Precisely because of these powerful human emotions, we have tried to involve masses of people in their own struggle. Participation and self-determination remain the best experience of freedom, and free men instinctively prefer democratic change and even protect the rights guaranteed to seek it. Only the enslaved in despair have need of violent overthrow.

This letter does not express all that is in my heart, Mr. Barr. But if it says nothing else it says that we do not hate you or rejoice to see your industry destroyed; we hate the agribusiness system that seeks to keep us enslaved, and we shall overcome and change it not by retaliation or bloodshed but by a determined nonviolent struggle carried on by those masses of farm workers who intend to be free and human.

Sincerely yours,
Cesar E. Chavez

United Farm Workers Organizing
  Committee, A.F.L.-C.I.O.
Delano, California.

Source: *Christian Century* 86 (April 23, 1969): 539.

For Further Reading:

J. Craig Jenkins, *The Politics of Insurgency* (New York: Columbia University Press, 1985).
Jacques E. Levy, *Cesar Chavez* (New York: Norton, 1975).
Peter Matthiessen, *Sal Si Puedes* (New York: Random House, 1969).

98. Judge John J. Sirica, Excerpt from "Order and Opinion on Presidential (Watergate) Tapes" (1973)

1972   Break-in at Watergate complex
1973   Story of break-in and cover-up unfolds in press and
        congressional hearings
1974   House Judiciary Committee votes to impeach President
        Nixon; Nixon resigns
1975   Nixon pardoned by President Gerald Ford

In 1972, President Richard Nixon was reelected, defeating Senator George McGovern, an outspoken critic of the war in Vietnam, in a landslide. Yet in the midst of the campaign a bizarre event took place that ultimately led to President Nixon's resignation. In the midst of the campaign, several burglars, with ties to the Committee to Re-Elect the President (CREEP), were arrested for breaking into the Democratic Party's headquarters at the Watergate hotel and office complex in Washington, D.C. At the time, President Nixon and his aides denied any connection to the incident. After the election, however, newspaper reports led many to see clear links between Nixon's top aides and the burglars. Further investigations by House and Senate subcommittees convinced the public that the President himself was either involved in the burglary or in a cover-up of it.

Still, as of the spring of 1973, no concrete evidence had been found linking the President to the crime or the cover-up. But then one of Nixon's top aides revealed that the President had secretly tape-recorded all of his conversations in the Oval Office, including those in which he had allegedly ordered a cover-up. Hence a crucial legal battle ensued for the tapes. Before it was all over, President Nixon had fired a series of Attorneys General and the federal courts were determining whether the President could be compelled to turn over the tapes to congressional investigators.

Ultimately, District Court Judge John J. Sirica ordered President Nixon to release the tapes. Higher courts upheld his decision. Nixon complied. But then investigators discovered large and crucial gaps, seeming erasures, in the tapes. Even without the proverbial smoking gun, the House Judiciary Committee voted in favor of impeaching the President and a week later Nixon resigned. A constitutional crisis had been averted. By issuing the order, Judge Sirica had demonstrated that no man is above the law. By resigning, Nixon showed that he would not challenge this principle.

This said, when Vice President Ford assumed the presidency, he imme-

diately pardoned Nixon, which, in turn, left many feeling that Nixon still saw himself above the law. In fact, in the years following the Watergate scandal, Nixon argued that he had been forced to resign for political rather than legal reasons.

ORDER

This matter having come before the Court on motion of the Watergate Special Prosecutor made on behalf of the June, 1972 grand jury of this district for an order to show cause, and the Court being advised in the premises, it is by the Court this 29th day of August, 1973, for the reasons stated in the attached opinion,

ORDERED that respondent, President Richard M. Nixon, or any subordinate officer, official or employee with custody or control of the documents or objects listed in the grand jury subpoena *duces tecum* of July 23, 1973, served on respondent in this district, is hereby commanded to produce forthwith for the Court's examination *in camera*, the subpoenaed documents or objects which have not heretofore been produced to the grand jury; and it is

FURTHER ORDERED that the ruling herein be stayed for a period of five days in which time respondent may perfect an appeal from the ruling; and it is

FURTHER ORDERED that should respondent appeal from the ruling herein, the above stay will be extended indefinitely pending the completion of such appeal or appeals.

(signed) John J. Sirica
Chief Judge

The Court has found it necessary to adjudicate but two questions for the present: (1) whether the Court has jurisdiction to decide the issue of privilege, and (2) whether the Court has authority to enforce the subpoena *duces tecum* by way of an order requiring production for inspection *in camera*. A third question, whether the materials are in fact privileged as against the grand jury, either in whole or in part, is left for subsequent adjudication. For the reasons outlined below, the Court concludes that both of the questions considered must be answered in the affirmative.

A search of the Constitution and the history of its creation reveals a general disfavor of government privileges, or at least uncontrolled privileges. Early in the Convention of 1787, the delegates cautioned each other concerning the dangers of lodging immoderate power in the executive department. This attitude persisted throughout the Convention, and executive powers became a major topic in the subsequent ratification debates. The Framers regarded the legislative department superior in power and importance to the other two and felt the necessity of investing it with some privileges and immunities, but even here an attitude of restraint, as expressed by James Madison, prevailed. . . . The upshot . . . regarding a definition of executive privileges was that none were deemed necessary, or at least that the Constitution need not record any.

. . . Are there, then, any rights or privileges consistent with, though not mentioned in, the Constitution which are necessary to the Executive? One answer may be found in the Supreme Court decision, *United States v. Reynolds*, 346 U.S. 1 (1953). The Court recognized an executive privilege, evidentiary in nature, for military secrets. *Reynolds* held that when a court finds the privilege is properly invoked under the appropriate circumstances, it will, in a civil case at least, suppress the evidence. Thus, it must be recognized that there can be executive privileges that will bar the production of evidence. The Court is willing here to recognize and give effect to an evidentiary privilege based on the need to protect Presidential privacy.

The Court, however, cannot agree with Respondent that it is the Executive that finally determines whether its privilege is properly invoked. The availability of evidence including the validity and scope of privileges, is a judicial decision. . . . In all the numerous litigations where claims of executive privilege have been interposed, the courts have not hesitated to pass judgment. Executive fiat is not the model of resolution. . . .

The measures a court should adopt in ruling on claims of executive privilege are discussed under Part III herein.

If after judicial examination *in camera*, any portion of the tapes is ruled not subject to privilege, that portion will be forwarded to the grand jury at the appropriate time. To call for the tapes *in camera* is thus tantamount to fully enforcing the subpoena as to any unprivileged matter. Therefore, before the Court can call for production *in camera*, it must have concluded that it has authority to order a President to obey the command of a grand jury subpoena as it relates to unprivileged evidence in his possession. The Court has concluded that it possesses such authority.

Analysis of the question must begin on the well established premises that the grand jury has a right to every man's evidence and that for purposes of gathering evidence, process may issue to anyone. . . . The important factors are the relevance and materiality of the evidence. . . . The burden here then, is on the President to define exactly what it is about his office that court process commanding the production of evidence cannot reach there. To be accurate, court process in the form of a subpoena *duces tecum* has already issued to the President, and he acknowledges that . . . courts possess authority to direct such subpoenas to him. A distinction is drawn, however, between authority to issue a subpoena and authority to command obedience to it. It is this second compulsory process that the President contends may not reach him. The burden yet remains with the President, however, to explain why this must be so. What distinctive quality of the Presidency permits its incumbent to withhold evidence? To argue that the need for

Presidential privacy justifies it, is not persuasive. On the occasions when such need justifies suppression, the courts will sustain a privilege. The fact that this is a judicial decision has already been discussed at length, but the opinion of Chief Justice Marshall (*United States v. Burr*, 25 Fed. Cas. 30, 1807) on the topic deserves notice here. When deciding that a subpoena should issue to the President, the Chief Justice made it clear that if certain portions should be excised, it being appropriate to sustain a privilege, the Court would make such a decision upon return of the subpoena. . . .

To argue that it is the constitutional separation of powers that bars compulsory court process from the White House, is also unpersuasive. Such a contention overlooks history. Although courts generally, and this Court in particular, have avoided any interference with the discretionary acts of co-ordinate branches, they have not hesitated to rule on non-discretionary acts when necessary. Respondent points out that these and other precedents refer to officials other than the President, and that this distinction renders the precedents inapplicable. Such an argument tends to set the White House apart as a fourth branch of government. . . .

The Special Prosecutor has correctly noted that the Farmers' intention to lodge the powers of government in separate bodies also included a plan for interaction between departments. A "watertight" division of different functions was never their design. The legislative branch may organize the judiciary and dictate the procedures by which it transacts business. The judiciary may pass upon the constitutionality of legislative enactments—and in some instances define the bounds of Congressional investigations. The executive may veto legislative enactments, and the legislature may override the veto. The executive appoints judges and justices and may bind judicial decisions by lawful executive orders. The judiciary may pass on the constitutionality of executive acts. . . .

That the Court has not the physical power to enforce its order to the President is immaterial to a resolution of the issues. Regardless of its physical power to enforce them, the Court has a duty to issue appropriate orders. The Court cannot say that the Executive's persistence in withholding the tape recordings would "tarnish its reputation," but must admit that it would tarnish the Court's reputation to fail to do what it could in pursuit of justice. In any case, the courts have always enjoyed the good faith of the Executive Branch, even in such dire circumstances as those presented by *Youngstown Sheet & Tube Co. v. Sawyer*, 343 U.S. 579 (1952), and there is no reason to suppose that the courts in this instance cannot again rely on that same good faith. Indeed, the President himself has publicly so stated.

It is important also to note here the role of the grand jury. Chief Justice Marshall, in considering whether a subpoena might issue to the President of the United States, observed:

In the provisions of the constitution, and of the statute, which give to

the accused a right to the compulsory process of the court, there is no
exception whatever. (*United States v. Burr, 25 Fed. Cas. 20, 1807*)

Aaron Burr, it will be remembered, stood before the court accused though
not yet indicted. The Chief Justice's statement regarding the accused is
equally true with regard to a grand jury: "there is no exception whatever"
in its right to the compulsory process of the courts. The Court, while in a
position to lend its process in assistance to the grand jury, is thereby in a
position to assist justice. . . .

In all candor, the Court fails to perceive any reason for suspending the
power of courts to get evidence and rule on questions of privilege in criminal
matters simply because it is the President of the United States who holds
the evidence. The Burr decision left for another occasion a ruling on whether
compulsory process might issue to the President in situations such as this.
In the words of counsel, this is "a new question," with little in the way of
precedent to guide the Court. But Chief Justice Marshall clearly distinguished the amenability of the King to appear and give testimony under
court process and that of this nation's chief magistrate. The conclusion
reached here cannot be inconsistent with the view of that great Chief Justice
nor with the spirit of the Constitution.

In deciding whether these tape recordings or portions thereof are properly
the objects of a privilege, the Court must accommodate two competing
policies. On the one hand, as has been noted earlier, is the need to disfavor
privileges and narrow their application as far as possible. On the other hand,
lies a need to favor the privacy of Presidential deliberations; to indulge a
presumption in favor of the President. To the Court, respect for the President, the Presidency, and the duties of the office, gives the advantage to
this second policy. This respect, however, does not decide the
controversy. . . .

The teaching of *Reynolds* is that a Court should attempt to satisfy itself
whether or not a privilege is properly invoked without unnecessarily probing
into the material claimed to be privileged. A decision on how far to go will
be dictated in part by need for the evidence. . . .

The grand jury's showing of need here is well documented and imposing.
The Special Prosecutor has specifically identified by date, time and place
each of the eight meetings and the one telephone call involved. Due to the
unusual circumstances of having access to sworn public testimony of participants to these conversations, the Special Prosecutor has been able to provide
the Court with the conflicting accounts of what transpired. He thus identifies
the topics discussed in each instance, the areas of critical conflict in the
testimony, and the resolution it is anticipated the tape recordings may render
possible. The relative importance of the issues in doubt is revealed. . . .

The point is raised that, as in *Reynolds*, the sworn statements of witnesses
should suffice and remove the need for access to documents deemed priv-

ileged. Though this might often be the case, here, unfortunately, the witnesses differ, sometimes completely, on the precise matters likely to be of greatest moment to the grand jury. Ironically, need for the taped evidence derives in part from the fact that witnesses *have* testified regarding the subject matter, creating important issues of fact for the grand jury to resolve. It will be noted as well in contradistinction to *Reynolds*, that this is a criminal investigation. Rather than money damages at stake, we deal here in matters of reputation and liberty. Based on this indisputably forceful showing of necessity by the grand jury, the claim of privilege cannot be accepted lightly.

In his Brief in Support, the Special Prosecutor outlines the grand jury's view regarding the validity of the Respondent's claim of privilege. Its opinion is that the right of confidentiality is improperly asserted here. Principally, the Special Prosecutor cites a substantial possibility, based on the sworn testimony of participants, that the privilege is improperly invoked as a cloak for serious criminal wrongdoing. . . .

If the interest served by a privilege is abused or subverted, the claim of privilege fails. Such a case is well described in *Clark v. United States*, 289 U.S. 1 (1933), a decision involving the privilege of secrecy enjoyed by jurors. . . .

These principles are, of course, fully applicable throughout government. A court would expect that if the privacy of its deliberations, for example, were ever used to foster criminal conduct or to develop evidence of criminal wrongdoings, any privilege might be barred and privacy breached. So it is that evidentiary privilege asserted against the grand jury may be ruled inapplicable if the interest served by the privilege is subverted.

Nevertheless, without discrediting the strength of the grand jury's position, the Court cannot, as matters now stand, rule that the present claim of privilege is invalid. The President contends that the recorded conversations occurred pursuant to an exercise of his duty to "take care that the laws be faithfully executed." Although the Court is not bound by that conclusion, it is extremely reluctant to finally stand against a declaration of the President of the United States on any but the strongest possible evidence. Need for the evidence requires that a claim not be rejected lightly. The Court is simply unable to decide the question of privilege without inspecting the tapes. . . .

It is true that if material produced is properly the subject of privilege, even an inspection *in camera* may constitute a compromise of privilege. Nevertheless, it would be an extremely limited infraction and in this case an unavoidable one. If privileged and unprivileged evidence are intermingled, privileged portions may be excised so that only unprivileged matter goes before the grand jury (which also meets in secret proceedings). If privileged and unprivileged evidence are so inextricably connected that separation becomes impossible, the whole must be privileged and no disclosure made to the grand jury.

Source: "Order and Opinion on Presidential Tapes," 487 F2nd 700 (1973).

For Further Reading:

Stanley I. Kutler, *The Wars of Watergate* (New York: Knopf, 1990).
Jonathan Schell, *The Time of Illusion* (New York: Knopf, 1975).
Bob Woodward and Carl Bernstein, *All the President's Men* (New York: Simon & Schuster, 1974).

99. Ronald Reagan, Excerpt from "Speech at Moscow State University" (1988)

1975   South Vietnamese government falls
1979   Second oil crisis
1978–80 Double-digit inflation
1980–81 Iran hostage crisis
1980   Ronald Reagan elected President

By 1980 the United States lay mired in a deep sense of crisis or malaise. The Vietnam War, urban race riots, Watergate, oil shortages, and the Iran hostage crisis had shaken America's faith in its institutions and leadership. Ronald Reagan, a former movie actor and governor of California, ran against the incumbent, President Jimmy Carter, in 1980, promising to return the nation to its prior glory. He would get the government off of people's backs and stand tall against the Soviet Union. Reagan defeated Carter and quickly launched a massive defense build-up, a tax cut, and an attack on what he referred to as the welfare state.

President Reagan's record and legacy will be a matter of debate for years to come. By the end of his second term, the nation had enjoyed nearly five years of sustained economic growth and communism was on its deathbed in Eastern Europe. Yet the deficit had soared, the number of poor had risen, and the middle class was barely holding onto its status. None of these problems, however, ever shook Reagan's faith in the free-market economy. Indeed, in the last year of his presidency he traveled to the Soviet Union, where he proudly defended his record and the principles of economic and political freedom. On May 31, 1988, with a portrait of Lenin in the background, President Reagan touted the spread of democracy and the virtues of freedom in a speech to students at Moscow State University. Ironically, in the question-and-answer session that followed, Reagan invented a mythical past, one in which the Indians had not been subjugated by the whites but had chosen to live a life of deprivation and degradation. Yet, as we have seen, the rights of whites had often come at the expense of the rights of nonwhites (see documents 1, 8, 28, 29, 33, and 41).

Standing here before a mural of your revolution, I want to talk about a very different revolution that is taking place right now, quietly sweeping the globe, without bloodshed or conflict. Its effects are peaceful, but they will fundamentally after our world, shatter old assumptions, and reshape our lives.

It's easy to underestimate because it's not accompanied by banners or fanfare. It has been called the technological or information revolution, and as its emblem, one might take the tiny silicon chip—no bigger than a fingerprint. One of these chips has more computing power than a roomful of old-style computers.

As part of an exchange program, we now have an exhibition touring your country that shows how information technology is transforming our lives— replacing manual labor with robots, forecasting weather for farmers, or mapping the genetic code of DNA for medical researchers. These microcomputers today aid the design of everything from houses to cars to spacecraft— they even design better and faster computers. They can translate English into Russian or enable the blind to read—or help Michael Jackson produce on one synthesizer the sounds of a whole orchestra. Linked by a network of satellites and fiber-optic cables, one individual with a desktop computer and a telephone commands resources unavailable to the largest governments just a few years ago.

Like a chrysalis, we're emerging from the economy of the Industrial Revolution—an economy confined to and limited by the Earth's physical resources—into . . . an era in which there are no bounds on human imagination and the freedom to create is the most precious natural resource.

Think of that little computer chip. Its value isn't in the sand from which it is made, but in the microscopic architecture designed into it by ingenious human minds. Or take the example of the satellite relaying this broadcast around the world, which replaces thousands of tons of copper mined from the Earth and molded into wire. In the new economy, human invention increasingly makes physical resources obsolete. We're breaking through the material conditions of existence to a world where man creates his own destiny. Even as we explore the most advanced reaches of science, we're returning to the age-old wisdom of our culture, a wisdom contained in the book of Genesis in the Bible: In the beginning was the spirit, and it was from this spirit that the material abundance of creation issued forth.

But progress is not foreordained. The key is freedom—freedom of thought, freedom of information, freedom of communication. The renowned scientist, scholar, and founding father of this University, Mikhail Lomonosov, knew that. "It is common knowledge," he said, "that the achievements of science are considerable and rapid, particularly once the yoke of slavery is cast off and replaced by the freedom of philosophy.". . .

The explorers of the modern era are the entrepreneurs, men with vision, with the courage to take risks and faith enough to brave the unknown. These entrepreneurs and their small enterprises are responsible for almost all the economic growth in the United States. They are the prime movers of the technological revolution. In fact, one of the largest personal computer firms in the United States was started by two college students, no older than you, in the garage behind their home.

Some people, even in my own country, look at the riot of experiment that is the free market and see only waste. What of all the entrepreneurs that fail? Well, many do, particularly the successful ones. Often several times. And if you ask them the secret of their success, they'll tell you, it's all that they learned in their struggles along the way—yes, it's what they learned from failing. Like an athlete in competition, or a scholar in pursuit of the truth, experience is the greatest teacher.

And that's why it's so hard for government planners, no matter how so-phisticated, to ever substitute for millions of individuals working night and day to make their dreams come true. . . .

We Americans make no secret of our belief in freedom. In fact, it's some-thing of a national pastime. Every four years the American people choose a new president, and 1988 is one of those years. At one point there were 13 major candidates running in the two major parties, not to mention all the others, including the Socialist and Libertarian candidates—all trying to get my job.

About 1,000 local television stations, 8,500 radio stations, and 1,700 daily newspapers, each one an independent, private enterprise, fiercely inde-pendent of the government, report on the candidates, grill them in inter-views, and bring them together for debates. In the end, the people vote— they decide who will be the next president.

But freedom doesn't begin or end with elections. Go to any American town, to take just an example, and you'll see dozens of churches, representing many different beliefs—in many places synagogues and mosques—and you'll see families of every conceivable nationality, worshipping together.

Go into any schoolroom, and there you will see children being taught the Declaration of Independence, that they are endowed by their Creator with certain inalienable rights—among them life, liberty, and the pursuit of hap-piness—that no government can justly deny—the guarantees in their Con-stitution for freedom of speech, freedom of assembly, and freedom of religion.

Go into any courtroom and there will preside an independent judge, beholden to no government power. There every defendant has the right to a trial by a jury of his peers, usually 12 men and women—common citizens, they are the ones, the only ones, who weigh the evidence and decide on guilt or innocence. In that court, the accused is innocent until proven guilty, and the world of a policeman, or any official, has no greater legal standing than the word of the accused.

Go to any university campus, and there you'll find an open, sometimes heated discussion of the problems in American society and what can be done to correct them. Turn on the television, and you'll see the legislature conducting the business of government right there before the camera, debating and voting on the legislation that will become the law of the land. March in any demonstration, and there are many of them—the people's right of assembly is guaranteed in the Constitution and protected by the police. Go into any union hall, where the members know their right to strike is protected by law. . . .

But freedom is even more than this: Freedom is the right to question, and change the established way of doing things. It is the continuing revolution of the marketplace. It is the understanding that allows us to recognize shortcomings and seek solutions. It is the right to put forth an idea, scoffed at by the experts, and watch it catch fire among the people. It is the right to follow your dream, to stick to your conscience, even if you're the only one in a sea of doubters.

Freedom is the recognition that no single person, no single authority or government has a monopoly on the truth, but that every individual life is infinitely precious, that every one of us put on this earth has been put here for a reason and has something to offer. . . .

Democracy is less a system of government than it is a system to keep government limited, unintrusive: A system of constraints on power to keep politics and government secondary to the important things in life, the true sources of value found only in family and faith.

But I hope you know I go on about these things not simply to extol the virtues of my own country, but to speak to the true greatness of the heart and soul of your land. Who, after all, needs to tell the land of Dostoevsky about the quest for truth, the home of Kandinsky and Scriabin about imagination, the rich and noble culture of the Uzbek man of letters, Alisher Navio, about beauty and heart?

The great culture of your diverse land speaks with a glowing passion to all humanity. Let me cite one of the most eloquent contemporary passages on human freedom. It comes, not from the literature of America, but from this country, from one of the greatest writers of the twentieth century, Boris Pasternak, in the novel *Dr. Zhivago.* He writes, "I think that if the beast who sleeps in man could be held down by threats—any kind of threat, whether of jail or of retribution after death—then the highest emblem of humanity would be the lion tamer in the circus with his whip, not the prophet who sacrificed himself. But this is just the point—what has for centuries raised man above the beast is not the cudgel, but an inward music—the irresistible power of unarmed truth."

The irresistible power of unarmed truth. Today the world looks expectantly to signs of change, steps toward greater freedom in the Soviet Union. . . .

Your generation is living in one of the most exciting, hopeful times in Soviet history. It is a time when the first breath of freedom stirs the air and the heart beats to the accelerated rhythm of hope, when the accumulated spiritual energies of a long silence yearn to break free.

I am reminded of the famous passage near the end of Gogol's *Dead Souls*. Comparing his nation to a speeding troika, Gogol asks what will be its destination. But he writes, "There was no answer save the bell pouring forth marvelous sound."

We do not know what the conclusion of this journey will be, but we're hopeful that the promise of reform will be fulfilled. In this Moscow spring, this May 1988, we may be allowed that hope—that freedom, like the fresh green sapling planted over Tolstoi's grave, will blossom forth at last in the rich fertile soil of your people and culture. We may be allowed to hope that the marvelous sound of a new openness will keep rising through, ringing through, leading to a new world of reconciliation, friendship, and peace. . . .

Source: *Public Papers of the Presidents of the United States, Ronald Reagan, 1988, Book I* (Washington, D.C., 1990), p. 683.

For Further Reading:

David Stockman, *The Triumph of Politics* (New York: Harper & Row, 1986).
Garry Wills, *Reagan's America* (Garden City, N.Y.: Doubleday, 1987).

100. Jesse Jackson, Excerpt from "Common Ground and Common Sense" (1988)

1984 and 1988   Jesse Jackson runs for President
1990   Douglas Wilder becomes governor of Virginia
1992   Riots erupt in Los Angeles

In 1988 the Reverend Jesse L. Jackson, a protégé of Martin Luther King, Jr., addressed the American people in a moving speech to the Democratic National Convention. Earlier in the year, he had mounted a vigorous campaign for his party's presidential nomination. Even though he lost, his effort won him distinction as the first black person to run a serious campaign for the presidency.

In his address, Jackson reminded the nation that its struggle to attain democracy was still unfulfilled. He observed that African Americans constituted a disproportionate share of the poor and that many seemed trapped in a vicious cycle of poverty and despair. Women, small farmers, blue-collar workers, and other minorities, Jackson asserted, still had not attained the democratic ideal. Jackson recognized the great strides that had been made in the recent past, but he also insisted that inequality persisted and in some cases was getting worse.

Two events in the following four years illustrated Jackson's points. In 1990, Douglas Wilder, a black man who was not allowed to vote when he reached voting age, was elected governor of Virginia. Such an event had seemed impossible just twenty-five years before. And in 1992, Los Angeles, the nation's second largest city, exploded in one of the worst riots in American history, as minorities and poor people displayed their despair with the system. The riot was precipitated by the verdict in the Rodney King trial, in which Los Angeles policemen were acquitted of assaulting King in spite of the fact that a video cameraman had filmed them beating King into submission. For many blacks and whites, the verdict in the trial demonstrated the persistence of racism in American society, and the riot that followed proved that a large gap between blacks and whites continued to exist.

Tonight we pause and give praise and honor to God for being good enough to allow us to be at this place at this time. . . . We're really standing on someone's shoulders. Ladies and gentlemen. Mrs. Rosa Parks. . . .

Twenty-four years ago, the late Fannie Lou Hamer and Aaron Henry—who sits here tonight from Mississippi—were locked out on the streets of Atlantic City, the head of the Mississippi Freedom Democratic Party. But tonight, a black and white delegation from Mississippi is headed by Ed Cole, a black man, from Mississippi.

. . . Many were lost in the struggle for the right to vote. Jimmy Lee Jackson, a young student, gave his life. Viola Liuzzo, a white mother from Detroit, called nigger lover, had her brains blown out at point blank range. Schwerner, Goodman and Chaney—two Jews and a black—found in a common grave, bodies riddled with bullets in Mississippi. The four little girls in the church in Birmingham, Alabama. They died that we might have a right to live.

Dr. Martin Luther King, Jr. lies only a few miles from us tonight. Tonight he must feel good as he looks down upon us. We sit here together, a rainbow, a coalition—the sons and daughters of slave masters and the sons and daughters of slaves sitting together around a common table, to decide the direction of our party and our country. His heart would be full tonight.

As a testament to the struggles of those who have gone before; as a legacy for those who will come after . . . their work has not been in vain, and hope is eternal; tomorrow night my name will go into nomination for the presidency of the United States of America.

We meet tonight at a crossroads, a point of decision. Shall we expand, be inclusive, find unity and power; or suffer division and impotence.

We come to Atlanta, the cradle of the old south, the crucible of the new South. Tonight there is a sense of celebration because we are moved, fundamentally moved, from racial battlegrounds by law, to economic common ground, tomorrow we will challenge to move to higher ground.

Common ground! . . .

Many people, many cultures, many languages—with one thing in common, the yearning to be free.

Common ground! . . .

The good of our nation is at stake—its commitment to working men and women, to the poor and vulnerable, to the many in the world. With so many guided missiles, and so much misguided leadership, the stakes are exceedingly high. Our choice, full participation in a Democratic government, or more abandonment and neglect. And so this night, we choose not a false sense of independence, not our capacity to act and unite for the greater good. The common good is finding commitment to new priorities, to expansion and inclusion. A commitment to expanded participation in the Democratic Party at every level. . . .

Common ground. Easier said than done. Where do you find common ground at the point of challenge? . . .

We find common ground at the plant gate that closes on workers without notice. We find common ground at the farm auction where a good farmer loses his or her land to bad loans or diminishing markets. Common ground at the schoolyard where teachers cannot get adequate pay, and students cannot get a scholarship and can't make a loan. Common ground at the hospital admitting room where somebody tonight is dying because they cannot afford to go upstairs to a bed that's empty, waiting for someone with insurance to get sick. We are a better nation than that. We must do better. . . .

America's not a blanket woven from one thread, one color, one cloth. When I was a child growing up in Greenville, S.C., and grandmother could not afford a blanket, she didn't complain and we did not freeze. Instead, she took pieces of old cloth—patches, wool, silk, gabardine, crockersak on the patches—barely good enough to wipe off your shoes with.

But they didn't stay that way very long. With sturdy hands and a strong cord, she sewed them together into a quilt, a thing of beauty and power and culture. Now, Democrats, we must build such a quilt. Farmers you seek fair prices and you are right, but you cannot stand alone. Your patch is not big enough. Workers, you fight for fair wages. You are right. But your patch labor is not big enough. Women you seek comparable worth and pay equality. You are right. But your patch is not big enough. Women, mothers, who seek Head Start and day care and pre-natal care on the front side of life, rather than jail care and welfare on the back side of life, you are right, but your patch is not big enough. . . .

But don't despair. Be as wise as my grandma. Pool the patches and the pieces together, bound by a common thread. When we form a great quilt of unity and common ground we'll have the power to bring about health care and housing and jobs and education and hope to our nation.

We the people can win. We stand at the end of a long dark night of reaction. We stand tonight united in a commitment to a new direction. For almost eight years, we've been led by those who view social good coming from private interest, who view public life as a means to increase private wealth. They have been prepared to sacrifice the common good of the many to satisfy the private interest and the wealth of a few. We believe in a government that's a tool of our democracy in service to the public, not an instrument of the aristocracy. . . .

Wherever you are tonight, I challenge you to hope and to dream. Don't submerge your dreams . . . dream of things as they ought to be. Dream. Face pain, but love, hope, faith, and dreams will help you rise above the pain. . . . Don't surrender and don't give up. Why can I challenge you this way? Jesse Jackson, you don't understand my situation. . . . I understand. . . . I wasn't always on television. Writers were not always outside my door. When I was born late one afternoon, October 8th, in Greenville, S.C., no writers asked my mother her name. Nobody chose to write down our address. My mama was not supposed to make it. And I was not supposed to make it. You see, I was born to a teen-age mother who was born to a teen-age mother.

I understand. I know abandonment. . . . I wasn't born in the hospital. . . . I was not born with a silver spoon in my mouth. I had a shovel programmed for my hand. My mother, a working woman. . . . I was born in the slum, but the slum was not born in me. And it wasn't born in you, and you can make it. . . .

You must not surrender. You may or may not get there, but just know that you're qualified and you hold on and hold out. We must never surrender. America will get better and better. Keep hope alive. . . . On tomorrow night and beyond, keep hope alive.

Source: Jesse Jackson, "Common Ground and Common Sense," address on July 20, 1988, *Vital Speeches*, Vol. LIV, no. 21 (August 15, 1988), pp. 649–53.

For Further Reading:

Gerald M. Jaynes and Robin M. Williams, eds., *Common Destiny* (Washington, D.C.: National Academy Press, 1989).

Adolph L. Reed, *The Jesse Jackson Phenomenon* (New Haven, Conn.: Yale University Press, 1986).

William J. Wilson, *The Truly Disadvantaged* (Chicago: University of Chicago Press, 1987).

Appendix A. The Declaration of Independence

The Unanimous Declaration of the Thirteen United States of America

W hen in the Course of human events it becomes necessary for one people to dissolve the political bands which have connected them with another, and to assume among the Powers of the earth, the separate and equal station to which the Laws of Nature and of Nature's God entitle them, a decent respect to the opinions of mankind requires that they should declare the causes which impel them to the separation.

We hold these truths to be self-evident, that all men are created equal, that they are endowed by their Creator with certain unalienable Rights, that among these are Life, Liberty and the pursuit of Happiness. That to secure these rights, Governments are instituted among Men, deriving their just Powers from the consent of the governed. That whenever any Form of Government becomes destructive of these ends, it is the Right of the People to alter or to abolish it, and to institute new Government, laying its foundation on such principles and organizing its Powers in such form, as to them shall seem most likely to effect their Safety and Happiness. Prudence, indeed, will dictate that Governments long established should not be changed for light and transient causes; and accordingly all experience hath shewn, that mankind are more disposed to suffer, while evils are sufferable, than to right themselves by abolishing the forms to which they are accustomed. But when a long train of abuses and usurpations, pursuing invariably the same Object evinces a design to reduce them under absolute Despotism, it is their right, it is their duty to throw off such Government, and to provide new Guards for their future security. Such has been the patient sufferance of these Colonies; and such is now the necessity which constrains them to alter their former Systems of Government. The history of the present King of Great Britain is a history of repeated injuries and usurpations, all having in direct object the establishment of an absolute Tyranny over these States. To prove this, let Facts be submitted to a candid world.

Reprinted from the facsimile of the engrossed copy in the National Archives. The original spelling, capitalization, and punctuation has been retained. Paragraphing has been added.

Drafting of The Declaration of Independence. The Committee—Franklin, Jefferson, Adams, Livingston, and Sherman (National Archives).

He has refused his Assent to Laws, the most wholesome and necessary for the public good.

He has forbidden his Governors to pass Laws of immediate and pressing importance, unless suspended in their operation till his Assent should be obtained; and when so suspended, he has utterly neglected to attend to them.

He has refused to pass other Laws for the accommodation of large districts of people, unless those people would relinquish the right of Representation in the Legislature, a right inestimable to them and formidable to tyrants only.

He has called together legislative bodies at places unusual, uncomfortable, and distant from the depository of their Public Records, for the sole Purpose of fatiguing them into compliance with his measures.

He has dissolved Representative Houses repeatedly, for opposing with manly firmness his invasions on the rights of the People.

He has refused for a long time, after such dissolutions, to cause others to be elected; whereby the Legislative Powers, incapable of Annihilation, have returned to the People at large for their exercise; the State remaining in the mean time exposed to all the dangers of invasion from without, and convulsions within.

He has endeavored to prevent the Population of these States; for that purpose obstructing the Laws for Naturalization of Foreigners; refusing to pass others to encourage their migrations hither, and raising the conditions of new Appropriations of Lands.

He has obstructed the Administration of Justice, by refusing his Assent to Laws for establishing Judiciary Powers.

He has made Judges dependent on his Will alone, for the tenure of their offices, and the amount and payment of their salaries.

He has erected a multitude of New Offices, and sent hither swarms of Officers to harass our People, and eat out their substance.

He has kept among us, in times of peace, Standing Armies without the consent of our legislatures.

He has affected to render the Military independent of and superior to the Civil Power.

He has combined with others to subject us to a jurisdiction foreign to our constitution, and unacknowledged by our laws; giving his Assent to their Acts of pretended Legislation:

For Quartering large bodies of armed troops among us:

For protecting them, by a mock Trial, from Punishment for any Murders which they should commit on the Inhabitants of these States:

For cutting off our Trade with all parts of the world:

For imposing Taxes on us without our Consent:

For depriving us in many cases, of the benefits of Trial by Jury:

For transporting us beyond Seas to be tried for pretended offenses:

For abolishing the free System of English Laws in a neighbouring Province, establishing therein an Arbitrary government, and enlarging its Boundaries so as to render it at once an example and fit instrument for introducing the same absolute rule into these Colonies:

For taking away our Charters, abolishing our most valuable Laws, and altering fundamentally the Forms of our Governments:

For suspending our own Legislatures, and declaring themselves invested with Power to legislate for us in all cases whatsoever.

He has abdicated Government here, by declaring us out of his Protection, and waging War against us.

He has plundered our seas, ravaged our Coasts, burnt our towns, and destroyed the lives of our people.

He is at this time transporting large Armies of foreign Mercenaries to compleat the works of death, desolation and tyranny, already begun with circumstances of Cruelty and perfidy scarcely paralleled in the most barbarous ages, and totally unworthy the Head of a civilized nation.

He has constrained our fellow Citizens taken Captive on the high Seas to bear Arms against their Country, to become the executioners of their friends and Brethren, or to fall themselves by their Hands.

He has excited domestic insurrections amongst us, and has endeavoured to bring on the inhabitants of our frontiers, the merciless Indian Savages, whose known rule of warfare, is an undistinguished destruction of all ages, sexes and conditions.

In every stage of these Oppressions We have Petitioned for Redress in the most humble terms: Our repeated Petitions have been answered only by repeated injury. A Prince, whose character is thus marked by every act which may define a Tyrant, is unfit to be the ruler of a free People.

Nor have We been wanting in attentions to our British brethren. We have warned them from time to time of attempts by their legislature to extend an unwarrantable jurisdiction over us. We have reminded them of the circumstances of our emigration and settlement here. We have appealed to their native justice and magnanimity, and we have conjured them by the ties of our common kindred to disavow these usurpations, which, would inevitably interrupt our connections and correspondence. They too have been deaf to the voice of justice and of consanguinity. We must, therefore, acquiesce in the necessity, which denounces our Separation, and hold them, as we hold the rest of mankind, Enemies in War, in Peace Friends.

We, therefore, the Representatives of the United States of America, in General Congress, Assembled, appealing to the Supreme Judge of the world for the rectitude of our intentions, do, in the Name, and by Authority of the good People of these Colonies, solemnly publish and declare, That these United Colonies are, and of Right ought to be FREE AND INDEPENDENT STATES; that they are Absolved from all Allegiance to the British Crown, and that all political connection between them and the State of Great Britain, is and ought to be totally dissolved; and that, as Free and Independent States, they have full Power to levy War, conclude Peace, contract Alliances, establish Commerce, and to do all other Acts and Things which Independent States may of right do. And for the support of this Declaration, with a firm reliance on the protection of divine Providence, we mutually pledge to each other our Lives, our Fortunes and our sacred Honor.

Appendix B. The Constitution of the United States of America[1]

We the People of the United States, in Order to form a more perfect Union, establish Justice, insure domestic Tranquility, provide for the common defence, promote the general Welfare, and secure the Blessings of Liberty to ourselves and our Posterity, do ordain and establish this Constitution for the United States of America.

Article. I.

Section. 1. All legislative Powers herein granted shall be vested in a Congress of the United States, which shall consist of a Senate and House of Representatives.

Section. 2. The House of Representatives shall be composed of Members chosen every second Year by the People of the several States, and the Electors in each State shall have the Qualifications requisite for Electors of the most numerous Branch of the State Legislature.

No Person shall be a Representative who shall not have attained to the Age of twenty five Years, and been seven Years a Citizen of the United States, and who shall not, when elected, be an Inhabitant of that State in which he shall be chosen.

Representatives and direct Taxes[2] shall be apportioned among the several States which may be included within this Union, according to their respective Numbers, which shall be determined by adding to the whole Number of free Persons, including those bound to Service for a Term of Years, and excluding Indians not taxed, three fifths of all other Persons.[3] The actual Enumeration shall be made within three Years after the first Meeting of the Congress of the United States, and within every subsequent Term of ten Years, in such Manner as they shall by Law direct. The Number of Representatives shall not exceed one for every thirty Thousand, but each State shall have at least one Representative; and until such enumeration shall be made, the State of New Hampshire shall be entitled to chuse three; Massachusetts eight; Rhode Island and Providence Plantations one; Connecticut

---

1. From the engrossed copy in the National Archives. Original spelling, capitalization, and punctuation have been retained.
2. Modified by the Sixteenth Amendment.
3. Replaced by the Fourteenth Amendment.

Signing of The Constitution. Painting by Howard Christy (National Archives).

five; New York six; New Jersey four; Pennsylvania eight; Delaware one; Maryland six; Virginia ten; North Carolina five; South Carolina five; and Georgia three.

When vacancies happen in the Representation from any State, the Executive Authority thereof shall issue Writs of Election to fill such Vacancies.

The House of Representatives shall chuse their Speaker and other Officers; and shall have the sole Power of Impeachment.

Section. 3. The Senate of the United States shall be composed of two Senators from each State, chosen by the Legislature thereof, for six Years; and each Senator shall have one Vote.[4]

Immediately after they shall be assembled in Consequence of the first Election, they shall be divided as equally as may be into three Classes. The Seats of the Senators of the first Class shall be vacated at the Expiration of the second Year, of the second Class at the Expiration of the fourth Year, and of the third Class at the Expiration of the sixth Year, so that one third may be chosen every second Year; and if Vacancies happen by Resignation, ot otherwise, during the Recess of the Legislature of any State, the Executive thereof may make temporary Appointments until the next Meeting of the Legislature, which shall then fill such Vacancies.[5]

No Person shall be a Senator who shall not have attained to the Age of thirty Years, and been nine Years a Citizen of the United States, and who shall not, when elected, be an Inhabitant of that State for which he shall be chosen.

The Vice President of the United States shall be President of the Senate, but shall have no Vote, unless they be equally divided.

The Senate shall chuse their other Officers, and also a President pro tempore, in the Absence of the Vice President, or when he shall exercise the Office of President of the United States.

The Senate shall have the sole Power to try all Impeachments. When sitting for that Purpose, they shall be on Oath or Affirmation. When the President of the United States is tried, the Chief Justice shall preside: And no Person shall be convicted without the Concurrence of two thirds of the Members present.

Judgment in Cases of Impeachment shall not extend further than to removal from Office, and disqualification to hold and enjoy any Office of honor, Trust or Profit under the United States: but the Party convicted shall nevertheless be liable and subject to Indictment, Trial, Judgment and Punishment, according to Law.

Section. 4. The Times, Places and Manner of holding Elections for Senators and Representatives, shall be prescribed in each State by the Legislature

---

4. Superseded by the Seventeenth Amendment.
5. Modified by the Seventeenth Amendment.

thereof, but the Congress may at any time by Law make or alter such Regulation, except as to the Places of chusing Senators.

The Congress shall assemble at least once in every Year, and such Meeting shall be on the first Monday in December, unless they shall by Law appoint a different Day.[6]

Section. 5. Each House shall be the Judge of the Elections, Returns and Qualifications of its own Members, and a Majority of each shall constitute a Quorum to do Business; but a smaller Number may adjourn from day to day, and may be authorized to compel the Attendance of absent Members, in such manner, and under such Penalties as each House may provide.

Each House may determine the Rules of its Proceedings, punish its Members for disorderly Behaviour, and, with the Concurrence of two thirds, expel a Member.

Each House shall keep a Journal of its Proceedings, and from time to time publish the same, excepting such Parts as may in their Judgment require Secrecy; and the Yeas and Nays of the Members of either House on any question shall, at the Desire of one fifth of those Present, be entered on the Journal.

Neither House, during the Session of Congress, shall, without the Consent of the other, adjourn for more than three days, nor to any other Place than that in which the two Houses shall be sitting.

Section. 6. The Senators and Representatives shall receive a Compensation for their Services, to be ascertained by Law, and paid out of the Treasury of the United States. They shall in all Cases, except Treason, Felony and Breach of the Peace, be privileged from Arrest during their Attendance at the Session of their respective Houses, and in going to and returning from the same; and for any Speech or Debate in either House, they shall not be questioned in any other Place.

No Senator or Representative shall, during the Time for which he was elected, be appointed to any civil Office under the Authority of the United States, which shall have been created, or the Emoluments whereof shall have been encreased during such time; and no Person holding any Office under the United States, shall be a Member of either House during his Continuance in Office.

Section. 7. All Bills for raising Revenue shall originate in the House of Representatives; but the Senate may propose or concur with Amendments as on other bills.

Every Bill which shall have passed the House of Representatives and the Senate shall, before it become a Law, be presented to the President of the United States; If he approve he shall sign it, but if not he shall return it, with his Objections to that House in which it shall have originated, who shall enter the Objections at large on their Journal, and proceed to reconsider

---

6. Superseded by the Twentieth Amendment.

it. If after such Reconsideration two thirds of that House shall agree to pass the Bill, it shall be sent, together with the Objections, to the other House, by which it shall likewise be reconsidered, and if approved by two thirds of that House, it shall become a Law. But in all such Cases the Votes of both Houses shall be determined by yeas and Nays, and the Names of the Persons voting for and against the Bill shall be entered on the Journal of each House respectively. If any Bill shall not be returned by the President within ten Days (Sundays excepted) after it shall have been presented to him, the Same shall be a Law, in Manner as if he had signed it, unless the Congress by their Adjournment prevent its Return, in which Case it shall not be a Law.

Every Order, Resolution, or Vote to which the Concurrence of the Senate and House of Representatives may be necessary (except on a question of Adjournment) shall be presented to the President of the United States; and before the Same shall take Effect, shall be approved by him, or being disapproved by him shall be repassed by two thirds of the Senate and House of Representatives, according to the rules and Limitations prescribed in the Case of a Bill.

Section. 8. The Congress shall have Power To lay and collect Taxes, Duties, Imposts and Excises, to pay the Debts and provide for the common Defence and general Welfare of the United States; but all Duties, Imposts and Excises shall be uniform throughout the United States;

To borrow Money on the credit of the United States;

To regulate Commerce with foreign Nations, and among the several States, and with the Indian Tribes;

To establish an uniform Rule of Naturalization, and uniform Laws on the subject of Bankruptcies throughout the United States;

To coin Money, regulate the Value thereof, and of foreign Coin, and fix the Standard of Weights and Measures;

To provide for the Punishment of counterfeiting the Securities and current Coin of the United States;

To establish Post Offices and post Roads;

To promote the Progress of Science and useful Arts, by securing for limited Times to Authors and Inventors the exclusive Right to their respective Writings and Discoveries;

To constitute Tribunals inferior to the supreme Court;

To define and punish Piracies and Felonies committed on the high Seas, and Offences against the Law of Nations;

To declare War, grant Letters of Marque and Reprisal, and make Rules concerning Captures on Land and Water;

To raise and support Armies, but no Appropriation of Money to that Use shall be for a longer Term than two Years;

To provide and maintain a Navy;

To make Rules for the government and Regulation of the land and naval Forces;

To provide for calling forth the Militia to execute the Laws of the Union, suppress Insurrections and repel Invasions;

To provide for organizing, arming, and disciplining, the Militia, and for governing such Part of them as may be employed in the Service of the United States, reserving to the States respectively, the Appointment of the Officers, and the Authority of training the Militia according to the discipline prescribed by Congress;

To exercise exclusive Legislation in all Cases whatsoever, over such District (not exceeding ten Miles square) as may, by Cession of particular States, and the Acceptance of Congress, become the Seat of the Government of the United States, and to exercise like Authority over all Places purchased by the consent of the Legislature of the State in which the Same shall be, for the Erection of Forts, Magazines, Arsenals, dock-Yards, and other needful Buildings;—And

To make all Laws which shall be necessary and proper for carrying into Execution the foregoing Powers, and all other Powers vested by this Constitution in the Government of the United States, or in any Department or Officer thereof.

Section. 9. The Migration or Importation of such Persons as any of the States now existing shall think proper to admit, shall not be prohibited by the Congress prior to the Year one thousand eight hundred and eight, but a Tax or Duty may be imposed on such Importation, not exceeding ten dollars for each Person.

The Privilege of the Writ of Habeas Corpus shall not be suspended, unless when in Cases of Rebellion or Invasion the public Safety may require it.

No Bill of Attainder or ex post facto Law shall be passed.

No Capitation, or other direct, Tax shall be laid, unless in Proportion to the Census or Enumeration herein before directed to be taken.

No Tax or Duty shall be laid on Articles exported from any State.

No Preference shall be given by any Regulation of Commerce or Revenue to the Ports of one State over those of another: nor shall Vessels bound to, or from, one State, be obliged to enter, clear, or pay Duties in another.

No Money shall be drawn from the Treasury, but in Consequence of Appropriations made by Law, and a regular Statement and Account of the Receipts and Expenditures of all public Money shall be published from time to time.

No Title of Nobility shall be granted by the United States: And no Person holding any Office of Profit or Trust under them, shall, without the Consent of the Congress, accept of any present, Emolument, Office, or Title, of any kind whatever, from any King, Prince, or foreign State.

Section. 10. No State shall enter into any Treaty, Alliance, or Confederation; grant Letters of Marque and Reprisal; coin Money; emit bills of Credit; make any Thing but gold and silver Coin a Tender in Payment of Debts; pass any

Bill of Attainder, ex post facto Law, or Law impairing the Obligation of Contracts, or grant any Title of Nobility.

No State shall, without the Consent of the Congress, lay any Imposts or Duties on Imports or Exports, except what may be absolutely necessary for executing its inspection Laws: and the net Produce of all Duties and Imposts, laid by any State on Imports or Exports, shall be for the Use of the Treasury of the United States; and all such Laws shall be subject to the Revision and Controul of the Congress.

No State shall, without the Consent of Congress, lay any Duty of Tonnage, keep Troops or Ships of War in time of peace, enter into any Agreement or Compact with another State, or with a foreign Power, or engage in War, unless actually invaded, or in such imminent Danger as will not admit of delay.

Article. II.

Section. 1. The executive Power shall be vested in a President of the United States of America. He shall hold his Office during the Term of four Years, and, together with the Vice President, chosen for the same Term, be elected, as follows:

Each State shall appoint, in such Manner as the Legislature thereof may direct, a Number of Electors, equal to the whole Number of Senators and Representatives to which the State may be entitled in the Congress: but no Senator or Representative, or Person holding an Office of Trust or Profit under the United States, shall be appointed an Elector.

The Electors shall meet in their respective States, and vote by Ballot for two Persons, of whom one at least shall not be an Inhabitant of the same State with themselves. And they shall make a List of all the Persons voted for, and of the Number of Votes for each; which List they shall sign and certify, and transmit sealed to the Seat of the Government of the United States, directed to the President of the Senate. The President of the Senate shall, in the Presence of the Senate and House of Representatives, open all the Certificates, and the Votes shall then be counted. The Person having the greatest Number of Votes shall be the President, if such Number be a Majority of the whole Number of Electors appointed; and if there be more than one who have such Majority, and have an equal Number of Votes, then the House of Representatives shall immediately chuse by Ballot one of them for President; and if no Person have a Majority, then from the five highest on the List the said House shall in like Manner chuse the President. But in chusing the President, the Votes shall be taken by States, the Representation from each State having one Vote; A quorum for this Purpose shall consist of a Member or Members from two thirds of the States, and a Majority of all the States shall be necessary to a Choice. In every Case, after the

Choice of the President, the Person having the greatest Number of Votes of the Electors shall be the Vice President. But if there should remain two or more who have equal Votes, the Senate shall chuse from them by Ballot the Vice President.[7]

The Congress may determine the Time of chusing the Electors, and the Day on which they shall give their Votes; which Day shall be the same throughout the United States.

No Person except a natural born Citizen, or a Citizen of the United States, at the time of the Adoption of this Constitution, shall be eligible to the Office of President, neither shall any Person be eligible to that Office who shall not have attained to the Age of thirty five Years, and been fourteen Years a Resident within the United States.

In Case of the Removal of the President from Office, or of his Death, Resignation, or Inability to discharge the Powers and Duties of the said Office, the Same shall devolve on the Vice President, and the Congress may by Law provide for the Case of Removal, Death, Resignation or Inability, both of the President and Vice President, declaring what Officer shall then act as President, and such Officer shall act accordingly, until the Disability be removed, or a President shall be elected.[8]

The President shall, at stated Times, receive for his Services, a Compensation, which shall neither be encreased nor diminished during the Period for which he shall have been elected, and he shall not receive within that Period any other Emolument from the United States, or any of them.

Before he enter on the Execution of his Office, he shall take the following Oath or Affirmation:— "I do solemnly swear (or affirm) that I will faithfully execute the Office of President of the United States, and will to the best of my Ability, preserve, protect and defend the Constitution of the United States."

Section. 2. The President shall be Commander in Chief of the Army and Navy of the United States, and of the Militia of the several States, when called into the actual Service of the United States; he may require the Opinion, in writing, of the principal Officer in each of the executive Departments, upon any Subject relating to the Duties of their respective Offices, and he shall have Power to grant Reprieves and Pardons for Offences against the United States, except in cases of Impeachment.

He shall have Power, by and with the Advice and Consent of the Senate, to make Treaties, provided two thirds of the Senators present concur; and he shall nominate, and by and with the Advice and Consent of the Senate, shall appoint Ambassadors, other public Ministers and Consuls, Judges of the supreme Court, and all other Officers of the United States, whose Appointments are not herein otherwise provided for, and which shall be es-

---

7. Superseded by the Twelfth Amendment.
8. Modified by the Twenty-fifth Amendment.

tablished by Law; but the Congress may by Law vest the Appointment of such inferior Officers, as they think proper, in the President alone, in the Courts of Law, or in the Heads of Departments.

The President shall have Power to fill up all Vacancies that may happen during the Recess of the Senate, by granting Commissions which shall expire at the End of their next Session.

Section. 3. He shall from time to time give to the Congress Information of the State of the Union, and recommend to their Consideration such Measures as he shall judge necessary and expedient; he may, on extraordinary Occasions, convene both Houses, or either of them, and in Case of Disagreement between them, with Respect to the Time of Adjournment, he may adjourn them to such Time as he shall think proper; he shall receive Ambassadors and other public Ministers; he shall take Care that the Laws be faithfully executed, and shall Commission all the Officers of the United States.

Section. 4. the President, Vice President and all civil Officers of the United States, shall be removed from Office on Impeachment for, and Conviction of, Treason, Bribery, or other high Crimes and Misdemeanors.

Article. III.

Section. 1. The judicial Power of the United States, shall be vested in one supreme Court, and in such inferior Courts as the Congress may from time to time ordain and establish. The Judges, both of the supreme and inferior Courts, shall hold their Offices during good Behaviour, and shall, at stated Times, receive for their Services, a Compensation, which shall not be diminished during their Continuance in Office.

Section. 2. The judicial Power shall extend to all Cases, in Law and Equity, arising under this Constitution, the Laws of the United States, and Treaties made, or which shall be made, under their Authority;—to all Cases affecting Ambassadors, other public Ministers and Consuls;—to all Cases of admiralty and maritime Jurisdiction;—to Controversies to which the United States shall be a Party;—to Controversies between two or more States;—between a State and Citizens of another State;[9]—between Citizens of different States,—between Citizens of the same State claiming Lands under Grants of different States, and between a State, or the Citizens thereof, and foreign States, Citizens or Subjects.

In all Cases affecting Ambassadors, other public Ministers and Consuls, and those in which a State shall be Party, the supreme Court shall have original Jurisdiction. In all the other Cases before mentioned, the supreme Court shall have appellate Jurisdiction, both as to Law and Fact, with such Exceptions, and under such Regulations as the Congress shall make.

---

9. Modified by the Eleventh Amendment.

The Trial of all Crimes, except in Cases of Impeachment, shall be by Jury; and such Trial shall be held in the State where the said Crimes shall have been committed; but when not committed within any State, the trial shall be at such Place or Places as the Congress may by Law have directed.

Section. 3. Treason against the United States, shall consist only in levying War against them, or in adhering to their Enemies, giving them Aid and Comfort. No Person shall be convicted of Treason unless on the Testimony of two Witnesses to the same overt Act, or on Confession in open Court.

The Congress shall have Power to declare the Punishment of Treason, but no Attainder of Treason shall work Corruption of Blood, or Forfeiture except during the Life of the Person attainted.

Article. IV.

Section. 1. Full Faith and Credit shall be given in each State to the public Acts, Records, and judicial Proceedings of every other State. And the Congress may by general Laws prescribe the Manner in which such Acts, Records and Proceedings shall be proved, and the Effect thereof.

Section. 2. The Citizens of each State shall be entitled to all Privileges and Immunities of Citizens in the several States.

A Person charged in any State with Treason, Felony, or other Crime, who shall flee from Justice, and be found in another State, shall on Demand of the executive Authority of the State from which he fled, be delivered up, to be removed to the State having Jurisdiction of the Crime.

No Person held to Service or Labour in one State, under the Laws thereof, escaping into another, shall, in Consequence of any Law or Regulation therein, be discharged from such Service or Labour, but shall be delivered up on Claim of the Party to whom such Service or Labour may be due.

Section. 3. New States may be admitted by the Congress into this Union; but no new State shall be formed or erected within the Jurisdiction of any other State, nor any State be formed by the Junction of two or more States, or Parts of States, without the Consent of the Legislatures of the States concerned as well as of the Congress.

The Congress shall have Power to dispose of and make all needful Rules and Regulations respecting the Territory or other Property belonging to the United States; and nothing in this Constitution shall be so construed as to Prejudice any Claims of the United States, or of any particular State.

Section. 4. The United States shall guarantee to every State in this Union a Republican Form of Government, and shall protect each of them against Invasion; and on Application of the Legislature, or of the Executive (when the Legislature cannot be convened) against domestic Violence.

Article. V.

The Congress, whenever two thirds of both Houses shall deem it necessary, shall propose Amendments to this Constitution, or, on the Application of the Legislatures of two thirds of the several States, shall call a Convention for proposing Amendments, which, in either Case, shall be valid to all Intents and Purposes, as Part of this Constitution, when ratified by the Legislatures of three fourths of the several States, or by Conventions in three fourths thereof, as the one or the other Mode of Ratification may be proposed by the Congress; Provided that no Amendment which may be made prior to the Year One thousand eight hundred and eight shall in any Manner affect the first and fourth Clauses in the Ninth Section of the first Article; and that no State, without its Consent, shall be deprived of its equal Suffrage in the Senate.

Article. VI.

All Debts contracted and Engagements entered into, before the Adoption of this Constitution, shall be as valid against the United States under this Constitution, as under the Confederation.

This Constitution, and the Laws of the United States which shall be made in Pursuance thereof; and all Treaties made, or which shall be made, under the Authority of the United States, shall be the supreme Law of the Land; and the Judges in every State shall be bound thereby, any Thing in the Constitution or Laws of any State to the Contrary notwithstanding.

The Senators and Representatives before mentioned, and the Members of the several State Legislatures, and all executive and judicial Officers, both of the United States and of the several States, shall be bound by Oath or Affirmation, to support this Constitution; but no religious Test shall ever be required as a Qualification to any Office or public Trust under the United States.

Article. VII.

The Ratification of the Conventions of nine States, shall be sufficient for the Establishment of this Constitution between the States so ratifying the Same.

done in Convention by the Unanimous Consent of the States present the Seventeenth Day of September in the Year of our Lord one thousand seven hundred and Eighty seven and of the Independence of the United States of America the Twelfth. In *witness* whereof We have hereunto subscribed our Names,

Articles in Addition to, and Amendment of, the Constitution of the United States of America, Proposed by Congress, and Ratified by the Legislatures of the Several States, Pursuant to the Fifth Article of the Original Constitution.

Amendment I[10]

Congress shall make no law respecting an establishment of religion, or prohibiting the free exercise thereof; or abridging the freedom of speech, or of the press; or the right of the people peaceably to assemble, and to petition the Government for a redress of grievances.

Amendment II

A well regulated Militia, being necessary to the security of a free State, the right of the people to keep and bear Arms shall not be infringed.

Amendment III

No Soldier shall, in time of peace, be quartered in any house, without the consent of the Owner, nor in time of war, but in a manner to be prescribed by law.

Amendment IV

The right of the people to be secure in their persons, houses, papers, and effects, against unreasonable searches and seizures, shall not be violated, and no Warrants shall issue, but upon probable cause, supported by Oath or affirmation, and particularly describing the place to be searched, and the persons or things to be seized.

Amendment V

No person shall be held to answer for a capital or otherwise infamous crime, unless on a presentment or indictment of a Grand Jury, except in cases arising in the land or naval forces, or in the Militia, when in actual service in time of War or public danger; nor shall any person be subject for the same offence to be twice put in jeopardy of life or limb; nor shall be compelled in any criminal case to be a witness against himself, nor be deprived of life, liberty, or property, without due process of law; nor shall private property be taken for public use, without just compensation.

---

10. The first ten amendments were passed by Congress September 25, 1789. They were ratified by three-fourths of the states December 15, 1791.

Amendment VI

In all criminal prosecutions, the accused shall enjoy the right to a speedy and public trial, by an impartial jury of the State and district wherein the crime shall have been committed, which district shall have been previously ascertained by law, and to be informed of the nature and cause of the accusation; to be confronted with the witnesses against him; to have compulsory process for obtaining witnesses in his favor, and to have the Assistance of Counsel for his defence.

Amendment VII

In suits at common law, where the value in controversy shall exceed twenty dollars, the right of trial by jury shall be preserved, and no fact tried by a jury, shall be otherwise reexamined in any Court of the United States, than according to the rules of the common law.

Amendment VIII

Excessive bail shall not be required, nor excessive fines imposed, nor cruel and unusual punishments inflicted.

Amendment IX

The enumeration in the Constitution, of certain rights, shall not be construed to deny or disparage others retained by the people.

Amendment X

The powers not delegated to the United States by the Constitution; nor prohibited by it to the States, are reserved to the States respectively, or to the people.

Amendment XI[11]

The Judicial power of the United States shall not be construed to extend to any suit in law or equity, commenced or prosecuted against one of the United States by Citizens of another State, or by Citizens or Subjects of any Foreign State.

---

11. Passed March 4, 1794. Ratified January 23, 1795.

Amendment XII[12]

The Electors shall meet in their respective States and vote by ballot for President and Vice-President, one of whom, at least, shall not be an inhabitant of the same State with themselves; they shall name in their ballots the person voted for as President, and in distinct ballots the person voted for as Vice-President, and they shall make distinct lists of all persons voted for as President, and of all persons voted for as Vice-President, and of the number of votes for each, which lists they shall sign and certify, and transmit sealed to the seat of the government of the United States, directed to the President of the Senate;—The President of the Senate shall, in the presence of the Senate and House of Representatives, open all the certificates and the votes shall then be counted;—The person having the greatest number of votes for President, shall be the President, if such number be a majority of the whole number of Electors appointed; and if no person have such majority, then from the persons having the highest numbers not exceeding three on the list of those voted for as President, the House of Representatives shall choose immediately, by ballot, the President. But in choosing the President, the votes shall be taken by states, the representation from each state having one vote; a quorum for this purpose shall consist of a member or members from two-thirds of the states, and a majority of all the states shall be necessary to a choice. And if the House of Representatives shall not choose a President whenever the right of choice shall devolve upon them, before the fourth day of March next following, then the Vice-President shall act as President, as in the case of the death or other constitutional disability of the President.—The person having the greatest number of votes as Vice-President, shall be the Vice-President, if such number be a majority of the whole number of Electors appointed, and if no person have a majority, then from the two highest numbers on the list, the Senate shall choose the Vice-President; a quorum for the purpose shall consist of two-thirds of the whole number of Senators, and a majority of the whole number shall be necessary to a choice. But no person constitutionally ineligible to the office of President shall be eligible to that of Vice-President of the United States.

Amendment XIII[13]

Section. 1. Neither slavery nor involuntary servitude, except as a punishment for crime whereof the party shall have been duly convicted, shall exist within the United States, or any place subject to their jurisdiction.

---

12. Passed December 9, 1803. Ratified June 15, 1804.
13. Passed January 31, 1865. Ratified December 6, 1865.

Section. 2. Congress shall have power to enforce this article by appropriate legislation.

Amendment XIV[14]

Section. 1. All persons born or naturalized in the United States, and subject to the jurisdiction thereof, are citizens of the United States and of the State wherein they reside. No State shall make or enforce any law which shall abridge the privileges or immunities of citizens of the United States; nor shall any State deprive any person of life, liberty, or property, without due process of law; nor deny to any person within its jurisdiction the equal protection of the laws.

Section. 2. Representatives shall be apportioned among the several States according to their respective numbers, counting the whole number of person in each State, excluding Indians not taxed. But when the right to vote at any election for the choice of electors for President and Vice-President of the United States, Representatives in Congress, the Executive and Judicial officers of a State, or the members of the Legislature thereof, is denied to any of the male inhabitants of such State, being twenty-one years of age, and citizens of the United States, or in any way abridged, except for participation in rebellion, or other crime, the basis of representation therein shall be reduced in the proportion which the number of such male citizens shall bear to the whole number of male citizens twenty-one years of age in such state.

Section. 3. No person shall be a Senator or Representative in Congress, or elector of President and Vice-President, or hold any office, civil or military, under the United States, or under any State, who, having previously taken an oath, as a member of Congress, or as an officer of the United States, or as a member of any State legislature, or as an executive or judicial officer of any State, to support the Constitution of the United States, shall have engaged in insurrection or rebellion against the same, or given aid or comfort to the enemies thereof. But Congress may by a vote of two-thirds of each House, remove such disability.

Section. 4. The validity of the public debt of the United States, authorized by law, including debts incurred for payment of pensions and bounties for services in suppressing insurrection or rebellion, shall not be questioned. But neither the United States nor any State shall assume or pay any debt or obligation incurred in aid of insurrection or rebellion against the United States, or any claim for the loss or emancipation of any slave; but all such debts, obligations, and claims shall be held illegal and void.

14. Passed June 13, 1866. Ratified July 9, 1868.

Section. 5. The Congress shall have the power to enforce, by appropriate legislation, the provisions of this article.

Amendment XV[15]

Section. 1. The right of citizens of the United States to vote shall not be denied or abridged by the United States or by any State on account of race, color, or previous condition of servitude—
Section. 2. The Congress shall have power to enforce this article by appropriate legislation.

Amendment XVI[16]

The Congress shall have power to lay and collect taxes on incomes, from whatever source derived, without apportionment among the several States, and without regard to any census or enumeration.

Amendment XVII[17]

The Senate of the United States shall be composed of two Senators from each State, elected by the people thereof, for six years; and each Senator shall have one vote. The electors in each State shall have the qualifications requisite for electors of the most numerous branch of the State legislatures.

When vacancies happen in the representation of any State in the Senate, the executive authority of such State shall issue writs of election to fill such vacancies: *Provided,* That the legislature of any State may empower the executive thereof to make temporary appointments until the people fill the vacancies by election as the legislature may direct.

This amendment shall not be so construed as to affect the election or term of any Senator chosen before it becomes valid as part of the Constitution.

Amendment XVIII[18]

Section. 1. After one year from the ratification of this article the manufacture, sale, or transportation or intoxicating liquors within, the importation thereof into, or the exportation thereof from the United States and all territory subject to the jurisdiction thereof for beverage purposes is hereby prohibited.
Section 2. The Congress and the several States shall have concurrent power to enforce this article by appropriate legislation.

---

15. Passed February 26, 1869. Ratified February 2, 1870.
16. Passed July 12, 1909. Ratified February 3, 1913.
17. Passed May 13, 1912. Ratified April 8, 1913.
18. Passed December 18, 1917. Ratified January 16, 1919.

Section 3. This article shall be inoperative unless it shall have been ratified as an amendment to the Constitution by the legislatures of the several States, as provided in the Constitution, within seven years from the date of the submission hereof to the States by the Congress.

Amendment XIX[19]

The right of citizens of the United States to vote shall not be denied or abridged by the United States or by any State on account of sex.

Congress shall have power to enforce this article by appropriate legislation.

Amendment XX[20]

Section. 1. The terms of the President and Vice-President shall end at noon on the 20th day of January, and the terms of Senators and Representatives at noon on the 3d day of January, of the years in which such terms would have ended if this article had not been ratified; and the terms of their successors shall then begin.

Section. 2. The Congress shall assemble at least once in every year, and such meeting shall begin at noon on the 3d day of January, unless they shall by law appoint a different day.

Section. 3. If, at the time fixed for the beginning of the term of the President, the President elect shall have died, the Vice-President elect shall become President. If a President shall not have been chosen before the time fixed for the beginning of his term, or if the President elect shall have failed to qualify, then the Vice-President elect shall act as President until a President shall have qualified; and the Congress may by law provide for the case wherein neither a President elect nor a Vice-President elect shall have qualified, declaring who shall then act as President, or the manner in which one who is to act shall be selected, and such person shall act accordingly until a President or Vice-President shall have qualified.

Section. 4. The Congress may by law provide for the case of the death of any of the persons from whom the House of Representatives may choose a President whenever the right of choice shall have devolved upon them, and for the case of the death of any of the persons from whom the Senate may choose a Vice-President whenever the right of choice shall have devolved upon them.

Section. 5. Sections 1 and 2 shall take effect on the 15th day of October following the ratification of this article.

Section. 6. This article shall be inoperative unless it shall have been ratified

---

19. Passed June 4, 1919. Ratified August 18, 1920.
20. Passed March 2, 1932. Ratified January 23, 1933.

as an amendment to the Constitution by the legislatures of three-fourths of the several States within seven years from the date of its submission.

Amendment XXI[21]

Section. 1. The eighteenth article of amendment to the Constitution of the United States is hereby repealed.

Section. 2. The transportation or importation into any State, Territory, or possession of the United States for delivery or use therein of intoxicating liquors, in violation of the laws thereof, is hereby prohibited.

Section. 3. This article shall be inoperative unless it shall have been ratified as an amendment of the Constitution by conventions in the several States, as provided in the Constitution, within seven years from the date of the submission hereof to the States by the Congress.

Amendment XXII[22]

No person shall be elected to the office of the President more than twice, and no person who has held the office of President, or acted as President, for more than two years of a term to which some other person was elected President shall be elected to the office of the President more than once.

But this Article shall not apply to any person holding the office of President when this Article was proposed by the Congress, and shall not prevent any person who may be holding the office of President, or acting as President, during the term within which this Article becomes operative from holding the office of President or acting as President during the remainder of such term.

Amendment XXIII[23]

Section. 1. The district constituting the seat of Government of the United States shall appoint in such manner as the Congress may direct:

A number of electors of President and Vice President equal to the whole number of Senators and Representatives in Congress to which the District would be entitled if it were a State, but in no event more than the least populous State; they shall be in addition to those appointed by the States, but they shall be considered, for the purposes of the election of President and Vice President, to be electors appointed by the State; and they shall meet in the District and perform such duties as provided by the twelfth article of amendment.

---

21. Passed February 20, 1933. Ratified December 5, 1933.
22. Passed March 12, 1947. Ratified March 1, 1951.
23. Passed June 16, 1960. Ratified April 3, 1961.

Section. 2. The Congress shall have power to enforce this article by appropriate legislation.

Amendment XXIV[24]

Section. 1. The right of citizens of the United States to vote in any primary or other election for President or Vice President, or for Senator or Representative in Congress, shall not be denied or abridged by the United States or any State by reason of failure to pay any poll tax or other tax.
Section. 2. The Congress shall have power to enforce this article by appropriate legislation.

Amendment XXV[25]

Section. 1. In case of the removal of the President from office or of his death or resignation, the Vice President shall become President.
Section. 2. Whenever there is a vacancy in the office of the Vice President, the President shall nominate a Vice President who shall take office upon confirmation by a majority vote of both Houses of Congress.
Section. 3. Whenever the President transmits to the President pro tempore of the Senate and the Speaker of the House of Representatives his written declaration that he is unable to discharge the powers and duties of his office, and until he transmits to them a written declaration to the contrary, such powers and duties shall be discharged by the Vice President as Acting President.
Section. 4. Whenever the Vice President and a majority of either the principal officers of the executive department or of such other body as Congress may by law provide, transmit to the President pro tempore of the Senate and the Speaker of the House of Representatives their written declaration that the President is unable to discharge the powers and duties of his office, the Vice President shall immediately assume the powers and duties of the office of Acting President.

Thereafter, when the President transmits to the President pro tempore of the Senate and the Speaker of the House of Representatives his written declaration that no inability exists, he shall resume the powers and duties of his office unless the Vice President and a majority of either the principal officers of the executive department or of such other body as Congress may by law provide, transmit within four days to the President pro tempore of the Senate and the Speaker of the House of Representatives their written declaration that the President is unable to discharge the powers and duties of his office. Thereupon Congress shall decide the issue, assembling within

24. Passed August 27, 1962. Ratified January 23, 1964.
25. Passed July 6, 1965. Ratified February 11, 1967.

forty-eight hours for that purpose if not in session. If the Congress, within twenty-one days after receipt of the latter written declaration, or if Congress is not in session, within twenty-one days after Congress is required to assemble, determines by two-thirds vote of both Houses that the President is unable to discharge the powers and duties of his office, the Vice President shall continue to discharge the same as Acting President; otherwise, the President shall resume the powers and duties of his office.

Amendment XXVI[26]

Section. 1. The right of citizens of the United States, who are eighteen years of age or older, to vote shall not be denied or abridged by the United States or by any State on account of age.
Section. 2. The Congress shall have power to enforce this article by appropriate legislation.

---

26. Passed March 23, 1971. Ratified July 5, 1971.

Index

About the Editor and the Advisory Board

About the Editor

PETER B. LEVY is Assistant Professor in the Department of History and Political Science at York College. He is the author of *Let Freedom Ring: A Documentary History of the Modern Civil Rights Movement* (Greenwood/ Praeger, 1992) and *The New Left and Labor in the 1960s*.

About the Advisory Board

KATHLEEN W. CRAVER is Head Librarian at the National Cathedral School in Washington, D.C. She holds a Ph.D. in Library and Information Studies from the University of Illinois. She is the author of numerous articles on the management of school libraries and is a reviewer for *American Reference Books Annual*.

DAVID J. GARROW is a Senior Fellow of the Twentieth Century Fund and is presently Visiting Distinguished Professor of History at The Cooper Union in New York. His book *Bearing the Cross: Martin Luther King, Jr., and the Southern Christian Leadership Conference* (1986) won the 1987 Pulitzer Prize in Biography. He is the author of three other books on the civil rights movement and served as a senior advisor to "Eyes on the Prize," the award-winning PBS television history of the American black freedom struggle. His new book, *Liberty and Sexuality: The Right to Privacy and the Making of Roe v. Wade*, will be published in early 1994.